ROMAN
CATHOLICS
AND
EVANGELICALS

ROMAN CATHOLICS

AND

EVANGELICALS

AGREEMENTS AND DIFFERENCES

NORMAN L. GEISLER

AND

RALPH E. MACKENZIE

BakerBooks
Grand Rapids, Michigan

©1995 by Norman L. Geisler and Ralph E. MacKenzie

Published by Baker Books
a division of Baker Book House Company
P.O. Box 6287, Grand Rapids, MI 49516-6287
www.bakerbooks.com

Tenth printing, February 2006

Printed in the United States of America

Library of Congress Cataloging-in-Publication Data
Geisler, Norman L.
    Roman Catholics and Evangelicals : agreements and differences / Norman L. Geisler and Ralph E. MacKenzie.
        p.   cm.
    Includes bibliographical references and index.
    ISBN-10: 0-8010-3875-8 (pbk.)
    ISBN 978-0-8010-3875-4 (pbk.)
    1. Evangelicalism—Relations—Catholic Church. 2. Catholic Church—Relations—Evangelicalism. 3. Catholic Church—Doctrines. 4. Evangelicalism. I. MacKenzie, Ralph E. II. Title.
    BR1641.C37G45   1995
    280'.042—dc20   95-18062

This book is dedicated to the memory of
Johannes von Staupitz,
the vicar-general of the Augustinian Hermits
and Luther's father confessor, and others
who, throughout church history, have kept
alive the Pauline and Augustinian doctrine
of salvation by grace

CONTENTS

APPENDIXES

Acknowledgments

The authors wish to single out the following persons for special mention in the formation of this volume. Dr. Harold O. J. Brown for his foreword and careful critique of our manuscript; Dr. Robert B. Strimple for material on St. Anselm; Dr. John N. Akers, who supplied information concerning Roman Catholic involvement in Billy Graham crusades; and Fr. James Barkett, pastor of St. George Orthodox Church, San Diego, who examined Appendix A and pronounced it historically and theologically accurate. Dr. David Wells, James White, William Watkins, and Kenneth R. Samples also read the manuscript and made valuable suggestions. We especially appreciate the help of *Catholic Answers*, who allowed us the use of their resources. One of their staff members, James Akin, delivered a time-consuming and invaluable effort of evaluation and critique of Parts One and Two. Librarians Marjorie Knight and Mary Lou Bradbury were helpful in tracking down hard-to-find works and Stephanie Turek was involved in word processing and manuscript formation. Lastly, we wish to thank our wives: Barbara Geisler for her careful proof-texting and Donna MacKenzie for her many hours of editing and word processing.

FOREWORD

Co-belligerents, competitors, or fratricidal brethren? As so often happened in the Soviet gulags, Christians of varying denominations and emphases are discovering that they have more in common with each other than with the secular world that denies God. Indeed, committed "traditional" or "orthodox" believers from various denominations have more in common with each other than with "liberals," revisionists, and modernists within their own groups. As the late Georges Florovsky said when queried why he, an Eastern Orthodox refugee from both Communism and Nazism, would turn up in an evangelical, even fundamentalist Calvinist circle: "The Christian is never a stranger where our blessed Lord is loved and worshiped."

Roman Catholics and conservative evangelical Protestants often find themselves fighting the same enemies. Enemies are those who do not merely attack traditional Christian beliefs and what today are called "family values," but who wish to ban every expression of faith in God, every trace of the moral standards of the Bible, from an increasingly secularistic, self-righteous, and—if God's Word is true—self-condemning and doomed society.

How is it possible that Protestants and Catholics could rally together for the same cause? Both have memories and traditions of bitter conflict. Protestants can recall the martyrdoms under Queen Mary—"Bloody Mary"—in England and the Duke of Alva in the Low Countries; persecutions in Germany, Austria, and Spain; the St. Barthelomew's Day massacre in France; and even incidents in recent years, in countries where a reactionary kind of Catholicism prevailed. But Protestants have not only been victims. Where the machinery of the state was in Protestant hands it has frequently been employed against Catholics, albeit perhaps less brutally (e.g., England, after it became Protestant, Sweden, the North American colonies). Where there was no outright persecution, there has often been discrimination; until the election of John F. Kennedy in 1960 it was commonly held that no Roman Catholic could ever become president of the United States. And we must not forget the wars of religion, the terrible Thirty Years' War that devastated central Europe being only the longest and most destructive example.

Of course there are misunderstandings that have divided Christendom. Catholics do not worship the Pope, and evangelicals do not think that it is fine to divorce at will a spouse with whom one is no longer pleased (or, in the case of Henry VIII, that king who embarrassingly began the rule of Protestantism in England, to cut off her head). But by no means are all the differences that divide based on misunderstandings. There are some real and fundamental-sounding differences in interpretation and application, where each side thinks itself right, but where the final and conclusive word is not apt to be pronounced until judgment day. In addition, some of the misunderstandings are all but impossible to clear away, because both sides have a long tradition of commitment to them and investment in them. Nevertheless, when all is said and done, evangelical Protestants and traditionalist, believing Roman Catholics have so many convictions and commitments in common that it would be foolish as well as wrong in the sight of the One whom we all claim as our Lord Jesus Christ to wrangle with each other in the face of the common enemy.

The Christian church has an incredibly rich spiritual and intellectual tradition. Simply in terms of volume, a tremendous part of this tradition has its repository in the Roman Catholic Church. Most of the great theologians of the early church wrote in Greek, but they were soon joined by the Latin speakers, and after the time of John of Damascus in the seventh century, virtually all of the major works of theology were written in Latin. Even Luther wrote in Latin, and the most important work in the Reformed tradition, John Calvin's *Institutes,* was written in Latin, although Calvin later produced a translation in his mother-tongue of French. Although Luther, Calvin, and the other great thinkers of the Reformation era and later criticized Roman Catholic doctrine and various interpretations of the Fathers and doctors of the church, they nevertheless learned much from them and relied extensively on them. It is impossible to reject Roman Catholicism and the teachers it honors *(tout court)*—for example, Augustine, Anselm, and Aquinas—without also discarding much of the rich treasure of Christian faith, morals, and life.

When dealing with a rich intellectual and spiritual history that fills hundreds of volumes and contains much that is vital—as well as a significant amount of material that is superfluous, misleading, or actually harmful—it requires virtually infinite patience, care, and attention to detail to sort the wheat from the chaff, the wholesome from the harmful. The authors have approached this monumental task with energy and patience. They have done so, as they confess, not merely out of intellectual curiosity, or in order to present a more perfect and complete presentation of the fundamental core of the Christian faith, but because the hour demands and the Lord requires that we who name his name and claim his allegiance devote ourselves primarily to proclaiming him and defending his cause and his people, rather than wrangling among ourselves.

It is vitally important for those who love and worship the same sovereign Lord, Catholic and Protestant, to stand together against the forces of unbelief and moral evil that beset us on every side. In order to be able to do this, however, it is important for us to understand the foundational things that we have in common, as well as to identify the irreducible differences that remain, and to be able to assign these differences a proper place on a scale that ranges from matters of taste and style in worship to basic doctrines on which the gospel and salvation may depend. Professor(s) Geisler and MacKenzie, with dedication, delicacy, and skill, have undertaken the monumental task of showing us how to do this. Almost two thousand years of Christian history have produced a vast number of witnesses, testimonies, arguments, polemics, dogmatics, worship styles, spiritual communities, and parachurch organizations, scattered across several major and minor confessions and innumerable denominations. The authors display an encyclopedic knowledge of Christian life and thought through the centuries, and handle it with understanding, sympathy, and clarity.

This volume has the size and comprehensiveness of a reference tool. Issues are handled systematically and with elaborate, detailed footnoting. It would be a shame, however, to treat it merely as a source or tool; those who read it from cover to cover will find it informative, edifying, and stimulating. It will help them to see that while evangelical Protestants and Roman Catholics have and will continue to have differences that cannot be swept under the table, in the words of Cardinal Suenens, "the walls of separation do not reach up to heaven." He that is with us is stronger than those that are against us.

Harold O. J. Brown
Zermatt, Switzerland
Holy Week, 1994

INTRODUCTION

Before Vatican II, Roman Catholics and Protestants had little contact with each other. On the Protestant side, many thought that the Pope was the anti-Christ, that Catholics worshiped Mary, and that even Unitarians were to be preferred to Roman Catholics.

A case in point is that of Paul Blanshard, a well-known Catholic "basher" of a generation ago. Blanshard, author of *American Freedom & Catholic Power,* assured fundamentalists and evangelicals that the Vatican has sinister designs on our freedoms in general and religious liberty in particular. Blanshard was later revealed to be a garden variety secular humanist, and evangelical Christians probably had more spiritual common ground with Fulton J. Sheen, the popular Roman Catholic television preacher, who was a contemporary of Blanshard.

There were, to be sure, similar mistaken notions on the Catholic side. Some regarded Protestants as little better than pagans. We were perceived as ignoring the value of works and disregarding church history prior to the Reformation. The intervening years have seen some changes take place in the perceptions between these two groups. With the coming to the fore of the secularist agenda (e.g., anti-family values, abortion on demand, gay rights), some Catholics and evangelicals have been doing some soul searching and re-evaluation.

The purpose of this book is to examine some of our common spiritual roots and see if we have any theological or moral bridges upon which we both can travel. We will examine similarities and differences in both doctrine and practice. Special attention will be given to the doctrine of salvation by grace. We will also speak to some interesting relationships and alliances that have developed between Catholics and Protestants, and address the issue of whether cooperation or conflict should characterize these unions.

This work will concern itself with traditional Roman Catholicism, which is expressed in the dogmas and authoritative pronouncements of the Roman Catholic Church. We take this approach for two reasons. First, this is the official Catholic position, however much other expressions of Catholicism may deviate from it. Second, evangelicals have less in common with the folk, cultural, or liberal varieties that exist in the Roman Catholic Church (see Appendixes C and D).

This work is divided into three parts. Part One (chaps. 1–8) deals with what Roman Catholics and evangelicals have in common. This contains surprises for many of our evangelical brethren who are unaware of the common core of doctrinal belief that permeates the two systems. Part Two (chaps. 9–16) discusses our differences with Roman Catholic teachings. No attempt has been made to downplay these significant differences on infallibility, Mariology, purgatory, the role of works in salvation, the Apocrypha, transubstantiation, and others. In Part One, we agree. In Part Two, we must agree to disagree with Roman Catholicism. In Part Three, however, we wish to build bridges between mainline evangelicals and Catholics wherever possible. We acknowledge that, as long as Roman Catholics hold as dogma the kinds of things enumerated in Part Two, there is no hope for ecclesiastic union with Catholicism. However, we believe this should not be an unsurpassable obstacle to cooperation on common moral, social, and educational efforts. Rather, in view of the devastating effects of both Western secularism and Eastern mysticism on our culture, the time is overdue for Catholics and Protestants to hang together before we hang separately.

If you are a Catholic, we recommend you read Part One and Part Three of this book first. If you are an evangelical, particularly a conservative one, you should read Part Two first and then Part One and Part Three. This will help maximize the message we wish to convey and eliminate any unnecessary bias before being exposed to the conclusions of the book. If you are neither Catholic nor evangelical, read the book in the order in which it is written. But by all means, from whatever persuasion you may come, we urge you to get the whole message by reading it all!

PART 1

AREAS OF
DOCTRINAL
AGREEMENT

*"One should believe only what has been
held 'always, everywhere and by all.'"*
Vincent of Lerins (died before A.D. 450)

In these chapters we try to put our best foot forward in Roman Catholic and evangelical relations by stressing what we have in common. Some of this will come as a surprise to many evangelicals, particularly those of a more conservative bent, who are used to stressing differences with Roman Catholics. The central thesis of these chapters is that both Catholics and orthodox Protestants have a common creedal and Augustinian doctrinal background. Both groups accept the creeds and confessions and councils of the Christian church of the first five centuries. Both claim Augustine as a mentor.

The doctrinal unity with Roman Catholics includes far more in common than many evangelicals have been wont to admit, including virtually all the so-called Fundamentals, such as the inspiration of the Bible, the virgin birth, the Trinity, the deity of Christ, his substitutionary death, his bodily resurrection, and his second coming. In addition, both Catholics and evangelicals hold to an Augustinian concept of salvation by grace. Our important differences notwithstanding (see Part Two), we believe this is too great a shared doctrinal heritage to ignore.

1

REVELATION

Catholics and evangelicals hold much more in common than is often recognized. In this section we will examine that body of doctrine shared by Roman Catholics and evangelicals.[1] In this endeavor, the following diagram (source unknown) is helpful. We hold in common:

1. Sources used will for the most part be the church fathers and/or Roman Catholic writers. Scripture cited throughout this work, unless otherwise indicated, will be from the *New American Bible*, St. Joseph Edition—with helps (New York: Catholic Book Publishing, 1986). This is a good translation, especially the New Testament, and it provides common ground with Catholics.

The standard reference for articles of faith and morals of the Roman Catholic Church has been Henry Denzinger's *Enchiridion Symbolorum*. The original volume was written in Latin and Greek and has gone through more than thirty editions. It is arranged in chronological order beginning with the Apostolic Creed and covers the Christian creeds, councils, and documents of the Roman pontiffs.

One problem facing the modern scholar is that the indexing of the various documents changes with the more recent editions. In the present work, we will use the following edition and hence all indexing numbers used in the notes will pertain to this edition: Henry Denzinger, *The Sources of Catholic Dogma*, trans. by Roy J. Deferrari from the Thirtieth Edition of Henry Denzinger's *Enchiridion Symbolorum* (St. Louis: B. Herder Book Co., 1957).

In a more recent work, J. Neuner, S.J., and J. Dupuis, S.J., eds., *The Christian Faith: Doctrinal Documents of the Catholic Church*, 5th rev. (New York: Alba House, 1990), the documents have been organized in chronological order under themes for easy reference.

Many traditional Roman Catholics favor a current study Bible that is now in process: *The Navarre Bible*, 2d ed., commentary by the members of the Faculty of Theology of the University of Navarre, Spain (Dublin: Four Courts Press, 1991). This work is presently available in twelve volumes, New Testament only. Scriptural text is from the *Revised Standard Version*, Catholic Edition (RSVCE), and the New Vulgate Version.

The first official catechism since the Council of Trent (A.D. 1545–63) was published in 1994: *Catechism of the Catholic Church: Libreria Editrice Vaticana* (Boston: St. Paul Books and Media, 1994). This new catechism is divided into four major parts: (1) the creed (what the Church believes); (2) the sacraments (what the Church celebrates); (3) the commandments (what the Church lives); and (4) the "Our Father" (what the Church prays). There is an internal cross-referencing system among the paragraphs that makes it simple to find all the passages in the catechism that treat a particular subject.

One Bible

Two Testaments	Old and New
Three Creeds	*Apostles Creed* (c. A.D. 150). Distinguished true believers from those who followed Gnosticism and Marcionism. *Nicene Creed* (A.D. 326). Condemned Arius, who was anti-trinitarian, denying the deity of Christ. *Athanasian Creed* (A.D. 428). Taught the doctrines of the trinity and the incarnation.
Four Councils	*First Nicea* (A.D. 325). Taught that Jesus Christ is the Son of one substance with the Father. *First Constantinople* (A.D. 381). Taught the divinity of the Holy Spirit. *Ephesus* (A.D. 431). Mary is *theotokos:* "bearer of God." *Chalcedon* (A.D. 451). Affirmed that there are two natures in Christ: divine and human.
Five Centuries	From the Apostolic era to the end of the fifth century.

During these early centuries,[2] the church was concerned with the person of Christ, *who he was*. Later they discussed the subject of *what he did*. As a contemporary handbook of the official documents of Roman Catholic doctrine puts it: "The early professions of faith result, therefore, from the merger of two enunciations, one Trinitarian and one Christological, both of which are based on the New Testament."[3] Concerning later development it adds: "To those primitive data, later creeds have in the course of the centuries added such further precisions as concrete circumstances made necessary to maintain the primitive faith."[4]

All cults and heresies depart theologically from doctrine which developed in this time period. For both Catholics and Protestants revelation is central to the understanding of Christianity. As a traditional Roman Catholic catechism states, "The object is to introduce the child even at an early age to the Bible itself where we have the Person and message of Our Lord Jesus Christ

2. Valuable yet concise treatments of the doctrines that emerged from this formative period of church history can be found in J. N. D. Kelly, *Early Christian Doctrines*, rev. (San Francisco: Harper Collins, 1978), and Gerald Bray, *Creeds, Councils and Christ* (Downers Grove, Ill.: InterVarsity Press, 1984).

3. Neuner and Dupuis, *Christian Faith*, p. 1. A current volume which includes contributions from evangelical scholars such as R. C. Sproul and Walter Martin says about the importance of the creeds: "Protestants, Roman Catholics, and Orthodox Christians have managed to embrace the creeds, even though they have diverse views on many issues; schismatics and heretics have denied them." For evangelicals, the Scripture remains the only infallible authority for arriving at theological orthodoxy, but the creeds are important in that "they have formed the commonly, historically accepted summary of the Scripture's teaching on the most fundamental points." "Appendix A: The Ecumenical Creeds," in *The Agony of Deceit: What Some TV Preachers Are Really Teaching*, ed. Michael Horton (Chicago: Moody Press, 1990), p. 253.

4. Ibid., p. 2.

presented by the Holy Spirit Himself" *(The Baltimore Catechism).*[5] Concerning the uniqueness of Christian revelation, one theologian added, "Throughout man's history and of all the religions in the world, the Judeo-Christian religion is the only one with a basis *in history.*"[6]

Although many Catholic theologians see tradition as a second source of revelation (see chap. 10), Roman Catholic scholar Louis Bouyer notes that "according to both the Council of Trent and *Vaticanum* Scripture *alone* can be said to have God as its author."[7] In this we can see a basic accord concerning the central place that revelation has in Christian theological formation.[8] We will now move directly to the Scriptures.

THE BIBLICAL DATA

That the Scriptures are central to an understanding of God's revelation is a truth stated throughout the documents of the Roman Catholic Church. While Catholics and Protestants differ over whether the apocryphal (Deutero-canonical) books belong in the Old Testament (see chap. 9), there is unanimous agreement on all the sixty-six books of the Bible. The First Vatican Council held that the Roman Catholic Church, "relying on the belief of the apostles, holds that the books of both the Old and New Testament in their entirety, . . . are sacred and canonical because, having been written under the inspiration of the Holy Spirit . . . they have God as their author."[9]

Augustine reflects the mind of the church—from the Apostolic era through the Medieval period—when he said that truth is that "which God wanted put into the sacred writings for the sake of our salvation."[10] Also, the First Vatican Council states: "It is to be ascribed to this divine revelation that such truths among things divine . . . can . . . be known by everyone."[11] The apostle Paul put it this way: "All scripture is inspired by God and is useful for teaching, for refutation, for correction, and for training in righteousness, so that one who belongs to God may be competent, equipped for every good work" (2 Tim. 3:16–17).

---

5. Official Revised Edition, No. 1, explained by Rev. Bennet Kelley, C.P. (New York: Catholic Book Publication, 1964), p. 4.

6. Ignace de la Potterie, "Exegesis: Truth as Event," *30 Days,* no. 2, 1993, p. 64.

7. Gustaf Aulén, *Reformation and Catholicity* (Edinburgh and London: Oliver and Boyd, 1962), p. 21.

8. Differences in how Roman Catholics and evangelicals view the extent of the canon and problems concerning authority will be addressed in chaps. 9 and 10.

9. Augustine, *Dogmatic Constitution on the Catholic Faith,* quoted in Denzinger, *Sources of Catholic Dogma,* no. 1787, p. 444.

10. Cf. St. Augustine, *"Gen ad Litt"* 2.9.20: PL 34, 270–71.

11. Denzinger, *Sources of Catholic Dogma,* 1786, chap. 2, "Revelation."

Concerning the purpose of Holy Writ: "All Sacred Scripture is but one book, and that one book is Christ, because all divine Scripture speaks of Christ, and all divine Scripture is fulfilled in Christ."[12]

THE OLD TESTAMENT

In the Old Testament God laid the foundation for salvation. First, a covenant was established with Abraham, declaring, "To your descendants I give this land, from the Wadi of Egypt to the Great River [the Euphrates]" (Gen. 15:18). In obedience to God, Moses "took the blood and sprinkled it on the people, saying, 'This is the blood of the covenant which the Lord has made with you in accordance with all these words of his'" (Exod. 24:8). Therefore, "The plan of salvation, foretold by the sacred authors, recounted and explained by them, is found as the true word of God in the books of the Old Testament."[13]

Although the New Covenant was established through Christ, the church has always recognized that the gospel finds its roots in the Old Testament. Augustine caught this sense when he declared that "The New is in the Old concealed, the Old is in the New revealed."[14]

THE NEW TESTAMENT

For both Catholics and Protestants it is in the New Testament that God's plan of salvation enters its final phase. In the prologue of his Gospel, John writes: "And the Word became flesh and made his dwelling among us, and we saw his glory, the glory as of the Father's only Son, full of grace and truth" (John 1:14).[15] This occurred in "the fullness of time" mentioned by Paul in Galatians 4:4. The writer of the Book of Hebrews describes the salvific transition as follows: "In times past, God spoke in partial and various ways to our ancestors through the prophets; in these last days, he spoke to us through a son, whom he made heir of all things and through whom he created the universe" (Heb. 1:1–2).

In the Gospels Christ is revealed as the Son of God and the one who will usher in the kingdom of God. His nature is revealed in particular to the apostles, and Jesus in turn reveals the Father: "All things have been handed over to me by my Father. No one knows who the Son is except the Father, and

---

12. "Hugh of St. Victor," *De arca Noe* 2.8: PL 176, 642; quoted in *Catechism 1994*, p. 37.
13. Walter M. Abbott, S.J., ed., *The Documents of Vatican II* (New York: Guild Press, 1966), p. 122.
14. *Quest in Hept* 2.73: PL 34, 623.
15. The NAB study note on the above verse has the following: "*Flesh:* the whole person, used probably against docetistic tendencies (cf. 1 John 4:2; 2 John 7). *Made his dwelling:* literally, pitched his tent/tabernacle."

who the Father is except the Son and anyone to whom the Son wishes to reveal him" (Luke 10:22). The Second Vatican Council states: "The Christian dispensation, therefore, being the new and definitive covenant, will never pass away, and we now await no new public revelation before the glorious manifestation of our Lord Jesus Christ (cf. 1 Tim. 6:14; Titus 2:13)."[16]

In the Pauline Epistles, the emphasis is on the "mystery" of Christ. Paul considers the truth of salvation in Christ, although previously hidden, as having now been revealed by God (Eph. 3:5). "Now to him who can strengthen you, according to my gospel and the proclamation of Jesus Christ, according to the revelation of the mystery kept secret for long ages" (Rom. 16:25). It is worth noting in passing that Jesus' gospel and Paul's are one and the same.[17] Paul also treats the last stage of this revelation, the "Day of the Lord," the parousia, "when he comes to be glorified among his holy ones and to be marveled at on that day among all who have believed, for our testimony to you was believed" (2 Thess. 1:10).[18]

THEOLOGICAL DEVELOPMENT

If God had not taken the initiative through general and special revelation we would have known nothing about him. "In his goodness and wisdom, God chose to reveal himself and make known to us the hidden designs of his will."[19] This revelation comes to us on two levels, first in the world of creation which he brought into existence through the direction of the Word, that is, Christ. The apostle John informs us that "In the beginning was the Word, and the Word was with God, and the Word was God. He was in the beginning with God. All things came to be through him" (John 1:1–3). This God of creation has revealed himself in nature so that all can "clearly" see. Those who refuse are "without excuse" (Rom. 1:19–20). Indeed, God has written his law upon the hearts of all people (Rom. 2:12–15). Second, God speaks to us through the Bible. This has been termed "special" revelation.

GENERAL REVELATION

General revelation is prior to special revelation, and does not consist of verbal communication. The psalmist said, "The heavens declare the glory of

16. Ibid., Dogmatic Constitution *Dei Verbum*, "Revelation," 4.

17. See G. G. Machen, *The Origin of Paul's Religion* (1925; reprint, Grand Rapids: Eerdmans, 1976).

18. Cf. "Concept of Revelation," *New Catholic Encyclopedia*, vol. 12 (New York: McGraw-Hill, 1967), pp. 438–39.

19. John A. Hardon, S.J., *The Catholic Catechism* (New York: Image Books, 1966), p. 30.

God, and the firmament proclaims his handiwork. Day pours out the word to day, and night to night imparts knowledge" (Ps. 19:2–3). Concerning general revelation Pius IX states: "But how many, how wonderful, how lucid are the arguments at hand by which reason ought to be thoroughly convinced that Christ's religion is divine."[20]

Primitive Revelation. Roman Catholics also use the concept of "primitive revelation" to identify supernatural truths revealed at the beginning of human history.[21] The "passing down" of this revelation may account for the elements of truth to be found in primitive/non-Christian religions. Thus, these concepts inherent in primitive revelation can serve as pointers to faith.[22]

Natural Law. When humans turn from God's general revelation, in nature and in the human heart, they end in moral disaster. Paul describes it this way: "they became vain in their reasoning, and their senseless minds were darkened. While claiming to be wise, they became fools and exchanged the glory of the immortal God for the likeness of an image of mortal man or of birds or of four-legged animals or of snakes" (Rom. 1:21–23). Paul's somber recital has been graphically demonstrated throughout human history. When the glory of God is ignored idolatry is the result. But there is more: "Therefore, God handed them over to impurity through the lusts of their hearts for the mutual degradation of their bodies. They exchanged the truth of God for a lie and revered and worshiped the creature rather than the creator, who is blessed forever. Amen" (Rom. 1:24–25).

The Bishop of Hippo, an astute observer of the human condition, spoke to this issue. "As St. Augustine was later to explain in his *Confessions,* there is a grim recompense for man's refusal to acknowledge God as his master. God allows a man's spirit to lose mastery over his own body. Lust is the normal consequence of pride."[23] Paul continued to develop this sorry scenario by introducing the doctrine of natural law: "For when the Gentiles who do not have the law by nature observe the prescriptions of the law, they are a law for themselves even though they do not have the law. They show that the demands of *the law are written in their hearts,* while their conscience also bears witness and their conflicting thoughts accuse or even defend them" (Rom. 2:14–15, emphasis added).

In the moral arena, general revelation has been termed "natural law." Thomas Aquinas developed this subject at length. Concerning natural law as a guideline in society, Aquinas taught that "since natural law is common

20. Denzinger, *Sources of Catholic Dogma,* 1638, p. 411, Encyclical Letter, *"Qui Pluribus"* (1846).

21. Ludwig Ott, *Fundamentals of Catholic Dogma* (Rockford, Ill.: Tan Books, 1960), pp. 15f.

22. *New Catholic Encyclopedia,* 12:440.

23. Ibid., p. 31.

to all people, not just believers, it can be used as a basis for civil law in religiously pluralistic societies."[24] In fact, "natural right is contained in the eternal law primarily, and in the natural judicial faculty of human reason secondarily."[25] Natural law is the human participation in eternal law by way of reason. It is "the natural light of reason, by which we discern what is right and wrong." In it is "naught else but the impression on us of divine light."[26] All rational creatures, not just believers, share in natural law. It is the law that is written on human hearts of which Paul speaks in Romans 2:12–15.

For Catholics, as well as many Protestants, natural law is the moral basis from which social issues are addressed. Issues such as abortion, euthanasia, and homosexuality can and are dealt with from the perspective of natural law. One of the authors made a convincing argument against euthanasia to the medical staff of a large hospital, using the natural law concept exclusively.[27] Clarence Thomas invoked the reality of "natural law" in his defense during his contentious confirmation for a seat on the Supreme Court.[28]

A discussion of natural law is the task Pope John Paul II set for himself in his recent encyclical letter to Roman Catholic bishops. *Veritatis Splendor* ("the splendor of Truth") is a finely reasoned thesis offering a restatement of the Church's argument against moral relativism.[29] The encyclical "takes on anthropologists who believe that morality has no meaning outside the culture that defines it." John Paul does not list a number of specific moral rules but rather describes "the universal law of nature that is discoverable by human reason; it exists in all people, regardless of culture, and leads us inevitably to judge actions as right or wrong—whatever their intentions and whether or not they help or harm others."[30]

Natural Theology. It is because of general revelation that the Catholic church believes that a natural theology is possible. Thus, the Council of Vatican I declared that "the beginning and end of all things can be known with certitude by the natural light of human reason from created things" for

---

24. Norman L. Geisler, *Thomas Aquinas: An Evangelical Appraisal* (Grand Rapids: Baker, 1991), pp. 164–70, 174.

25. Aquinas, *Summa Theologiae*, 1a2ae. 71, 6, ad 4.

26. Ibid., 1a2ae. 91, 2.

27. Norman L. Geisler, *"To Die or Not to Die: That Is the Fatal Question,"* paper presented at Naval Hospital, San Diego, Calif. (7 December 1992). Also see Francis Beckwith and Norman L. Geisler, *Matters of Life and Death* (Grand Rapids: Baker, 1991). For a treatment of homosexuality from this perspective, see Harry V. Jaffa, *Homosexuality and the Natural Law* (Montclair: Claremont Institute, 1990).

28. Charles Colson, *The Body* (Dallas: Word, 1992), p. 169.

29. "Encyclical Letter of John Paul II," *The Splendor of Truth: Veritatis Splendor* (Boston: St. Paul Books and Media, 1993). In one week after the original publication the Daughters of St. Paul in San Diego sold 1,200 copies of the encyclical, mostly to lay people.

30. James Q. Wilson, "'Calvin and Hobbes' and the Pope's Case for Morality," *The San Diego Union-Tribune* (29 November 1993).

"the invisible things of him, from the creation of the world, are clearly seen, being understood by the things that are made" (Rom. 1:20).[31] Vatican II added that "God, who creates and conserves all things by his Word (cf. John 1:3), provides men with constant evidence of himself in created realities (cf. Rom. 1:19–20)."[32] It is on the basis of this general revelation of God available to all men that Aquinas built his natural theology with proofs for the existence of God.[33]

Natural theology examines what human reason can know about God apart from special revelation. It is therefore to be contrasted with "revealed theology." The principal distinctions were established in the Middle Ages by scholasticism.[34] Both traditional Roman Catholics and conservative Protestants agree that general revelation is insufficient to lead one to a saving knowledge of the gospel. The entrance of sin into God's creation has prevented humans from adequately grasping our desperate spiritual condition. While the *imago Dei* is not *erased*, it is *effaced*. For Aquinas, although the knowledge *that* God exists can be demonstrated by reason (general revelation), belief *in* God only comes through special/supernatural revelation.[35]

The Nature and Value of General Revelation. The apostle Paul spelled out the nature of general revelation in Romans 1, insisting that it was both clear and rendered all human beings, even those with the aid of special revelation, without excuse.

> The wrath of God is indeed being revealed from heaven against every impiety and wickedness of those who suppress the truth by their wickedness. For what can be known about God *is evident to them*, because *God made it evident to them*. Ever since the creation of the world, his invisible attributes of eternal power and divinity *have been able to be understood and perceived* in what he has made. As a result, *they have no excuse;* for although *they knew God* they did not accord him glory as God or give him thanks (Rom. 1:18–20, emphasis added).

Even though it is limited, general revelation is not valueless. The general revelation of God forms the background for his message to us contained in sacred Scripture. Paul used general revelation to good effect when he preached to Epicurean and Stoic philosophers at the Areopagus in Athens. Since his address clearly shows the purpose of general revelation and also the transition to special revelation, we reproduce the sermon in its entirety.

31. Denzinger, *Sources of Catholic Dogma*, 1785. Vatican I, "Dogmatic Constitution Concerning the Catholic Faith," p. 443.

32. *Vatican Council II*, vol. 1, p. 751.

33. See Geisler, *Thomas Aquinas*, chap. 9.

34. F. L. Cross, ed., *The Oxford Dictionary of the Christian Church*, rev. (Oxford: Oxford University Press, 1983), p. 956.

35. Geisler, *Thomas Aquinas*, pp. 37–38, 43–49.

Then Paul stood up at the Areopagus and said: You Athenians, I see that in every respect you are very religious. For as I walked around looking carefully at your shrines, I even discovered an altar inscripted, "To an Unknown God." What therefore you unknowingly worship, I proclaim to you. The God who made the world and all that is in it, the Lord of heaven and earth, does not dwell in sanctuaries made by human hands, nor is he served by human hands because he needs anything. Rather it is he who gives to everyone life and breath and everything. He made from one the whole human race to dwell on the entire surface of the earth, and he fixed the ordered seasons and the boundaries of their regions, so that people might seek God, even perhaps grope for him and find him, though indeed he is not far from any one of us. For "In him we live and move and have our being," as even some of your poets have said, "For we too are his offspring." Since therefore we are the offspring of God, we ought not to think that the divinity is like an image fashioned from gold, silver, or stone by human art and imagination. God has overlooked the times of ignorance, but now he demands that all people everywhere repent because he has established a day on which he will "judge the world with justice" through a man he has appointed, and he has provided confirmation for all by raising him from the dead (Acts 17:22–31).

Clearly Paul believed that one could reason with unbelievers on the basis of general revelation because it can provide an opening for a more complete presentation of truth emanating from special revelation. This has been termed "pre-evangelism" by the late Francis Schaeffer.[36]

SPECIAL REVELATION

In spite of his emphasis on natural theology, even Aquinas argued that special revelation is made necessary because of the limitations of the human mind and the sinfulness springing from the human will. Aquinas asserted emphatically that "human reason is very deficient in things concerning God. A sign of this is that philosophers, in their inquiry into human affairs by natural investigation, have fallen into many errors, and have disagreed among themselves." Consequently, "in order that men might have knowledge of God, free of doubt and uncertainty, it was necessary for divine truths to be delivered to them by way of faith, being told to them as it were, by God Himself Who cannot lie."[37]

The grace of special revelation is needed to overcome the effects of sin on human reason. Aquinas concluded that "if for something to be in our power means that we can do it without the help of grace, then we are bound to many

---

36. See also Norman L. Geisler and Ron Brooks, *When Skeptics Ask* (Wheaton: Victor, 1990), pp. 9–10.

37. Aquinas, *Summa Theologiae*, 2a2ae. 2, 4.

things that are not within our power without healing grace—for example to love God or neighbor." Further, "the same is true of believing in the articles of faith. But with the help of grace we do have this power. As Augustine says, to whomever this help is given by God it is given in mercy; to whomever it is denied, it is denied in justice, namely because of previous sin, even if only original sin."[38] However, Aquinas did not believe that sin completely destroyed people's rational ability. Rather, he insisted that "sin cannot destroy man's rationality altogether, for then he would no longer be capable of sin."[39]

Vatican II, in its *Dogmatic Constitution on Divine Revelation,* concludes that "It pleased God, in his goodness and wisdom, to reveal himself and to make known the mystery of his will (cf. Eph. 1:9)." Further, "wishing to open up the way to heavenly salvation, he manifested himself to our first parents from the very beginning. After the fall, he buoyed them up with the hope of salvation, by promising redemption (cf. Gen. 3:15); and he has never ceased to take care of the human race. For he wishes to give eternal life to all those who seek salvation by patience in well-doing (cf. Rom. 2:6–7)."[40]

The Council also stated that "By divine Revelation God wished to manifest and communicate both himself and the eternal decrees of his will concerning the salvation of mankind."[41] Concerning the Church's attitude toward the Scriptures, "The Church has always venerated the divine Scriptures." As to the need for Christians to read the Bible, the Council affirmed that "access to sacred Scripture ought to be open wide to the Christian faithful."[42] Therefore, "all clerics, particularly priests of Christ and others who, as deacons or catechists, are officially engaged in the ministry of the Word, should immerse themselves in the Scriptures by constant sacred reading and diligent study."[43] In the same context, Jerome is quoted as saying: "Ignorance of the Scriptures is ignorance of Christ."[44] So official Roman Catholicism seems to take seriously the presence of special revelation in the form of Holy Scripture. The study and preaching of the Bible are mandatory, not optional.

In the first part of this chapter we have identified spiritual roots of revelation in the Old and New Testaments. We now turn to some concepts that flow from a theological understanding of special revelation.

The Progressive Nature of Revelation. Special revelation is revelation about the history of redemption. It has for its purpose the redemption of hu-

---

38. Ibid., 2a2ae. 2, 6, ad 1.
39. Ibid., 1a2ae. 85, 2.
40. Austin Flannery, O.P., *Vatican Collection: Vatican Council II*, vol. 1, rev. (North Port: Costello Publishing, 1992), pp. 750–51.
41. Ibid., p. 752.
42. Ibid., p. 762.
43. Ibid., p. 764.
44. Jerome, *Commentary in Isais*, Prol: PL 24, 17.

manity. It renews, illumines, and inclines the disposition to that which is good. It fills with holy affections and finally prepares us to partake of the beatific vision (blessed vision of God in heaven).

Such revelation is clearly progressive in nature. During biblical times new redemptive truths appeared that cast new light on previous ones. Finally they stand out, fully exposed, in the New Testament. In discussing the development of dogma, Catholic theologian Ludwig Ott says that "in the communication of the Truths of Revelation to humanity, a substantial growth took place in human history until Revelation reached its apogee and conclusion in Christ (cf. Heb. 1:1)."[45] In the same context, he quotes Gregory the Great: "With the progress of the times, the knowledge of the spiritual Fathers increased; for, in the Science of God, Moses was more instructed than Abraham, the Prophets more than Moses, the Apostles more than the Prophets."[46]

One can also speak of stages of revelation. Aquinas divided sacred history into three great periods—before the Mosaic law, under the law, and under grace—and united them with the revelations given to Abraham, Moses, and the apostles respectively.[47]

The Authoritative Nature of Revelation. "Concerning the authority of the Scriptures," Augustine asserted, "the authority of these books has come down to us from the Apostles . . . [and] claims the submission of every faithful and pious mind."[48] Aquinas, Augustine's medieval successor, also believed that "we are bound to believe all the contents of Sacred Scripture."[49] The Bible is as authoritative as the voice of God because it is the Word of God. For what the sacred authors affirmed, God affirms. The Scriptures are, therefore, as infallible and inerrant as is God.

The Inerrant Nature of Revelation. The twentieth century has seen in Christendom the rise of theologies which have attacked the integrity and authoritativeness of the Scriptures. Various approaches have been taken: (1) The Bible is inerrant in what it *teaches,* not necessarily in everything it *says,* and (2) The Bible is inerrant on matters of *faith and morals,* but perhaps faulty on issues of *history and science.* Traditional Roman Catholics have happily avoided these dangerous deviations. Augustine said, "it seems to me that most disastrous consequences must follow upon our believing that *anything* false is found in the sacred books."[50] Elsewhere he adds, "If we are perplexed by an apparent contradiction in Scripture, it is not allowable to say,

---

45. Ott, *Fundamentals of Catholic Dogma*, pp. 6–7.
46. Ibid., p. 7. (In Ezechielem lib. 2, hom. 4, 12.)
47. Cited by *New Catholic Encyclopedia* from vol. 12, ST 2a2ae, 174.6, p. 443.
48. *Against Faustus* 11.5; quoted in Norman L. Geisler, *Decide for Yourself* (Grand Rapids: Zondervan, 1982), p. 34.
49. Aquinas, *Summa Theologiae* 1.61, ibid., p. 38.
50. *Letters* 23.3.3, ibid., p. 36. Emphasis added.

the author of this book is mistaken; but either the manuscript is faulty, or the translation is wrong, or you have misunderstood."[51] Aquinas backs up his theological predecessor, contending that "it is heretical to say that any falsehood whatever is contained either in the gospels or in any canonical Scripture."[52]

Moving to the current situation, a contemporary Roman Catholic Scripture scholar affirms the Bishop of Hippo and the "Doctor Anglicus" (Thomas Aquinas): Inspiration rules out any sort of error in the Bible whatsoever. Thus Pope Leo XIII, in his Encyclical *Providentissimus Deus,* wrote that since God is the author, "It follows that they who think any error is contained in the authentic passages of the Sacred Books surely either pervert the Catholic notion of divine inspiration, or make God Himself the source of error."[53]

The Council of Vatican I proclaimed the inerrancy of the Scriptures, saying, "they contain revelation without error . . . because having been written by the inspiration of the Holy Spirit they have God as their author."[54] Leo XIII affirmed that "it would be entirely wrong either to confine inspiration only to some parts of Scripture, or to concede that the sacred author himself has erred."[55] Vatican II added that, "since, therefore, all that the inspired authors, or sacred writers, affirm should be regarded as affirmed by the Holy Spirit, we must acknowledge that the books of Scripture, firmly, faithfully and without error, teach that the truth which God, for the sake of our salvation, wished to see confided to the sacred Scriptures."[56] More liberal Catholic theologians see a caveat in the phrase "for the sake of our salvation," arguing that inerrancy covers only salvific truths, but this is contrary to the whole of the Catholic tradition up to modern times. All agree, however, that inspiration and inerrancy are limited to the meaning the sacred authors "intended to express and did in fact express, through the medium of contemporary literary forms." For "rightly to understand what the sacred author wanted to affirm in his work, due attention must be paid both to the customary and characteristic patterns of perception, speech and narrative which prevailed at the age of the sacred writer, and to the conventions which the people of his time followed in their dealing with one another."[57]

Public vs. Private Revelation. The last topic to be addressed in this section is the matter of "public" vs. "private" revelation. Concerning the former,

---

51. *Against Faustus* 11.5, ibid., p. 37.
52. *Job 13*, lect. 1, Geisler, *Thomas Aquinas,* p. 47.
53. William G. Most, *Free from All Error* (Libertyville: Prow Books, 1985), p. 37.
54. Denzinger, *Sources of Catholic Dogma,* 1787, "The Source of Revelation," p. 444.
55. Ibid., 1950, Encyclical, *"Providentissimus Deus"* (1893), p. 492.
56. *Documents of Vatican II,* "On Revelation," p. 757.
57. Ibid., pp. 757–58.

"St. Thomas holds that prophetic revelation, insofar as it is ordered to doctrine, ceased with the Apostles."[58] Private revelation differs from public revelation in that "whatever God has communicated since apostolic times to privileged souls can add nothing to the deposit of Christian faith."[59] Further, "Throughout the ages, there have been so-called private revelations, some of which have been recognized by the authority of the church. They do not belong, however, to the deposit of faith."[60] Differences between Roman Catholics and evangelicals over the relationship between public and private revelation, and also Scripture and tradition, will be addressed in chapter 10.

THE CHURCH FATHERS AND SCRIPTURE

We have mentioned Augustine and Aquinas and examined their approach to Scripture. Many lesser church leaders also held God's word written in highest esteem.

The Patristic Period. The *Didache* (c. A.D. 70), "The Teaching of the Lord through the Twelve Apostles," is an early church manual on morals and practices. It instructs the church to test the authenticity of teachers and leaders by comparing their words with sacred Scripture. Clement of Rome (A.D. 30–100) exhorted believers to "look carefully into the Scriptures, which are the true utterances of the Holy Spirit."[61]

Justin Martyr (A.D. 100–165) published his *First Apology* and addressed it to Emperor Antoninus Pius. It was a defense of Christianity and in it he gave an account of a regular worship service and the place of prominence given to the Scriptures: "And on the day called Sunday, all who live in cities or in the country gather together in one place, and the memoirs of the apostles or the writings of the prophets are read."[62] Irenaeus (c. A.D. 130–200) declared that "the Scriptures are indeed perfect, since they were spoken by the Word of God (Christ) and His Spirit."[63]

Clement of Alexandria (A.D. 150–215) called the Bible the "infallible criterion of faith," noting that "God is the cause of all good things; but of some primarily, as of the Old and the New Testaments; and of others by consequence, as philosophy."[64] Tertullian (A.D. 160–225) insisted that "we are united. . . . Divine Scripture has made us concorporate; the very letters are

---

58. *New Catholic Encyclopedia*, 12:444.

59. Ibid. Also see Most, *Free from All Error*, p. 2.

60. *Catechism 1994*, no. 67, p. 23.

61. *The First Epistle of Clement to the Corinthians*, p. 45; quoted in Geisler, *Decide for Yourself*, p. 24.

62. Chapter LXVII in *Ante-Nicene Fathers*, vol. 7, p. 378; quoted in Stott, *Between Two Worlds*, pp. 18–19.

63. *Against Heresies* 2.28.2; quoted in Geisler, *Decide for Yourself*, p. 25.

64. *Stomata* 5.5, ibid., p. 31.

our glue."[65] Pope Gelasius (d. A.D. 496), in a decree attributed to him, addressed the nature of Scripture: "The line of thought is clear. Holy Writ, in the proper sense, ensures the basis of the Church, being dependent on Jesus Himself."[66] Indeed: "The clearest token of the prestige enjoyed by [Scripture] is the fact that almost the entire theological effort of the Fathers, whether their aims were polemical or constructive, was expended upon what amounted to the exposition of the Bible. Further, it was everywhere taken for granted that, for any doctrine to win acceptance, it had first to establish its Scriptural basis."[67]

The Medieval Period. John Scotus Erigena (c. A.D. 810–877) affirmed that "in everything the authority of Sacred Scripture is to be followed."[68] The following prayer also indicates Erigena's devotion to Scripture: "O Lord Jesus, no other reward, no other blessedness, no other joy do I ask than a pure understanding, free of mistakes, of thy words which were inspired by the Holy Spirit."[69] Rupert of Deutz (c. A.D. 1075–1129) taught that "Whatever may be arrived at, or concluded from arguments, outside that of Holy Scripture . . . does in no way belong to the praise and confession of almighty God. . . . Whatever may be arrived at outside of the rule of the Holy Scriptures, no body can lawfully demand from a Catholic."[70] Anselm (A.D. 1033–1109) declared that "the God-man himself originates the New Testament and approves the Old. And, as we must acknowledge him to be true, so no one can dissent from anything contained in these books."[71]

CONCLUSION

In the examination of the topic of revelation, we have covered the thinking of the church from the Apostolic Era through the Middle Ages. We have seen the honor and devotion that the early and later church fathers extended to sacred Scripture. Both Catholics and Protestants share this important tradition. On this subject, Donald G. Bloesch notes that "For the most part both the patristic fathers and the medieval theologians before the fourteenth century taught that the Bible is the unique and sole source of revelation."[72]

65. *On Modesty* 5, ibid., p. 27.

66. George H. Tavard, *Holy Writ or Holy Church* (New York: Harper and Brothers, 1959), p. 7.

67. Kelly, *Early Christian Doctrine,* p. 46.

68. *De Divina Natura,* bk. l, ch. 64; PL, 122, 509; quoted in ibid., p. 12.

69. Ibid., bk. 5; PL, 122, 1010, pp. 12, 13.

70. *De Omnipotentia Dei,* 27; PL, 170, 477–78, ibid., p. 13.

71. Anselm, *Cur Deus Homo* 22, in *St. Anselm: Basic Writings,* trans. S. W. Deane (La Salle, Ill.: Open Court Publishing, 1962), p. 288.

72. *Essentials of Evangelical Theology,* vol. 1 (New York: Harper & Row, 1978), p. 57. Also, see Tavard, *Holy Writ or Holy Church,* pp. 22f.

Bloesch continues: "The priority of Scripture over tradition was clearly enunciated by Thomas Aquinas: 'Arguments from Scripture are used properly and carry necessity in matters of faith; arguments from other doctors of the Church are proper, but carry only probability; for our faith is based on the revelation given to the apostles and prophets who wrote the canonical books of the Scriptures and not on revelation that could have been made to other doctors.'"[73]

Concerning *sola Scriptura*, at least in the material sense, there is more unanimity than one would expect. Of course, Roman Catholics deny the formal sufficiency of Scripture, insisting on the need for the infallible teaching magisterium of the Church (see chap. 11). Regarding this doctrine which was to become the "linchpin" of the Reformation, Harold O. J. Brown writes: "The principle that Scripture alone has the final authority in matters of faith and morals is an old one in Christendom, one that has never really been repudiated, *not even by the Roman Church*."[74] Even some great Catholic theologians, such as Aquinas, can be cited in support of this position: "we believe the successors of the apostles and prophets *only in so far as they tell us those things which the apostles and prophets have left in their writings*."[75]

As for the basis for Christian faith in Scripture, a modern Roman Catholic work emphasizes "that faith is not a leap into the dark but has an unshakable foundation."[76] Of course the question arises as to the relationship between the Scriptures and the church. This will be addressed in chapter 10.

In conclusion, concerning the goal of revelation official Roman Catholicism states that "By revealing himself God wishes to make them [humankind] capable of responding to him, and knowing him, and of loving him far beyond their own natural capacity."[77] Supernatural revelation is necessary to fulfill man's supernatural end.

73. Aquinas, *Summa Theologiae* I, 1.8.

74. *Heresies: The Image of Christ in the Mirror of Heresy and Orthodoxy from the Apostles to the Present* (Grand Rapids: Baker, 1984), p. 308, italics added.

75. Aquinas, *De veritate* XIV, 10, ad 11, emphasis added.

76. Neuner and Dupuis, *Christian Faith*, p. 62. Comment on Pope John Paul II, *Catechesi Tradendae*, 16 October 1979.

77. *Catechism 1994*, no. 52, p. 19.

2

GOD

Catholics and evangelicals hold the same basic view of God. From the very earliest formulations of the faith Christians confessed the belief "in the Father almighty,—and in Jesus Christ, our Savior;—and in the Holy Spirit."[1] Other forms of this Apostolic Creed read, "I believe in God the Father almighty creator of heaven and earth and in Jesus Christ, His only son, our Lord."[2] The Eastern form of this creed was even more explicit, confessing "We believe in one God the Father Almighty. The creator of heaven and earth and of all things visible and invisible and in one Lord Jesus Christ the only begotten Son of God."[3] It soon became necessary to make explicit the trinitarian implications of the Christian confession. The Creed of the Council of Toledo (A.D. 400) declared: "We believe in one true God, Father, and Son and Holy Spirit, maker of the visible and the invisible, by whom were created all things in heaven and on earth. This God alone and this Trinity alone is of divine name [divine substance]." Further, "this Trinity, though distinct in persons, is one substance, virtue, power, majesty indivisible, not different."[4] Later, in the Athanasian Creed, more attributes of God emerged, such as "eternal," "uncreated," "immense," "omnipotent," and undivided in substance.[5]

DEFINITION OF GOD

From a religious perspective two affirmations can be made concerning God: he is and he may be known. That God *exists* is a statement of faith. That God

---

1. Denzinger, *Sources of Catholic Dogma*, 1, "The most ancient form of the Apostolic Creed," p. 3.
2. Ibid., 6, p. 7.
3. Ibid., 9, p. 8.
4. Ibid., 19, p. 13.
5. Ibid., 39, p. 15.

may be *known* is a statement of experience. The following definition of God is from *The New Catholic Encyclopedia*, with which orthodox Protestants have no difficulty:

> [God is] The Supreme Being, Pure Act, First Cause of all, provident conserver and governor of the universe; the Absolute—infinite, eternal, immutable, intelligent, omniscient, all-powerful, and free; the Creator, to whom creatures owe homage, respect, and obedience; the Sovereign Good, diffusive of all goodness, toward which everything tends as to its ultimate final cause; the supernatural source of revelation; the Godhead composed of three Divine Persons in one divine nature—Father, Son and Holy Spirit.[6]

GOD IN PRIMITIVE RELIGIONS

Since Darwin, it has been fashionable to understand primitive religious concepts in an evolutionary sense: humanity has moved from an initial polytheism toward monotheism. This theory, however, has encountered difficulties. For many primitive peoples believe in a "high god" in addition to a number of lesser gods. "Such a high god appears early in the creation myths of such people as the Australian aborigines and primitive Indians."[7] We find creation accounts contained in religious ideas coming from Egypt, Mesopotamia, and Samaria. These myths have parallels in early Hellenistic cultures. So this once popular, nineteenth-century evolutionary view has given way to recent critiques.[8] Further, this evolutionary view of the development of the concept of God is contrary to Scripture (cf. Rom. 1:18–23). Also, it overlooks the early monotheistic views of God in other cultures. The Ebla Archives which contain hundreds of tablets to patriarchal times (no. 239), for example, tell of a monotheistic God who created the world from nothing: "Lord of heaven and earth: the earth was not, you created it, the light of day was not, you created it, the morning light you had not [yet] made exist."[9]

According to Catholic scholars, Greek philosophers introduced a higher concept of God. In Plato, the role of the "supreme being" became more prominent. "Certainly the overall impression given by Plato's writings is an atmosphere of great reverence for the divine, an exalted notion of it, and a strong desire for assimilation to it in some intimate personal relationship. To be more precise than this would be to state explicitly what Plato merely hints at implicitly."[10] To be sure, Plato's Demiurgos (God) falls short of Judeo-Chris-

6. "God," *New Catholic Encyclopedia*, 6:535.
7. Ibid.
8. See Lewis M. Hopfe, *Religions of the World* (New York: Macmillan, 1991), p. 10.
9. See Eugene H. Merrill, "Ebla and Biblical Historical Inerrancy," *Bibliotheca Sacra* (October–December 1983): 302–21.
10. *New Catholic Encyclopedia*, 6:537.

tian monotheism, since for him God is limited and is subject to the Good which is beyond him. Nonetheless, Plato transcended traditional polytheisms.

Aristotle developed arguments for the existence of God from motion or change in the world. The move from potentiality to actuality can only be under the influence of an actualizer (cause). Hence, there must have been a First Cause. So for Aristotle, God is the "Uncaused Cause."[11] Later Augustine, using Platonic terms,[12] and Aquinas, using Aristotelian concepts, would develop arguments for the existence of one supreme God.[13] Of course, whatever the philosophical language used to express their convictions, Catholic theologians believe that their concept of God is based on His self-revelation in Scripture. Two tasks faced the church concerning the concept of God: "First among these is the right conception of God as compared to the distorted ideas found in the world surrounding the Christian fold." The second problem adheres to the concept of the Holy Trinity: "The Christian concept of God unfolds itself in the mission and revelation of the Son and the Spirit. . . . Together with the Father they are truly divine. . . . This mystery became from the beginning the object of theological reflection."[14] God, through his mercy, "willed both to reveal himself to man and give him the grace of being able to welcome this revelation in faith."[15] Now we turn to "salvation history" as expressed in the Judeo-Christian Scriptures—the Old and New Testaments.

THE CONCEPT OF GOD IN SCRIPTURE

THE OLD TESTAMENT

The Judeo-Christian concept of the person and work of God is derived from the Old Testament. We addressed the "progressive" quality of revelation in chapter 1. The concept of God gradually unfolded in much the same way. During its history more and more was revealed to Israel about God's nature and work.

It is interesting to note that nowhere in the Scripture is a formal philosophical argument presented as to God's existence. Rather, Old Testament believers were content simply with the evidence God presented of himself in

11. See Aristotle, *Metaphysics* 12.8.1073b–74a, in *The Basic Works of Aristotle,* trans. Richard McKeon (New York: Random House, 1941), pp. 882–83.

12. See Augustine, *On Free Will* 2.6, in *The Fathers of the Church,* ed. Ludwig Schopp et al. (New York: CIMA, 1948–54).

13. See Aquinas, *Summa Theologiae* 1.2.3.

14. Neuner and Dupuis, *The Christian Faith,* p. 103.

15. *Catechism of the Catholic Church: Libreria Editrice Vaticana* (Boston: St. Paul Books and Media, 1994), p. 16.

nature and by supernatural messages and events (cf. Exod. 4:1–9). "The heavens declare the glory of God; the sky proclaims its builder's craft" (Ps. 19:1). Even the great agnostic philosopher, Immanuel Kant, after offering criticisms of all the traditional proofs for the existence of God, confessed: "Two things fill the mind with ever new and increasing admiration and awe, the oftener and more steadily we reflect on them: the starry heavens above me and the moral law within me."[16]

Genesis reveals God to be the creator of heaven and earth and also the sustainer of his work, expecting obedience from the man and woman whom he made. God dealt with our physical ancestors, Adam and Eve, face-to-face (Gen. 2:16–19; 3:8). With Abraham (known as the father of the faithful, Gal. 3:7–8), God began to deal with humanity in a new way. The Lord said to Abraham:

> Go forth from the land of your kinsfolk and from your father's house to a land that I will show you. "I will make of you a great nation, and will bless you; I will make your name great, so that you will be a blessing. I will bless those who bless you and curse those who curse you. All the communities of the earth shall find blessing in you" (Gen. 12:1–3).

God had become the God of Abraham, and would later be the God of Isaac and Jacob (Exod. 6:3).

In the Mosaic Period, God installed Moses as the leader of Israel's religion. Yahweh caused their liberation from Egypt, entered into a covenant with them, and demanded that they renounce the pagan deities that surrounded them and worship him alone (cf. Exod. 4; 12; 20). Although Moses and the leaders in Israel who followed him recognized Yahweh to be the supreme Deity, this knowledge was to come more slowly to the average Israelite. The fertility gods of the Canaanites were very attractive to the popular mind. However, in the seventh century B.C., when Jerusalem became the official center of worship, Israelite religion became more defined and centralized. The people came to realize more fully the great Shema of monotheistic Judaism: "Hear, O Israel! The LORD is our God, the LORD alone! Therefore, you shall love the LORD, your God, with all your heart, and with all your soul, and with all your strength" (Deut. 6:4–5). "Mosaic monotheism implied that God was one, unique, holy, pleased at up-rightness, and deeply interested in Israel. But exactly where did Yahweh stand in relation to other gods and other nations? Was there more to His justice than vindictiveness? Much light was to be diffused upon these and other points during the prophetic period."[17]

---

16. Immanuel Kant, *Critique of Practical Reason*, trans. Lewis White Beck (New York: The Bobbs–Merrill Company, 1956), p. 166.
17. *New Catholic Encyclopedia*, 6:539.

In the Prophetic Period, from the ninth to the sixth century B.C., the concept of God became even clearer. Elijah (9th century), Amos (8th century), Isaiah and Hosea (8th century) all stressed God's majesty and dominion over all nations and his steadfast love for his particular people. Isaiah asks: "To whom can you liken God? With what equal can you confront him? . . . He sits enthroned above the vault of the earth, and its inhabitants are like grasshoppers. . . . Do you not know or have you not heard? The Lᴏʀᴅ is the eternal God, creator of the ends of the earth" (Isa. 40:18, 22, 28).

Concerning the goal of the prophets, the *New Catholic Encyclopedia* says the prophetic mission "did not consist in the formulation of a new belief, but in the restoration and understanding of traditional belief. The Prophets insisted on the moral qualities of God, but aside from this offered little that was original."[18]

Israel's experience during the exile and the destruction of Jerusalem (including the temple) proved to be the final victory in the battle against idolatry. "Its political autonomy ended, Israel's mind turned inward."[19] The Jewish community as a whole has avoided idolatry since that time.

All attempts by proponents of the "evolutionary hypothesis" to identify Israel's concept of God with the alleged monotheism of such cults as Akhnaton (c. B.C. 1364–47) and Zoroaster (c. B.C. 500) have failed. "In its monotheism, Israel was utterly unique."[20]

Tʜᴇ Nᴇᴡ Tᴇsᴛᴀᴍᴇɴᴛ

Israel's monotheism is carried over into the New Testament. When speaking of God, the New Testament writers use Greek words for "God" or for "Lord" (Hb: *Yahweh*). Jesus often refers to God as his Father: "My Father is at work until now, so I am at work" (John 5:17). Our Lord also encourages his followers to address God as Father: in Matthew 6 the phrases "your heavenly Father," "your Father," and "Our Father" occur ten times. This term is used sparingly in the Old Testament and is narrowly applied: God as Father of David's line (2 Sam. 7:14) and God as Father of orphans (Ps. 68:6) are two examples.

In the midst of his prayer in the garden prior to his betrayal, Jesus addresses the Father saying, "Abba, Father, all things are possible to you" (Mark 14:36). Concerning Jesus' use of "Abba," the *New American Bible* notes: "An Aramaic term, here also translated by Mark, Jesus' special way of addressing God was filial intimacy. The word 'abba' seems not to have been used in earlier or contemporaneous Jewish sources to address God

18. Ibid., p. 540.
19. Ibid.
20. Ibid.

without some qualifier. Cf. Rom. 8:15; Gal. 4:6 for other occurrences of the Aramaic word in the Greek New Testament."[21]

Although the concept of "God as love" is found throughout the Old Testament (e.g., Exod. 20:6; Lev. 19:18), Jesus takes it to new heights. And even though God's concern was that "all the communities of the earth" (Gen. 12:3) would be blessed through them, in the Old Testament the focus of his love was toward Israel. In the New Testament God's love is extended to all: "God so loved the world that he gave his only Son, so that everyone who believes in him might not perish but might have eternal life" (John 3:16). Thus, Jesus commanded his disciples to "make disciples of all nations" (Matt. 28:19). Further, the New Testament provides "the supreme illustration of God's love, the Incarnation of the Word, His Passion, death, and Resurrection, are to be matched, on man's part, by love of neighbor."[22] In view of this love, we are to love others as he has loved us (cf. John 15:13; 2 Cor. 5:14–15).

BIBLICAL NAMES FOR GOD

"The oldest name used for the deity by almost all Semitic peoples was 'El' (perhaps from a root meaning strong). The *El* of Israel stood alone, supreme, without consort."[23] Pagan cultures that surrounded Israel depicted *El* as the Father of the gods, lord of heaven, the force of nature, and a local deity. In Scripture, however, God is the everlasting *El*. For "Abraham planted a tamarisk at Beersheba, and there he invoked by name the LORD, God the Eternal" (Gen. 21:33). He is also the living *El*, since "This is how you will know that there is a living God in your midst" (Josh. 3:10).

Elohim, as a name for God, is an often-recurring plural form in the Old Testament (Gen. 1:1). The plural usage should not be understood as indicating a polytheistic element in early Israelite theology but as expressing the intensity, power, and majesty of God.

El Elyon means "Most High God." This idea is developed in Abraham's encounter with Melchizedek (Gen. 14:18–22). *El Shaddai* has been translated "the Mighty One." This title comes out of God's discussion with Moses concerning his original covenant with Abraham, Isaac, and Jacob (Exod. 6:3). God was also called *Adonai* which connotes the idea of "King" (Num. 23:21; Deut. 33:5) and "Lord" (Ps. 110:1).

By the Mosaic period, the name most frequently used for God was *Yahweh*, which Catholic scholars have traditionally taken to mean "He who is" or the self-existent One, the source of all other being (Exod. 3:14–15; cf. John 8:58). Commenting on Exodus 3:14, the *New American Bible* says, "It

---

21. Footnote on Mark 14:36, *New American Bible*.
22. *New Catholic Encyclopedia*, 6:561.
23. Ibid., p. 538.

is commonly explained in reference to God as the absolute and necessary Being. It may be understood of God as the Source of all created being." When Moses asked God what his name was he replied: "I AM WHO I AM." Concerning Christian names for God, "The New Testament takes over the Old Testament designations for God as found in the Septuagint, and makes the appellation Father, which occurs only in a few places in the Old Testament, the centre of the Christian Revelation."[24]

THEOLOGICAL DEVELOPMENT OF THE CONCEPT OF GOD

Catholic as well as evangelical understanding of God is derived from both general and special revelation. General revelation provides a natural knowledge of God available to all persons.

NATURAL KNOWLEDGE OF GOD

The existence of a "natural" knowledge of God has already been discussed in chapter 1 under general revelation. Concerning this possibility, Catholic theologian Ludwig Ott says, "God, our Creator and Lord, can be known with certainty, by the natural light of reason from created things (De fide)."[25] Scripture states that God may be known naturally in the following ways: from nature (cf. Rom. 1:20); from conscience (cf. Rom. 2:14ff.); and from history (cf. Acts 17:28).

The Fathers, drawing from the aforementioned concepts and their commensurate scriptural proofs, stated the possibility of a "natural" understanding of God. Tertullian said, "O testimony of the soul, which is by nature Christian."[26] Theophilus of Antioch writes: "God has called everything into existence from nothing, so that His greatness might be known and understood through His works. Just as the soul in man is not seen, as it is invisible, but is known through the movement of the body, so God cannot be seen with human eyes; but He is observed and known through providence and His works."[27]

Because of our creaturely limitations, we cannot know God "directly" but by "analogical cognition"; that is, we know God by way of analogy, we

---

24. Ott, *Fundamentals of Catholic Dogma*, p. 24. Also see *New Catholic Encyclopedia*, 6:538–39.

25. Ibid., p. 13. In Catholic theology, *"de fide"* means that the proposition expressed is an article of the Catholic faith.

26. *Apology* 17; quoted in ibid., p. 14.

27. *Ad Autolycom* 1:4–5.

reason from created things to him. "There is a relation of analogy between the creature and the Creator which is founded on the fact that the creature is necessarily made to the likeness of the Creator. This analogy is the basis of all natural knowledge of God."[28] Although we may come to some understanding of God through the above method, it must be stated that this knowledge is, at best, imperfect. Augustine says: "More true than our speech about God is our thinking of Him, and more true than our thinking is His Being."[29]

Finally, concerning the function of the natural understanding of God, Aquinas held "that while man can by his reason alone know *that* God is . . . , man's reason cannot grasp *what* He is."[30] A natural knowledge of God is useful to point us in the right direction. To enter the kingdom of God, however, and experience its fullness and blessings, we are in need of the Scriptures which can give us "wisdom for salvation" (2 Tim. 3:15).

GOD AS TRINITY

While it can be known from general revelation that God exists and that he is one, the knowledge of God as a Trinity is known only through special revelation. Although not itself a biblical term, the term *Trinity* was used by the early church to describe the God who is one in essence, eternally revealed in three Persons: Father, Son, and Holy Spirit. As Oxford scholar and Anglican cleric Alister McGrath writes:

> The doctrine of the Trinity is basically an attempt to bring together the incredible richness of the Christian understanding of God. It is the distillation of the kaleidoscopic Christian experience of God in the light of its scriptural foundations. The scriptural witness to and Christian experience of God came first, and reflection on it came later.[31]

Christianity has always understood the Trinity as one of the most profound doctrines of the Christian faith. It comes to us through the vehicle of special revelation—the teaching is above reason. The early church stressed the mystery and also the necessity of the Trinity. John Damascene said: "It is known and adored in Faith (the Trinity), not by investigating, examining and proving. . . . You have to believe that God is in three Persons. How sublime is this above all questions. For God is inconceivable."[32]

28. Ott, *Fundamentals of Catholic Dogma*, p. 19.
29. Augustine, *De Trinitate*, VII 4.7; quoted in ibid., p. 20.
30. *New Catholic Encyclopedia*, 6:541.
31. Alister McGrath, *Understanding the Trinity* (Grand Rapids: Zondervan, 1990), p. 116.
32. As cited by Ott, *Fundamentals of Catholic Dogma*, p. 74.

The 11th Council of Toledo (A.D. 675) was a local council, yet it produced a confession of faith that reflected the thinking of the patristic theology of the West. Concerning the Trinity, it states: "We confess and believe that the holy and ineffable Trinity, Father, Son and Holy Spirit, is one God by nature, of one substance, of one nature as also of one majesty and power."[33] Concerning the Father, "we profess that the Father is not begotten, nor created, but unbegotten."[34] The Son "was born, but not made, from the substance of the Father, without beginning, before all ages. . . ."[35] As to the Holy Spirit, "we also believe that the Holy Spirit, the third person in the Trinity, is God, one and equal with God the Father and the Son."[36]

Many feel that the understanding of the Trinity involves a mathematical mystery: how to conceive of one equaling three. This is a misunderstanding. Roman Catholic lay apologist Frank Sheed spoke to this point: "There is no question of arithmetic involved. We are not saying three persons in one person, or three natures in one nature; we are saying three persons in one nature."[37] Others have noted that the wrong kind of arithmetic is involved, for we do not *add* but *multiply* the Persons of the Trinity. God is not $1+1+1=3$. He is $1 \times 1 \times 1 = 1^3$. He is one God in essence who is eternally expressed in three different persons simultaneously. We see, then, that the question becomes one of understanding the meaning of the terms *nature* and *person*. Sheed notes that "Nature answers the question *what* we are; person answers the question *who* we are."[38] Thus in God there is one What (essence) and three Whos (persons).[39]

We mentioned earlier in this chapter that although the Old Testament portrays God's unity (Deut. 6:4), we also find intimations of plurality (Ps. 110:1; Prov. 30:4; Isa. 63:7–10; Zech. 1:12). In the New Testament, trinitarian evidence is overwhelming. Jesus proclaims his own deity (John 8:58) and accepts worship (Matt. 16:16; John 20:28). The Holy Spirit or Comforter is also a member of the Trinity (Matt. 28:20; John 14–16; Acts 5:3–4; 2 Cor. 13:13). All three Persons of the Godhead are mentioned in many passages (cf. Matt. 3:15–17; Eph. 1:3, 13; 1 Thess. 1:1–5; 1 Pet. 1:2).

Deviations from the Catholic concept of the Trinity are numerous, and both Catholics and Protestants consider these heresies. Several have arisen concerning the nature of God. One such heresy, *tritheism,* dates back to the

---

33. Denzinger, *Sources of Catholic Dogma*, 275, p. 106.
34. Ibid.
35. Ibid., 276, p. 106.
36. Ibid., 277, p. 107.
37. Frank Sheed, *Theology and Sanity*, enlarged ed. (Huntington: Our Sunday Visitor, 1978), p. 52.
38. Ibid.
39. See Norman L. Geisler and William Watkins, "The Incarnation and Logic: Their Compatibility Defended," *Trinity Journal* (1985).

sixth century, and asserts that there are three equal, closely related Gods. *Modalism* is the heresy that postulates one God who plays three different roles but is not three co-eternal, co-equal persons existing simultaneously in one nature. The Trinity is not three gods but one. Likewise, the Trinity is not one person in God but three persons in one God.

The difference between essence and office is crucial to understanding the Trinity. The three Persons are equal in essence, but not in function. The Son is subordinate to the Father and receives his generation from him. The Athanasian Creed states: "The Son is from the Father alone not made not created but generated."[40] The Holy Spirit is also equal to the Father in essence but proceeds from the Father and the Son. Eastern Orthodoxy teaches that the Holy Spirit proceeds from the Father alone, and this disagreement was one cause of the East/West rupture of A.D. 1054 (see Appendix A).

As some of the heresies involved in the nature of the Godhead have direct implications concerning the Person and nature of Christ, we will address them in chapter 4 which deals with Christology.[41] The evangelical can take comfort that, as John W. Montgomery states, "the Roman Catholic Church and the Orthodox Eastern Churches have never ceased to stand uncompromisingly for the Trinitarian core of the Christian faith."[42]

GOD AS CREATOR

Christianity (along with orthodox Judaism) believes that God created *ex nihilio,* "out of nothing." Roman Catholic dogma states: "All that exists outside God was, in its whole substance, produced out of nothing by God *(De fide)."*[43] Scriptural support for this doctrine is provided in the first verse of the Bible: "In the beginning, when God created the heavens and the earth" (Gen. 1:1). While the Hebrew word for "create" *(bara)* does not always mean to make something from nothing (cf. Ps. 104:30), nonetheless, in the context of God's initial production of the entire universe it certainly takes on this meaning. The statement "heavens and earth" indicates the whole universe, all extra-divine things. A contemporary Roman Catholic scholar states: "That God alone created the world is an article of the Catholic faith, found in all the Christian creeds and solemnly taught by several ecumenical councils, notably, the Fourth Lateran and First Vatican. The basis in revelation for the doctrine spans the whole of Scripture, from Genesis to the writings of St. John."[44]

40. Denzinger (D) 39; quoted in Ott, *Fundamentals of Catholic Dogma,* p. 62.
41. For a comprehensive treatment of the many concepts that were pronounced heretical by the early church, see ibid., pp. 50–75.
42. John W. Montgomery, *Ecumenicity, Evangelicals and Rome* (Grand Rapids: Zondervan, 1969), p. 20.
43. Ott, *Fundamentals of Catholic Dogma,* p. 79.
44. Hardon, *Catholic Catechism,* p. 70.

The church fathers testify that God, motivated by his goodness, created the world for his glorification: "We are because He is good,"[45] and "God does not act for His own profit, but only for His own Goodness."[46] It is important to note that what God created was "good." The Council of Florence held that "there is no nature bad in itself, as all nature in so far as it is nature, is good."[47] This statement was directed against the Manichaean heresy, and would have later theological ramifications when the church grappled with the question of the nature of sin.

God not only created but also preserves and sustains his creation. We have proof of this from the Scriptures: "My Father is at work until now, so I am at work" (John 5:17). Concerning Christ in this work of preservation, the writer of Hebrews states that he "sustains all things by his mighty word" (Heb. 1:3). Augustine, commenting on John 5:17, said, "Let us therefore believe that God works constantly, so that all created things would perish, if His working were withdrawn."[48] Paul declared not only that "all things were created through him [Christ]" but also that "in him all things hold together" (Col. 1:16–17). Further, "Though the work of creation is attributed to the Father in particular, it is equally a truth of faith that the Father, Son, and Holy Spirit together are the one, indivisible principle of creation."[49]

A word must be said about the method by which God created. Difficulties have arisen from apparent contradictions between the results of modern science and the creation narrative in Genesis. Although much latitude is given concerning the *how* of creation, official Roman Catholic teaching on these matters holds that "The first three Chapters of Genesis contains narratives of real events . . . , no myths, no mere allegories or symbols of religious truths, no legends."[50] Further, they insist that, whatever natural (evolutionary) process may have been utilized by God to produce the first human body, God directly created Adam's soul and, indeed, creates every rational human soul in their mother's womb from the very inception of life. As Ott puts it, "Every individual soul was immediately created out of nothing by God."[51] Although earlier Catholic theologians, like Aquinas, believed that this happened some weeks after conception, in the light of modern science, Catholic theology "holds that the creation and infusion of the spiritual soul coincides with the moment of conception."[52]

45. Augustine, *De doctr. christ.* I 32, 35; quoted in Ott, *Fundamentals of Catholic Dogma*, p. 81.

46. Aquinas, *Summa Theologiae* I 44, 4 ad I, ibid.

47. *Decretum pro Jacobitis* (1441), ibid., p. 84.

48. *De Gen. Ad Litt.* [Literal Commentary on Genesis] V20, 40., ibid., p. 87.

49. *Catechism* 1994, no. 316, p. 84.

50. D.2122, ibid., p. 92. This position on the inerrancy of Holy Writ would prove to be the downfall of Pierre Teilhard de Chardin and his "new age" understanding of creation.

51. Ott, *Fundamentals of Catholic Dogma*, p. 100.

52. Ibid.

THE ATTRIBUTES OF GOD

Ludwig Ott affirms that "the attributes or properties of God are perfections which, according to our analogical mode of thinking, proceed from the metaphysical substance of God and belong to it."[53] Other Catholic theologians have defined the attributes "as an absolutely simple perfection that exists in God necessarily and formally, and that, according to man's imperfect mode of knowing, either constitutes the essence of the Divine Being or is deduced from this essence."[54]

Protestants and Catholics agree that the classical attributes of God fall into two broad categories: incommunicable and communicable. The former are those only God possesses and the latter are those he can communicate to his creatures (2 Pet. 1:4). The former are sometimes called metaphysical attributes and the latter, non-metaphysical (moral) attributes.

GOD'S INCOMMUNICABLE (METAPHYSICAL) ATTRIBUTES

God Is Self-Existent. The formal constituent of the divine essence is God's self-existence (or "aseity"). Of this attribute "it is commonly taught that God is Being itself, subsistent by itself, and that this aseity *(aseitas),* or 'by-itself-ness,' is a constitutive perfection of God."[55] God is the "I AM" who exists in and of himself. He is totally uncaused and independent in his existence. As Aquinas put it, God is pure Actuality with no potentiality for non-existence. He is a necessary being who cannot not be. It is important to note that this does not mean that God is *self*-caused. A self-caused being is impossible, since something cannot be ontologically prior to itself as a cause is to its effect. Rather, God is *un*caused. He is the uncaused Cause of all else that exists.

God Is Infinite. God is not finite or limited. He is "in every way without limit."[56] He has no boundaries or restrictions on his being. He has no limiting potential. As Aquinas put it, God is unlimited and unique unless conjoined with passive potency (potentiality). God has active potency (powers) but he has no unactualized potentials. He is fully actual and, as such, has no limitations whatsoever on his being.

God Is Simple. God is undivided in his being; he has no parts. "It [God's nature] is called simple because it is that which it has, except that which is said of one Person in relation to the Other."[57] Thus, the only plurality God has is relational, not essential.

---

53. Ibid., p. 28.
54. *New Catholic Encyclopedia,* 6:557.
55. Ibid., p. 558.
56. Gregory of Nyssa, *Quod non sint tres dii:* PG 45, 129.
57. Augustine, *De civ. Dei [City of God]* XI 10, I.

God Possesses Unicity. God is absolute one in his nature, not many. "The true God is one alone."[58] God is not only indivisible in himself (simplicity) but he is unmultiplied in terms of others. There is only one of him (Deut. 6:4).

God Is Immutable. God is by nature unchangeable. "I, the LORD, do not change" (Mal. 3:6). Even though the universe will change, being rolled up like a garment, God is "the same" (Heb. 1:12). There is not even the slightest "alteration" in God's nature. He is "immutable" (Heb. 6:18).

God Is Eternal. God is above and beyond all time. "The eternity of God is His Essence itself."[59] He has no "before" or "after" in his being. He is the "first and the last" (Isa. 41:4; cf. Rev. 1:8). God is "before all ages."

God Is Omnipresent. God is everywhere present at all times and in the fullness of his being. In view of this, the psalmist declared, "Where can I hide from your spirit? From your presence, where can I flee?" As the Cause of all being, Aquinas understood God to be intrinsically present in everything as long as it exists.[60]

God Is Omniscient. "All things are naked and open to his eyes [cf. Heb. 4:13], even those things that will happen through the free actions of creatures."[61]

God Is Omnipotent. God has all power. He is the "almighty" (cf. Job 6:14; Rev. 1:8; 19:6). He can do all things that are not intrinsically impossible or contradictory. For example, God cannot make a square circle. Thus when Jesus said, "for God all things are possible" (Matt. 19:26), he meant all *non-contradictory* things.

GOD'S COMMUNICABLE (MORAL) ATTRIBUTES

There are also attributes that God can give to others. These include moral qualities, such as truth, goodness, justice, and mercy.

God Is Perfect. God is the summation of all perfection, both metaphysically and morally, lacking in absolutely nothing. "The Divine Essence is perfect, (it) is in no way deficient in goodness."[62] He is supremely good, the ultimate in all that is of value. "God is infinite in every perfection."[63]

God Is Truthful. Truth is the correspondence of thought and thing. It is the adequation of word and reality. God is absolutely truthful. He can neither deceive nor be deceived.[64] As Holy Writ declares, "it was impossible for God to lie" (Heb. 6:18; cf. Titus 1:2).

---

58. The Fourth Lateran Council (1215), D. 428; cf. 1782.
59. Augustine, *Enarr. in Ps.* 101, 2, 10.
60. Aquinas, *Summa Theologiae* I 8, 1.
61. Vatican I, D. 1784; cf. D. 3017.
62. John of Damascus, *De fide orth.* I, 5.
63. Vatican I, D. 1782.
64. Augustine, *Enarr. in Ps.* 123, 2. Cited in Ott, *Fundamentals of Catholic Dogma*, p. 34.

God Is Benevolent. Indeed, God is all-benevolent or omni-benevolent. He is essentially good. That is, God is desirable for his own sake. He is the ultimate End desired, wittingly or unwittingly, by all rational creatures. He has ultimate intrinsic value within himself.

God Is Holy. "Holy, holy, holy" is what the angels sing (Isa. 6:3; cf. Rev. 4:8). "You shall be holy, because I am holy" (Lev. 11:45), said the Lord. Holiness (Hb: *kadosh*), according to Ott, expresses not only "God's sublimity over all worldliness (objective holiness) but also his sublimity over all sinfulness (subjective holiness)."[65]

God Is Just. God possesses ultimate justice. He will give to all their due. As Paul taught, "There is no partiality with God" (Rom. 2:11) for he "will give to each according to his deeds" (Rev. 22:12).

God Is Merciful. The psalmist declares, "The LORD is good to all and compassionate toward all his works" (Ps. 145:9).[66] To Moses God said, "I, the LORD, your God am a jealous God . . . bestowing mercy down to the thousandth generation" (Exod. 20:5). The psalmists repeatedly proclaimed that God's mercy endures forever (e.g., Ps. 136).

TESTIMONY OF THE EARLY FATHERS ABOUT GOD'S NATURE

The following statements from the early church fathers concerning God and his nature are helpful.[67] They form a basis not only for the basic Catholic concept of God but also for the evangelical heritage rooted in them. The essential attributes of the Triune God emerge from their collective wisdom.

IGNATIUS OF ANTIOCH (C. A.D. 35–107)

There is one God, who manifested himself through his Son, Jesus Christ, who is his Word proceeding from silence, and who was in all respects pleasing to him that sent him.[68]

IRENAEUS (C. A.D. 130–200)

For the Church, although dispersed throughout the whole world even to the ends of the earth, has received from the apostles and from their disciples the faith in one God, Father Almighty, the creator of heaven and earth and sea and all that is in them; and in one Jesus Christ, the Son of God.[69] Nor is he moved by anyone; rather, freely and by his Word he made all things. For he

---

65. Ibid., p. 35.
66. Material on the aforementioned attributes taken from ibid., pp. 30–49.
67. The quotes are taken from "The Fathers Know Best," *This Rock,* December 1992, pp. 26–27. Their original source was Jurgens, *Faith of the Early Church.*
68. Ignatius, *Letter to the Magnesians* 8.1 (c. A.D. 110), ibid.
69. Irenaeus, *Against Heresies* 1.10.1 (inter A.D. 180–199), ibid.

alone is God, he alone is Lord, he alone is creator, he alone is Father, he alone contains all and commands all to exist.[70]

TERTULLIAN (C. A.D. 160–230)

The object of our worship is the one God, who, by the word of his command, by the reason of his plan, and by the strength of his power, has brought forth from nothing for the glory of his majesty this whole construction of elements, bodies and spirits; whence also the Greeks have bestowed upon the world the name "cosmos."[71] There is only one God, and none other besides him, the creator of the world who brought forth all things out of nothing through his Word, first of all sent forth.[72]

EPIPHANIUS (C. A.D. 315–403)

We believe in one God, the Father almighty, maker of all things, both visible and invisible.[73]

FULGENTIUS (A.D. 468–533)

True religion consists in the service of the one true God. For it is truth itself that there is one God; and just as besides the one truth, there is no other truth, so too, besides the one true God there is no other true God. For the one truth itself is naturally one true divinity. And thus one cannot speak truthfully of two true gods, because it is not possible for the truth itself, naturally one, to be divided.[74]

AUGUSTINE (A.D. 354–430)

By the time of Augustine the Christian doctrine of God had reached full bloom. His book *On The Trinity* is a classic expression of the doctrine of God. It has been definitive for orthodox expression of this truth since his time. To summarize, Augustine spoke of "All those Catholic expounders of the divine Scriptures, both of Old and New, whom I have been able to read, who have written before me concerning the Trinity who is God." These, he said, have taught according to the Scriptures:

The Father, and the Son, and the holy Spirit intimate a divine unity of one and the same substance in an indivisible equality; and therefore that they are not three Gods, but one God: although the Father hath begotten the Son, and so He who is the Father is not the Son; and the Son is begotten by the Father,

70. Ibid., 2.1.1.
71. Tertullian, *Apology* 17.1 (A.D. 197).
72. Tertullian, *The Demurrer Against the Heretics* 13.1 (c. A.D. 200).
73. Epiphanius, *The Man Well-Anchored* 120 (A.D. 374).
74. Fulgentius, *Letter to Donatus* 8.10 (post A.D. 512–ante A.D. 527).

and so He who is the Son is not the Father; and the Holy Spirit is neither the Father nor the Son, but only the Spirit of the Father and of the Son, Himself also co-equal with the Father and the Son, and pertaining to the unity of the Trinity.[75]

CONCLUSION

We have attempted in this chapter to reveal the common Catholic and evangelical understanding of the nature of God. God is one in his eternal and unchangeable essence, yet three Persons. The divine essence is common to the three Persons, they are not separable. Also, the trinitarian mystery is revealed in the ministry and work of the Son and the Spirit for human salvation: "the entire work of salvation is unfolded . . . with the conclusion, borrowed from St. Cyprian, that 'the Church is clearly a people whose unity derives from that of the Father, the Son, and the Holy Spirit.'"[76]

These beliefs are shared equally by both Catholics and evangelical Protestants. The essentials of Christian orthodoxy are reflected in the Vatican Council II:

> The dignity of man rests above all on the fact that he is called to communion with God. The invitation to converse with God is addressed to man as soon as he comes into being. For if man exists it is because God has created him through love, and through love continues to hold him in existence.[77]

Moreover, concerning the relationship between the doctrine of God and the reality of salvation: "It is true that there has always been a more or less extensive optimism that one could know or have a notion of God apart from and independent of the Christian faith." Further, "One might be convinced of the existence of God, but God is God in reality only when one can say of him that God is salvation."[78]

Contemporary Roman Catholic philosopher Peter Kreeft says:

> the creed does not speak of a God, only of God. The God of Abraham, Isaac, and Jacob, the God of Jesus Christ, is the absolute, the Alpha and Omega, the

75. Augustine, *On the Trinity* 1.4.7; quoted in Schaff, *Nicene and Post-Nicene Fathers,* 3:20.

76. Neuner and Dupuis, *Christian Faith,* pp. 120–21.

77. *Vatican Collection,* vol. 2, ibid., p. 918.

78. Otto Hermann Pesch, *The God Question in Thomas Aquinas and Martin Luther,* trans. Gottfried G. Krodel (Philadelphia: Fortress, 1972), p. 30. Pesch concludes concerning the "God question" that "if one looks, first of all, at the material from a purely statistical point of view, he will not be able to state that any specific discrepancy exists between Luther and Thomas on the doctrine of God" (p. 17).

point and pinnacle of all reality. He is not an it or object; his name is I AM, the absolute subject. He is not our object, we are his. He is the I and we are his Thou, not vice versa.[79]

Evangelicals can stand together with Roman Catholics on this most basic doctrine of the Christian faith. As the *New Catholic Encyclopedia* states: "Since man's knowledge of God is that of the beginning and end of all creation, it is a knowledge that makes possible and reasonable the order of morality and its laws in life. This must include the idea of a personal and provident God, a God to be worshipped and obeyed."[80]

79. Peter Kreeft, *Fundamentals of the Faith* (San Francisco: Ignatius Press, 1988), p. 118.
80. *New Catholic Encyclopedia*, 6:562.

3

Human Beings

Introduction

Catholics and evangelicals share a common view of the origin, nature, and fall of human beings. Both believe God is the creator, human beings are made in his image and likeness, and human beings are immortal. From this common heritage many other things follow, including our duty to God our creator and to our fellow creatures and to God's creation. The Roman Catholic Church teaches: "As to man, it is the sacred duty of the Church throughout the ages to defend his [humanity's] spiritual nature and his destiny reaching beyond the material processes of nature."[1]

The Definition of Humanity

Classically, the term "man" meant humanity in general, females as well as males. The etymology of the term "man" in various languages is interesting. The Sanskrit root means "to think." The Greek understanding of the word applies "to one that looks up (i.e., to the gods) from below; if so, this would express both a distinction and a certain kinship between man and God."[2] The Latin *homo* is derived from *humus*, which seems to indicate a certain kinship with the earth. These concepts, stemming from various language groups, give us insights into the basic "stuff" of humanity. Humans have an essential connection to the earth but also, by virtue of their minds, possess a transcendency that marks them as different from the nature that surrounds them and orients them toward God.

1. Neuner and Dupuis, *Christian Faith*, p. 126.
2. *New Catholic Encyclopedia*, 9:125.

THE ORIGIN OF HUMANITY

Catholic dogma teaches that "the First Man was created by God *(De fide)*."[3] The Fourth Lateran and Vatican I Councils made this statement forcefully. In 1968 Pope Paul VI stated: "We believe in one God, Father, Son and Holy Spirit, creator of things visible . . . and things invisible . . . and creator in each man of his spiritual and immortal soul."[4] (The question of humanity's connection to the materialistic theory of evolution will be considered below.) The Book of Genesis (which literally means "in the beginning") contains two complimentary accounts of the creation of the first human being. The first account relates human creation to creation in general: "Then God said: 'Let us make man in our image, after our likeness. Let them have dominion over the fish of the sea, the birds of the air, and the cattle, and over all the wild animals and all the creatures that crawl on the ground'" (Gen. 1:26). Further, "The first man was not only created good, but was also established in friendship with his Creator and in harmony with himself and with the creation around him, in a state that would be surpassed only by the glory of the new creation in Christ."[5]

The *New American Bible* says, "Man is here presented as the climax of God's creative activity; he resembles God primarily because of the dominion God gives him over the rest of creation."[6] Another Catholic authority comments: "According to the immediate, literal sense, God created the body of the first man immediately out of inorganic material ('from the slime of the earth') and vivified it by breathing into it a spiritual soul."[7]

Lastly, concerning the origin of man, the Roman Catholic Church teaches that there is a basic unity of the human race: "The whole human race stems from one single human pair."[8] This, of course, is based in the New Testament teaching about the origin of the human race in one man, Adam. Paul, addressing the Greek philosophers at the Areopagus, argued that God "made from one the whole human race to dwell on the entire surface of the earth" (Acts 17:26). Furthermore, since all people die and inherit original sin because of Adam's sin, all must be organically connected with Adam, their head (cf. Rom. 5:12).

THE NATURE OF HUMANITY

We human beings, upon reflection, understand ourselves as dualities. We have bodies and physical characteristics that resemble creatures around us,

---

3. Ott, *Fundamentals of Catholic Dogma*, p. 94.
4. Neuner and Dupuis, *Christian Faith*, p. 22.
5. *Catechism of the Catholic Church: Libreria Editrice Vaticana* (Boston: St. Paul Books and Media, 1994), no. 374, p. 95.
6. Study note on Gen. 1:26.
7. Ott, *Fundamentals of Catholic Dogma*, p. 95.
8. Ibid., p. 96.

but the transcendent element in our nature indicates a duality in our being. The early Greek thinkers drew their idea of humanity from mythology (activity on the part of gods) and also from a rational examination of the existing world.

Aristotle held that humans were supreme in the creation and consisted of two parts, a material body and a "spiritual soul" that constitutes the driving force within the whole person. Plato stressed humanity's spiritual nature, asserting that we essentially are souls who merely have bodies. "This explains why the Platonic view appealed more than that of Aristotle to thinkers with a spiritualist orientation, particularly among the early Christians."[9] Augustine, taking his philosophical direction from Plato, tended to elevate the spiritual and down play the physical side of humanity.

In the Middle Ages, scholastic philosophy in general and Aquinas in particular developed a more complete view of humanity. Relying on special revelation and drawing from Aristotelian principles, Aquinas fashioned a more balanced view of human nature as a unity of soul and body but, nonetheless, with a belief that the soul consciously survived death awaiting the resurrection in its body. Thus, Catholics believe that "the body is an essential part of man, and has a positive value. Yet the body exists, not in its own right, but by virtue of the spiritual soul, which is a form in the most real sense and the unique substantial form of the body."[10] That is, "Man consists of two essential parts—material body and a spiritual soul *(De fide)*."[11] Further, "the rational soul is per se the essential form of the body *(De fide)*."[12] Personal immortality presupposes the individuality of the soul. Jesus warned, "Do not be afraid of those who kill the body but cannot kill the soul; rather, be afraid of the one who can destroy both soul and body in Gehenna" (Matt. 10:28).

Concerning the creation of the soul, Roman Catholicism teaches that this occurs at the moment of its unification with the body. In spite of some question on the part of some of the church fathers concerning just when the fetus becomes human, "Modern Christian philosophy generally holds that the creation and infusion of the spiritual soul coincides with the moment of conception."[13] (This position of course has serious implications regarding the Christian attitude toward issues like abortion.)

Summing up the Roman Catholic understanding of the nature of humans, Vatican II stated: "Man, though made of body and soul, is a unity. Through his very bodily condition, he sums up in himself the elements of the material

---

9. *New Catholic Encyclopedia*, 9:125.
10. Ibid.
11. Ott, *Fundamentals of Catholic Dogma*, p. 96.
12. Ibid.
13. Ibid., p. 100; cf. Denzinger, *Sources of Catholic Dogma*, no. 1185.

world. Through him they are thus brought to their highest perfection and can raise their voice in praise freely given to the creator."[14]

BIBLICAL DATA

Like evangelicals, the basic Catholic view of human beings is rooted in Scripture, both Old and New Testaments. From the earliest chapters of the Bible there is a clear picture of the origin, nature, and fall of the human race. There is also a sense of the unity of the human race: "All peoples form a single community; their origin is one, for God made the whole human race to dwell over the entire face of the earth (cf. Acts 17:26)."[15]

OLD TESTAMENT

At first glance (and at first glance only), the two accounts of humanity's origin in Genesis might seem to some to be in conflict. The first declares that humans are made in the image of God (Gen. 1:27). The second account says they are made from "the clay of the ground" into which God breathed life: "the LORD God formed man out of the clay of the ground and blew into his nostrils the breath of life, and so man became a living being" (Gen. 2:7). Upon closer analysis, however, we discover that this second account is a fuller and more developed description of human creation. First, humanity, although the product of a special creation ("made in God's image"), retains a connection with the general creation by virtue of being formed from "the clay of the ground." Second, this account (the whole of chap. 2) indicates that the Garden of Eden was prepared for human habitation and was a literal physical place where they could enjoy fellowship with God and each other.

The second account also details the emergence of the first woman, who was formed from the body of the first man. "So the LORD God cast a deep sleep on the man, and while he was asleep, he took out one of his ribs and closed up its place with flesh. The LORD God then built up into a woman the rib that he had taken from the man" (Gen. 2:21–22). Ott notes that "this account, which is starkly anthropomorphistic, was understood by the generality of the Fathers in the literal sense. . . . According to a decision of the Bible commission, the literal historical sense is to be adhered to in regard to the formation of the first woman out of the first man."[16]

---

14. Austin Flannery, O.P., *Vatican Collection: Vatican Council II*, vol. 2 (North Port: Costello Publishing, 1982), pp. 914–15.

15. Neuner and Dupuis, *Declaration Nostra Aetate* (1965), 424, p. 138.

16. Ott, *Fundamentals of Catholic Dogma*, p. 95.

Men and women alone are made in the image of God (Gen. 1:26–27). Adam alone was given the task of naming the animals around him. Human beings, not animals, enjoy fellowship with God and, in short, are the center of creation. The Old Testament further comments that the creation of humanity was a marvelous event. Job confessed to God: "Your hands have formed me and fashioned me; will you then turn and destroy me?" (Job 10:8–9). As the psalmist said, "Yet you have made them [humans] a little less than a god, crowned them with glory and honor" (Ps. 8:6).

God also set up rules of conduct for his special creation. From the very beginning he was enjoined to obey God's command (Gen. 2:16–17). Later, God's people were given the Ten Commandments (Exod. 20). The Lord told Moses to command the Israelite community: "You shall be holy, because I am holy" (Lev. 11:45). The prophet Micah summed up our duty to God, saying, "You have been told, O man, what is good, and what the LORD requires of you: Only to do the right and to love goodness, and to walk humbly with your God" (Mic. 6:8).

NEW TESTAMENT

The New Testament reaffirms the Old Testament teaching on the origin, nature, and fall of human beings. There are general references to the creation of "all things," including human beings (John 1:3; Col. 1:16; Rev. 4:11). But Jesus referred specifically to the creation of Adam and Eve when he reminded them, "Have you not read that from the beginning the Creator 'made them male and female?'" (Matt. 19:4). Likewise, Paul said, "Adam was first formed, then Eve" (1 Tim. 2:13) and "man did not come from woman, but woman from man" (1 Cor. 11:8).

As to the spiritual nature of human beings, called "soul" or "spirit," the New Testament is clear that there is conscious existence after death. The dying thief was told that his soul would be in paradise that very day (Luke 23:43). Paul said, "We would rather leave the body and go home to the Lord" (2 Cor. 5:8), and "I long to depart this life and be with Christ, [for] that is far better" (Phil. 1:23). John speaks of "the souls of those who had been slaughtered" being in heaven in conscious bliss (Rev. 6:9–11). The word "immortality," as used of human beings, is reserved in the New Testament for humans in their final resurrected state (cf. 1 Cor. 15:53). Nevertheless, the Scriptures are clear that there is a spiritual dimension to human beings that survives death and goes eventually either into the blessing of God's presence or into the conscious suffering of the place called hell (cf. Matt. 25:41; Luke 16:22–31) to await the resurrection of their bodies when Jesus returns (cf. John 5:29; 1 Cor. 15:22–23; Rev. 20:4–5).

Catholics and evangelicals also agree that human beings are fallen. Not only does the New Testament teach the origin and nature of human beings from God; it also affirms that they fell and are in a state of original sin, as Paul declared: "through one person sin entered the world, and through sin, death, and thus death came to all, inasmuch as all sinned" (Rom. 5:12). Thus we are "by nature children of wrath" (Eph. 2:3) and must be born again, since "what is born of flesh is flesh and what is born of spirit is spirit" (John 3:6).

THEOLOGICAL DEVELOPMENT OF THE DOCTRINE OF HUMANITY

The common Catholic-evangelical doctrine of human beings is not only rooted in Scripture; it also finds similar theological expression. Both, for example, believe in original sin.

ORIGINAL SIN

The official Roman Catholic position on original sin is evangelical at the core. It asserts: "If anyone does not confess that the first man, Adam, when he transgressed the commandment of God in paradise, immediately lost the holiness and justice in which he had been constituted, and through the offence of that prevarication incurred the wrath and indignation of God, . . . and that the entire Adam through that offence of prevarication was changed in body and soul for the worse, let him be anathema."[17]

Likewise, the final remedy for this woeful situation is the same as the common evangelical view: "If anyone asserts that this sin of Adam, which in its origin is one, and by propagation, not by imitation, transfused into all, which is in each one something that is his own, is taken away either by the forces of human nature or by a remedy other than the merit of the one mediator, our Lord Jesus Christ . . . let him be anathema."[18]

The Roman Catholic Church teaches that our first parents in the Garden of Eden lost sanctity by their disobedience. God's commandment to them was probationary in nature, and the entire sorry scenario happened in space/time and must not be relegated to the realm of myth or saga. "Since Adam's sin is the basis of the dogma of Original Sin and Redemption the historical accuracy of the account as regards the essential facts may not be impugned."[19] Also, original sin is not to be understood as having been sexual

---

17. *Canons and Decrees of the Council of Trent,* trans. Rev. H. J. Schroeder, O.P. (Rockford, Ill.: Tan Books, 1978), p. 21.
18. Ibid., p. 22.
19. Ott, *Fundamentals of Catholic Dogma,* p. 106.

in nature. It was a sin of disobedience. "The theory that original sin was a sexual sin (Clement of Alexandria, Ambrose) cannot be accepted."[20]

The transgression of Adam and Eve resulted in the loss of sanctifying grace (i.e., the spiritual life of the soul). Further, they became subject to death and the tyranny of the devil. The Catholic church also teaches that Adam's sin and its consequences are transmitted to his descendants by inheritance, not by example, as David lamented, "Indeed, in guilt was I born, and in sin my mother conceived me" (Ps. 51:7).

The central question in the debate between Catholics and Protestants is this: Does grace *perfect* nature (the Roman Catholic position) or does it *change* nature (the Reformed view)? Richard John Neuhaus touches on this issue in his important and provocative book, *The Catholic Movement,* written before he became a Roman Catholic. Drawing the insights of Fr. Carl Peter, a theologian at Catholic University, Neuhaus states: "Protestantism, so insistent upon the worship owed to God alone, tends to neglect or despise the holy that is less than Absolute." On the other hand, "Roman Catholicism, so sensitive to the myriad manifestations of the sacred, tends to worship the holy that is less than God" (p. 14).

In the New Testament, Ott notes that "The passage which contains the classical proof is Rom. 5:12–21, in which the Apostle draws a parallel between the first Adam, from whom sin and death are transmitted to all humanity, and Christ, the second Adam, from whom justice and life are transmitted to all men."[21]

While Catholics and evangelicals share belief in the *fact* of original sin there are differences concerning the remedy for Adam and Eve's transgression. Although based in Christ's atoning death, the Catholic understanding of original sin is that it is remedied by the sacrament of baptism and what remains is *concupiscence,* which is not sin proper but a tendency toward sin. "Thus although concupiscence is not itself, strictly speaking, sinful, it is as it were, a weight dragging even the regenerate downwards into sin."[22] Although the Catholic view on the extent of depravity is not significantly different from that of most Arminian Protestants, it does differ from a strongly Reformed position. The latter, in contrast to Catholicism, places a stronger emphasis on people's total inability to even cooperate with God's grace by their free will in the process of their salvation. Even here, however, the differences are often exaggerated, since Catholicism has its own "Calvinists" (called Thomists) in contrast to its "Arminians" (called Molinists) who differ strongly on the relationship between free will and predestination.

20. Ibid., p. 107.
21. Ibid., p. 109.
22. Bernard M. G. Reardon, "Counter-Reformation: The Council of Trent," in *Religious Thought in the Reformation* (London and New York: Longman, 1981), p. 307.

THE IMAGE OF GOD

Although there are some differences between Catholics and many evangelicals as to the doctrine of the *imago Dei,* or "image of God," nevertheless, there are essential similarities. Speaking to humanity's creation, Pope John Paul II states: "The primordial affirmation of this anthropology is that man is God's image and cannot be reduced to a mere portion of nature or a nameless element in the human city."[23] Catholic scholars following several church fathers (notably Tertullian and Irenaeus) developed the distinction between the likeness of God *(similitudo)* and the image of God *(imago).* Sin has caused us to lose communion with God and our state of righteousness. This formed the basis of the distinction between *pura naturalia* and a *donum supernaturale,* a special gift in addition to his natural endowment. Catholics believe that "original righteousness" has been lost in the fall, but a natural justice remains. Human beings still retain some freedom and some sense of moral law. The Reformers took issue with this view on the grounds that it did not indicate the extent of the damage humanity has suffered as a result of sin. Luther goes beyond Aquinas and even Augustine in his understanding of people as *totus depravatus,* "totally depraved." Luther says: "Not only is he, as Augustine held, *curvatus,* 'bent' (toward the things of the world) but *curvatus in se,* 'bent in upon himself,' enclosed in a vicious circle of egocentricity."[24] This developed into what the Reformers would call "total depravity," according to which the effects of sin are felt in all areas: spiritual, physical, social, and intellectual.[25]

THE CONSEQUENCES OF SIN

However, both Roman Catholics and evangelicals realize the far-reaching effects of sin, not only on individual human beings, but on the creation as a whole. The psalmist lamented the state of humanity: "The fool says in his heart, 'There is no God.' . . . All alike have gone astray; they have become perverse; there is not one who does good, not even one" (Ps. 53:2–4). Thus, human beings are totally unredeemable apart from the grace of God. As Ott notes, "Internal supernatural grace is absolutely necessary for the beginning of faith and of salvation."[26] In fact, it is a matter of Catholic dogma that "in adults the beginning of that justification must be derived from the predisposing grace of God through Jesus Christ . . . whereby without any existing mer-

---

23. Neuner and Dupuis, *Christian Faith,* p. 138.
24. WA, LVI, 356, 4; quoted in Reardon, *Religious Thought in the Reformation,* p. 84.
25. Total depravity has, in our opinion, been misunderstood and frequently caricatured in Roman Catholic literature. See chap. 12, pp. 246, 247.
26. Ott, *Fundamentals of Catholic Dogma,* p. 229.

its on their part they are called." Indeed, a person cannot "of his own free will without the grace of God move himself to justice before Him [God]."[27] And, "By his sin Adam, as the first man, lost the original holiness and justice he had received from God, not only for himself but for all human beings."[28] That is, grace is absolutely necessary for salvation.

In addition to sins committed by individuals, the blight of original corruption extends to sins performed by groups in society. In the Old Testament God tells Israel: "Wash yourselves clean! Put away your misdeeds from before my eyes; cease doing evil; learn to do good. Make justice your aim: redress the wronged, hear the orphan's plea, defend the widow" (Isa. 1:16–17). In short, there is corporate guilt as well as individual guilt. History has revealed countless examples of group sin: oppression by the strong over the weak, wars, and the like. Unfortunately, the church, as it manifests itself in various jurisdictions, has not been without blame. We all need to confess and repent in this matter. Current social aberrations such as abortion, euthanasia, and passivity toward homosexuality are clear examples of complete depravity.[29]

HUMANITY AND GOD'S CREATED WORLD

Throughout recorded history we find people pondering their connection to the rest of creation that surrounds them. In fact, "in every conception of man from primitive Greek thought to the present, man's special relation to the cosmos has been stressed."[30]

Relationship with Creation. Earlier in this chapter we discussed the notion that while we are the result of a special creative act on the part of God, we nevertheless also have a kinship with the cosmos around us. The first creation account in Genesis (1:26–27) stresses the spiritual aspect and the second (2:7) records humanity's ties with the rest of creation.

Science has discovered that human bodies are composed of the same chemical elements as the rest of the material universe. However, an examination of man's relationship with the rest of creation reveals "a hierarchical cosmic structure with man at the top, possessing in his own being the various

27. From the Council of Trent, "On the Necessity of Preparation for Justification of Adults, and Whence It Proceeds"; quoted in Denzinger, *Sources of Catholic Dogma*, no. 797, p. 250.

28. *Catechism 1994*, no. 416, p. 105.

29. Of course there are other disagreements between Roman Catholics and many evangelicals (viz. Calvinists), such as the traditional Catholic distinction between venial and mortal sin. Mortal sin is defined as that which "kills" grace in the soul. For Catholics, this grace may be renewed by the sacrament of penance. Venial sin is less serious and does not destroy grace (see chap. 12).

30. *New Catholic Encyclopedia*, 9:127.

levels or grades of other beings, yet transcending all of them by his humanity."[31] Human beings enjoyed the status of being considered at the top of the
hierarchical ladder by the Greeks and also the ancient and medieval Fathers.
Thus Aquinas could write, "the highest grade of the whole order of generation is the human soul, to which matter tends as toward an ultimate form."[32]
He goes on to say that "summarizing the whole of reality in his mind, accepting and using it by his will, transforming and so spiritualizing it through his
activity, man is not only the ontological achievement but also the dynamic
fulfillment of the entire cosmos."[33]

The great Christian thinkers understood that men and women, by virtue
of their special position within creation, have unique gifts which can be
brought to bear on the world around them. "Through his work, his technol-
ogy, his art, and his moral activity man can actualize virtualities of the material world that otherwise would never be realized. This too is part of the
task imposed on man by his place in the cosmos: he has to humanize the material world, to fill it with his spirit."[34] Vatican Council II also speaks of the
value of human activity: "Considered in itself, human activity, individual
and collective—all that tremendous effort which man has made through the
centuries to better his living conditions—is in keeping with God's design."[35]
For God said to Adam, "Fill the earth and subdue it" (Gen. 1:28).

The apostle Paul, in his theological *tour de force,* includes these intriguing
verses:

> For the creation awaits with eager expectation the revelation of the children
> of God; for creation was made subject to futility, not of its own accord but
> because of the one who subjected it, in hope that creation itself would be set
> free from slavery to corruption and share in the glorious freedom of the chil-
> dren of God. We know that all creation is groaning in labor pains even until
> now (Rom. 8:19–22).

Concerning this passage, the Roman Catholic *New American Bible* says,
"Paul considers the destiny of the created world to be linked with the future
that belongs to the believers. As it shares in the penalty of corruption brought
about by sin, so also will it share in the benefits of redemption and future
glory that comprise the ultimate liberation of God's people."[36]

In addition to Paul, the writer of Hebrews addresses both the insignifi-
cance and the greatness of humanity by quoting Psalm 8:4–6: "What is man

---

31. Ibid.
32. Aquinas, *Summa contra Gentiles* 3.22.
33. Ibid., 3.78.
34. Ibid.
35. Neuner and Dupuis, *Christian Faith*, p. 137.
36. *New American Bible*, notes on Rom. 8:19–22.

that you are mindful of him, or the son of man that you care for him? You made him for a little while lower than the angels; you crowned him with glory and honor, subjecting all things under his feet" (Heb. 2:6–8). Thus the author identifies our position and responsibility in and to the creation in general. We are not the product of a mindless and purposeless force in the universe. This brings us to the subject of evolution and how its tenets affect a Christian understanding of humanity.

EVOLUTION

The concepts surrounding the modern notion of evolution began to take shape toward the end of the eighteenth century. After Charles Darwin (1809–82) published his *Origin of Species* (1859), the theory of evolution became a cornerstone of modern science. Since humans were now believed to be the product of this naturalistic process, it was inevitable that the church would be forced to examine this theory and judge its compatibility, or the lack thereof, with Holy Writ. Catholic scholars have offered a way to reconcile the apparent conflicts of evolution and the biblical account of creation. Catholics are permitted to believe in evolution (in both the micro and macro senses). But all Catholics must agree that "the first three Chapters of Genesis contain narratives of real events . . . no myths, no mere allegories or symbols of religious truths, no legends *(D. 2122).*"[37] Further, they must believe in the creation of the human soul.

Catholics are also given freedom in their interpretation of the days of Genesis. The theories which have been put forward to explain the biblical hexahemeron (the six days of creation) have been of two sorts: those who held a "literal" (realistic) approach and those who preferred a more "symbolic" (idealistic) understanding. Early and medieval church fathers can be found on both sides of the issue, with Origen being the father of those in the symbolic camp.

Concerning biological evolution, Augustine allowed for a certain development of living creatures. However, as Ott says about the creation of humanity, "a special creation by God is demanded, which must extend at least to the spiritual soul *(creato hominis peculiaris, D. 2123).*"[38] According to some modern Catholic sources, "the inspired writers of Genesis did not intend to produce a scientific cosmology, nor did they intend to indicate *how* God accomplished His creation. That God is the author, creator, and governor of the universe is the religious truth imported; it remains for science to discover, if possible, the times, the places, and the modes of origins."[39]

---

37. Ott, *Fundamentals*, p. 92. Also see Denzinger, *Sources of Catholic Dogma*, no. 2123, p. 546.
38. Ibid., p. 94.
39. *New Catholic Encyclopedia*, 5:694.

However, even these broad criteria have been disregarded by certain avant-garde Catholic thinkers. The name of Teilhard de Chardin comes to mind. Many anti-Christian philosophies of evolution, existentialism, and historicism—which tended to alter orthodox theological precepts—came to the attention of Pope Pius XII. In 1950 he issued an encyclical, *Humani Generis,* to address the situation. The purpose was twofold—to combat certain heterodox opinions and to restate traditional Catholic teachings that had been put in jeopardy by the innovators. Concerning the Scripture he wrote: "the encyclical condemned as specific errors the exegesis of Scripture that ignores or is opposed to the analogy of faith . . . and that which is marked by either ignorance or contempt for the literal meaning of the text in favor of a purely spiritual interpretation."[40] Finally, concerning historical speculations, "the encyclical condemns those who empty the Genesis accounts in the Old Testament of any historical sense."[41] The above quoted statements sound as if they could have been taken from a number of contemporary evangelical treatments concerning the inerrancy of Scripture.[42]

CONCLUSION

Despite some differences on the extent of sin and the possible use of evolutionary processes by God in producing the human body, there are essential similarities in the Roman Catholic and evangelical understanding of human beings. We find significant overlap on the views of humanity's origin, nature, fall, and destiny. Some differences exist, at least with Reformed Protestants, on such issues as the extent to which sin has corrupted the human condition. Also, the distinction between mortal and venial sins is a problem for most evangelicals. In spite of this, the early and medieval Fathers would agree that, as concerns salvation, God must take the initiative. Certainly that troika of theological giants, Augustine, Anselm, and Aquinas, would stand fast on the proposition that God's grace to humanity is absolutely necessary for salvation (see chap. 5).

In short, concerning the spiritual understanding of our beginning, the Roman Catholic Church teaches, and evangelicals agree, that "We believe that in Adam all have sinned. From this it follows that on account of the original offence committed by him human nature, which is common to all men, is reduced to that condition in which it must suffer the consequences of that fall."[43] As to the dignity of human beings because of being made in the image

40. Ibid., 7:215.
41. Ibid.
42. See Norman L. Geisler, ed., *Inerrancy* (Grand Rapids: Zondervan, 1979).
43. Flannery, *Vatican Collection: Vatican Council II,* p. 391.

of God, "God did not create man a solitary being. From the beginning 'male and female he created them' (Genesis 1:27). This partnership of man and woman constitutes the first form of communion between persons. For by his innermost nature man is a social being; and if he does not enter into relations with others he can neither live nor develop his gifts."[44]

Finally, both Catholics and evangelicals agree that the doctrine of God as creator cannot be ignored in a discussion about human beings. "Without a creator there can be no creature. . . . Besides, once God is forgotten, the creature is lost sight of as well."[45] Sin has had its baleful effect on human beings. "Although set by God in a state of rectitude, man, enticed by the evil one, abused his freedom at the very start of history. He lifted himself up against God, and sought to attain his goal apart from him."[46]

44. Ibid., pp. 913–14.
45. Ibid., p. 935.
46. Ibid., p. 914.

4

CHRIST

INTRODUCTION

There is a common biblical and creedal source for both Catholics and evangelicals on the doctrine of Christ. This christological core is found in the Athanasian and Chalcedonian creeds. Here too both orthodox Protestants and Catholics share the insights of the great troika of Christian theologians: Saints Augustine, Anselm, and Aquinas. The Christian tradition down through the centuries has proclaimed that Jesus Christ is God in the flesh.

The unique and altogether singular event of the incarnation of the Son of God does not mean that Jesus Christ is part God and part man, nor does it imply that he is the result of a confused mixture of the divine and the human. He became truly man while remaining truly God. Jesus Christ is true God and true man. During the first centuries, the Church had to defend and clarify this truth of faith against the heresies that falsified it.[1]

DEFINITION OF THE DOCTRINE OF CHRIST

Christianity indicates by its very name the central place that Christ has in its theology. Concerning the mission of Jesus Christ: "The eternal Son of God, 'one of the Trinity,' became man in order to save men."[2] Christ accomplished this by "recapitulating all things in himself, He re-united the whole human race with God through the mystery of His death and resurrection, and reconciled all things among themselves."[3] Martin Luther has caused Roman Catholics much heartburn, but we trust they would agree with him when he

---

1. *Catechism of the Catholic Church*, no. 464, p. 117.
2. Neuner and Dupuis, *Christian Faith*, p. 155.
3. Ibid.

states: "I have found and noted in all histories of the whole Christian Church that all those who have maintained the central doctrine of Jesus Christ in its integrity have remained safe and sound in the true Christian faith. Although they erred and sinned in other respects, yet they were finally saved. For if anyone stands firm and right on this point, that Jesus Christ is true God and true man, all the other articles of the Christian faith will fall in place for him and firmly sustain him."[4]

The study of Christ historically has been divided into two areas of investigation: who Christ was and what Christ did. The latter subject, soteriology, we will treat in chapter 5. The former topic is called Christology and will be addressed here.

Christology also is closely connected with "anthropology"—the study of humanity. Anthropology begins with people and investigates their origin, nature, and initial contact with sin (see chap. 3). This discipline ends with a cry for divine help. Christology is the first step in the answer to that cry.

CHRIST IN THE OLD TESTAMENT

Catholics, like evangelicals, point to the evidence in the Old Testament concerning Christ that are made clear from Jesus' repeated statements in the New Testament. Our Lord made this evident to the disciples on the road to Emmaus. Jesus, remaining unrecognized by the two men, questioned them about the events that had transpired concerning the crucifixion. When they indicated their misunderstanding of the nature of the messianic mission, Christ said: "'Oh, how foolish you are! How slow of heart to believe all that the prophets spoke! Was it not necessary that the Messiah should suffer these things and enter into his glory?' Then beginning with Moses and all the prophets, he interpreted to them what referred to him in all the scriptures" (Luke 24:25–27).

Later in the same chapter Jesus said, "These are my words that I spoke to you while I was still with you, that everything written about me in the law of Moses and in the prophets and psalms must be fulfilled" (Luke 24:44). Indeed, Jesus had already declared in the Sermon on the Mount: "Do not think that I have come to abolish the law and the prophets. I have come not to abolish but to fulfill" (Matt. 5:17). To the Jews he declared, "You search the scriptures, because you think you have eternal life through them; even they testify on my behalf" (John 5:39). And the writer of Hebrews cites Jesus saying, "As is written of me in the scroll, Behold, I come to do your will, O God" (Heb. 10:7). The entire Old Testament speaks of Christ; so claimed our Lord on several occasions.

4. WA, 50.266f.; quoted in James Atkinson, *Martin Luther: Prophet to the Church Catholic* (Grand Rapids: Eerdmans, 1983), p. 184.

Information concerning Jesus in the Old Testament is both typological and prophetic in nature. That is to say, the messianic material there is anticipatory in nature and requires the further development of the New Testament. As Catholic scholars note, "The Old Testament is indispensable . . . for an understanding of the categories and terms in which both Jesus and the Apostolic Church expressed themselves."[5] To paraphrase Augustine, the New is in the Old concealed and the Old is in the New revealed. That is, Christ is seen in the Old Testament by way of anticipation and in the New Testament by way of realization.[6]

Historically, it has become customary to refer to three offices connected to the work of Christ. These are the offices of Prophet, Priest, and King. All of these designations find their origin in the Old Testament. Concerning the office of Prophet, Moses said, "A prophet like me will the Lord, your God, raise up for you from among your own kinsmen; to him you shall listen" (Deut. 18:15). Concerning this verse the *New American Bible* (NAB) says: "*A prophet like me:* from the context (opposition to the pagan soothsayers) it seems that Moses is referring in general to all the true prophets who were to succeed him. But since Christ is the Great Prophet in whom the prophetic office finds its fulfillment and completion, this passage was understood in a special Messianic sense both by the Jews (John 6:14; 7:40) and by the Apostles (Acts 3:22; 7:37)."[7]

Christ also fulfills the office of Priest. In the Old Testament, a priest was one in whom authority was vested and, almost without exception, designated an ecclesiastical position. The following verse has been understood by the church as having implications concerning the ministry of Jesus: "The Lord has sworn, and he will not repent: 'You are a priest forever, according to the order of Melchizedek'" (Ps. 110:4). Again, the study notes from the *New American Bible* are helpful to identify the Roman Catholic position: "*According to the order of Melchizedek:* in the same way as Melchizedek was a priest. There are three main points of resemblance between Melchizedek, the prophetic type, and Christ who fulfilled this prophecy: both are Kings as well as priests, both offer bread and wine to God, and both have their priesthood directly from God and not through Aaron, since neither belongs to the tribe of Levi. Cf. Gen. 14:18; Heb. 7."[8] Christ our high priest is distinguished from his Old Testament forerunners in that the sacrifice that he offered was himself. (This gets us into the crucial question concerning the atonement, which we will address; as well as Anselm's significant

---

5. *New Catholic Encyclopedia*, 7:909.
6. For further discussion, see Norman L. Geisler, *To Understand the Bible, Look for Jesus* (Grand Rapids: Baker, 1979).
7. *New American Bible*, notes on Deut. 18:15.
8. Ibid., notes on Ps. 110:4.

contribution, in chap. 5. The office of priesthood as it impacts the sacerdotalism of the Roman Catholic system will be discussed in chap. 14.)

Concerning the office of King, Roman Catholics believe that Christ rules over his people as a spiritual King, a rule established in the hearts and lives of his people the church. The prophet Isaiah foresaw the "King of Kings": "For to us a child is born, to us a son is given, and the government will be on his shoulders and he will be called Wonderful Counselor, Mighty God, Everlasting Father, Prince of Peace" (Isa. 9:6 NIV).[9]

CHRIST IN THE NEW TESTAMENT

Concerning Christ and the New Testament it has been said that "it is impossible to exaggerate the personalist character of the Christian Scriptures, whose object, in the words of the Lord at the Last Supper, is 'everlasting life, that they may know you, the only true God and him whom you have sent, Jesus Christ.'"[10] As to the origin of Jesus, Cardinal Joseph Ratzinger states, "St. John's gospel emphasizes again and again that the real origin of Jesus is the 'Father,' that he comes from him more totally than any previous envoy of God's, and in a different way."[11]

The early apostolic church was made up largely of Jews who were convinced that the expected Messiah had come. The facts of Jesus' life, death, and resurrection were central to their understanding. Hence, the New Testament, which is a product of the apostolic church, is replete with information about the life and ministry of Jesus.

Concerning the necessity of both faith and history in the formation of the apostolic tradition the *New Catholic Encyclopedia* notes: "Those who formulated and preserved the tradition just described were conscious of the necessity that it be based on historical occurrence. See, e.g., 1 Cor. 15:14–15: 'If Christ has not risen, vain is our preaching, vain too is your faith. Yes, and we are found false witnesses as to God, in that we have borne witness against God that he raised Christ.'"[12]

Roman Catholics draw their understanding of Christ and his mission from the pages of the New Testament. "He who is the 'image of the invisible God' (Col. 1:15), is himself the perfect man who has restored in the children of Adam that likeness to God which had been disfigured ever since the first sin. Human nature, by the very fact that it was assumed, not absorbed, in him, has been raised in us also to a dignity beyond compare."[13]

---

9. Many Protestants, particularly amillennialists, hold the same view. Premillennialists, however, insist that there will be a future, literal reign of Christ on earth (cf. Rev. 20:1–7).

10. Hardon, *Catholic Catechism,* p. 111.

11. Cardinal Joseph Ratzinger, *Introduction to Christianity,* trans. J. R. Foster (San Francisco: Ignatius Press, 1990), p. 205.

12. *New Catholic Encyclopedia,* 7:910.

13. Flannery, *Vatican Collection: Vatican Council II,* p. 922.

THE TWO NATURES OF CHRIST

THE DEITY OF CHRIST

Belief in the deity of Christ has been foundational to the Christian church from the beginning (cf. Acts 2:31–36; Rom. 10:9; Heb. 1:8). It forms the framework from which springs Christian theology. It was the crucial issue that split "followers of the Way" from their Judaistic compatriots. This division is vividly illustrated in Acts 7, which records Stephen's speech before the Sanhedrin and his subsequent martyrdom. Concerning this incident, the *New American Bible* states: "With Stephen, who thus perceived the fuller implications of the teachings of Jesus, the differences between Judaism and Christianity began to appear."[14]

Less than three hundred years after the close of the Apostolic era, the church was faced with a profusion of ideas challenging the New Testament's teaching about Christ. The first four general councils responded to these speculations and laid the groundwork for Christian orthodoxy.

At the Ecumenical Council of Nicea (A.D. 325) the church addressed the nature of the relationship between the Father and the Son with the resulting condemnation of Arianism. An Alexandrian priest named Arius (d. A.D. 250) held that, since God the Father was immutable and unique, the Son had to be a created being. Thus Arius rejected the orthodox view that Jesus was of the "same substance" as the Father. Under the influence of Athanasius, the Council made it clear that Jesus was of the same, not just similar, substance as the Father: "begotten not made." Constantinople I (A.D. 381) confirmed Nicea and stated the divinity of the Holy Spirit and his inclusion in the Godhead while further refining the doctrine of the Trinity. Ephesus (A.D. 431) concerned itself primarily with the incarnation, and Chalcedon (A.D. 451) distinguished the two natures—divine and human—in Christ. Nestorius, a priest in Antioch, is credited with the distinction of the two natures in Christ as involving also a distinction of persons. He was vigorously opposed by Cyril, Bishop of Alexandria (c. A.D. 380–440). In a letter to Nestorius, Cyril argued: "Can. 1. If anyone does not confess that God is truly Emmanuel . . . let him be anathema." And, "Can. 5. If anyone ventures to say that Christ is a man inspired by God, and not rather that He is truly God, as a son by nature, as the Word was made flesh . . . let him be anathema."[15]

The Roman Catholic dogma concerning the divinity of Christ agrees with orthodox Protestants: "Jesus Christ is True God and True Son of God *(De*

---

14. Study notes on Acts 7.
15. Denzinger, *Sources of Catholic Dogma*, 113/115, p. 50.

fide)."[16] Furthermore, "He is God and man. He is God begotten of the substance of the Father before all ages and man born in time of the substance of His Mother. He is perfect God and perfect man."[17] Concerning the Old Testament testimony on this matter: "The Divine dignity of the Messiah is indicated by the appellations: Emmanuel = God with us (Isa. 7:14; 8:8). Wonderful, Counsellor, God the Mighty, the Father of the world to come, the Prince of Peace (Isa. 9:6)."[18]

In the New Testament, we have the testimonies of the baptism of Jesus (Matt. 3:17) and his transfiguration (Mark 9:7): "At His baptism Christ is inducted by His heavenly Father into His Messianic office, and His Divine Sonship is attested by means of a solemn Revelation to St. John. In the transfiguration on Tabor this Divine attestation is repeated before the chief Apostles."[19]

Christ is addressed as "God" in the New Testament. "The Apostle St. Paul gives further expression to his conviction of faith in the Godhead of Christ by directly calling Him God (Rom. 9:5)."[20] This he did also in other passages (cf. Titus 2:13). Jesus is also called *Kyrios* or "Lord." Although this term does not always designate deity, given the context in which it is used, "to the Apostle St. Paul the designation Kyrios was tantamount to a confession of Christ's Godhead."[21] For example, in Philippians Paul speaks of every knee bowing and confessing him as Lord (Phil. 2:10–11), and this is taken from Isaiah 45:23 which says that every knee will bow to *Yahweh,* a term that always means "God." Indeed, Jesus often claimed to be Yahweh, sometimes citing the very words Yahweh to refer to himself. For example, Jesus said, "I am the Alpha and Omega," that is, the First and the Last—something Yahweh claims in Isaiah 44:6. Jesus also said he shared the Father's glory with him before the foundation of the world and prayed, "Now glorify me, Father, with you, with the glory that I had with you before the world began" (John 17:5). Yahweh explicitly said, "I am the LORD, this is my name; *my glory I give to no other*" (Isa. 42:8, emphasis added). Jesus clearly claimed to be one with Yahweh.[22]

Christ's deity also is verified by verses that state his preexistence. John declared emphatically that "In the beginning . . . the Word [Jesus] was with God" (John 1:1). To the Jews who were determined to stone him, Christ said: "Abraham your father rejoiced to see my day; he saw it and was glad." And, Jesus said to them, "Amen, amen, I say to you before Abraham came

---

16. Ott, *Fundamentals of Catholic Dogma,* p. 127.
17. Ibid.
18. Ibid., p. 128.
19. Ibid.
20. Ibid., p. 136.
21. Ibid., p. 137.
22. God does share his *reflective* glory (his image, Gen. 1:27) with humans (cf. Pss. 8:5–6; 84:11), but not his *essential* glory, spoken of here.

to be, *I AM*" (John 8:56–58). The apostle Paul spoke of the preexistence of Christ "Who, though he was in the form of God, did not regard equality with God something to be grasped. Rather, he emptied himself" by coming to earth in the form of a servant (Phil. 2:6–7). John too says "the Word [Christ] *became* flesh," though he was God from all eternity (John 1:14, emphasis added; cf. 1:1).

THE HUMANITY OF CHRIST

That the "Eternal Word," the second Person in the Godhead, took upon himself a real human nature has been a crucial doctrine of classic Christianity. The gulf between God and humanity has been bridged by the Son of God, who has taken our humanity and joined it to his eternal divinity. Indeed, "in the mysterious union of the incarnation, the church was led over the course of centuries to confess the full reality of Christ's human soul, with its operations of intellect and will, and of his human body."[23]

The Incarnation. The doctrine that leads any discussion of the humanity of Christ is the incarnation. The biblical basis for this doctrine is found most clearly in the prologue of John's Gospel: "the Word became flesh and made his dwelling among us, and we saw his glory, the glory as of the Father's only Son, full of grace and truth" (John 1:14). The *kenosis* (emptying) passage (Phil. 2:5–11) addresses the deity of Christ. It also speaks to Christ's humanity when it says "he emptied himself, taking the form of a slave, coming in human likeness; and found human in appearance" (2:7). In Peter's first Epistle we read that Jesus "suffered in the flesh" (1 Pet. 4:1) and was "put to death in the flesh" (3:18). Lastly, the Johannine Epistles speak of his coming "in the flesh" (1 John 4:2; 2 John 7). The present and perfect tenses used here respectively indicate that Jesus came in a fleshly human nature in the past and remains in one in the present. Indeed, the creeds speak of him being raised and ascending in the same body of flesh and bones in which he died.[24]

It is important to note that when he became man, Christ did not cease being God. To paraphrase Athanasius, in the incarnation we do not have the subtraction of deity but the addition of humanity. As to the fact of the incarnation, Pope Leo the Great, writing to Flavian of Constantinople (A.D. 449), states: "Consequently, the Son of God entered into these lowly conditions of the world, after descending from His celestial throne, and though He did not withdraw from the glory of the Father, He was generated in a new order and in a new nativity." Further, "For He who is true God, is likewise true man, and there is no falsehood in this unity."[25]

---

23. *Catechism 1994*, no. 470, p. 119.
24. See Norman L. Geisler, *Battle for the Resurrection* (Nashville: Nelson, 1992), chap. 4.
25. Denzinger, *Sources of Catholic Dogma*, no. 144, p. 58.

Concerning the purpose of the incarnation, the Roman Catholic Church teaches that "the Son of God became man in order to redeem men *(De fide)*."[26] This understanding would in the Medieval period be expanded by Anselm in his important work *Cur Deus Homo (Why the God-Man)*.[27] We will address this in chapter 5.

The second article of the Nicene Creed emphasizes the incarnation. The purpose of these statements is to give equal balance to both the divine and human natures that made up Christ's person. Two false notions are rejected. First, the idea that Christ was a mere human being; the creed declares him to be "of one substance with the Father." Christ was *homoousious* (of the same substance), as opposed to *homoiousious* (of like substance), as the Arians held. This addresses the Marcionite and Gnostic attempts to distinguish between the God of creation and the God of redemption. "The God who becomes incarnate in Christ and through him carries out the work of redemption is no one else than the God of creation."[28] Second, "the Nicene confession of Christ also rejects all tendencies to regard Christ as a kind of theophany or divinity wandering around incognito on earth. The humanity of Christ is true humanity. . . ."[29]

The early church fathers refused to separate the two natures of Christ. "Unless man had overcome the enemy of man, the enemy would not have been legitimately vanquished. And again, unless it had been God who had freely given salvation, we could never have possessed it securely. And unless man had been joined to God, he could never have become a partaker of incorruptibility."[30]

Many contemporary Catholics support the early church fathers. Peter Kreeft quotes Pascal concerning Christ and the Christian believer: "Not only do we only know God through Jesus Christ, but we only know ourselves through Jesus Christ. We only know life and death through Jesus Christ. Apart from Jesus Christ we cannot know the meaning of our life or our death, of God, or of ourselves."[31] Harold O. J. Brown observes that, "by dividing the deity and the humanity from one another, free rein is also given to the imagination to deal with Christ not as a historic, human person but rather as a cosmic spiritual or idealistic principle."[32] G. K. Chesterton, a noted lay Roman Catholic author of the early 1900s, understood the importance of the incarnation: "As compared with a Jew, a Moslem, a Buddhist, a Deist, or

26. Ibid., p. 175.
27. Or, *Why God Became Man.*
28. Gustaf Aulén, *Reformation and Catholicity* (Edinburgh and London: Oliver and Boyd, 1962), p. 105.
29. Ibid.
30. Irenaeus, *Adversus haereses* III.18.7; quoted in ibid.
31. Kreeft, *Fundamentals of the Faith*, p. 129.
32. Brown, *Heresies: The Image of Christ*, p. 327.

more obvious alternatives, a Christian means a man who believes that deity or sanctity has attached itself to matter or entered the world of the sense."[33]

The Virgin Birth. The Roman Catholic Church, in keeping with the witness of Holy Writ and the testimony of all the church fathers, attests to the virgin birth of Christ. "This dogma of the Church declares that Christ, the Son of God, was born by external generation of but one parent, the Blessed Virgin Mary, and that she being a virgin did not lose her virginity, either physical or spiritual."[34] Another authority states, "The gospel accounts understand the virginal conception of Jesus as a divine work that surpasses all human understanding and possibility (cf. Mt. 1:18–25; Lk. 1:26–38)."[35]

Evangelicals typically believe only in the doctrine of the virgin *conception*.[36] Roman Catholics, however, believe that Mary was a virgin *before, during, and after* the birth of Jesus Christ.[37] We will address this more fully in chapter 15.

The Union of the Two Natures. In a discussion of the relationship between the divine and human natures of Christ we must first examine the role of the Virgin Mary. "Christ was truly generated and born of a daughter of Adam, the Virgin Mary *(De fide)*. The reality and integrity of Christ's human nature is especially guaranteed by the fact that Christ was truly generated and born of a human mother. Through His descent from a daughter of Adam, He was, as to His humanity, incorporated into the posterity of Adam. He had identity of essence with man and community of race; Christ became our Brother."[38]

Also, Christ is one person, not two as the Nestorian heresy held. Hence, Mary was only the "Mother of Christ" not "the Mother of God." The church, however, stated that "the Divine and human natures are united hypostatically in Christ, this is, joined to each other in one Person *(De fide)*. The dogma asserts that there is in Christ a person, who is the Divine Person of the Logos, and two natures, which belong to the One Divine Person."[39] Hence, Mary may be understood as being the "Mother of God," since her Son is only one person. Protestants can affirm this also. More will be said concerning Mary's title in chapter 15.

The heresy of the Monophysites denied the duality of the two natures; Christ was not only one person but also one single nature. The church, how-

33. G. K. Chesterton, *Saint Thomas*, pp. 41–42; quoted in *Antithesis*, vol. 1, no. 6 (Nov./ Dec. 1990): 27.

34. Robert C. Broderick, M.A., ed., *The Catholic Concise Encyclopedia* (St. Paul: Simon and Schuster, 1956), p. 327.

35. *Catechism 1994*, no. 497, p. 126.

36. Brown, *Heresies*, p. 173.

37. Ott, *Fundamentals of Catholic Dogma*, pp. 203–7.

38. Ibid., p. 142.

39. Ibid., p. 144.

ever, taught that, "in the Hypostatic Union each of the two natures of Christ continues unimpaired, untransformed and unmixed with each other *(De fide)*. According to the testimony of Holy Writ, Christ is true God and true Man that is, possessor of the unimpaired Divine Nature and an unimpaired human nature."[40]

The heresy of Monothelitism taught that while Christ had two natures he had but one divine will. The church responded that "Each of the two natures in Christ possesses its own natural will and its own natural mode of operation *(De fide)*. In spite of the real duality of wills, a moral unity subsisted and subsists, because Christ's human will is, in the most perfect fashion, in harmony with, and in free subordination to, the Divine Will."[41]

The Roman Catholic Church teaches that "The Hypostatic Union of Christ's human nature with the Divine Logos took place at the moment of conception *(De fide)*." Augustine said, "From the moment in which He began to be man, He is also God. (De Trin. XIII, 17,22.)."[42] The Church designates that point by as conception.

We must not neglect the relationship between the Hypostatic Union and the Trinity. "The Hypostatic Union was effected by the Three Divine Persons acting in common. *(De fide.)* The Creed of the Eleventh Synod of Toledo (A.D. 675) states: 'It is to be believed that the Whole Trinity effected the Incarnation of the Son of God, because the works of the Trinity are indivisible.'"[43] Also, it is to be believed that "Only the Second Divine Person became Man *(De fide)*."[44] The union occurs not in the nature, but in the person; specifically, in the Person of the second member of the Godhead, Christ.

THE RESURRECTION OF CHRIST

The Roman Catholic communion holds, with all of Christendom, the reality of Christ's resurrection. "On the third day after His death Christ rose gloriously from the dead *(De fide)*. The Resurrection of Christ is a basic truth of Christianity, which is expressed in all the symbols of Faith and in all rules of Faith of the ancient Church."[45] According to the understanding of the apostles Peter (Acts 2:24) and Paul (Acts 13:35), the Old Testament attests to the resurrection: "Because you will not abandon my soul to the nether world, nor will you suffer your faithful one to undergo corruption" (Ps. 16:10).

As it did in the Protestant churches, modernism in the early twentieth century threatened the foundations of Roman Catholic Christology. Pius X

---

40. Ibid., p. 147.
41. Ibid., p. 148.
42. Ibid., p. 150.
43. Ibid., p. 155.
44. Ibid.
45. Ibid., p. 192.

(1835–1914) condemned a number of errors concerning Christ. The effort to separate the resurrection from historical fact was firmly rejected.[46] Some liberal Catholic scholars offer theological views that appear to deny this. Edward Schillebeeckx is prominent among them. He argues that after the resurrection of Christ, "what is normally invisible [i.e., his body] was made to appear: that the invisible makes itself seen is expressed on lines of human perceiving."[47] Certain evangelical scholars also have deviated from the historical creedal view of the Christian church[48] which from the beginning has made the apostolic confession: "I believe . . . in the resurrection of the flesh."

The nature of the body of the risen Christ is of vital importance, since if it was not the same physical body in which he died, then God's purposes in both creation and redemption would be thwarted. Of late, some have stressed the non-materiality of the resurrection body and have down played its connection with the pre-resurrection body of Christ.[49] This is a rebirth of a similar controversy centered in the views of Origen that plagued the early church. Official Roman Catholic theology holds that "the Body of the Risen Christ was in a state of glory as is apparent from a study of the circumstances of the appearances, and from the Risen Christ's supremacy over the bonds of space and time. The Risen Christ retained the wounds in His transfigured body as tokens of His triumph over death."[50] As Augustine declared: "The world has come to the belief that the *earthly body* of Christ was received up into heaven. Already both the learned and unlearned have believed in the resurrection of the *flesh* and its ascension to the heavenly places, while only a very few either of the educated or uneducated are still staggered by it."[51] With this conclusion, both creeds and councils of the Christian church have repeatedly agreed.[52]

Finally, concerning Christ's return to heaven, "Christ ascended body and soul into Heaven and sits at the right hand of the Father *(De fide)*."[53] The early church leaders stressed Christ's return to the Father: "The Fathers give unanimous testimony of Christ's Ascension. All the ancient rules of Faith mention it together with the Death and the Resurrection."[54]

---

46. Neuner and Dupuis, *Decree Lamentabili*, pp. 192–93.

47. Edward Schillebeeckx, *Jesus: An Experiment in Christology*, trans. Hubert Hoskins (New York: Seabury, 1979), p. 353.

48. See Geisler, *Battle for the Resurrection*, chap. 6.

49. See Murray Harris, *From Grave to Glory*, pp. 401–6.

50. Ott, *Fundamentals of Catholic Dogma*, p. 193. Also cf. "The Resurrection of the Body," in *Catechism of the Council of Trent for Parish Priests* (Rockford, Ill.: Tan Books, 1982), pp. 124–31.

51. Augustine, *City of God;* quoted in Geisler, *Battle for the Resurrection*, p. 57.

52. See Geisler, *Battle for the Resurrection*, chap. 4, and Geisler, *In Defense of the Resurrection* (Chico, Calif.: Witness Inc., 1993), chap. 9.

53. Ott, *Fundamentals of Catholic Dogma*, p. 194.

54. Ibid. Cf. Irenaeus, *Adv. haer. 110,I; I11 4,2;* Tertullian, *De praesr.* 13; *De Virg. vel I; Adv. Prax.* 2; Origen, *De princ.* 1 praef. 4.

TITLES OF CHRIST

Earlier in this chapter we discussed the manner in which Christ fulfilled the requirements of the offices of prophet, priest, and king. There are several other titles attached to the person and work of Christ: Messiah, Son of God, Son of man, Lord, and Savior.

Jesus seldom spoke directly of himself as Messiah, probably because he wanted to avoid confusion with the mistaken political notion of the Messiah that was current at the time. However, "Jesus' reluctance to use the title was not shared by the first Christians. By the end of the Apostolic Age, the term *Christ* (the Greek translation of the Hebrew, *messiah*) had lost its character as a title and was considered part of the personal name, Jesus Christ. The early Church must have found no better title by which to present the meaning of Jesus to the Jews as the fulfillment of the destiny of Israel."[55]

Concerning Jesus as the *Son of God,* we again find Jesus shying away from applying the title to himself. The early church, however, used this title and it is found in almost all the books of the New Testament in one form or another.

Jesus' favorite title for himself was *Son of Man.* It is used approximately eighty times in the Gospels. The title actually connotes divinity: "In Dn 7:13 . . . the term is applied to an apocalyptic figure that represents the messianic Kingdom of God, a transcendent figure coming on the clouds of heaven surrounded by the exalted symbols of divine majesty."[56]

The title of *Lord* is closely related with the titles Christ and Son of God. "The disciples had called Jesus Lord in the secular sense of master. With the Easter experience, they saw a much deeper meaning in this term."[57]

Finally, we have the title of Jesus as *Savior.* In the Old Testament, God was often designated as Savior (cf. Isa. 43:3, 11, 15; 49:26; 63:8). The title was used of Jesus early on but was more popular with the later New Testament writers. "Because of the connotations the word had in the Hellenistic world, which was looking for savior gods, and especially in pagan ruler worship, this title was a rich one. . . . It may have been found more useful than the Suffering Servant concept to explain the meaning of the death of Jesus to the Gentile world."[58]

CONCLUSION

We have traced the development of Christology from the Scriptures to the present citing mainly Roman Catholic sources. Christology's major task is to

55. *New Catholic Encyclopedia,* 7:915.
56. Ibid., p. 917.
57. Ibid.
58. Ibid. Also see *Catechism 1994,* ibid., Index, "Jesus: names and designations," pp. 776–77.

address the relationship of the divine and the human in Christ.[59] From the early church fathers through the Medieval Doctors to the Reformers, we find basic agreement concerning doctrines addressing Christ's person and work. Modern orthodox Roman Catholic scholars agree with this assessment: "By and large, the mainstream of traditional Protestantism stemming from the Reformation agrees with Catholic teaching in basic Christology."[60]

Modern Reformed theologian Louis Berkhof, commenting on the history of the doctrines dealing with the two natures of Christ, observed that "rationalistic attacks on the doctrine were not entirely wanting, but the Church remained firm in the confession of this truth, in spite of the fact that it was once and again declared to be contrary to reason. In this confession, Roman Catholics and Protestants stand shoulder to shoulder."[61]

Another Reformed scholar, writing about the Chalcedonian Christology, notes: "Shedd in his *History of Christ Doctrine*, writes, 'Another important implication in the Chalcedon Christology is that it is the Divinity, and not the humanity, which constitutes the root and basis of Christ's personality. The incarnation is the humanizing of deity, and not the deification of humanity.' Shedd continues, 'The redemption of mankind is accomplished, not by the elevation of the finite to the infinite, but by the humiliation of the infinite to the finite.'"[62]

Modern Roman Catholic popes have been mindful of the need to preserve the classical formulations concerning Christology. Paul VI declared that it was "not enough to believe that Christ is a man in whom God is fully present; the faith as formulated in the great Christological Councils implies that He is God's eternal Son who in time became man to reveal the Father fully."[63]

In 1990, Pope John Paul II issued an encyclical entitled *"Redemptoris Missio"* (Mission of the Redeemer). Its purpose was to stress the importance of Christian missionary evangelization. In it the Pope rejected "any anthropocentric views of salvation and mission that would focus on humanity's earthly needs while remaining 'closed to the transcendent.'"[64] As to the centrality of Christ in this endeavor, he affirmed that "if we go back to the beginnings of the Church, we find a clear affirmation that Christ is the one savior of all, the only one able to reveal God and lead to God."[65] Indeed, "for

59. Kelly, *Early Christian Doctrines*, p. 138. This is an excellent work addressing the study of Christology as well as other subjects in the early history of Christian doctrine.

60. Hardon, *Catholic Catechism*, p. 111.

61. Louis Berkhof, *Systematic Theology* (Grand Rapids: Eerdmans, 1965), pp. 315–16.

62. J. Marcellus Kik, *Ecumenism and the Evangelical* (Philadelphia: Presbyterian and Reformed, 1958), p. 57.

63. Neuner and Dupuis, Declaration *Mysterium Filii Dei* (21 February 1972), p. 204.

64. "John Paul II/Encyclical on Missionary Activity," *Origins: Catholic News Service Documentary Service*, vol. 20, no. 34, 31 January 1991.

65. Ibid., p. 544.

all people—Jews and gentiles alike—salvation can only come from Jesus Christ."[66]

A current evangelical work declares: "If Christ has not truly suffered, why should we? Because Christ invites us to Himself through His passion, those who will not be branches of His cross will bear no fruit—rather their fruit is deadly, and one who eats of it dies eternally."[67]

In closing, we can do no better than to reproduce a portion of the Symbol of Chalcedon (A.D. 451):

> Following therefore the holy Fathers, we unanimously teach to confess one and the same Son, our Lord Jesus Christ, the same perfect in divinity and perfect in humanity, the same one is being *(homoousios)* with the Father as to the divinity and one in being with us as to the humanity, like unto us in all things but sin (cf. Heb. 4:15). The same was begotten from the Father before the ages as to the divinity and in the later days for us and our salvation was born as to His humanity from Mary the Virgin Mother of God.[68]

We have examined here the common orthodox Catholic and evangelical Protestant view of who Christ *was*. In chapter 5 we will look at what he *did* for us.

---

66. Ibid.
67. Thomas J. Nettles, "One, Holy, Catholic, Apostolic Church," in John Armstrong, ed., *Roman Catholicism: Evangelical Protestants Analyze What Divides and Unites Us* (Chicago: Moody Press, 1994), p. 40.
68. Neuner and Dupuis, *Christian Faith*, p. 166.

5

SALVATION

Catholics and evangelicals share a common core of beliefs about salvation. The roots of this common heritage are found in the early church fathers and flowered in Augustine. These first teachers of the church grappled primarily with the issues concerning the *Person* of Christ (Christology) rather than questions about the *work* of Christ (soteriology). It is only later that theologians addressed the doctrine of what Christ accomplished, agreeing that salvation is based on God's grace. As a current catechism puts it, "Believing in Jesus Christ and in the One who sent him for our salvation is necessary for obtaining that salvation (cf. Mk. 16:16; Jn. 3:36; 6:40 et al.)."[1]

After nearly twenty years of dialogue between Catholic and Lutheran scholars searching for common understanding they agreed that "our entire hope of justification and salvation rests on Christ Jesus and on the gospel whereby the good news of God's merciful action in Christ is made known; we do not place our ultimate trust in anything other than God's promise and saving work in Christ." Although they acknowledge that "this Christological affirmation does not necessarily involve full agreement between Catholics and Lutherans on justification by faith,"[2] nonetheless, it does express the surprisingly significant core of salvation beliefs shared by Catholics and evangelicals.

THE EARLY PATRISTIC PERIOD

The basis for our common heritage is, of course, the Old and New Testaments. Beyond these, the writings of the early Fathers, as well as the creeds

1. *Catechism of the Catholic Church*, no. 161, p. 44.
2. H. Georges Anderson et al., eds., *Justification by Faith* (Minneapolis: Augsburg, 1985), p. 16.

81

and confessions of the church form a common basis for all orthodox believers, Roman Catholic and Protestant.

REACTION TO GNOSTICISM

The most serious threat to early Christian faith was Gnosticism.[3] This was not a clearly defined movement but was made up of various subgroups drawn from Hellenic as well as oriental sources. The term *Gnosticism* comes from the Greek word *gnosis*, which means "knowledge." One of Gnosticism's central doctrines was the belief that those who embraced the movement possessed a special mystical knowledge which led to salvation.

Gnosticism also held to a form of dualism, a view of reality which posits two fundamental principles: matter is evil and spirit is good. Gnostics believed that salvation was the escape from the physical body (which is evil) achieved by special knowledge *(gnosis)*. The understanding of the body as evil led some Gnostics to stress control of the body and its passions (asceticism), while others left the body to its own devices and passions (libertinism). Both forms of these Gnostic-like practices (which existed in embryonic form in the New Testament), were addressed in several books, including Colossians, 1 and 2 Timothy, Titus, 2 Peter, and the Epistles of John.

Harold O. J. Brown offers this succinct summation of the effects of Gnosticism: "Gnosticism was a response to the widespread desire to understand the mystery of being: it offered detailed, secret knowledge of the whole order of reality, claiming to know and to be able to explain things of which ordinary, simple Christian faith was entirely ignorant."[4]

Gnostics rejected the notion that Christ had a body like ours. Docetists held a similar view. Docetism—named from the Greek word meaning "to seem"—held that the body of Jesus appeared to be fully human but was not. This does serious damage to the doctrine of the incarnation and this error has recently reappeared.[5] Marcion, a second-century heretic, represented the most dangerous movement associated with Gnosticism. According to him, the Father of Jesus is not the same as Yahweh, the God of the Old Testament. If this is true, Christianity is severed from its historic roots.

Fatalism, the belief that everything is controlled by an impersonal force, was also an element of Gnostic thinking. The early church fathers opposed

3. For a general discussion of the subject, see Kurt Rudolph, *Gnosis: The Nature and History of Gnosticism* (Edinburgh: T. and T. Clark, 1984). On the subject of Gnosticism and the New Testament documents, see Edwin M. Yamauchi, *Pre-Christian Gnosticism: A Survey of the Proposed Evidence,* 2d ed. (Grand Rapids: Baker, 1983).

4. Brown, *Heresies: The Image of Christ,* p. 39. This volume examines Gnosticism in great detail.

5. See the "nature of Christ's resurrection body" controversy in Geisler, *Battle for the Resurrection,* and a proponent of the "spiritual body" theory in Murray Harris, *Raised Immortal* (Grand Rapids: Eerdmans, 1985).

fatalism by stressing the freedom of the human will. Justin Martyr and John Chrysostom argued that good and evil come not from the individual's nature but from the will and choice. In response to the Gnostic libertarians Tertullian focused on the importance of works and righteousness, going so far as to say that "the man who performs good works can be said to make God his debtor."[6] This unfortunate phrase set the stage for centuries to come.

The "works-righteousness" concept, which seemed to be so ingenuous in combating Gnosticism, was popular for the first 350 years of the church's history. However, a controversy which would produce a more precise definition of the theological elements involved was needed. This dispute came on the scene in the system of Pelagius and the Christian thinker to confront it was Augustine of Hippo.[7]

AUGUSTINE, BISHOP OF HIPPO

Augustine (A.D. 354–430) was an intellectual giant. Born in Tagaste, North Africa (now Algeria), his mother was a Christian and his father a pagan. In his youth, Augustine sought after intellectual wisdom and thus was drawn to Manichaeism, a third-century religion that blended Persian, Christian, and Buddhist concepts. Augustine taught in Carthage for a time and then moved to Rome and Milan (A.D. 384), where he became disenchanted with Manichaeism and began to investigate Neoplatonism.

This new philosophical orientation convinced him that the existence of evil could be reconciled with the doctrine of creation. His understanding that evil was not a positive, created thing, but a privation or lack in things proved to be of great theological significance. Hence, concerning substance and evil, he wrote: "Therefore, as they are, they are good; therefore whatsoever is, is good. That evil, then, which I sought whence it was, is not any substance; for were it a substance, it would be good."[8] Further, "When accordingly it is inquired, whence is evil, it must first be inquired, what is evil, which is nothing else than corruption, either of the measure, or the form, or the order, that belong to nature."[9]

---

6. Tertullian, *De paenitentia* 2; 1.323.44–46.

7. An excellent historical analysis of this period can be found in Alister E. McGrath, *Iustitia Dei: A History of the Christian Doctrine of Justification*, vol. 1 (Cambridge: Cambridge University Press, 1986), pp. 1–23. For data on the church's preaching during this period, see Michael Green, *Evangelism in the Early Church* (Grand Rapids: Eerdmans, 1970). Although we have taken great pains throughout this work to point out that official Roman Catholic theology rejects Pelagianism (and semi-Pelagianism), it must be noted that impulses due to these heresies keep surfacing; see chap. 12 and Appendix B. The international Roman Catholic journal *30 Days* has addressed this issue; see "The Canons of Carthage: The Error of Pelagius," no. 1, 1994, pp. 37–44, and "Small Roman Catechism," no. 2, 1994, pp. 66–71.

8. *Confessions* 7.12; quoted in Norman L. Geisler, ed., *What Augustine Says* (Grand Rapids: Baker, 1982), p. 188.

9. *On the Nature of Good* 4; quoted in ibid., p. 189.

Through the preaching of Ambrose of Milan, his study of the New Testament, and the life of the desert father Antony of Egypt, Augustine was prepared for Christian conversion and was baptized at Easter in A.D. 387. He was ordained a priest in A.D. 391, was a bishop four years later, and succeeded to the See of Hippo in A.D. 396. Augustine died during the siege of the city by the Vandals in A.D. 430.

The thought of this intellectual and spiritual giant is crucial to the central investigation of this present work in that Augustine's contributions have been embraced by both Roman Catholics and Protestants. Our primary concern here is with Augustine's soteriological contributions. No one has exercised a greater influence over the development of Western Christian thought than the Bishop of Hippo. Anselm of Canterbury equated theological orthodoxy as he knew it with conformity to the writings of Augustine of Hippo, as did Thomas Aquinas after him.

In dealing with Augustine's doctrine of justification, it is important to note that his thinking on this most vital of issues underwent significant development. Early on Augustine stressed the role of the human will in matters of salvation, a view he would later modify in his disputations with the British monk, Pelagius. His mature doctrine, however, came down decidedly on the side of grace alone (sola gratia). We are saved by grace, not by the law, "for the law gives its prescriptions to this end alone that when one has failed to fulfill these commandments, he will not be filled with pride; thus, by frightening him, the law fulfills its purpose of pedagogue, leading him to love Christ."[10] Augustine was fond of saying: "The justice of God is not that by which God himself is just but that which God gives to man so that he might be just through God."[11] In short, it is totally by God's grace that we are justified. Salvation is neither initiated nor obtained by human action. Even the faith by which we obtain salvation is the gift of God.

SUMMING UP SALVATION IN THE EARLY PERIOD

After reflecting on Pauline insights, Augustine came to the following conclusions. First, the eternal decree of God's predestination determines one's election. "I speak thus of those who are predestined to the Kingdom of God, whose number is so certain that one can neither be added to them nor taken from them."[12]

Second, God's offer of grace (salvation) is itself a gift (John 6:44a). Commenting on Paul's statement in 2 Timothy 4, Augustine wrote: "His last

10. Augustine, De perfectione iustitae hominis 5.11; quoted in Anderson, Justification by Faith, p. 123.
11. Augustine, Tractatus Johannem 26.1; quoted in ibid.
12. Augustine, On Rebuke and Grace 39; quoted in ibid., p. 127.

clause runs thus: 'I have kept the faith.' But he who says this is the same who declares in another passage, 'I have obtained mercy that I might be faithful.' He does not say, 'I obtained mercy because I was faithful' but 'in order that I might be faithful,' thus showing that even faith itself cannot be had without God's mercy, and that it is the gift of God."[13]

Third, the human will is completely unable to initiate or attain salvation. This concept squares quite well with the later doctrine of total depravity—which surfaced more than a millennium later as the first point of the Reformed mnemonic device, TULIP: Total depravity, Unconditional election, Limited atonement, Irresistible grace, and Perseverance of the saints. These five points of Calvinist soteriology were adopted at the Synod of Dort (A.D. 1618–19).

Fourth, Augustine maintained that the justified sinner does not merely receive the *status* of sonship, but *becomes* one. For Augustine, justification included both the beginnings of one's righteousness before God and its subsequent perfection—the event and the process. What later became the Reformation concept of "sanctification" then is effectively subsumed under the aegis of justification.[14] Although he believed that God initiated the salvation process, it is incorrect to say that Augustine held to the concept of "forensic" justification. This understanding of justification is a later development of the Reformation (see chap. 12).

Fifth, a feature in Augustinianism which Protestants will no doubt find interesting is that God may regenerate a person without causing that one to finally persevere.[15] This is Calvinism without the perseverance of *all* the saints. Thus Reformed scholar Louis Berkhof comments: "The [Reformed] doctrine [of perseverance] is not merely the effect that the elect will certainly be saved in the end, though Augustine has given it that form, but teaches very specifically that they who have once been regenerated and effectually called by God to a state of grace, can never completely fall from that state and thus fail to attain to eternal salvation."[16]

Despite the later Protestant emphasis on forensic justification, there is a common core of teaching on salvation that unites Catholics and Protestants; namely, that *salvation is by God's grace*.[17] That is, no good works precede justification (regeneration). Recently, some have claimed that the common core is "salvation by grace through faith,"[18] but this is misleading since

---

13. Augustine, *On Grace and Free Will* 17, ibid., p. 167.

14. McGrath, *Iustitia Dei*, 1:32.

15. Augustine, *City of God* 10.8.

16. Berkhof, *Systematic Theology*, p. 546.

17. The Protestant view is often contrasted with this as being salvation by grace alone and faith alone, *sola gratia, sola fide* (see chap. 12).

18. See the "Evangelicals and Catholics Together" joint statement released 29 March 1994 by Chuck Colson, Richard John Neuhaus, and others.

Roman Catholics believe that justification occurs at baptism when the infant is too young to express any conscious or explicit faith in Christ. Further, they believe works are necessary for salvation (see chap. 12), whereas Protestants believe salvation is by faith alone. Often the views are distinguished by saying both Catholics and Protestants believe salvation is by grace alone *(sola gratia)*, while Protestants add that it is also by faith alone *(sola fide)*. But even here different things are meant by "grace alone,"[19] for *sola gratia* does not mean the same thing for Catholics as it does for Reformed Protestants. For normative Catholicism, *sola gratia* means only the primacy and necessity of grace, but not the exclusivity of grace. Official Catholicism teaches that works are also necessary for salvation. And while all Catholics believe these works are prompted by grace, they also believe in the meritorious nature of good works, which Protestants deny (see chap. 12).

Nonetheless, both Catholics and Protestants believe in the *necessity of grace.* That is, without God's grace there would be no salvation. And even man's good works, which are the necessary fruit of regeneration, are produced by God's grace. This teaching was made clear by Augustine, Aquinas, and even the Council of Trent. Augustine said emphatically of Pelagius's error, "should he consent that we receive love from the grace of God, he must not suppose that any merit of our own preceded our reception of the gift," for "what merit could we possibly have had at the time when we loved not God?" Hence, "that grace of God, whereby 'His love is shed abroad in our hearts through the Holy Ghost, which is given to us,' must be so confessed . . . that nothing whatever in the way of goodness pertaining to godliness and real holiness can be accomplished without it."[20] The third canon of the Second Council of Orange (A.D. 529) was emphatic: "If anyone says that the grace of God can be conferred because of human prayer, and not rather that it is grace itself that prompts us to pray, he contradicts the prophet Isaiah, or the apostle Paul who says the same thing: 'I have been found by those who did not seek me; I have shown myself to those who did not ask for me' (Rom. 10:20; Isa. 65:1)."[21] Canon 18 adds, "Whatever good works we do are deserving of reward, not through any merit anterior to grace; their performance, rather, is due to a prior gift of grace to which we have no claim."[22]

In concluding this section on the early church's view of salvation, it is fitting to mention the tension between Augustine's doctrine of the church—which had sacramental and sacerdotal elements—and his soteriological concerns. In addressing this point, B. B. Warfield wrote, "the Reformation, in-

---

19. Anderson, *Justification by Faith*, pp. 15–16, 22.

20. Augustine, *On the Grace of Christ*, I.27 [26], in *A Select Library of the Nicene and Post-Nicene Fathers*, pp. 227–28.

21. Neuner and Dupuis, *Christian Faith*, p. 606.

22. Cited by Louis Bouyer, *The Spirit and Forms of Protestantism* (Westminster, Md.: Newman Press, 1961), p. 49.

wardly considered, was just the ultimate triumph of Augustine's doctrine of grace over Augustine's doctrine of the Church."[23] While the sacraments of baptism and penance, the concept of merit, and the relationship between predestination and justification can be found in Augustinianism, they become more clearly defined later, and we will address them in Part Two. Augustine has been regarded as both the last of the church fathers and the first medieval theologian. He marks the end of one era and the beginning of another.

THE EARLY MEDIEVAL PERIOD

The medieval period (the "middle ages") is commonly dated from Augustine (or slightly later) to the 1500s. During this period the balance of power in the church shifted from the East (where Christianity began) to the West (or Latin) wing of the church.

Many heresies emerged during this time. Pelagianism was officially condemned by the church at the Council of Ephesus (A.D. 431) and again at the Second Council of Orange (A.D. 529) which declared that "If anyone says that the grace of God can be bestowed by human invocation, but that the grace itself does not bring it to pass that it be invoked by us, he contradicts Isias the Prophet . . . [cf. Isa. 65:1]."[24] This heresy, however, along with its close relative semi-Pelagianism[25] (also condemned at the Council of Orange), keeps recurring in church history. It seems that the natural inclination leans toward Pelagianism rather than Augustine's Pauline emphasis on the grace of God.

Leo the Great, who was the Roman Pontiff from A.D. 440 to 461, is designated by many non-Catholic historians as the first "pope" in the modern sense. Many Roman Catholic dogmas (which may have existed in germ form earlier) now solidified: the supreme authority of the Roman bishop in the church, sacramentalism, sacerdotalism, and the change of emphasis in the Eucharistic Feast from celebration to sacrifice, to name a few.[26] These doctrines impacted medieval soteriology in several ways.

JUSTIFICATION AND THE SACRAMENTS

During the medieval period, baptism and penance were linked with justification. God's righteousness was *begun* (infused) in baptism and *continued*

---

23. B. B. Warfield, *Calvin and Augustine* (Philadelphia: Presbyterian and Reformed, 1956), pp. 312ff., p. 322.

24. Denzinger, *Sources of Catholic Dogma,* no. 176, p. 76.

25. Semi-Pelagianism held that humanity cooperated with God by ordinarily taking the first step toward salvation. The term was also applied by Dominco Báñez (1528–1604) to the theology of the Jesuit Luis De Molina (1535–1600).

26. These distinctives of Roman Catholicism will be dealt with more at length in Part Two.

(perfected) through penance. Augustine stated: "'Who forgiveth all thine iniquities': this is done in the sacrament of baptism."[27] To circumvent the fact that it is impossible to please God without faith (which infants cannot possess), Bernard of Clairvaux held that God justified children on account of the faith of others.[28]

Although this understanding of the nature and purpose of baptism can be found from the earliest of times, the same is not true of the concept of penance. The idea of confession to a priest for the remission of sin existed until the second century but did not become a widespread practice in the early medieval period. Indeed, some applied the term "the second baptism" to sacerdotal confession. Baptism addressed the problem of *original* sin, while confession cleansed the effect of *actual* sin. Some theologians of this era took pains to stress that the sacraments were the *means* God used to mediate grace to us. However, this theological nicety was often lost on the laity, who became entangled in a works-righteousness system.

THE CONCEPT OF MERIT

Closely related to the sacraments in general is the concept of *merit*. The term is first used by Tertullian (A.D. 160–225) and then fully developed by the Schoolmen in the medieval period. There was a pastoral intention connected to the concept of merit. As McGrath points out: "It can be shown that a distinction came to be drawn between the concepts of *merit* and *congruity*; while man cannot be said to merit justification by any of his actions, his preparation for justification could be said to make his subsequent justification 'congruous' or 'appropriate.'"[29]

An example of this thinking by Roman Catholics is mentioned by a contemporary Catholic historian who says concerning Martin Luther: "As a monk, he had found no peace in trying to clear his guilty conscience through penance and self-denial but experienced freedom when he realized that man is justified by faith alone, as Paul explains in his letter to the Romans."[30] Unfortunately, as with the sacraments, this distinction did not always filter down to the common folk.

PREDESTINATION AND JUSTIFICATION

As in most of the theological concepts surrounding the doctrine of justification, we must go back to Augustine to find the earliest treatment of predes-

---

27. Augustine, *On Forgiveness of Sins and Baptism* 1.44; quoted in Geisler, p. 151.
28. Anselm of Canterbury also taught this. See McGrath, *Iustitia Dei*, 1:92.
29. Ibid., 1:110.
30. Alan Schreck, *The Compact History of the Catholic Church* (Ann Arbor: Servant Books, 1987), p. 63.

tination this side of Paul. The context was Augustine's dispute with Pelagius, whose theological system—among other things—denied original sin. Pelagius taught that people are free in their natural state to do good, apart from God's grace.

Augustine disagreed, arguing that, before the fall, humanity was free both to sin and not to sin. Between the fall and the cross, we were free only to sin. When we are redeemed, the Holy Spirit works in our hearts, freedom is restored, and we are again free both to sin and not to sin. Ultimately, in heaven we shall still be free, but only free not to sin. It is important to note that, through all this, Augustine does not deny the freedom of the human will.[31]

Augustine took great pains to distinguish between predestination and fatalism. He resisted the notion of double predestination, which argues that God not only decides to elect some to eternal life but also actively predestines others to eternal destruction. Nonetheless, the predestination controversy came to the fore during the medieval period. Peter Lombard, Thomas Aquinas, and Duns Scotus held the Augustinian position that grace was extended to man by God without consideration of any existing merit. William of Ockham, on the other hand, seems to have based predestination on the reality of perseverance, which to the Reformed mind is putting the cart before the horse.

THE ARCHBISHOP OF CANTERBURY

Anselm of Canterbury (A.D. 1033–1109) was arguably the most penetrating theological thinker between Augustine and Aquinas. He was born in Aosta, Northern Italy. At age fifteen Anselm gave his life to God and decided to become a monk.

He entered the Benedictine monastery of Bec in Normandy. Exposed to the rigors of theological investigation, he developed into a philosophical/religious thinker of first rank. He answered an invitation to come to England, and on his arrival was appointed archbishop of Canterbury, where he served with distinction until his death in A.D. 1109.

Anselm's earliest literary efforts were prayers, meditations, and letters of consolation and reproof, directed to those under his spiritual care. His facile mind soon turned to profound theological themes and his efforts would change the soteriological landscape forever.[32] Anselm wrote on a number of

---

31. See Justo L. González, *The Story of Christianity*, vol. 1 (San Francisco: Harper and Row, 1984), pp. 214f.

32. The following volumes on Anselm are helpful: John J. Delaney and James Edward Tobin, eds., *Dictionary of Catholic Biography* (Garden City, N.Y.: Doubleday, 1961); F. L. Cross, ed., *Oxford Dictionary of the Christian Church* (Oxford: Oxford University Press, 1983); John D. Woodbridge, ed., *Great Leaders of the Christian Church* (Chicago: Moody Press, 1988).

themes during his career: the existence and attributes of God, the incarnation, the atonement, evil, free will, and predestination.

Like Aquinas, Anselm owed a great deal to Augustine. The guiding principle in his theological investigations was *fides quarens intellectum* ("faith seeking understanding"). For Anselm, "faith is not only the foundation of true understanding; it is the *stimulus* to understanding. Faith seeks completion in an understanding which stands midway between faith and vision."[33] According to Anselm, Christianity is "intrinsically and preeminently rational; and a Christian lacking an understanding of his faith would be a stunted Christian indeed."[34]

Anselm rejects fideism. Faith is not without reasons. In fact, "one believes *in order that* one may understand."[35] However, the faith that opens the door to understanding cannot be defined simply as an intellectual acceptance of certain truths. The faith that introduces man to God, and thus to all of reality, must be defined primarily in terms of *relationship* with God.[36]

One of Anselm's great theological treatises was *Cur Deus Homo* ("Why the God-man").[37] In it he addressed the relationship between the incarnation and the atonement and redirected thinking on the nature and purpose of the atonement that had been in place since the apostolic era.

Augustine had plumbed the depths of depravity and grace, but even he had not addressed the ultimate question posed by Anselm. A popular theory in the early church was the so-called *ransom* theory. This "classic view" understood the atonement as an antidote over the forces of sin and evil, as a deliverance of humanity from the clutches of Satan. Augustine also held this view. Anselm's contribution to the doctrine of the atonement is called the *satisfaction* theory. It understands the atonement as compensation to the Father; sin is failing to give God his due.[38]

Cur Deus Homo consists of two parts, having twenty-five and twenty-two chapters respectively. In the first part, Anselm attempts to show that no one is saved apart from Christ: "The man who thinks that he can make satisfaction for his own sin has simply 'not yet considered what a heavy weight sin is' (1:21)."[39]

In Part Two, Anselm states that man is destined for salvation and examines how this purpose was carried out by the God-man. "The *Cur Deus*

---

33. Robert B. Strimple, *Anselm and the Theology of Atonement*, unpublished Master of Theology thesis (Philadelphia: Westminster Theological Seminary, 1964), p. 79.

34. Ibid.

35. Ibid., pp. 79, 80.

36. Ibid., p. 81.

37. Or "Why God Became Man," *The Library of Christian Classics*, vol. 10, ed. and trans. Eugene R. Fairweather (Philadelphia: Westminster Press, 1951).

38. Careful treatment of Anselm's view can be found in McGrath, *Iustitia Dei*, pp. 55–60.

39. Strimple, *Anselm*, p. 91.

Homo performed a valuable service for the Church in dealing the death-blow to the notion that Christ's death was a ransom paid to the devil in order to satisfy the latter's just claim upon men."[40] Anselm exhibited "a profound sense of the sinfulness of sin and the necessity of atonement."[41]

Finally, "*Cur Deus Homo* places in the forefront of consideration the *objective* efficacy of the Atonement—Christ's death as removing that obstacle which our sin had placed in the way of God's extending his favor toward us."[42] *Cur Deus Homo* has been called "the truest and greatest book on the atonement that has ever been written."[43]

One further theory concerning the atonement should be mentioned—the *moral-influence* theory. This position was advanced by Peter Abelard (A.D. 1070–1142). A younger contemporary of Anselm, Abelard promoted the view that the atonement is best understood as a demonstration of God's love. Hence, "the major effect of Christ's death was upon man rather than upon God."[44] Abelard's moral-influence theory, however, proved to be less satisfactory than Anselm's.[45]

SOME CENTRAL THEMES IN MEDIEVAL SOTERIOLOGY

It may be helpful at this point to summarize some important developments in the doctrine of salvation in the Middle Ages. First, there was an increased interest in Pauline studies for theological formulations; hence, new attention was paid to moral and legal concepts of redemption.

Second, with the brilliant work of Anselm, the medieval notion of the "devil's rights" over sinful humanity—known as the ransom theory of the atonement—was replaced by the satisfaction theory. The Reformers were later to build on Anselm's insights and would develop a forensic perspective on justification.

Third, the distinction between justification and sanctification—which came to the fore in the Reformation—is almost totally absent from the medieval period. Instead, the idea that man's *status,* not his *nature,* was affected by justification was later developed by the Reformers.

40. Ibid., p. 109.
41. Ibid.
42. Ibid.
43. James Denney, *The Atonement and the Modern Mind* (New York: A. C. Armstrong and Son, 1903), p. 116.
44. Millard J. Erickson, *Christian Theology* (Grand Rapids: Baker, 1986), p. 785.
45. It is of interest to note that this great Christian scholar, Anselm (who was declared a Doctor of the Church in A.D. 1720), was also concerned with practical issues as well as academic theological formulations. In 1102 at a domestic council at Westminster, he made an impassioned plea against the slave trade in England.

Fourth, although Pelagianism (and semi-Pelagianism) were not completely absent from the theological scene during this period it is incorrect to hold that these deviations dominated the soteriological scene. Most theological concepts were Augustinian in nature, to a greater or lesser degree.

THE LATE MEDIEVAL PERIOD

One figure dominated the late medieval period, the Angelic Doctor. St. Thomas Aquinas (A.D. 1225?–74) considered himself Augustinian in his theology, although he preferred to express his philosophical views in Aristotelian terms rather than the Platonic language of Augustine. Aquinas seldom differed from Augustine in theology, and then only with great deference to his theological mentor. This is certainly true on the doctrine of justification.

Like Augustine, Aquinas believed that regeneration occurs at baptism, asserting that "Baptism cleanses only the individual person who receives it [baptism] from original sin; his children must also be baptized."[46] Likewise, he held that not all the regenerate will persevere. Contrary to a widespread misunderstanding among Protestants, Aquinas believed that humankind is unable to initiate or attain salvation except by the grace of God. While man can do "natural" good (i.e., loving one's family, kindness toward those who do good to us, etc.), he is completely dependent on God for salvation. Aquinas asserted emphatically that

> Human reason is very deficient in things concerning God. A sign of this is that philosophers, in their inquiry into human affairs by natural investigation, have fallen into many errors, and have disagreed among themselves. [Consequently] . . . in order that men might have knowledge of God, free of doubt and uncertainty, it was necessary for divine truths to be delivered to them by way of faith, being told to them as it were, by God Himself Who cannot lie.[47]

Aquinas also believed that human beings are fallen. Commenting on Ephesians 2:3, he wrote, "Original sin is hinted at in [this phrase] *and we were by nature children of wrath.* This sin of the first parents was not only passed on to the Gentiles but also to the Jews also. . . ." Thus, "*we were by nature,* that is, from the earliest beginning of nature—not of nature as nature since this is good and from God, but of nature as vitiated—*children of* an avenging *wrath,* aimed at punishment and hell."[48] As a result of the effects of sin on

---

46. Aquinas, *Commentary on Saint Paul's Epistle to the Ephesians by St. Thomas Aquinas,* trans. Matthew L. Lamb (Albany, N.Y.: Magi Books, 1966), p. 89.

47. Aquinas, *Summa Theologiae,* 2a2ae. 2, 4, in *The Basic Writings of Thomas Aquinas,* ed. Anton C. Pegis (New York: Random House, 1944), p. 1079.

48. Ibid.

man, grace is necessary. Commenting on the great text on grace in Ephesians 2:8–9, Aquinas even asserted that faith is a gift of God:

> *He* [St. Paul] eliminates two errors. . . . The first of these is that, since he has said we are saved by faith, any one can hold the opinion that faith originates within ourselves and that to believe is determined by our own wishes. Therefore to abolish this he states *and that not of yourselves.* Free will is inadequate for the act of faith since the contents of faith are above human reason.[49]

Aquinas added, "The second error he [St. Paul] rejects is that anyone can believe that faith is given by God to us on the merit of our predestined actions. To exclude this he adds *Not of* preceding *works* that we merited at one time to be saved." Aquinas concluded that "if for something to be in our power means that we can do it without the help of grace, then we are bound to many things that are not within our power without healing grace—for example to love God or neighbor." Further, he stated:

> The same is true of believing in the articles of faith. But with the help of grace we do have this power. As Augustine says, to whomever this help is given by God it is given in mercy; to whomever it is denied, it is denied in justice, namely because of previous sin, even if only original sin.[50]

Whatever can be said of others, the two greatest theologians of the Catholic church, Augustine and Aquinas, clearly believed that *salvation is completely dependent on God's grace.* In fact in their case, though not infallibly normative for Catholics, it is by grace alone *(sola gratia)* in the sense that every human action connected with salvation is not only prompted by but is produced by God's grace. Grace is operative, not merely cooperative, in effecting our salvation.[51]

However, Aquinas, like Augustine, did not speak of forensic justification as understood by the Reformers. Justification for him meant not simply to *declare* the sinner righteous but to *make* him righteous. Whereas the Reformers distinguished forensic justification and progressive sanctification, Augustine and Aquinas did not. This does not mean that the Reformers' distinction is incompatible with Aquinas's view, but simply that Aquinas did not state it this way. Both can be true. Some contemporary Roman Catholic scholars believe that declarative justification is included in the thinking of Augustine and Aquinas, at least implicitly.

---

49. Ibid., p. 96.
50. Aquinas, *Summa Theologiae,* 2a2ae. 2, 6, ad 1.
51. Of course, Aquinas did believe in the doctrine of merit and the necessity of good works. So in this sense he would fall short of the Protestant understanding of salvation by faith alone. But since these good works come in the overall context of God's operative grace, some evangelicals have embraced Aquinas as "Protestant."

THE PRE-REFORMATION PERIOD

IMPORTANT PRE-REFORMATION EVENTS

The end of the fifteenth century proved to be a turning point in Western history. Not only the church but culture in general was to be forever changed. Columbus's arrival in America (A.D. 1492), Henry VIII and his matrimonial difficulties, and the spreading influence of the Renaissance were but a few of the incidents marking this period. Virtually all historians—Roman Catholic and Protestant alike—agree that the church had become morally corrupt and in need of reform. The "Babylonian Captivity" at Avignon (A.D. 1309–77) and the Great Schism (1378–1417) with its scandal of anti-popes (competing claims to the papacy) exposed cracks in the papal edifice.

While clerical celibacy was officially the law of the church, many priests and bishops ignored this rule. Pope John XXII (A.D. 1316–34) officially condemned the distortions that had crept into the church concerning the ideal of poverty promoted by Francis of Assisi (1182–1226), a man so revered by his contemporaries that he was called "the second Christ."[52] The ecclesiastical situation is aptly summed up by Sebastian Brant (1457–1521): "St. Peter's bark is tempest-tossed, I fear the vessel may be lost."

The two major figures prior to the Reformation were John Wycliffe (A.D. 1329–84) and John Hus (A.D. 1373–1415). Wycliffe was a brilliant Oxford scholar whose insistence on the superiority of Scripture in religious affairs earned him the title of the "morning star of the Reformation." As a philosopher, he attacked nominalism and upheld an Augustinian realism. Hus was ordained in A.D. 1401 and soon became the rector of the University of Prague. He was an admirer of Wycliffe's views in general, while not quite as "anti-Roman" as the Oxford thinker. His views, however, led to him being called a heretic, and he was burned at the stake in A.D. 1415.

SUMMING UP SALVATION PRIOR TO THE REFORMATION

It is important to note that concerning the soteriological doctrines of the men we have been examining were Augustinian. The following features characterize the medieval theological tradition prior to the Reformation period.

First, justification was regarded as both an initial act and a continual process.

---

52. Jaroslav Pelikan, *Jesus through the Centuries* (New York: Harper and Row, 1987), p. 133.

Second, the view of man's standing before God and his basic nature underwent change.

Third, a firm anti-Pelagianism permeated late medieval thought and this view passed into the early theology of the Reformation.

Fourth, a works-righteousness position emerged which was to become a focal point in the Reformation controversy.

THE REFORMATION PERIOD

Many volumes have been written covering both sides of this controversy.[53] The passage of time since the event in question has caused the stridency and emotional trauma associated with the rupture to subside. On both sides of the debate those of a progressive and traditional bent have of late taken a more sympathetic look at the causes and events that led to the Reformation. Much study and dialogue have occurred recently between Roman Catholics and Protestants concerning core theological issues in general and soteriological concerns (i.e., justification by faith) in particular. We will examine the degree of continuity—or lack of it—between the Augustinianism of the early church and later medieval period, and that of the major movers and shakers of the Reformation.

MARTIN LUTHER

Born in A.D. 1483, in Eisleben, Germany, of middle-class parents, Martin Luther entered the Augustinian monastery at Erfurt in 1505. The themes of salvation and damnation—which were central to the culture of the day— concerned him greatly. Luther became aware of the presence of sin in his life and the ineffectiveness of the penance provided by the church to bring relief to this situation. In addition to penance, divine "grace" was dispensed by the church through the six other sacraments, the most important of these being, in addition to penance, baptism and the Eucharistic observance (Holy Communion).[54]

Listen to Luther as years later he recalls his experience in the monastery:

---

53. Two good Protestant treatments are: R. Tudur Jones, *The Great Reformation* (Downers Grove, Ill.: InterVarsity, 1985), and Bernard M. G. Reardon, *Religious Thought in the Reformation* (London: Longman, 1981). A short but balanced Roman Catholic work is Alan Schreck, *The Compact History of the Catholic Church* (Ann Arbor: Servant, 1987). Also see William Durant's *The Reformation* (New York: Simon and Schuster, 1957), Part VI of "The Story of Civilization" series.

54. Protestants should be aware that Luther's view of the sacraments of baptism and the Eucharist was very close to that of the Roman Catholic church. See Paul Althaus, *The Theology of Martin Luther* (Philadelphia: Fortress Press, 1966), pp. 345–74.

> I was a good monk and kept my order so strictly that I could claim that if ever a monk were able to reach heaven by monkish discipline I should have found my way there. All my fellows in the house, who know me, would bear me out in this. For if it had continued much longer I would, what with vigils, prayers, readings and other such works, have done myself to death.[55]

A Dominican scholar recalls Luther's word during this time of spiritual anguish: "I wanted to live so devoutly that I could appear before God and say: 'here you have holiness.'"[56]

In 1511 Luther was transferred from Erfurt to Wittenberg. He lived in the Augustinian cloister and was fortunate to have as his spiritual confessor a godly man who was also the vicar-general of the monastery: Johannes von Staupitz (1469–1524). Staupitz, aware of the intense spiritual struggles that enveloped his young charge, directed Luther to study Scripture. Luther was graduated Doctor of Theology on October 19, 1512, and commenced teaching theology and biblical studies at Wittenberg on August 16, 1513. It was in the context of his assignment at the university that Luther developed his initial ideas concerning justification by faith.

Luther had been influenced by nominalism, the form of theology and philosophy advocated by William of Ockham. It was known as the *via moderna* in contrast to Thomism and Scotism, which were called the *via antiqua*. Nominalism removed most of the data of faith from the realm of reason and was one of the antecedents of modern fideism.

Luther seems to have had little contact with the early Dominican school (which had Thomism as its theological rudder) and it is interesting to speculate on how exposure to the Augustinian core of Thomistic thought might have influenced his early spiritual and exegetical investigations.

The decisive role in the formulation of Luther's theology was played by St. Paul and Augustinianism. It was shortly after his exegesis of Paul's phrase in Romans 1:17, "the righteousness of God" (*iustitia Dei* in the Latin), that Luther stated that justification is a gift of God, appropriated by faith:

> Now I felt as though I had been immediately born anew and had entered Paradise itself. From that moment the face of Scripture as a whole became clear to me. My mind ran through the sacred books, as far as I was able to recollect them, seeking analogies in other phrases, such as *opus Dei,* that which God works in us; *virtus Dei,* that by which God makes us strong; *sapienta Dei,* that by which he makes us wise; *fortitudo Dei, salus Dei, gloria Dei*—the strength, the salvation, the glory of God.[57]

---

55. WA, Tischreden, IV, 303.16.

56. Quoted in Stephanus Pfurtner, *Luther and Aquinas—a Conversation: Our Salvation, Its Certainty and Peril,* trans. Edward Quinn (London: Darton, Longman and Todd, 1964), p. 19.

57. WA, LIV, 179–87.

Luther's understanding of God's justice and grace had undergone a drastic change. He wrote: "Because God is almighty and rich in mercy and turns as such to me, I can—indeed, I must—trust in him, I can and must be certain of my salvation in spite of my own sinfulness!"[58]

The beginning of Martin Luther's problems with Rome has often been identified with his posting of the *Ninety-five Theses* on the eve of All Saints, October 31, 1517. These theses dealt with the doctrine of purgatory, the penitential system, papal authority, but primarily with the sale of indulgences. Pastoral concern prompted Luther to act. People who showed no signs of sincere repentance for their sins would come to him for confession. They would produce copies of indulgences that they had purchased and thought of them as licenses to sin without spiritual consequences. Luther declined to grant them absolution. With the public display of the *Ninety-five Theses* the die was cast; the Reformation began and Christendom changed forever.[59]

Among the points raised in the *Ninety-five Theses* were the following:

1. A true Christian who is repentant has remission from both the guilt and penalty of sin because he participates in the benefits of Christ (theses 16–17).
2. A Christian has no need of letters of pardon and the purchase of such is wrong when it is clearly better to give the money to the poor (theses 41–45).
3. "The Pope can remit no guilt, but only declare and confirm that it has been remitted by God" (thesis 6).
4. Concerning the "treasury of the accumulated merits of the saints," the "true treasure of the Church is the holy Gospel of the glory and the grace of God" (thesis 62).

In the *Ninety-five Theses,* Luther did not "challenge the doctrine of purgatory. He [did] not question the scriptural basis of the sacrament of penance. He [did] not demand the abolition of indulgences."[60] What he did was address the abuses of the doctrines that had become commonplace in the culture of his day.

Indicating how deeply his evangelical (Augustinian) principles influenced the theses, Luther was later to write:

And this is the confidence that Christians have and our real joy of conscience, that by faith our sins become no longer ours but Christ's upon whom God

---

58. Pfurtner, *Luther and Aquinas*, p. 22.
59. It should be pointed out that the pope agreed with many of these theses, primarily those which dealt with moral issues.
60. Jones, *Great Reformation*, p. 36.

placed the sins of all of us. He took upon himself our sins. . . . All the righteousness of Christ becomes ours. . . . He spreads his cloak and covers us.[61]

Some reevaluation has been going on among contemporary Catholic theologians concerning Luther's reaction to the state of the church in his day. For example, Louis Bouyer (who had been a Lutheran pastor before his conversion to Roman Catholicism) does not view Luther as a revolutionary, but as a truly spiritually sensitive pastor seeking to reform the church from within. Bouyer argues that the Lutheran doctrine of justification by faith alone is not a heresy but is consistent with Catholic tradition and in harmony with the teachings of Augustine, Anselm, and Aquinas.[62] Other Catholic theologians hold similar views.

Another quote from a modern Roman Catholic source is in order: "The irony of the Protestant Reformation is that much of what Luther believed and taught was authentic Catholic doctrine that had been distorted by abuses and incorrect practices in the Church, such as the mercenary selling of indulgences. Unfortunately, Luther's criticism of real abuses was not heeded."[63]

The Council of Trent (A.D. 1545–63) would, during the Counter-Reformation, address these same issues and provide needed reforms, such as banning the sale of indulgences. This was done to avoid the corrupt practices that had developed.

In addressing the similarities and differences of Augustinianism and Luther, the following may be stated.

First, Luther and Augustine both believed that *iustitia Dei* (righteousness of God) is a righteousness that is a gift from God to us, rather than the righteousness that God possesses in his own Person.[64]

Second, Luther, following Augustine, did not make the distinction between forensic justification and progressive sanctification that would emerge in later Protestantism.[65] Indeed, "It is important to note that Luther does not employ forensic [legal] terms to explain this imputation of alien righteousness. This development will come later, from others."[66]

---

61. Martin Luther, *Explanations of the Ninety-five Theses,* published August 1518.

62. Louis Bouyer, *The Spirit and Forms of Protestantism,* trans. A. V. Littledale (Westminster: Newman Press, 1961). See chaps. 1 through 6 covering such topics as salvation as a free gift, justification by faith, and the sovereign authority of Scripture.

Harry McSorley, in his book *Luther: Right or Wrong?* (Minneapolis: Augsburg Publishing House, 1969), is another Roman Catholic scholar who is of the opinion that Luther rightly reacted to the semi-Pelagianism of Biel and Ockham which had corrupted scholasticism. He feels that Luther's protest was in full accord with Augustine, Anselm, Bernard, Aquinas, and the Councils of Trent and Vatican II are quoted to support his thesis.

63. Schreck, *Compact History,* pp. 63f.

64. McGrath, *Iustitia Dei,* 2:7ff.

65. Paul Althaus, *The Theology of Martin Luther* (Philadelphia: Fortress Press, 1966), pp. 237ff.

66. Peter Toon, *Justification and Sanctification* (Westminster: Crossway Books, 1983), p. 58.

Third, Augustine and the medieval church had believed in a "theology of glory." This is the result of natural theology and claims to know God through his works. Its antithesis is Luther's "theology of the cross" concept, which elevates the cross as the most important place of encounter between God and man. There God is seen in weakness (1 Cor. 1:18–25) and suffering and our preconceived concepts of divine glory are shattered. Luther said:

> That person does not deserve to be called a theologian who looks upon the invisible things of God as if it were clearly perceptible in those things in which have actually happened. He deserved to be called a theologian, however, who comprehends the visible and manifest things of God seen through suffering and the cross.[67]

A contemporary orthodox Roman Catholic theologian comments on these two "paths" in Christology:

> In the history of the Christian faith, two divergent lines of approach to the contemplation of Jesus have appeared again and again: the theology of the incarnation (glory), which sprang from Greek thought and became dominant in the Catholic tradition of East and West, and the theology of the cross, which based itself on St. Paul and the earliest forms of Christian belief and made a decisive break-through in the thinking of the Reformers.[68]

Ratzinger goes on to develop these two themes and states that they are not contradictory but "must remain present as polarities which mutually correct each other and only by complementing each other point toward the whole."[69]

Finally, Augustine never held the doctrine of "double" predestination. "This means an unconditional, eternal predestination both to salvation and to damnation."[70] Although Augustinianism might be said to imply logically such a concept, the bishop of Hippo never took that step and actually argued against it.

It seems clear that in spite of significant differences in their systems, Luther and Augustine were united in their belief that man is spiritually destitute and, apart from God's grace, is incapable of producing any semblance of spiritual merit. Luther was, indeed (at least concerning the basic tenets of justification), a spiritual son of the bishop of Hippo and of the "Doctor Angelicus."

---

67. WA, 361f.; LW 31, 52. Theses 19 and 20 of the Heidelberg Disputation; quoted in ibid. Good treatment of the "Theology of the Cross" is found on pp. 25–34.

68. Joseph Cardinal Ratzinger, *Introduction to Christianity*, trans. J. R. Foster (San Francisco: Ignatius Press, 1990), p. 170.

69. Ibid., p. 171. This section, "Theology of the Incarnation and Theology of the Cross" (pp. 170–72), is excellent.

70. WA, DB, 7, 23; LW 35, 378; quoted in ibid., p. 275. Also see chap. 20 in its entirety.

PHILIPP MELANCHTHON

Philipp Melanchthon was born in Bretten in A.D. 1497. He was a mere twenty-one years of age when, teaching at Tübingen, he was appointed to the newly founded Chair of Greek in Luther's University of Wittenberg. Two men could not be less alike than Melanchthon and Luther. Luther was a tempestuous religious revolutionary; Melanchthon, a quiet systematic theologian. Luther was contemptuous of philosophy and Christian humanism[71] while Melanchthon enjoyed the support and friendship of the greatest Christian humanist of the day, Erasmus.

Even though they were opposites in temperament and somewhat different in theological methodology, "Magister Philipp," as Luther called him, became Luther's trusted friend and first lieutenant. The major theological work of Lutheranism, the Augsburg Confession (1530), was mainly the work of Melanchthon. His irenic nature in contrast to his superior's bombast made him a natural candidate to effect a rapprochement between Rome and Wittenberg, but efforts in this direction came to naught.

Melanchthon represented many differences with his mentor and earlier Lutheran thinking. For one thing, he had a more positive approach to the freedom of the human will. For another, Melanchthon was more conciliatory toward Calvin and Zwingli, appreciating their view on the sacraments and their approach to the disciplines of the Christian life. Then, too, Melanchthon seems to abandon an important aspect of Luther's understanding of justification: the personal union of Christ and the believer. Thus, extrinsic justification overwhelmed intrinsic justification. Indeed, it was Melanchthon, not Luther, who first spoke of justification in forensic terms.[72] In short, concerning issues of soteriology, Melanchthon was less Augustinian than Luther and much a product of his earlier training in humanistic studies.[73]

JOHN CALVIN

Without a doubt, the most important Reformed theology to come out of the Protestant Reformation was that of John Calvin. He was born in Noyon, France, on July 10, 1509. Calvin studied in Paris, where he encountered humanism as well as the conservative reaction to it. Calvin was familiar with

---

71. Christian humanists, unlike secular humanists, were God-centered, being theists in their philosophy. Nonetheless, they believed the focus of history was on human beings. Hence, they stressed the importance of the humanities as a field of study. See Norman L. Geisler, *Is Man the Measure?* (Grand Rapids: Baker, 1983), chap. 8.

72. See Anderson, *Justification by Faith*, p. 279.

73. Melanchthon introduces forensic terms that were absent in Luther's treatment of justification. For an examination of this and other differences between Luther and Melanchthon, see Toon, *Foundations for Faith*, pp. 61–63.

the writings and theology of Wycliffe, Hus, and Luther. He drew his deepest inspiration, however, from Augustine. Calvin believed that he was doing nothing more than reproducing "that holy man's own plain and uncompromising teachings."[74] "If I wanted to compile a whole volume from Augustine, I would readily show my readers that I need no other language than his."[75]

Calvin's theological system begins, as did Augustine's and Aquinas's before him, with man's present condition—one of complete moral corruption. For "Even though we grant that God's image was not totally annihilated and destroyed in man, yet was it so corrupted that whatever remains is a horrible deformity."[76]

Calvin held that "Predestination we call the eternal decree of God, which he has determined in himself, what he would have to become of every individual of mankind."[77] Election is prior to faith, for "While the elect receive the grace of adoption by faith, their election does not depend on faith, but is prior in time and order."[78]

Calvin refers to justification as the "main hinge upon which religion turns." It "consists in remission of sins and the imputation of Christ's righteousness."[79] Departing at this point from Augustine, Aquinas, and the medieval tradition, Calvin does not see justification as involving an *infusion* of grace. "We are justified by God solely by the intercession of Christ's righteousness."[80] What place, then, do good works have in the life of the believer? "To the charge that justification thus understood obviates the need for good works Calvin's firm reply is, like Luther's, that although in no respect can good works become the ground of our holiness a living faith is never devoid of such works. Thus justification necessarily has its consequence in sanctification."[81]

Christian salvation includes both justification and sanctification. Calvin kept these doctrines in balance, writing, "We confess that, when God reconciles us to himself by means of the justice of Christ, and by the free remission of our sins, reputes us to be just, he joins to this mercy a further benefit, namely, he dwells in us by his holy Spirit, by whose virtue the lusts of our flesh are daily more and more mortified, and we are ourselves sanctified, that is, consecrated to God in true purity of life, our hearts once moulded to the obedience of the Law."[82]

---

74. Reardon, *Religious Thought*, p. 190.
75. Calvin, *Institutes*, III, xxii, 8.
76. Ibid., I, xv, 4.
77. Ibid., II, i.
78. J. K. S. Reid, trans., *Calvin: Theological Treatises*, vol. 22, in *The Library of Christian Classics* (Philadelphia: Westminster Press, 1954), Article 5.
79. Calvin, *Institutes*, III, xi, 2.
80. Ibid., xi, 23.
81. Reardon, *Religious Thought*, p. 196.
82. Calvin, *Institutes*, chap. 24.

Hence, "God's justification of the sinner must lead to ethical, eternal sanctification; but justification can never be based on man's ethical attainments. God's justification must lead to righteousness of life, but such righteousness of life is never the basis for God's justification."[83]

In closing the discussion of Calvin and his contributions to Christian thought, let us hear the words of another Reformed theologian:

> The fundamental interest of Calvin as a theologian lay, it is clear, in the region broadly designated soteriological. Perhaps we may go further and add that, within this broad field, his interest was most intense in the application to the sinful soul of the salvation wrought out by Christ . . . and we have been told that the main fault of the *Institutes* . . . lies in its too subjective character. Its effect, at all events, has been to constitute Calvin pre-eminently "the theologian of the Holy Spirit."[84]

For Calvin, justification was an aspect of the greater question of man's relation to God in Christ.

HULDREICH ZWINGLI

Zwingli was born New Year's Day, 1484, about forty miles from Zurich. He was the dominant force in the Swiss Reformation. He was much influenced by the Christian humanist Erasmus. Zwingli was more rationalistic and seems to have lacked the intense personal religious conversion in his life Luther experienced.

Whereas Luther searched for a gracious God, Zwingli emphasized a sovereign God. On another key principle of Zwingli's theology, he was one with the other Reformers: "We call God Father because he can do what he pleases with us." As to the divine image, "it has been obscured, but not obliterated."[85]

Zwingli and Luther differed over the issue of the "actual presence" in the Eucharistic controversy, and Zwingli seems to include a "works-righteousness" element in his understanding of justification. In this, a similarity with Erasmus can be noted. Thus, "It is this aspect of Zwingli's theology which led Melanchthon to hint darkly at Marburg of the works-righteousness of the Swiss Reformers."[86]

Concerning Christian doctrine, it is important to note that "The Reformers never claimed to have an exhaustive knowledge of biblical truth,

83. Toon, *Foundations for Faith*, p. 42.
84. Benjamin B. Warfield, *Calvin and Augustine* (Philadelphia: Presbyterian and Reformed, 1956), p. 484.
85. Zwingli, *Apolegeticus Architeles*, IV, 307. This is Zwingli's major statement concerning his beliefs.
86. McGrath, *Iustitia Dei*, 2:33.

but they did maintain that any 'new truth' arises out of the Spirit's application of the Word in the Christian's life. The 'new truth' in no way adds to that in Scripture."[87]

SUMMING UP OUR COMMON SOTERIOLOGICAL ROOTS

Our differences on the doctrine of salvation notwithstanding,[88] a survey of both Roman Catholics and Protestant Reformers leads to the following conclusions regarding Roman Catholic and evangelical agreement in this area.

First, both believe salvation is historical. The Old Testament view of salvation as effected through historic, divine intervention is affirmed in the New Testament. Against Gnosticism, we jointly affirm that man is not saved by wisdom; as against Judaism, man is not saved by moral and religious merit apart from the grace of God. Over against the Hellenistic mystery religions, man is not saved by mere religious practices, but by God's action in history in the person of Jesus Christ (Rom. 4:25; 5:10; 2 Cor. 4:10f.; Phil. 2:6f.; 1 Tim. 1:15; 1 John 4:9–10, 14).

Second, both evangelicals and Catholics believe salvation is moral and spiritual. Salvation is related to a deliverance from sin and its consequences and hence from guilt (Rom. 5:1; Heb. 10:22), from the curse of the law (Gal. 3:13; Col. 2:14), from death (1 Pet. 1:3–5), from judgment (Rom. 5:9), from fear (Heb. 2:15); and, finally, from bondage (Gal. 5:1f.; Titus 2:11–3:6).

Third, salvation is eschatological for both Catholics and evangelicals. The future perspective of salvation is crucial (Rom. 8:24; 13:11; 1 Cor. 5:5; Phil. 3:20; Heb. 1:14; 9:28; 1 Pet. 1:5–9). All that is now known about salvation is preliminary and a foretaste of the fullness which awaits the completing of the kingdom at the *parousia* of the Lord.

Fourth, initial justification is unmerited. As the new *Catechism of the Catholic Church* puts it, "Our justification comes from the grace of God" (1996) and even "the merits of our good works are gifts of the divine goodness" (2009).[89] Although the forensic aspect of justification stressed by Reformed theology is scarcely found prior to the Reformation, there is continuity concerning salvation between medieval Catholicism and the Reformers. Thus, Colin Brown can speak of "the Augustinian orthodoxy of Geneva and Rome."[90] For both groups salvation is by grace and is not prompted by

---

87. David F. Wells, *Revolution in Rome* (Downers Grove, Ill.: InterVarsity, 1972), p. 44.

88. The differences between Catholic and evangelical views on salvation will be discussed in Part Two. For a treatment of salvation doctrines beyond the scope of this work, see Peter Toon, *Born Again: A Biblical and Theological Study of Regeneration* (Grand Rapids: Baker, 1987).

89. (*Libreria Editrice Vaticana*, 1994), pp. 483, 487.

90. Colin Brown, *Christianity and Western Thought*, vol. 1 (Downers Grove, Ill.: InterVarsity, 1990), p. 165.

human works. It comes as a gift of God to undeserving humanity. Harold O. J. Brown states, "We must not oversimplify and create an artificial and forced consensus between great Christians of the past and present. Yet if one thing stands out when one studies the writings and lives of such men, it is that they knew and served the same Lord, and that they shared one faith and one hope."[91]

This is not to say that there are no important differences between Catholics and evangelicals on the topic of salvation (see chap. 12). However, perhaps the bishop of Hippo, the archbishop of Canterbury, the Angelic Doctor, the monk from Erfurt, and the theologian of the Holy Spirit have more in common than has hither-to-fore been granted.

---

91. Harold O. J. Brown, *The Protest of a Troubled Protestant* (New Rochelle: Arlington House, 1969), p. 107.

6

THE CHURCH

Despite some major differences between Catholics and evangelicals on the nature of the church (see chaps. 13 and 14), there are also some significant similarities. Even the great Reformer Martin Luther said, "the Roman Church is holy, because 'it has God's holy name, the gospel, baptism, etc.'"[1] And despite his strong criticisms of the Roman Catholic Church, John Calvin, writing to a cardinal of his time, added that this does not mean "that Roman Catholics are not also Christians. 'We indeed, Sadoleto, do not deny that those over which you preside are Churches of Christ.'"[2]

Common doctrinal beliefs warrant including the topic of the church in this section on "agreements." This common heritage includes, interestingly enough, Catholic beliefs about the foundation, nature, and function of the church. Therefore, "The Church is not primarily an object of theology, but its subject."[3] Among the areas of commonality are the origin and nature of the Christian church. Both Catholics and Protestants believe the church was built on Christ, the chief cornerstone (1 Cor. 3:11; Eph. 2:20). Both believe there is a continuity between the people of God in the Old Testament and the New Testament. And both believe that there is an invisible dimension to the

1. Cited by Gustaf Aulén, *Reformation and Catholicity*, trans. Eric H. Wahlstrom (Edinburgh and London: Oliver and Boyd, 1962), p. 76.
2. Cited by Alan Thomson, *New Movements, Reform, Rationalism: Revolution 1500–1800* (London: SPCK, 1976), pp. 28–29. Moving closer to our time, Abraham Kuyper, the famous Dutch Reformed scholar, was clearly ecumenical in his view of the church and can serve as an example for evangelicals today. During his 1898 Princeton Lectures, he stated: "Calvin in his day already acknowledged that, as against a spirit from the Great Deep, he considered Romish believers his allies. A so-called orthodox Protestant need only perceive immediately that what we have in common with Rome concerns precisely those fundamentals of our Christian creed. . . . I for my part am not ashamed to confess that on many points my views have been clarified through my study of the Romish theologians." *Lectures on Calvinism* (Grand Rapids: Eerdmans, 1931), pp. 183–84; quoted in J. Daryl Charles, "Evangelical-Catholic Dialogue: Basis, Boundaries, Benefits," *Pro Ecclesia* 3, no. 3, p. 303. Of course, after Trent the Reformers believed that Rome had apostasized.
3. Neuner and Dupuis, *Christian Faith*, p. 229.

church wherein all the regenerate are united. Indeed, "it is Christ who, through the Holy Spirit, makes Church one, holy, catholic, and apostolic, and it is he who calls her to realize each of these qualities."[4]

In a broad sense, the community of believers on earth, which many Catholics and Protestants call "the church," can be said to have had its beginning with the inception of humanity. The Christian church did not begin until after Christ said, "I will build [future tense] my church" (Matt. 16:18).[5] The Second Council of Lyons (A.D. 1274) states: "We believe that the true Church is holy, Catholic, apostolic, and one, in which is given one holy baptism and true remission of all sins."[6] Nonetheless, God did have a covenant community in the Old Testament which many call "the church." Whatever the title— let us call them the people of God—it is evident that God has always been interested in dealing with individuals in the context of a community of believers. Indeed, the Second Vatican Council declared: "It has not been God's resolve to sanctify and save men individually with no regard for their mutual relationship. Rather he wants to establish them as a people who would give him recognition in truth and service in holiness."[7] Thus, we find socialization to be an important factor in the unfolding of the people of God in history.

The English word "church" developed through the German *Kirche*. The Latin word *ecclesia* is derived from the Greek and means "the assembly/community." In the secular sense, the word means "an assembly of the people, the civil community." As Ott observes, "The Roman Catechism (I. 10,2), supported by St. Augustine (Enarr. in Ps. 149:3), gives the following definition of the concept: 'The Church is the faithful of the whole world.'"[8]

THE BIBLICAL FOUNDATION

THE PEOPLE OF GOD IN THE OLD TESTAMENT

We have already spoken about the origin of the human race in chapter 3. Humans were to reproduce themselves, control (or better, "husband") nature

---

4. *Catechism of the Catholic Church*, no. 811, p. 214.

5. Many evangelicals distinguish God's earthly people, Israel in the Old Testament, from his heavenly people, the church, which they believe did not begin until after Christ came (cf. Matt. 1:16–18). They believe it began on the day of Pentecost (Acts 2) when Christ fulfilled his promise to baptize them in the Holy Spirit (Acts 1:8) which, according to Paul, places believers in one body (1 Cor. 12:13), the church (Eph. 1:22–23). Nonetheless, they acknowledge that both Old and New Testament believers are part of a broader category that may be called the people of God.

6. Denzinger, *Sources of Catholic Dogma*, para. 464, p. 184.

7. Second Vatican Council, *Dogmatic Constitution on the Church*, II, 9. See also Hardon, *Catholic Catechism*, p. 206.

8. Ott, *Fundamentals of Catholic Dogma*, p. 270. Also see *New Catholic Encyclopedia*, 3:678.

around them, and enjoy fellowship with God (Gen. 2:8–25). This special relationship was shattered by the entrance of sin, which resulted in alienation from God and caused a rupture between human beings (Gen. 4:8; 6:11) and the manifestation of selfishness and pride (Gen. 11:8–9).

The events and pronouncements surrounding the election and call of Abram are of great importance concerning the origins of the people of God in the Old Testament, who came to be known as Israel. About this we read:

> The Lord said to Abram: "Go forth from the land of your kinsfolk and from your father's house to a land that I will show you. I will make of you a great nation, and I will bless you; I will make your name great, so that you will be a blessing. I will bless those who bless you and curse those who curse you. All the communities of the earth shall find blessing in you" (Gen. 12:1–3).

This special relationship between God and the people which he was forming was sealed with a covenant. The concept of covenant involved "a bond entered into voluntarily by two parties by which each pledges himself to do something for the other. The idea of the covenant between the God of Israel and His people is fundamental to the religion of the O.T."[9]

This covenant was renewed with Abraham's descendants when, under Moses' direction, they left Egypt (Exod. 19–24). In spite of God's grace and care, time and again Israel was unfaithful and violated the precepts of God's law. The prophets foretold that only the portion of the people who remained faithful would experience the benefits of God's promises.

> The days are coming, says the LORD, when I will make a new covenant with the house of Israel and the house of Judah. It will not be like the covenant I made with their fathers the day I took them by the hand to lead them forth from the land of Egypt. . . . But this is the covenant which I will make with the house of Israel after those days, says the LORD. I will place my law within them, and write it upon their hearts; I will be their God and they shall be my people (Jer. 31:31–33).

While many evangelicals believe that this awaits a final future fulfillment in the restored nation of Israel, it is clear that the results of this new covenant, which is based on Christ's death, are applied in the New Testament to the church (cf. Heb. 8) which Christ said he would found (Matt. 16). However, through the remaining Old Testament period, "These two ideas, the faithful remnant and the new covenant, were reaffirmed during the centuries following the Babylonian Exile, and they nourished the messianic hopes of Israel (Isa. 54:9, 10)."[10]

---

9. F. L. Cross, ed., *The Oxford Dictionary of the Christian Church* (Oxford: Oxford University Press, 1983), pp. 353–54.

10. *New Catholic Encyclopedia*, 3:678.

Despite intramural evangelical differences on the time of origin and nature of the church, all acknowledge that believers of both Testaments are in one sense the spiritual seed of Abraham, inasmuch as they, like him, are justified by faith. The apostle Paul made the connection between the redeemed of the New Testament and father Abraham: "Thus Abraham 'believed God, and it was credited to him as righteousness.' Realize then that it is those who have faith who are children of Abraham. Scripture, which saw in advance that God would justify the Gentiles by faith, foretold the good news to Abraham, saying, 'Through you shall all the nations be blessed.' Consequently, those who have faith are blessed along with Abraham who had faith" (Gal. 3:6–9).

THE CHURCH OF CHRIST IN THE NEW TESTAMENT

Pope Leo the Great, commenting on the birth of the Christian Church and the rending of the temple's veil, stated: "To such an extent was there effected a transfer from the Law to the Gospel, from the Synagogue to the Church, from many sacrifices to one Victim, that, as our Lord expired, the mystical veil which shut off the innermost part of the temple and its sacred secret was rent violently from top to bottom."[11]

The legitimacy of the new covenant was announced by the death and resurrection of Jesus Christ. The nature of this new society, the church, was gradually revealed. The new community was seen as separate from Judaism and having its own structure (cf. Rom. 9:3–4; 1 Cor. 10:32). After Christ's ascension, with the coming of the Holy Spirit at Pentecost, the apostles began to preach to the Jews and to baptize all converts (Acts 2:4–41; 4:2). Concerning Christ's purpose in sending the Holy Spirit, Pope Pius XII declared:

> He wished to make known and proclaim his spouse through the visible coming of the Holy Spirit with the sound of a mighty wind and tongues of fire. For just as he himself, when he began to preach, was made known by his eternal Father through the Holy Spirit descending and remaining on him in the form of a dove, so likewise, as the apostles were about to enter on their ministry of preaching, Christ our Lord sent the Holy Spirit down from heaven, to touch them with tongues of fire and to point out, as by the finger of God, the supernatural mission and office of the Church.[12]

In the Book of Acts, Luke details the conversion of Paul, formerly a persecutor of the church. Through the efforts of Paul the gospel was proclaimed to the Gentiles and tensions between Jewish members of the church and these

---

11. Leo, *Sermon LXVIII, 3*; quoted in *Catholic Catechism*, p. 207.
12. Pius XII, encyclical, *Mystici Corporis Christi*, I, 33; quoted in *Catholic Catechism*, p. 208.

new converts from paganism increased (Acts 15:1–2). The content of the Pauline corpus reveals much about the nature of the church. From Paul's conversion experience on the road to Damascus he came to identify the Christian community with Jesus Christ.

The apostles had designated certain members as "deacons" to be in charge of duties such as charitable works, preaching, and prayer (Acts 6:1–7). The believing community "was composed of various local churches whose members were 'saints,' chosen by God (1 Cor. 1:2). There was authority in the Church: Peter (Gal. 1:18; 2:6–14); the twelve and Paul himself (1 Cor. 15:1–11); Timothy, Titus, and the 'bishops' (1 Tim. 1:3–5; 3:2; Titus 1:7; Phil. 1:1; Acts 20:28) . . . elders or presbyters (Titus 1:5; 1 Tim. 5:17), and deacons (Phil. 1:1)."[13] These religious communities (called "churches") were to observe the traditions that Paul brought to them (1 Cor. 11:2, 23–24; 15:1–3; Gal. 1:6–10). These doctrines, of course, had their roots in the ministry and teaching of Jesus (1 Cor. 7:10; 11:23; 2 Cor. 4:5). The rituals of baptism and the Lord's Supper were practiced (Gal. 3:26–27; Eph. 4:5; 1 Cor. 11:23–24). Baptism provided an identification between the believer and the risen Lord, and participation in the Eucharistic Feast provided similar unity (1 Cor. 10:16–17). Baptism and the conversion experience went hand in hand (Gal. 3:26–27). Faith came through the preaching of the "good news" and its acceptance.[14]

THEOLOGICAL DEVELOPMENT OF THE DOCTRINE OF THE CHURCH

Building on this biblical foundation, both Catholics and evangelicals have developed a systematic doctrine of the church, or ecclesiology. While there are significant differences (see chaps. 13 and 14), particularly in the make-up of the visible body of Christ on earth, nonetheless, there is more agreement than many evangelicals realize over the nature of the mystical or spiritual body of Christ.

THE MYSTICAL BODY OF CHRIST

When examining the church and its nature and function perhaps the place to start is the church as "the body of Christ." Pope Pius XII declared: "To describe this true Church of Christ—which is the Holy, Catholic, Apostolic, Roman Church—there is no name more noble, none more excellent, none

13. *New Catholic Encyclopedia*, 3:679.
14. Ibid.

more Divine, than the expression, 'the Mystical Body of Jesus Christ.'"[15] With the exception of singling out the Roman jurisdiction for special mention, most evangelicals would agree with the above statement. (We will address questions concerning the supremacy of the Roman See in chap. 11.) The Second Vatican Council states: "Reflection on the pilgrim status of the Church leads naturally to the theme of the Church as the People of God of the new and eternal Covenant."[16]

In the New Testament, we find the apostle Paul using the term "the body of Christ" to depict the spiritual link between Christ and his church. Speaking of God the Father, he says that "he put all things beneath his feet and gave him as head over all things to the church, which is his body, the fullness of the one who fills all things in every way" (Eph. 1:22–23). And concerning Christ: "He is the head of the body, the church" (Col. 1:18), and "Now you are Christ's body and individually parts of it" (1 Cor. 12:27).

This teaching from Scripture is reflected in the church fathers and later in the Middle Ages. Clement said, "It is not unknown to you that I believe that the living Church is the body of Christ." Augustine, when asked "What is the church?" answered, "The Body of Christ. Add to this, the Head (Christ) and it becomes a man. The head and the body, a man."[17] In the Middle Ages, the scholastics employed the term "Mystical Body of Christ" to describe the Lord's Supper. Later, however, the appellation became used in a general sense for the church: "The word 'mystical' (full of mystery, i.e., hidden things) indicates the mysterious character of the communion of grace between Christ and the faithful."[18] Roman Catholics use the term in two senses: "In the wider sense, the designation 'Mystical Body of Christ' means the communion of all those made holy by the grace of Christ" including those in heaven. And secondly, "In the narrower sense, the 'Mystical Body of Christ' means the visible Church of Christ on earth."[19]

THE FOUNDATION OF THE CHRISTIAN CHURCH

CHRIST AS FOUNDER OF THE CHURCH

Contrary to a popular misunderstanding among many Protestants, Roman Catholicism teaches that "The Church was founded by the God-Man Jesus Christ *(De fide.).*"[20] Indeed, the Vatican Council declared in the Dogmatic

---

15. Encyclical, *Mystici Corporis*, 1943; quoted in Ott, *Fundamentals of Catholic Dogma*, p. 270.
16. *"Lumen Gentium,"* Neuner and Dupuis, *Christian Faith*, p. 261.
17. Augustine, *Sermon* 45.5.
18. Ibid., p. 271.
19. Ibid.
20. Ott, *Fundamentals of Catholic Dogma*, p. 272.

Constitution on the Church of Christ that "the eternal Shepherd and Bishop of our souls (1 Peter 2:25) resolved, in order to give permanent duration to the saving work of the Redemption, to establish the Holy Church, in which all the faithful would be welded together as in the house of the Living God, by the bond of the one Faith and of the one Charity."[21] Pope Pius X stated in 1910 that "the Church was founded immediately and personally by the true and historical Christ during the time of His earthly life."[22]

The question surrounding Christ's statement to Peter "Thou art Peter and upon this rock I will build my Church" (Matt. 16:18) will be briefly addressed later in this chapter. Roman Catholicism takes this statement as a reference to Peter. Some Protestants agree but deny that this proves the primacy of Peter. Most Protestants take the "rock" to mean Peter's firm testimony about Christ. A number of different interpretations were held by the church fathers (see chap. 11).

THE HOLY SPIRIT AND THE CHURCH

Whenever the person and/or the work of the Holy Spirit has been ignored or undervalued, the church has suffered. Many believe that it may well be that God has raised up the charismatic renewal movement (which has impacted both Roman Catholic and Protestant churches) to address this situation. It is of interest then to observe the official position of Roman Catholicism concerning the role of the Holy Spirit vis-à-vis the church: "The Holy Ghost is the Soul of the Church *(Sent. communis.)*." In the encyclical *Divinum illud* (1897), Leo XIII declared, "Let the one proposition suffice: Christ is the Head of the Church, the Holy Ghost her soul." Pius XII confirmed this doctrine in the encyclical *Mystici Corporis*,[23] asserting that, like the soul in the body, the Holy Ghost is the principle of being and life in the church.[24]

The Fathers clearly speak to the intimate relationship that exists between the Holy Spirit and the church. Irenaeus said, "Where the Church is, there also the Spirit of God is, there is the Church and all grace *(Adv. haer. III 24,1.)*." Augustine, speaking about the Holy Spirit's operation in the church: "As the soul quickens every member of the body and bestows a definite function on each, so the Holy Ghost, by His grace, quickens every member of the Church, and allocates to each a definite activity in the service of the whole *(Sermo 267. 4,4).*"[25] We certainly cannot lay the blame for the neglect of the person and work of the Holy Spirit at the feet of the early church fathers.

---

21. Denzinger, *Sources of Catholic Dogma*, no. 1821, p. 451.
22. Ibid.; see also no. 2145.
23. See ibid., no. 2288, p. 616.
24. Ibid., p. 294.
25. Ibid., p. 295.

THE NATURE OF THE CHURCH

The Church has two dimensions, visible and invisible. The invisible is the spiritual (mystical) body of Christ composed of all true believers. The visible church is the community of Christ's followers on earth.

Our discussion thus far has centered on properties which speak to the inner, invisible side of the church. Its purpose—addressing our spiritual needs—is invisible. The "Energizer" (the Holy Spirit) of the church operates "behind the scenes." Thus Pius XII states: "If we examine closely this divine principle of life and power given by Christ . . . we easily see that it is nothing else than the Holy Spirit, the Paraclete who proceeds from the Father and the Son."[26]

The external, visible side of the church is a doctrine that is intrinsic to an understanding of the Roman Catholic concept of the church. Concerning the nature of the church, "Catholics are willing to admit that there is an invisible side to the Church, but prefer to reserve the name 'church' for the visible communion of believers."[27] Augustine, in comparing the church to a city on a mountain (Matt. 5:14), said, "The Church stands clear and visible before all men, for she is the city on the mountain which cannot be hidden."[28] Evangelicals also believe that the church is visible, existing now in the world. What is at issue is the claim that the Roman Catholic jurisdiction is the only true manifestation of the body of Christ on earth. This is the question of authority over which Catholics and Protestants disagree, which will be addressed in chapter 11.

BIBLICAL IMAGES FOR THE CHURCH

In addition to the title "the body of Christ," we find other names in the New Testament used to describe the reality called "the church." The Body of believers is likened to a sheepfold. In John's Gospel Jesus says, "I am the gate for the sheep" (10:7). Of course, if the people of God are the sheepfold, then Christ is the Shepherd. He said, "I am the good shepherd. A good shepherd lays down his life for the sheep" (v. 11).

Paul uses the images of a field and a building to describe the church. In discussing the role of Christian ministers, he says: "For we are God's coworkers; you are God's field, God's building" (1 Cor. 3:9). Elaborating on the concept of the church as a building, Paul states that it is "built upon the foundation of the apostles and prophets, with Christ Jesus himself as the cap-

---

26. Encyclical, "Mystici Corporis" (1943), Neuner and Dupuis, Christian Faith, p. 255.
27. Berkhof, Systematic Theology, p. 562.
28. Augustine, Contra Clesonium II.36.45; quoted in ibid.

stone" (Eph. 2:20). This is a pivotal verse when attempting to understand the nature of the church and will be examined in chapter 11.

THE CONSTITUTION OF THE CHURCH

The visible church is constituted of all the regenerate but it has a structure. Not all have the same gifts, and not all have the same authority. In New Testament language, there are "bishops," "elders," "deacons," and just plain "brethren" (laity). Catholics call "elders" ministers and priests.

It is evident that the church which Christ founded was to have a visible manifestation. Evangelicals, along with Catholics, believe that the church is composed not only of laity (who Catholics acknowledge are called "saints" [Eph. 1:1] and "priests" [1 Pet. 2:9] in Scripture) but of ministers. These ministers lead, teach, and offer sacraments (or ordinances) in the church.

Roman Catholics, in contrast to most Protestants (high Anglicans excepted), base their hierarchical structure on the premise of "apostolic succession." This doctrine is: "The sequence, following from the apostles themselves down to the bishops of the present time. This is marked (a) by lawful, valid ordination conferred on bishops of the Church; (b) by the giving over or delegating directly the powers entrusted to the apostles of ordaining, or ruling, and of teaching, which powers were given by Christ to the apostles."[29]

The underpinning which holds the structure of Roman Catholicism together is the doctrine that designates the apostle Peter as the chief of all the apostles. Further, Catholics believe this primacy was conferred on the bishops of Rome, Peter's successors: "The invisible Head of the Church is the risen Christ. St. Peter represents the position of Christ in the external government of the militant Church, and is to this extent 'the representative of Christ' on earth *(Chrisi vicarius; D. 694)*."[30]

The scriptural support used by Roman Catholics for the doctrine of the primacy of Peter is found in Matthew 16. After Peter confesses that Jesus is "the Messiah, the Son of the living God," Jesus states: "Blessed are you, Simon son of Jonah. For flesh and blood has not revealed this to you, but my heavenly Father. And so I say to you, you are Peter, and upon this rock I will build my church, and the gates of the netherworld shall not prevail against it" (Matt. 16:17–18).

The problem here turns on the meaning of the word "rock." Because Peter is called *Petros* (which means "rock" in Greek) Roman Catholics believe Jesus was designating Peter in a special way as the human foundation for the visible church. This authority, they claim, was passed on to his suc-

---

29. Robert C. Broderick, M.A., ed., "Apostolic Succession," in *The Catholic Concise Encyclopedia* (St. Paul: Simon & Schuster, 1956), p. 43.
30. Ott, *Fundamentals of Catholic Dogma*, p. 279.

cessors, the bishops of Rome. Most Protestants believe that Jesus was declaring here that the church will be built upon the confession that Jesus Christ is Lord (cf. Matt. 16:18; Eph. 2:20). This is an area rife with difficulties, not only for evangelicals but also Eastern Orthodox communities. The issue will be explored more fully in chapter 11.

THE PURPOSE OF THE CHURCH

Roman Catholicism teaches that "as the local Church must represent the universal Church as perfectly as possible, it must remember that it has been sent to those who live in the same territory as itself, but do not believe in Christ so that it might be for them, by the example of the lives of the faithful and of the whole community, a sign indicating Christ."[31] Concerning the mission of redemption that the church must exercise, Catholics claim that, "while Christ acquired the fruits of the Redemption by His own efficacy, the task of the Church consists in the application of the fruits of the Redemption to mankind." Of course "this is achieved by the exercise of the three-fold office delegated to the Church by Christ—the teaching office, the pastoral office and the sacerdotal office. Thus the Church is Christ continuing and perpetually working on earth."[32] Although some of the ecclesiastical machinery involved in the Roman Catholic understanding of the above task may be problematic, the general goal would be acceptable to most evangelicals. Pope John Paul II stated in his first encyclical that the central purpose of the church was to help the believer to "realize and fulfill his full human destiny in Christ."[33]

As to the purpose of the church, the most recent catechism states: "The mission of Christ and the Holy Spirit is brought to completion in the Church, which is the Body of Christ and the Temple of the Holy Spirit. This joint mission henceforth brings Christ's faithful to share in his communion with the Father in the Holy Spirit."[34]

AREAS OF CATHOLIC AND PROTESTANT AGREEMENT[35]

We have found much in common with our Roman Catholic friends concerning the nature and mission of the church. This unity begins with a common confession of the great ecumenical creeds.

31. Austin Flannery, O.P., *Vatican Collection: Vatican Council II*, vol. 2 (North Port: Costello Publishing, 1982), p. 836.
32. Ott, *Fundamentals of Catholic Dogma*, p. 274.
33. *"Redemptor Hominis"* (1979), Neuner and Dupuis, *Christian Faith*, p. 266.
34. *Catechism 1994*, no. 737, p. 194.
35. Of course, the Roman Catholic (and Orthodox) understanding of unity includes not only invisible/spiritual unity but also visible/institutional unity.

CREEDAL UNITY

There is, of course, a basic doctrinal unity between Catholics and Protestants at the foundation of the church. "Each of the major churches accepted the great ecumenical creeds, the Apostles', Nicene, and Chalcedonian symbols [creeds], and was persuaded that the doctrine they express is both true and necessary. They differed among themselves about *what else* might be required, but there was no doubt among them that at least the doctrines of the ecumenical creeds were required."[36] Historically, four marks of the true church have been identified by Protestant scholars.

The church is one. The church is one because Christ is one. "One body and one Spirit, . . . one Lord, one faith, one baptism" (Eph. 4:4–5) appears in both Protestant and Roman Catholic Bibles. Both agree that the final ground for the unity of the church is not in anything people have done or ever can do for themselves, but in what God has done for people in Christ.[37]

The church is holy. Indeed, the attribute of holiness seems to have been the earliest term applied to the church, for a very early version of the creed reads: "I believe in the Holy Ghost, the holy church." All Christians, Roman and non-Roman, would agree that the church is holy, but they would disagree about the specific meaning and content of its holiness.[38]

The church is catholic. "Catholicity . . . means identity plus universality. The ancient church became the catholic church when it achieved this combination."[39] Evangelicals who recite the Apostles' Creed understand catholicity as indicating the broad scope of the body of Christ, extending to the ends of the earth and encompassing every "tribe and tongue and people and nation" (Rev. 5:9).

The church is apostolic.[40] "Protestants . . . tend to say that the criterion of apostolic authority is loyalty to the apostolic scriptures of the New Testament. The church is apostolic because and insofar as it obeys the apostolic message in the Scriptures."[41] Evangelicals can learn much from church history and the Catholic tradition. A Reformed pastor, commenting on some of the superficial examples of worship forms in some evangelical churches, said, "worship is not entertainment for believers. It is not designed to make us feel

---

36. Brown, *Heresies: The Image of Christ,* p. 411.

37. Jaroslav Pelikan, *The Riddle of Roman Catholicism* (New York: Abingdon, 1960), p. 178. This work is highly recommended for its balanced approach to the development of Roman Catholicism.

38. Ibid., p. 181.

39. Ibid., p. 184.

40. It should be noted that the Roman Catholic and Orthodox understanding of apostolicity is not only apostolic Scripture/doctrine but also apostolic succession.

41. Ibid., p. 187.

good, though it can and often does. Worship is designed to be entertaining to God, to please and delight Him. God is the audience in worship."[42]

CONCLUSION

As we have seen, Catholics and evangelicals have much in common on the origin, nature, and purpose of the church. This is true both doctrinally and organically, especially with regard to the invisible church.

One of the burning issues of the Reformation was the nature of the church. The notion was that "the church of the sixteenth century was seen by Rome as an institution that stood *between* the people and God, whereas Luther and others argued that the church indeed was the very people of God."[43]

Even given their somewhat different understanding of the function of the *visible* church, Roman Catholics are not unaware of the sinfulness of the church. Cardinal Ratzinger states, "the Second Vatican Council itself ventured to the point of speaking no longer merely of the holy Church but of the sinful Church, and the only reproach it incurred was that of still being far too timorous."[44] Not all evangelicals are prepared to go as far as one contemporary evangelical theologian, Donald Bloesch, who claims that "in addition to upholding evangelical distinctives, we need to regain catholic substance, which means continuity with the tradition of the whole church, including its sacramental side." Even noted Reformed apologist R. C. Sproul observes the absence of incense in Protestant churches. Why should not our sensibilities to worship God be stimulated by our senses as well as our eyes (beautiful buildings) and ears (beautiful music)?

As to the role of the church, Bloesch notes that "the Church is not a mediator between God and man, but it is a veritable means of grace to man. It cannot dispense grace as though it were in control, but it can function as an instrument of the Holy Spirit who does convey the grace of Christ to a sinful world."[45] Unfortunately, the current situation finds the church (in all of its

---

42. Peter J. Leithart, "A Presbyterian Appreciation of Liturgy," *Crisis* (October 1992): 30–32.

43. J. Daryl Charles, "Evangelical-Catholic Dialogue: Basis, Boundaries, Benefits," *Pro Ecclesia*, vol. III, no. 3, 1994, p. 295 n. 20.

44. Cardinal Ratzinger, *Introduction to Christianity*, trans. J. R. Foster (San Francisco: Ignatius Press, 1990), p. 262.

45. Donald G. Bloesch, *Essentials of Evangelical Theology*, vol. 2 (San Francisco: Harper and Row, 1978), p. 278. Many evangelicals view confession as an unnecessary Roman Catholic accretion. However, at least one evangelical scholar who is a specialist in Patristics finds much value in the function of auricular confession. See Thomas C. Oden, *Corrective Love: The Power of Communion Discipline* (St. Louis: Concordia Press, 1995), pp. 57, 60, 73–77.

various manifestations) struggling to preserve doctrinal integrity and ecclesiastical orderliness. As evangelical thinker Harold O. J. Brown puts it: "In today's intellectual climate, the ordinary safeguards of church membership qualifications, ordination, theological degrees, and the like mean virtually nothing."[46] The purity of the church is still crucial, however, for "the responsibility for preserving it is no longer adequately exercised by church officials, and now devolves upon the individual believer."[47] We will be addressing this situation in Parts Two and Three.

Finally, concerning the church and her relationship with Christ, a contemporary Roman Catholic layman offers the following observation: "The Church, the Bride, should be speaking of her beloved, the Bridgroom: about how wonderful he is, about how she owes everything to him, about how good he is and how truthful and faithful and powerful and glorious."[48]

46. Brown, *Protest of a Troubled Protestant,* p. 239.
47. Ibid.
48. Ralph Martin, *The Catholic Church at the End of an Age: What Is the Spirit Saying?* (San Francisco: Ignatius Press, 1994), p. 199.

7

ETHICS

Catholic and evangelical ethics have the same Augustinian roots. Both are absolutistic, and both are anchored in the nature and will of God. Since Augustine's ethics were amplified by his brightest follower, Thomas Aquinas, we will elaborate the common core of Catholic/evangelical ethics in the writings of both. They have set the standard for Catholic ethics during the subsequent centuries.

EARLY MEDIEVAL ROOTS OF CATHOLIC ETHICS

The Bishop of Hippo was well ahead of his time when he unfolded his divine command ethic in terms of the essential attribute of God's love which, like all his attributes, is essential to his being. Augustine, in contrast to much of contemporary love ethics,[1] spelled out the absolute nature and knowable content of this truly Christian ethic of love.

LOVE IS THE SUPREME LAW

According to Augustine, "the supreme law is love."[2] Not only is love the supreme virtue; in a sense it is the only one. "Therefore hold fast [to] love, and set your mind at rest." For "who does evil to the man he loves? Love thou: it is impossible to do this without doing good."[3]

The love of God is the greatest love possible. Augustine said, "it is a perversion for people to want to enjoy money, but merely to make use of God. Such people do not spend money for the sake of God, but worship God for

---

1. See Joseph Fletcher, *Situation Ethics: The New Morality* (Philadelphia: Westminster Press, 1966).
2. Augustine, *City of God* 15.16.
3. Augustine, *Epistle of John* 10.7.

the sake of money."[4] Only God should be loved for his own sake. Therefore, "you ought not to love even yourself for your own sake, but for Him in whom your love finds its most worthy object."[5]

Augustine also believed in a proper self-love. He believed that "Man . . . ought to be taught the due measure of loving, that is, in what measure he may love himself so as to be of service to himself." For "that he does love himself and desire to do good to himself, nobody but a fool would doubt." But "he is to be taught in what measure to love his body, so as to care for himself wisely and within due limits."[6] This proper self-love is evident in the command to love our neighbor *as ourself*.[7] For "Whoever loves another as himself ought to love that in him which is his real self. . . . Whoever, then loves in his neighbor anything but his real self does not love him as himself."[8]

There is, of course, bad self-love or selfishness. This is the love of one's self in an improper measure. This evil self-love is pride, and it is the moral essence of the City of Man as opposed to the City of God (i.e., the domain of God on earth), which is based in the love of God. Augustine believed that "what we see, then, is that two societies have issued from two kinds of love. Worldly society has flowered from a selfish love which dared to despise even God, whereas the communion of saints is rooted in a love of God that is ready to trample on self."[9] In fact, "this is the main difference which distinguishes the two cities of which we are speaking. The humble City of God is the society of holy men and good angels; the proud city is the society of wicked men and evil angels. The one city began with love; the other had its beginnings in the love of self."[10]

Loving others is a divine command. "For this is the law that has been laid down by Divine authority. 'Thou shalt love thy neighbor as thyself.'"[11] In fact, love is to be manifest on four levels: "first, that which is above us [God]; second, ourselves; third, that which is on a level with us; fourth, that which is beneath us."[12]

LOVE AND THE VIRTUES

All virtues can be defined in terms of love. For Augustine, virtue was "nothing else than perfect love of God."[13] For "the fourfold division of virtue I re-

---

4. Augustine, *City of God* 11.25.
5. Augustine, *On Christian Doctrine* 1.22.
6. Ibid., 1.25.
7. Ibid., 1.26.
8. Augustine, *Of True Religion* 46 TR.
9. Augustine, *City of God* 14.28.
10. Ibid., 14.13.
11. Ibid.
12. Ibid., 1.23.
13. Augustine, *On the Morals of the Catholic Church* 15.

gard as taken from four forms of love." For example, "temperance is love giving itself entirely to that which is loved; fortitude is love readily bearing all things for the sake of the loved object; justice is love serving only the loved object, and therefore ruling rightly; prudence is love distinguishing with sagacity between what hinders it and what helps it."[14] Thus, for Augustine, "it is a brief but true definition of virtue to say it is the order of love."[15]

Since God is the ultimate object of love, Augustine redefined the traditional virtues in a theocentric way. "Temperance is love keeping itself entire and incorrupt for God; justice is love serving God only, and therefore ruling well all else, as subject to man; prudence is love making a right distinction between what helps it toward God and what might hinder it."[16]

Prudence. Prudence is love acting wisely. "It is the part of prudence to keep watch with most anxious vigilance, lest any evil influence should stealthily creep in upon us."[17] It is for this reason that God instructs us to "watch" and "walk while ye have the light, lest darkness come upon you."[18]

Fortitude. Fortitude is love standing firm in the face of danger. While temperance is love burning in desire for God and not seeking earthly things, fortitude bears the loss of these temporal things for the love of God. It is love bearing all things. For "there is nothing, though iron hardness, which the fire of love cannot subdue. And when the mind is carried up to God in this love, it will soar above all torture free and glorious, with wings beauteous and unhurt, on which chaste love rises to the embrace of God."[19]

Temperance. Temperance is love keeping itself pure for God. It "promises us a kind of integrity and incorruption in the love by which we are united to God. The office of temperance is in restraining and quieting the passions which make us pant for those things which turn us away from the laws of God." In short, "the whole duty of temperance, then, is to put off the old man, and to be renewed in God . . . and to turn the whole love to things divine and unseen."[20]

LOVE AND THE GREATER GOOD

Although Augustine was a staunch defender of never telling a lie, even to save a life,[21] he nonetheless believed that there were occasions when the obliga-

14. Ibid.
15. Augustine, *City of God* 15.22.
16. Augustine, *On the Morals of the Catholic Church* 15.
17. Ibid., 24.
18. Ibid.
19. Ibid., 22.
20. Ibid., 19.
21. Augustine, *On Lying* 22–23.

tions to love came into unavoidable conflict. Stated positively, there are some things we should love more than others. God, of course, should be loved supremely. Further, a faithful person does not love improperly, "nor loves that more which ought to be loved less, nor loves that equally which ought to be loved either less or more, nor loves that less or more which ought to be loved equally."[22] Negatively put, there are greater and lesser sins. In the words of our Lord, there are "weightier matters of the law" (Matt. 23:23). Unlike contemporary situationalism, "what sins are trivial and what grand, however, is not for human but for divine judgment to determine."[23] For "there are some sins which would be considered very trifling, if the Scripture did not show that they are really very serious."[24]

LOVE AND SEX

Augustine, like the apostles and church fathers before him, condemned sex before and outside of a monogamous marriage as ethically wrong. He incited "that no lapse occur into damnable sins; that is, into fornication and adulteries."[25] Homosexuality and bestiality were considered abhorrent or, to borrow the biblical term, "an abomination" (Lev. 18:22–23). Other forms of lust, such as gluttony, were likewise condemned, noting that, in matters of this kind, "it is not the nature of the things we use, but our reason for using them, and our manner of seeking them, that make what we do either praiseworthy or blamable."[26]

LOVE AND WAR

Augustine also provided the basis for the traditional Christian view of a "just" war, which both Catholics and most Protestants have shared in common ever since. "For it is the wrong-doing of the opposing party which compels the wise man to wage just wars; and this wrong-doing even though it gives rise to no war would still be a matter of grief to man because it is man's wrong-doing."[27] He adds, "it is therefore with the desire for peace that wars are waged. . . . And hence it is obvious that peace is the end sought by war. For every man seeks peace by waging war; but no man seeks war by waging peace."[28]

22. Augustine, *On Christian Doctrine* 1.28.
23. Augustine, *Enchiridion* 78.
24. Ibid., 79.
25. Augustine, *On Marriage and Concupiscence* 1.16.
26. Augustine, *On Christian Doctrine* 3.12.
27. Augustine, *City of God* 19.7.
28. Ibid.

LOVE AND LIFE

Augustine held that human life not only should be lived in a saintly way but that human life itself is sacred from its very inception.[29] Hence abortion is condemned as immoral. Abortion is the intentional taking of an innocent life and, as such, it is murder. Unborn human life is just as human as the life of a young child or an adult. David said, "Surely I was sinful at birth, sinful from the time my mother conceived me" (Ps. 51:5 NIV). And of Jesus in the Blessed Virgin's womb it was said, "that which is conceived in her is of the Holy Spirit" (Matt. 1:20). Since both science and the Bible (general revelation and special revelation) teach that life begins at conception, it is not a matter of divine law alone but also of natural law for all people that forbids abortion.

LATE MEDIEVAL ARTICULATION OF CATHOLIC ETHICS

Although Augustine believed in natural law,[30] it was left to Aquinas to spell it out in greater detail.[31] His view is amazingly relevant to the current discussion, cutting between the two extremes of theonomy and utilitarianism. Theonomists hold that all law is divine law, contending that human governments should be based on divine law as expressed in the Bible.[32] Utilitarians, on the other hand, argue that there are no moral absolutes, reducing all law to human law. Traditional Catholic ethics offered an answer that most of classical Protestantism accepted and of which an increasing number of contemporary evangelicals are coming to see the relevance.

THE NATURE OF MORAL LAW

Like his mentor Augustine, Thomas Aquinas believed that ethics is based in moral law which flows from God, the Moral Law Giver. It flows from his will and is rooted in his nature. Catholic ethics is essentialistic. As Catholic ethicist Germain Grisez affirms, "By wisdom God makes us what we are and thus determines the true requirements for our fulfillment. . . . He does not

29. Based on an outmoded Aristotelian view, Aquinas believed the rational soul was not created until several weeks after conception. But the Catholic church, along with modern science, has affirmed that life begins at the moment of conception (fertilization).
30. Terry Miethe, "Natural Law, The Synderesis Rule," *Augustinian Studies* 2 (1980): 91–97.
31. The discussion here follows that in Norman L. Geisler, *Thomas Aquinas: An Evangelical Appraisal* (Grand Rapids: Baker, 1991), chap. 12.
32. Greg L. Bahnsen, *Theonomy in Christian Ethics* (Nutley, N.J.: Craig Press, 1979).

make things right or wrong by an additional arbitrary choice."[33] God wills something because it is right (based on his unchangeably good nature); it is not good simply because God wills it to be so. God is not arbitrary in what he wills to be good.

Aquinas defined law as "measure or rule by which we are led to act or withheld from acting."[34] It is "an ordinance of reason made for the common good by the public personage who has charge of the community, and [is] promulgated."[35] Thus, law is the basic rule or principle by which actions of persons are directed.

LAW AS FIRST PRINCIPLE

Law is a first principle for action. "The rule and measure of human activity is the reason, the first principle of human activity, whose function is to direct means to ends."[36] Each area of human activity has its own first principles. There are, for example, first principles of human thinking, such as the law of non-contradiction. Also, there are first principles of human acting. "The precepts of the natural law are to the practical reason what first principles of science are to the theoretical reason."[37] For "reason is the first principle of human acts."[38] The precepts of the natural law, of course, are not first principles of theoretical reason but of practical reason. That is, they are operative not in speculative matters but in practical matters. Hence, "the first principle of the practical reason is our ultimate end, or happiness; law is chiefly concerned with planning for this."[39] In brief, law is the rule directed toward the common good (happiness).

In order for law to be in effect it must be promulgated. "No one is obliged to obey a precept unless he be reasonably informed about it."[40] This follows from the nature of law as a duty of action for the common good. Thus, "to lay an obligation a law must be applied to the men who have to be regulated, and this means that it must be brought to their knowledge by promulgation."[41] In this sense, ignorance of the law is a legitimate excuse not to obey it. At the same time, "a man does not make up a law for himself, but by his very act of recognizing it as a law enacted for him he [thereby] binds himself

33. See Germain Grisez, *The Way of Our Lord*, vol. 1 (Chicago: Franciscan Herald, 1983), pp. 101–2.
34. Thomas Aquinas, *Philosophical Texts* (New York: Oxford University Press, 1960), p. 354.
35. Aquinas, *Summa Theologiae* 1a2ae. 90, 4.
36. Ibid., 90, 1 and ad 3.
37. Ibid., 90, 2.
38. Ibid.
39. Ibid.
40. Aquinas, *Disputations* 17, On Truth 3.
41. Aquinas, *Summa Theologiae* 1a2ae. 90, 4.

to its observance."[42] Aquinas illustrates this point: "If a mistaken reason bids a man sleep with another man's wife, to do this will be evil if based on ignorance of a divine law he ought to know; but if the misjudgment is occasioned by thinking that the woman is really his own wife, and she wants him and he wants her, then his will is free from guilt."[43]

In summation, law is by nature a measure for conduct. It is a first principle of human action. But in order to be in effect the law must be proclaimed. When it is proclaimed, a law is binding.

DIFFERENT KINDS OF LAW

Catholics and many Protestants following Thomas distinguish four different kinds of law: eternal law, natural law, human law, and divine law. Each is the measure or rule in a different sphere.

Eternal Law. Aquinas declared that eternal law is "the idea existing in God as the principle of the universe and lying behind the governance of things."[44] It is the source and exemplar of all other law, for "all laws derive from the eternal law to the extent that they share in right reason."[45] It is eternal "because naught in the divine reason is conceived in time, for the plan was set up from eternity."[46] So eternal law is the divine reason by which the universe is ruled. "All things subject to divine providence are ruled and measured by the eternal law, and consequently it is clear that somehow they share in the eternal law, for under it they have their propensities to their appropriate activities and ends."[47] This law is the eternal mind of God as it conceived and determined all that would be and how it would be run. From it flow all other kinds of law, whether natural, human, or divine.

Natural Law. Natural law is derived from eternal law. In fact, "natural right is contained in the eternal law primarily, and in the natural judicial faculty of human reason secondarily."[48] Natural law, then, is the human participation in eternal law by way of reason. It shares in the eternal reason. "This communication of the eternal law to rational creatures is called natural law." So natural law is "the natural light of reason, by which we discern what is right and wrong." It is "naught else but the impression on us of divine light."[49] All rational creatures, not just believers, share in natural law. It is the law written on their hearts of which Paul speaks in Romans 2:12–15.

---

42. Aquinas, *Disputations* 17, *On Truth* 3 ad 1.
43. Aquinas, *Summa Theologiae* 1a2ae. 19, 6.
44. Ibid., 91, 1.
45. Ibid., 93, 3.
46. Ibid.
47. Ibid., 91, 2.
48. Ibid., 71, 6 ad 4.
49. Ibid., 91, 2.

Natural law prescribes that all human beings do good and shun evil. But "good and evil should be set in the context of what is proper to humans as humans. This is his rational life."[50] A good act, then, is one in accordance with human (rational) nature, and an evil act is one contrary to reason. According to Aquinas, the sad fact is that "most men seem to live according to sense rather than reason";[51] their actions are based on feeling rather than good reasoning.

Living according to human (rational) nature, however, does not mean that human nature is the ultimate measure of all things. "In voluntary activity the proximate measure is the human reason, the supreme measure the eternal law." In other words, "the measure of human willing is double: one close and of the same nature, namely the human reason itself; the other, first and transcendent, namely the eternal law which is like the reason of God."[52] Thus, "when a human act goes to its end in harmony with the order of reason and eternal law then the act is right; when it turns away from that rightness it is termed sin."[53] However, human reason is the basis for natural law only insofar as it participates in the eternal reason which is God's. Hence, in this sense "to disparage the dictate of reason is equivalent to condemning the command of God."[54]

Human Law. Human law, also called positive law or civil law, is the attempt of human reason to make practical laws based on natural law. Human law results when "the practical reason proceeds to make concrete the precepts of the natural law."[55] It is a particularization of the general principles of natural law.

Human laws may be inferred from natural law in two ways. "Some precepts are inferred from the natural law as a conclusion, thus *thou shalt not kill* comes from *thou shalt not harm.*" Others, however, "relate to the natural law as determinate embodiments; for though it may be declared that criminals should be punished, the natural law does not settle the character of the punishment."[56] In short, human laws may be derived from natural law "either as a conclusion or as a particular application."[57] According to Aquinas, the first is like a demonstrative science and the second like an art. Hence, "laws that are declared as conclusions have their force from the natural law as well as from enactment. But laws that are decreed as applied decisions have their force from human legislation."[58]

50. Aquinas, *Disputations*, II de Malo, 4.
51. Aquinas, *Summa Theologiae* 1a. 49, 3 ad 5.
52. Ibid., 1a2ae. 71, 6.
53. Ibid., 21, 1.
54. Ibid., 19, 5 ad 2.
55. Ibid., 91, 3.
56. Ibid., 95, 2.
57. Ibid.
58. Ibid., 2a2ae. 57, 2 ad 3.

Unlike natural law, not everything forbidden by human law is essentially evil (e.g., driving on the right side of the road). For "some things are commanded because they are good, or forbidden because they are evil. Others again are good because they are commanded, or evil because forbidden."[59] Of course, "a human act that is faulty and a sinful kind of act is wrong under all circumstances whatsoever. An act of vice, forbidden by a negative precept is never to be committed by anyone." However, "in an act of virtue, which is commanded by an affirmative precept, many factors have to conspire to make it right. . . . [Thus, it] need not be complied with persistently and in every case, but only when the due conditions of person, time, place, and situation demand its observance."[60]

Human law is imposed on imperfect people. "Therefore it does not forbid all vices, from which the virtuous keep themselves, but only the graver ones which the majority can avoid, and chiefly those that are damaging to others and on prevention of which depends social stability."[61] That is, "human law cannot forbid all and everything that is against virtue; it is enough that it forbid deeds against community life; the remainder it tolerates almost as if they were licit, not indeed because they are approved, but because they are not punished."[62] In short, "every act of virtue is not commanded by human law, but only those that can be enjoined for the public good."[63] For "the immediate end of human law is men's own utility."[64]

According to Aquinas, not every human law is legitimate. For "every law is ordered for the common good, and a precept has the force of law only when it serves this community benefit."[65] Laws contrary to the common good, as demanded by the natural law, do not have the force of law. This leaves room for justifiable revolution, a belief held by most who follow Aquinas's natural law tradition, including John Calvin, John Locke, Samuel Rutherford, and the American founding fathers (e.g., the Declaration of Independence). Further, laws that are not promulgated, even if they are directed to the common good, are not binding. For, as Aquinas said, "no one is obligated to obey a precept unless he be reasonably informed about it."[66]

Divine Law. Divine law has a different purpose than the others. "The intent of the divine law given to man is to lead him to God"; that is, "the entire purpose of the lawgiver is that man may love God."[67] Divine law, therefore,

59. Ibid.
60. Gilby, PT, p. 361, from de Correctionne Fraterna, 1.
61. Aquinas, *Summa Theologiae* 1a2ae. 96, 2.
62. Ibid., 2a2ae. 77, 1 ad 1.
63. Ibid., 96, 3.
64. Ibid., 1a2ae. 95, 3.
65. Ibid., 90, 2.
66. Aquinas, *Disputations* 177, *On Truth* 3.
67. Aquinas, *III Summa contra Gentiles*, 111–16.

is not given to unbelievers but to believers. Natural law is for unbelievers. Divine law is binding on the church, but natural law is binding on society. Natural law is directed toward our temporal good, but divine law is directed toward our eternal good. Contemporary theonomy and reconstructionism fail to make this distinction.[68]

Inasmuch as natural law reflects the very character of God, it cannot change. Divine law, however, is based on God's will, and therefore can be changed. Hence, "in divine as in human law, some things are commanded because they are good. . . . Others again are good because they are commanded"[69] (e.g., worshiping on Sunday rather than Saturday for a Christian, or not eating pork for a Jew in Old Testament times). This is reflected in God's change in divine law from the Old Testament to the New Testament. The natural law, however, has not been altered; it remains the same from age to age and from person to person.

NATURAL LAW AND PROTESTANTS

Natural law is not unique to Catholic thinkers. John Calvin believed that natural law is ingrained by God in the hearts of all people. "That there exists in the human mind, and indeed by natural instinct, some sense of Deity, we hold to be beyond dispute." Calvin insisted that "there is no nation so barbarous, no race so brutish, as not to be imbued with the conviction that there is a God."[70] This "sense of Deity is so naturally engraven on the human heart, in fact, that the very reprobate are forced to acknowledge it."[71]

According to Calvin this innate knowledge of God includes a knowledge of his righteous law.[72] He argued that since "the Gentiles have the righteousness of the law naturally engraved on their minds, [so] we certainly cannot say that they are altogether blind as to the rule of life."[73] He explicitly called this moral awareness "natural law" which is "sufficient for their righteous condemnation"[74] but not for salvation. By means of this natural law "the judgment of conscience" is able to distinguish between "the just and the unjust."[75] God's righteous nature "is engraved in characters so bright, so dis-

---

68. See Craig Bahnsen, *Theonomy in Christian Ethics* (Phillipsburg, N.J.: Presbyterian and Reformed, 1984).

69. Aquinas, *Summa Theologiae* 2a2ae. 57, 2 ad 3.

70. John Calvin, *Institutes of the Christian Religion*, 1.3.1., vol. 1 (Grand Rapids: Eerdmans, 1957), p. 43.

71. Ibid., 1.4.4, vol. 1, p. 49.

72. Kenneth Kantzer, *John Calvin's Theory of the Knowledge of God and the Word of God* (Cambridge, Mass.: Harvard Divinity School, 1981).

73. Calvin, *Institutes*, 2.2.22, vol. 1, p. 241.

74. Ibid.

75. Ibid., p. 242.

tinct, and so illustrious, that none, however dull and illiterate, can plead ignorance as their excuse."[76]

Calvin believed that natural law is not only clear but also specific. It includes a sense of justice "implanted by nature in the hearts of men."[77] There "is imprinted on their hearts a discrimination and judgment, by which they distinguish between justice and injustice, honesty and dishonesty." Accordingly, it is what makes them "ashamed of adultery and theft."[78] According to Calvin, the natural law even governs "good faith in commercial transactions and contracts."[79] Even the heathen "prove their knowledge . . . that adultery, theft, and murder are evils, and honesty is to be esteemed."[80] He summarized our "natural knowledge of the law [as] that which states that one action is good and worthy of being followed, while another is to be shunned with horror."[81]

The roots of early American natural law views derive from John Locke, who in turn got it from the English Protestant Richard Hooker, whose roots are in both Calvin and Aquinas. Locke believed that the "law of Nature" teaches us that "being all equal and independent, no one ought to harm another in his life, health, liberty or possessions," because all people are "the workmanship of one omnipotent and infinitely wise Maker."[82] This same view was expressed by Thomas Jefferson in the Declaration of Independence (1776) when he wrote: "We hold these truths to be self-evident, that all men are created equal, that they are endowed by their Creator with certain unalienable Rights, that among these are Life, Liberty and the pursuit of Happiness."

Our founding fathers believed that these unalienable rights are rooted in the "Laws of Nature" which derive from "Nature's God." On the Jefferson Memorial in Washington, D.C., are inscribed these words he wrote: "God who gave us life gave us liberty. Can the liberties of a nation be secure when we have removed a conviction that these liberties are the gift of God?" Here again it is clear that Jefferson's America was based on the concept of God-given rights grounded in God-given moral rules called "Nature's Laws." For America's founders, too, natural law was not a descriptive "is" but a divinely prescriptive "ought."

76. Ibid., 1.5.1, vol. 1, p. 51.

77. John Calvin, *The Epistles of Paul the Apostle to the Romans and to the Thessalonians* (2:14), ed. David W. Torrance and Thomas F. Torrance, vol. 8 (Grand Rapids: Eerdmans, 1979), p. 48.

78. Ibid.

79. Ibid.

80. Ibid.

81. Ibid., p. 49.

82. John Locke, *An Essay* 2.6, in *The Great Books*, vol. 35 (Chicago: Encyclopaedia Britannica, 1952), p. 26.

THE PURPOSE OF LAW

God has a purpose in giving law. In general the purpose of law is to regulate human activity. Each kind of law, of course, has its own specific kind of regulation in mind. Eternal law is the means by which God regulates the entire universe, divine law is that by which he regulates the church, and natural law is the means of regulating the actions of all rational creatures. In addition to these spheres, Aquinas spells out several specific dimensions of God's purpose for giving law.

Friendship. One of the purposes of law is to promote friendship. "As the leading purpose of human law is to bring about friendship of men among themselves, so divine law is chiefly intended to establish men in friendship with God."[83] If human behavior is to be civil, it must be regulated. Apart from laws, friendship cannot function, since it is the measure of right relationships.

Love of God. Like Augustine before him, Aquinas believed that Jesus summarized all the laws into two: love God and love others. Thus, "the entire purpose of the lawgiver is that man may love God."[84] Hence, it is not either law or love; rather, it is the law of love. Thus "the intent of divine law given to man is to lead him to God."[85] For "love is our strongest union with God, and this above all is intended by the divine law."[86] God is love, and the highest duty is to love him. Thus the primary purpose of God's law is that we may love him.

Curing Evil. Aquinas realized that not everyone will obey God's laws. Hence, a secondary purpose in giving law is punishment. But even here "the value of human penalties is medicinal" for "they promote public security or the cure of the criminal."[87] This is also true of divine and natural law. The primary purpose is for our good, but the secondary purpose is to penalize those who disobey. The hope, of course, is that the punishment will help cure the violator, but this is not the purpose of it.

The Common Good. Human laws also have the purpose of achieving the common good. Aquinas recognized that "to make a rule fit every case is impossible." Hence, "legislators have to attend to what happens in the majority of cases and should frame their laws accordingly." For example, "the law commands that deposits [things borrowed] should be returned, but this, though just in most cases, may sometimes be damaging, as when a weapon is returned to a raging maniac."[88] So what is productive for the common good

---

83. Aquinas, *Summa Theologiae* 1a2ae. 99, 2.
84. Aquinas, *III Summa contra Gentiles*, 111–16.
85. Ibid.
86. Ibid.
87. Aquinas, *Summa Theologiae* 2a2ae. 68, 1.
88. Ibid., 120, 1.

is not always right in a specific case. Since lawmakers cannot take every specific exception into consideration, they must base laws on what happens in the majority of cases. For example, a zoologist says a human hand has four fingers and a thumb, realizing that in some cases persons have fewer or more.[89]

LAWS AND THEIR PRIORITY

Aquinas was not unaware of the fact that there are conflicts among various laws. In such unavoidable conflicts, however, he saw a priority among the conflicting laws that could resolve the problem. This is reflected in several issues he addresses.

The Priority of Natural Law over Human Law. As already indicated, Aquinas believed there were exceptions even to just human laws. Human laws are only general, not universal. Hence, at times the natural law overrides them. As just noted, even though the law of property rights demands that we return what we have borrowed when requested, nonetheless, we should not return a person's weapon to one who is in a murderous rage. In such a case, "to follow the law as it stands would be wrong; to leave it aside and follow what is demanded by fairness and the common benefit will then be right."[90] The virtue of justice of equity demands this. In other words, the moral law takes precedence over the human law in these special cases, even if the human law is a just law.

Laws Based on God's Nature over Those Based on His Will. Aquinas distinguished between laws that were based on the nature of God and those which flowed only from God's will. The latter can be changed but the former cannot.[91] Both divine law and human law fall into the latter category. Because they are based on God's will they can be changed. The natural law, however, is based on God's nature and cannot be changed.[92] Hence, it would follow that, whenever there is a conflict between unchangeable law and changeable law, the former would take priority over the latter. Such seems to be what Aquinas has in view when commenting on the fact that Jesus' disciples broke the Jewish law. For "when the disciples picked ears of corn on the sabbath they were excused from breaking the law by necessity of hunger." Likewise, "nor did David transgress the law when he took the loaves it was illegal for him to eat."[93]

The Letter versus the Spirit of the Law. How Aquinas would resolve conflict situations also emerged in his treatment of "letter of the law" issues. He

---

89. Commentary, V Ethics, lect. 16.
90. Aquinas, *Summa Theologiae* 2a2ae. 120, 1.
91. Ibid., 57, 2 ad 3.
92. Aquinas did not envision real conflicts within two or more absolute moral laws and, hence, did not offer a hierarchy of moral principles in this context.
93. Aquinas, *Summa Theologiae* 3a. 90, 4 ad 3.

observed that "the judgement that the letter of the law is not to be followed in certain given circumstances is not a criticism of the law, but an appreciation of a particular situation that has cropped up."[94] If one does not do this, then severity takes priority over equity. For "legal-mindedness should be directed by equity, which provides a higher rule for human activity."[95] From this it is clear that he believed that there is a "higher rule" or law which takes priority over lower laws. It is also evident that when they conflict one is obligated to take the higher over the lower.

The Principle of Double Effect. Catholic ethics are not unaware of moral conflicts. The time-honored way of dealing with them is the moral principle of double effect. Briefly, this rule states that when a given action brings about both good and bad results, it is our moral duty to will the good ones. For example, amputating a leg with gangrene will both mutilate a body and hopefully save a life. It is one's moral duty to will the saving of a life, even though one knows that a byproduct of this action will be the mutilation of a body. This principle is applied in the case of tubal pregnancies which will, apart from medical intervention, kill both the mother and her unborn child. In this case, one is obligated to will the saving of the mother's life, even though that action will indirectly result in the immediate inability of the baby to survive.

THE MORAL VIRTUES

According to Aquinas, there are four "cardinal" or reasonable virtues (prudence, courage, temperance, and justice) and three divine virtues (faith, hope, and love). The reasonable virtues are common to all rational creatures, being naturally attainable. The divine virtues, however, are supernaturally attained and received only by God's grace.

The Cardinal Virtues. There are four cardinal virtues. By "cardinal" Aquinas meant hinge (Lat: *cardo*); that is, these are not the only virtues, but they are the pivotal ones. Of these Aquinas believed that "prudence opens the way for the other virtues."[96]

Prudence. "Prudence [wisdom] furnishes the right plan for immediate conduct."[97] It is both thoughtful and practical. It is good sense applied to conduct.[98] Prudence chooses the best means to the good end.[99] Since prudence applies principles to particular cases, it does not establish moral purposes, "but contrives the means thereto."[100] Prudence does not establish a

---

94. Ibid., 2a2ae. 120, 1 ad 2.
95. Ibid., 120, 2.
96. Ibid., 47, 6 ad 3.
97. Ibid., 1a2ae. 57, 4.
98. Ibid., 2a2ae. 47, 1 ad 3.
99. Ibid., 47, 2 ad 3.
100. Ibid., 47, 6.

moral end but presupposes it. "That we should live according to right reason is presupposed to prudence. But how, and through what means, our conduct may keep the reasonable measure, that is the affair of prudence. Prudence does not determine our moral duty (the natural law does that), but it devises a plan of conduct to attain it. Since prudence also induces the right frame of mind, it is an intellectual virtue as well as a moral one."[101]

There are three kinds of prudence: "solitary prudence directed to one's own benefit; economic or domestic prudence directed to the good of a household or family; and political prudence ordered to the common good of the State."[102] Three stages are marked in prudent conduct. First, the wise man takes counsel and discusses the question. Next, he makes a judgment about the matter as to the best course of action. Finally, he applies the counsel and judgment to what must be done here and now.[103] Since "an infinity of singulars cannot be comprehended by the human reason," prudence does not deal with universals but with "what usually happens."[104] There is no absolute certainty with prudence. "Opinion [probability] is about things that could be otherwise, and so is prudence."[105] Wisdom, then, deals only with what is generally the case; it does not admit to universals. Only the natural law does that. Natural law deals with the good itself (as an end); prudence estimates the best way (means) to attain the good.

Courage. Courage is the virtue of "holding steady in the face of danger."[106] It includes patience.[107] Courage is both a general and a special virtue. As a general virtue courage is "a firmness of spirit, or a condition of every virtue" and as a special virtue courage is "a particular firmness in enduring and repulsing threats in situations fraught with conspicuous difficulty."[108] Like Augustine, Aquinas believed that courage is obtained by drawing close to God, for "the nearer a man is to God, who is ever constant, the more steadfast he is and the less fickle."[109] In the display of courage two characteristics should be considered: "the premeditated deliberateness and the habit of discipline."[110] It is the latter that manifests itself in emergencies. Courage is not to be confused with aggressiveness, since "holding steady in danger is more important than taking the offensive."[111] Courage, then, is the virtue that enables one to hold fast in the face of danger.

101. Ibid., 47, 4.
102. Ibid., 47, 11.
103. Ibid., 47, 8.
104. Ibid., 47, 3 ad 2.
105. Commentary, VI Ethics, lect. 4.
106. Aquinas, *Summa Theologiae* 2a2ae. 123, 6.
107. Aquinas, *On the Cardinal Virtues* 1 ad 14.
108. Aquinas, *Summa Theologiae* 2a2ae. 123, 2.
109. Aquinas, *III Summa contra Gentiles*, 62.
110. Aquinas, *Summa Theologiae* 2a2ae. 123, 9.
111. Ibid., 123, 6.

Temperance. Temperance is the virtue of moderation. The virtues of "justice and courage are more immediately related to the common good than temperance is, for justice controls transactions with others, while courage faces the dangers to be undergone for the common good." By contrast, "temperance moderates merely one's own personal lusts and pleasures. Therefore, the others are greater virtues, and prudence and the divine virtues are more potent still."[112]

The virtue of temperance "does not abolish all depraved lusts, but the temperate man does not tolerate them as does the intemperate man."[113] A temperate person is one who modifies sensual desires by reason. For these desires are "born to obey reason."[114] The intemperate person is childish on three grounds. First, both intemperate persons and children desire graceless things: "a child does not bother about counsels of moderation . . . ; neither does lust listen to sobriety." Second, both are spoiled when left to their own devices: "concupiscence grows with gratification." Third, "both require the same remedy, namely, the use of force." Thus, "when lusts are resisted they may be tamed to the due manner of decency."[115]

A temperate person, however, does not avoid all pleasure. "Nature provides pleasure in vitally necessary activities, and the natural order requires that a man should enjoy what is required for the well-being of the individual and the race." In fact, "were someone to avoid pleasure so far as to omit what is a natural necessity he would sin, as though resisting the design of nature." Indeed, "a man cannot lead a reasonable life if he avoids all pleasure. He who abhors pleasures because they are pleasurable is boorish and ungracious."[116] Jesting is a pleasure to be enjoyed, for "jokes and plays are words and gestures that are not instructive, but merely seek to give lively pleasure. We should enjoy them. They are governed by the virtue of witty gaiety . . . which we call pleasantness."[117]

Justice. Justice is virtue that "directs our deeds with regard to other people under the aspect of what is owing to them."[118] In other words, "justice stands out as rendering another man his due."[119] While art is the making of external things, "justice is the administration of external things."[120]

Human rights are "the special object of justice."[121] There are two kinds of rights: natural and positive. The former is one's rights "from the very na-

112. Ibid., 141, 8.
113. Disputations, *On Cardinal Virtues* 1 ad 6.
114. Aquinas, *Summa Theologiae* 3a. 18, 2.
115. Ibid., 2a2ae. 142, 2.
116. Ibid., 142, 1 ad 2.
117. Ibid., 148, 2.
118. Ibid., 23, 3 ad 1.
119. Ibid., 57, 1.
120. Ibid., 58, 3 ad 3.
121. Ibid.

ture of things." The other is a right "from agreement, either private or public."[122] Natural rights have priority over positive rights, and "what is contrary to natural rights cannot be made just by human will. *Woe to those who make iniquitous laws* [Isa. 11:1]."[123]

Aquinas believed there were "two main reasons why men fall short of justice—deference to magnates, deference to the mob." Both yield to might over right. In the first case it is a yielding to social power and in the other to physical power. Both subordinate fairness to force and principles to pressure.

The Divine Virtues. Following the apostle Paul (1 Cor. 13:14), Aquinas believed that the principal Christian virtues were faith, hope, and love, and that the greatest of these was love. These actions all take divine grace to perform; hence, they are not natural but divine. They are supernatural virtues since they "surpass human virtue; for they are virtues of men as made partakers in divine grace."[124] Further, "theological virtues shape a man to supernatural happiness in the same way as his natural bent shapes him to his connatural end."[125]

Faith. Faith is prior to hope and love, since "it is by faith that the mind apprehends what it hopes for and loves. And so in the sequence of coming to be, faith has to precede hope and charity." Faith is the substance of things hoped for and the evidence of things not yet seen (Heb. 11:1). Hence, faith is meritorious because it involves the will to believe. It "depends on the will according to its very nature. It is for this reason that to believe can be meritorious, and that faith . . . is a virtue for the theologian."[126] "For in science and opinion [probable arguments] there is no inclination because of the will, but only because of reason."[127] But "no act can be meritorious unless it is voluntary, as has been said."[128]

The supernatural virtue of faith does not destroy reason but complements it. In Aquinas's words, "grace does not destroy nature but completes it."[129] Faith goes beyond reason and "sees" by faith what unaided reason cannot see. Thus "faith is the foretaste of that knowledge which hereafter will make us happy."[130] In brief, the virtue of faith is directed toward our eternal happiness.

Hope. Hope is the virtue of expectation. It provides confidence for the content of faith that is perfected by love. "Hope denotes a movement toward

---

122. Ibid., 57, 2.
123. Ibid., 57, 2 ad 2.
124. Ibid., 1a2ae. 58, 3 ad 3.
125. Ibid., 62, 3.
126. Ibid., 62, 3 ad 5.
127. Aquinas, *On Truth*, XIV, 3, reply.
128. Ibid., 5, reply.
129. Aquinas, *Summa Theologiae* 1a. 1, 8 ad 2.
130. Aquinas, *Compendium of Theology*, 2.

that which is not possessed. . . . When, therefore, what is hoped for is possessed, namely the enjoyment of God, hope will no longer be possible."[131] Hope implies four things: "that it is good, future, arduous, possible. Hence, respectively, hope differs from fear, joy, simple desire, and despair."[132]

Like faith, hope precedes love, since "by basing his hopes on another, he proceeds to love him. Thus, in the sequence of coming to be, the act of hope precedes that of charity."[133] However, as we will see, love is prior to hope by its very nature, for both faith and hope need love to complete them.

Hope is the mean between the extremes of presumption and despair. Presumption results in "hoping to receive from God a good in excess of his condition, or [in] despair through failing to hope for what he could hope for according to his condition." However, "there can be no excess of hope in looking to God, for his goodness is infinite."[134] Thus, "the act of hope consists in reliance upon God for future beatitude."[135]

Love. Aquinas believed that "love is the form, mover, and root of the virtues."[136] However, unlike the natural virtues, "the object of charity is not the common good, but the highest good."[137] Following the words of Jesus, Aquinas held that "there are two precepts of charity: Thou shalt love the Lord thy God with thy whole heart. . . . And the second is like to it: thou shalt love thy neighbor as thyself."[138]

Faith and hope cannot be completed without love. Faith draws God to man, but "love draws man to God."[139] Of course, "faith and hope can in a way exist without charity, but they have not the perfect status of a virtue without charity." This is because "the work of God is to believe in God, and . . . to will otherwise than as one ought is not a perfect work of faith." But "to will as one ought is caused by charity, which perfects the will; for every right movement of the will proceeds from a right love, as Augustine says."[140]

As for Augustine's summary of the virtues in terms of love, Aquinas responds: "Augustine's saying is to be understood of virtue in its unqualified sense; not that every such virtue is simply love, but that it depends in some way on love, inasmuch as it depends on the will, the primordial motion of which is love."[141] Love is not the essence of each virtue but the essential mo-

131. Aquinas, *Summa Theologiae* 1a2ae. 67, 4 ad 1.
132. Disputations, de Spe, 1.
133. Aquinas, *Summa Theologiae* 1a2ae. 62, 4.
134. Ibid., 64, 4 ad 3.
135. Ibid., 65, 4.
136. Disputations, 6 de Caritate, 3.
137. Disputations, de Caritate, 5 ad 4.
138. Opusc. 29, de Perfectione Vitae Spiritualis, 1–8.
139. Disputations, 6 de Potentia, 9 ad 6.
140. Aquinas, *Summa Theologiae* 1a2ae. 65, 4.
141. Ibid., 56, 3 ad 1.

tive behind it. Without love, the other virtues are less virtuous. For instance, fortitude in hatred is vice, but fortitude in love is virtue.

THE ABIDING VALUE OF THE BASIC CATHOLIC ETHIC

Nothing of real significance has been added to the basic Catholic view of morality since the time of Aquinas. Like Augustine before him, Aquinas believed morality is absolutistic, anchored in the nature and will of an unchangingly perfect God. This morality can be expressed in terms of love: the love of God, self, and others. This love is manifest in many areas which sometimes conflict. God has commanded, however, that we love him supremely and uniquely over any human being or thing. Other conflicts are resolved by following the greater obligation of love.

With the exception of specific areas such as contraception, both Catholics and evangelicals share a common ethical heritage in Augustine and Aquinas. And contrary to a vocal minority of reconstructionists, basic Protestant ethic, especially as applied to civil government, is based in the Catholic natural law tradition.

Several values emerge from the Catholic view of ethics. First, the Catholic view of ethics avoids the extreme of situationism. Unlike much of modern ethical thought, it does not reduce all law to human (positive) law. Rather, human law ought to be based on natural law, from which it draws its legitimacy. Without an unchangeable anchor for civil law in moral law, human rights cannot be protected. As the Declaration of Independence puts it, there are "unalienable rights" of "the Creator" imbedded in "Nature's Laws" which come from "Nature's God." These include the unalienable "right to life," and government does not have the right to deprive anyone of these God-given rights. Rather, government should protect these rights.

Also, natural law is common to all men, not just believers and therefore can be used as the basis for civil law in religiously pluralistic societies. This avoids the problems of theonomy, wherein divine law is pronounced or practiced as the only legitimate basis for human government. The history of the Christian church gives ample testimony to the fatal consequences of a church-dominated state. Constantine, the Spanish Inquisition, Calvin's Geneva, and the Puritans' persecution of Roger Williams are examples from both sides of the spectrum.

Finally, since natural law is transnational, it provides a basis for international activity and commerce. Without natural law there is no objective basis for the condemnation of tyrants like Hitler and Stalin, for if civil law is the last word, then each nation can do what is right in its own eyes.

CONCLUSION

There is a common core to Catholic and evangelical ethics. Both are *absolutistic,* being rooted in the nature and will of God. Both are *essentialistic,* holding that God wills something because it is good; it is not good simply because God wills it. Both are *revelational,* being based on God's self-disclosure to humans in both nature (general revelation) and Scripture (special revelation). Likewise, at least for many Protestants, both are *universal,* insisting that God has revealed himself to all people via natural law. This universal moral law serves as a common basis for all human actions and for universal human rights. It at once avoids the extremes of both situationism and reconstructionism, that is, of those who have no moral law and those who would superimpose their "divine" or religious law on those of opposing religious beliefs. Thus, in a religiously pluralistic society, the basic Catholic moral system, embraced by much of evangelicalism, appears to be the best hope to save religious freedom without sacrificing moral absolutes.

8

LAST THINGS

INTRODUCTION

All religions, from the most primitive to the most advanced, have beliefs about the "endtime." This section in theology is called "eschatology." The term comes from the Greek *eschatos* which means "last." Indeed, from the very earliest Christian creeds convictions about the last things have been confessed. The Apostles' Creed declares: "From thence He shall come to judge the living and the dead" and "I believe in . . . the life everlasting." The Council of Toledo XI (A.D. 675) states: "There sitting at the right hand of the Father, He [Christ] awaits the end of time to be the judge of all the living and the dead."[1]

DEFINITION OF LAST THINGS

One Roman Catholic authority defines the doctrine of the last things as "the part of theology which treats of the final things: death, judgment, heaven and hell. More specifically this is concerned with a study of the Resurrection of Christ and His teaching to the disciples concerning His second coming (the *parousia*)."[2] A post-Vatican theologian observes that "the word *eschatology* means a doctrine about the last events and final circumstances toward which the history of mankind and the life of each individual are directed." Christian eschatology can be distinguished "by its transcendental character from that secular faith in progress which in modern times has become a dominant theme of the European outlook on history."[3]

1. Denzinger, *Sources of Catholic Dogma*, para. 287, p. 112.
2. Broderick, *Catholic Concise Encyclopedia*, p. 148.
3. Michael Schmaus, *Dogma 6: Justification and the Last Things* (London: Sheed and Ward, 1977), pp. 149–50.

Theologians distinguish between "individual" eschatology and "cosmic" or general eschatology. In the former they treat the end of every individual in the world, and in the latter they consider "the last things" as they apply to humanity and the world in general. We will discuss individual eschatology first, dealing with experiences that lie in the future for us such as death, the possibility of an intermediate state, heaven, and hell. Then we will move to cosmic eschatology, which impacts the future of humanity and the entire creation. We shall see that Catholics and evangelicals share common beliefs about the future.

INDIVIDUAL ESCHATOLOGY

In considering individual eschatology, Roman Catholics include heaven, hell, and purgatory. Of course, preparatory to this is belief about the nature of death.

THE REALITY AND SIGNIFICANCE OF DEATH

Catholic theology teaches that, "in the present order of salvation, death is a punishment for sin *(De fide)*. The Council of Trent teaches in the Decree on Original Sin that Adam became subject to sin by the transgression of the Divine commandment, that God had previously threatened him with death, and that he transmitted death to the whole of mankind."[4] Consequently, "All human beings subject to original sin are subject to the law of death *(De fide).*"[5] The writer of Hebrews declares that "it is appointed that human beings die once, and after this the judgment" (Heb. 9:27). While death is indeed a reality, "our Christian faith teaches that bodily death . . . will be overcome by the all-powerful mercy of the Saviour, when man will be restored to the salvation lost thru his own fault."[6]

The most important aspect of death is that with its arrival all possibility of conversion ends. Origen and a few of the early church fathers (notably Clement of Alexandria and Gregory of Nyssa) held what was known as the *Apocatastasis* doctrine. This was the belief that all free moral creatures—angels, humans, and devils—will ultimately be converted. The modern form of this teaching is "universalism." Contemporary theology is much enamored of this unfortunate notion, and it has affected both modern Roman Catholic and Protestant thought. Although the *Apocatastasis* doctrine was declared heretical by the Council of Constantinople (A.D. 543), once again we find the

4. Ott, *Fundamentals of Catholic Dogma,* p. 473.
5. Ibid., p. 474.
6. Neuner and Dupuis, *Christian Faith,* p. 774.

ancient church setting standards for orthodoxy which some in the modern church ignore.[7]

THE PARTICULAR JUDGMENT

Roman Catholicism teaches that "immediately after death the particular judgment takes place, in which, by a Divine Sentence of Judgment, the eternal fate of the deceased person is decided."[8] This particular judgment is preparatory to the general judgment which all will experience at the end of the world. Catholicism rejects the modern "soul-sleep" theory which holds that souls, after their separation from their bodies, are in an unconscious state until re-unified with their bodies. Among Scriptural passages that refute the notion of soul-sleep is the story of Lazarus and the rich man (Luke 16:19–31). Upon death the former is immediately exposed to bliss whereas the latter is in torment. Also, as Jesus was about to die on the cross he told the penitent thief, "I say to you, today you will be with me in Paradise" (Luke 23:43).[9] Paul said he would "rather leave the body and go home to the Lord" (2 Cor. 5:8), and the writer of Hebrews declared, "it is appointed that human beings die once and after this the judgment" (Heb. 9:27).

HEAVEN

The doctrine of heaven has great importance for the believing Christian. Heaven's very name "takes its meaning from the end to which it is directed, and grace is only the means required to reach what is unattainable by any created being without elevation to the family of God."[10] Concerning the location and nature of heaven, Roman Catholicism teaches that "heaven is a place and condition of perfect supernatural bliss, which consists in the immediate vision of God and the perfect love of God associated with it."[11] Support for the doctrine of heaven is provided by Catholic scholars from both Scripture and tradition.

The doctrine of heaven (as well as the future state in general) in the Old Testament is rudimentary in nature; it remained for the New Testament to fill out the details of our heavenly home. David mentioned the future state in Psalm 16 when he said, "You [God] will not abandon my soul to the nether world, nor will you suffer your faithful one to undergo corruption. You will

---

7. Cross, *Oxford Dictionary of the Christian Church*, pp. 69–70.
8. Ott, *Fundamentals of Catholic Dogma*, pp. 475–76.
9. Ibid.
10. Hardon, *Catholic Catechism*, p. 260.
11. Ott, *Fundamentals of Catholic Dogma*, p. 476.

show me the path of life, abounding joy in your presence, the delights at your right hand forever" (Ps. 16:10–11). Even before this Job declared, "I know that my Vindicator lives, and that he will at last stand forth upon the dust . . . and from [in] my flesh I shall see God" (Job 19:25–26). The Book of Daniel later affirmed that "Many of those who sleep in the dust of the earth shall awake; some shall live forever, others shall be an everlasting horror and disgrace" (12:2).

Heaven occupied a prominent place in Jesus' teaching. Heaven is depicted as a wedding feast (Luke 14:15–24). He also said, "In my Father's house there are many dwelling places. . . . And if I go and prepare a place for you, I will come back again and take you to myself, so that where I am you also may be" (John 14:2–3). In his famous Sermon on the Mount Jesus said, "Blessed are the clean of heart, for they will see God" (Matt. 5:8). The apostle John, commenting on the "Beatific Vision" (i.e., our vision of God in heaven) said, "Beloved, we are God's children now; what we shall be has not yet been revealed. We do know that when it is revealed we shall be like him, for we shall see him as he is" (1 John 3:2). Commenting on the imperfect nature of our present understanding Paul said, "At present we see indistinctly, as in a mirror, but then face to face" (1 Cor. 13:12).

Support for the doctrine of heaven is also found in tradition. The last phrase in the Apostles' Creed addresses the early church's belief in the future bliss of the redeemed: "I believe in . . . the life everlasting." The early Fathers and the later Schoolmen (especially Augustine and Aquinas) addressed the nature of the future heavenly bliss. In the *Constitution of Benedict XII* we find an authoritative statement on heaven: "We define that, since the passion and death of the Lord Jesus Christ, they (the souls in heaven) have seen and do see the divine essence with an intuitive and even face-to-face vision, without interposition of any creature in the function of the object seen."[12]

As to the duration of heaven Catholic dogma proclaims that "the bliss of Heaven lasts for all eternity *(De fide)*."[13] Augustine, on the concept of perfect bliss, also declared: "How can one speak of true bliss, when confidence in its eternal duration is lacking?"[14] There will also be a difference in reward: "The degree of perfection of the beatific vision granted to the just is proportioned to each one's merits *(De fide)*."[15] Every redeemed person will receive blessings in heaven commensurate to the degree to which each used their opportunities and gifts while on earth. The Fathers are fond of appealing to the

---

12. Benedict XII, Constitution *Benedictus Deus: Denzinger 693 (1304–6)*; quoted in Hardon, *Catholic Catechism*, pp. 261–62.
13. Ott, *Fundamentals of Catholic Dogma*, p. 478.
14. Ibid., p. 479; see Augustine, *City of God* XII 13, 1; cf. X 30 and XI 13.
15. Ibid.

words of Jesus concerning the many mansions in the Father's house (John 14:2). Tertullian remarked: "Why are there many mansions in the Father's house if not on account of the difference of the merits?"[16]

HELL

The topic of hell has caused great consternation among unbelievers and believers alike. One Catholic scholar noted that "There are few doctrines of Christianity that cause more scandal to those who do not share the Christian faith than the mystery of hell."[17] Relating to the latter group, one Catholic authority comments that, "among the faithful, belief in eternal punishment places a heavy burden on their minds, since it seems to run so counter to all that revelation tells us about the goodness and mercy of God."[18] The fact remains that our Lord spoke to the reality of hell more than most other theological truths (cf. Matt. 10:28; 13:40; 25:41; Mark 9:43).

The Roman Catholic Church has faithfully witnessed to the truthfulness of this stern but essential doctrine in its theological formulations. The official Roman Catholic position on hell is that "The souls of those who die in the condition of personal grievous sin enter Hell *(De fide)*. Hell is a place or state of eternal punishment inhabited by those rejected by God."[19] The unregenerate, upon physical death, go directly to hell. "Moreover we define that according to the general disposition of God, the souls of those who die in actual moral sin go down into hell immediately."[20] Some liberal Catholic scholars acknowledge that they must believe there is a hell but deny that anyone actually goes there! This is clearly contrary to Catholic dogma. More realistically, Roman Catholic philosopher Peter Kreeft says, "Fear of hell is not a base motive. As George MacDonald says, 'As long as there are wild beasts about, it is better to be afraid than secure.'"[21]

The New Testament presents the stark realities of the doctrine of hell held by both Catholics and evangelicals. Jesus issues the strong warning: "do not be afraid of those who kill the body but cannot kill the soul; rather, be afraid of the one who can destroy both soul and body in Gehenna" (Matt. 10:28). Modern Catholic scholars note that "this comes from the Hebrew 'Valley of Hinnom', a place near Jerusalem where ritual infant-sacrifices had been practiced (2 Chron. 28:3). The word became synonymous with the place of malediction (Jer. 7:31), and then in the New Testament with the abode of the

16. Ibid.
17. Hardon, *Catholic Catechism*, p. 268.
18. Ibid.
19. Ott, *Fundamentals of Catholic Dogma*, p. 479.
20. Neuner and Dupuis, Benedict XII, "Constitution *Benedictus Deus*" (1336), p. 769.
21. Kreeft, *Fundamentals of the Faith*, p. 162.

damned, a place of torment, unquenchable fire and the consuming worm (Matt. 5:29; 10:28; 18:8f.; Mark 9:44ff.)."[22]

Jesus describes hell as a place "where their worm does not die and the fire is not extinguished" (Mark 9:46). It is likened to a "furnace of fire" (Matt. 13:42, 50), where there is darkness (Matt. 8:12; 22:13; 25:30) and "wailing and gnashing of teeth" (Matt. 13:42, 50; 24:51; Luke 13:28). Paul (2 Thess. 1:9), Peter (2 Pet. 2:4–6), and John all mention the dreadful consequences of ending up in this place of torment.[23]

The church creeds support the witness of Scripture. The Athanasian Creed states: "those who have done evil will go into eternal fire."[24] The church fathers were united in their belief in the reality of hell. According to Ignatius of Antioch, the person who "corrupts the faith of God, for which Jesus Christ was crucified, by evil teaching, will go into the unquenchable fire; and so will the person who listens to him (Eph. 16:2)."[25]

Concerning the duration of hell, the official Catholic teaching states that "the punishment of Hell lasts for all eternity *(De fide)*." The Fourth Lateran Council (A.D. 1215) declared that "those [the rejected] will receive a perpetual punishment with the devil."[26] As to the degree of punishment, Roman Catholicism holds that "The punishment of the damned is proportioned to each one's guilt." Augustine taught that, "in their wretchedness, the lot of some of the damned will be more tolerable than that of others."[27] Just as there are levels of blessedness in heaven, there are degrees of wretchedness in hell.

The doctrine of hell can serve as a warning. A contemporary catechism states: "The affirmations of Sacred Scripture and the teachings of the Church on the subject of hell are a call to the *responsibility* incumbent upon man to make use of his freedom in view of his eternal destiny."[28]

PURGATORY

On the doctrine of purgatory Protestants part company with Roman Catholics. The Eastern Orthodox Church also rejects the concept of purgatory: "(According to the normal Roman teaching, souls in Purgatory undergo expiatory suffering, and so render 'satisfaction' or 'atonement' for their sins.) Today most if not all Eastern Orthodox theologians reject the idea of Purga-

---

22. *New American Bible*, p. 421.
23. Ott, *Fundamentals of Catholic Dogma*, p. 480.
24. See Denzinger, *Sources of Catholic Dogma*, no. 40, p. 16.
25. Ott, *Fundamentals of Catholic Dogma*, p. 480.
26. Ibid., p. 481.
27. Ibid., p. 482. See Augustine, *Enchiridion* III.
28. *Catechism of the Catholic Church*, p. 270.

tory at any rate in this form."[29] This topic will be addressed more fully in chapter 16.

COSMIC ESCHATOLOGY

In the later prophets of the Old Testament, notably Daniel, we find traditional elements of prophetic eschatology given a universalistic spin. Here, "Cosmic imagery and a concept of plan were now combined with a greater emphasis on the transcendent nature of the event that would be definitive for all history."[30] The Roman Catholic Church condemns the notion that the world will be destroyed "naturally."[31] In the following section we will deal with eschatology in its cosmic implications and effects on all of humanity and the created order.

THE SECOND COMING OF CHRIST

All orthodox Christians believe, in the words of the Apostles' Creed, that Christ will return bodily from heaven: "From thence He shall come to judge the living and the dead." There are differences on the specific order of events surrounding Christ's Second Advent, but all agree on the fact of it.

Reality of the Second Coming. Roman Catholicism teaches that, "at the end of the world, Christ will come again in glory to pronounce judgment *(De fide.)*."[32] The Apostles' Creed, and indeed the whole of church tradition, is united in the belief that Jesus Christ will return. The *Didache* (1st century), one of the earliest of all Christian sources outside the Bible, declares that at this time "the world shall see the Lord come on the clouds of Heaven."[33]

The New Testament contains numerous references to Christ's second coming (Gk.: *parousia*) as well. Jesus foretold his coming again in glory. Matthew records him declaring: "For the Son of Man will come with his angels in his Father's glory, and then he will repay everyone according to his conduct" (Matt. 16:27). Luke notes him saying that "they will see the Son of Man coming in a cloud with power and great glory" (Luke 22:27). Paul addresses the eschatological concerns of the church at Thessalonica (1 Thess.

29. Timothy Ware, *The Orthodox Church,* rev. (New York: Penguin Books, 1983), p. 259. Some Catholic scholars believe this is compatible with their view since they don't deny this but only affirm that purgatory is for the *temporal* consequences for sins, not for their guilt or spiritual consequences.
30. *New Catholic Encyclopedia,* 5:528.
31. Denzinger, "Errors of Zanini de Solcia," 717a., p. 232.
32. Ott, *Fundamentals of Catholic Dogma,* p. 485.
33. *Didache* 16, 8. cf. 10, 6; quoted in ibid., p. 486.

4:15–17; 2 Thess. 1:8). And Peter (2 Pet. 1:16), John (1 John 2:28), James (5:7f.), and Jude (v. 14) all deal with the second coming of Christ.

Signs of the Second Coming. Roman Catholics, along with evangelicals, recognize a number of events that can be understood as signs of the return of the Lord to earth. These include the evangelization of the world, the conversion of the Jews, the falling away from the faith, the appearance of the antichrist, and the tribulation period.

Concerning evangelization of the whole world, Scripture states that "this gospel of the Kingdom will be preached throughout the world as a witness to all nations and then the end will come" (Matt. 24:14). The point is made that there may be a length of time between this event and the final consummation.[34] The conversion of the Jews is another sign. Paul said that when all of the elect among the Gentiles have been called into the church then all "Israel will be saved" (Rom. 11:25–32).[35] What exactly is meant by "all" in the above verses is in dispute. The coming of Elijah, which was foretold by Malachi (3:23–24), is understood to have been fulfilled in the person of John the Baptist (Mark 9:13).[36]

Jesus also warned that there will be a proliferation of false prophets before the end comes (Matt. 24:4ff.). Paul mentions an event which he calls "the apostasy" (2 Thess. 2:3). This will cause a "falling away" prior to Christ's second coming.[37] This "falling away" is facilitated by a malevolent creature known as "the man of sin," "the lawless one," and "the son of perdition." These names all refer to the antichrist (2 Thess. 2:3; 1 John 2:18, 22; 4:3; 2 John 2:7). The antichrist is understood to be a real person who is at the service of Satan.[38] "Such specific personal titles and characteristics [mentioned in Holy Writ] cannot refer to an abstract ethical force for evil, or to a collective body or to movements of evil. An individual is specifically pointed out and identified by his supreme capacity and stunningly unique career in the pursuit of evil."[39]

Finally, Jesus warns that the endtimes will be accompanied by wars, famines, earthquakes, and persecution of the faithful. This period before Christ returns is known as the time of tribulation (Matt. 24:9, 29; cf. Isa. 13:10; 34:4).[40] It is a time of unprecedented suffering on the face of the earth. The belief in such an endtime apostasy is common to both Catholics and evangelicals.

34. Ott, *Fundamentals of Catholic Dogma*, p. 486.
35. Ibid.
36. Ibid., p. 487.
37. Ibid.
38. Ibid.
39. Vincent P. Miceli, S.J., *The Antichrist* (Harrison, N.Y.: Roman Catholic Books, 1981), p. 18. In the appendix Miceli quotes a number of Christians (including Aleksandr Solzhenitsyn, Rousas John Rushdoony, and C. S. Lewis) to the effect that the final confrontation between Christ and the antichrist may be at hand (pp. 273–82).
40. Ibid.

The Time of the Second Coming. As to the precise time of Christ's coming
Catholicism maintains the words of our Lord that "no one knows." Ott
notes that "the time of Jesus' second coming is unknown to men *(Sent.
certa.).* Jesus left the moment of the *parousia* indeterminate. At the conclusion of the *parousia* speech, He declared: 'But of that day and hour no man
knoweth, neither the angels in Heaven, nor the Son, but the Father' (Mark
13:32)."[41] Indeed, the last thing Jesus said before he ascended was, "No one
knows the times or the seasons" of his return (Acts 1:5). Paul tells the Thessalonians that they need not know the exact time of the parousia (1 Thess.
5:1–2), and Peter "ascribes the delay of the parousia to the patience of God
who wishes to give sinners time to repent."[42] However, Roman Catholics,
like most evangelicals, teach that the Lord could return at any time: "Since
the Ascension Christ's coming in glory has been imminent (cf. Rev. 22:20).
. . . This eschatological coming could be accomplished at any moment, even
if both it and the final trial that will precede it are 'delayed' (cf. Mt. 24:44;
1 Thess. 5:2; 2 Thess. 2:3–12)."[43]

As to whether Christ comes before or after the "thousand years" (millennium) mentioned in Revelation 20 the Roman Catholic Church has made no
official pronouncement. Many but not all of the early church fathers held to
a view called "chiliasm" (or "millennialism") which held that a long period
of time—one thousand years—would transpire until the final judgment was
rendered. By and large this view has been rejected by Catholics in favor of
"amillennialism," the position favored by Augustine and popularized in his
work *The City of God.* Augustine, however, admits that he himself, like most
earlier Fathers, once held this view but gave it up because he observed abuses
among some groups that took it literally.[44] Most Protestants, especially in
earlier centuries, being more concerned with soteriological differences with
Catholics, have been content not to deviate from the later Augustinian and
dominant Catholic view at this point. The twentieth century has experienced
a revival of the premillennial (that Christ will return before the thousand
years and literally reign over the earth) view held by the early Fathers. Few
Catholics, however, hold this position.

Many contemporary evangelicals have a special interest in the return of
the Jews to their ancient land. Some Roman Catholics are concerned that "a
one-sided advocacy of Israel disregards the Palestinians (some of whom happen to be Christians). But, as the Vatican and the American bishops have

41. Ibid., p. 488.
42. Ibid.
43. *Catechism 1994,* no. 673, p. 176.
44. See Norman L. Geisler, "A Pre-Millennial View of Law and Government," *Bibliotheca
Sacra* (July–Sept. 1985): 253–55. Others suggest that premillennialism was given up because the
Roman persecution failed to end in the second coming that was predicted by some. This too
would be an extra-biblical reason, based on an abuse of the doctrine, and not a proper use of it.

pointed out, basic principles of human rights apply equally to all nations, including Israel."[45]

THE RESURRECTION OF THE DEAD

At Christ's coming there will be a resurrection of the dead. All orthodox Christians confess with the *Apostles' Creed* to "believe . . . in the resurrection of the flesh." The fact of the bodily resurrection is not a matter of dispute between Catholics and evangelicals.

According to Catholic dogma, "All the dead will rise again on the last day with their bodies" *(De fide).*[46] The Athanasian Creed stresses resurrection: "On His coming all men with their bodies must arise."[47] As to the exact timing of this event, the last thing Jesus said before he ascended was, "It is not for you to know the times or seasons" of his return (Acts 1:7).

Argument from Scripture. Both Old and New Testaments speak repeatedly about the bodily resurrection of both believers and unbelievers from their graves. Old Testament passages on the resurrection of the body include Deuteronomy 32:39, 1 Samuel 2:6, Job 19:25–26, Isaiah 26:19, Ezekiel 37:12f., and Daniel 12:2. Daniel 12:2 declares that in the endtime "many of those who sleep in the dust of the earth shall awake; some shall live forever, others shall be an everlasting horror and disgrace." In the New Testament Jesus said explicitly that "the hour is coming in which all who are in the tombs will hear his voice and will come out, those who have done good deeds to the resurrection of life, but those who have done wicked deeds to the resurrection of condemnation" (John 5:28–29). John noted that those who follow Jesus "came to life and they reigned with Christ for a thousand years," but "the rest of the dead did not come to life until the thousand years were over" (Rev. 20:4–5). Paul also speaks of the resurrection of believers, insisting that "Christ has been raised from the dead, the firstfruits of those who have fallen asleep. For since death came through a human being, the resurrection of the dead came also through a human being . . . but each in proper order: Christ the firstfruits; then, at his coming, those who belong to Christ" (1 Cor. 15:20–21).

Argument from the Fathers. Irenaeus (c. A.D. 130–200) was one of the first great theologians of the Christian church. In his famous work, *Against Heresies*, he affirmed that, "Inasmuch as Christ did rise in our flesh, it follows that we shall be also raised in the same [flesh]; since the resurrection promised to us should not be referred to spirits naturally immortal, but to

---

45. "The Book of Revelation," *God's Word Today* (St. Paul: University of St. Thomas Press, 1993), p. 49.
46. Ott, *Fundamentals of Catholic Dogma*, p. 488.
47. Ibid., pp. 488–89.

bodies in themselves mortal."[48] Resurrecting the flesh, he insists, is no problem for God, for "since the Lord has power to infuse life into what He has fashioned, since the flesh is capable of being quickened, what remains to prevent its participation in incorruption, which is a blissful and never-ending life granted by God?"[49]

Tertullian (c. A.D. 160–230) declared that Jesus "will come with glory to take the saints to the enjoyment of everlasting life and of the heavenly promises, and to condemn the wicked to everlasting fire, after the resurrection of both these classes shall have happened, together with the restoration of their flesh."[50]

Justin Martyr (c. A.D. 100–165), a converted philosopher and one of the great apologists of the early church, spoke plainly: "the resurrection is a resurrection of the flesh which dies."[51] He adds, "Let the unbelieving be silent, even though they themselves do not believe. But in truth, He has even called the flesh to the resurrection, and promises to it everlasting life. For where He promises to save man, there He gives the promise to the flesh."[52]

Athenagoras, the second-century Christian teacher at Athens, wrote a treatise on "The Resurrection of the Dead." In it he affirmed in response to those who denied the physical resurrection: "Moreover also, that His power is sufficient of the raising of dead bodies, is shown by the creation of these same bodies. For if, when they did not exist, He made at their first formation the bodies of men, and their original elements, He will, when they are dissolved, in whatever manner that may take place, raise them again with equal ease: for this too, is equally possible to Him."[53]

The famous Latin bishop, Rufinus (A.D. 345–410), in his "Commentary on the Apostle's Creed," declared that even the lost particles of the dead body will be restored in the resurrection body. In his preface to "Pamphilus' Defense of Origen," he also emphasized the identity of the pre- and post-resurrection body, saying: "We believe that it is this very flesh in which we are now living which will rise again, not one kind of flesh instead of another, nor another body than the body of this flesh. . . . It is an absurd invention of maliciousness to think that the human body is different from the flesh."[54]

Epiphanius, in his *Second Creed of Epiphanius* (A.D. 374), an enlargement of the Nicene Creed, declared that "the Word became flesh . . . the same suffered in the flesh; rose again; and went up to heaven in the same body, sat

---

48. Irenaeus, *Against Heresies*, chap. 7, 1, p. 532.
49. Ibid., chap. 3, 3, p. 530.
50. Tertullian, *Prescription Against Heretics*; quoted in ibid., vol. 3, p. 249.
51. Justin Martyr, *On the Resurrection, Fragments* in Ante-Nicene Fathers, vol. 1, p. 298.
52. Ibid., p. 297.
53. Athenagoras, *The Resurrection of the Dead*; quoted in ibid., vol. 2, p. 150.
54. Cited by ibid., p. 225.

down gloriously at the right hand of the Father; is coming in the same body in glory to judge the quick and the dead."[55]

Cyril of Jerusalem (A.D. 315–386), in his famous *Catechetical Lectures* (chap. 18), argued that God is able to reconstitute flesh that has become dust into flesh again. "Let no heretic ever persuade thee to speak evil of the Resurrection." Belief in the physical resurrection of the body was part of the confession of the "one Holy Catholic Church." For "The Faith which we rehearse" contains in order the following, "And in one baptism of repentance for the remission of sins; and in one Holy Catholic Church; and in the resurrection of the flesh; and in eternal life."[56] Cyril referred to the resurrection body as "the very same body" we have before the resurrection.[57] Similar views were held by Gregory of Nazianzen (a president of the Constantinople Council), Gregory of Nyssa, and Basil the Great. From this it is evident that the early Eastern Church also confessed a literal, physical resurrection.

The greatest Christian thinker of the early Middle Ages was the Bishop of Hippo, Augustine. Augustine stressed the fact that resurrection is in the same physical body in which one lived before the resurrection. He believed that individuals would be raised in their same sex and even without any bodily loss, "lest the men who were largest here should lose anything of their bulk and it should perish, in contradiction to the words of Christ, who said that not a hair of their head should perish."[58] Along with the early Fathers, Augustine believed that God would reconstitute all of the decomposed parts of the body in the resurrection, saying: "Far be it from us to fear that the omnipotence of the Creator cannot, for the resuscitation and reanimation of our bodies, recall all the portions which have been consumed by beasts or fire, or have been dissolved into dust or ashes, or have decomposed into water, or even evaporated into the air."[59]

Anselm (A.D. 1033–1109), speaking to the topic "How man will rise with the same body which he has in this world," concluded that "From this the future resurrection of the dead is clearly proved. For if man is to be perfectly restored, the restoration should make him such as he would have been had he never sinned." Therefore, "as man, had he not sinned, was to have been transferred with the same body to an immortal state, so when he shall be restored, it must properly be with his own body as he lived in this world."[60]

---

55. Epiphanius, *Two Creeds of Epiphanius: Second Formula* (A.D. 374) in Schaff, *Creeds of Christendom: With a History and Critical Notes*, vol. 2 (Grand Rapids: Baker, 1983), p. 37.

56. Cyril of Jerusalem, *Catechetical Lectures* (18, 22) in Philip Schaff, *Nicene and Post-Nicene Fathers of the Christian Church* (Grand Rapids: Eerdmans, 1983), p. 139.

57. Ibid., Lecture 18, 18, p. 139.

58. Ibid., Lecture 22, 14, p. 495.

59. Ibid., 20, p. 498.

60. Anselm, *Cur Deus Homo* 2.3 in *St. Anselm: The Basic Writings*, S. W. Deane, trans. (La Salle, Ill.: Open Court Publishing, 1962), p. 241.

Aquinas affirmed explicitly that "the soul does not take an airy or heavenly body, or a body of another organic constitution, but a human body composed of flesh and bones and the same members enjoyed at present."[61] Commenting on those who deny a physical resurrection, he wrote: "They have not believed in the resurrection of the body, and have strained to twist the words of Holy Scripture to mean a spiritual resurrection, a resurrection from sin through grace. . . . That St. Paul believed in a bodily resurrection is clear. . . . To deny this, and to affirm a purely spiritual resurrection is against the Christian Faith."[62]

As for the seeming impossibility that a body that dies can be restored with numerical identity, Aquinas concluded that "by conjunction to a soul numerically the same the man will be restored to matter numerically the same." Therefore, "although this corporeality yields to nothingness when the human body is corrupted, it cannot, for all that, be an obstacle to the body's rising with numerical identity." Hence, "it is clear that man returns numerically the same both by reason of the permanence of the rational soul and by reason of the unity of matter."[63] The fact that human bodies have parts that are changing "is not an obstacle to his being numerically one from the beginning of his life to the end of it . . . for the form and species of its single parts remain continuously through a whole life."[64] From this "it is clear, also, that there is no obstacle to faith in the resurrection—even in the fact that some men eat human flesh," for in the resurrection "the flesh consumed will rise in him in whom it was first perfected by a rational soul." As for those who ate flesh that will not be part of their resurrection body, "what is wanting will be supplied by the Creator's omnipotence."[65] These unequivocal statements leave no doubt that Aquinas believed that the resurrection body was numerically identical to the pre-resurrection body.

The Reformers did not forsake their theological roots in Catholicism at this point. They too continued the unbroken confession of the resurrection of the physical flesh. The Lutheran *Formula of Concord* (A.D. 1576) confessed: "We believe, teach and confess . . . the chief articles of our faith (of Creation, of Redemption, of Sanctification, and of the Resurrection of the flesh)."[66] *The Belgic Confession* (A.D. 1561), adopted by the Reformed Synod at Emden (A.D. 1571) and the Synod of Dort (A.D. 1619), affirmed: "we believe, according to the Word of God . . . that our Lord Jesus Christ

---

61. Thomas Aquinas, *Compendium of Theology*, 153, in Thomas Gilby, *St. Thomas Aquinas: Philosophical Texts* (New York: Oxford University Press, 1964), no. 764.

62. Aquinas, *III Summa contra Gentiles*, 79 in Thomas Gilby, *St. Thomas: Theological Texts* (Durham, N.C.: Labyrinth Press, 1982).

63. Aquinas, *Summa contra Gentiles*, IV.81.6, 7, 10.

64. Ibid., IV.81.12.

65. Ibid., IV.81.12–13.

66. Schaff, *Creeds of Christendom*, 3:98.

will come from heaven, corporally and visibly as he ascended with great glory and majesty, to declare himself Judge of the quick [the living] and the dead. . . . For all the dead shall be raised out of the earth, and their souls joined and united with their proper bodies in which they formerly lived."[67] Likewise, the Westminster Confession of Faith declared: "At the last day, such as are found alive shall not die, but be changed: and all the dead shall be raised up, with the self-same bodies, and none other (although with different qualities) which shall be united again to their souls for ever."[68] *The New Hampshire Baptist Confession* (A.D. 1833) also acknowledged the material nature of the resurrection body, speaking of raising "the dead from the grave" where the material corpse was buried.[69] Other Anabaptist and Baptist groups also confessed the literal, physical nature of the resurrection body.

In brief, evangelical Protestants, following Catholics, confessed the physical bodily resurrection of believers in the day when Christ returns. Thus, a current trend among some scholars to approve as orthodox opposing views is totally out of line with historic orthodoxy,[70] for they deny the essential physical nature of the resurrection body. Such a view denies the historic Catholic (and evangelical) confession of a physical resurrection from the grave in the last days.

THE GENERAL JUDGMENT

Roman Catholicism teaches that there will be a general judgment at the end of time. This will be after Christ returns to earth. As a result of this judgment, persons will be sent to their final destiny. "Christ, on His second coming, will judge all men *(De fide.)*."[71] The Lateran Council (A.D. 655) declared: "If anyone does not properly and truly confess in accordance with the Holy Fathers that God the Word himself . . . will come again . . . to judge the living and the dead, let him be condemned."[72]

Further, Christ will function as judge upon his return is proclaimed by all of the creeds. In the New Testament Jesus says that the Father has assigned the Son the office of Judge: "Nor does the Father judge anyone, but he has given all judgment to his Son, so that all may honor the Son just as they honor the Father" (John 5:22–23). Peter preached that Christ is "the one appointed by God as judge of the living and the dead" (Acts 10:42). Paul also referred often to Christ as "judge" (Acts 17:31; Rom. 2:5–16; 2 Cor. 5:10).

---

67. Ibid., pp. 433–34.
68. Westminster Confession of Faith (Philadelphia: Great Commission Publications, n.d.), chap. 22, 2 (p. 19).
69. Ibid., p. 748.
70. See Geisler, *Battle for the Resurrection*, chap. 6.
71. Ott, *Fundamentals of Catholic Dogma*, pp. 492–93.
72. Denzinger, *Sources of Catholic Dogma*, Can. 2, 255, p. 102.

Catholics believe that the scope of judgment extends to "all the nations." Jesus said, "When the Son of Man comes in his glory, and all the angels with him, he will sit upon his glorious throne, and all the nations will be assembled before him" (Matt. 26:31–32). The purpose of the general judgment is "the glorification of God and of the God-Man Jesus Christ (2 Thess. 1:10) by revealing the wisdom of God in the government of the world, His goodness and patience towards sinners and above all His rewarding justice. The glorification of the God-Man achieves its apogee in the exercise of the office of Judge of the World."[73] The church fathers affirm this teaching. Polycarp, Clement, Augustine, and others, quoting from the Old and New Testaments, designate Christ as the Judge of the World.

THE END OF THE WORLD

Following the teaching of Scripture, Catholics and evangelicals believe that there will be an end to this world. Ott succinctly states the position of the Catholic church: "The present world will be destroyed on the Last Day."[74]

Jesus spoke of the "end of the age" (Matt. 24:3f.). He even promised his disciples that he would be with them (through the ministry of the Holy Spirit) "until the end of the age" (Matt. 28:20). Peter described the end of the world in graphic terms: "the day of the Lord will come like a thief, and then the heavens will pass away with a mighty roar and the elements will be dissolved by fire, and the earth and everything done on it will be burned up" (2 Pet. 3:10). That is the bad news.

The good news is that "the present world will be restored on the Last Day."[75] That which will be destroyed will also be renewed. The prophet Isaiah speaks of God's restoration: "Lo, I am about to create new heavens and a new earth" (Isa. 65:17). Jesus speaks of a "new age" (Matt. 19:28), and Paul teaches that the whole of the cosmos awaits redemption (Rom. 8:18–25). Peter tells of a "new Heaven and earth" (2 Pet. 3:13) and John describes this restoration concerning the nature of this "new creation" (Rev. 21:1–8). "St. Augustine teaches that the properties of the future world will be just as suited to the immortal existence of the transfigured human body as were the properties of the corruptible existence to the mortal body."[76] Thus, the general eschatology of Catholics and evangelicals is the same. Christ will return bodily to earth. There will be a resurrection of the dead, followed by eternal bliss for believers and eternal condemnation for unbelievers.

73. Ott, *Fundamentals of Catholic Dogma*, p. 493.
74. Ibid., p. 494.
75. Ibid., p. 495.
76. Ibid. See Augustine, *City of God* XX.16.

CONCLUSION

We have attempted to present the major points covered in Roman Catholic eschatology. Concerning these, Catholic scholars note that "The 'last things' in Biblical theology are not so much last as ultimate, and their chronological sequence does not correspond to their degree of definitiveness."[77]

Many evangelicals are quick to note that Roman Catholic eschatology has different emphases and tends to have "simpler" theological constructs. For instance, in dealing with the concept of judgment (and judgments) in Scripture, Roman Catholics speak of one general judgment. Many evangelicals, however, find more than one judgment in the Scriptures; some scholars identify at least five different judgments dealing with believers, Israel, the Gentiles, angels, and the "great white throne of judgment."[78] Many Protestants, however, particularly amillennialists, agree with the Catholic view of one general judgment.

As to the time of and the events surrounding the second coming of Christ Catholicism does not have the variety which exists among evangelical theologians; however, the major points of Christian eschatology are there.[79] The reality and significance of death are taught, as well as a conscious intermediate state. The reality of judgment and the identity of the Judge are established. There is a "heaven to gain and a hell to shun." Jesus is returning to claim his bride, the church, believers will be reunited with their bodies, and heaven and earth will be made anew. Augustine addressed this subject:

> [God] shall be the end of our desires Who shall be contemplated without ceasing, loved without cloy, and praised without weariness. There will be degrees of honour there, based on merit, but there will be no jealousy; and free will will not only continue to be exercised by the saints, but will be the more truly free because liberated from the delight in sinning.[80]

As Vatican II states: "The Church, to which all of us are called in Christ Jesus and in which, through God's grace, we acquire holiness, will reach her consummation only in the glory of heaven, when the time will come for the restoration of all things."[81] So here too, both Catholics and evangelicals share a common core of basic beliefs about the future.

77. *New Catholic Encyclopedia*, 5:532.
78. See John Walvoord, ed., *Lewis Sperry Chafer: Systematic Theology*, vol. 2, abridged edition (Wheaton, Ill.: Victor Books, 1988), pp. 500–504.
79. For a brief treatment of the differing views concerning the millennium, see Robert Clouse, *The Meaning of the Millennium: Four Views* (Downers Grove, Ill.: InterVarsity Press, 1977).
80. Ibid., 22, 30 I.2f.; quoted in Kelly, *Early Christian Doctrines*, p. 489.
81. Neuner and Dupuis, "Dogmatic Constitution," *Lumen Gentium* (1964), p. 772.

PART 2

AREAS OF
DOCTRINAL
DIFFERENCES

In the first part of this volume we have stressed what evangelicals have in common with Roman Catholics. In short, this includes the great fundamentals of the Christian faith, including a belief in the Trinity, the virgin birth, the deity of Christ, the creation and subsequent fall of humanity, Christ's unique atonement for our sins, the physical resurrection of Christ, the necessity of God's grace for salvation, the existence of heaven and hell, the second coming of Christ, and the verbal inspiration and infallibility of Scripture.

In spite of all these similarities in belief, however, there are some significant differences between Catholics and evangelicals on some important doctrines. Catholics affirm and evangelicals reject the immaculate conception of Mary, her bodily assumption, her role as corredemptrix, the veneration of Mary and other saints, prayers to Mary and the saints, the infallibility of the pope, the existence of purgatory, the inspiration and canonicity of the Apocrypha, the doctrine of transubstantiation, the worship of the transformed Host, the special sacerdotal powers of the Roman Catholic priesthood, and the necessity of works to obtain eternal life. Since all of these have been proclaimed as infallible dogma by the Roman Catholic Church, and since many are contrary to central teachings of evangelicalism, there appears to be no hope of ecumenical or ecclesiastical unity. Here we must recognize our differences and agree to disagree agreeably, knowing that there are many doctrines we hold in common (see Part One) and many things we can do together morally, socially, and educationally (see Part Three).

Donald G. Bloesch has put it thusly, "We are called to build bridges where bridges can be built and allow the cleavage to remain where it cannot be overcome."[1] Unlike some evangelicals, we believe that there is no need to exaggerate our differences or to condemn Catholics for holding beliefs they do not hold. Nor should our doctrinal differences keep us from personal fellowship with other believing Catholics and social cooperation with them on common moral, social, and educational causes. At the same time, these valuable things we hold in common should not hinder us from the necessary task of pointing out, as we do in this section, what we believe to be serious errors in the official teachings of the Roman Catholic Church.

1. "Is Spirituality Enough?" in Armstrong, *Roman Catholicism: Evangelical Protestants Analyze What Divides and Unites Us,* p. 158.

9

APOCRYPHA

The question of authority is fundamental to the difference between Catholics and Protestants. There are disagreements in two basic areas: the extent of biblical authority and the sufficiency of biblical authority (see chap. 10). In this chapter we will deal with the extent of biblical authority by looking at the apocryphal books.

THE ROMAN CATHOLIC DEFENSE
OF THE APOCRYPHA

As we have already seen in chapter 1, both Catholics and Protestants affirm the inspiration and divine authority of the sixty-six books of the Protestant canon (thirty-nine in the Old Testament and twenty-seven in the New Testament). A crucial difference emerges, however, over eleven pieces of literature (seven books and four parts of books) that the Roman Catholic Church infallibly pronounced part of the canon in A.D. 1546 at the Council of Trent. These books are known by Protestants as the Apocrypha and by Catholics as the deuterocanonical books (lit. "second canon"). It is important to note that, unlike some Protestant groups,[1] Catholics' use of this "second canon" does not imply that the Apocrypha is a secondary canon of inferior status. In spite of some current speculative usage by Catholic scholars to the contrary, the Council of Trent affords these books full canonical status and pronounces an anathema (excommunication) on any who reject them. After enumerating the books, including the eleven apocryphal books, the Council stated: "If anyone, however, should not accept the said books as sacred and canonical, entire with all their parts . . . and if both knowingly and deliber-

---

1. At the Reformation, Lutherans and Anglicans considered the apocryphal books to be of inferior status, believing they had ethical/devotional value but denying they had authority in matters of faith.

ately he should condemn the aforesaid tradition let him be anathema."[2] The same language affirming the Apocrypha is repeated by Vatican II.[3]

The differences over the canonicity of the Apocrypha are not minor. They are both doctrinal and canonical. Doctrinally, the Apocrypha supports prayers for the dead (which also entails a belief in purgatory). For instance, 2 Maccabees 12:46 reads: "Thus he made atonement for the dead that they might be freed from this sin." Canonically, the grounds on which the Apocrypha was accepted undermine the true test for canonicity—propheticity. In short, if the Apocrypha can be accepted in the canon, lacking, as it does, the characteristics that meet the true test of canonicity, then other noncanonical books could be accepted on the same grounds.

CATHOLIC ARGUMENTS IN FAVOR OF THE APOCRYPHA

The Apocrypha that Rome accepts includes eleven books—or twelve, depending on whether Baruch (1–6) is split into two books consisting of Baruch 1–5 and The Letter of Jeremiah (Baruch 6). These include all fourteen (or fifteen) books in the Protestant Apocrypha, except the Prayer of Manasseh and 1 and 2 Esdras (called 3 and 4 Esdras by Roman Catholics, since the Protestant Ezra and Nehemiah are called 1 and 2 Esdras by Catholics).

The Number of Books in Dispute

Revised Standard Version	New American Bible
1. The Wisdom of Solomon (c. 30 B.C.)	Book of Wisdom
2. Ecclesiasticus (Sirach) (132 B.C.)	Sirach
3. Tobit (c. 200 B.C.)	Tobit
4. Judith (c. 150 B.C.)	Judith
5. 1 Esdras (c. 150–100 B.C.)	3 Esdras*
6. 1 Maccabees (c. 110 B.C.)	1 Maccabees
7. 2 Maccabees (c. 110–70 B.C.)	2 Maccabees
8. Baruch (c. 150–50 B.C.)	Baruch chaps. 1–5
9. Letter of Jeremiah (c. 300–100 B.C.)	Baruch chap. 6
10. 2 Esdras (c. A.D. 100)	4 Esdras*
11. Additions to Esther (140–130 B.C.)	10:4–16:24
12. Prayer of Azariah (2nd or 1st cent. B.C.)	Daniel 3:24–90 (Song of Three Young Men)
13. Susanna (2nd or 1st cent. B.C.)	Daniel 13

2. Denzinger, *Sources of Catholic Dogma*, 784, p. 245.
3. See *Documents of Vatican II,* "Document on Revelation," chap. 3: "The Divine Inspiration and the Interpretation of Sacred Scripture."

14. Bel and the Dragon (c. 100 B.C.)   Daniel 14
15. Prayer of Manasseh (2nd or 1st cent. B.C.)   Prayer of Manasseh*
     * These books were rejected by the Council of Trent.

Although the Roman Catholic canon has eleven more books than the Protestant Bible, only seven extra books appear in the table of contents of Roman Catholic Bibles. This makes the total forty-six (the thirty-nine in the Protestant and Jewish Old Testament, plus seven more complete books). There are, however, four more books or pieces of literature that are added to other books that do not appear in the table of contents. There are the Additions to Esther, added at the end of the Book of Esther (Esth. 10:4f.); the Prayer of Azariah, inserted between the Jewish (and Protestant) Daniel 3:23 and 24 (making it Daniel 3:24–90 in Roman Catholic Bibles); Susanna, placed at the end of Daniel 12 in the Protestant and Jewish Old Testament (as chap. 13); and Bel and the Dragon, which became chapter 14 of Daniel. So with seven complete books and four other pieces of literature found in Daniel and Esther, the Roman Catholic canon has eleven more books than does the Jewish Bible and Protestant Old Testament.

REASONS ADVANCED FOR ACCEPTING THE APOCRYPHA

The larger canon is sometimes referred to as the "Alexandrian Canon," as opposed to the "Palestinian Canon" (which does not contain the Apocrypha) because they are alleged to have been part of the Greek translation of the Old Testament (the Septuagint or "Seventy" [LXX], which originated in Alexandria, Egypt). The reasons generally advanced in favor of this broader Alexandrian list accepted by Roman Catholics, which includes the apocryphal books, are as follows:

1. The New Testament reflects the thought of the Apocrypha, and even refers to events contained in it (cf. Heb. 11:35 with 2 Macc. 7, 12).
2. The New Testament quotes mostly from the Septuagint, which contained the Apocrypha. This gives tacit approval of the whole text, including the Apocrypha, from which they quoted.
3. Some of the early church fathers quoted and used the Apocrypha as Scripture in public worship.
4. Some of the early church fathers—Irenaeus, Tertullian, and Clement of Alexandria—accepted all the books of the Apocrypha as canonical.
5. Early Christian catacomb scenes depict episodes from the Apocrypha, showing it was part of the early Christians' religious life. If not their inspiration, this at least reveals a great regard for the Apocrypha.

6. The early Greek manuscripts (Aleph, A, and B) interpose the Apocrypha among the Old Testament books. This reveals that they were part of the Jewish-Greek translation of the Old Testament.

7. Several early church councils accepted the Apocrypha: the Council of Rome (A.D. 382), the Council of Hippo (A.D. 393), and the Council of Carthage (A.D. 397).

8. The Eastern Orthodox church accepts the Apocrypha, revealing that it is not simply a Roman Catholic dogma.

9. The Roman Catholic Church proclaimed the Apocrypha canonical at the Council of Trent (A.D. 1546). This was in accord with pronouncements at early councils (see point 7 above) and the Council of Florence not long before the Reformation (A.D. 1442).

10. The apocryphal books were included in the Protestant Bible as late as the nineteenth century. This indicates that even Protestants accepted the Apocrypha until very recently.

11. Some apocryphal books written in Hebrew have been found among other Old Testament canonical books in the Dead Sea community at Qumran. This shows that they were part of the Hebrew canon.

PROTESTANT RESPONSE TO CATHOLIC ACCEPTANCE OF THE APOCRYPHA[4]

In response to the alleged support for considering the apocryphal books as canonical, we will do two things. First, we will respond to each of the Roman Catholic arguments in favor of the Apocrypha, showing that they are unfounded. Second, we will build a positive case in favor of the Jewish and Protestant canon.

A RESPONSE TO CATHOLIC ARGUMENTS IN FAVOR OF THE APOCRYPHA

Our response will follow the order of the arguments given by Catholics discussed above. Thus, the numbering will correspond point by point.

1. There may be New Testament allusions to the Apocrypha, but there are no clear New Testament quotations from it. Not once is there a direct quotation from any apocryphal books accepted by the Roman Catholic Church.[5]

---

4. For a current critique of the so-called Alexandrian Canon, see Norman L. Geisler, "The Extent of the Old Testament Canon," in Gerald F. Hawthorne, ed., *Current Issues in Biblical and Patristic Interpretation* (Grand Rapids: Eerdmans, 1975).

5. There are, of course, allusions to pseudipigraphal (false writings) that are rejected by Roman Catholics as well as Protestants, such as the *Book of Enoch* (Jude 14–15) and the *Bodily Assumption of Moses* (Jude 9). There are also citations from pagan poets and philosophers

Further, although the New Testament cites the Hebrew Old Testament, it never once quotes any of the fourteen (or fifteen) apocryphal books as divinely authoritative or canonical. For example, they are never cited with introductory phrases like "thus says the Lord" or "as it is written" or "the Scriptures say," such as are typically found when canonical books are quoted.

2. The fact that the New Testament often quotes from the Greek Old Testament in no way proves that the apocryphal books contained in the Greek manuscript of the Old Testament are inspired. First, it is not certain that the Septuagint (LXX) of the first century contained the Apocrypha. The earliest Greek manuscripts that include them date from the fourth century A.D. Further, even if they were in the Septuagint of apostolic times, Jesus and the apostles never once quoted them, although they are supposed to have been included in the very version of the Old Testament (the LXX) that they usually cited. Finally, even the notes in the current Roman Catholic Bible (NAB) make the revealing admission that the apocryphal books are "religious books used by both Jews and Christians which were not included in the collection of inspired writings." Instead, they "were introduced rather late into the collection of the Bible. Catholics call them 'deuterocanonical' (second canon) books."[6]

3. Citations of the church fathers in support of the canonicity of the Apocrypha are selective and misleading. While some Fathers accepted their inspiration, others used them only for devotional or homiletical (preaching) purposes but did not accept them as canonical. As a recent authority on the Apocrypha, Roger Beckwith, observes,

> When one examines the passages in the early Fathers which are supposed to establish the canonicity of the Apocrypha, one finds that some of them are taken from the alternative Greek text of Ezra (1 Esdras) or from additions or appendices to Daniel, Jeremiah or some other canonical book, which . . . are not really relevant; that others of them are not quotations from the Apocrypha at all;[7] and that, of those which are, many do not give any indication that the book is regarded as Scripture.[8]

(Acts 17:28; 1 Cor. 15:33; Titus 1:12). But none of these are cited as Scripture nor as a divine authority. The New Testament simply refers to a truth contained in these books which otherwise may (and do) have many errors. Roman Catholics agree.

6. *New American Bible,* p. 413.

7. "Thus, *Epistle of Barnabas* 6.7 and Tertullian, *Against Marcion* 3.22.5, are not quoting Wisd. 2.12 but Isa. 3:10 LXX, and Tertullian, *On the Soul* 15, is not quoting Wisd. 1.6 but Ps. 139.23, as a comparison of the passages shows. Similarly, Justin Martyr, *Dialogue with Trypho* 129, is quite clearly not quoting Wisdom but Prov. 8.21–5 LXX. The fact that he calls Proverbs 'Wisdom' is in accordance with the common nomenclature of the earlier Fathers." See Roger Beckwith, *The Old Testament Canon of the New Testament Church and Its Background in Early Judaism* (Grand Rapids: Eerdmans, 1986), p. 427 n. 208.

8. Ibid., p. 387.

So unqualified Catholic appeal to the use of the Apocrypha is misleading. For, as Beckwith notes, in many cases the Fathers were not claiming divine authority for one or more of the eleven books infallibly canonized by the Council of Trent. Rather, they were either citing a book that was part of the Hebrew canon or not quoting the apocryphal books as Scripture.

4. Although some individuals in the early church had a high regard for the Apocrypha, there were many who vehemently opposed it.[9] For example, Athanasius, Cyril of Jerusalem, Origen, and the great Roman Catholic biblical scholar and translator of the Latin Vulgate, Jerome, all opposed the Apocrypha (see below). Even the early Syrian church did not accept the Apocrypha. In the second century A.D. the Syrian Bible (Peshitta) did not contain the Apocrypha.[10]

5. As even many Catholic scholars will admit, scenes from the catacombs do not prove the canonicity of the books whose events they depict. Such scenes need not indicate any more than the religious significance that the portrayed events had for early Christians. They may show a respect for the books containing these events without recognizing that they are inspired.

6. None of the great Greek manuscripts (Aleph, A, and B) contain all of the apocryphal books. In fact, only four (Tobit, Judith, Wisdom, and Sirach [Ecclesiasticus]) are found in all of them, and the oldest manuscripts (B or Vaticanus) totally exclude the books of Maccabees. Yet Catholics appeal to this manuscript for proof of their deuterocanonical books that include the Apocrypha! What is more, no Greek manuscript has the same list of apocryphal books accepted by the Council of Trent (A.D. 1545–63).[11]

7. There are some important reasons why citing these church councils does not prove the Apocrypha belonged in the canon of the Christian church. First, these were only local councils and were not binding on the whole church.[12] Local councils have often erred in their decisions and have been overruled later by the universal church.

Second, these books were not part of the Christian (New Testament period) writings and hence were not under the province of the Christian church to decide. They were the province of the Jewish community that wrote them and had centuries before rejected them as part of the canon, for books were

---

9. J. D. N. Kelly's comment that "For the great majority [of early fathers] . . . the deuterocanonical writings ranked as scripture in the fullest sense" is out of synch with the facts just cited by Beckwith.

10. See Norman L. Geisler and W. E. Nix, *General Introduction to the Bible, Revised and Expanded* (Chicago: Moody Press, 1986), chaps. 27–28.

11. See Beckwith, *Old Testament Canon*, pp. 194, 382–83.

12. Some Catholic apologists argue that even though the council was not ecumenical its results are binding since they were confirmed by a pope. However, they acknowledge that there is no infallible way to know which statements by popes are infallible and which are not. Indeed, they admit that other statements by popes were even heretical, such as the teaching of the monothelite heresy by Pope Honorius I (see chap. 11).

accepted by the contemporary generations who were in the best position to verify the prophetic claims of their authors (cf. Heb. 2:3–4).

Third, the books accepted by these Christian councils may not have been the same ones in each case. Hence, they cannot be used as evidence of the exact canon later infallibly proclaimed by the Roman Catholic Church in A.D. 1546.

Fourth, the local councils of Hippo and Carthage in North Africa were influenced by Augustine, who is the most significant voice of antiquity that accepted the same apocryphal books later canonized by the Council of Trent in A.D. 1546.[13] However, Augustine's position is ill-founded for several reasons. (a) His contemporary, Jerome, a greater biblical authority than Augustine, rejected the Apocrypha (see below). (b) Augustine himself recognized that the Jews did not accept these books as part of their canon.[14] (c) Augustine erroneously reasoned that these books should be in the Bible because of their mention "of extreme and wonderful suffering of certain martyrs."[15] On that ground one could argue that *Foxe's Book of Martyrs*[16] should also be in the canon! (d) Augustine was inconsistent, since he rejected books not written by prophets yet accepted a book that appears to deny being prophetic (1 Macc. 9:27).[17] (e) Augustine's acceptance of the Apocrypha seems to be connected with his mistaken belief in the inspiration of the Septuagint, whose later Greek manuscripts contained them.[18]

---

13. The Council of Rome did not list the same books accepted by Hippo and Carthage. It does not include Baruch, thus listing only six, not seven, of the apocryphal books later pronounced canonical by the Roman Catholic Church. Catholic scholars assume it was part of Jeremiah. However, Trent lists it as a separate book. See Denzinger, *Sources*, 84, p. 34.

14. Augustine, *City of God* 19.36–38.

15. Of the books of Maccabees Augustine said, "These are held to be canonical, not by the Jews, but by the Church, on account of the extreme and wonderful sufferings of certain martyrs" (*City of God* 18, 36).

16. John Foxe (1516–87), *Acts and Monuments of Matters Happening in the Church* (1563).

17. This verse denies there was a prophet *during the period it was written*, which would mean the author was not a prophet. In response, Catholics appeal to verses that say there were no prophetic visions in Israel *before* God raised up Samuel (1 Sam. 3:1). But this misses the point: the books of Samuel were not written *before* God began to speak to Samuel but *after*. Likewise, Psalm 74:9 refers to no prophet being left "in the land," since the Babylonians had destroyed the temple (v. 3) and the prophets were in exile (e.g., Daniel and Jeremiah). And Lamentations 2:9 does not say there were no prophets anywhere (Jeremiah, who wrote it, was a prophet) but that there were none in the land who were getting a "vision from the Lord." By contrast, the writer of 1 Maccabees was bemoaning the fact that there were no longer any prophets in Israel, even after they had returned to the land. Nor does 1 Maccabees state that the prophetic lull in Israel was to be only temporary. Indeed, Judaism has acknowledged that even before the time of Maccabees the prophetic spirit had departed from Israel (see Josephus, *Antiquities*, Against Apion 1.8: "From Artaxerxes until our time everything has been recorded, but has not been deemed worthy of like credit with what preceded, because the exact succession of the prophets ceased."

18. However, Augustine's later acknowledgment of the superiority of Jerome's Hebrew text over the Septuagint's Greek text should have led him to accept the superiority of Jerome's Hebrew canon as well, which did not include the Apocrypha.

8. The Greek church has not always accepted the Apocrypha, nor is its present position unequivocal. At the synods of Constantinople (A.D. 1638), Jaffa (1642), and Jerusalem (1672) these books were declared canonical. But even as late as 1839 their Larger Catechism expressly omitted the Apocrypha on the grounds that its books did not exist in the Hebrew Bible. This is still their position.

9. At the Roman Catholic Council of Trent (A.D. 1546) the infallible proclamation was made accepting the Apocrypha as part of the inspired Word of God.[19] Unfortunately, the proclamation came a millennium and a half after the books were written and in an obvious polemic against Protestantism.[20] Furthermore, the official infallible addition of books that support prayers for the dead is highly suspect, coming as it did only a few years after Luther protested against this very doctrine. It has all the appearance of an attempt to provide ecclesiastical support for Roman Catholic doctrines that lack biblical support (see chap. 16).

10. Apocryphal books did appear in Protestant Bibles prior to the Council of Trent, but were generally placed in a separate section because they were not considered of equal authority.[21] While Anglicans and some other non-Roman Catholic groups had a high regard for the devotional and historical value of the Apocrypha, they did not consider it inspired and of equal authority with Scripture. Even Roman Catholic scholars throughout the Reformation period made the distinction between the Apocrypha and the canon. Cardinal Ximenes made this distinction in his *Complutensian Polyglot* (A.D. 1514–17) on the very eve of the Reformation. Cardinal Cajetan, who later opposed Luther at Augsburg in 1518, published a *Commentary on All the Authentic Historical Books of the Old Testament* (A.D. 1532) many years after the Reformation began which did not contain the Apocrypha. Luther spoke against the Apocrypha in 1543, placing its books at the back of his Bible.[22]

11. The discovery at Qumran included not only the community's Bible (the Old Testament) but their library, with fragments of hundreds of books.

19. Some Catholic scholars claim that the earlier Council of Florence (A.D. 1442) made the same pronouncement. However, this is a disputed council, and its action here does not have any real basis in Jewish history, the New Testament, or early Christian history.

20. Even before Luther, the Council of Florence (A.D. 1442) had proclaimed the Apocrypha inspired, which helped bolster the doctrine of purgatory that had already blossomed in Roman Catholicism. However, the manifestations of this belief in the sale of indulgences came to full bloom in Luther's day, and Trent's infallible proclamation of the Apocrypha was a clear polemic against Luther's teaching.

21. Even knowledgeable Catholics acknowledge that the appearance of apocryphal books in Protestant bibles does not prove they were accepted as inspired but only that they were valued.

22. See Bruce Metzger, *An Introduction to the Apocrypha* (New York: Oxford University Press, 1957), pp. 181f. Luther also had some initial doubts about James, but he eventually placed it alongside the other New Testament books.

Among these were some Old Testament apocryphal books. But the fact that no commentaries were found on an apocryphal book and that only canonical books, not the Apocrypha, were found in the special parchment and script indicates that the Qumran community did not view the apocryphal books as canonical.[23] The noted scholar on the Dead Sea Scrolls, Millar Burroughs, concluded: "There is no reason to think that any of these works were venerated as Sacred Scripture."[24]

Actually, all that the arguments used in favor of the canonicity of the apocryphal books prove is that various apocryphal books were given varied degrees of esteem by different persons within the Christian church, usually falling short of canonicity. Only after Augustine and the local councils he dominated mistakenly pronounced them inspired did they gain wider usage and eventual acceptance by the Roman Catholic Church at Trent. This falls far short of the kind of initial, continual, and complete recognition of the canonical books of the Protestant Old Testament and Jewish Torah (which exclude the Apocrypha) by the Christian church. It exemplifies how the teaching magisterium of the Catholic church proclaims infallible one tradition to the neglect of strong evidence in favor of an opposing tradition because it supports a doctrine that lacks any real support in the canonical books.[25]

ARGUMENTS IN FAVOR OF THE PROTESTANT ("PALESTINIAN") CANON

The evidence indicates that the Protestant Old Testament canon, consisting of thirty-nine books identical to the Hebrew Bible and excluding the Apocrypha, is the true canon.[26] The Palestinian Jews represented Jewish orthodoxy. Therefore, their canon was recognized as the orthodox one. It was the

---

23. Menahem Mansoor, *The Dead Sea Scrolls*, p. 203, lists the following fragments of the Apocrypha and Pseudepigrapha: Tobit, in Hebrew and Aramaic; Enoch, in Aramaic; Jubilees, in Hebrew; Testament of Levi and Naphtali, in Aramaic; Apocryphal Daniel literature, in Hebrew and Aramaic; and Psalms of Joshua. See *New Catholic Encyclopedia*, 2:390.

24. Millar Burroughs, *More Light on the Dead Sea Scrolls*, p. 178.

25. The (proto) canonical books were received *immediately* by the people of God into the growing canon of Scripture (see Geisler and Nix, *General Introduction*, chap. 13). The subsequent debate was by those who were not in a position, as was the immediate audience, to know whether they were from an accredited apostle or prophet. Hence, this subsequent debate over the antilegomena was directly over their *authenticity*, not canonicity—they were already in the canon. What some individuals in subsequent generations questioned was whether they rightfully belonged there. Eventually, all of the antilegomena were retained in the canon. This is not true of the Apocrypha, for Protestants reject all of the books and even Roman Catholics reject some of them (e.g., 3–4 Esdras and The Prayer of Manasseh).

26. The numbering of thirty-nine books is reduced to twenty-four by combining the following two books into one each: 1–2 Samuel, 1–2 Kings, 1–2 Chronicles, Ezra–Nehemiah (thus reducing the number by four), and counting the Twelve Minor Prophets as one book (thus reducing the number by 11). Thus the total of 15 (4+11) from 39 leaves 24.

canon of Jesus,[27] Josephus, and Jerome. For that matter, it was the canon of many of the early church fathers, including, Origen, Cyril of Jerusalem, and Athanasius. The arguments in support of the Protestant canon can be divided into two categories: historical and doctrinal.

REASONS FOR ACCEPTING THE PROTESTANT CANON

The True Test of Canonicity. Contrary to the Roman Catholic argument from *Christian usage*, the true test of canonicity is *propheticity*. That is, propheticity determines canonicity. God determined which books would be in the Bible by giving their message to a prophet. So only books written by a prophet, that is, an accredited spokesperson for God, are inspired and belong in the canon of Scripture.

Of course, while God *determined* canonicity by propheticity, the people of God had to *discover* which of these books were prophetic. The evidence supports the thesis that this was done immediately by the people of God to whom the prophet wrote, not centuries later by those who had no access to him nor any way to verify his prophetic credentials. For example, Moses' books were accepted immediately and were stored in a holy place (Deut. 31:26). Likewise, Joshua's books were immediately accepted and preserved along with Moses' Law (Josh. 24:26). Samuel wrote a book and added it to the collection (1 Sam. 10:25). Daniel already had a copy of his contemporary Jeremiah (Dan. 9:2, 11, 13). Paul encouraged the churches to circulate his inspired epistles (Col. 4:16). And Peter had a collection of Paul's writings, which he called "Scripture" along with the Old Testament (2 Pet. 3:15–16).

There were a number of ways for the immediate contemporaries to confirm whether someone was a prophet of God. Among these were supernatural confirmation (cf. Exod. 3:1–3; Acts 2:22; 2 Cor. 12:12; Heb. 2:3–4). Sometimes this came in the form of feats of nature and other times in terms of predictive prophecy. Indeed, false prophets were weeded out if their predictions did not come true (Deut. 18:22). Of course, alleged revelations that contradicted previously revealed truths were rejected as well (Deut. 13:1–3).

The evidence that there was a growing canon of books that were accepted immediately by contemporaries who could confirm their prophetic authenticity is that succeeding books cited preceding ones. Moses' writings are cited throughout the Old Testament beginning with his immediate successor, Joshua (Josh. 1:7; 1 Kings 2:3; 2 Kings 14:6; 2 Chron. 17:9; Ezra 6:18; Neh. 13:1; Jer. 8:8; Mal. 4:4). Likewise, later prophets cited earlier ones (e.g., Jer. 26:18; Ezek. 14:14, 20; Dan. 9:2; Jon. 2:2–9; Mic. 4:1–3). In the New Testament Paul cites Luke (1 Tim. 5:18), Peter recognizes Paul's epistles (2 Pet.

---

27. See Geisler and Nix, *General Introduction,* chap. 5.

3:15–16), and Jude (4–12) cites 2 Peter. Also, the Book of Revelation is filled with images and ideas taken from previous Scripture, especially Daniel (cf. Rev. 13).

In fact, the entire Protestant Old Testament was considered prophetic. Moses, who wrote the first five books, was a prophet (Deut. 18:15). The rest of the Old Testament books were known as "the Prophets" (Matt. 5:17) since these two sections are called "all the Scriptures" (Luke 24:27).[28] The "apostles and [New Testament] prophets" (Eph. 3:5) composed the entire New Testament. Hence, the whole Bible is a prophetic book, including the final book (cf. Rev. 20:7, 9–10). As we will see, this cannot be said for the apocryphal books.

There is strong evidence that the apocryphal books are not prophetic. But since propheticity is the test for canonicity, this would eliminate the Apocrypha from the canon. First, no apocryphal books claim to be written by a prophet. Indeed, as already noted, one apocryphal book even disclaims being prophetic (1 Macc. 9:27). Second, there is no divine confirmation of any of the writers of the apocryphal books, as there is for prophets who wrote canonical books (e.g., Exod. 4:1–2). Third, there is no predictive prophecy in the Apocrypha, such as we have in the canonical books (e.g., Isa. 53; Dan. 9; Mic. 5:2) and which is a clear indication of their propheticity. Fourth, there is no new messianic truth in the Apocrypha. Thus, it adds nothing to the messianic truths of the Old Testament. Fifth, even the Jewish community, whose books they were, acknowledged that the prophetic gifts had ceased in Israel before the Apocrypha was written (see quotes above). Sixth, the apocryphal books were never listed in the Jewish Bible along with the "Prophets," or any other section for that matter. Seventh, never once is any apocryphal book cited authoritatively by a prophetic book written after it.[29] Taken together, this provides overwhelming evidence that the Apocrypha was not prophetic and, therefore, should not be part of the canon of Scripture.

The Continuous Testimony from Antiquity. In addition to the evidence for the propheticity of only the books of the Protestant Old Testament (which exclude the Apocrypha) there is virtually an unbroken line of support from ancient to modern times for rejecting the Apocrypha as part of the canon. This is true for both Jewish teachers and Christian Fathers.

28. "The Prophets" were later divided into Prophets and Writings. The reasons are not clear, but some believe this division was based on whether the author was a prophet by office or just by gift. Others claim it was for purposes of use at Jewish festivals. Some say they were arranged chronologically in descending order of size (see Geisler and Nix, *General Introduction*, pp. 244–45). Whatever the reason, it is clear that the original (cf. Dan. 9:2; Zech. 7:12) and continual way to refer to the entire Old Testament up to the time of Christ was the twofold division of the "Law and Prophets."

29. While not every canonical book manifests all those characteristics, they do possess one or more. However, none of the apocryphal books possess any essential prophetic characteristic, manifesting that they are not prophetic.

1. Philo, an Alexandrian Jewish teacher (20 B.C.–A.D. 40), quoted the Old Testament prolifically from virtually every canonical book. Never once, however, did he quote the Apocrypha as inspired text.

2. Josephus (A.D. 30–100), a Jewish historian, explicitly excluded the Apocrypha, numbering the Old Testament as twenty-two books (= thirty-nine books in the Protestant Old Testament). Neither does he quote an apocryphal book as Scripture, though he was familiar with them. In *Against Apion* he wrote:

> For we have not an innumerable multitude of books among us, disagreeing from and contradicting one another [as the Greeks have,] *but only twenty-two books, which are justly believed to be divine; and of them, five belong to Moses, which contain his law, and the traditions* of the origin of mankind till his death. This interval of time was little short of three thousand years; but as to the time from the death of Moses till the reign of Artaxerxes king of Persia, who reigned at Xerxes, *the prophets,* who were after Moses, wrote down what was done in their times in *thirteen books.* The remaining *four books contain hymns to God,* and precepts for the conduct of human life.[30]

These correspond exactly to the present Protestant Old Testament, which excludes the Apocrypha.

3. Jewish teachers acknowledged that their prophetic line ended in the fourth century B.C. Yet, as even Catholics acknowledge, the apocryphal books were written after this time. Josephus wrote: "From Artaxerxes until our time everything has been recorded, but has not been deemed worthy of like credit with what preceded, because the exact succession of the prophets ceased."[31] Numerous rabbinical statements on the cessation of prophecy support these.[32] Seder Olam Rabbah 30 declares: "Until then [the coming of Alexander the Great] the prophets prophesied through the Holy Spirit. From then on, 'Incline thine ear and hear the words of the wise.'" Baba Bathra 12b declares: "Since the day when the Temple was destroyed, prophecy has been taken from the prophets and given to the wise." Rabbi Samuel bar Inia said, "The Second Temple lacked five things which the First Temple possessed, namely, the fire, the ark, the Urim and Thummin, the oil of anointing and the Holy Spirit [of prophecy]." Thus, the Jewish fathers (rabbis) acknowledged that the time period during which their Apocrypha was written was not a time when God was giving inspired writings.

4. Jesus and the New Testament writers never once quoted the Apocrypha as Scripture, even though they were aware of these books and possibly

---

30. See Josephus, *Antiquities*, Against Apion 1.8, emphasis added.
31. Ibid.
32. The following citations are found in Beckwith, *Old Testament Canon*, p. 370.

even alluded to them at times.[33] This point is reinforced by the fact that the New Testament writers have hundreds of citations from all but a few canonical books in the Old Testament. And the manner in which they are cited with authority indicates that they were believed to be part of the "Law and Prophets" [i.e., the whole Old Testament] which was believed to be the inspired and infallible Word of God (Matt. 5:17–18; cf. John 10:35). In fact, Jesus specifically quoted books from each of the parts of the Old Testament "Law and Prophets," which he called "all the Scriptures" (Luke 24:27).[34]

5. The Jewish scholars at Jamnia (c. A.D. 90) did not accept the Apocrypha as part of the divinely inspired Jewish canon.[35] Since the New Testament explicitly states that Israel was entrusted with the oracles of God and was the recipient of the covenants and the Law (Rom. 3:2), the Jews should be considered the custodians of the limits of their own canon. And they have always rejected the Apocrypha.

6. No canonical list or general council accepted the Apocrypha as inspired for nearly the first four centuries of the Christian church. This is especially significant since all the lists available and most of the Fathers from this period rejected the Apocrypha. The first councils to accept the Apocrypha were only local ones without ecumenical force.[36]

7. Many of the early Fathers of the Christian church spoke out against the Apocrypha, including Origen, Cyril of Jerusalem, Athanasius, and the great Roman Catholic Bible translator, Jerome.

8. Jerome (A.D. 340–420), the greatest biblical scholar of the early medieval period and translator of the Latin Vulgate, explicitly rejected the Apocrypha as part of the canon.[37] He said the church reads these books "for ex-

---

33. For example, Heb. 11:35 may allude to 2 Macc. 7, 12, though this may be a reference to the canonical Book of Kings.

34. There was also a threefold division of the Old Testament into Law, Prophets, and Writings, but this simply divided the "prophets" into two sections called "prophets and writings." See Geisler and Nix, *General Introduction,* chap. 14.

35. See Beckwith, *Old Testament Canon,* pp. 276–77, for a summary of recent scholarship on Jamnia.

36. The Catholic contention that the Council of Rome (A.D. 382), though not an ecumenical council, had ecumenical force because Pope Damasus ratified it is without grounds. First, it begs the question, assuming that Damasus was a pope with infallible authority. Second, even Catholics acknowledge this council was not an ecumenical one. Third, not all Catholics agree that statements like this by popes are infallible. As noted in chap. 11, there are no infallible lists of infallible statements by popes. Nor are there any universally agreed upon criteria that yield conclusions on issues like this that even all Catholics agree on. Finally, appealing to a pope to make a statement by a local council infallible is a double-edged sword; even Catholic scholars admit that some popes taught error and were even heretical at times!

37. In view of these clear quotations showing Jerome's rejection of the Apocrypha, recent Catholic argument that Jerome "occasionally quotes from them as scripture in accordance with the common practice" and thus "becomes an involuntary witness to their established position" is without foundation (see *A Catholic Commentary on Holy Scripture* [New York: Nelson, 1953], par. 15f.).

ample and instruction of manners" but does not "apply them to establish any doctrine."[38] In fact, Jerome disputed Augustine's unjustified acceptance of these books. He even refused at first to translate the Apocrypha into Latin, but later made a hurried translation of a few books. After listing the exact books of the Jewish Bible and Protestant Old Testament (which exclude the Apocrypha), Jerome concluded:

> "Thus altogether there come to be 22 books of the old Law [according to the letters of the Jewish alphabet], that is, five of Moses, eight of the Prophets, and nine of the Hagiographa. Although some set down . . . Ruth and Kinoth among the Hagiographa, and think that these books ought to be counted (separately) in their computation, and that there are thus 24 books of the old Law; which the Apocalypse of John represents as adoring the Lamb in the number of the 24 elders." . . . Then St. Jerome adds, "This prologue can fitly serve as a Helmed (i.e., equipped with a helmet, against assailants) *introduction to all the biblical books* which have been translated from Hebrew into Latin, so that we may know that *whatever is not included in these is to be placed among the apocrypha.*"[39]

In his preface to Daniel, Jerome clearly rejected the apocryphal additions to Daniel (Bel and the Dragon, Susanna) and argued only for the canonicity of those books found in the Hebrew Bible that excluded all the Apocrypha. He wrote:

> The stories of Susanna and of Bel and the Dragon are not contained in the Hebrew. . . . For this same reason when I was translating Daniel many years ago, I noted these visions with a critical symbol, showing that they were not included in the Hebrew. . . . After all, both Origen, Eusebius and Appolinarius, and other outstanding churchmen and teachers of Greece acknowledge that, as I have said, these visions are not found amongst the Hebrews, *and therefore they are not obliged to answer to Porphyry for these portions which exhibit no authority as Holy Scripture.*[40]

---

38. As cited by Beckwith, *Old Testament Canon,* p. 343, who cites Jerome's preface to his Vulgate version of the *Book of Solomon.*

39. Jerome, main preface to Vulgate, as cited in Beckwith, *Old Testament Canon,* pp. 119–20, emphasis added.

40. Jerome, Preface to *Jerome's Commentary on Daniel,* trans. by Gleason Archer (Grand Rapids: Baker, 1977), p. 17, emphasis added. The suggestion that Jerome really favored the apocryphal books but was only arguing that the Jews rejected them is groundless. First, he said clearly in the above quotation that these books *"exhibit no authority as Holy Scripture."* Second, he never retracted his rejection of the Apocrypha. Further, he stated in his work *Against Rufinus* (33) that he had "followed the judgment of the churches" on this matter. And his statement "I was not following my own personal views" appears to refer to "the remarks that they [the enemies of Christianity] are wont to make against us." In any event, he nowhere retracted his many statements against the Apocrypha. Finally, the fact that Jerome cited apocryphal books is no proof that he accepted them. This was a common practice by many Fathers. What is

9. Even noted Roman Catholic scholars during the Reformation period rejected the Apocrypha, such as Cardinal Cajetan, who opposed Martin Luther. As already noted, he wrote a *Commentary on All the Authentic Historical Books of the Old Testament* (A.D. 1532), which excluded the Apocrypha. If he believed they were authentic, they certainly would have been included in a book on "all the authentic" books of the Old Testament.

10. Martin Luther, John Calvin, and other Reformers rejected the canonicity of the Apocrypha. Lutherans and Anglicans used it only for ethical/devotional matters but did not consider it authoritative in matters of faith. Reformed churches followed the Westminster Confession of Faith (A.D. 1647), which states: "The Books commonly called Apocrypha, not being of divine inspiration, are not part of the canon of the Scriptures; and therefore are of no authority in the Church of God, nor to be any otherwise approved, or made use of, than any other human writings."

In short, the Christian church (including Anglican, Lutheran, Reformed, and others) has rejected the Apocrypha as part of the canon to this date. They do so because it lacks the primary determining factor of canonicity: propheticity; that is, the apocryphal books lack evidence that they were written by accredited prophets of God. Further supporting evidence is found in the facts that the Apocrypha is never cited as authoritative in Scripture in the New Testament; it was never part of the Jewish canon whose books they are; and the early church as a whole did not accept the Apocrypha as inspired.

THE MISTAKE OF THE COUNCIL OF TRENT

The infallible pronouncement by the Council of Trent that the Apocrypha is part of the inspired Word of God is unjustified for many reasons. It reveals how fallible an allegedly infallible statement can be, since it is historically unfounded, being a polemical overreaction, and entailing an arbitrary decision that involved a dogmatic exclusion.

1. *Prophetically Unverified.* The true test of canonicity is propheticity. There is no evidence that the apocryphal books were prophetic. They lack prophetic authorship, content, and confirmation.
2. *Historically Unfounded.* The council's pronouncement went against a continuous line of teaching, including noted Jewish and Christian fathers, such as Philo, Josephus, Cyril of Jerusalem, Athanasius, and Jerome. Certainly, it is not based on any "unanimous consent of the Fathers" Catholics claim for their dogma.

---

important is that he never retracted his statement that the church reads them "for example and instruction of manners" but does not "apply them to establish any doctrine."

3. *Polemical Overreaction.* The occasion of Trent's infallible pronouncement on the Apocrypha was part of a polemical action against Luther, supporting teaching that he had attacked, such as prayers for the dead (cf. 2 Macc. 12:45–46).

4. *Arbitrary Decision.* Not all the Apocrypha was accepted at Trent. In fact, they arbitrarily accepted a book favoring their belief in prayers for the dead (2 Maccabees) and rejected one opposing such prayers (2 [4] Esdras; cf. 7:105). Thus, Trent's acceptance of the Apocrypha was unfounded. There were fourteen books and yet they selected only eleven. On what grounds did they reject the three?

5. *Dogmatic Exclusion.* In fact, the very history of this section of 2 (4) Esdras reveals the arbitrariness of Trent's decision.[41] It was written in Aramaic by an unknown Jewish author (c. A.D. 100) and circulated in Old Latin versions (c. A.D. 200). The Latin Vulgate printed it as an appendix to the New Testament (c. A.D. 400). It disappeared from Bibles until Protestants, beginning with Johann Haug (1726–42), began to print it in the Apocrypha based on Aramaic texts, since it was not in Latin manuscripts of the time. However, in 1874 a long section (seventy verses of chap. 7) was found by Robert Bently in a library in Amiens, France. Bruce Metzger noted: "It is probable that the lost section was deliberately cut out of an ancestor of most extant Latin Manuscripts, because of dogmatic reasons, for the passage contains an emphatic denial of the value of prayers for the dead."[42]

In spite of the testimony of antiquity against them, in A.D. 1546, just twenty-nine years after Luther had posted his ninety-five theses,[43] the Roman Catholic Church infallibly and irrevocably proclaimed that the apocryphal books were on the same level as Scripture, declaring: "The Synod . . . receives and venerates . . . all the books [including the *Apocrypha*] both of the Old

---

41. Some Catholics argue that this was not arbitrary because: (1) it was not part of earlier deuterocanonical lists; (2) it was written after the time of Christ; (3) it was relegated to an inferior position in the Vulgate; and (4) it was only included among the Apocrypha by Protestants in the eighteenth century. This line of argument is not convincing. First, 2 [4] Esdras was part of earlier lists of books not considered fully canonical, as even Catholics acknowledge. Second, the date of the book has nothing to do with whether it should be in the Jewish Apocrypha but whether it was used by early Christians, and it was used, just as the other apocryphal books were. Third, if it was rejected because it was reduced to an inferior position in the Vulgate, then Catholics would have to reject all the Apocrypha, since Jerome, who translated the Vulgate, relegated all the Apocrypha to an inferior position. Fourth, the reason it did not reappear until the eighteenth century is because early on a Catholic monk apparently cut out the section against praying for the dead!

42. Metzger, *Introduction to the Apocrypha*, p. 23.

43. For information concerning the occasion and content of the *Ninety-Five Theses*, see chap. 5.

and the New Testaments—seeing that one God is the Author of both . . . as having been dictated, either by Christ's own word of mouth or by the Holy Ghost. . . . If anyone receives not as sacred and canonical the said books entire with all their parts, as they have been used to be read in the Catholic Church . . . let him be anathema."[44]

The Wrong Test for Canonicity. When all is said and done, the Roman Catholic Church uses the wrong test for canonicity. The true and false views of what determines canonicity can be contrasted as follows.[45]

Incorrect View of Canon	Correct View of Canon
Church Determines Canon	Church Discovers Canon
Church Is Mother of Canon	Church Is Child of Canon*
Church Is Magistrate of Canon	Church Is Minister of Canon
Church Regulates Canon	Church Recognizes Canon
Church Is Judge of Canon	Church Is Witness of Canon
Church Is Master of Canon	Church Is Servant of Canon

* Of course the whole canon was not completed before the New Testament church came into existence.

In spite of the fact that Catholic sources can be cited supporting what looks very much like the "correct view" above, Catholic apologists often equivocate on this issue. Peter Kreeft, for example, argues that the church must be infallible if the Bible is, since the effect cannot be greater than the cause and the church caused the canon. But if the church is regulated by the canon, not ruler over it, then the church is not the cause of the canon. Other defenders of Catholicism make the same mistake, giving lip-service to the fact that the church only discovers the canon, yet constructing an argument that makes the church the determiner of the canon. They neglect the fact that it is God who caused (by inspiration) the canonical Scriptures, not the church.

This misunderstanding is sometimes evident in the equivocal use of the word "witness." When we speak of the later church as being a "witness" to the canon, we do not mean in the sense of being an eyewitness to first-hand evidence. Only the people of God contemporary to the events were first-hand witnesses. Rather, the later church is a witness of the canon in the sense that it testifies to the historical *evidence* for the authenticity of the canonical books as coming from prophets and apostles. Yet when Roman Catholics speak of the role of the church in determining the canon they endow it with an evidential role it does not have. Several points will clarify the proper role of the Christian church in discovering which books belong in the canon.

44. Schaff, *Creeds of Christendom,* 2:81.
45. The chart comes from Geisler and Nix, *General Introduction,* p. 221.

First, *only the people of God contemporary to the writing of the biblical books are actual eyewitnesses to the evidence.* They alone were witnesses to the canon as it was developing. Only they are qualified to testify to the evidence of the propheticity of the biblical books, which is the determinative factor of canonicity.

Second, *the later church is not an evidential witness for the canon.* The later church does not create or constitute evidence for the canon. It is only a discoverer and observer of the evidence that remains for original confirmation of the propheticity of the canonical books. Assuming that the church itself is evidence is the mistake behind the view favoring the canonicity of the Apocrypha.

Third, *neither the earlier nor later church is the judge of the canon.* The church is not the final authority for the criteria of what will be admitted as evidence in the way that judges are. That is, it does not determine the rules of canonicity. Since the Bible is the Word of God, only God can determine the criteria for our discovery of what is his Word. Or, to put it another way, what is of God will have his "fingerprints" on it, and only God is the determiner of what his "fingerprints" are like. It is up to the people of God simply to discover these divine characteristics that God has determined.

Fourth, *both the early and later church is more like a jury than a judge.* The role of a jury is to listen to the evidence, not create it or try to be it. They weigh the evidence, not make it or constitute it. Then, they render a verdict in accord with the evidence. This, as we have shown, is precisely what the Christian church has done in rendering its verdict that the Apocrypha is not part of sacred Scripture. The first-century church looked at the first-hand evidence for *propheticity* (miracles, etc.), and the subsequent historic church has reviewed the evidence for the *authenticity* of these prophetic books that were directly confirmed by God when they were written.

There is, of course, a certain sense in which the church is a "judge" of the canon. It is called upon, as all juries are, to engage in an active use of the mind in sifting and weighing the evidence and in rendering a verdict. But this is not what Roman Catholics believe, in practice, if not in theory. For the Roman Catholic Church plays a magisterial role in determining the canon. After all, this is what is meant by the "teaching magisterium" of the church, which it exercised at Trent and reaffirmed at Vatican I and II. The Roman Catholic hierarchy is not merely ministerial, it is magisterial. It has a judicial role, not just an administrative one. It is not just a jury looking at evidence, but a judge determining what counts as evidence and what does not. And herein is the problem.

In exercising its magisterial role, the Roman Catholic Church chose the wrong course in rendering its decision about the Apocrypha. First, it chose to follow the wrong criterion: *Christian usage* rather than *propheticity.* Second, it used *second-hand evidence* of later writers rather than *first-hand ev-*

idence for canonicity (divine confirmation of the author's propheticity). Third, it did not use *immediate confirmation* by contemporaries of the events but *later statements* by people often separated from the events by generations or centuries. All of these mistakes arose out of a misconception of the very role of the church as judge rather than jury, as magistrate rather than minister, as sovereign over rather than servant of the canon. By contrast, the Protestant rejection of the Apocrypha was based on a proper understanding of the role of the contemporary eyewitnesses to the evidence of propheticity and the succeeding church as being possessor of historical evidence for the authenticity of these prophetic books.

CONCLUSION

Differences over the Apocrypha are crucial to Roman Catholics and Protestants. Opposing doctrines held firmly by both sides are at stake, such as purgatory and prayers for the dead. As we have seen, there is no evidence that the apocryphal books are inspired and, therefore, should be part of the canon of inspired Scripture. They do not claim to be inspired nor does the Jewish community that produced them claim they were. Indeed, they are never quoted as Scripture in the New Testament, and many early Fathers, including the great Roman Catholic biblical scholar, Jerome, categorically rejected them. Adding them to the Bible with an infallible decree at the Council of Trent has all the markings of a dogmatic and polemical pronouncement, geared by Roman Catholicism to bolster support for doctrines for which they cannot find clear support in any of the sixty-six canonical books.

In view of the strong evidence against the Apocrypha, the decision by the Roman Catholic Church to pronounce them canonical is unfounded and unanimously rejected by all orthodox Protestants. Tragically, the Roman Catholic view has been pronounced *ex cathedra* and is therefore an official, infallible, and irrevocable part of the Roman Catholic faith. As such, it is an insurmountable obstacle to any union between Catholics and Protestants on a fundamental teaching: the extent of Scripture. Furthermore, it is a very serious error to admit nonrevelational material into the written Word of God, since it corrupts the revelation of God and thereby undermines the divine authority of Scripture.[46]

---

46. See Bernard Ramm, *The Pattern of Religious Authority* (Grand Rapids: Eerdmans, 1959), p. 65.

10

SCRIPTURE

In addition to basic differences over the extent of the authority of Scripture, Catholics and Protestants differ over the limits of infallible authority. The Protestant Reformation stressed two principles: a formal principle *(sola Scriptura)* and a material principle *(sola fide)*:[1] The Bible alone and faith alone.[2] When properly defined, both of these are affirmed by Protestants and denied by Catholics, although there is some question about whether the differences are as great as once thought on the question of justification (see chaps. 5 and 12).

CATHOLIC ARGUMENTS
FOR INFALLIBLE APOSTOLIC TRADITION

There is, however, no doubt about the irresolvable differences on whether the Bible alone is the infallible guide for faith and practice. This is certainly true in the formal sense in which Protestants mean it, though modern Catholics allow the belief that the content of the Bible contains all the revelation God has given (at least implicitly). But even this more progressive view has-

---

1. More properly, it is salvation by grace alone and faith alone (*sola gratia* and *sola fide*). Some Reformed theologians specify the material principle as "in Christ alone" and say that "faith alone" is the means of access.

2. Some strict Calvinists maintain that the phrase *sola fide* can be somewhat misleading in this context. They state that *sola Christos* would be more precise in that faith (like good works) is the *fruit* of God's grace in our hearts; the Holy Spirit produces faith in us on the basis of the Father's election and the Son's atonement. See Stephen Charnock, *The Doctrine of Regeneration* (Grand Rapids: Baker, reprinted 1980), pp. 214–27; Loraine Boettner, *The Reformed Doctrine of Predestination* (Grand Rapids: Eerdmans, 1954), pp. 97–104; Berkhof, *Systematic Theology* (1965). Berkhof states, "Strictly speaking, it is not the act of faith as such, but rather that which is received by faith, which justifies and therefore saves the sinner" (p. 506).

tens to add that an infallible teaching magisterium is still necessary to formally interpret the Bible correctly.

THE PROTESTANT UNDERSTANDING OF *SOLA SCRIPTURA*

By *sola Scriptura* orthodox Protestants mean that Scripture alone is the primary and absolute source of authority, the final court of appeal, for all doctrine and practice (faith and morals). It is important to repeat that Catholics often misunderstand the Protestant principle of *sola Scriptura* to exclude any truth outside the Bible. This, of course, is untrue, as is revealed by Luther's famous quote about being "convinced by the testimonies of Scripture *or evident reason*" (emphasis added). Most Protestants accept the general revelation declared in the heavens (Ps. 19:1) and inscribed on the human heart (Rom. 2:12–15). However, classical Protestantism denies any salvific value of natural (general) revelation, believing one can only come to salvation through special revelation. What Protestants mean by *sola Scriptura* is that the Bible alone is the infallible written authority for faith and morals. Natural revelation as such is not a written revelation, nor does it cover all matters of faith and morals (it only overlaps with some). Good reason can and should be used apologetically (to defend against attacks on orthodoxy from without), polemically (to defend against attacks on orthodoxy from within), and theologically (to define orthodox doctrines within).

Sola Scriptura implies several things. First, the Bible is a direct revelation from God. As such, it has divine authority, for what the Bible says, God says.

Second, Scripture is the sufficient and final written authority of God. As to sufficiency, the Bible—nothing more, nothing less, and nothing else—is all that is necessary for faith and practice. In short, "the Bible alone" means "the Bible only" is the final authority for our faith. Further, the Scriptures not only have sufficiency but they also possess final authority. They are the final court of appeal on all doctrinal and moral matters. However good they may be in giving guidance, all the church fathers, popes, and councils are fallible (see chap. 11). Only the Bible is infallible.

Third, the Bible is clear (perspicuous). The perspicuity of Scripture does not mean that everything in the Bible is perfectly clear, but rather the essential teachings are. Popularly put, in the Bible the main things are the plain things and the plain things are the main things. This is not to say that Protestants obtain no help from the Fathers and early councils. Indeed, Protestants accept the pronouncements of the first four ecumenical councils (see chap. 1) as helpful but not infallible. What is more, most Protestants have high regard for the teachings of the early Fathers, though obviously they do not believe they are without error. So this is not to say that there is no usefulness to Christian tradition, but only that it is of secondary importance. As John Jefferson Davis notes, "*Sola Scriptura* meant the primacy of Scripture

178

as a theological norm over all tradition rather than the total rejection of tradition."[3]

Calvin does not dismiss the role of authority in the church. That authority, however, must be subservient to the Scriptures. "Ours be the humility which . . . yields the highest honor and respect to the Church, in subordination, however, to Christ the Church's head." The church "tests all obedience by the Word of God . . . whose supreme care it is humbly and religiously to venerate the Word of God, and submit to its authority."[4]

Fourth, Scripture interprets Scripture. This is known as the analogy of faith principle.[5] When we have difficulty in understanding an unclear text of Scripture, we turn to other biblical texts, since the Bible is the best interpreter of the Bible. In the Scriptures, clear texts should be used to interpret the unclear ones.[6]

COMPARISON AND CONTRAST OF VIEWS ON *SOLA SCRIPTURA*

A good bit of confusion exists between Catholics and Protestants on *sola Scriptura* due to a failure to distinguish two aspects of the doctrine: the formal and the material. *Sola Scriptura* in the material sense simply means that all the content of salvific revelation exists in Scripture. Many Catholics hold this in common with Protestants,[7] including well-known theologians from John Henry Newman to Cardinal Joseph Ratzinger. French Catholic theologian Yves Congar states: "we can admit *sola Scriptura* in the sense of a material sufficiency of canonical Scripture. This means that Scripture contains, in one way or another, all truths necessary for salvation."[8] What Protestants affirm and Catholics reject is *sola Scriptura* in the formal sense that the Bible

3. John J. Davis, *Foundations of Evangelical Theology* (Grand Rapids: Baker, 1994), p. 227. For a discussion of tradition from Irenaeus to *Humani Generis*, see Heiko A. Oberman, *The Dawn of the Reformation* (Grand Rapids: Eerdmans, Reprinted, 1992), pp. 269–96.

4. John C. Olin, ed., *A Reformation Debate* (New York: Harper Torchbooks, 1966), p. 75.

5. Catholics use this principle but do not limit it to Scripture interpreting Scripture; they include tradition as well. In view of this, perhaps it would be better for Protestants to call this the "analogy of Scripture" principle.

6. Reformed theologians also believe that the Spirit of God brings divine assurance that the Bible is the Word of God. This is known as the witness of the Spirit. Only the God of the Word can bring full assurance that the Bible is the Word of God. Further, Reformed theologians acknowledge the aid of the Holy Spirit in understanding and applying the Scriptures to our lives. But he does not do this contrary to the Bible or contrary to good rules of biblical interpretation.

7. Catholic scholar Louis Bouyer even goes so far as to claim: "It is none the less true that no Catholic theologian worthy of the name, today any more than in the Middle Ages, would place any doctrinal authority on the level of Scripture" (*Spirit and Forms of Protestantism*, p. 130).

8. Cited by James Akin, "Material and Formal Sufficiency," *This Rock* 4, no. 10 (October 1993): 15.

alone is sufficiently clear that no infallible teaching magisterium of the church is necessary to interpret it.

The differences can be charted as follows:

Sola Scripture: Two Views

Material Sufficiency	Formal Sufficiency
Content	Form
Revelation	Interpretation
Protestantism Affirms	Protestantism Affirms
Catholicism Allows	Catholicism Denies
Traditional Catholicism Denies	
Progressive Catholicism Affirms	

ARGUMENTS FOR THE BIBLE PLUS TRADITION

One of the basic differences between Catholics and Protestants is over whether the Bible alone or the Bible plus extra-biblical apostolic tradition[9] is the sufficient and final authority for faith and practice. Roman Catholics affirm the latter and Protestants the former. For, while Catholics allow the Protestant teaching on the material sufficiency of Scripture, they deny its formal sufficiency. Catholics insist that there is a need for a teaching magisterium to rule on just what is and is not authentic apostolic tradition.

Catholics are not all agreed on their understanding of the relation of tradition to Scripture. Some understand it as two sources of revelation. Others understand apostolic tradition as a lesser form of revelation. Still others understand tradition in an almost Protestant way, namely, as merely an interpretation of revelation (albeit, an infallible one) that is found only in the Bible. Traditional Catholics, such as Ludwig Ott and Henry Denzinger, tend to be in the first category, and more modern Catholics, such as John Henry Newman and Cardinal Joseph Ratzinger, in the latter.

The language of the Council of Trent seems to favor the traditional understanding. It claimed, for example, that "this truth and instruction are contained in the written books *and* in the unwritten traditions, which have been received by the apostles from the mouth of Christ Himself, or from the apostles themselves, *at the dictation*[10] *of the Holy Spirit,* have come down to us." Consequently, Trent "receives and holds in veneration with an equal affection or piety and reverence all the books of the Old and of the New Testa-

---

9. Protestants, of course, believe all apostolic tradition is inscriptured in the Bible.

10. The use of this term does not imply that Catholics believe in the "dictation theory" of inspiration, but only that the Scriptures come by the dictates of the Holy Spirit, utilizing of course the personalities, vocabularies, and literary styles of the human writers of Scripture.

ment, since one God is the author of both, *and also the traditions themselves,* those that appertain both to faith and to morals, *as having been dictated either by Christ's own word of mouth, or by the Holy Spirit.*"[11] Indeed, in Denzinger's "Systematic Index" he speaks of "the Sources [plural] of Revelation": "The written source of revelation is the canonical books of both Testaments. . . . Another source of revelation is ecclesiastical tradition."[12] The original draft of Trent left no doubt it intended two sources of revelation, speaking of the gospel being contained "partly in written books, partly in unwritten tradition." This, however, was changed at the last minute, omitting the word "partly" in both cases. Many post-Vatican II Catholic scholars claim it is improper to speak of two sources of revelation, since the "De Verbum" [the Word] document speaks of "a single sacred deposit of the Word of God." This is not an infallible pronouncement, however, and it leaves it undefined as to whether each may contain elements not found in the other. The debate continues as to whether the words "partly" were omitted from Trent's declaration for theological or stylistic reasons.

David Wells provides a good summary of the new (more progressive) view: "1) There is only one source of revelation, not two; 2) Scripture and tradition both mediate this common revelation; 3) Scripture and tradition can never be in conflict since they arise from the same source of revelation; 4) Scripture is generically no different in nature from tradition since both contain and communicate the same revelation, but it is more important."[13] Wells likens the Catholic belief in the relation of Scripture and tradition to that of two eyes. "The second eye adds no new knowledge of the outside world to that brought by the first eye, but with the two eyes the world is perceived with greater clarity than with one."[14]

Whether or not extra-biblical apostolic tradition is considered a second source of revelation, there is no question that both sides agree that the Roman Catholic Church believes apostolic tradition is both authoritative and infallible. The Council of Trent was emphatic in proclaiming that the Bible alone is not sufficient for faith and morals; God has ordained tradition in addition to the Bible to faithfully guide the church. The basic arguments in favor of the Bible plus tradition fall into several categories.

Infallible guidance in interpreting the Bible comes from the church. One of the criteria used to determine this is the "unanimous consent of the Fathers."[15] In accordance with "The Profession of Faith of the Council of

---

11. Denzinger, *Sources of Catholic Dogma,* p. 244, emphasis added. From the Council of Trent, Session 4 (1546).

12. Ibid., pp. 11–12.

13. David F. Wells, "Tradition: A Meeting Place for Catholic and Evangelical Theology?" *The Christian Scholar's Review* 5, no. 1 (1975): 60.

14. Ibid.

15. Denzinger, *Sources of Catholic Dogma,* "Systematic Index," p. 11.

Trent," the faithful Catholic must be able to state: "I shall never accept nor interpret it ["Holy Scripture"] otherwise than in accordance with the unanimous consent of the Fathers."[16] The same council declared (1546) that no one should dare to interpret "Sacred Scripture . . . contrary to the unanimous consent of the Fathers."[17] Vatican I (1870) repeated this same decree that "no one is permitted to interpret Sacred Scriptures . . . contrary to the unanimous agreement of the Fathers."[18]

Catholic scholars advance several arguments in favor of the Bible and tradition, as opposed to the Bible as the only final authority. One of their primary arguments is that even the Bible does not teach that the Bible is our final and only authority for faith and morals.

Nowhere does the Bible teach sola Scriptura. A common Catholic claim is that nowhere in Scripture does it teach that the Bible alone is sufficient for faith and morals. Thus they conclude that even on Protestant grounds there is no reason to accept *sola Scriptura.* Indeed, they believe it is inconsistent or self-refuting, since the Bible does not teach that the Bible alone is the basis of faith and morals.

The Bible teaches that traditions should be followed. In point of fact, argue Catholic theologians, the Bible teaches that the "traditions" as well as the written words of the apostles should be followed. Paul exhorted the Thessalonian Christians to "stand fast and hold the traditions which you were taught, whether by word or epistle" (2 Thess. 2:15; cf. 3:6).

The Bible states a preference for oral tradition. One Catholic apologist even went so far as to argue that one apostle, John, even stated his preference for oral tradition: "I have much to write to you, but I do not wish to write with pen and ink. Instead, I hope to see you soon when we can talk face to face" (3 John 13). This Catholic writer adds, "why would the apostle emphasize his preference for oral Tradition over written Tradition . . . if, as proponents of *sola Scriptura* assert, Scripture is superior to oral Tradition?"[19]

The Bible cannot be properly understood without tradition. Another argument offered by Catholic apologists is that it is insufficient to have an infallible Bible unless we have an infallible interpretation of it. No chain is stronger than its weakest link. And if we have only a fallible interpretation of the Bible what good does it do us to believe the Bible is infallible? Hence, God preserved apostolic traditions (teachings) as defined by the teaching magisterium of the Roman Catholic Church to serve as an infallible guide to understanding the Bible.

16. Ibid., 995, p. 303.
17. Ibid., 786, p. 245.
18. Ibid., 1788, p. 444. Pope Leo XIII (1893) agreed: "Now, the authority of the Fathers . . . is the highest authority, as often they all in one and the same way interpret a Biblical text, as pertaining to the doctrine of faith and morals" (ibid., 1944, p. 489).
19. See *This Rock* (August 1992), p. 23.

Tradition and Scripture are inseparable. Roman Catholic apologist Peter Kreeft lists several arguments against *sola Scriptura* which in turn are arguments for tradition: "First, it separates Church and Scripture. But they are one. They are not two rival horses in the authority race, but one rider (the Church) on one horse (Scripture)." He adds, "We are not taught by a teacher without a book or by a book without a teacher, but by one teacher, the Church, with one book, Scripture."[20]

Excluding tradition is self-contradictory. Kreeft insists that to exclude the need for tradition "is self-contradictory, for it says we should believe only Scripture, but Scripture never says this! If we believe only what the Scripture teaches, we will not believe *sola Scriptura,* for Scripture does not teach *sola Scriptura.*"[21]

Excluding tradition violates the principle of causality. Kreeft also argues that "*sola Scriptura* violates the principle of causality; that an effect cannot be greater than its cause," for "the successors of the apostles, the bishops of the Church, decided on the canon, the list of books to be declared scriptural and infallible. . . . If the Scripture is infallible, then its cause, the Church, must also be infallible."[22]

Rejecting tradition leads to denominationalism. According to Kreeft, "denominationalism is an intolerable scandal by scriptural standards—see John 17:20–23 and I Corinthians 1:10–17." But "let five hundred people interpret the bible without Church authority and there will soon be five hundred denominations."[23] So rejection of authoritative apostolic tradition leads to the unbiblical scandal of denominationalism.

Rejecting tradition is unhistorical. Kreeft argues that "the first generation of Christians did not have the New Testament, only the Church to teach them."[24] This being the case, using the Bible alone without apostolic tradition was not possible.

PROTESTANT ARGUMENTS FOR *SOLA SCRIPTURA*

As convincing as these arguments may seem to be to a devout Catholic, they fail to refute the Protestant view of *sola Scriptura.* As we will see, they fail to provide any substantial basis for the Catholic dogma of an infallible teaching magisterium.

20. Kreeft, *Fundamentals of the Faith,* pp. 274–75.
21. Ibid.
22. Ibid.
23. Ibid.
24. Ibid.

RESPONSE TO THE CATHOLIC ARGUMENTS FOR TRADITION

We will argue here that each of the Roman Catholic arguments attempting to invalidate the Protestant doctrine of *sola Scriptura* fails. The responses will be taken in the same order that the arguments were given.

The Bible teaches sola Scriptura. Two points must be made here. First, as Catholic scholars themselves recognize, it is not necessary that the Bible explicitly and formally teach *sola Scriptura* in order for this doctrine to be true. Many Christian teachings are a necessary logical deduction of what is clearly taught in the Bible. For example, nowhere does the Bible formally and explicitly state the doctrine of the Trinity. The Bible does, however, clearly teach two truths from which the necessary logical deduction is the doctrine of the Trinity: (1) There is only one God, not many (Exod. 20:1–2; Deut. 6:4; Mark 12:29); (2) There are three distinct persons who are God: the Father, the Son, and the Holy Spirit (Matt. 3:16–17; 28:18–20; Acts 5:3–4; 2 Cor. 13:14). The only possible valid conclusion from this is (3) God is a trinity of three persons in one essence. This is not to say that philosophy and theology play no role in *expressing* and *defending* this truth. It is only to observe that the doctrine of the Trinity is validly *based* in Scripture alone. Likewise, it is possible that *sola Scriptura* could be a necessary logical deduction from what is taught in Scripture.

Second, the Bible does teach implicitly and logically, if not formally and explicitly, that the Bible alone is the only infallible basis for faith and practice. This it does in a number of ways. Scripture states that it is "inspired" and "competent" for a believer to be "equipped for every good work" (2 Tim. 3:16–17). If the Bible alone is sufficient to do this, then nothing else is needed. Also, this text teaches that the Bible alone is inspired and capable of saving, edifying, and equipping believers. This is evident from several things stated in the text. First, only the Scriptures are "inspired" or God-breathed. Second, while the reference here is only to the Old Testament (v. 15), other passages show that the New Testament Gospels (1 Tim. 5:18; cf. Luke 10:7) and Epistles were considered "Scripture" too (2 Pet. 3:15–16). Third, the use of the word "competent" or "thoroughly" (KJV, NKJV), in connection with the ability to save (v. 15) and sanctify (vv. 16–17), implies the sufficiency of Scripture for faith and practice. Fourth, the total absence of reference to any other instrument or source of authority than the written Word (Gk. *graphē*) reveals that the locus of this sufficient authority is in the written Word (= Scripture). Fifth, Paul repeatedly stresses the need to cling to the Scriptures (1:13; 2:15; 3:15–16; 4:2). Finally, given that this was his last book (4:6–8), if there was some other apostolic authority other than the written Word of God the apostle surely would have mentioned it.

The fact that Scripture, without tradition, is said to be "God-breathed" *(theopneustos)* and thus by it believers are *"competent, equipped for every good work"* (2 Tim. 3:16–17, emphasis added) supports the doctrine of *sola Scriptura*. This flies in the face of the Catholic claim that the Bible is formally insufficient[25] without the aid of tradition. Paul declares that the God-breathed writings are sufficient.[26] And contrary to some Catholic apologists, limiting this to only the Old Testament is wrong, since the New Testament is also called "Scripture" (2 Pet. 3:15–16; 1 Tim. 5:18; cf. Luke 10:7); thus, it is inconsistent to argue that God-breathed writings in the Old Testament were sufficient, but the inspired writings of the New Testament are not.

Third, Jesus and the apostles constantly appealed to the Bible as the final court of appeal. This they often did by the introductory phrase "It is written," which is repeated some ninety times in the New Testament. Jesus used this phrase three times when appealing to Scripture as the final authority in his dispute with Satan (Matt. 4:4, 7, 10). Of course, Jesus (Matt. 5:22, 28, 31; 28:18) and the apostles (1 Cor. 5:3; 7:12) sometimes referred to their own God-given authority, but it begs the question for Roman Catholics to claim that this supports their belief that the Roman church still has infallible authority today outside the Bible since even they admit that no new revelation is being given today. In other words, the only reason Jesus and the apostles could appeal to an authority outside the Bible was that God was still giving normative revelation for the faith and moral of believers. But, as we will see, apostolic revelation ceased when apostolic miracles ceased—in the first century (see chap. 11). Therefore, it is not legitimate to appeal to any oral revelation in New Testament times as evidence that non-biblical infallible authority exists today.

What is more, Jesus made it clear that the Bible was in a class of its own, exalted above all tradition. He rebuked the Pharisees for negating the final authority of the Word of God with their religious traditions, saying, "why do you break the commandment of God for the sake of your tradition? . . . You have nullified the word of God, for the sake of your tradition" (Matt. 15:3, 6). It is important to note that Jesus did not limit his statement to mere *human* traditions but applied it specifically to the traditions of the religious authorities who used their tradition to misinterpret the Scriptures. Further, he is not negating the value of all tradition but simply not giving it authority equal to or greater than Scripture. Tradition (= teaching about Scripture) is not wrong as such, only tradition that "nullifies" Scripture. There is a direct parallel with the religious traditions of Judaism that grew up around (and obscured, even negated) the Scriptures and the Christian traditions which have

25. Catholicism allows, and some Catholics believe, that the Bible is materially sufficient (namely, it contains at least the seeds of all revelation), but Catholics insist that the Bible is not formally sufficient. They believe that the teaching magisterium is necessary to infallibly interpret doctrine and to enable us to understand doctrines that are not clear in Scripture.

26. While 2 Tim. 3:16–17 does not use the word "sufficient" it does use the equivalent in the phrase "competent, equipped for every good work."

grown up around (and obscured, even negated) the Scriptures since the first century. Indeed, since Catholic scholars make a comparison between the Old Testament religious authority (i.e., the high priesthood) and the Roman Catholic papacy, this seems to be a good analogy.

In addition, the Bible constantly warns us "not to go beyond what is written" (1 Cor. 4:6).[27] This kind of exhortation is found throughout Scripture. Moses was told not to "add to what I command you nor subtract from it" (Deut. 4:2). Solomon reaffirmed this in Proverbs, saying, "Every word of God is tested. . . . Add nothing to his words, lest he reprove you, and you be exposed as a deceiver" (Prov. 30:5–6). Indeed, John closed what is widely held to be the last words of the Bible with the same exhortation: "I warn everyone who hears the prophetic words in this book: if anyone adds to them, God will add to him the plagues described in this book, and if anyone takes away from the words in this prophetic book, God will take away his share in the tree of life" (Rev. 22:18–19). As Jesus declared (Matt. 15:3–6), tradition sometimes adds to the words of Scripture teachings that make void what Scripture affirms. *Sola Scriptura* could hardly be stated more emphatically.

Of course, none of these are absolute prohibitions on all future revelations. God could speak anytime he chooses to do so. They do, however, apply to the point of difference between Protestants and Catholics, namely, whether there exists today any authoritative normative teachings outside those revealed to apostles and prophets and inscripturated in the Bible. And this is precisely what these texts affirm. Indeed, even the prophet himself was not to add to the revelation God gave him, for prophets were not infallible whenever they spoke but only when giving God's revelation. Now, since both Catholics and Protestants agree that there is no new revelation beyond the first century, and since even what the apostles said apart from these revelations could not make them void, it would follow that these texts support the Protestant principle of *sola Scriptura*. For if there is no normative revelation after the time of the apostles and even the prophets themselves were not to add their teachings to the revelations God gave them in the Scriptures, then it follows that the Scriptures are the only infallible source of divine revelation.

Further, the Bible teaches *sola Scriptura* by stressing that it is a revelation from God (Gal. 1:12; cf. 1 Cor. 2:11–13) as opposed to the words of men. A revelation from God is a divine unveiling or disclosure. Paul's contrast vividly illustrates the difference: "Now I want you to know, brothers, that the gospel preached by me is not of human origin. For I did not receive it from a human being, nor was I taught it, but it came through a revelation of Jesus Christ" (Gal. 1:11–12). It is important to note here that "human being" in-

27. There is some debate even among Protestant scholars as to whether Paul is referring here to his own previous statements or to Scripture as a whole. Since the phrase used here is reserved only for sacred Scripture (cf. 2 Tim. 3:15–16) it is not inappropriate to imply the latter.

cludes the other apostles, of whom Paul adds, "nor did I go up to Jerusalem to those who were apostles before me" (1:17). So even the preaching of an apostle is not on the same level as the "revelation" (disclosure) from God; neither are the words of an angel (Gal. 1:8). This is argument for *sola Scriptura*. True, the New Testament speaks about "receiving" revealed teaching of apostles or prophets in an oral manner (cf. 2 Thess. 2:2), but these were *revelations,* not mere teachings about revelations.

Finally, although written revelation was progressive, both Catholics and Protestants agree that normative revelation ended by the time of the completion of the New Testament. Indeed, Jesus told the apostles he would "lead *them* [not their successors] into 'all truth'" (John 14:26; 16:13, emphasis added), and to be an apostle one had to have been an eyewitness of the resurrected Christ (cf. Acts 1:22; 1 Cor. 9:1; 15:4–8).[28] But, as we will see shortly, the only infallible record we have of apostolic teaching is in the New Testament. Therefore, it follows that Jesus predicted that the Bible alone would be the summation of "all truth" that he desired for his followers. This being the case, then, since canonical revelation ceased at the end of the first century, *sola Scriptura* means that the Bible—nothing more, nothing less, and nothing else"—has infallible authority.

Roman Catholics admit that the New Testament is the only infallible record of apostolic teaching we have from the first century. They do not seem to appreciate, however, the significance of this fact for the Protestant argument for *sola Scriptura.* Even many early Fathers testified to the fact that all apostolic teaching was put in the New Testament. While acknowledging the existence of apostolic tradition, J. D. N. Kelly concluded: "Admittedly there is no evidence for beliefs or practices current in the period which were not vouched for in the books later known as the New Testament."[29] Indeed, church history shows that many early Fathers, including Athanasius, Cyril of Jerusalem, Chrysostom, and Augustine, believed that the New Testament was the only infallible basis for all Christian doctrine (see "Conclusion" below). Further, if the New Testament is the only infallible record of apostolic teaching, then every other record from the first century is not infallible (i.e., is fallible). The fact that the teaching magisterium has pronounced some extra-biblical tradition (such as the bodily assumption of Mary) as infallibly true is immaterial because it does not have an infallible record from the first century on which to base such a decision. And if the New Testament is the only infallible record we have for apostolic teaching, then it follows that the Bible alone teaches that the Bible alone is the infallible Word of God.

All apostolic "traditions" are in the Bible. It is true that the New Testament speaks of following the "traditions" (= teachings) of the apostles,

---

28. For differences between "public" and "private" revelations, see chap. 1.
29. Even the *Didache* was not considered on a par with Scripture.

whether oral or written. This is because the apostles were living authorities set up by Christ (Matt. 18:18; Acts 2:42; Eph. 2:20). However, when they died there was no longer a living apostolic authority since, as already noted, only those who were eyewitnesses of the resurrected Christ could have apostolic authority (Acts 1:22; 1 Cor. 9:1). There is no more evidence for derived or indirect apostolic authority (i.e., apostolic succession) than there is that the "signs of an apostle" were possessed by non-apostles. That is, even non-apostles in the New Testament could not give the gifts of an apostle (1 Tim. 1:6) or pass on the special gifts of healing all kinds of sickness and even raising the dead (Matt. 10:8). For to have apostolic authority one must be able to perform apostolic signs (2 Cor. 12:12; Heb. 2:3–4). But since these special apostolic signs have ceased, there is no longer apostolic authority, except in the inspired writings of the apostles. And since the New Testament is the only inspired (infallible) record of what the apostles taught, it follows that, since the death of the apostles, the only apostolic authority we have today is the inspired record of their teaching in the New Testament. That is, all apostolic tradition (teaching) on faith and practice is in the New Testament. This does not necessarily mean that everything the apostles ever taught is in the New Testament, any more than everything Jesus said is there (cf. John 20:30; 21:25). Jesus did promise that "all the truth" he had taught them would be brought to their remembrance (John 14:26; 16:13), but he no doubt said the same truth in different ways at different times. Further, the understood context of Jesus' statement probably means all truth necessary for faith and morals (cf. 2 Tim. 3:15–17). So all apostolic teaching which God deemed necessary for the faith and practice (morals) of the church was preserved. It is only reasonable to infer that God would preserve what he inspired.

The fact that the apostles sometimes referred to "traditions" they gave orally as authoritative in no way diminishes the Protestant argument for *sola Scriptura*. First, it is not necessary to claim that all these oral teachings were inspired or infallible, only that they were authoritative. The believers were asked to "maintain" them (1 Cor. 11:2) and "stand fast in them" (2 Thess. 2:15). But oral teachings *about* Christ (not the words *of* Christ) and the apostles' affirmations were not called inspired or unbreakable or the equivalent unless they were inscripturated in the Bible (2 Tim. 3:16). The apostles were living authorities, but not everything they said was infallible. Catholics understand the difference between authoritative and infallible, since they make the same distinction with regard to non-infallible and [infallible (*ex cathedra*)] statements made by the pope.

Second, the traditions (teachings) of the apostles that were revelations were written down and are inspired and infallible. They comprise the New Testament. What the Catholic must prove (and cannot) is that the God who deemed it so important for the faith and morals of the faithful to inspire the inscripturation of twenty-seven books of apostolic teaching would have left out some important revelation in this book. So, however authoritative the apostles were by their office, only their inscripturated words are inspired and infallible (2 Tim. 3:16–17; cf. John 10:35). There is no evidence that all the revelation God gave them to express was not inscripturated in the twenty-seven books of the New Testament.

Further, the Bible makes it clear that God from the very beginning desired that his normative revelations be written down and preserved for succeeding generations. "Moses then wrote down all the words of the Lord" (Exod. 24:4). Indeed, Moses wrote in Deuteronomy, "these are the words of the covenant which the Lord ordered Moses to make with the Israelites" (Deut. 28:69), and Moses' book was preserved in the ark of the covenant (Deut. 31:26). "So Joshua made a covenant with the people that day and made statutes and ordinances for them . . . which he recorded in the book of the law of God" (Josh. 24:25–26) along with Moses' (cf. Josh. 1:7). Likewise, "Samuel next explained to the people the law of royalty and wrote it in a book, which he placed in the presence of the Lord" (1 Sam. 10:25). Isaiah was commanded by the Lord to "take a large cylinder-seal, and inscribe on it in ordinary letters" (Isa. 8:1) and to "inscribe it in a record; That it may be in future days an eternal witness" (30:8). Daniel had a collection of "the books" of Moses and the prophets right down to his contemporary, Jeremiah (Dan. 9:2). Jesus and the New Testament writers used the phrase "Scripture has it" (cf. Matt. 4:4, 7, 10) over ninety times, stressing the importance of the written Word of God. When Jesus rebuked the Jewish leaders is was not because they did not follow the traditions but because they did not "understand the Scriptures" (Matt. 22:29). The apostles were told by Jesus that the Holy Spirit would "guide . . . [them] to all truth" (John 16:13). But Jesus said in the very next chapter "Your word is truth" (John 17:17) and the apostles claimed their writings to the churches were "Scripture . . . inspired of God" (2 Tim. 3:16; cf. 2 Pet. 3:15–16). Clearly God intended from the very beginning that his revelation be preserved in Scripture, not in extra-biblical tradition. To claim that all God's revelation was not written down is to claim that the prophets were not obedient to their commission not to subtract a word from what God revealed to them.

The Bible does not state a preference for oral tradition. The Catholic use of 3 John to prove the superiority of oral tradition is a classic example of taking a text out of context. John is not comparing oral and written tradition about the past but a written (as opposed to a personal) communication in the present. Notice carefully what John says: "I have much to write to you, but I do not wish to write with pen and ink. Instead, I hope to see you soon when we can talk face to face" (3 John 13). Who would not prefer a face-to-face talk with a living apostle over a letter from him? But that is not what oral tradition gives. Rather, it provides a mere oral tradition (which is known to be unreliable [see below]) as opposed to an infallible written one. *Sola Scriptura* contends that the latter is preferable.

The Bible has perspicuity apart from traditions. The Bible is clear without the aid of traditions to help us understand it. This is known as the Protestant doctrine of the perspicuity (clarity) of Scripture. Contrary to a misunderstanding by many Catholics, perspicuity does not mean that everything in the Bible is absolutely clear but that the main message of salvation is clear; that is, that all doctrines essential for salvation are sufficiently clear.[30] Nor does perspicuity mean that those who are unwilling to "receive" or "welcome" (Gk. *dekomai*) the message will not become blinded (1 Cor. 2:14; cf. Rom. 1:21; 2 Cor. 4:3–4). For one can *perceive* the truth even if he does not *receive* it (cf. Rom. 1:18), know it in the mind (i.e., understand it) but not know it by experience (1 Cor. 2:14; Gk. *ginosko*). Jesus said that only the one who "chooses to do his will shall know whether my teaching is from God" (John 7:17). Indeed, to assume that oral traditions of the apostles not recorded in the Bible are necessary to interpret what is recorded under inspiration is to argue in effect that the uninspired is more clear than the inspired.[31] It is utterly presumptuous to assert that what fallible human beings write is clearer than what the infallible Word of God declares! Further, it insists that words of the apostles that were not written down are more clear than the ones they did write! We all know from experience that this is not so.

One final comment is in order. Catholic apologists sometimes make the assertion that "Protestants must prove . . . that Scripture is so clear that no outside information or authority is needed in order to interpret it."[32] They insist this is so since Catholics can, and many do (e.g., John Henry Newman and Cardinal Joseph Ratzinger), claim that the content of revelation is in the Scriptures alone (i.e., material sufficiency). But Protestants affirm (and Catholics deny) the formal sufficiency of Scripture, namely, that one needs nothing else to interpret Scripture. However, this argument is misleading for several reasons.

---

30. Roman Catholics, by contrast, believe that the Bible, apart from any outside information or authority, is not sufficient to explain all essential points of doctrine. That is why they believe an infallible teaching magisterium is necessary.

31. On the surface, creeds and commentaries may seem more clear than the Bible, but this is misleading for several reasons. First, they are only summaries of what the Bible teaches, and good summaries are often clearer than the whole text. Second, when the Bible summarizes a truth it is as clear, if not clearer, than any statement someone can make about the Bible (cf. Matt. 7:12; 1 John 5:12). Third, the comparison is false, since the Bible does not systematize most doctrines, as do human creeds and theologies. Hence, they cannot be clearer systematic statements than the non-systematic ones in the Bible for the simple reason that no fair comparison can be made between systematic and non-systematic statements. Finally, unless the Bible were clear enough to begin with, no one would be able to summarize or systematize it.

32. See Akin, "Material and Formal Sufficiency," p. 15.

First, even the translation of Scripture involves interpretation, and Protestants do not deny the need for good linguistic scholarship to make good translations of Scripture. Indeed, Catholic Bible translators use this kind of "outside information" to translate their Bibles without depending on the authority of the church to do so, at least with regard to all the truths essential to our salvation.

Second, Protestants do not hold, as Catholic scholars sometimes assert, that the Bible is formally sufficient without any outside help on everything taught. Perspicuity only covers the main (essential) truths of salvation, not everything.

Third, when orthodox Protestants utilize outside "information" to properly interpret Scripture they ought to do so with two very important restrictions in mind: (1) no information should be used to conflict with any clearly taught doctrine of Scripture, and (2) the outside information should only be used as a material cause, not a formal cause, of the interpretation.[33] The form of meaning must come from the text itself, as placed there by the author, not from outside the text. One may get material on the meaning of words, archaeology, culture, and so on from outside the text, but this is only data to help understand the text; the determination of its meaning must come from the text itself. In a piece of literature, any interpretive framework (formal cause) taken from outside the text and alien to the meaning of the text that is used to interpret the text is illegitimate and will invariably lead to error. This, of course, is not necessarily true in oral communication, where gestures and tones can give context for meaning. One may use whatever information is available from linguistics, history, and culture, but the structure of meaning must be found in the text itself.

Of course, all of this is not to say that Protestant interpreters cannot utilize traditional commentaries, confessions, and creeds as aids in understanding the text. They can use scholarly sources in their interpretation, but in order to remain true to the principle of *sola Scriptura* they must not use them in a magisterial way. Otherwise, they are just replacing the Roman Catholic teaching magisterium with a magisterium of Protestant scholarship, an unfortunate error into which more than one Protestant scholar has fallen.

The restriction on the use of outside "authorities" flows from the principle of *sola Scriptura* itself. First, no outside authorities, however trustworthy, should be afforded infallible status. Further, their teaching should never be used if they contradict the clear teaching of Scripture. Finally, scholars should use them as the occasional cause, not the formal cause, of the real meaning of a text. These authorities may be used only to help us *discover* the meaning of the text of Scripture, not *determine* its meaning. The determiner

---

33. When Protestants violate this principle, they go astray from one of their own basic principles *(sola Scriptura)* and often err as a result.

(efficient cause) of the meaning of all Scripture is its primary author (God), who used its secondary author (prophets and apostles) to write it. The formal cause of the meaning of Scripture is in the text itself, as expressed by its author(s).[34] To take any meaning structure from beyond the text, rather than that which is expressed in the text, is inconsistent with the principle of *sola Scriptura*. It is not difficult to understand Scripture without a teaching magisterium, at least not with regard to the essential salvific (salvation) teachings of Scripture. Normal people do it all the time in normal discourse. The difference between legitimate and illegitimate use of extra-biblical sources can be outlined as follows.

Tradition and Scripture are not inseparable.[35] First of all, even Kreeft's illustration of the horse (Scripture) and the rider (tradition) suggests that Scripture and tradition are separable. Further, even if it is granted that tradition is necessary, the Catholic inference that it has to be infallible tradition, indeed, the infallible tradition of the church of Rome is unfounded (see chap. 11). Protestants who believe in *sola Scriptura* accept tradition; they simply do not believe it is infallible. Finally, Kreeft's argument wrongly assumes that the Bible was produced by the Roman Catholic Church. The next point shows that this is not the case.

The principle of causality is not violated. Kreeft's argument that *sola Scriptura* violates the principle of causality (an effect cannot be greater than its cause) is invalid for one fundamental reason: it is based on a false assumption. He wrongly assumes, on the basis of what Vatican II says about the canon,[36] that the church determined the canon. This is not the case. God *determined* the canon by inspiring these books and no others. The church merely *discovered* which books God had determined (inspired) to be in the canon. Vatican I appears to agree, declaring these "books to be sacred and canonical, not because, having been carefully composed by mere human industry, they were afterward approved by her authority . . . but because, having been written by inspiration of the Holy Ghost, they have God for their author, and have been delivered as such to the Church herself."[37] If this is the case, then Kreeft's argument that the cause must be equal to its effect (or greater) fails. For even Catholic dogma admits that the church only received and recognized the canon but did not actually cause or produce it.

As F. F. Bruce correctly noted, "One thing must be emphatically stated. The New Testament books did not become authoritative for the Church be-

---

34. For further elaboration, see Norman L. Geisler, "Purpose and Meaning: The Cart and the Horse," *Grace Theological Journal* 5 (1984): 229–45.

35. For this section criticizing Kreeft's arguments I am indebted to Kenneth Samples' excellent unpublished paper, "Does the Bible Teach the Principle of *Sola Scriptura?*" (1993).

36. See *The Documents of Vatican II,* "De Verbum."

37. See Denzinger, *Sources of Catholic Dogma,* 1787, p. 444.

cause they were formally included in a canonical list; on the contrary, the Church included them in her canon because she already regarded them as divinely inspired."[38] Thus, the correct view of the canon is that the church is only a witness, not a judge of the canon, that is, all books which the apostles and prophets wrote (see chap. 9).

Rejection of tradition does not necessitate scandal. Kreeft's argument that the rejection of the Roman Catholic view on infallible tradition leads to denominationalism does not follow for many reasons. First, this implies that all denominationalism is scandalous, which is not necessarily so. As long as the denomination does not deny the essential doctrines of the Christian church and true spiritual unity with other believers in contrast to mere external organizational uniformity, it is not scandalous. It also implies that unbelievers are not able to see spiritual unity. Jesus declared: "This is how all [people] will know that you are my disciples, if you have love for one another" (John 13:35), not if we belong to the same ecclesiastical organization.

Second, as orthodox Catholics know well, the scandal of liberalism is as great inside the Catholic church as it is outside of it. One author had a Catholic teacher at a Catholic university who claimed to be an atheist. When Catholic apologists claim there is significantly more doctrinal agreement among Catholics than Protestants they must mean between *orthodox Catholics* and *all* Protestants (orthodox and unorthodox), which clearly is not a fair comparison. Only when one chooses to compare things like the mode and candidate for baptism, church government, and other doctrines are there greater differences among orthodox Protestants. When, however, we compare the differences with orthodox Catholics and orthodox Protestants or all Catholics and all Protestants on the classical creedal doctrines, Catholicism enjoys no significant edge. This fact negates the value of an infallible teaching magisterium for the Roman Catholic Church. In point of fact, Protestants seem to do about as well as Catholics on unanimity of essential doctrines with only an infallible Bible and no infallible interpreters of it! In fact, Protestants do much better at not deviating from biblical truth, as is evident in the Catholic belief in the Apocrypha, infallibility of the church, meritorious works for salvation, the exaltation and veneration of Mary, purgatory, and other extrabiblical doctrines (see chaps. 9–16).

Third, orthodox Protestant "denominations," though there be many, do not differ much more significantly than do the various "orders" (such as Dominicans, Franciscans, and Jesuits) and factions of the Roman Catholic Church. Orthodox Protestants differ largely over secondary issues, not primary (fundamental) doctrines, so this Catholic argument against Protestantism is rather self-condemning.

---

38. F. F. Bruce, *The New Testament Documents: Are They Reliable?* (Downers Grove, Ill.: InterVarsity Press, 1960), p. 27.

Fourth, as J. I. Packer noted, "the real deep divisions have been caused not by those who maintained *sola Scriptura,* but by those, Roman Catholic and Protestant alike, who reject it." Further, "when adherents of *sola Scriptura* have split from each other the cause has been sin rather than Protestant biblicism."[39] This is certainly often the case. A bad hermeneutic is more crucial to deviation from orthodoxy than is the rejection of infallible tradition from the Roman Catholic Church.

Rejecting tradition is not unhistorical. Kreeft's argument that the first generation of Christians did not have the New Testament but only the church to teach them forgets several basic facts. First, the early first-century Christians did have a Bible; it was the Old Testament, as the New Testament itself declares (cf. Rom. 15:4; 1 Cor. 10:6; 2 Tim. 3:15–17). Second, as for the further revelation through the apostles, early first-century believers did not need it in written form for one very simple reason—*they still had the apostles to teach them!* As soon as the apostles died, however, it became imperative that the written record of their infallible teaching be available. And it was—in the apostolic writings known as the New Testament. Third, Kreeft's argument assumes wrongly that there was apostolic succession (see below). The only infallible authority that succeeded the apostles was their infallible apostolic writings, that is, the New Testament.

PROTESTANT ARGUMENTS AGAINST INFALLIBLE TRADITION

There are many reasons why Protestants reject the Roman Catholic claim that they possess an infallible teaching magisterium that can unerringly interpret Scripture. The following are some of the more significant ones.

Oral traditions are unreliable. In point of fact, oral traditions are notoriously unreliable.[40] They are the stuff of which legends and myths are made. What is written is more easily preserved in its original form. Dutch theologian Abraham Kuyper notes four advantages of a written revelation: (1) it has durability whereby errors of memory or accidental corruptions, deliberate or not, are minimized; (2) it can be universally disseminated through translation and reproduction; (3) it has the attribute of fixedness and purity;

39. J. I. Packer, "*Sola Scriptura:* Crucial to Evangelicalism," in *The Foundations of Biblical Authority,* ed. James Boice (Grand Rapids: Zondervan, 1978), p. 103.

40. As a written record traceable to the very apostles themselves who were confirmed by miracles (Heb. 2:3–4), the New Testament is not unreliable, as are oral traditions. Hence, the attempt by Catholic apologists to compare the New Testament Scriptures to those of other religions to show that one needs a teaching magisterium to guide them in determining which Scriptures are from God fails. All that is necessary is the historical evidence we have to show that the New Testament was produced by apostles and prophets who were miraculously confirmed by God.

(4) it is given a finality and normativeness that other forms of communication cannot attain.[41] By contrast, what is not written is more easily polluted, as the New Testament illustrates. John 21:22–23 records how an unwritten "apostolic tradition" (i.e., one coming from the apostles) was based on a misunderstanding of what Jesus said. The disciples wrongly assumed that Jesus said that John would not die. John, however, debunked this false tradition in his authoritative written record.

If traditions are so reliable it is strange that Jesus spent so much time debunking the false traditions of the Jews that had grown up around the Old Testament Scriptures. On one occasion Jesus said, "You do err, not knowing the Scriptures . . ." (Matt. 22:29). In his sermon on the Mount Jesus rebuked what the Jewish leaders had "said" (Matt. 5:21, 27, 31, 33, 38, 43), in contrast to what was "written" (cf. Matt. 4:4, 7, 10).[42] On another occasion Jesus declared, "why do you break the commandment of God for the sake of your traditions? . . . You have nullified the word of God for the sake of your traditions" (Matt. 15:3). These words apply with equal force to many of the teachings of the church of Rome, such as the infallibility of the pope, the need for meritorious works, the addition of the Apocrypha, and the veneration of Mary.

Common sense and historical experience inform us that the generation alive when an alleged revelation was given is in a much better position to know if it is a true revelation than are succeeding generations—especially those hundreds of years later. They can apply the tests for propheticity (Deut. 13, 18) or apostolicity (Matt. 10:1; 2 Cor. 12:12; Heb. 2:3–4) which no succeeding generation can do directly. But many traditions proclaimed to be divine revelation by the Roman Catholic magisterium were done centuries, even a millennium or so, after they were allegedly given by God; in the case of some of these, there is no incontrovertible evidence that the tradition was believed by any significant number of orthodox Christians until centuries after they occurred. Those removed in time are greatly handicapped as compared to contemporaries, such as those who wrote the New Testament, to know what was truly a revelation from God. To affirm otherwise is like arguing that historians of a trial generations earlier are in a better position than the eyewitnesses who saw who committed the crime.

41. Cited by Bruce Milne, *Know the Truth* (Downers Grove, Ill.: InterVarsity Press, 1982), p. 28.

42. It is clear that Jesus is not contrasting his view with that of the Old Testament but with the Jewish leaders' misinterpretation of it. First, Jesus had just said he came to fulfill, not destroy, the Old Testament (Matt. 5:17–18). Second, it was what the Jewish leaders "said," not what was "written" in the Old Testament with which Jesus disagreed. Third, at least some of what they "said" is found nowhere in the Old Testament, such as "hate your enemy" (5:43). Indeed, the Old Testament taught that one should love everyone (Lev. 19:18), including one's enemies (Ps. 109:4–5).

Protestant conviction is built on the kind of view Luther expressed at the Council of Worms (A.D. 1521): "Unless I am convinced by the testimonies of Scripture or evident reason—for I believe neither the Pope nor Councils alone, since it is established that they have often erred and contradicted themselves—I am the prisoner of the Scriptures." Here we stand; we can do no other. The Catholic response that Luther was 1500 years after the New Testament and sometimes erred himself misses the point. Of course, interpreters often err. This is why we should trust only the Scriptures, which do not err, as our final authority.

There are contradictory traditions. It is acknowledged by all, even by Catholic scholars, that there are contradictory Christian traditions.[43] In fact, Abelard noted hundreds of differences. For example, some church fathers (like Augustine) supported the Apocrypha, while others (like Jerome) opposed it (see chap. 9). Some great teachers (like Aquinas) opposed the immaculate conception of Mary, while others (like Scotus) favored it. Indeed, some church fathers opposed *sola Scriptura,*[44] but others favored it.[45] This very fact makes it impossible to trust tradition, certainly in any ultimately authoritative sense, for the question always arises: *Which of the contradictory traditions should be accepted?* To say, "The one pronounced authoritative by the church" begs the question, since tradition is a necessary link in the argument for the very doctrine of the infallible authority of the church.

The fact is that there are so many contradictory traditions that tradition, as such, is rendered unreliable as an authoritative source of dogma. Nor does it suffice to argue that while particular scholars cannot be trusted, nonetheless, their "unanimous consent" can be. For, as we have shown elsewhere (in chaps. 9 and 15), *there is no unanimous consent among the church fathers on many doctrines which are proclaimed to be infallibly true by the Roman Catholic Church. Indeed, in some case there is not even a majority consent!* Thus, to appeal to the teaching magisterium of the Catholic church to settle the issue begs the question.[46]

43. By contrast, there are no contradictions in Scripture, as even Catholics acknowledge. Hence, the Catholic argument that a teaching magisterium is needed to judge which traditions are from God and which are not, just like which Scriptures are and are not from God, is a false analogy. We have strong historical evidence that the New Testament documents come from the apostles and their associates. We do not have this same kind of evidence for extra-biblical traditions.

44. At least in the material sense, if not the formal.

45. Some Catholic theologians favor *sola Scriptura* in the material sense (that all revelation is found at least in seminal form in Scripture) but reject it in the formal sense (that no infallible teaching magisterium is necessary). However, it can be argued that some Catholic scholars (like Augustine and Aquinas) favored *sola Scriptura* in both senses. See quotations under "Conclusion."

46. Ironically, while Catholics do not measure up to their own principle of "unanimous consent" of the Fathers, even Catholic scholar Louis Bouyer notes that "Protestants, in the positive statements [on Scripture] we refer to, say no more than the unanimous ecclesiastical tradition" (p. 129).

One Catholic response is to claim that the early church fathers were closer to the apostles. Hence, when they agreed generally (or unanimously?), that should be considered to be apostolic truth. But there are several serious problems with this reasoning. First, it does not help the Roman Catholic position, since they have sometimes proclaimed as infallibly true a less than unanimous position (e.g., the bodily assumption of Mary). Further, as is well known, truth is not determined by majority (or even unanimous) vote. What is more, when we add to this the knowledge that many heresies existed even in apostolic times (see Col. 2; 1 Tim. 4; 2 Tim. 2; 1 John 4), then simply because a tradition is earlier does not make it true. Heresy was very early, even in apostolic times.

Another Catholic response to this is that, just as the bride recognizes her husband's voice in a crowd, even so the church recognizes the voice of her Husband in deciding which traditions are authentic. The analogy, however, is flawed. It assumes (without proof) that there is some divinely appointed post-apostolic way to decide which teachings were from God. During the period of divine revelation ending with the apostles the God-ordained way to do this was by special miraculous confirmation (Acts 2:22; 2 Cor. 12:12; Heb. 2:3–4). Admittedly these apostolic sign-gifts do not exist today.[47]

Also, the Catholic attempt to provide non-miraculous objective evidence to support its view fails. Protestants use historical evidence (miracles) to support the New Testament and thereby the deity of Christ, and then use Christ to verify the divine authority of the New Testament. The historical evidence that supports the reliability of the New Testament is not the same as the religious tradition used by Roman Catholics. The former is objective and verifiable; the latter is not. There is, for example, no good evidence supporting first-century eyewitnesses (who were confirmed by miracles) that affirms the traditions pronounced infallible by the Roman Catholic Church. Indeed, many of them are based on traditions that only emerge several centuries later and which are disputed by both other traditions and the Bible (e.g., the bodily assumption of Mary).

Finally, the whole argument seems to be reduced to a subjective mystical experience which is given plausibility only because the analogy is false. Neither the Catholic church as such, nor any of its leaders, has experienced down through the centuries anything like a continual hearing of God's audible voice, so that it can recognize it again whenever he speaks. Thus it would appear that the alleged recognition of her Husband's voice is nothing more than mystical faith in the teaching magisterium of the Roman Catholic Church.

The Catholic use of tradition is not consistent. Not only are there contradictory traditions, but the Roman Catholic Church is arbitrary and inconsis-

---

47. See Norman L. Geisler, *Signs and Wonders* (Wheaton, Ill.: Tyndale House, 1988).

tent in its choice of which traditions to pronounce infallible. This is evident in a number of areas. First, as discussed earlier in this chapter, the Council of Trent chose to follow the tradition that has less support in pronouncing the apocryphal books inspired. The earliest and best authorities, including the translator of the Roman Catholic Latin Vulgate Bible, Jerome, opposed the Apocrypha (see chap. 9).

Second, support from tradition for the dogma of the bodily assumption of Mary is late and weak. Yet in spite of the lack of any real evidence from Scripture (see chap. 15) or any substantial evidence from the teachings of early church fathers, Rome chose to pronounce this an infallible truth of the Catholic faith. In short, Roman Catholic dogmas are not the product of rationally weighing the evidence of tradition but rather of arbitrarily choosing which of the many conflicting traditions they wish to pronounce infallible. The so-called unanimous consent of the Fathers to which Trent commanded allegiance is a fiction; no such consent actually exists since the Fathers often held diametrically opposing views.[48] In fact, not even a majority, to say nothing of unanimous consent, can be found among the early fathers on some traditions that were later pronounced infallibly true.

Third, apostolic tradition is nebulous. As has often been pointed out, "Never has the Roman Catholic Church given a complete and exhaustive list of the contents of oral tradition. It has not dared to do so because this oral tradition is such a nebulous entity."[49] That is to say, even if all extra-biblical revelation definitely exists somewhere in some tradition (as Catholics claim), which ones these are has nowhere been declared.[50]

Finally, if the method by which Catholics chose which tradition to canonize were followed in the practice of textual criticism, one could never arrive at a sound reconstruction of the original manuscripts, for it involves weighing the evidence as to what the original actually said, not reading back

---

48. Some Catholic apologists vainly attempt to avoid the clear language of Trent by reducing "unanimous consent" to "moral unanimity." First, anything less than unanimous consent is not really unanimous, whatever it is called. Second, "moral" unanimity is never definitively spelled out, certainly not in an infallible pronouncement. Finally, it does not even mean "majority" in some cases, since a majority of the Fathers, at least the early ones, did not even hold some doctrines later pronounced as infallibly true (e.g., the bodily assumption of Mary).

49. Ramm, *Pattern of Authority,* p. 68.

50. The Catholic claim that this is the same as the Protestant idea of doctrinal development is misdirected for several reasons. First, doctrinal development is in the *understanding* of revealed doctrines that are already there in the inspired text, not in the *creation* of new ones (like papal infallibility, Mary's bodily assumption, and the veneration of images) which are not, as even many Catholic scholars admit. Second, the discovery of "new" truths in the Bible do not involve any fundamentals of the faith, whereas the new proclamations by Roman Catholicism involve what they believe to be *de fide,* infallible dogma. Third, for Protestants the newness is in the formulization of the fundamental truth, not in its fact. For example, the fact of the Trinity was always in Scripture; the *terms* used to describe it and creedal *formulization* of the doctrine were progressively unfolded.

into it what subsequent generations would like it to have said. Indeed, even most contemporary Catholic biblical scholars do not follow such an arbitrary procedure when determining the original text of Scripture to be translated (as in the *New American Bible*).

SUMMARY AND CONCLUSION

The question of authority is crucial to the difference between Catholics and Protestants. One of these is whether the Bible alone has infallible authority. We have examined carefully the Catholic arguments in favor of an infallible tradition and found them all wanting. Further, we have advanced many reasons for rejecting any claim to an infallible tradition in favor of the Bible alone as the sufficient authority for all matters of faith and morals. These are supported by Scripture and sound reason. Indeed, the words of early church fathers and some of the greatest Catholic theologians seem to support the Protestant view that the Bible alone has infallible authority.[51] As J. N. D. Kelly noted:

> "the holy and inspired Scriptures," wrote Athanasius "are fully sufficient for the proclamation of the truth"; while his contemporary, Cyril of Jerusalem, laid it down that "with regard to the divine and saving mysteries of faith no doctrine, however trivial, may be taught without the backing of the divine Scriptures. . . . for our saving faith derives its force, not from capricious reasoning, but from what may be proved out of the Bible." Later in the same century John Chrysostom bade his congregation seek no other teacher than the oracles of God; everything was straightforward and clear in the Bible, and the sum of necessary knowledge could be extracted from it.[52]

What is more, Augustine declared that "it is to *the canonical Scriptures alone* that I am bound to yield such implicit subjection as to follow their teaching, without admitting the slightest suspicion that in them any mistake or any statement intended to mislead could find a place."[53] This is not an isolated statement, taken out of context, where Augustine gives supreme authority to Scripture alone. In *The City of God* Augustine declared that "He [God] also inspired the Scripture, which is regarded as canonical and of *supreme authority* and to which we give credence concerning all the truths we ought to know and yet, of ourselves, are unable to learn" (11.3). In his *Reply*

---

51. See Leonard R. Kline, "Lutherans in Sexual Commotion," *First Things*, no. 43 (May 1994): 35, for a Lutheran confirmation of this point.

52. Kelly, *Early Christian Doctrine*, pp. 42–43.

53. Augustine, *Letters* 82.3, in Schaff, *A Select Library of the Nicene and Post-Nicene Fathers*, emphasis added.

199

to *Faustus the Manichean* Augustine insisted that "Scripture has a sacredness peculiar to itself. . . . But in consequence of the sacred writing, we are bound to receive as true whatever the canon shows to have been said by even one prophet, or apostle, or evangelist" (11.5). This is not true of any tradition. Speaking in contrast to "the succession of bishops" after the time of the apostles, Augustine said that "there is a distinct boundary line separating all productions subsequent to apostolic times from the authoritative canonical books of the Old and New Testaments," for "the authority of these books has come down to us from the apostles . . . and, from a position of lofty supremacy, claims the submission of every faithful and pious mind." Hence, *"in the innumerable books that have been written latterly we may sometimes find the same truth as in Scripture, but there is not the same authority. Scripture has a sacredness peculiar to itself."*[54]

This is not to say that Augustine did not believe in tradition; he did,[55] as do most Protestants. It is only to note that he did not place tradition on the same level of authority as the Bible. As one scholar notes, "Tradition has only a derivative authority (based on its faithfulness to the prior authority of the Scriptures rather than an intrinsic authority equal to Scripture in its own right)." Further, "while the church is a witness to, and a guardian of, the inspired Word of God, the declaration of canonicity by the church is only a pronouncement about an already existing state of affairs."[56] Even Augustine's famous statement that he "should not believe the gospel except as moved by the authority of the Catholic Church"[57] should be understood historically, not magisterially, for several reasons. First, the overall context is a rational defense of historic Christianity against the attack of Manichaeism, not a defense of the authority of the church (as against the Donatists). Second, the immediate context speaks of having "no clear proof" or "incontrovertible testimony to the apostleship of Manichaeus," such as he had for the apostles of Christ who wrote the Gospels. Third, he speaks of that which was "inaugurated by miracles," which can only refer to the teachings of the apostles as recorded in the New Testament, since he refers to it being "inaugurated" and believed that these miracles ceased with the apostles. In brief, Augustine argues that, were it not for the historic apostolic truths preserved by the Catholic church, which contain the revelation given to the apostles and confirmed by miracles, he would not have known the gospel. In this sense the church which has preserved apostolic testimony for us in the New Testament which Augustine considered infallible, has thereby unerringly mediated the

---

54. Augustine, *Reply to Faustus* 11.5.

55. See Augustine, *On Baptism* 2.7.12; 4.24.31; *Letters* 54.1.1

56. Kim Riddlebarger, "No Place Like Rome: Why Are Evangelicals Joining the Catholic Church?" in John Armstrong, ed., *Roman Catholicism: Evangelical Protestants Analyze What Divides and Unites Us* (Chicago: Moody Press, 1994), pp. 238–39.

57. Augustine, *Against the Epistle of Manichaeus* 4.5.

gospel to us. So, the "authority" of the church is meant historically, not magisterially. Thus, this kind of authority is not infallible but only reliable.

For Augustine, the Bible alone is an infallible and inerrant authority. Of course, like Protestants who followed him, Augustine did not exclude "arguments addressed to . . . reason," for he accepted the truths of reason or general revelation. However, there is no infallible or written revelation of these. In this connection it is important to repeat that Catholics often misunderstand the Protestant principle of *sola Scriptura* to exclude any truth outside the Bible. This, of course, is untrue, as is revealed by both Augustine's quote here and Luther's famous quote earlier about being "convinced by the testimonies of Scripture *or evident reason.*" What Protestants mean by *sola Scriptura* is that the Bible alone is the infallible written authority for faith and morals. Natural revelation as such is not infallible, written, nor does it cover all matters of faith and morals (it only overlaps with many).

Following Augustine, Aquinas declared that "we believe the successors of the apostles and prophets *only in so far as they tell us those things which the apostles and prophets have left in their writings,*"[58] and "it is heretical to say that any falsehood whatsoever is contained either in the gospels or in any canonical Scripture."[59] From these statements and from his use of the Fathers only to help understand the Scriptures and not to supplement them, it is clear that Aquinas believed in the material, if not formal, sufficiency of Scripture—something many conservative Catholics believe is contrary to the Council of Trent. If so, the greatest theologian of the Catholic church stands against what was later proclaimed to be an infallible dogma of that church.

---

58. Thomas Aquinas, *De veritate* XIV, 10, ad 11, emphasis added.
59. Thomas Aquinas, *Commentary on the Book of Job* 13, lect. 1.

11

INFALLIBILITY

According to Roman Catholic dogma the teaching magisterium is infallible when officially defining faith and morals for believers. One manifestation of this doctrine is popularly known as the "infallibility of the Pope," which was pronounced a dogma in A.D. 1870 at Vatican I. This is a major bone of contention between Catholics and Protestants and thus merits attention here.

THE DOCTRINE OF INFALLIBILITY EXPLAINED

Roman Catholic authorities define infallibility as "immunity from error, i.e., protection against either passive or active deception. Persons or agencies are infallible to the extent that they can neither deceive nor be deceived."[1]

THE STATEMENT OF THE DOCTRINE OF INFALLIBILITY

Vatican I pronounced that all the faithful of Christ must believe

> that the Apostolic See and the Roman Pontiff hold primacy over the whole world, and that the Pontiff of Rome himself is the successor of the blessed Peter, the chief of the apostles, and is the true vicar of Christ and head of the whole Church and faith, and teacher of all Christians; and that to him was handed down in blessed Peter, by our Lord Jesus Christ, full power to feed, rule, and guide the universal Church, just as is also contained in the records of the ecumenical Councils and in the sacred canons.[2]

Furthermore, the Council went on to speak of "the Infallible 'Magisterium' of the Roman Pontiff," declaring that:

1. Avery Dulles, "Infallibility: The Terminology," in *Teaching Authority*, ed. by Empie, p. 71.
2. Also see Denzinger, *Sources of Catholic Dogma*, pp. 455–56.

the Roman Pontiff, when he speaks *ex cathedra,* that is, when carrying out the duty of the pastor and teacher of all Christians in accord with his *supreme apostolic authority* he explains a doctrine of faith or morals to be held by the Universal Church, through the divine assistance promised him in blessed Peter, *operates with that infallibility* with which the divine Redeemer wished that His church be instructed in defining doctrine on faith and morals; and so such definitions of the Roman Pontiff from himself, but not from the consensus of the Church, *are unalterable.*[3]

This declaration is followed by the traditional condemnation of any who reject papal infallibility: "But if anyone presumes to contradict this definition of Ours, which may God forbid: let him be anathema" [i.e., excommunicated].[4]

QUALIFICATIONS ON THE DOCTRINE OF INFALLIBILITY

Roman Catholic scholars have expounded significant qualifications on the doctrine of papal infallibility. First, they acknowledge that the pope is not infallible in everything he teaches but only when he speaks *ex cathedra,* as the official interpreter of faith and morals. Avery Dulles, an authority on Catholic dogma, states that, for a pronouncement to be *ex cathedra,* it must:

1. fulfill his office as supreme pastor and teacher of all Christians;
2. accord with his supreme apostolic authority, i.e., as a successor of Peter;
3. determine a doctrine of faith and morals, i.e., a doctrine expressing divine revelation;
4. impose a doctrine to be held definitively by all.[5]

Dulles notes that "Vatican I firmly rejected one condition . . . as necessary for infallibility, namely, the consent of the whole church."[6]

Second, the pope is not infallible when pronouncing on matters that do not pertain to "faith and morals." On these matters he may be as fallible as the next person.

Third, the pope is infallible but not absolute. As Dulles observes, "Absolute infallibility (in all respects, without dependence on another) is proper to God. . . . All other infallibility is derivative and limited in scope."[7]

3. Ibid., 1839, p. 457, emphasis added.
4. Ibid., 1840
5. Dulles, "Infallibility," pp. 79–80.
6. Ibid., p. 79.
7. Ibid., p. 72.

Fourth, infallibility entails irrevocability. A pope cannot, for example, declare void previous infallible pronouncements of the church.

Finally, in contrast to Vatican I, many (usually liberal or progressive) Catholic theologians believe that the pope is not infallible independently of the bishops but only as he speaks in one voice with and for them in collegiality. As Dulles noted, infallibility "is often attributed to the bishops as a group, to ecumenical councils, and to popes."[8] Conservatives argue that Vatican I condemned this view.[9]

ARGUMENTS FOR PAPAL INFALLIBILITY

In his widely used work, *Fundamentals of Catholic Dogma,* Ludwig Ott offers the two standard arguments for the infallibility of the bishop of Rome: the proof from Scripture and the proof from tradition.

Argument from Scripture. Ott argues that "Christ made Peter the foundation of His Church, that is, the guarantor of her unity and unshakable strength, and promised her a duration that will not pass away (Mt. 16, 18). . . . However, the unity and solidarity of the Church is not possible without the right Faith. Peter is, therefore, also the supreme teacher of the Faith. As such he must be infallible in the official promulgation of Faith, in his own person and in his successors."[10]

Ott appeals to John 21:15–17 to prove that "Christ installed Peter (and his successors) as the supreme pastor over the whole flock." He argues that "the task of teaching Christian truth and of protecting it from error is part of the function of the supreme pastor. But he could not fulfill this task if, in the exercise of his supreme teaching office, he himself were subject to error."[11] For further support, he appeals to Luke 22:31 where Christ said to Peter, "I have prayed for thee, that thy faith fail not," insisting that "the reason for Christ's praying for Peter especially was that Peter, after his own conversion, should confirm his brethren in their faith, which clearly indicates Peter's position as head of the Apostles."[12]

John 11:49–52 also is used to defend the infallibility of the pope. Caiaphas the high priest, in his official capacity as high priest, unwittingly prophesied about Christ dying for the nation of Israel so that they would not perish. They argue that, just as in the Old Testament the high priest had an official revelatory function connected with his office, the same would be ex-

---

8. Ibid.
9. They appeal to Denzinger, *Sources of Catholic Dogma,* 1839, to support their view.
10. Ott, *Fundamentals of Catholic Dogma,* p. 287.
11. Ibid., pp. 287–88.
12. Ibid., p. 288.

pected in the New Testament. This, they say, is manifest in the bishop of Rome.

Argument for Infallibility from Tradition. Catholics also base their belief in papal infallibility in the early church fathers, who "attest the decisive teaching authority of the Roman Church and its Pontiff." Irenaeus said, "with this Church on account of its special eminence, every other Church must agree . . . in her apostolic traditions has always been kept pure."[13] Ott further argues that "the teaching Primacy of the Pope from the earliest times was expressed in practice in the condemnation of heretical opinions."[14] He then supports his view by citing the great medieval theologian, Thomas Aquinas, who argued that it was the official power of the papal office "finally to decide questions of faith, so that they may be held with unshakable faith by all."[15] Of course, Ott and all Catholic theologians admit that papal infallibility was not officially proclaimed as dogma by the Roman church until A.D. 1870. And, as we shall see, even then it was done under questionable circumstances and with significant opposition.

A RESPONSE TO THE ARGUMENTS FOR INFALLIBILITY

Not only Protestants but the rest of Christendom, Anglicans and Eastern Orthodox included, reject the doctrine of papal infallibility.[16]

> In every age there have been those who considered the claims of a single bishop to supreme authority to be a sure identification of the corruption of the church, and perhaps even the work of the Antichrist. Pope Gregory I (A.D. 590–604) indignantly reproached Patriarch John the Faster of Constantinople for calling himself the universal bishop; Gregory did so to defend the rights of all the bishops, himself included, and not because he wanted the title for himself.[17]

Protestants accept the infallibility of Scripture but deny that any human being or institution is the infallible interpreter of Scripture. The classic refutation of papal infallibility was written by George Salmon, *The Infallibility of the Church* (1914). It has never really been answered by the Catholic church.

The doctrine of papal infallibility has opponents even within the modern

13. Irenaeus, *Against Heresies* 3, 3, 2.
14. Ott, *Fundamentals of Catholic Dogma*, p. 288.
15. Ibid., p. 289.
16. Eastern Orthodoxy is willing to accept the bishop of Rome as "first among equals," i.e., a place of honor coming short of the total superiority of the pope.
17. Statement by Gregory the Great, in Brown, *Protest of a Troubled Protestant*, p. 122.

Roman Catholic Church. Hans Küng wrote a pointed critique of it in his work, *Infallible? An Inquiry,*[18] for which he was censured and forbidden to teach under the auspices of the Roman Catholic Church. First, let us point out the flaws in the arguments given in favor of papal infallibility.

A RESPONSE TO THE BIBLICAL ARGUMENTS FOR INFALLIBILITY

There are several texts used by Catholics to defend the infallibility of the pope. In response, Protestants note several things.

Matthew 16:18f. Roman Catholics use Jesus' statement to Peter in Matthew 16:18 that "upon this rock I will build my church" to support papal infallibility. When properly understood, however, this verse falls far short of support for papal infallibility.

First, many Protestants insist that Christ was not referring to Peter being the foundation of the church when he spoke of "this rock." (1) Whenever Peter is referred to in this passage it is in the second person ("you"), but "this rock" is in the third person. (2) "Peter" (Gk: *petros*) is a masculine singular term but "rock" *(petra)* is feminine singular, hence they do not have the same referent, and even if Jesus did speak these words in Aramaic (which does not distinguish genders), the inspired Greek original does make such distinctions. (3) What is more, the same authority Jesus gave to Peter (Matt. 16:18) is given later to all the apostles (Matt. 18:18). (4) No Catholic commentator gives Peter primacy in evil simply because he was singled out in Jesus' rebuke a few verses later: "Get behind me, Satan! You are an obstacle to me. You are thinking not as God does, but as human beings do" (v. 23). Why then should Peter be given primacy in authority because of Jesus' affirmation? Jesus replied to Peter because only Peter spoke, even though he represented the group. (5) Great authorities, some Catholic, agree with this interpretation, including John Chrysostom and Augustine. Augustine wrote: "On this rock, therefore, He said, which thou hast confessed. I will build my Church. For the Rock *(petra)* is Christ; and on this foundation was Peter himself built."[19]

Second, even if Peter is the rock referred to by Christ, as some Protestant scholars believe, he was not the *only* rock in the foundation of the church, as many early church fathers point out. Whatever this may mean, Jesus gave all the apostles the same power ("keys") to "bind" and "loose" that he gave to Peter (cf. Matt. 18:18). Some argue that these were common rabbinic phrases

18. Hans Küng, *Infallible? An Inquiry,* trans. by Edward Quinn (Garden City, N.Y: Doubleday, 1971).

19. Augustine, "On the Gospel of John," Tractate 12435; quoted in White, *Answers to Catholic Claims,* p. 106.

used of "forbidding" and "allowing." These "keys" were not some mysterious power given to Peter alone but the power granted by Christ to his church by which, when they proclaim the gospel, they can proclaim God's forgiveness of sin to all who believe. As John Calvin noted, "Since heaven is opened to us by the doctrine of the gospel, the word "keys" affords an appropriate metaphor. Now men are bound and loosed in no other way than when faith reconciles some to God, while their own unbelief constrains others the more."[20] Others believe Jesus was speaking of non-salvific binding of a brother in probable sin (cf. Matt. 18:18). Whatever the case, all the apostles, not just Peter, possessed this power.

Further, Scripture affirms that the church is "built on the foundation of the apostles and prophets, with Christ Jesus himself as the capstone" (Eph. 2:20). Two things are clear from this: all the apostles—not just Peter—are the foundation of the church, and the only one who was given a place of uniqueness or prominence was Christ, the capstone. Indeed, Peter himself referred to Christ as "the cornerstone" of the church (1 Pet. 2:7) and the rest of believers as "living stones" (v. 4) in the superstructure of the church. Peter gives no indication that he was given a special place of prominence in the foundation of the church above the rest of the apostles and below Christ. He is just one "stone" along with the other eleven apostles (Eph. 2:20).

Third, Peter's role in the New Testament falls far short of the Catholic claim that he was given unique authority among the apostles.[21] (1) While Peter did preach the initial sermon on Pentecost, his role in the rest of Acts is scarcely that of the chief apostle but at best *one* of the "most eminent apostles" (plural, 2 Cor. 21:11 NKJV). (2) In fact, by God's inspiration the apostle Paul taught that no apostle was really superior: "I was in no way inferior to these [so-called] 'superapostles'"(2 Cor. 12:11).[22] (3) No one reading Galatians carefully can come away with the impression that any apostle, including Peter, was inferior to the apostle Paul. For Paul claimed to get his revelation independently of the other apostles (Gal. 1:12; 2:2), to be on the same level as Peter (Gal. 2:8) and even used his revelation to rebuke Peter (Gal. 2:11–14)! (4) Likewise, the fact that both Peter and John were sent by the apostles on a mission to Samaria reveals that Peter was not *the* superior apostle (Acts 8:4–13), otherwise he would have been doing the sending. (5) Indeed, if Peter was the God-ordained superior apostle it is strange that Acts gives more attention to Paul's ministry than to Peter's. Peter is the focus only in chapters 1–12, but Paul is the dominant figure in

20. Calvin, *Institutes*, 4:6, 4, p. 1105.
21. Many of the following critiques are found in White's helpful book, *Answers to Catholic Claims*, pp. 101–2.
22. Paul was referring here in 2 Cor. 12:11 to true apostles like Peter, not to false ones as earlier (11:13–14), since he implies that they could do genuine miracles which confirmed their apostleship such as he did (2 Cor. 12:12; cf. Heb. 2:3–4).

13–28.[23] (6) Furthermore, though Peter addressed the first council (Acts 15), he exercised no primacy over the others. The decision came from "the apostles and presbyters, in agreement with the whole church" (Acts 15:22; cf. v. 23). Many scholars believe that James, not Peter, presided over the council, since he was the one who gave the final words (cf. vv. 13–21).[24] (7) By Peter's own admission he was not *the* pastor of the church but only a "*fellow* presbyter [elder]" (1 Pet. 5:1–2, emphasis added). And while he did claim to be "*an* apostle" (1 Pet. 1:1), he nowhere claimed to be "*the* apostle" or the chief apostle. He certainly was a leading apostle, but even then he was only one of the "pillars" (plural, Gal. 2:9) of the church along with James and John, not *the* pillar.

Fourth, however the early church understood Peter's role, *there is absolutely no reference to any alleged infallibility he possessed.* Indeed, the word "infallible" never occurs in the New Testament. When parallel words or phrases do occur they refer to Scripture alone, not to any person's ability to interpret it. Jesus said, for example, "scripture cannot be set aside" (John 10:35), and "until heaven and earth pass away, not the smallest letter or the smallest part of a letter will pass from the law" (Matt. 5:18).

This is not to say that Peter did not have a significant role in the early church; he did. He even seems to have been the initial leader of the apostolic band. As already noted, along with James and John he was one of the "pillars" of the early church (Gal. 2:9). It was Peter who preached the great sermon at Pentecost when the gift of the Holy Spirit was given, welcoming many Jews into the Christian fold. And it was Peter who spoke when the Spirit of God fell on the Gentiles (Acts 10). However, from this point on, Peter fades into the background and Paul becomes the dominant figure, carrying the gospel to the ends of the earth (Acts 13–28), writing approximately half of the New Testament (as compared to Peter's two Epistles), and even rebuking Peter for his hypocrisy (Gal. 2:11–14). In short, there is no evidence in Matthew 16 or any other text for the Roman Catholic dogma of the superiority or infallibility of Peter.

Finally, and most importantly, whatever apostolic powers Peter and the others possessed, it is clear that they were not passed on to anyone after their death. The repeated criterion for being an apostle was that one had to be a first-century eyewitness of the resurrected Christ (cf. Acts 1:22; 1 Cor. 9:1;

---

23. One cannot, as some Catholic scholars do, dismiss this dominant focus on Paul rather than Peter on the circumstantial fact that Luke wrote more about Paul because he was his travel companion or that he was defending Christianity against Roman accusations so he focused on Paul. After all, it was the Holy Spirit who inspired what Luke wrote here! And if Peter has supreme authority, then surely Acts would have made this clear by stressing Peter's unique role. But it does not.

24. See F. F. Bruce, *Peter, Stephen, James and John* (Grand Rapids: Eerdmans, 1979), pp. 86ff.

15:5–8). Therefore, there could be no true apostolic succession in the pope or anyone else.

Further, these select individuals known as apostles were given certain unmistakable "signs of an apostle" (2 Cor. 12:12). These sign-gifts included the ability to raise the dead (Matt. 10:8), heal diseases (Matt. 10:8; John 9:1–7), perform exorcisms (Matt. 10:8; Acts 16:16–18), speak messages in languages they had never studied (Acts 2:1–8; cf. 10:44–46), and pass on supernatural gifts to others so that they could be assisted in their apostolic mission of founding the church (Acts 6:6; cf. 8:5–6; 2 Tim. 1:6). On one occasion Peter pronounced a supernatural death sentence on two people who had "lied to the Holy Spirit," and they immediately dropped dead (Acts 5:1–11)!

These miraculous powers ceased during the apostles' lifetime. The writer of Hebrews (c. A.D. 69) referred to the special sign-gifts of an apostle as having already past when he spoke of the message "announced originally through our Lord, it *was confirmed* [past event[25]] for us by those who had heard him [namely, the apostles]. God added his testimony by signs, wonders, various acts of power, and distributing of the gifts of the Holy Spirit according to his will" (Heb. 2:3–4, emphasis added). Jude, writing late in the first century (after A.D. 70), spoke of "the faith that was *once for all handed down* to the holy ones" (v. 3), and exhorted his hearers to "remember the words spoken *beforehand* by the apostles of our Lord Jesus Christ" (v. 17, emphasis added). In contrast to the profusion of apostolic miracles (cf. Acts 28:1–10) up to the end of the Book of Acts (c. A.D. 60–61), there is no record of any apostolic miracle in Paul's later Epistles after this time.[26] Indeed, some of his trusted helpers were sick and Paul apparently was not able to heal them (Phil. 2:26; 2 Tim. 4:20),[27] asking for prayer for them or recommending that they take medicine (1 Tim. 5:23). The special apostle-confirming miracles apparently ceased even before some apostles had died.

---

25. While the use of the aorist tense here does not in itself prove this was a past event it does strongly indicate it. This is especially so in view of the fact that the writer puts himself in a class that is not one of the twelve apostles and is writing after Paul, Peter, and most apostles were martyred and/or scattered (viz., c. A.D. 69).

26. This argument from the later and sudden *absence* of miracles after their earlier abundance is not to be confused with the fallacious "argument from *silence*." The Bible is not silent on the nature, purpose, and function of these special apostolic miracles (cf. 2 Cor. 12:12; Heb. 2:3–4), and this function (of confirming apostolic revelation) fits with their cessation, since they were not needed once the revelation was confirmed.

27. The fact that Paul was inflicted with a "physical infirmity" (Gal. 4:13) during the time God was still doing miracles (cf. 3:5) does not disprove this thesis. If Galatians was written early, this could have been the divinely inflicted infirmity resulting from his being blinded by God (Acts 9:17–18; cf. Gal. 6:11) or, if Galatians was written later, the infliction God sent to humble him (2 Cor. 12). Further, there is no indication in the New Testament that those with the gift of healing exercised it on themselves. These special gifts were given to confirm the truth of revelation to others (Heb. 2:3–4), not to benefit one's personal needs.

In addition, these special miraculous signs were given to the apostles to establish their authority as the representatives of Christ in founding his church. Jesus had promised them special "power" to be his witnesses (Acts 1:8). Paul pointed to "the signs of an apostle" to confirm his authority to the Corinthians, some of whom had challenged it (2 Cor. 12:12). Hebrews 2:3–4 speaks of the special apostolic miracles as being given to confirm their witnesses to Christ. Indeed, from the time of Moses to the apostles, God gave special miracles to his servants to confirm that their revelations were from him (Exod. 4; 1 Kings 18; John 3:2; Acts 2:22).

In summation, since to be an apostle one had to be an eyewitness of the resurrected Christ, and since these select individuals known as apostles were given certain unmistakable "signs of an apostle" to establish their authority—which ceased during their lifetime—it follows that no one since the first century has possessed apostolic authority. In brief, the absence of these special apostolic gifts proves the absence of the special apostolic authority. What remains today is the *teaching* of the apostles (in the New Testament), not the *office* of an apostle or its authority. The authority of *living* apostles has been replaced by the authority of the *writings* of the apostles.

John 21:15–17. In this passage Jesus says to Peter, "Feed my lambs" and "Tend my sheep" and "Feed my sheep" (vv. 15–17). Roman Catholic scholars believe this shows that Peter, and Peter alone, was given infallible authority to be *the* pastor of the whole Christian church. A careful examination of the text reveals that this is a serious overclaim for the passage.

First, whether the passage is taken of Peter alone or of all the disciples, there is absolutely no reference here to any infallible authority. It is simply a matter of pastoral care that concerns Jesus here. "Feeding" is a God-given pastoral function that even non-apostles had in the New Testament (cf. Acts 20:28; Eph. 4:11–12; 1 Pet. 5:1–2). One does not have to be an infallible shepherd in order to feed his flock properly.

Second, if Peter had infallibility (i.e., the ability to not mislead in faith and practice), then why did he mislead believers and have to be rebuked by the apostle Paul (Gal. 2:11)? The infallible Scriptures, accepted by Roman Catholics, declare that Peter "clearly was wrong" and "stood condemned."[28] Peter "acted hypocritically . . . with the result that even Barnabas was carried away by their hypocrisy," hypocrisy here being defined as "pretense, play-acting; moral insincerity" (2:11–13). It is difficult to exonerate Peter from the charge that he led believers astray—something the infallible pastor of the church would never do! The Catholic response that Peter was only infallible in his *ex cathedra* words and not his actions, rings hollow when we remember that "actions speak louder than words." Actions are the domain of mor-

---

28. This is the literal rendering of Gal. 2:11 given in the *New American Bible*.

als, and the pope is alleged to be infallible in faith *and* morals. In view of this, even Roman Catholic admission of the despicable behavior of some of its popes is revealing.[29] The fact is that Peter could not be both an infallible guide for faith and morals and at the same time mislead believers on the important matter of faith and morals of which Galatians speaks.

Third, contrary to the Catholic claim, the overall import of the passage in John speaks more to Peter's weakness and need for restoration than to his unique authority. The reason Peter is singled out for restoration, being asked three times by Jesus "Do you love me more than these [other disciples]?" was that *only Peter denied the Lord three times and so only Peter needed to be restored.* Thus Jesus was not exalting Peter above the other apostles here but bringing him back up to their level![30]

Finally, in view of the New Testament titles used of Peter it is clear that he would never have accepted the terms used of the pope today: "Holy Father" (cf. Matt. 23:9) or "Supreme Pontiff" and "Vicar of Christ." The only vicar of Christ on earth is the blessed Holy Spirit (John 14:16, 26). Jesus said this of the Holy Spirit of God, not of Peter (John 16:13–14). As noted earlier, Peter referred to himself in much more humble terms as "an apostle" (1 Pet. 1:1) not the apostle and "fellow-presbyter [elder]" (1 Pet. 5:1), not the supreme Bishop, the Pope, or the Holy Father.

John 11:49–52. The argument that, since in the Old Testament the high priest had an official revelatory function connected with his office it is therefore to be expected that there be an equivalent New Testament figure (namely, the pope), is seriously flawed. First, this is merely an argument from analogy and is not based on any New Testament affirmation that this is so. And it is a weak or extrinsic analogy since unlike the analogy between God and creatures (Acts 14:15–17; Rom. 1:19–20) there is no intrinsic connection between cause and effect. Second, the New Testament affirmations made about the Old Testament priesthood would reject the analogy, for they say explicitly that the Old Testament priesthood has been abolished! The writer to the Hebrews declared that "there is a change of priesthood" from that of Aaron (Heb. 7:12). The Aaronic priesthood has been fulfilled in Christ who is a priest forever after the order of Melchizedek (Heb. 7:15–17). Third, even Catholics acknowledge that there is no new revelation after the

29. To appeal to David's sin is not helpful, since (1) he did not claim to be infallible, (2) he confessed his sin (Ps. 51), and (3) God forgave and restored him (Ps. 32) to his fallible position as king. And, unlike the Catholic view of Peter, both Moses' and Paul's great sins were before God called them and neither of them claimed infallibility.

30. The fact that Peter was asked whether he loved Jesus "more" than the others does not prove Jesus gave him more authority than they were given. For this would imply that the amount of Peter's love is the basis for the amount of authority God graciously gave to him. God's grace is not conditioned on the amount of our works of love (Rom. 4:4–5). Furthermore, even Roman Catholics admit that God gave infallible authority to popes who were more evil than others who they say do not have this authority.

time of the New Testament. So no one (popes included) after the first century can have a revelatory function in the sense of giving new revelations. Finally, there is a New Testament revelatory function like that of the Old, but it is in the New Testament "apostles and prophets" (cf. Eph. 2:20; 3:5) and it ceased when they died. To assume a revelatory (or even infallible defining) function was passed on after them and is resident in the bishop of Rome is to beg the question.

In addition to the total lack of support from the Scriptures and equivocal support from tradition there are many other arguments against papal infallibility. We will divide them into theological, philosophical, and historical arguments.

THEOLOGICAL PROBLEMS WITH INFALLIBILITY

There are serious theological problems with papal infallibility. One is the question of heresy being taught by an infallible pope.

The Problem of Heretical Popes. Pope Honorius I (A.D. 625–638) was condemned by the Sixth General Council for teaching the monothelite heresy (that there was only one will in Christ).[31] Even Roman Catholic expert Ludwig Ott admits that "Pope Leo II (682–683) confirmed his anathematization."[32] This being the case, we are left with the incredible situation of an infallible pope teaching a fallible, yea, heretical, doctrine. If the papal teaching office is infallible, that is, if it cannot mislead on doctrine and ethics, then how could a papal teaching be heretical? What is more, this was a serious heresy—one relating to the nature of Christ. To claim that the pope was not infallible on this occasion is only to further undermine the doctrine of infallibility. How can one know when his doctrinal pronouncements are infallible and when they are not? There is no infallible test.[33] And without such a test, how can the Roman Catholic Church provide infallible guidance on doctrine and morals? If the pope can be fallible on one doctrine, then why not others?

Further, the contention that Pope Leo did not condemn Pope Honorius with heresy "but with negligence in the suppression of error" is ineffective as a defense.[34] It still raises serious questions as to how Pope Honorius could

---

31. Bernhard Lohse, *A Short History of Christian Doctrine*, trans. F. Ernest Stoeffler (Philadelphia: Fortress Press, 1985), p. 208.

32. Ott, *Fundamentals of Catholic Dogma,* p. 150.

33. Catholic apologists claim that there are objective tests, such as asking, was the pope speaking (1) to all believers, (2) on faith and morals, and (3) in his official capacity as pope (see ibid., p. 287)? However, this is not definite as to which pronouncements are infallible. First, there is no infallible statement on just what are the criteria. Second, there is not universal agreement on the criteria. Third, there is no universal agreement on how to apply these or any criteria to all cases.

34. Ibid.

be an infallible guide in faith and morals, since he taught heresy. And the Catholic response that he was not speaking *ex cathedra* when he taught this heresy is convenient but inadequate. Indeed, invoking such a distinction only tends to undermine the authority of the far more numerous occasions when the pope is speaking with authority but not with infallibility. Also, it does not explain how the Sixth General Council could condemn Honorius as a heretic, as even Ott admits.[35] Finally, by disclaiming the infallibility of the pope on this and like situations the number of occasions such pronouncements actually were made is relatively rare. For example, the pope has spoken *ex cathedra* only one time this whole century (on the bodily assumption of Mary)! If infallibility is exercised this rarely then its value for all practical purposes is nil. This being the case, since the pope speaks with only fallible authority on most occasions, the Catholic is bound to accept his authority on faith and morals when he may be (and sometimes has been) wrong. In short, the alleged infallible guidance of the papacy is negligible at best. Indeed, on the vast majority of occasions there is no infallible guidance at all.

The Problem of Revelational Insufficiency. One of the chief reasons Catholic authorities offer to argue the need for an infallible teaching magisterium is that we need infallible guidance to understand God's infallible revelation. Otherwise it is misinterpreted as the many Protestant sects do.

There are two problems with this rationale. For one thing, how is an infallible interpretation any better than the infallible revelation? Divine revelation is a disclosure or unveiling by God. To claim that God's infallible unveiling in the Bible needs further infallible unveiling by God says that it was not unveiled properly to begin with. To be sure, there is a difference between objective disclosure (revelation) and subjective discovery (understanding). But the central problem in this regard is not in the *perception* of God's truth. Even his general revelation is "evident" and "able to be understood" (Rom. 1:19–20). Our most significant problem with regard to the truth of God's revelation is *reception.* Paul declared that "the natural [unregenerate] person does not accept [Gk: *dekomai,* welcome, receive] what pertains to the Spirit of God" (1 Cor. 2:14). He cannot "know" (Gk: *ginosko,* know by experience) them because he does not receive them into his life, even though he understands them in his mind. Indeed, what he clearly perceives (Rom. 1:19–20) he does not openly receive but suppresses (Rom. 1:18). This is why there are atheists in their minds because they have rejected the truth about God in their hearts (Ps. 14:1). So even though there is a difference between objective disclosure and subjective understanding people are "without excuse" for failing to understand the objective revelation of God, whether in nature or in Scripture (cf. Rom. 1:20).

35. Ibid.

It is interesting to note here that Catholic theology maintains that unbelievers should and can understand the truth of natural law apart from the teaching magisterium. Why then should they need an infallible teaching magisterium in order to understand properly divine law? Furthermore, it seems singularly inconsistent for Catholic scholars to claim they need another mind to help them interpret Scripture correctly for them when the mind God gave them is sufficient to interpret everything else, including some things much more difficult than Scripture. Many Catholic scholars, for example, are experts in interpreting classical literature, involving both the moral and religious meaning of those texts. Yet these same educated minds are said to be inadequate to obtain a reliable religious and moral interpretation of the texts of their own Scriptures.

The Catholic response that Protestants have their own teaching magisterium of modern scholarship misses the mark. First, the Catholic magisterium depends on scholarship just as much as Protestants do. Otherwise, they would not be able to translate the texts and understand them in their proper cultural context. Second, Protestants do not claim that it is necessary to have infallible scholarship in order to interpret the Bible. Further, the kind of scholarship necessary to understand the Bible does not provide a theological framework to *interpret* the Bible, as does the teaching magisterium of the Roman Catholic Church. Rather, it provides merely the necessary linguistic tools to *translate* the Bible. Finally, the skills of interpretation are the same as those for any other document, namely, to understand the meaning the author expressed in the text. For example, Catholic attorneys and judges are experts at interpreting the Constitution, and yet these same experts are told that their skills in understanding the Constitution are not adequate to obtain a reliable interpretation of the Scriptures. Why is the Roman Catholic teaching magisterium necessary for the latter while their own ability is adequate for the former?

Furthermore, it does not take an expert to interpret the essential teachings of the Bible. The New Testament was written in the vernacular of the times, the trade language of the first century, known as koine Greek. It was a book written in the common, everyday language for the common, everyday person. Likewise, the vast majority of English translations of the Bible are also written in plain English, including Catholic versions. The essential truths of the Bible can be understood by any literate person. In fact, it is an insult to the intelligence of the common person to suggest that he or she can read and understand the daily newspaper but needs an infallible teaching magisterium in order to understand God's good news in the New Testament.

Problem of Indecisiveness of the Teaching Magisterium. If an infallible teaching magisterium is needed to overcome the conflicting interpretations of Scripture, why is it that even these supposedly infallibly decisive declarations of the magisterium are also subject to conflicting interpretations? There are many hotly disputed differences among Catholic scholars on just what *ex cathedra* statements mean, including those on Scripture, tradition, Mary, and justification. Even though there may be future clarifications on some of these, the problem remains for two reasons. It shows the indecisive nature of supposedly infallible pronouncements, and, judging by past experience, even these future declarations will not settle all matters completely. Pronouncements on the inerrancy of Scripture are a case in point. In spite of infallible statements on the nature and origin of Scripture there is strong disagreement on whether the Bible is really infallible in all matters or only on matters of salvation (see Appendix D).

PHILOSOPHICAL PROBLEMS WITH INFALLIBILITY

Philosophical problems emerge from the Catholic claim of the need for an infallible teaching magisterium. Both are in the realm of epistemology, that is, how we know.

The Epistemic Problem. The supposed need for an infallible magisterium is an epistemically (Fr: *episteme*, to know) insufficient basis for rising above the level of probable knowledge. Catholic scholars admit, as they must, that they do not have infallible evidence that there is an infallible teaching magisterium. They have merely what even they believe to be only probable arguments. But if this is the case, then epistemically or apologetically there is no more than a probable basis for Catholics to believe that a supposedly infallible pronouncement of their church is true. The bottom line, then, is that they are in no better position to be certain about matters of faith and morals than are Protestants who accept only the infallibility of the Scriptures on the basis of probable arguments.

So the Catholic claim to have an infallible interpretation of the infallible Scriptures, in contrast to the Protestant claim to have only a fallible but reliable interpretation of the infallible Scriptures, only *sounds* more certain. In actuality, their basis for believing what is truly from God is no better than the Protestant, since both are based only on probable evidence, not on absolute certainty.[36]

The Problem of Death by Qualification. Once all the qualifications are placed on infallibility, both in theory and in practice, it is defrocked of its glory. For example, the pope is infallible only when:

1. speaking in fulfillment of his office as supreme pastor and teacher of all Christians;

---

36. Claiming moral certainty or the guidance of the Holy Spirit will not help either position here, since both can claim it, in which case they are mutually self-canceling claims. Further, the claim is subjective, without objective evidence to support it. Or, if objective evidence is claimed in association with it, then it is only probable evidence, and we are back to square one.

2. speaking in virtue of his supreme apostolic authority (i.e., as successor of Peter);
3. determining a doctrine of faith and morals (i.e., a doctrine expressing divine revelation);
4. imposing a doctrine to be held definitively by all;[37]
5. he is the real pope (as opposed to rival popes); and
6. his decision is ratified by an ecumenical council.[38]

Not only are all these criteria not infallibly pronounced but all are not universally accepted among Catholics. What is more, when one tries to apply these criteria to the doctrine of papal infallibility it begins to suffer "death by a thousand qualifications." For example, if the pope was not infallible when excommunicating Galileo or when teaching heresy (see examples below), then how can we be sure when he really acts infallibly? And if we cannot ever be sure, then what good is the doctrine of infallibility? Once all the qualifications are placed on it, the aura of infallibility has been stripped of its glory and stands as nakedly fallible as any other human teaching.

Historical Problems with Infallibility

In addition to biblical and philosophical problems, there are serious historical problems with the Catholic claim for infallibility. Two are of special note here.

The Problem of the Anti-Popes. Another riddle of Roman Catholicism is the scandalous specter of having more than one infallible pope at the same time—a pope and an anti-pope. *The Oxford Dictionary of the Christian Church* says "there have been about thirty-five anti-popes in the history of the Church."[39] How can there be two infallible and opposing popes at the same time? Which is the true pope? Since there is no infallible list of popes or even an infallible way to determine who is the infallible pope, the system has a serious logical problem. Further, this difficulty has had several actual historical manifestations which bring into focus the whole question of an infallible pope.[40]

Catholic apologists claim that there were not really two popes, since only one can be infallible. This is at best only a theoretical solution, not an actual one, since the faithful have no way to know for sure which one is the right one. Which one should they look to for guidance, since each pope can ex-

---

37. Dulles, "Infallibility," pp. 79–80.
38. Many Catholic scholars believe the pope speaks infallibly only in concert with all the bishops (with collegiality).
39. Cross, *Oxford Dictionary,* p. 66; A. Mercati, "The New List of the Popes," *Medieval Studies,* 9 (1947): 71–80.
40. See Pelikan, *Riddle of Roman Catholicism,* p. 40.

communicate the other—and sometimes has? Claiming that only one is the real pope does not solve the practical problem of which pope should actually be followed as the infallible guide in faith and morals.

The Problem of Galileo. Perhaps the greatest embarrassment to the self-claimed infallible church is its fallible judgment about Galileo Galilei (A.D. 1564–1642). Threatened by the implications of Galileo's discovery, the Catholic church sided with the scientifically outdated Ptolemaic geocentric universe. The church's condemnation and banishment of Galileo has caused pause for any subsequent infallible pronouncements on scientific matters. Perhaps this explains the reluctance of Rome to condemn macroevolutionary theory, allowing belief in it for fear it might prove to be true.

Galileo, using his telescope to view the heavens, adopted the Copernican view that the sun, not the earth, was the center of the solar system. This, of course, was opposed to the prevailing theological position of an earth-centered system held by the Roman Catholic Church. Trouble arose when Galileo wrote his *Letters on Sunspots* in A.D. 1613. Attention shifted from discussions of science to scriptural difficulties: "People wanted to know why Josue [Joshua] would command the sun to stand still if it never moved anyway. (See Josh. 10:12–13.) They wondered how a moving earth could be reconciled with the statement that God 'fixed the earth upon its foundation, not to be moved forever' (Ps 103:5)."[41]

In A.D. 1616, the Copernican theory was condemned at Rome.[42] The drama unfolded with Galileo writing tracts and lobbying for his cause. Aristotelian scientists, Jesuits, Dominicans, and three popes (Paul V, Gregory XV, and Urban VIII) played key roles in the conflict. Galileo was summoned by the Inquisition in 1632, tried, and on June 21, 1633, pronounced "vehemently suspected of heresy." By way of punishment, he was ordered to repeat once a week the seven penitential psalms for three years. After five months, Pope Urban VIII allowed Galileo to return to Florence, where he remained under house arrest until his death in 1642.[43]

---

41. *New Catholic Encyclopedia,* 6:252.

42. It should be noted that although the Protestant Reformers were not directly involved in this controversy, "Luther and Melanchthon condemned the work of Copernicus in unmeasured terms" (Herbermann et al., *Catholic Encyclopedia,* 6:344). Also, "Calvin and Luther accepted the Ptolemaic system, as did most astronomers in the decades following Copernicus" (Charles E. Hummel, *The Galileo Connection: Resolving Conflicts between Science and the Bible* [Downers Grove, Ill.: InterVarsity Press, 1986], p. 161). The problem, however, is more acute for Catholics since, unlike Protestants, they claim infallibility for the teaching magisterium.

43. It should be observed that Galileo was a believing Christian who had high regard for sacred Scripture. He believed that "the Holy Bible can never speak untruth—whenever its true meaning is understood" (Hummel, *Galileo Connection,* p. 105). However, he did tend to undermine the inerrancy of Scripture by focusing on its salvific purpose: "the Bible is written for 'the primary purpose of the salvation of souls and the service of God' and not to teach science" (p. 106). A similar tack is taken by contemporary liberal Catholics to deny that the Bible is inerrant in scientific matters.

After suffering many centuries of embarrassment for the church's condemnation of Galileo, in 1979 Pope John Paul II spoke to the Pontifical Academy of Science. In the address titled "Faith, Science and the Galileo Case" the pope called for a reexamination of the whole episode.[44] In 1983, while addressing the subject of the church and science, John Paul II conceded that "Galileo had 'suffered from departments of the church.'"[45] This, of course, is not a clear retraction of the condemnation, nor does it solve the problem of how an infallible pronouncement of the Catholic church could be in error.

Roman Catholic responses to this question leave something to be desired. One Catholic authority claims that, while both Paul V and Urban VIII were committed anti-Copernicans, their pronouncements were not *ex cathedra*. The decree of A.D. 1616 "was issued by the Congregation of the Index, which can raise no difficulty in regard of infallibility, this tribunal being absolutely incompetent to make a dogmatic decree."[46] As to the second trial in 1633, which also resulted in a condemnation of Galileo, this sentence is said to be of lesser importance because it "did not receive the Pope's signature."[47] Another Catholic authority states that although the theologian's treatment of Galileo was inappropriate, "the condemnation was the act of a Roman Congregation and in no way involved infallible teaching authority."[48] Still another source observes that "the condemnation of Galileo by the Inquisition had nothing to do with the question of papal infallibility, since no question of faith or morals was papally condemned *ex cathedra*."[49] Still another Catholic apologist suggests that, although the decision was a "regrettable" case of "imprudence," there was no error made by the pope, since he was not really condemned of heresy but only strongly suspected of it.

None of these ingenious solutions is very convincing, having all the earmarks of after-the-fact tinkering with the pronouncements that resulted from this episode. Galileo and his opponents would be non-plussed to discover that the serious charges leveled against him were not *"ex cathedra"* in force. And in view of the strong nature of both the condemnation and the punishment, he would certainly be surprised to hear Catholic apologists claim that he was not really being condemned for false teaching but only that "his 'proof' did not impress even astronomers of that day—nor would they impress astronomers today"![50] At any rate, the pope's condemnation of Galileo

44. Colin Brown, p. 177 n. 4.

45. Ibid. See also "Discourse to Scientists on the 350th Anniversary of the Publication of Galileo's 'Dialoghi,'" in Neuner and Dupuis, *Christian Faith*, p. 68.

46. Herbermann et al., *Catholic Encyclopedia*, p. 345.

47. Ibid., p. 346.

48. *New Catholic Encyclopedia*, 6:254.

49. John J. Delaney and James E. Tobin, "Galileo Galilei," *Dictionary of Catholic Biography* (New York: Doubleday, 1961), p. 456.

50. See William G. Most, *Catholic Apologetics Today: Answers to Modern Critics* (Rockford, Ill.: Tan Books, 1986), pp. 168–69.

only undermines the alleged infallibility of the Catholic church. Catholic apologists can always invoke their apologetic warehouse—that the pope was not really speaking infallibly on that occasion—but constant appeal to this non-verifiable distinction only weakens their case for infallibility. For it leaves us with the question of just how we can know when the church is speaking infallibly.

CONCLUSION

Despite the common creedal and doctrinal heritage of Catholics and Protestants, there are some serious differences.[51] None of these is more basic than the question of authority. Catholics affirm *de fide,* as an unchangeable part of their faith, the infallible teaching authority of the Roman church as manifested in the pope. But what Catholics affirm infallibly Protestants deny emphatically. This is an unresolvable roadblock to any ecclesiastical unity between Roman Catholicism and orthodox Protestantism. No talk about "first among equals" or "collegiality" will solve the problem. For the very concept of an infallible teaching magisterium, however composed, is contrary to the basic Protestant principle of *sola Scriptura,* the Bible alone (see chap. 10). Here we must agree to disagree. For while both sides believe the Bible is infallible, Protestants deny that the church or the pope has an infallible interpretation of it.

51. Interestingly, the problem areas for evangelicals have also been addressed by some well-known Roman Catholic authorities, such as Athanasius, Jerome, and Aquinas. The evangelical case could be made from these writers on a number of issues. For example, Jerome did not accept the Catholic apocryphal (deuterocanonical) books (see chap. 9) and Aquinas rejected the doctrine of the immaculate conception of Mary.

12

JUSTIFICATION

In spite of the common core of Augustinian belief in salvation by grace (see chap. 5), Roman Catholics and Protestants have had strong disagreement over the doctrine of justification. For one thing, while Catholics believe in the primacy and necessity of grace, Protestants believe in the exclusivity of grace; that is, only Protestants believe salvation is by grace alone *(sola gratia)* apart from any good works. Likewise, while Catholics believe in the necessity of faith (at least for adults) for justification,[1] only Protestants believe in the exclusivity of faith. The heart cry of the Reformation was "justification by faith alone" *(sola fide).*[2] The distinguishing salvation doctrines of the Reformation, then, are grace alone and faith alone (*sola gratia* and *sola fide*) through Christ alone and based on the Bible alone (see chap. 10).[3]

The Roman Catholic Church responded with the Council of Trent, declaring: "By his good works the justified man really acquires a claim to su-

1. See Bouyer, *Spirit and Forms of Protestantism,* p. 52, where he notes that, for Catholics, faith is necessary for salvation but not totally sufficient; works prompted by grace are also necessary for salvation.

2. Indeed, justification provides the foundation for the Christian life: "Luther's ETHICS is determined in its entirety, in its starting point and all its main features, by the heart and center of his theology, namely, by the justification of the sinner through the grace that is shown in Jesus Christ and received through faith alone" (Paul Althaus, *The Ethics of Martin Luther* [Philadelphia: Fortress, 1972], p. 3).

3. Lutheran scholar George Linkbeck may have allowed his ecumenical zeal to obscure his theological judgment when he suggests that, since both Catholics and Protestants accept *sola gratia,* there is no reason they can't also accept *sola fide.* This might be true were it not for the fact that Catholicism has pronounced infallibly that works are a necessary condition of final salvation. Another Lutheran scholar allows that "There is a sense in which the other two 'alones'— grace alone and Christ alone—could be accepted by the old scholastics, as Melanchthon acknowledged. The *sola fide,* Melanchthon said, was 'the chief issue on which we clash with our opponents and which we believe Christians must understand'" (Robert W. Bertram; quoted in Carl E. Braaten, *Justification: The Article by Which the Church Stands or Falls* [Minneapolis: Fortress Press, 1990], pp. 16–17).

pernatural reward from God."[4] Are we justified by faith alone or are good works a necessary condition for salvation? These questions are at the heart of the differences between Roman Catholics and evangelicals. In order to understand the issue we must first examine what the Reformers taught and how the Council of Trent responded.

ROMAN CATHOLIC TEACHING ON JUSTIFICATION

The Catholic position on justification was made infallible dogma at the Council of Trent in reaction to Martin Luther's proclamation that the just shall live by faith alone! Needless to say, Luther's view hit like a lightning bolt in an institution known for its stress on good works as necessary for salvation.[5] His initial reaction was to the Roman Catholic sale of indulgences. An overzealous salesman named Tetzel is said to have promised the potential purchasers of indulgence, "When in the box the penny rings, the soul from purgatory springs."

LUTHER'S POSITION ON JUSTIFICATION

Before Luther, the standard Augustinian position on justification stressed intrinsic justification (see chap. 5). Intrinsic justification argues that the believer is *made* righteous by God's grace, as compared to extrinsic justification, by which a sinner is forensically *declared* righteous (at best, a subterranean strain in pre-Reformation Christendom). With Luther the situation changed dramatically, although "Luther does not employ forensic terms to explain this imputation or alien righteousness. This development will come later, from others."[6] Melanchthon, Luther's great systematic theologian, did use forensic terms to describe justification. Luther, however, did hold that believers are given the alien righteousness of Christ by which alone they are able to stand before God, and not in their own righteousness. Such an imputed righteousness is extrinsic to the believer.

When Martin Luther was reassigned from Erfurt to Wittenberg he came under the influence of Johann von Staupitz (to whom this volume is dedicated). Staupitz, in addition to being the director of the cloister at Wittenberg, had a mystical bent and was a sympathetic spiritual guide. About Staupitz, Luther said, "If it had not been for Dr. Staupitz . . . I should have

---

4. Ott, *Fundamentals of Catholic Dogma*, p. 264.

5. Roman Catholics are quick to point out that the works necessary for salvation are prompted by God's grace. Nevertheless, they are meritorious works that are a necessary condition of salvation, which is precisely what the Protestant objection is.

6. Peter Toon, *Foundations for Faith: Justification and Sanctification* (Westchester, Ill.: Crossway, 1983), p. 58.

sunk in hell."[7] During the course of counseling and receiving Luther's confessions Staupitz recognized his subject's deep spiritual difficulties and inability to experience God's forgiveness. To expose Luther to the scriptural antidote for his problems Staupitz assigned Luther to the chair of Bible at the local university—a position that Staupitz himself had once occupied. Luther lectured on Paul's letters to the Romans and Galatians from the fall of A.D. 1515 to 1517. The result of his study led Luther to a new view of God: the All Terrible is also the All Merciful.

Luther discovered that in the Greek used by the apostle Paul, the word "justice" has a double meaning: the first is a strict enforcement of the law; the second is "a process of the sort which sometimes takes place if the judge suspends the sentence . . . and thereby instills such resolve that the man is reclaimed."[8] This latter meaning of justice is necessary because "The sinner cannot ever attain any righteousness of his own: he merits or deserves only condemnation." But God has "freely opted to receive us to Himself . . . to a fellowship that we from our side had broken and could never mend."[9]

When studying the meaning of Romans 1:16–17 Luther came to a revolutionary discovery.

> Night and day I pondered until I saw the connection between the justice of God and the statement that "the just shall live by faith." Then I grasped that the justice of God is that righteousness by which through grace and sheer mercy God justifies us through faith. Thereupon I felt myself to be reborn and to have gone through open doors into paradise. The whole of Scripture took on new meaning, and whereas before the "justice of God" had filled me with hate, now it became to me inexpressibly sweet in great love. This passage became to me the gate to heaven.[10]

Amid the Protestant stress on Luther's discovery it is sometimes forgotten that Luther also believed in a progressive sense of the word "justification." For example, he said: "For we understand that a man who is justified is not already righteous but moving toward righteousness (WA 391, 83; LW 34, 152)." Further, "Our justification is not yet complete. . . . It is still under construction. It shall, however, be completed in the resurrection of the dead (WA 391, 252)."[11] This sense of progressive justification is what many Protestants call "sanctification," the process by which we are *made* righteous, not an act

---

7. Roland H. Bainton, *Here I Stand: A Life of Martin Luther* (Nashville: Abingdon, 1978), p. 40. This is a valuable short work on the life and ministry of Martin Luther.

8. Ibid., p. 49.

9. James Atkinson, *Martin Luther: Prophet to the Church Catholic* (Grand Rapids: Eerdmans, 1983), p. 133.

10. Cited by Bainton, *Here I Stand*, p. 65.

11. Cited by Paul Althaus, *The Theology of Martin Luther* (Philadelphia: Fortress, 1984), p. 237 n. 63.

by which one is *declared* righteous. Toon adds, "Justification by faith is both an event and a process. What later Protestants were to divide, Luther kept together. He is quite clear that there is a moment when a sinner is actually justified by faith. He then has the righteousness of another, the alien righteousness of Christ, imputed to him." However, "this is the beginning of a journey toward a time (following the resurrection of the dead in the age to come) when he will in fact possess a perfect righteousness created in him by the Spirit of God."[12]

Luther also suggested that the believer is righteous in the eyes of God and yet sinful at the same time. "For Luther, faith is the right (or righteous) relationship to God. Sin and righteousness thus coexist; we remain sinners inwardly, but we are righteous extrinsically in the sight of God."[13] However, "Luther is not necessarily implying that this co-existence of sin and righteousness is a permanent condition." Instead, for Luther, "the existence of sin does not negate our status as Christians."[14]

THE CATHOLIC CHURCH'S RESPONSE TO LUTHER

The Council of Trent was the Catholic response to Lutheranism. No proper understanding of the Catholic view of justification is possible apart from an understanding of the decrees of the Council of Trent. The council considered six questions concerning justification. (1) Is justification only judicial in nature (extrinsic) or is there also an intrinsic (sanctifying) work involved? (2) What is the relationship between faith and good works? (3) Does the will have an active role in justification? (4) How are justification and sacraments such as the Eucharist, baptism, and penance related? (5) Can believers know with certainty they are justified? (6) Can people incline themselves toward justification, and if so, is this inclination to be understood as meritorious?[15]

Study on these questions began in June 1546. In January 1547 the council participants agreed on a final formula for justification. The process had been long and arduous and all of the theological schools weighed in with opinions on a great variety of complicated scholastic theological distinctions. We will examine the conclusions to the six questions mentioned above.

First, although several council members recognized an extrinsic element in justification (thereby approaching the Reformers on this point),[16] the con-

---

12. Toon, *Foundations for Faith*, pp. 58–59.

13. Joanna McGrath and Alister McGrath, *The Dilemma of Self-Esteem: The Cross and Christian Confidence* (Wheaton: Crossway, 1992), p. 98.

14. Ibid., p. 99. This is a helpful volume dealing with the tensions between the gospel and modern psychological theories of self-esteem.

15. McGrath, *Iustitia Dei*, 2:69.

16. See Hans Küng, *Justification: The Doctrine of Karl Barth and a Catholic Reflection* (New York: Nelson, 1964), p. 218. It would be proper to say that Trent allows for but does not teach forensic justification as one element in the overall process of justification.

sensus view was that "the opinion that a sinner may be justified *solely* as a matter of reputation or imputation . . . is rejected."[17] Therefore, "Justification is thus defined in terms of a man becoming, and not *merely* being reputed as, righteous."[18]

Second, in that Trent understands justification in two senses (the second corresponding to the Reformed doctrine of sanctification), this second justification requires good works as a condition for ultimate justification. "It is thus both possible and necessary to keep the law of God."[19]

Third, taking into account original sin, Trent states that sin has affected the human race. Therefore, "man is incapable of redeeming himself. Free will is not destroyed, but is weakened and debilitated by the Fall,"[20] something which Luther rejected in his *Bondage of the Will*. According to Trent, "If anyone shall say that man's free will moved and aroused by God does not cooperate by assenting to God who looses and calls . . . let him be anathema."[21] (It is important to note that "anathema" is a decree of excommunication, not automatic damnation.) So as one Catholic author puts it, "the sinner indeed cooperates with this grace, at least in the sense of not sinfully rejecting it."[22] Of course, most Protestants agree with this. Many Protestants, however, Calvinists in particular, quickly add (as would Catholic Thomists) that it is God by his grace who brings about this cooperation. But he does this without destroying our free choice.

Fourth, in order to understand the pronouncements on the sacraments, one must remember that Trent understood justification in two ways: the first and second phases which Catholic scholars refer to as "initial" and "progressive" justification respectively. Baptism is operative in the first or initial justification, since grace to overcome original sin is "mediated" to us through baptism.[23] Both the Eucharist and penance pertain to the second or progressive sense of justification, and such justification (i.e., righteousness) is said to be "increased" by participation in these sacraments. There is, of course, a

---

17. McGrath, *Iustitia Dei*, 2:72, emphasis added. The words "solely" and "merely" in these quotes indicate that Trent did not reject forensic justification as such.

18. Ibid., emphasis added.

19. Ibid., p. 84.

20. Ibid., p. 81.

21. Denzinger, 814, p. 258. For a good treatment of the Council of Trent from a Roman Catholic view, see H. Jedin, *History of the Council of Trent*, trans. F. C. Eckhoff (St. Louis and London, 1947). The standard Protestant work is Martin Chemnitz (1522–86), *Examination of the Council of Trent* (St. Louis: Concordia, 1971).

22. H. George Anderson, *Justification by Faith* (Minneapolis: Augsburg, 1985), p. 34.

23. A detailed treatment of the sacrament of baptism is beyond the scope of this chapter. There are differences concerning it, not only between Roman Catholics and evangelicals, but within the Protestant community as well. It should be noted that Luther had difficulty formulating his understanding of baptism in light of his concept of justification. On Luther and baptism, see Paul Althaus, *The Theology of Martin Luther* (Philadelphia: Fortress, 1966), pp. 353–74, and Appendix E.

third or "ultimate" stage of justification by which—providing one had not committed a mortal sin—one is allowed into heaven.

Fifth, due to the stress that the Reformers placed on the concept of assurance of salvation, Trent was forced to deal with the subject. McGrath claims that they issued "an explicit condemnation of the Lutheran doctrine of assurance as an assertion contrary to proper Christian humility."[24] However, the explicit condemnation deals with "infallible certainty," which many Catholic scholars point out is not necessary, if indeed it is possible. In fact, "In many ways Roman [Catholic] dogmatics have pointed out that Rome's rejection of personal assurance of salvation does not mean the proclamation of a religion of uninterrupted anxiety."[25] For the Roman Catholic there is "an intermediate position between the assurance of faith and doubt. This position is that of moral certainty which excludes any anxiety and despair."[26] Thus, Christians can be said to have "relative," not absolute (i.e., infallible), certainty of salvation.[27]

Sixth, Trent states that our initial justification must be seen as a "gift." Thus, it comes as a surprise to many Protestants that Roman Catholics believe that *"If anyone shall say that man can be justified before God by his own works which are done . . . without divine grace through Christ Jesus: let him be anathema."*[28] Further, *"nothing that precedes justification, whether faith or works, merits the grace of justification. For if it is by grace, it is no more by works; otherwise, as the apostle says, grace is no more grace."*[29] The new *Catechism of the Catholic Church* says clearly: "The merits of our good works are gifts of the divine goodness" (2009).[30]

It is only fair to point out here that when Catholic scholars cite James 2:24 ("we are justified by works") they do not mean this initial justification which comes only by grace. Rather, they are referring to progressive justification (growth in righteousness) which Protestants call sanctification. Trent does assert, however, that works are necessary for salvation in the progressive and eventual senses, making it dogma that "by his good works the justified man really acquires a claim to supernatural reward from God."[31] It is precisely here that Catholics and evangelicals disagree.

---

24. McGrath, *Iustitia Dei*, 2:78.

25. Gerrit C. Berkouwer, *The Conflict with Rome* (Philadelphia: Presbyterian and Reformed, 1958), p. 114.

26. Bernhard Bartmann, *Lehrbuch der Dogmatik*, II, p. 109; quoted in ibid., p. 115.

27. One Dominican theologian suggests that Luther and Trent are not as far apart as is often thought, contending that "a very different picture from that offered by the controversial theology of the past would emerge if the real content of the teachings of both confessions were once given expression" (Stephanus Pfürtner, *Luther and Aquinas—A Conversation: Our Salvation, Its Certainty and Peril*, trans. Edward Quinn [London: Darton, Longman and Todd, 1964], p. 11).

28. Trent, as cited in Denzinger, *Sources of Catholic Dogma*, no. 811, emphasis added.

29. Trent, as cited in ibid., no. 801, emphasis added.

30. (*Libreria Editrice Vaticana*, 1994), p. 487.

31. Ott, *Fundamentals of Catholic Dogma*, p. 264.

CATHOLIC ARGUMENTS
FOR MERITORIOUS JUSTIFICATION

Since the defense of forensic justification goes hand-in-hand with the rejection of the Catholic teaching on merit, the doctrine of good works will be discussed first. The arguments will be divided into theological, biblical, and traditional ones.

THEOLOGICAL ARGUMENTS FOR THE DOCTRINE OF MERIT

Catholic dogma states: "By his good works the justified man really acquires a claim to supernatural reward from God."[32] Of course, this demand is not intrinsic; it is only because God has placed himself in this situation because of his promise to reward good works. Further, eternal life is given to us on the grounds of our good works.[33] Thus the Council of Trent declared that "those who work well 'unto the end' [Matt. 10:22], and who trust in God, life eternal is to be proposed, both as a grace mercifully promised to the sons of God through Christ Jesus, 'and as a recompense' which is . . . to be faithfully given to their good works and merit."[34] It adds, "If anyone shall say that the good works of the man justified are in such a way the gift of God that they are not also the good merits of him who is justified, or that the one justified by the good works . . . does not truly merit increase of grace, eternal life, and the attainment of eternal life (if he should die in grace), and also an increase of glory; let him be anathema."[35]

ARGUMENT FROM SCRIPTURE

Ott argues that "According to Holy Writ, eternal blessedness in heaven is the reward for good works performed on this earth, and rewards and merit are correlative concepts."[36] He offers the following Scripture in support: "'Be glad and rejoice, for your reward is very great in heaven' (Mt. 5, 12). . . . 'Come, ye blessed of my Father, possess you the kingdom prepared for you from the foundation of the world. For I was hungry, and you gave me to eat' (Mt. 25, 34 et seq.)." He adds, "St. Paul, who stresses grace so much, also em-

---

32. Ibid.
33. While Protestants sometimes speak of the "reward" of eternal life in the sense of something graciously given by God, they do not believe this reward is based on our works but only on God's grace received through our faith alone.
34. Denzinger, *Sources of Catholic Dogma*, no. 809, p. 257.
35. Ibid., no. 842, p. 261.
36. Ott, *Fundamentals of Catholic Dogma*, p. 264.

phasized on the other hand, the meritorious nature of good works performed with grace, by teaching that the reward is in proportion to the works: 'He [God] will render to every man according to his own labour' (Rom. 2, 6)."[37] Other similar passages are cited (1 Cor. 3:8; Col. 3:24; Heb. 10:35; 11:6). He concludes, "he thereby shows that the good works of the just establish a legal claim *(meritum de condigno)* to reward on God. Cf. Hebr. 6, 10."[38]

ARGUMENTS FROM TRADITION

Catholic theology claims: "From the times of the Apostolic Fathers, Tradition attests the meritoriousness of good works." For example, Ignatius of Antioch wrote to Polycarp, "Where there is great effort there is rich gain" (I, 3). Justin and Tertullian are also cited in defense of merit. Tertullian asserted that "the man who performs good works can be said to make God his debtor."[39] Even though God is not indebted in any intrinsic sense, nonetheless, works are said to be the basis for getting this merit.[40] Ott claims that "natural reason cannot prove the reality of supernatural merit since this rests on the free Divine promise of reward." However, "the general conscience of men bears witness to the appropriateness of a supernatural reward for supernaturally good deeds freely performed."[41]

AN EVANGELICAL RESPONSE
TO CATHOLIC ARGUMENTS FOR SALVATION BY MERIT

We have already noted that the Council of Trent declared that no works prior to justification are meritorious.[42] Nonetheless, several significant differences between the official Roman Catholic and orthodox Protestant views on salvation remain. Before stating the basis for the Protestant position, a response to the Catholic arguments in favor of merit is in order.

A CRITIQUE OF THE ROMAN CATHOLIC
VIEW OF JUSTIFICATION

With all due recognition to the common Augustinian core of salvation by grace (see chap. 5), there are some important differences between the Roman Cath-

---

37. Ibid., p. 265.
38. Ibid.
39. Tertullian, *De paenitentia* 2; 1.323.44–46.
40. Of course, in Catholic theology these works grow out of faith, but it is the works that are the basis for the merit and which are necessary for obtaining eternal life.
41. Ott, *Fundamentals of Catholic Dogma*, p. 265.
42. Council of Trent, "Decree on Justification," chap. 8.

olic and evangelical views of justification. Unfortunately the noble but unsuccessful recent statement by "Evangelicals and Catholics Together" lacked precision in this very area, speaking of a common belief that "we are justified by grace through faith."[43] What it failed to note, however, is what the Reformation was fought over, namely, that Scripture teaches, as Protestants affirm, that *we are saved by grace alone through faith alone.* As we will see, there is a common belief in salvation by grace, but Roman Catholics hold that justification takes place at baptism of infants, which is long before they can believe in any conscious sense. Further, as the Catholic doctrine of merit reveals, they do not believe that salvation is by grace alone *(sola gratia),* since meritorious works are also necessary, at least for those that live beyond infancy. Further, for evangelicals, salvation is not simply "through faith" but "by faith *alone" (sola fide).* Since this was at the very heart of the Reformation, many evangelicals refuse to sign the statement since they believe it would betray the Reformation. Indeed, their protest led to a follow-up statement which strikes a more distinctively Protestant note: "We understand the statement that 'we are justified by grace through faith because of Christ,' in terms of the substitutionary atonement and imputed righteousness of Christ, leading to full assurance of eternal salvation; we seek to testify in all circumstances and contexts to this, the historic Protestant understanding of salvation by faith alone *(sola fide).*"

Many criticisms of the Catholic view of justification revolve around the concept of merit that was made into infallible dogma of the Roman Catholic Church at the Council of Trent. The Catholic doctrine of meritorious works has been a target of Protestants since the Reformation. For Luther and his followers, it is "misleading to speak of any rewards as 'merited.'"[44] Indeed, the Reformers believed that at Trent the Roman Catholic Church apostatized and denied the true gospel. "For I thoroughly believe, more firmly than I believe in God, that they are acquainted with more human doctrine, and also with more villainy, because they are proving it before my very eyes by the things they are doing, and so they are apostles, evangelists, and prophets just as little as they are the church; that is to say, they are the devil's apostles, evangelists, and prophets. The true apostles, evangelists, and prophets preach God's word, not against God's word."[45]

---

43. "Evangelicals and Catholics Together: The Christian Mission in the Third Millennium," final draft (29 March 1994). This statement was signed by noted Catholics like James Hitchcock, William Bentley Ball, Peter Kreeft, Cardinal John O'Connor, and Richard Neuhaus. Evangelicals signing it included Chuck Colson, Os Guinness, J. I. Packer, Bill Bright, and Richard Land. Conspicuous by their absence were the names of top evangelical theologians who are experts on Roman Catholicism, such as Harold O. J. Brown, Carl Henry, David Wells, and R. C. Sproul. Many of these have expressed criticism of the statement (see Appendix F).

44. Anderson, *Justification by Faith,* p. 54 (citing the *Apology for the Augsburg Confession,* 4:194).

45. George Salmon, *The Infallibility of the Church* (London: John Murray Publishing, 1914), p. 347.

It confuses reward and merit. While Catholics wish to remind us that the whole doctrine of merit should be viewed in the context of grace,[46] they overlook the fact that Scripture teaches that grace and meritorious works are mutually exclusive. Part of the reason for the difficulty is that the Catholic use of the word "reward" has an equivocal sense that leads to a confusion between a reward based on grace and one based on merit (i.e., on works), albeit prompted by grace. Often the problem seems to stem from a fallacious inference that simply because something is prompted by grace it is not obtained by merit. Just because the previous graciousness of a friend may prompt one to do a job for him that one would not otherwise have accepted does not mean that the wages earned from it were not at least partly merited, even if they were higher wages than one deserved. Thus, neither merit in the strict sense of what is justly earned nor merit which is based in part on what is earned but goes beyond that by God's goodness is compatible with grace.

Catholic theology rightly points out that the Bible sometimes speaks of eternal life as a reward (e.g., Gal. 6:8) that one can "inherit" (Luke 18:18).[47] In this sense, however, works are not a condition of salvation;[48] salvation is a gift of grace received by faith alone apart from meritorious works. None of us works for an inheritance; it is something graciously *given* to us by a benefactor. If, however, we are "rewarded" for our work by salvation or eternal life, then it is not truly and solely God's grace, despite Catholic protests to the contrary. When one is rewarded for works, the reward is not a matter of grace, since the payment is *owed* (at least in part) for work done. As Paul said emphatically, "But if by grace, it is no longer because of works; otherwise grace would no longer be grace" (Rom. 11:6). It is in this latter sense that the New Testament clearly speaks against obtaining salvation (whether justification or sanctification) as a reward (i.e., wage)[49] for work done. For the Scriptures insist that "a worker's wage is credited not as a gift, but as something due" (Rom. 4:4). If the Catholic concept of merit (that progressive justification [= sanctification] is obtained by good works) is true, then the grace of sanctification would be bestowed, at least in part, on the basis of good works. But what is worked for is not of grace, and what is

---

46. See Avery Dulles in Anderson, *Justification by Faith*, p. 274.

47. The New Testament also speaks of eternal life in the sense of the kind or degree of reward one will inherit, based on the kind of faith that produces works which one performs. Gal. 6:6–10 seems to fit in this category, since it speaks of believers reaping "eternal life" by what they sow in their life.

48. While works are not a condition of faith they are a concomitant and fruit of true faith (James 2:24).

49. This is true whether the wage is an equal payment or an overpayment for work done. Salvation is a complete gift from God for which no work can be done to merit it (Rom. 4:4–5). Otherwise, Christ's sacrifice was not the complete payment for our sin and we have some ground for boasting, both of which are rejected by Scripture (cf. John 19:30; Eph. 2:8–9; Heb. 10:11–18).

grace, and what is given by grace is not obtained by works (Rom. 4:4; Eph. 2:8–9). So the Catholic concept of merit as a necessary condition for obtaining eternal life or ultimate justification is contrary to this clear affirmation of Holy Writ.

It makes works a condition of eternal life. The Council of Trent declared clearly that "those who work well 'unto the end' [Matt. 10:22], and who trust in God, life eternal is to be faithfully given to their good works and merit."[50] Even the new *Catechism of the Catholic Church* which tends to state doctrine in a way less objectionable to Protestants declares that *"the merit of good works is to be attributed* in the first place to the grace of God, then *to the faithful"* (2008, emphasis added, p. 486). Hence, it is grace *plus* good works. By contrast the Bible declares clearly and emphatically that "the wages of sin is death, but *the gift of God is eternal life* in Christ Jesus our Lord" (Rom. 6:23, emphasis added). Further, in direct opposition to the Catholic position, the Bible guarantees that eternal life is a present possession of those who believe. Jesus said: "I say to you, whoever hears my words and believes in the one who sent me has [present tense] eternal life and will not come into condemnation, but is [currently] passed from death to life" (John 5:24). But according to the Roman Catholic view, one must await a final justification at death to know whether one has eternal life and will not see God's condemnation. This same truth that eternal life is a present possession of the believer is repeated over and over in Scripture. John records Jesus proclaiming, "Whoever believes in the Son *has* eternal life" (John 3:36), and later adds, "I write these things to you so that you may *know* that you *have* eternal life" (1 John 5:13, emphasis added). Catholic dogma excludes Catholics from claiming that they can know with assurance that, if they were to die, they would have eternal life.[51]

In the Gospel of John only one condition is laid down for obtaining eternal life: belief (e.g., John 3:16, 36; 5:24; 20:31). If salvation were not by faith alone then John's whole message would be misleading, since it states that there is only one condition for salvation when actually there are two: faith plus works. Indeed, John states explicitly that the only "work" necessary for salvation is to believe. When asked, "What can we do to accomplish the works of God?" Jesus replied, "This is the work of God, that you *believe* in the one he sent" (John 6:29, emphasis added). There simply is nothing else we may do in exchange for our salvation. Jesus did it all (John 19:30; Heb. 10:14).

---

50. Denzinger, *Sources of Catholic Dogma*, no. 809, p. 257.

51. But Protestantism teaches that we can know with assurance right now that we have eternal life. This is true of Calvinists (and even Armenians, who believe they could later commit a serious sin and lose the gift of eternal life). But this is not true for a Catholic that cannot know with confidence that he possesses eternal life right now.

It makes works of sanctification a condition of ultimate salvation. The Council of Trent affirmed: "When he [Paul] characterizes the eternal reward as 'the crown of justice which the Lord, the just judge, will render' (2 Tim. 4, 8), he thereby shows that the good works of the just establish a legal claim to reward on God."[52] Of course, this "legal" claim is not intrinsic but only because God has promised it. Nonetheless, it is a promise to give us salvation based in part on our works. "If anyone shall say that the good works of the man justified are in such a way the gifts of God that they are not also the good merits of him who is justified, or that the one justified by the good works, which are done by him through the grace of God and the merit of Jesus Christ (whose living member he is), does not truly merit increase of grace, eternal life, and the attainment of that eternal life (if he should die in grace), and also an increase of glory: let him be anathema."[53] But one cannot work for a gift (Rom. 4:4–5). We work *from* our salvation but never *for* it (Gal. 3:11; Eph. 2:8–10). We are not saved *by* our works but in order to *do* good works.

Even granting that, for infants, works are not a condition for receiving initial righteousness (= justification), nonetheless, Catholic theology makes works a condition for progressive righteousness (= sanctification). In other words, one cannot receive a right standing before God by which one has the divine promise of salvation (eternal life) without engaging in works of righteousness. But this is precisely what Scripture says is not the case: It is "not because of any righteous deeds that we had done but because of his mercy, he saved us" (Titus 3:5).[54] "It is not from works, so no one may boast," wrote Paul (Eph. 2:9). To repeat the apostle, "if by grace, it is no longer because of works; otherwise grace would no longer be grace" (Rom. 11:6). A right standing before God comes by grace through faith alone! Grace means unmerited favor, and reward based on works is merited. Hence, grace and works are no more compatible than is an unmerited merit! Trent overreacted to Luther, and in so doing, obfuscated the purity and clarity of the gospel of God's grace.

The Catholic response that not all Protestants agree that one has the promise of heaven on the basis of initial justification[55] alone (Arminians believe people can lose their salvation) misses the mark. For the question is not how we *keep* salvation after we get it, but how we *get it* to begin with. It is a fact that some Protestants (evangelicals) do believe like Catholics that one can *lose* his or her salvation (a belief the authors do not share), but this

---

52. Cited in Ott, *Fundamentals of Catholic Dogma*, p. 265.

53. Denzinger, *Sources of Catholic Dogma*, no. 842, p. 809.

54. This cannot apply only to initial justification as Catholics claim, since the present tense ("renewing") is used in this text.

55. That is, by initial (forensic) justification and its concomitant benefits, such as sonship, the forgiveness of sins, imputed (alien) righteousness, etc.

in no way justifies the Catholic belief that eternal life cannot be *obtained* without meritorious works. But as we have seen, the Bible makes it clear that eternal life, not just initial (and some say forfeitable) justification, is a *present* gift that believers possess (Luke 23:42–43; John 3:16; 5:24; Rom. 6:23). So the fact that some Protestants believe people can lose their salvation (eternal life) in no way justifies making works a condition for *obtaining* this salvation. The fact is that, even once the confusing terminology is cleared up and we understand that by eventual justification Catholics mean what Protestants call justification and sanctification, the official Catholic position is unbiblical. For it insists that works are necessary for salvation; that is, *they are a condition for obtaining a right standing before God that entails the promise of heaven.*[56] This is precisely what the Reformation rejected.

It confuses working for *and working* from *salvation.* Put in traditional terms, Catholicism fails to recognize the important difference between working *for* salvation and working *from* salvation. We do not work in order to get salvation; rather, we work because we have already gotten it. God works salvation *in* us by justification, and by God's grace we work it *out* in sanctification (Phil. 2:12–13). But neither justification nor sanctification can be merited by works; they are given by grace. Gifts cannot be worked for, only wages can. As Paul declared, "when one does not work, yet believes in the one who justifies the ungodly, his faith is credited for righteousness" (Rom. 4:5).

In spite of the fact that the Catholic understanding of salvation does not logically eliminate forensic justification, it nevertheless obscures it. For when one fails to make a clear distinction between forensic *justification* and practical *sanctification,*[57] then the good works Catholics believe are needed

56. Catholic insistence that a right standing can be obtained without works is insufficient because, for Catholics, this standing does not entail the gift of eternal life. The Catholic argument that this gift is merited by works (though not deservedly earned) also is wanting. For even if one is given, say, a million dollars in exchange for a loaf of bread, the person obviously did not earn it but did do *some* work and, hence, it was not by grace alone. Likewise, if someone spends a *lifetime of works* (however long) as a condition for receiving eternal life, then it was clearly not by grace alone. Furthermore, the argument by some Catholic apologists that one need not work for eternal life but simply avoid mortal sin misses the mark for two important reasons. First, the question is not how one *loses* salvation but how he *obtains* it to begin with. Second, and most importantly, regardless of whether one only loses salvation by a mortal sin (and not by lack of works) or not, if he lives after initial justification he still has to work as a condition for receiving eternal life. If this is so, then salvation is not totally by grace.

57. Of course there can be forensic or positional aspects of sanctification as well (cf. 1 Cor. 1:2; Heb. 10:10). We speak here of forensic justification in the sense of the legal aspect of the initial act of salvation, namely, God's graciously saving us from the *penalty* of sin. Sanctification, at least in the practical sense, is salvation from the *power* of sin in our lives ("glorification" is being saved from the very *presence* of sin when we enter heaven). There are also non-forensic (or actual) aspects of the initial state of salvation, such as our being made a "new creation" (2 Cor. 5:17) and becoming "sons of God" (John 1:12) at the initial moment of salvation.

for sanctification tend to obscure the fact that works are not needed for justification. Perhaps this is why hundreds of thousands of Catholics are coming to know Christ personally outside of the Catholic church. Indeed, this may be why Catholicism has not produced any of the great evangelists (such as Wesley, Whitfield, Sunday, Moody, and Graham) and has no widely circulated equivalent to "The Four Spiritual Laws" or other simple plan of salvation.

It makes a false distinction between "works" and "works of the law." The New Testament verses against salvation by works are clearly opposed to the Catholic teaching that salvation can be merited. In order to counter this Roman Catholic scholars have made an artificial distinction between "works of the law" (which they admit are not a condition for salvation) and works (which they insist are a condition of salvation). But contrary to the Catholic claim, Paul's statements against "works" cannot be limited to only "works of the [Mosaic] law" (such as circumcision) but extend equally to all kinds of meritorious good works, for all such works will in one way or another be works in accordance with God's law. They would not be *good* works if they were not in accordance with God's standard of goodness, namely, his law. Since God is the standard of all righteousness, it follows that all true works of righteousness will be according to his law and nature. It is only *our* righteousness (= self-righteousness) that is abhorrent in God's eyes (cf. Isa. 64:6; Rom. 10:3). It makes no difference whether these works are prompted by grace; they are still meritorious works as a condition for eternal life. They are not based on grace and *grace alone*. That is, part of the basis for obtaining eternal life is meritorious works.

Further, when condemning works for salvation Paul does not limit himself to "works of the law" but sometimes simply refers to "works" or "works of righteousness" (cf. Eph. 2:8–9; Titus 3:5–7). Contrary to the Catholic view, the Ephesians passage is clearly aimed at Gentiles with no suggestion of works of the Jewish law such as circumcision.[58] Nor does the Jew-Gentile conflict diminish the fact that he is speaking to Gentiles about "works" other than those unique to the Jewish law. And the argument offered by some Catholics that the boasting mentioned in Ephesians 2:9 is an indication that it is Jewish boasting (since they boasted about works of the law) is implausible for many reasons. First, unbelieving Jews are not the only ones who boast in their good works; pride is a condition of all fallen creatures, not just Jewish ones. Furthermore, in this context Paul explicitly addresses the issue of Gentiles who were "alienated from the community of Israel" (Eph. 2:11–12), not Jews. Likewise, Titus 3:5–7 does not refer to "works of the law" but simply

---

58. This is evident from the fact that Paul's audience is (predominantly) Gentiles (Eph. 2:11) who were "alienated from the community of Israel" (2:12).

"works of righteousness."[59] The fact that the tense being applied to salvation refers to the past does not help the Catholic explanation that this refers only to what Protestants call justification, not to sanctification. Paul is speaking to people who have already been saved and therefore his words would naturally be in the past tense.[60]

Also, the Catholic claim that "works" are sometimes an abbreviation of "works of the law" (e.g., Rom. 3:27–28) fails for several reasons. Even if "works of the law" were sometimes summarized as "works," it would not mean the reverse is necessarily true. All works of the law are works, but not all works are works of the law.

Further, when Paul is speaking to Gentiles (who, as Rom. 2:14 says, "do not have the [Mosaic] law"), he does not speak of them performing works of the Mosaic law as such but simply to "works" (e.g., Eph. 2:8–9). They too are said not to be justified by works (Rom. 3:21–24). To be sure, in the New Testament "works" often arise in the context of circumcision (cf. Rom. 4; Gal. 3). But this is only because that was the specific situation that occasioned Paul's condemnation of any kind of works deemed necessary for salvation (cf. Acts 15). To limit all of his condemnations of "works" to only works of the Mosaic law is like limiting God's condemnation of homosexuality in the Old Testament (cf. Lev. 18:22; 20:13)[61] to Jews since these passages occur only in the Jewish law which was written to Jews! And to grant that a moral law (e.g., natural law) exists outside the law of Moses is to grant the Protestant point that "works" here are not just limited to works of the Mosaic law. The truth is that the condemnations are more broadly applicable than the immediate context in which they arose. The same is true of Paul's condemnation of meritorious "works" as a means of salvation. To limit Paul's condemnation to works of self-righteousness as opposed to meritorious works is reading into the text a distinction that is not there. What is more, if our works contributed anything to our obtaining salvation, then we would have grounds to boast and would still come under Paul's condemnation.

Finally, the basic moral character of God expressed in the Ten Commandments is the same as that expressed through the natural law to all people. The fact that someone is not consciously or deliberately doing works according to the law of Moses does not mean that the basic moral standard is

---

59. Some Catholics argue that this refers to works of Jewish almsgiving, since the concepts parallel Jewish literature. This is implausible since it is contrary to the context of the Titus passage, almsgiving not being in view. Further, even if Jewish almsgiving was a work of righteousness, not all works of righteousness were acts of Jewish almsgiving.

60. Further, this stretched interpretation is contrary to the Catholic claim that the "washing of regeneration" in this passage is baptism. Since they practice infant baptism, this would have to refer to initial justification, not to progressive justification (= righteousness), which evangelicals call sanctification.

61. In fact, God said that the pagans, who do not have the Mosaic law, would be condemned for homosexual practices as well (cf. Lev. 18:24–26).

not the same. In one sense all moral "works" are "works of the law," in that they are in accord with the moral principles expressed in the law. This is why the apostle Paul said that "when the Gentiles who do not have the law [of Moses], by nature observe the prescriptions of the law . . . they show that the demands of the law written in their hearts" (Rom. 2:14–15). In the final analysis, when it comes to the *moral*[62] demands of the law, there is no substantial difference between "works of righteousness" and the "works of the law." Thus, the Catholic argument that Paul meant the latter but not the former is a formal distinction without a real difference. The simple truth is that no works of any kind merit salvation. Eternal life is a gift received only by faith (John 3:16, 36; 5:24; Rom. 6:23).

It is similar to the error of Galatianism. By insisting that works are not a condition for obtaining initial justification (righteousness) but only for sanctification (progressive righteousness) Catholics do not avoid the charge of soteriological error. Claiming that sanctification is by works, even if justification is not, seems akin to the error that Paul addressed in the Book of Galatians. The Galatian Christians were already justified, or declared righteous, in the forensic sense (or, to use Catholic terminology, they had already received "initial justification"). They were "brethren" (Gal. 1:11; 6:1). They were "in Christ" (Gal. 2:4). Otherwise, they would not have been in danger of "falling from grace" (Gal. 5:4) as a way of living the Christian life. They had initial (forensic) justification but were in danger of losing their sanctification (progressive justification).

Paul's warning to them clearly related to their sanctification. His fear was not that they would *lose* their initial (forensic) justification but that they would fall back into bondage to the law (Gal. 2:4). Even if Paul did mean that they would lose their justification (as Arminians say) it merely intensifies the problem with the Catholic view, for then the failure to do good works results in the loss of both sanctification and justification. In this indirect sense, failure to do good works is a means of forfeiting one's (initial) justification too! Paul was afraid they would fall from grace as a means of *continuing* in the Christian life, not as a means of *obtaining* it to begin with, since they already had it (Gal. 3:3). To state it another way, if their initial righteousness was given by grace though faith, why should they think they could progress in righteousness in any other way than by grace through faith? In short, he did not want them to replace grace with works as the means of sanctification. This is evident from his pivotal plea: "Having *begun*

---

62. This, of course, is not true of what are often called ceremonial or civil aspects of the Mosaic law; they were unique to Israel. And it is only true of the *duty* to obey God's moral precepts, not the *punishment* for not obeying them which was often more severe in the Old Testament (e.g., capital punishment for fornication, adultery, homosexuality, rape, and even an incorrigible child).

236

in the Spirit, are you *now* being made perfect in the flesh?" (Gal. 3:3 NKJV, emphasis added).

Clearly, the message of Galatians is: You are not only justified by faith alone, but you are also being sanctified by faith alone. For "without faith it is impossible to please him [God]" (Heb. 11:6). Melanchthon articulated this Reformation principle when he argued that "the importance of faith not be restricted to the beginning of justification."[63] Neither initial righteousness (justification) nor progressive righteousness (sanctification) is conditioned on meritorious works. Rather, both are received by grace through faith apart from any works of righteousness. Failure to understand that sanctification *and* justification are by grace through faith alone is the error of Galatianism. It seems to be the same error made by the Council of Trent.

It should be noted that Paul's reference to "false brothers" *(pseudadelphos)* is not to the believers in Galatia who had adopted their erroneous teaching about needing to keep the law of Moses as a means of sanctification. Paul was referring to false teachers (Judaizers) who were "secretly brought in" from the outside (Gal. 2:4). Since the Galatians had already been justified by faith alone, the danger of the Judaizers' teaching was that the true believers at Galatia would adopt this view as a means of progressive sanctification. This would have been a serious error, since it would have obscured the necessity of the pure grace of God as the condition for their progressive sanctification, just as it was the condition for their initial justification.[64]

It confuses salvation and service. All the texts cited by Catholics about reward for works are not really speaking about reward of *salvation* (whether it be justification or sanctification); they are talking about rewards for *service*. Justification is by faith alone and not by works (Rom. 4:5). It is true that all who are saved by God's grace through faith will be rewarded for their works in Christ (1 Cor. 3:10–14; 2 Cor. 5:10). These works, however, have nothing to do with *whether* we will be in heaven, but only with *what status* we will have there. As Jesus said, some of the saved will reign over ten cities and others over five (Luke 19:17–19), but all believers will be in his kingdom. The reward-for-works verses all speak of *rewards* for those who will be in the kingdom, not whether one will *be* in the kingdom. By contrast, in Roman Catholic theology one's progressive sanctification does affect whether one will make it to heaven. What a person receives at the moment of initial justification, apart from progressive sanctification, does not suffice to get one into heaven (unless, of course, the person dies immediately after regenera-

---

63. Melanchthon, *Apology of the Augsburg Confession* 4.71; quoted in Anderson, p. 226.
64. We call the error of "Galatianism" (namely, works are necessary for sanctification) a "serious error." If it is a heresy, then many Protestants are heretical at this point too, since, at least in practice if not in theory, they too teach works are a condition for progressive sanctification.

tion). In this sense, for Catholics works are necessary for salvation, even if they are works subsequent to initial justification. Actually, works are only necessary for the degree of reward we receive in heaven; they are not a condition for getting into heaven.

Works-for-reward come under sanctification, not justification. They are what we do *as a result of* being saved, not what we do *in order to be* saved (i.e., to receive the gift of eternal life). In other words, merit makes sense if understood in the context of those who already are justified before God and simply are *working out* their salvation with fear and trembling (Phil. 2:12), not *working for* it. Even here the works are not a condition for being sanctified but a manifestation of it. Thus Catholics are left with a de facto denial of the grace that they officially claim is necessary for both justification and sanctification.

It adds works into its concept of faith. Roman Catholic biblical scholars admit "the absence of any reference to sacraments and good works in Paul's thesis in [Romans 1] 16f." To this they respond by redefining faith to include works, saying, "Omission causes no difficulty if faith be understood in the sense of dogmatic faith, which accepts all the doctrines of the Gospel as true and obeys all its precepts as divine commandments. For in this faith sacraments and good works are included."[65] This is a classic example of eisegesis, that is, reading into the text what is not there, indeed, in this case, the exact opposite of what is there. For Paul goes on to say that "when one does not work, yet believes in the one who justifies the ungodly, his faith is credited as righteousness" (Rom. 4:5), and "a person is justified by faith apart from works of the law" (Rom. 3:28). Yet when commenting on this verse *A Catholic Commentary on Holy Scripture* says emphatically that "Another conclusion from [Romans 1:]28 that had to be rejected by the Council of Trent is that *before* justification only faith is necessary as a preparation and no other good works." Faith, the commentary insists, is only the "immediate" preparation for justification; a "remote" preparation is also necessary, including "a resolution to receive the Sacrament of baptism and *to keep the commandments.*"[66] In other words, faith is only a necessary initial condition but not a sufficient condition for receiving the gift of salvation. However, the evident meaning of the Romans text (1–4) is that nothing in addition to faith is necessary for salvation (cf. Rom. 1:17; 4:4–5).

In spite of the commendable insistence on the necessity of grace for salvation and the need for explicit faith in adults as a precondition for justification, it is still true that Catholicism teaches that even justification (in adults) is preconditioned on faith plus the resolution to do good works. Hence, the

---

65. See "Romans," in *A Catholic Commentary on Holy Scripture*, ed. by Dom Bernard Orchard et al. (Nashville: Nelson, 1953), p. 1049.
66. Ibid., p. 1055.

promise to do good works is a condition of initial justification. Thereby sanctification is frontloaded into justification. That is, the promise to live a godly life is a condition for receiving the gift of eternal life. But if this is so then it is not of grace but works. And for Roman Catholics, salvation in the ultimate sense, not just initial justification, always requires faith plus works to obtain eternal life.

AN EVANGELICAL RESPONSE
TO THE ARGUMENT FROM TRADITION

As to Catholic arguments from tradition they too confuse reward of *salvation* and reward for *service*. In an attempt to stress the need for good works, as over against antinomians and others, some church fathers, like Tertullian, stated the importance of works so strongly that it left the impression that works were a condition for salvation rather than an inevitable consequence of it. This obscures the clear plan of salvation by grace alone through faith alone.

Protestants have responded in a much more biblical and balanced way. They insist that while we are *saved by faith alone,* nevertheless, *the faith that saves us is not alone.* Faith inevitably produces good works; that is, we are saved *by faith* and *for works.* Works are not a *condition* of justification but a *consequence* of it. As James put it, we show our faith by our works (2:18). Further, as Paul taught in Galatians, good works are not a condition of sanctification. We are saved by grace and we are sanctified by grace (Titus 2:11–13). Also, we are justified by faith alone as well as sanctified by faith alone. Of course, as already noted, works flow from true faith. Thus, someone who is truly saved will manifest good works. If no good works are present there is no reason to believe that genuine faith is there. James said "faith without works is dead." Such faith cannot save. "Can [mere intellectual] faith save him?" Only the kind of faith that produces good works can save. So, we are not saved (i.e., do not get eternal life) by works, but we are saved by the kind of faith that produces good works. Demons have mere intellectual faith (mere mental assent) and are not saved (James 2:19). And since works always flow from living faith (real heart commitment), it is appropriate that the Bible should declare that we will be rewarded according to our faith-produced works (1 Cor. 3:11–14; 2 Cor. 5:10).

Protestant theology clearly distinguishes between forensic justification[67]

---

67. By "forensic justification" we do not mean to exclude the other positional things bestowed on us at the same moment, namely, sonship, forgiveness of sins, imputation of alien righteousness, etc. Our status is not merely legal (as in forensic justification) but also ontological (real), for we become the actual children of God at the initial moment of salvation (John 1:12; 1 John 3:1), a new creation (2 Cor. 5:17), and our sins are actually washed away (Acts 13:38; Eph. 1:7).

(by which alone one is promised a place in heaven) and sanctification (which determines how high a place one will have in heaven). Catholic theology does not agree. Further, Protestants affirm that justification is a forensic act by which God *declares* a person righteous legally, while practical sanctification is a process by which one is *made* righteous morally.[68] The initial acts of salvation received the moment one believes, which for Protestants include forensic justification, are not only a necessary requirement for heaven (as Catholics also believe);[69] they are a sufficient condition (which Catholics do not believe). While practical sanctification flows inevitably from positional justification, sanctification (at least in any complete sense) is not necessary to get into heaven. This is evident from those who die the moment after they are justified, like the thief on the cross.[70] Jesus said the thief would be in paradise that very day, even though he had no time to perform good deeds. This is also true of believers who do not live a very sanctified life (such as Lot).[71] Sanctification is the actual process by which one is *made* righteous after being *declared* righteous (by justification). The failure of Trent to make this distinction obscures the doctrine of justification. For if we must live a life of sanctification as a condition for our ultimate justification (i.e., to get to heaven), then works have nullified grace. Works have become a de facto condition for heaven. But we cannot work *for* our salvation (Rom. 4:5; Eph. 2:8–9); we can only work *from* it (Eph. 2:10). The failure to see this obfuscates the very grace which even Catholics admit is necessary for sanctification.

Works are not necessary for re-justification. Catholic teaching on re-justification makes it clear that works are a condition for receiving salvation—at least the second time. (Catholicism, like Arminianism, teaches that we can lose our salvation or initial justification.) When this happens we have to be re-justified. Since the Roman Catholic Church believes that one should not be rebaptized, they have to offer another way to come back into the fold. This is the function of penance. The Council of Trent declared that the sacrament of penance "is necessary (normatively) for the salvation of those who have fallen after baptism, as baptism itself is for those as yet not regenerated (can. 6)."[72] And even though Trent declared that justification "in adults is to be understood as the result of antecedent grace . . . without any previous merit on their part,"[73] nevertheless, there is a real sense in which

---

68. Of course, at the moment of forensic justification one is also made righteous in an ontological sense (cf. 2 Cor. 5:17, 21). But practical sanctification refers to a moral process by which one becomes more like Christ in an ethical or behavioral sense (cf. Heb. 5:14; 6:1).

69. According to Catholic theology initial justification is not sufficient for salvation, at least not for those who live after they are regenerated.

70. See Luke 23:43.

71. Lot is an example, since the Bible calls him "righteous" and yet teaches that his righteous soul was marred by his constant commerce with the wicked Sodomites (2 Pet. 2:7).

72. Denzinger, *Sources of Catholic Dogma*, no. 895, p. 273.

73. Council of Trent, chap. 5; cited in Bouyer, p. 51.

works are a condition for this initial re-justification, since the work of penance is necessary as a condition for obtaining it. For doing penance is explicitly listed as a precondition for adults who wish to be saved.[74] The Council of Trent cited both Jesus and Peter to prove their point: "The Lord also said: 'Except you do penance, you shall all likewise perish' (Luke 13:3). And the prince of the apostles, Peter, recommending penance to sinners about to receive baptism said: 'Do penance and be baptized every one of you' (Acts 2:38)."[75]

Stressing the need for good works decreases motivation to do them. The Catholic insistence on good works to attain progressive and final justification does not provide the proper motive toward sanctification, namely, God's love and grace working in our lives (cf. Rom. 5:5). Recognizing this grace by God, which declares one righteous apart from any meritorious works on his part, a believer is more highly motivated to do good works. For the love of Christ "impels us" (2 Cor. 5:14), and "we love because [we realize that] he first loved us" (1 John 4:19).[76] As Paul said, the grace of God not only brings us salvation (Titus 2:11) but it *trains* us "to reject godless ways" (2:12). By contrast, keeping laws in order to obtain grace only brings one into further bondage (cf. Rom. 8:2–3; Gal. 4:3–7; Col. 2:22).

The areas of agreement and disagreement may be summarized as follows:

Justification (Righteousness)

	Initial Act	*Progressive*	*Final Act*
Legal (Extrinsic)	R.C. allow Prot. affirm	R.C. allow Prot. deny	R.C. affirm Prot. deny
Actual (Intrinsic)	Both affirm*	Both affirm	Both affirm
Grace Needed	Both affirm	Both affirm	Both affirm
*Works Needed***	Both deny	R.C. affirm Prot. deny	R.C. affirm Prot. deny

*Though Protestants insist this is not the basis of justification.
**Works are needed normatively but not absolutely.

74. Of course, the work of penance is to spring from a penitent heart.

75. Denzinger, *Sources of Catholic Dogma*, no. 894, p. 272. Peter is not speaking here of the sacrament of penance but of the fact of penance. Nonetheless, Catholics believe that, for adults, works are a necessary precondition of salvation. Of course, so is faith, but it is faith plus works that are the condition of salvation. Only infants are not required to have works as a precondition of salvation because they receive baptism (justification) before they can do any works.

76. A Catholic response might be that the Protestant stress on grace produces libertarians. The abuse of grace, however, does not prevent the proper use of grace. Paul's response is still appropriate: "God forbid! How shall we who have died to sin live any longer in it?" (Rom. 6:2 KJV). The fear of Protestant libertarianism does not justify Catholic legalism. (Of course, neither is the fear of legalism an excuse for antinomianism.)

OTHER PROBLEMS WITH SALVATION BY MERITORIOUS WORKS

There are many difficulties with the Roman Catholic position that salvation is merited. Three important ones will be discussed here.

The Catholic Arguments for Salvation by Sacraments. While Roman Catholic theology claims that there is no salvation apart from God's grace, their view of the sacraments tends to take away in practice what they have affirmed in principle. The Catholic view of a sacrament, unchanged by Vatican II, is that it is given "not merely as a sign but as a cause of grace."[77] Catholic dogma states: "If anyone shall say that the sacraments of the New Law do not contain the grace which they signify, or that they do not confer that grace on those who do not place any obstacle in the way, as though they were only outward signs of grace or justice, received through faith . . . let him be anathema."[78] Furthermore, it is anathema to believe that "grace is not conferred from the work which has been worked" but has come from "faith alone."[79] This being the case, salvation is by sacraments. God's normative way of saving sinners is, according to Catholic dogma, through the Catholic sacramental system (see chap. 13).

Sacraments are effective objectively, whether or not their efficacy is experienced subjectively. "Sacraments confer grace immediately, without the mediation of fiducial faith."[80] In order to designate the objective efficacy of a sacrament, Catholic theology coined the phrase *ex opere operato* (by the work that is worked); that is, "the Sacraments operate by the power of the completed sacramental rite." The Council of Trent adopted this phrase, which the Reformers vigorously opposed, for sacraments were said to "move God to bestow the grace by their objective value. As soon as the sacramental sign is validly accomplished God bestows the grace."[81] This being the case, salvation is dependent on performing the works of the sacramental system. It is not really by grace alone through faith alone.

The Roman Catholic Church is an institution of salvation. The sacraments are mediated through the Roman Catholic Church, which bestows the grace of God on its recipient in seven stages from birth (baptism) to death (extreme unction). Roman Catholicism recognizes the validity of two Protestant sacraments practiced outside its jurisdiction, namely, baptism and

---

77. Ott, *Fundamentals of Catholic Dogma*, p. 325.
78. Denzinger, *Sources of Catholic Dogma*, no. 849, p. 262.
79. Ibid., no. 851, p. 263.
80. However, "it is true that in the adult recipient, faith is an indispensable pre-condition or a disposing cause, but it is not an efficient cause of grace" (Ott, *Fundamentals of Catholic Dogma*, p. 329). But in babies no actual (conscious) faith is necessary to receive the sacrament of baptism; the sacrament works its work automatically. Of course, if an adult profanes the sacrament it can bring condemnation (cf. 1 Cor. 11:30).
81. Ibid., p. 331.

marriage.[82] It also believes grace can be dispensed through the Lord's Supper, though not in the way it is dispensed in the Catholic Eucharist.[83] More important, the sacraments, institutionalized as they are in the Roman Catholic Church, are necessary for salvation. The Council of Trent reminded Catholics that "If anyone shall say that the sacraments of the New Law are not necessary for salvation, but are superfluous, and that, although all are not necessary individually, without them or without the desire of them through faith alone men obtain from God the grace of justification: let him be anathema."[84]

The Catholic church also teaches that, "Except for Baptism and Matrimony, a special priestly or episcopal power, conferred by Holy Orders, is necessary for the valid ministration of the Sacraments."[85] True, Catholic lay persons (e.g., nurses or doctors) and even Protestant ministers may administer baptism in the name of the Trinity. However, the Council of Trent soundly condemned the belief that "all Christians have the power to administer all the sacraments."[86] Only the Catholic church has the right to do this. Trent made it infallible dogma that the Catholic church is God's chosen organization to mete out all God's sacramental grace piece-by-piece from birth to death; the Roman Catholic Church is an institution of salvation. Protestants take strong exception to this view.

The sacrament of the Eucharist (see chap. 13) is a classic case in point. Not only is the Roman Catholic Church, through its priesthood, the only divinely instituted organization on earth to administer this sacrament, but they also have the divinely granted power to perform the ceremony by which the physical earthly elements of bread and wine are transformed into the actual body and blood of Christ! Perhaps one has to stand outside the Roman Catholic system to be properly impressed with the utter presumption that any institution on earth possesses such powers. Nowhere is the institutionalization of salvation more apparent than in this sacrament.

The Catholic view of the Eucharist as a sacrifice vitiates salvation by grace. Roman Catholics view the eucharistic feast as a "sacrifice" (although a bloodless one).[87] This idea of the Eucharist as a sacrifice is found in some

---

82. Roman Catholicism accepts the validity of all seven sacraments practiced by Eastern Orthodoxy since they have retained valid ordination.

83. Catholics believe that in the Protestant version of the Eucharistic Feast grace is only dispensed *ex opere operantis* [by the work of the worker], not *ex opere operato* [by the work that is worked]. That is, grace is given only due to the proper disposition of the receiver, not by the work of the sacrament itself.

84. Denzinger, *Sources of Catholic Dogma*, no. 847, p. 262.

85. Ott, *Fundamentals of Catholic Dogma*, p. 341.

86. Ibid.

87. It should be noted that Eastern Orthodoxy agrees with Roman Catholicism on this point: "At the Eucharist, the sacrifice offered is Christ himself, and it is Christ himself, who in the Church performs the act of offering" (Ware, *Orthodox Church*, pp. 292–93).

early medieval Fathers.[88] Gregory the Great (c. A.D. 540–604) was elected pope in 590 and is considered the father of the medieval papacy.[89] He held that at every mass Christ was sacrificed afresh, consequently, "this notion of the mass as sacrifice eventually became standard doctrine of the Western church—until it was rejected by Protestants in the sixteenth century."[90]

Protestants reject the concept of the mass as a sacrifice (see chap. 13). For example, Lutheran theology declares: "Since Christ died and atoned for sin once and for all, and since the believer is justified by faith on the basis of that one-time sacrifice, there is no need for repeated sacrifices."[91] Sacerdotalism or the need for priestly consecration is also rejected: "The presence of Christ's body and blood is not a result of the priest's actions. It is instead a consequence of the power of Jesus Christ."[92] Of course, it is to be understood that the priest does not do this by his own power but by the power of God invested in him. The Protestant point is not whether the priest is an efficient cause or just a secondary or instrumental cause of God working through him. What Protestants object to is the Catholic belief that such divine power is invested in the Roman Catholic priesthood to both consecrate the elements (transforming them into the actual body and blood of Christ) and properly administer them. Here again, Roman Catholicism has institutionalized salvation, and thus corrupted the pure grace of God by placing it in control of a human institution and its hierarchy.

THE PROTESTANT DEFENSE OF FORENSIC JUSTIFICATION

The heart cry of the Reformation was "justification by faith alone!" This formula was strongly opposed by the Roman Catholic Counter-Reformation, where they insisted on justification by faith *and* works. Interestingly, some modern Catholics have come to acknowledge that "Luther's famous formula 'faith alone' . . . can have a good Catholic sense."[93] However, it is not the same sense in which Protestants believe it, for, as we have seen, works are added to faith as a condition for ultimate justification. In order to appreciate the significant contribution of the Reformers it is necessary to examine the biblical background of the term *justification*. As we will see there are solid biblical grounds for arguing that the Protestant doctrine of forensic justifica-

88. See Ott, *Fundamentals of Catholic Dogma,* pp. 405–7.

89. Cross, *Oxford Dictionary,* pp. 594–95.

90. Justo L. González, *The Story of Christianity,* vol. 1 (San Francisco: Harper and Row, 1984), p. 247.

91. Martin Luther, *Babylonian Captivity,* p. 140; quoted in ibid.

92. Ibid.

93. *A Catholic Catechism for Adults: The Church's Confession of Faith* (San Francisco: Ignatius Press, 1989), p. 199.

tion is correct. This doctrine is found in both the Old and New Testaments, and was expounded by the great Reformers and their followers.

THE BIBLICAL BASIS FOR FORENSIC JUSTIFICATION

Old Testament Use of Forensic Justification. The background for the doctrine of forensic justification (as with other New Testament doctrines) is found in the Old Testament. The Old Testament word *hitsdiq,* usually rendered "justify," more often than not it is "used in a forensic or legal sense, as meaning, not 'to make just or righteous,' but 'to declare judicially that one is in harmony with the law.'"[94] Another scholar notes, "He is righteous who is judged to be in the right (Ex. 23:7; Deut. 25:1); i.e., who in judgment through acquittal thus stands in a right relationship with God."[95] Therefore, the majority of Reformed scholars would agree that "in the Old Testament, the concept of righteousness frequently appears in a forensic or juridical context. A righteous man is one who has been declared by a judge to be free from guilt."[96] This thinking on the forensic nature of the Old Testament terms for justification and righteousness is not restricted to evangelicals. Hans Küng agrees that, "according to the original biblical usage of the term, 'justification' must be defined as a *declaring just by court order.*"[97]

New Testament Use of Forensic Justification. In the New Testament, the verb translated "to justify" is *dikaioó.* Paul used this word in a forensic or legal sense: the sinner is declared to be righteous (cf. Rom. 3–4). It is the opposite of condemnation. As Hoekema notes, "The opposite of condemnation, however, is not 'making righteous' but 'declaring righteous.'" Therefore, by *dikaiō,* Paul means the "legal imputation of the righteousness of Christ to the believing sinner."[98]

When a person is justified, God pronounces that one acquitted—in advance of the final judgment. "The resulting righteousness is not ethical perfection; it is 'sinlessness' in the sense that God no longer counts a man's sin against him (II Cor. 5:19)."[99] Thus we find in the New Testament that "jus-

---

94. Anthony A. Hoekema, *Saved by Grace* (Grand Rapids: Eerdmans, 1989), p. 154.

95. George E. Ladd, *A Theology of the New Testament* (Grand Rapids: Eerdmans, 1974), p. 440.

96. Millard J. Erickson, *Christian Theology* (Grand Rapids: Baker, 1987), p. 955.

97. Hans Küng, *Justification* (New York: Nelson, 1964), p. 209. For an extended treatment of the Old Testament understandings of these terms and the difficulties inherent in translating from the Hebrew into Greek and Latin, see Alister E. McGrath, *Iustitia Dei,* vol. 1 (Cambridge: Cambridge University Press, 1986), pp. 4–16.

98. Hoekema, *Saved by Grace.*

99. Ladd, *A Theology of the New Testament,* p. 446. This is not to imply that Catholics believe that ethical perfection is received by justification; they do not. They distinguish complete ontological righteousness received at justification with perfect ethical (behavioral) righteousness which is not then received, although a measure of it is since the love of God is shed in our hearts (Rom. 5:5).

tification is the declarative act of God by which, *on the basis of the suffi-ciency of Christ's atoning death,* he pronounces believers to have fulfilled all of the requirements of the law which pertain to them."[100]

A THEOLOGICAL EXPOSITION OF FORENSIC JUSTIFICATION

Next to Martin Luther, John Calvin is usually regarded as the most important figure in the Reformation. On the subject of forensic justification Calvin stated: "Man is not made righteous in justification, but is accepted as righteous, not on account of his own righteousness, but on account of the righteousness of Christ located outside of man."[101] The reason human beings need justification is that they are "totally depraved." This Reformed doctrine has been misunderstood by some Protestants as well as Roman Catholics. The Reformed view is that although humans are lost, they are not nothing. On the one hand, "In constructing a Christian anthropology, we must not ignore the basic nobility of man." On the other hand, "There is a glaring contrast between what man is truly and essentially and what he has become. Because man lives in opposition to his own God-given nature, his present nature signifies an existence in contradiction."[102]

Reformed theology teaches that total depravity involves several aspects. First, corruption is present at the center of our being. Second, depravity has extended to every aspect of humanity: physical, social, and spiritual. Third, it prevents us from being able to please God unless enabled by grace. Fourth, depravity extends to every corner and culture of the human race.[103] Total depravity does not mean that human beings are destitute of all natural goodness; the *imago Dei* has been "effaced" but not "erased." This is often misunderstood by Catholics. For example, Karl Keating—who ordinarily is quite careful and precise in his criticisms—writes concerning Calvin's understanding of the natural person and his or her works: "Your own acts are entirely worthless. Everything you do is worthless. Reason is unavailing since it can't bring you closer to God. Worse, everything you do is a sin."[104] However, Calvin (along with the other Reformers) was too careful an exegete not to be aware of Jesus' statement: "If you then, who are wicked, know how to give good gifts to your children, how much more will the Father in Heaven

100. Erickson, *Christian Theology,* p. 956.
101. McGrath, *Iustitia Dei,* 2:36.
102. Donald G. Bloesch, *Essentials of Evangelical Theology,* vol. 1 (San Francisco: Harper and Row, 1978), p. 89.
103. Ibid., p. 90.
104. Karl Keating, *What Catholics Really Believe: Setting the Record Straight* (Ann Arbor: Servant Publications, 1992), p. 102.

give the holy Spirit to those who ask him?" (Luke 11:13).[105] Calvin acknowledged that people can do good socially and horizontally, but spiritually they are dead in their trespasses and sins (Eph. 2:1) and can initiate no meritorious action toward God on behalf of their sinful condition. They can receive eternal life by faith and faith alone.

Early Princeton Calvinistic theologian Charles Hodge indicates that sin has predisposed humanity against any move toward God and his salvation. Hence, "Every man should bow down before God under the humiliating consciousness that he is a member of an apostate race; the son of a rebellious parent; born estranged from God, and exposed to his displeasure."[106] Likewise, for Calvin, the need for justification follows from the spiritual reality of total depravity, that is, our total inability to initiate or attain salvation. This justification is judicial, or forensic, in nature. Küng defines the term *justification* as "a declaring just. It really implies a declaring just, in the sense of a leaving out of the account, a not imputing."[107] In the Old Testament, David put it this way: "Happy is he whose fault is taken away, whose sin is covered. Happy the man to whom the LORD imputes not guilt" (Ps. 32:1–2). In the New Testament, Paul said that "God was reconciling the world to himself in Christ, not counting their trespasses against them" (2 Cor. 5:19). A contemporary Lutheran scholar has put it thusly: "Justification by grace alone through faith alone on account of Christ alone is the absolute truth by which the church stands or falls. It is this truth that makes Christianity Christian and the church really the church, preserving it from idolatry, preventing its secularization, providing the charter of its career, and offering believers a solid basis and direction for their daily life."[108]

As we have shown, these valuable insights into the doctrine of justification had been largely lost throughout much of Christian history, and it was the Reformers who recovered this biblical truth. And although some contemporary Catholics are beginning to acknowledge the Protestant contribution of forensic justification, it was not spelled out by the Council of Trent. Indeed, while there may be no logical incompatibility of forensic justification with the Roman Catholic concept of initial justification, there are serious problems with the Catholic concept of progressive justification. In short, in spite of its insistence on the need for grace, it is a system of works based on merit that tends to negate in practice what has been affirmed in theory about (initial) justification by grace apart from works.

---

105. Bloesch also comments on the Reformed doctrine of common grace: "It is not only the *imago Dei* but also the common grace of God that accounts for sinful man's ability to arrive at a modicum of justice" (*Essentials of Evangelical Theology,* 1:91).

106. Ibid., p. 92.

107. Küng, *Justification,* p. 212.

108. Braaten, *Justification,* p. 82.

SUMMARY AND CONCLUSION

We have shown that the characteristically Protestant concept of forensic justification is grounded in both the Old and New Testaments. However, during the patristic, and especially the later medieval periods, forensic justification was largely lost to an emphasis on the need for good works as a ground for justification in the progressive and final sense of the term, if not for initial justification. Still, the theological formulations of such figures as Augustine, Anselm, and Aquinas did not preclude a rediscovery of this "judicial" element in the Pauline doctrine of justification. Indeed, some scholars see at least implied forensic justification in these early Fathers.

The Reformers, however, recovered the biblical view of divine imputation of the alien righteousness of Christ to the believer and of forensic justification, that a person is legally declared righteous by God on the basis of faith alone. In so doing, their principle of "salvation by grace alone through faith alone" gave a more biblical specificity to the common Augustinian view of "salvation by grace" held by Catholics and Protestants alike. However, the Catholic view of justification, made dogma by the Council of Trent, obscured the pure grace of God, if not at times negating it in practice. Indeed, it was condemned as heretical by the Reformers. Both sacramentalism and sacerdotalism vitiated and institutionalized grace so that it was incorporated into a system of works. Nonetheless, at least officially, though not in practice, Rome has not always held the common Augustinian belief of salvation by grace. In this way they have avoided even more serious doctrinal error.

13

SACRAMENTALISM

The sacraments are at the heart of Roman Catholic religious practices. It is not possible to understand the essence of Catholicism without them, especially the sacrament of the mass. According to Catholic dogma there are seven sacraments, all of which are causes of God's grace on his church.

THE ROMAN CATHOLIC VIEW OF THE SACRAMENTS

The Council of Trent proclaimed infallibly of the sacraments that "If anyone shall say that the sacraments of the New Law were not all instituted by Jesus Christ our Lord . . . let him be anathema."[1] This excommunication includes almost all Protestants,[2] since most affirm that there are less than seven sacraments. This condemnation has never and can never be revoked since it is an infallible *ex cathedra* pronouncement of the Roman Catholic Church.

THE NATURE OF THE SACRAMENTS

A sacrament is a cause of grace. According to Roman Catholic authority Ludwig Ott, by "its etymology the word 'sacramentum' means a sacred or holy thing."[3] Early scholastic theologians, such as Hugo of St. Victor and Peter Lombard, defined it "not merely as a sign but as a cause of grace,"[4] which is the meaning it retains today in Catholic theology. Ott informs us that "The Roman Catechism (II, I, 8) defines a Sacrament as 'a thing perceptible to the

---

1. Denzinger, *Sources of Catholic Dogma*, no. 844, p. 262.
2. High church Anglicans and "Old Catholics" are an exception since they believe in the same seven sacraments that Roman Catholics do.
3. Ott, *Fundamentals of Catholic Dogma*, p. 325.
4. Ibid.

senses, which on the grounds of Divine institution possesses the power both of effecting and signifying sanctity and righteousness' (= sanctifying grace)."[5]

By decree of the Roman Catholic Church, "If anyone shall say that the sacraments of the New Law do not contain the grace which they signify, or that they do not confer that grace on those who do not place any obstacle in the way, as though they were only outward signs of grace or justice, received through faith . . . let him be anathema."[6] Furthermore, it is wrong to deny "that grace, as far as concerns God's part, is not given through the sacraments always and to all men. . . ."[7] According to Catholic dogma it is anathema to claim that "grace is not conferred from the work which has been worked [ex opere operato] but that faith alone . . . suffices to obtain grace."[8]

A sacrament has two aspects: the outward sign and the inner grace conveyed by it. An outward sacramental sign has two dimensions: matter and form. "The outward sign of the sacrament is composed of two essential parts, namely, thing and word."[9] The "thing" (matter) is either a physical substance (such as water or oil) or an action that is perceptible to the senses (such as absolution or marriage). The "word" (form) is usually a spoken word at the time the sacrament is administered. The second aspect, that of conveying inner grace, concerns the function of the sacraments.

THE FUNCTION OF THE SACRAMENTS

It is through the outward sacramental sign that the inner workings of God's grace occur. It is essential to Catholic faith to affirm that "the Sacraments of the New Covenant contain the grace which they signify, and bestow it on those who do not hinder it."[10] Sacraments are effective objectively, whether or not their efficacy is felt subjectively. "Sacraments confer grace immediately, without the mediation of fiducial faith." However, "it is true that in the adult recipient, faith is an indispensable pre-condition or a disposing cause, but it is not an efficient cause of grace."[11] In order to designate the objective efficacy of a sacrament, Catholic theology coined (and Trent adopted) the phrase *ex opere operato* (by the work that has been worked); that is, "the Sacraments operate by the power of the completed sacramental rite."[12] The Reformers vigorously opposed this phrase since they believed it demeaned the grace of God. Nonetheless, Catholics hold that "The sacraments . . . not

5. Ibid., p. 326.
6. Denzinger, *Sources of Catholic Dogma*, no. 849, p. 262.
7. Ibid., no. 850, p. 263.
8. Ibid., no. 851, p. 263.
9. Ott, *Fundamentals of Catholic Dogma*, p. 327.
10. Ibid., p. 328.
11. Ibid., p. 329.
12. Denzinger, *Sources of Catholic Dogma*, no. 851, p. 263.

only point externally to salvation; they contain and bestow the salvation they signify."[13]

Catholic scholars differ as to precisely how the sacraments work. According to the "moral mode of operation" view (following after Scotus), the sacraments

> move God to bestow the grace by their objective value. As soon as the sacramental sign is vividly accomplished God bestows the grace, [either] because He has bound Himself by a treaty to do so by the institution of the Sacraments (thus the older Scotists), or because the sacramental signs possess an imprecatory power similar to the intercession of Christ, since in a certain sense, they are the actions of Christ.[14]

According to this explanation, "God gives grace *immediately* on account of the moral pressure exercised on Him by the Sacrament."[15] Another view, favored by many Catholic scholars (following after Aquinas), is the "physical mode of operation" which states:

> The sacraments operate physically if, through the power received from God indwelling in them, they cause the grace which they signify. God, as *causa principalis* [principal cause] of grace, makes use of the sacramental sign as a physical instrument in order to produce through it the sacramental grace in the soul of the recipient. God conveys the grace *mediately* [not immediately] through the Sacrament.[16]

Each particular sacrament confers a specific grace on the recipient, corresponding to its special purpose. Most Catholic theologians believe that God conveys the same measure of grace on each of the sacrament's recipients. This grace continues until the death of its receiver.[17]

With respect to the sacraments of baptism, confirmation, and holy order, "there is imprinted on the soul a sign, that is, a certain spiritual and indelible mark, on account of which they cannot be repeated."[18] Of course, this grace is not conferred unless the priest administers it with good intentions and in accord with the intentions of the church.[19] And no priest may, without sinning, disdain or omit the administration of any sacrament.[20]

---

13. Stephen W. Arndt and Mark Jordan, *A Catholic Catechism for Adults: The Church's Confession of Faith* (San Francisco: Ignatius Press, 1987), p. 265.
14. Ott, *Fundamentals of Catholic Dogma*, p. 331.
15. Ibid., emphasis added.
16. Ibid., p. 330, emphasis added.
17. Ibid., p. 335.
18. Denzinger, *Sources of Catholic Dogma*, no. 852, p. 263.
19. Ibid., no. 854, p. 263 (cf. canon 12).
20. Ibid., no. 856, p. 263.

THE NECESSITY OF THE SACRAMENTS

The purpose of a sacrament is to bestow the grace of God through the Roman Catholic Church[21] to its recipient in seven stages from birth (baptism) to death (extreme unction). Thus, the sacraments are necessary for salvation. The Council of Trent reminded Catholics that "If anyone shall say that the sacraments of the New Law are not necessary for salvation, but are superfluous, and that, although all are not necessary individually, without them or without the desire of them through faith alone men obtain from God the grace of justification: let him be anathema."[22] Protestants, of course, take exception with this.

THE NUMBER AND DEFENSE OF THE SACRAMENTS

The Council of Trent proclaimed that "If anyone shall say that the sacraments of the New Law were not all instituted by Jesus Christ our Lord, or that there are more or less than seven, namely baptism, confirmation, Eucharist, penance, extreme unction, [holy] order, and matrimony, or even that any one of these seven is not truly and strictly a sacrament: let him be anathema."[23] In brief, there are seven and only these seven sacraments.

According to Catholic theology, "Holy Scripture attests that Christ immediately instituted the Sacraments of Baptism, Eucharist, Penance and Consecration. The other Sacraments . . . were [already] in existence in apostolic times."[24] The apostles simply became the dispensers of these sacraments.

Acknowledging that neither the Bible nor the Fathers enumerate these seven sacraments as such, Roman Catholic scholars seek other—theological, historical, speculative—grounds. Theologically, they argue that "the existence of seven Sacraments has been regarded as a truth of Faith since the middle of the 12th century." Later, it was confirmed by the official teaching of the Church from the 13th century on.[25] Historically, they point to the fact that "The Greek-Orthodox Church . . . agrees that there are seven Sacraments."[26] According to Ott, even the Nestorian and Monophysite sects of the fifth century "held firmly to the sevenfold number of the Sacraments."[27] Speculatively, grounds for the seven sacraments is sought in "The appropri-

---

21. Protestant baptism and the Orthodox church's eucharistic celebration may be exceptions, since it is a debatable point whether the grace given through these comes by way of the Roman Catholic Church.
22. Denzinger, *Sources of Catholic Dogma,* no. 847, p. 262.
23. Ibid., no. 844, p. 262.
24. Ott, *Fundamentals of Catholic Dogma,* p. 337.
25. Ibid., p. 338.
26. Ibid., p. 339.
27. Ibid.

ateness of the number seven of the Sacraments [which] flows from the analogy to the supernatural life of the soul with the natural life of the body." For example, "The supernatural life [by analogy with the natural life] is *generated* by Baptism; *brought to growth* by Confirmation; *nourished* by the Eucharist; *cured from the diseases of sins* and [*cured*] *from the weakness* arising from these by Penance and Extreme Unction." And "By the two social Sacraments of Holy Order and Matrimony the congregation of the Church is *guided,* and spiritually and corporeally *preserved* and increased."[28] Thus, Roman Catholics insist that for these reasons there are seven and only seven sacraments—the ones their church has infallibly proclaimed and enumerated.

THE ADMINISTRATION OF THE SACRAMENTS

Ott notes that, "Except for Baptism and Matrimony, a special priestly or Episcopal power conferred by Holy Orders, is necessary for the valid ministration of the Sacraments."[29] Both Catholic lay persons (e.g., nurses or doctors) and even Protestants may administer baptism in the name of the Trinity. The Council of Trent, however, soundly condemned the view that "all Christians have the power to administer all the sacraments."[30] Further, "The validity and efficacy of the Sacraments is independent of the minister's orthodoxy and state of grace."[31] That is, the priest does not have to be holy or heresy-free in order for the sacraments to convey grace.

Only human beings are valid recipients of sacraments. And, "excepting the Sacrament of Penance, neither orthodox belief nor moral worthiness is necessary for the validity of the Sacrament, on the part of the recipient."[32] Heretics and immoral people can be valid recipients. In adults, however, "the intention of receiving the Sacrament is necessary."[33] Also, in adults, moral worthiness in the sense of removing any obstacle to grace "is necessary for the worthy or fruitful reception of the Sacraments."[34]

A DISCUSSION OF SOME CRUCIAL SACRAMENTS

From a Catholic point of view, all the sacraments are crucial, but from an evangelical Protestant perspective, baptism, communion, and holy orders are

28. Ibid., emphasis added.
29. Ibid., p. 341.
30. Ibid.
31. Ibid.
32. Ibid., p. 345.
33. Ibid.
34. Ibid., p. 346.

especially important to our differences with Catholics. (Since holy orders is the subject of the next chapter, we will concentrate on the first two here.) Although Catholics and Protestants disagree about the number of the sacraments, the latter generally affirming only baptism and communion, the difference on the nature of the sacraments is more crucial.

THE SACRAMENT OF BAPTISM

The Council of Trent declared that the sacrament of baptism must be administered with literal water and not merely symbolically. "If anyone shall say that natural water is not necessary for baptism, and on that account those words of our Lord Jesus Christ: 'Unless a man be born again of water and the Holy Spirit' (John 3:5), are distorted into some sort of metaphor: let him be anathema."[35] And, "If anyone shall say that baptism is optional, that is, not necessary for salvation: let him be anathema."[36] Baptism properly administered is a once-for-all act, not to be repeated.[37] However, baptism is not a guarantee of salvation, for even the regenerate can lose their salvation.[38]

Even baptism done by Protestants and other non-Catholics (including heretics) in the name of the Trinity is valid.[39] But the denial of infant baptism (such as Baptists and many other Christian groups do deny) is a heresy.[40] For Trent declared that "If anyone shall say that infants, because they have not actual faith,[41] after having received baptism are not to be numbered among the faithful, and therefore, when they have reached the years of discretion, are to be rebaptized . . . let them be anathema."[42] This, of course, anathematizes all Baptists and like groups, including the authors of this book!

Crucial to the debate between Catholics and evangelicals is the Catholic belief that "baptism confers the grace of justification."[43] Since this is an *ex cathedra* pronouncement of the Catholic church it is not negotiable. The Council of Trent declared: "If anyone denies that by the grace of our Lord Jesus Christ which is conferred in Baptism, the guilt of original sin is remit-

---

35. Denzinger, *Sources of Catholic Dogma*, no. 858, p. 263.
36. Ibid., no. 861, p. 264.
37. Ibid., no. 867, p. 264.
38. Ibid., no. 862, p. 264.
39. Ibid., no. 860, p. 263.
40. Roman Catholics distinguish between material and formal heresy, the latter being only those who obstinately doubt or deny an article of faith and are thus morally culpable.
41. Some Catholic scholars speak of infants having "implicit faith," but it is difficult to determine precisely what this means. How can they have faith when the faculties for believing (e.g., rationality and volitionality) are not yet developed? Some Catholic apologists suggest this cannot operate the way original sin operates, since everyone inherits original sin and we have no choice, but not everyone has faith and we do have a choice about that.
42. Denzinger, *Sources of Catholic Dogma*, no. 869, p. 264.
43. Ott, *Fundamentals of Catholic Dogma*, p. 354.

ted; or even assert that the whole of that which has the true and proper nature of sin is not taken away . . . let him be anathema."[44] This does not mean that the tendency to sin (concupiscence) is removed but that the actual (ontological) stain of the guilt of our sins is taken away by baptism.

Elaborating on the Catholic dogma of justification by baptism Ott comments:

> As justification consists, negatively, in the remission of sin, positively, in the sanctification and renewal of the inner man (D 799), so Baptism, provided that the proper dispositions (Faith and sorrow for sin) are present, effects: a) the eradication of sins, both original sin and, in the case of adults, also all personal moral or venial sins; b) inner sanctification by the infusion of sanctifying grace, with which the infused theological and moral virtues and the gifts of the Holy Ghost are always joined.[45]

A host of proof tests are offered in support of the belief in infant salvation by baptism. For a complete discussion of them, and a response to them, see Appendix E.

THE SACRAMENT OF THE EUCHARIST (COMMUNION)

Few issues better illustrate the difference between Catholics and Protestants than the doctrine of communion. This is especially true with regard to the Catholic dogma of transubstantiation, which holds that, during communion, the wine and bread are transformed into the actual body and blood of Christ.

Different Understandings Concerning the Lord's Supper. Christians have historically taken different approaches toward the "eucharistic feast." The Eastern Orthodox view dates back to the earliest times in Christendom, and interprets communion in much the same way as do Roman Catholics—with one important difference. Orthodox believers agree that when the priest consecrates the elements (the bread and wine), they become the very body and blood of Christ. However, "while Orthodoxy has always insisted on the *reality* of the change, it has never attempted to explain the *manner* of the change."[46] Eastern Orthodoxy has always held that Western Christianity (both Roman Catholic and Protestant)—under the influence of thinkers such as Augustine and Aquinas—has preempted the faith of mystery (see Appendix A).

The Lutheran view of the Lord's Supper, sometimes called "consubstantiation," is that Christ's body and blood are in, with, and under the elements.

---

44. Denzinger, *Sources of Catholic Dogma,* no. 792, p. 247.
45. Ott, *Fundamentals of Catholic Dogma,* p. 354.
46. Timothy Ware, *The Orthodox Church,* rev. (New York: Penguin Books, 1983), p. 290.

Luther believed that the actual body of Christ, being in and under the elements, penetrates the elements in the same way that fire penetrates metal.[47] He rejected Catholic "transubstantiation," stating: "It is not that the bread and wine have become Christ's body and blood, but that we now have the body and blood in addition to the bread and wine."[48] Thus, as we will discuss later, Lutheran theology rejects the concept of the mass as a sacrifice.[49]

The Reformed view of the Lord's Supper is that the bread and the wine contain the body and blood of Christ *spiritually*. Christ is found in the sacrament in a spiritual or dynamic sense, rather than a physical or bodily way. John Calvin used the sun as an illustration, stating that "The sun remains in the heavens, yet its warmth and light are present on earth. So the radiance of the Spirit conveys to us the communion of Christ's flesh and blood."[50]

Finally, we have the "memorial" view of the Lord's Supper. This position states that communion is primarily a commemoration of Christ's death on the cross, following Jesus' words "Do this in remembrance of me." Adherents of this view included the Anabaptists and modern Baptist (and "baptistic") churches. These groups often prefer to use the term "ordinance" rather than "sacrament" when referring to the eucharistic event (i.e., communion).

The crucial difference in the various views is whether the communion bread and the wine are the body and blood of Christ physically, spiritually, or only symbolically. We now move to the Roman Catholic "transubstantiation" view, which holds that the communion elements are transformed into the literal physical body and blood of Christ.

The Holy Eucharist Defined. Catholic theology (transubstantiation) defines this sacrament as follows: "The Eucharist is that Sacrament, in which Christ, under the forms of bread and wine, is truly present, with His Body and Blood, in order to offer Himself in an unbloody manner to the Heavenly Father, and to give Himself to the faithful as nourishment for their souls."[51] In the words of the irrevocable pronouncement of the Council of Trent,

---

47. Luther, *Babylonian Captivity*, in *Three Treatises* (Philadelphia: Muhlenberg, 1943), p. 140. Some Lutheran theologians are uneasy with the term "consubstantiation." Luther himself never used the term *consubstantiatio*, which is of scholastic origin. Given his intense dislike of philosophy in general (he once called it a "whore") and metaphysical formulations applied to theology in particular, he probably would be content to say that "the actual body and blood of Christ exist 'in, with, or under' the elements of bread and wine." A. Skevington Wood, "Consubstantiation," in Everett F. Harrison, ed., *Baker's Dictionary of Theology* (Grand Rapids: Baker, 1960), p. 138. Also see Bernard M. G. Reardon, *Religious Thought in the Reformation* (London and New York: Longman, 1981), p. 78. One of the forerunners of the Reformation, John Wycliffe (c. 1328–84), seems to have held to a view which would be later characterized as substantiation. See Williston Walker, *A History of the Christian Church*, 3d ed. (New York: Charles Scribner's Sons, 1970), pp. 269–70.

48. Erickson, *Christian Theology*, p. 1117.

49. Luther, *Babylonian Captivity*, p. 140; quoted in ibid.

50. Calvin, *Institutes*, 4.17.12; quoted in ibid., p. 1119.

51. Ott, *Fundamentals of Catholic Dogma*, p. 370.

"First of all the holy Synod teaches and openly and simply professes that in the nourishing sacrament of the Holy Eucharist after the consecration of the bread and the wine our Lord Jesus Christ, true God and man, is truly, really, and substantially (can. 1) contained under the species of those sensible things."[52]

Because of its nature in presenting the very body and blood of Christ, the Eucharist is the most important of all sacraments to Catholics. Trent commented, "this, indeed, the most Holy Eucharist has in common with the other sacraments, that it is a 'symbol of a sacred thing and a visible form of an invisible grace'; but this excellent and peculiar thing is found in it, that the other sacraments first have the power of sanctifying, when one uses them, but in the Eucharist there is the Author of sanctity Himself before it is used (can. 4)."[53] The reason the Eucharist is the greatest sacrament for Catholics is found in the doctrine of transubstantiation. Trent made it an official part of Catholic faith that "by the consecration of the bread and wine a conversion takes place of the whole substance of the bread into the substance of the body of Christ our Lord, and of the whole substance of the wine into the substance of His blood. This conversion is appropriately called transubstantiation by the Catholic Church."[54]

Since in transubstantiation the elements become the actual body and blood of Christ, Catholics believe that it is appropriate to worship the consecrated elements as God. Trent pronounced emphatically that "There is, therefore, no room left for doubt that all the faithful of Christ . . . offer in veneration (can. 6) the worship of *latria* [the act of adoration] which is due to the true God, to this most Holy Sacrament."[55] Catholic reasoning for this is that since Christ in his human form is God and, therefore, appropriately worshiped (e.g., John 20:28), and since in the mass the bread and wine are transformed into the actual body and blood of Christ, there is no reason that the elements should not be worshiped as God. Thus, Trent declared that "If anyone says that in the holy sacrament of the Eucharist the only-begotten Son of God is not to be adored even outwardly with the worship of *latria* (the act of adoration) . . . and is not to be set before the people publicly to be adored, and that the adorers are idolaters: let him be anathema."[56]

Transubstantiation Defended. The Catholic defense of the doctrine of transubstantiation is based primarily on the words of Christ when he instituted this sacrament at the Last Supper: "This is my body" (Matt. 26:26; cf. 1 Cor. 11:24). Other passages are sometimes used, especially John 6:53,

52. Denzinger, *Sources of Catholic Dogma,* no. 874, p. 265.
53. Ibid., no. 876, p. 267.
54. Ibid., no. 877, pp. 267–68.
55. Ibid., no. 878, p. 268.
56. Ibid., no. 888, p. 271.

where Jesus said, "unless you eat the flesh of the Son of Man and drink his blood, you do not have life within you." Of course, the key to the Roman Catholic view is interpreting Jesus' words literally rather than symbolically. Ott summarizes the argument as follows:

> The necessity of accepting a literal interpretation in this case is however evident:
>
> a) From the nature of the words used. One specially notes the realistic expressions *alathas brosis* = true, real food (v. 55); *alathas posis* = true, real drink (v. 55); *trogein* = to gnaw, to chew, to eat (v. 54 et seq.).
>
> b) From the difficulties created by a figurative interpretation. In the language of the Bible to eat a person's flesh and drink his blood in the metaphorical sense means to persecute him in a bloody fashion, to destroy him. Cf. Ps. 26, 2; Is. 9, 20; 49, 26; Mich. 3, 3.
>
> c) From the reactions of the listeners, which Jesus does not correct, as He had done previously in the case of misunderstandings (cf. John 3, 3 et seq.; 4, 32 et seq.; Mt. 16, 6 et seq.). In this case, on the contrary He confirms their literal acceptance of His words at the risk that His Disciples and His Apostles might desert Him (v. 60 et seq.).

THE EVANGELICAL RESPONSE TO THE CATHOLIC VIEW OF THE SACRAMENTS

THE NUMBER OF THE SACRAMENTS

Ott frankly admits that "Holy Writ . . . does not summarize them in the figure seven. Again no formal enumeration of the seven Sacraments is found in the Fathers." In fact, "This [enumeration of seven] emerged only around the middle of the 12th century."[57] Further, Catholic scholars openly acknowledge that "it cannot be shown that any one of the seven Sacraments was at any particular time instituted by a Council, a Pope, a Bishop or a Community." How, then, did belief in them arise? According to Ott, "the doctrinal decisions of the Church, the Fathers and the theologians *presuppose* the existence of the individual Sacraments as something handed down from antiquity. From this one may *infer* that the seven Sacraments existed in the Church from the very beginning."[58]

The argument for seven sacraments scarcely needs critique; the lack of scriptural and historical support speaks for itself. There is no real basis in the Bible, the Fathers, or church councils for the enumeration of seven. The decision to recognize seven and only seven was late (13th century). The other

---

57. Ott, *Fundamentals of Catholic Dogma*, p. 338.
58. Ibid., pp. 338–39, emphasis added.

argument is the weak one from analogy. Catholic scholars claim that seven sacraments exist in Scripture implicitly like the Trinity does. This is a false analogy since all the premises from which the Trinity is derived are taught explicitly in Scripture, namely: (1) there is one God, and (2) there are three persons who are God: Father, Son, and Holy Spirit. Hence, (3) there must be three persons in the one God. But nowhere does the Bible explicitly teach that marriage, penance, and confirmation, for example, are sacraments. These activities are no more sacraments than Bible reading, which is also a means of receiving grace (Ps. 119; Rom. 10:17; Rev. 1:3). At best, Catholic scholars can point to the acts or events corresponding to these seven sacraments in Scripture, but proving they were sacraments as Catholicism understands them (namely, as a cause of grace) is another matter.

THE NATURE AND NECESSITY FOR SACRAMENTS

Catholic theology claims that sacraments are an actual cause of grace to the recipient. Baptism, for example, causes the grace of justification and sanctification to occur in the infant recipient's life, even though the child has not exercised any actual faith in God.[59] Likewise, the Eucharist actually conveys the literal physical body and blood of Christ to the recipient. Evangelical Protestants reject this view in favor of a view we believe is grounded in Scripture.

The Catholic concept of a sacrament causing grace *ex opere operato* (by the work that has been worked) is a mystical, if not magical, view of sacraments. It is as though they are inherently endowed with powers to produce grace in the recipient. As Ronald Nash noted of pagan rites, "The phrase *ex opere operato* describes the pagan belief that their sacraments had the power to give the individual the benefits of immortality in a mechanical way without his undergoing any moral or spiritual transformation. This certainly was not Paul's view, either of salvation or of the operation of the Christian sacraments." By contrast, sacraments "were considered to be primarily *dona data,* namely blessings conveyed to those who by nature were unfit to participate in the new order inaugurated by the person and work of Jesus Christ. Pagan sacraments, on the contrary, conveyed their benefits *ex opere operato.*"[60]

---

59. The Catholic view of the "implicit faith" of infants is significantly different from the belief of many Protestants who hold that God elects infants apart from actual faith, knowing that they will exercise faith in God when their faculties are quickened by God (presumably before death) so that they are able to believe. Further, it differs from Protestants who hold that God actually saves infants who *can't* believe (because their faculties are not yet developed), knowing that they *would have* believed if they could have. God sees the potential as well as the actual, and he can act accordingly, even in advance of the actual events (see Appendix E).

60. Ronald Nash, *Christianity and the Hellenic World* (Grand Rapids: Zondervan, 1984), p. 153.

BAPTISMAL JUSTIFICATION/SANCTIFICATION

Since our response to Roman Catholic use of Scripture to support baptismal regeneration is found in Appendix E, here we will concentrate on other problems with viewing baptism as a saving sacrament. The following critiques are offered from a Reformed/Baptist view. The Lutheran/Anglican belief in baptismal regeneration admittedly causes tension with the Protestant principle of justification by faith alone (see Appendix E). Thus from a Reformed/ Baptistic perspective:

Baptismal regeneration appears to be contrary to grace. The belief that baptism brings regeneration seems inconsistent with the biblical teaching on God's grace, namely, that salvation comes by grace through faith and not by any works of righteousness, including baptism. Baptism is called a work of "righteousness" in Matthew 3:15, but Paul declared that it was "not because of any righteous deeds we have done but because of his mercy, he saved us" (Titus 3:5). He also said that it is "by grace you have been saved through faith, and this is not from you; it is the gift of God; it is not from works, so no one may boast" (Eph. 2:8–9). So, baptism appears to be no more necessary for being saved than is any other "work of righteousness." Indeed, any work of righteousness to obtain salvation is contrary to grace.

Baptismal regeneration is in conflict with the need for faith. Throughout the Bible it is faith and faith alone[61] that is commanded as a condition for receiving God's gift of salvation. When the Philippian jailor asked, "What must I do to be saved?" Paul answered, "Believe in the Lord Jesus Christ and you and your household will be saved" (Acts 16:30–31). In the entire Gospel of John belief is the only thing required to receive eternal life. Jesus said, "God so loved the world that he gave his only Son, so that everyone who believes in him might not perish but might have eternal life" (John 3:16). He added, "Whoever believes in the Son has eternal life" (John 3:36), and "whoever hears my word and believes in the one who sent me has eternal life and will not come to condemnation, but has passed from death to life" (John 5:24). If baptism—or anything in addition to belief—is necessary for salvation, then it seems difficult to exonerate Jesus from misleading his audience.

Baptismal regeneration is contrary to the teaching of Paul. The great apostle called of God to take the gospel to the Gentiles said emphatically, "Christ did not send me to baptize but to preach the gospel" (1 Cor. 1:17), thus putting the "gospel" and "baptism" in opposition. Clearly, baptism is not part of the gospel. But the gospel "is the power of God for the salvation of everyone who believes" (Rom. 1:16). Since, then, the gospel saves us and

---

61. Repentance is sometimes mentioned (cf. Luke 13:3; Acts 17:30) but the two are one: there is no true faith without repentance (a change of mind) and there is no true repentance without faith (1 Thess. 1:8–9).

baptism is not part of the gospel, it follows that baptism cannot be part of what saves us. Baptism, rather, is an outward sign of what saves us, namely, the regeneration of the Holy Spirit in the lives of those who believe the gospel.

"Baptism of desire" proves baptism is not essential to salvation. According to Roman Catholic theology someone can be saved who has never been baptized, providing the desire was present. Ott claims that "Baptism of desire, it is true, replace[s] Sacramental Baptism in so far as the communication of grace is concerned."[62] Even the great Catholic theologian, Thomas Aquinas, conceded that "a person may be saved extrasacramentally by baptism of desire and therefore [there is] the possibility of salvation without actual membership . . . in the Church."[63]

The same applies to those who suffered and were not baptized—the so-called baptism of blood. As Augustine acknowledged, "I find not only suffering for the sake of Christ can replace that which is lacking in Baptism, but also faith and conversion of the heart, if perhaps the shortness of time does not permit the celebration of the mystery of Baptism."[64] So even within Catholic theology there can be salvation without baptism, proving that baptism is not essential to salvation. Indeed, the thief on the cross was saved by faith alone apart from baptism or other good works (Luke 23:43).

Of course, as already noted, this is also an intramural Protestant debate, since many Protestants also believe in baptismal regeneration. Further, the outcome of this debate is not crucial to the argument against the Catholic sacramental system. For to them, all sacraments cause grace and are not merely a sign or means of grace. With this Protestants disagree.

TRANSUBSTANTIATION

More important than the differences over baptism is the disagreement about communion. Roman Catholic scholars argue that Jesus' words should be taken in a physical sense when he said of the bread and wine "This is my body" and when he said "unless you eat the flesh of the Son of Man and drink his blood, you do not have life within you." But evangelicals believe there are several good reasons for rejecting this interpretation.

It is not necessary to take these phrases literally. Jesus' words need not be taken in the literal sense of ingesting his actual physical body and blood. Jesus often spoke in metaphors and figures of speech.[65] He said, "I am the gate" (John 10:9) and "I am the true vine" (John 15:1), and Roman Catholic

---

62. Ott, *Fundamentals of Catholic Dogma*, p. 311.
63. Aquinas, *Summa Theologiae* III 68, 2; cited in ibid., p. 313.
64. Augustine, *On Baptism* IV 22, 29; cited in ibid., p. 357.
65. The intensity with which Jesus spoke when challenged does not prove that his words are to be taken literally. Jesus called the Pharisees "blind guides" (Matt. 23:24) and labeled Herod a "fox" (Luke 13:32), both strong metaphors not meant to be taken literally.

scholars do not take these statements literally, even though they come from the same book that records "This is my body"! It is, therefore, not necessary to take Jesus literally when he said "this is my body" or "eat my flesh." Jesus often spoke in graphic parables and figures, as he himself said (Matt. 13:10–11). As we shall see, these can be understood from the context.

It is not plausible to take Jesus' words literally. In response to the Catholic argument, first of all, the vividness of the phrases are no proof of their literal intent. The Psalms are filled with vivid figures of speech. God is depicted as a rock (Ps. 18:3), a bird (Ps. 63:7), a tower (Prov. 18:10), and many other ways in Holy Writ. Yet Catholic scholars do not take these to have a literal, physical referent. Further, the Bible often uses the language of ingesting in a figurative sense. "O taste and see that the Lord is good" is a case in point (Ps. 34:9 NKJV). The apostle John himself was told to eat a scroll (God's word) in the Apocalypse: "Take and swallow it." John did and said, "when I had eaten it, my stomach turned sour" (Rev. 10:9–10). What could be more vivid? This, however, was all part of a vision John had referring to his receiving God's word (the scroll). Even Peter tells young believers, "like newborn infants, long for pure spiritual milk" (1 Pet. 2:2). And the writer of Hebrews speaks of mature Christians eating "solid food" (5:14) and of others who "tasted the heavenly gift" (6:4).

Neither is it necessary, as Catholic scholars suggest, to take flesh and blood literally because this phrase was used that way in many places in other contexts. The same words have different meanings in different contexts. The word "flesh" (Gk: *sarx*) is often used in the New Testament in a spiritual, non-physical sense of the fallen nature of human beings, such as when Paul said, "I know that good does not dwell in me, that is, in my flesh" (Rom. 7:18; cf. Gal. 5:17). Meaning is discovered by context, not simply by whether the same or similar words are used. The same words are used in very different ways in different contexts. Even the word "body" (Gk: *soma*), which means a physical body when used of an individual human being sometimes means the mystical body of Christ, the church, in other contexts (cf. Eph. 1:22–23), as both Catholics and Protestants acknowledge.

The fact that some of Jesus' listeners apparently took his words literally (John 6:52) without his explicit and immediate rebuke is not a good argument. Jesus rebuked their understanding, at least implicitly, when he said later in the same discourse, "It is the spirit that gives life, while the flesh is of no avail. The words I have spoken to you are spirit and life" (John 6:63).[66] To borrow a phrase from Paul, Jesus' words are to be "judged spiritually" (1 Cor. 2:14; cf. Matt. 16:17), not in a gross physical sense. Also, Jesus did

66. Ott's argument that "In V, 63 ('It is the spirit that quickeneth: the flesh profiteth nothing') Christ does not reject the literal, but only the grossly sensual (Capharnaitic) interpretation" is implausible for reasons given above.

not have to rebuke them explicitly in order for their interpretation to be wrong, since a literalistic understanding in this context would have been so unreasonable that no disciple would have expected the Lord to be making such an absurd statement. After all, if the disciples had taken these words literally they could have thought he was suggesting cannibalism.

Neither is the appeal to an alleged miraculous transformation of the elements called for in this context. The only miracle in this connection is the feeding of the five thousand (John 6:11), which was the occasion for this discourse on the bread of life (John 6:35). An appeal to miracles of transubstantiation here is *deus ex machina;* that is, it is a vain attempt to evoke God to keep an implausible interpretation from collapsing.

Finally, appeal to the church fathers to support the Trentian dogma of transubstantiation is poorly grounded for many reasons. First, as even Catholic scholars admit, the Fathers were by no means unanimous in their interpretation, and yet Trent speaks of the "unanimous consent of the Fathers" as the means of determining true apostolic tradition. But some Fathers clearly opposed the idea of taking literally the phrase "this is my body." Second, many of the Fathers simply supported the idea of Jesus' real presence in the communion, not that the elements were literally transformed into the actual body and blood of Christ. So the later dogma of transubstantiation cannot be based on any early or unanimous consent of the Fathers which Catholics claim for it.

The Eastern Orthodox Church, whose roots are at least as old as the Roman church, has always held a mystical view of Christ's presence in the communion but never the Roman Catholic dogma of transubstantiation (see Appendix A).[67] Likewise, the Lutheran understanding, which rejects transubstantiation, appeals to the same Fathers in support of their view over against Catholicism. Finally, as noted before, the Fathers had only a fallible interpretation of the infallible Word. They could be—and often were— wrong. So there is no reason why they could not be wrong on this issue as well.

The Catholic church's use of the Fathers to proclaim a doctrine as infallibly true is not always consistent with the evidence. For sometimes their proclamation of a view as apostolic truth is not as well supported in the early fathers. In the final analysis, the decision of the teaching magisterium to proclaim a view on an article of faith is not based on the evidence, and its appeal to the Fathers and councils is uneven and after the fact. For example, when the Catholic church pronounces infallible a view that earlier Fathers and councils condemned, it ignores their statements against it, but when only a

---

67. The Orthodox church permits but does not require that real presence be understood in terms of transubstantiation which Roman Catholicism proclaims infallibly as the only way to properly understand it.

few early fathers and councils support a view they desire to pronounce *de fide*, then they point triumphantly to this minority voice. The truth is that the Catholic church's use of the Fathers is not only inconsistent but also circular. For the Fathers are used as a basis for the infallible teaching of the church, but the infallible teaching of the church is the basis for the use of the Fathers.

It is not possible *to take a literal view*. In at least one important respect it is logically impossible (inconsistent) for an orthodox Christian to hold to a literal interpretation of Jesus' words at the Last Supper. For, *when Jesus said of the bread in his hand "this is my body," no disciple present could possibly have understood him to mean that the bread was actually his physical body since he was still with them in his physical body, the hands of which were holding that very bread*. Otherwise, we must believe that Christ was holding his own body in his own hands. This reminds one of the medieval myth of the saint whose head was cut off yet he put it in his mouth and swam across the river!

Jesus could not have been speaking literally when he said, "this is my body" because ever since his incarnation he had always been a human being and also had always dwelt continuously in a human body (except for three days in a grave). *If the bread and the wine he held in his hands at the Last Supper were actually his body and blood, then he would have been incarnated in two different places at the same time!* One physical body cannot, however, be in two different locations at the same time; it takes two different bodies to do that. Hence, despite Catholic protest to the contrary,[68] transubstantiation logically would involve two bodies and two incarnations of Christ, which is contrary to the orthodox doctrine of *the* Incarnation.

It is idolatrous to worship the host. As we have seen, it is an official dogma of Roman Catholicism that the consecrated Eucharist can and should be worshiped. But many Protestants believe this is a form of idolatry.[69] For it is the worship of something which the God-given senses of every normal human being inform them is a finite creation of God, namely, bread and wine. It is to worship God under a physical image which is clearly forbidden in the Ten Commandments (Exod. 20:4).

---

68. Catholic scholars speak of Christ being in only one body but two locations, holding to bilocation but not bicorporation. But this is a distinction without a difference, since one of the essential properties of a physical earthly body, such as Jesus had, is that it has one particular location in space and time and cannot have another at the same time.

69. Catholics are quick to point out that some Protestants (e.g., Anglicans) and Eastern Orthodox also venerate the host and genuflect before it. This does not prove it is correct; at best it may only show that these views are also wrong. However, there is a difference that makes the criticism more severe for Roman Catholics, since they alone believe that the host is actually the body of Christ and can and should be worshiped as God. Others may believe that Christ is really present *in* the host, but this is very different from saying he *is* the host and should be worshiped as such.

Furthermore, the appeal to some kind of ubiquitous presence of the body of Christ or omnipresence of Christ as God in the host does not resolve the problem. That is, to consider the eucharistic elements to be only the "accidental clothing" under which Christ is somehow localized does not avoid the difficulty, for, using the same argument, one could justify pagans worshiping stones or statues, since God is everywhere present, even in their objects of worship. So by the same kind of argument that Roman Catholics would use to justify their worship of the host, pagan and other non-Christian idolatry also can be justified. After all, no animistic pagan really worships the stone. What he worships is the spirit that animates it.

Finally, to claim that the consecrated host is anything but a finite creature undermines the very epistemological basis by which we know anything in the empirical world and, indirectly, the very historical basis of support for the truth about the incarnate Christ, his death, and resurrection. For if the senses cannot be trusted when they experience the communion elements then the disciples could not have even verified Christ's claims to be resurrected. Jesus said, "*Look* at my hands and my feet, that it is I myself. *Touch* me and *see,* because a ghost does not have flesh and bones as you can see I have" (Luke 24:39, emphasis added; cf. John 20:27). John said of Christ that he was "What was from the beginning, what we have *heard,* what we have *seen* with our eyes, what we *looked upon* and *touched* with our hands" (1 John 1:1, emphasis added).

The mass shows no evidence of the miraculous. The Roman Catholic response to the foregoing arguments is that the mass is a miracle and, therefore, appealing to the normal, natural way of observing things is irrelevant. Miracles are not normal occurrences. This strategy, however, will not work, since the mass shows absolutely no evidence of being a miracle.

First, using the same kind of reasoning to try to justify an invisible material substance miraculously replacing the empirically obvious signs of bread and wine, one could justify the belief in Santa Claus at Christmas or a little invisible gremlin moving the hands on one's watch. Transubstantiation is literally not sensible, even though its object is a sensible (i.e., physical) body. Philosophically, it is an empirically unknowable event in the empirical world, and theologically, it is a matter of pure faith. Catholics must simply believe what the teaching magisterium tells them, namely, that the host is really Jesus' body, even though their senses tell them otherwise.

Second, if the mass is a miracle, then virtually any natural empirical event could also be a miracle, since miracles could be happening without any empirical evidence they were. This is like a physical resurrection without an empty tomb. If this is true, then nothing is a miracle. Hence, claiming that the mass is a miracle undermines the very nature of miracles themselves, at least as special events with apologetic value.

Third, it is futile for Catholic apologists to appeal to special divine appearances (theophanies) in an attempt to avoid these criticisms, for in so doing they overlook a very important difference. When God himself appears in a finite form it is an obvious miraculous appearance that one knows clearly is not a normal event. That is, there are supernatural manifestations, voices, prophecies, or unusual events of nature connected with it (cf. Exod. 3:1–6). The mass has no such events associated with it. Indeed, nowhere in the New Testament are the normal words for miracle (sign, wonder, power) used of the communion. There is absolutely no evidence that it is anything but a natural event with natural elements on which Christ places special spiritual blessings (and/or presence) as we "remember" his death (1 Cor. 11:25).

THE MASS AS A SACRIFICE

Roman Catholics (and Anglicans)[70] view the eucharistic feast as a sacrifice (albeit an unbloody one).[71] This term is found as early as Gregory the Great (c. A.D. 540–604), who was elected pope in A.D. 590.[72] Gregory held that at every mass Christ was sacrificed afresh and consequently "This notion of the mass as sacrifice eventually became standard doctrine of the Western church—until it was rejected by Protestants in the sixteenth century."[73]

In A.D. 831, a Frankish monk, Paschasius Radbertus (d. ca. 860), in a work titled *On the Body and Blood of the Lord*, addressed this issue. Radbertus taught that Christ is "corporeally" present during communion. The early church had considered the Eucharist a fellowship meal. Hence, "The new emphasis on the corporeal presence of Christ permitted the Church to begin to treat Christ as a victim, rather than as the host [of the feast], to think of itself as offering him to the Father, rather than as coming to be nourished at his table."[74] Thus, the Lord's Supper—which the early church viewed as a *fellowship* meal—became a *sacrifice*. The *remembrance* of a sacrifice becomes a new *enactment* of that sacrifice.[75] While, as Roman Catholics point out, the New Testament term "remembrance" (Gk: *anamnesis*) is often used in a sacrificial context, it does not justify their contention that communion is

---

70. Roman Catholics and Anglicans have issued a 600-word, five-point statement on common eucharistic beliefs, including viewing the Eucharist as a sacrifice. See "Catholics, Anglicans Agree," *The Southern Cross* (27 January 1994): 10.

71. It should be noted that Eastern Orthodoxy agrees with Roman Catholicism on this point: "At the Eucharist, the sacrifice offered is Christ himself, and it is Christ himself, who in the Church performs the act of offering" (Ware, pp. 292–93).

72. Cross, *Oxford Dictionary*, pp. 594–95.

73. González, *Story of Christianity*, 1:247.

74. Brown, *Heresies: The Image of Christ*, p. 233.

75. Ibid., emphasis added.

a sacrifice. What Jesus said was that, in participating in communion, we are *remembering* his sacrifice on the cross, not *reenacting* it.

Lutheran theology also rejects the concept of the mass as a sacrifice: "Since Christ died and atoned for sin once and for all, and since the believer is justified by faith on the basis of that one-time sacrifice, there is no need for repeated sacrifices."[76] Sacerdotalism is also rejected: "The presence of Christ's body and blood is not a result of the priest's actions. It is instead a consequence of the power of Jesus Christ."[77] But even granting that God is the primary cause of the transformation, Protestants still object to the Roman Catholic sacerdotal belief that the priest is a secondary cause or instrument through which God accomplishes such a transformation. It is contrary to the known ways of God revealed in Scripture to grant any creature the power to transform a creation (the bread and wine) into the actual body of the Creator (Christ).[78] The whole concept of re-enacting and re-presenting Christ's sacrifice on the cross is contrary to the clear teaching of Hebrews that this sacrifice occurred once for all time (Heb. 10:12–14). Thus, when the Council of Trent speaks of Christ being "immolated" (sacrificed)[79] again and again in the mass, it violates the clear teaching of Scripture.

THE CORPOREAL PRESENCE OF CHRIST

As mentioned earlier, the doctrine of the corporeal presence of Christ during the eucharistic feast poses another problem for most evangelicals.[80] Brown summarizes the difficulty that Roman Catholics (and Lutherans) face: "In order to be bodily present at thousands of altars, the body of Christ must possess one of the so-called attributes of the majesty of God, namely, omnipresence or ubiquity."[81] Simply put, "To believe that Jesus was in two places at once is something of a denial of the incarnation, which limited his physical human nature to one location."[82] This eucharistic understanding is fraught

---

76. Luther, *Babylonian Captivity*, p. 140.

77. Ibid.

78. While God granted human instruments (e.g., Moses, Elijah, and the apostles) the power to do miracles, some of which transformed water into wine, there is no evidence that he ever gave them the power to transform wine into the actual blood of the Son of God!

79. The Catholic observation that "immolate" does not necessarily mean "kill" (cf. Num. 8:11–21) but merely to "sacrifice" does nothing to counter the Scripture that affirms there is only one "sacrifice" forever (Heb. 10:10–14).

80. We use the word "most" because this difficulty is also inherent in Lutheran theology with their understanding that, in communion, the physical body and blood of Christ are "contained in" or are "under" the communion elements. In spite of "denials of various facets of the Catholic position, Luther insisted upon the concept of *manducation*. There is a real eating of Jesus' body" (Erickson, *Christian Theology*, p. 1118).

81. Brown, *Heresies: The Image of Christ*, p. 229.

82. Erickson, *Christian Theology*, p. 1121.

with difficulties. In an effort to preserve the "actual presence," one comes perilously close to "monophysitism," which held that, following the incarnation, Christ possessed only one incarnate divine nature—combining and co-mingling his two natures. Monophysitism was condemned by the Council of Ephesus (A.D. 431), and this official condemnation was reaffirmed at Chalcedon (A.D. 451).[83] Thus, by the same logic, should not the co-mingling of the divine and human in the substance of the communion elements also be condemned as unorthodox?

THE SACRAMENTALS

Lastly, we briefly mention something that the Roman Catholic Church calls the "Sacramentals"—not to be confused with the sacraments. Sacramentals include blessed ashes on Ash Wednesday, holy water, the sign of the cross, candles, the rosary, fasts, and the like. They are defined as "things or actions which the church uses in a certain imitation of the Sacraments, in order, in virtue of her prayers, to achieve effects, above all of the spiritual nature."[84] Sacramentals differ from sacraments in that Roman Catholics believe that the latter were instituted by Christ and the former by the church. Sacramentals also differ from sacraments "in the effects they produce. Unlike the sacraments, they do not confer sanctifying grace directly but merely dispose a person to its reception."[85]

Because sacramentals are not thought to be grace-producing in themselves, they are less problematic for evangelicals than the sacraments. The difference between Catholics and evangelicals here is more ceremonial than substantial.

SUMMARY AND CONCLUSION

The sacraments, especially the Eucharist, are at the heart of Roman Catholic belief and practice. Indeed, they have institutionalized them and, hence, are deserving of the title "an institution of salvation." Salvation is dispensed by the Catholic church to each recipient piece by piece from birth to death. Luther's heartbeat was to liberate the Christian soul from the heavy burden of institutionalized salvation. Even Catholic scholar Louis Bouyer asserted that Luther's *Babylonian Captivity* had "the sole, fundamental aim" of separating the individual soul, in its living relation with God, from all the complexities of an ecclesiastical organism which would stifle it, once the means

---

83. Brown, *Heresies: The Image of Christ*, pp. 168–72, 181–85.
84. Ott, *Fundamentals of Catholic Dogma*, p. 348.
85. Hardon, *Catholic Catechism*, p. 549.

of grace were either misdirected or made an end in themselves.[86] What Bouyer seems to forget, however, is that this is precisely what happened in Roman Catholicism.

Few things involve greater differences between Catholics and Protestants than the sacraments. Catholics believe that a sacrament is a cause of grace. For example, they hold that the grace of justification and sanctification are conveyed through baptism. Most Protestants do not.[87] Further, Catholics believe in transubstantiation; all historic orthodox Protestants do not.[88] We have examined both the arguments from the Bible and tradition in support of the Roman Catholic view and found them wanting. In fact, some dimensions of Roman Catholic teaching on the sacraments clearly contradict Scripture, other orthodox Christian teaching, and even fact and logic. Even Luther—who was the least radical of the Reformers with regard to church practices—retained many of the external ceremonies "so as not to disturb people."[89]

In view of these significant differences between Roman Catholic and evangelical Protestant doctrine, realism demands one take a less optimistic view than the ecumenical call, "Rome is home." As long as Roman Catholics maintain that these are unnegotiable dogmas, we will have to find ecclesiastical lodging elsewhere, in spite of all the other doctrines on which we agree (see Part One) and the practical areas in which we can cooperate (see Part Three).

---

86. Bouyer, *Spirit and Forms of Protestantism*, p. 100.

87. Lutherans are an exception, retaining the Catholic view at this point but manifesting a great deal of tension between it and the doctrine of justification by faith alone (see chap. 12 and Appendix E).

88. One can always find some exception somewhere, such as Howard Erwin, a charismatic Protestant who claims to believe in transubstantiation. But then again there are unorthodox Protestant charismatics who believe God the Father has a physical body and that Jesus was born again in hell! (see Hank Hanegraaff, *Christianity in Crisis* [Eugene, Oreg.: Harvest House, 1993]).

89. Toon, *Born Again*, p. 91.

14

ECCLESIOLOGY

Some of the greatest differences between Catholics and evangelicals concern the doctrine of the church, or ecclesiology. Of course, here too there are areas of common agreement, such as the foundation of the church by Christ, Christ being the head of the church (which has a visible as well as invisible dimension to it), that the sacraments (ordinances) include baptism and communion, that the purpose of the church is redemptive and evangelistic, and others (see Part One).[1] Our purpose here, however, is to explore some of the significant differences. In chapter 11 we discussed such differences as the primacy of Peter, apostolic succession, and the infallibility of the church of Rome. The main areas of dispute left for discussion here are the visibility, unity, priestly authority, and constituency of the church.

THE VISIBILITY OF THE CHURCH

According to Catholic doctrine, the church is not merely an invisible mystical body but also a visible organization on earth whose headquarters is in Rome. This they attempt to support by arguments from both Scripture and sacred tradition.

CATHOLIC DEFENSE OF THE VISIBILITY OF THE CHURCH

Pope Leo XIII declared that "When one visualizes the ultimate purpose of the Church and the proximate causes of effecting sanctity, she is, in fact, spiritual. But when one considers the members of the Church and the means which lead to the spiritual gifts, then she is externally and necessarily visi-

---

1. See Ott, *Fundamentals of Catholic Dogma*, pp. 270–76, 292.

ble."[2] Pope Pius XII confirmed this teaching that the church is visible in his encyclical "Mystici Corporis," where he rejected the view that the church is "a mere spiritual entity, joining together by an invisible link a number of communities of Christians, in spite of their difference in Faith."[3] The Council of Trent declared that, "Since in the New Testament the Catholic Church has received from the institution of the Lord the holy, visible sacrifice of the Eucharist, it must also be confessed that there is in this Church a new visible and external priesthood [can. 1], into which the old has been translated [Heb. 7:12]."[4] Thus, "If anyone says that there is not in the New Testament a visible and external priesthood, or that there is no power of consecrating and offering the true body and blood of the Lord, and of forgiving and retaining sins, but only the office and bare ministry of preaching the Gospel, or that those who do not preach are not priests at all: let him be anathema."[5]

Roman Catholics explicitly reject another view of the Reformers, insisting that "without an authoritative teaching office there is no certain norm for the purity of doctrine or for the administration of the Sacraments. The rejection of the hierarchy inevitably led to the doctrine of the invisible Church."[6] Catholics believe that the doctrine of the visibility of the church is based in both Scripture and tradition.

ARGUMENT FROM SCRIPTURE

A widely used source on Catholic dogma argues that "The biblical proof of the visibility of the Church springs from the Divine institution of the hierarchy." And "The teaching office demands from its incumbents the duty of obedience to the faith (Rom. 1, 5) and the confession of faith (Mt. 10, 32 et seq.; Rom. 10, 10)." Further, "To the sacerdotal office corresponds, on the part of the faithful, the duty of using the means of grace dispensed by it (John 3, 5; 6, 54)." Also, "To the pastoral office corresponds, on the part of those shepherded, the duty of being subject to the Church Authority (Mt. 18, 17 et seq.; Luke 10, 16)." In addition, it is argued that "The Prophets of the Old Covenant depict the Messianic Kingdom symbolically by the simile of a high mountain visible from afar, which overtowers all other mountains, and to which all people converge (Is. 2, 2 et seq.; Micah 4, 1 et seq.)." And "According to the parables of Jesus, the Church is like an earthly kingdom, a flock, a building, a vine, a city on a mountain. St. Paul compares the Church to the human body."[7]

2. Cited by Ott, *Fundamentals of Catholic Dogma*, p. 301.
3. Ibid.
4. Denzinger, *Sources of Catholic Dogma*, no. 957, p. 293.
5. Ibid., no. 961, pp. 294–95.
6. Ott, *Fundamentals of Catholic Dogma*, p. 301.
7. Ibid., pp. 301–2.

Some contemporary Catholic scholars argue that in Matthew 16 Jesus made Peter the head of a visible universal church, not just a visible local church or an invisible universal one.[8] They affirm that: (1) Jesus was not making Peter the head of an invisible church, which was his prerogative (Eph. 5:23), but of a visible earthly church; (2) the fact that Jesus gave the keys to exercise governmental authority over the church indicates it must have been a visible church; (3) the fact that the power of binding and loosing (Matt. 18:18) was to be exercised on earth shows that a visible earthly church was in view; (4) the power given to the disciples in Matthew 18:18 involves excommunication from a visible earthly church; and (5) the fact that the gates of hell would not prevail against it reveals that it would not pass out of existence, which would be superfluous to say of a heavenly church.

ARGUMENT FROM TRADITION

Catholic theologians note that even early Fathers like Irenaeus (2nd century) held to the visibility of the church, since "He compares the Church . . . to a seven-branched candlestick, which, visible to all, bears the light of Christ."[9] Further, "St. Augustine compares the Church to a city on a mountain (Mt. 5, 14): 'The Church stands clear and visible before all men; for she is the city on the mountain which cannot be hidden.'"[10] Some Catholic theologians believe, however, that "The final reason for the visibility of the Church lies in the Incarnation of the Divine Word."[11] That is, just as Christ was visible in incarnation, even so his body, the church, is visible in his absence. J. N. D. Kelly adds, "What these early Fathers were envisioning was almost always the empirical, visible society: they had little or no inkling of the distinction between a visible and invisible Church."[12]

PROTESTANT RESPONSE TO CATHOLIC ARGUMENT FOR THE VISIBILITY OF THE CHURCH

Evangelical Protestants reject the Roman Catholic insistence that the church which Christ and the apostles spoke of must be manifested in a visible organization, namely, the Roman Catholic Church. They reject both the Catholic interpretation of Scripture and their use of tradition on this matter.

---

8. Permission was granted to cite the material here which appears in an unpublished manuscript by James Akin titled *A Defense of Catholic Theology* (San Diego, 1994).

9. Irenaeus, *Against Heresies* V, 20, 1, as summarized by Ott, *Fundamentals of Catholic Dogma*, p. 302.

10. Augustine, *Contra Cresconium* II, 36, 45; cited in Ott, *Fundamentals of Catholic Dogma*, p. 302.

11. Ott, *Fundamentals of Catholic Dogma*, p. 302.

12. Kelly, *Early Christian Doctrine*, pp. 190f.

RESPONSE TO ARGUMENT FROM SCRIPTURE

A careful examination of the context of the text used to support the Catholic insistence on a visible earthly organization that is Christ's true church reveals a misuse of these passages. A brief examination of the crucial texts will reveal the invalidity of their conclusions.

Romans 1:5. Based on this text, Catholics claim that "The teaching office [of the Roman Catholic Church] demands from its incumbents the duty of obedience to the faith." This is not, however, supported by this text which states: "Through him [Christ] we have received the grace of apostleship, to bring about the obedience of faith." First, Paul is speaking here about his apostleship (v. 1), not that of Peter, to say nothing of Peter's alleged successors, Roman Catholic popes. Further, to be an apostle one had to be an eyewitness of the resurrected Christ (Acts 1:22; 1 Cor. 9:1; 15:5–7), which clearly disqualifies anyone after the first century, and thus negates the claim that the teaching office of the Roman Catholic Church is somehow implied here. It should be noted that the added requirement of being a witnesses of Jesus' earthly ministry (Acts 1:22) was only to be one of the twelve apostles who have a special place in the foundation of the church (Eph. 2:20), their very names being written on the foundation (Rev. 21:14) and their reigning with Christ on twelve thrones when he returns (Matt. 19:28). Paul was not one of the twelve and, hence, need not fulfill this requirement. However, he was an apostle (Gal. 1:1) who received direct revelation from God (Gal. 1:12), who compared his apostolic authority with that of the other apostles (Gal. 1:17; 2:5–9) and who manifested the "signs of an apostle" (2 Cor. 12:12). Further, Paul explicitly listed the appearance of the resurrected Christ to him as qualifying him for being an apostle. He wrote: "Am I not an apostle? Have I not seen Jesus our Lord?" (1 Cor. 9:1). Likewise, he listed Jesus' resurrection appearance to him along with that of the other apostles, saying, "After that he [Jesus] appeared to James, then to all the apostles. Last of all . . . he appeared to me" (1 Cor. 15:7–8).

What is more, it is evident from several texts there were no more appearances of Christ to confirm apostolic authority after Paul. First, there are no other appearances listed in the 1 Corinthians 15 list after that of Paul, which he describes as "last of all." Second, the miraculous signs which confirmed an apostle are referred to as past events by A.D. 69 when the book of Hebrews was written (Heb. 2:3–4). Third, Jude, who wrote his book after Paul's death, refers to the apostles as having lived in the past (Jude 17) and speaks of the faith as having been "once for all" handed down to the church by them (v. 3).

Finally, Paul and the other apostles manifested the "signs of an apostle"

(2 Cor. 12:12), which included the ability to heal *all diseases*,[13] even naturally incurable ones, *immediately* (cf. Acts 3:7), to exorcise demons on command (Matt. 10:8; cf. Acts 16:16–18), strike dead some who lied to the Holy Spirit (Acts 5:1–11), and even perform resurrections from the dead (Matt. 10:7; cf. Acts 20). This automatically excludes anyone alive today, including the pope, since no one possesses the power to perform these kinds of apostolic signs. Without these kinds of apostolic signs there is no proof of apostolic authority. Of course, the authority of the New Testament apostles existed after their miracles had ceased, but only because these apostolic signs had confirmed their authority expressed in the abiding apostolic writings. Once these confirmed apostles died, however, there was no living apostolic authority. The only apostolic authority present today is that of the apostolic writings (namely, the New Testament) that were confirmed by apostolic signs. Since we possess no traditions that can be evidentially and documentarily traced to the apostles, as can the New Testament, it follows that only the New Testament contains this apostolic authority (see chap. 11).

Matthew 10:32 (and Rom. 10:10). According to these passages it is the obligation of believers to confess Christ openly before humanity, but neither of them speaks of the necessity of doing it in connection with the visible organization known as the Roman Catholic Church. Indeed, in the first century, when this was written, even baptism was performed in public, not in churches (cf. Acts 2:38; 10:46–48; 16:31–33). It is a big leap in logic to argue that from the practice of public testimony and baptism one must accept the visible hierarchy of the church of Rome.

13. Scripture clearly says that Jesus gave the apostles the ability "to heal every kind of disease and every kind of sickness" (Matt. 10:1). Indeed, it is written that after the apostle Paul performed a healing, "the rest of the sick on the island came to Paul and were cured" (Acts 28:9). The fact that Paul at a later time (1 Tim. 5:23; 2 Tim. 4:20) did not heal some companions does not prove that the apostolic sign gifts failed but merely that they had ceased to exist by that time or that it was not "according to his [God's] will" to exercise healing on that occasion (cf. Heb. 2:4). Since their function was only a temporary one to confirm the apostolic message (Heb. 2:3–4), thus laying the foundation of the church (Eph. 2:20), it is understandable that once the new revelation had been confirmed and the foundation laid there would be no more need for these sign gifts. And this is what Hebrews 2:3–4 says happened, since by then (A.D. 69) these gifts had already passed (see Geisler, *Signs and Wonders,* chap. 9 and appendixes 2 and 8).

Likewise, Paul's reference to his "physical illness" (Gal. 4:13) during the period when apostolic signs were still in effect does not prove that the apostles did not have the ability to heal all sicknesses on command. The apostle may not have desired to use his miraculous powers for his own good, following the example of Christ who refused to turn stones to bread to satisfy his own hunger (Matt. 4). Or it may not have been God's will (cf. Heb. 2:4) to exercise it on that occasion. It is also possible that Paul's condition was a result of his being blinded by the dazzling light from Christ when he was converted (Acts 9), an impaired visual condition he may have been alluding to in his reference to writing in large letters (Gal. 6:11). At any rate, it is clear that the age of apostolic miracles was still in effect at this time (Gal. 3:5) that did entail special supernatural abilities (2 Cor. 12:12) to perform miracles that confirmed the apostles' new revelation (Heb. 2:3–4), even if this did not necessarily mean they would heal everyone all the time, including themselves.

John 3:5 (and 6:54). Catholics argue that these texts speak of baptism and the Eucharist. To argue, however, that they prove that participation in the sacraments supports the Catholic doctrine that the church is a visible earthly organization is unwarranted for several reasons. First, even Catholic theology acknowledges that baptism done by lay persons and even heretics (including Protestant ministers)[14] is valid. It does not have to be done in connection with the visible church of Rome. Second, as we show elsewhere (see Appendix E), baptism is not essential to salvation. If it is not necessary for salvation, then it is not an essential sacrament in the visible church. Indeed, even Catholic theology (in its "baptism of blood" [martyrs] and "baptism of desire" doctrines)[15] acknowledges that baptism is not absolutely essential for salvation. Namely, that those who are not baptized but would have been (had they known and could have) can be saved without it. So here again the necessity of an outward sign done in connection with the visible church has not been proven from these texts.

Matthew 16:16–18. Contrary to Catholic dogma, this passage does not prove that the Roman Catholic Church is the one true visible church of Christ on earth. First, the argument wrongly assumes that Christ is not the head over the earthly church as he is the heavenly one. The Bible, however, clearly teaches that even though Christ is not visibly present today he is still head over all things to the church (his body) part of which is still on earth. After reminding the Ephesian Christians that Christ is "head over all things to the church, which is his body" (Eph. 1:22–23), Paul goes on to say that the apostles (who were alive then) were part of the "foundation" of the church (2:19–20) of which the Ephesians were a part (see "you," v. 19). Paul is saying that Christ was the head of the church at Ephesus as well as the head of the invisible church. There is no need for an earthly head of the church.

Second, the Catholic argument that Christ made Peter the head of a visible earthly church begs the question. As we have already shown (in chap. 11), Jesus did not make Peter the unique head of anything. Jesus gave the same powers to bind and loose to all the apostles (Matt. 18:18). The church is "built upon the foundation of the apostles [plural] and prophets, with Christ Jesus himself as the capstone" (Eph. 2:20). Whatever role Peter had in the foundation he shared with the other apostles. Christ alone is unique in being the cornerstone.

Third, it is true that when the body of Christ began it was all visible since no believers had died and gone to heaven, so of course it was a visible church

14. Catholic scholars note that not all Protestant ministers are formally heretical but only materially heretical, since their error is not culpable, unless they are fully informed and obstinate.

15. See Ott, *Fundamentals of Catholic Dogma*, pp. 114, 311, and especially where he says, "Baptism of desire works *ex opere operantis*. It bestows Sanctifying Grace, which remits original sin, all actual sins, and the eternal punishment for sin." The repentant thief on the cross was saved by the baptism of desire.

when Christ founded it. The invisible church only grew as Christians died and went to heaven. Protestants do not deny that there was a visible Christian church on earth that traces back to the apostles who exercised authority over it, including excommunication. What Protestants object to (and Catholics have not proven) is that Roman Catholic jurisdiction is the sole heir to this original visible church that began with the apostles and will continue until Christ comes without the gates of hell destroying it.

Matthew 18:17. Jesus said, "If he [the offender] refuses to listen to them [the offended and his witnesses], tell the church." This statement cannot be used to support the Roman Catholic claim that this text proves the divine authority of the Roman See. First, "the church" referred to was a local assembly of believers, such as they were no doubt accustomed to having in their local synagogue. There is no reference here to a universal (catholic) church.

Second, the New Testament church, as a united, gifted, and empowered body of believers, did not come into existence until the day of Pentecost (Acts 1:8; 2:1–4, 42–47). So, whatever "church" means in the context of Matthew 18, it does not refer to what Roman Catholics mean by a visible church that administers the sacraments and infallibly teaches and disciplines the faithful.

Third, this passage does not speak of any universal apostolic authority to settle all disputes of faith and practice. It refers only to cases involving "sins" and "faults" by which one "brother" has offended another (18:15). This falls short of what Catholics claim for the divine authority of the visible Roman church.

Finally, even if this text did speak about the need for submission to God-ordained authority in all matters of doctrine and conduct, it would not support the Catholic argument for a visible church. For clearly this passage does not show that this authority is to be found in the visible Roman Catholic Church, as opposed to other visible churches, some of which, like the Eastern Orthodox, are as old or even older.

Luke 10:16. Jesus said to his apostles, "Whoever listens to you listens to me. Whoever rejects you rejects me." This does not, however, prove the duty to be subject to the Catholic church's authority—at least not in the sense that Catholics believe. The passage is not speaking about any authority limited to Peter or the apostles but about "seventy" disciples (Luke 10:1–3) sent on a mission to preach the kingdom of God. Also, the passage says nothing about exercising ecclesiastical authority such as binding and loosing (cf. Matt. 18:18) but simply about pronouncing God's judgment on those who reject Christ's evangels of his kingdom (Luke 10:10–11). Neither does the phrase "whoever listens to you listens to me" refer to any organizational structure of the visible church but to the authority given to every pair of evangelists sent out to proclaim Christ's message in his name. Finally, whatever else this passage entails it certainly does not refer to the authority of a visible church over which Peter has primacy, even in the first century. For the "you" (Gk:

humas) is plural not singular, referring to all the disciples. The same is true, as we have seen, with Jesus' statement to Peter in Matthew 16, since he gave the same authority to bind and loose to all the disciples (Matt. 18:18).

Isaiah 2:2 (Mic. 4:1). The fact that the Old Testament prophets spoke of Israel's future kingdom in terms of a mountain is significantly different from the Roman Catholic doctrine of the visibility of the church. For one thing, according to Catholic authority Ludwig Ott, the prophet is speaking only "symbolically." Further, even if the passage is taken to depict a literal outward kingdom, it is not the Roman Catholic Church. Rather, it is the literal Davidic kingdom promised to the nation of Israel wherein they will dwell with their Messiah (Jesus) in the land of Palestine promised to their father Abraham (Gen. 12:1–3; 13:14–17; 15:1–16). During this time "the Son of Man [Jesus] is seated on his throne . . . judging the twelve tribes of Israel" (Matt. 19:28). This will occur, as Jesus indicated, when he returns "to restore the kingdom to Israel" (Acts 1:6) at which time "all Israel will be saved" (Rom. 11:26) when they are "grafted back into their own olive tree" (Rom. 11:24).

Finally, even if there were some anticipation of a visible manifestation of the Christian church in these Old Testament passages, as even some Protestants believe, it does not imply that this would be manifested in the organizational Roman Catholic Church. So in no way can the claims of Roman Catholicism be justified from these passages.

The Parables of Jesus. Jesus does depict his future believers on earth as a flock, a building, a vine, a human body, and a city on a mountain, but none of these either anticipates or necessitates what Catholic scholars infer from them. They are simply depictions of the manifestation of Jesus' followers in a corporate way. Some passages may not even be speaking of Christ's universal church but only of a local church (e.g., 1 Cor. 14:1–4). Others refer to the invisible church, not the visible church (Eph. 1:22–23). None of them speak of the visible church being manifest in what we know as the Roman Catholic church.[16]

RESPONSE TO ARGUMENT FROM TRADITION

The argument from the Fathers is less than convincing for many reasons. Even Catholic scholars acknowledge that the church fathers were not unanimous on this topic. As Kelly noted, not all the Fathers clearly envisioned a visible organizational unity in the church. Some recognized, as did the New Testament (cf. Eph. 1–4), an invisible church as well. Furthermore, even those who believed in a visible unity did not do so in the same way Roman Catholics envision it, namely, as centered in the hierarchy of the Catholic

16. Ibid., pp. 301–2.

church, with its apex in the primacy of the bishop of Rome. Eastern church fathers, to which Eastern Orthodoxy traces its lineage and who are as early as any in the Western church, clearly did not think it would or should be. Finally, the papacy as it is known today is a relatively late institution, having assumed its shape under Pope Leo I (d. A.D. 461). The visible unity stressed by the early Fathers is not identical to the organizational unity under the headship of an infallible pope in Rome. Roman Catholicism's conclusion goes well beyond even a consensus view of the early Fathers, to say nothing of the "unanimous" one they claim.

THE UNITY OF THE CHURCH

In addition to a visible unity of Christians in the Roman Catholic Church, Catholics also believe there is a God-ordained unity to the church. This unity is manifested in two ways: a unity of faith and a unity of communion.

CATHOLIC DEFENSE OF THE UNITY OF THE CHURCH

Roman Catholicism teaches that "The unity both of faith and communion is guaranteed by the Primacy of the Pope, the Supreme Teacher and Pastor of the Church. One is cut off from the unity of Faith by heresy and from the unity of communion by schism."[17] In his 1896 encyclical *(Satis gognitum)* Pope Leo XIII declared: "Surely it is well established among all according to clear and manifold testimony that *the true Church of Jesus Christ is one*, that no Christian dare contradict it."[18] The nature of this unity was clearly specified by the pope: "Jesus did not arrange and organize such a Church as would embrace several communities similar in kind, but distinct, and not bound together by those bonds that make the Church indivisible and unique after the manner clearly in which we profess the symbols of faith, 'I believe in one Church.'" He continued, *"The Church of Christ, therefore, is one and perpetual;* whoever go apart [from it] wander away from the will and prescription of Christ the Lord and, leaving the way of salvation, digress to destruction." Consequently, "Jesus Christ instituted in the Church a living, authentic, and likewise permanent *Magisterium*, which He strengthened by His own power, taught by the Spirit of Truth, and confirmed by miracles." In addition, "When the divine Founder decreed that the Church be one in faith, and in government, and in communion, *He chose Peter and his successors in whom should be the principle and as it were the center of unity.*"[19]

17. Ibid., p. 303.
18. Denzinger, *Sources of Catholic Dogma*, no. 1954, p. 494, emphasis added.
19. Ibid., nos. 1955–57, 1960, emphasis added.

In defending the visible unity of the church under the Roman jurisdiction Catholic theologians appeal to both Scripture and church tradition. The argument from Scripture is based in a variety of texts, some of which are directed at the unity of faith and others at the unity of communion. Catholic scholars believe that the unity of faith "consists in the fact that all members of the Church inwardly believe the truths of faith proposed by the teaching office of the Church, at least implicitly and outwardly confess them." Of course, "Unity of Faith leaves room for various opinions in those controversial questions which the Church has not finally decided."[20] The unity of communion "consists, on the one hand, in the subjection of the members of the Church to the authority of the bishops and of the Pope (unity of government or hierarchical unity); on the other hand, in the binding of the members among themselves to a social unity by participation in the same cult and in the same means of grace (unity of cult or liturgical unity)."[21]

ARGUMENT FROM SCRIPTURE

Scriptural evidence offered by Catholic scholars can be summarized as follows: "Christ gives the Apostles the mandate to promulgate His teaching to all peoples, and demands unconditional assent to its promulgation (Mt. 28, 19 et seq.; Mk. 16, 15 et seq.)." Also, "In the prayer of the High Priest He insistently asks the Father for the unity of the Apostles and of the future faithful [John 17:20]." Further, "Paul symbolically represents the unity of the Church by picturing it as a house (I Tim. 3, 15) and again as a human body (Rom. 12, 4 . . .). He expressly enjoins internal and outward unity . . . (Eph. 4, 3–6). He warns insistently against schism and heresy . . . (I Cor. 1, 10 . . . Tit. 3, 10)."[22]

ARGUMENT FROM TRADITION

Catholic theology depends heavily on tradition to support its concept of the ecclesiastical unity of communion. They appeal especially to the early Fathers' struggle against heresy, particularly to Irenaeus and Tertullian. "St. Cyprian, impelled by the secession from the Church in Carthage and in Rome, wrote the first monograph on the unity of the Catholic Church."[23] Later, Augustine, in his *Anti-Donatist Writings,* took a strong stand against schism, arguing that the Catholic church has the right to force conformity to its essential doctrines.[24]

20. Ott, *Fundamentals of Catholic Dogma,* p. 303.
21. Ibid.
22. Ibid., p. 304.
23. Ibid.
24. See Augustine, *Correction of the Donatists* 6.22–24.

PROTESTANT RESPONSE TO CATHOLIC ARGUMENT FOR THE UNITY OF THE CHURCH

Protestants confess the Apostles' Creed which affirms one "Catholic [universal] Church" but they do not mean the same thing by it that Roman Catholics do. The common denominator of the Protestant concept of unity is doctrinal and spiritual, not organizational.

RESPONSE TO ARGUMENT FROM SCRIPTURE

Evangelicals reject the Catholic interpretation of Scripture to support their doctrine of a visible, organizational, ecclesiastical unity. They insist that the basis of true unity is found in the spiritual (mystical) body of Christ, the invisible church, not in a visible church.

Matthew 28:19 (Mark 16:15). While Christ did give the disciples a mandate to proclaim the gospel to all people, they were not instructed to demand an "unconditional assent to its promulgation," at least not in the sense in which Rome has interpreted this.[25] Rather, they were told simply to "*teach* them to observe" Christ's teaching (Matt. 28:20). But their willingness to be taught is a necessary condition made clear by the fact that they were asked to "believe" (Mark 16:16). As Augustine acknowledged, you cannot force people in matters of faith, for "God judged that men would serve him better if they served him freely. That could not be if they served him by necessity and not by free will."[26]

Furthermore, even if in some qualified sense the "demand for unconditional assent" is required for discipleship, this does not mean that Christ intended here that it must be given to any earthly organization. Clearly, the "commands" to be "observed" were those of Christ (Matt. 28:20), not those of any alleged representative of Christ on earth (like Peter). This is to say nothing of the extra-biblical doctrines the Catholic church has added to them since that time, such as the infallibility of the pope (see chap. 11), the bodily assumption of Mary (chap. 15), and the Apocrypha (chap. 9).

Finally, the unity envisioned here is not organizational but doctrinal and spiritual. It is a unity in Christ's "teaching" and of his presence (Matt. 28:20), not in an earthly institution. Institutional unity is not envisioned in this passage, at least not in the explicit or monolithic sense in which Roman Catholics hold it.

---

25. Ott, *Fundamentals of Catholic Dogma,* p. 303.

26. Augustine, *Of True Religion* 14. See also Denzinger, *Sources of Catholic Dogma,* no. 1875. Augustine, however, seemed to be inconsistent with his own principle when he argued that the Donatist heretics should be coerced into conformity with the Catholic church (see his *Anti-Donatist Writings*).

John 17:20–21. Jesus did pray for his followers, "that they may all be one," but evangelicals insist that he was not speaking about *organizational* unity but *organic* unity. He was not referring to an *external uniformity* but to the visible manifestation of our *spiritual unity,* for example, in our love for one another which Jesus said unbelievers can detect (John 13:35). After all, Jesus only prayed that all *believers* be one, not that all *churches* belong to one. Certainly the unity should be *visible,* but it need not be *organizational.* In this regard the recent statement by "Evangelicals and Catholics Together" has been criticized for not making the historic Protestant view more clear, sometimes blurring the distinction between the visible and invisible dimensions of the church crucial to the Protestant view.[27] That the unity was truly spiritual is evident in what was said of early Christians, "Behold, how they love one another!" Christ's true followers are one in faith, hope, and love, not in denomination, synod, or jurisdiction.

Furthermore, even though the immediate discussion concerns a visible unity of the church, it is clear that Jesus did not envision this organizational unity, such as that claimed by the Roman See from the facts that: (1) no such governmental unity is mentioned anywhere in the passage; (2) Jesus is speaking of "all those who will believe" in him in the future too, which includes those who couldn't be seen (v. 20)—a description of the whole spiritual body of believers, not simply the organized believers on earth; (3) the unity for which he prayed is compared to that among the persons of the Godhead ("as you, Father, are in me and I in you"), a unity that is clearly spiritual and invisible, not visible and organizational; (4) the primary sense in which the world was to observe the manifestation of this unity was by "love" (v. 23), a spiritual tie, not an organizational one. Indeed, Jesus said, "This is how all will know that you are my disciples, if you have love for one another" (John 13:35). The kind of unity envisioned here clearly is not a visible organization, as Catholics claim, but a true spiritual unity.

Ephesians 4:3–6. Paul speaks here of "striving to preserve the unity of the spirit" in "one body." It is evident, however, that he does not have an organizational unity of the Christian church in mind, certainly not the kind claimed by the Roman Catholic church. For one thing, according to the New American Bible it is not an organizational unity, since he spoke of "unity of the spirit" (v. 3). Even if it is rendered "the unity of the [Holy] Spirit" (NIV, RSV), there is no indication that it is more than a spiritual unity wrought by the source of all true spiritual unity, the Holy Spirit. Further, the spiritual unity is made by God, not people. Christians are merely urged to strive to *maintain* this unity that God has *made* in the body. What is more, the "one body" is the body (cf. 1 Cor. 12:13) into which believers are

27. See "Evangelicals and Catholics Together: The Christian Mission in the Third Millennium," final draft (29 March 1994). See Appendix F.

baptized by "one Spirit" (v. 4). This must be the spiritual body of Christ that is the only body to which all believers belong, since many believers belonging to that body (namely, those who are dead) are not part of the visible church. Further, this is clearly baptism by the Spirit, which unites one with the invisible (spiritual) body of Christ, and not water baptism (which is different, cf. Acts 1:5; 10:47), which unites one with part of the visible body of Christ on earth. So the unity here is a unity of faith, not of communion, since Paul refers to "one Lord, one faith, one baptism," all of which are a matter of confession. There is nothing in this text about unity of government or organization, certainly not on the universal scale that Roman Catholics believe.

Romans 12:4. The "body" referenced in these texts is not necessarily the visible organization of a universal Church, such as is claimed by Catholicism. In context it is the spiritual unity to be found in the local congregation. This is evident from the fact that Paul is addressing "all the beloved of God *in Rome*" (Rom. 1:7, emphasis added), not the whole visible Christian church. True, he gives truths that are applicable to the whole church, but this does not mean that when he speaks of "body" (in 12:4) that he necessarily has visible, organizational unity in mind. Further, the context in which he speaks of "one body" is the exercise of the individual members' gifts to edify this local congregation (vv. 6–8). Although what is true for one local body of believers will be true for others, there is no reference here to any visible authority that governs all these churches.[28] The context indicates that the one body is not the universal church but the local church in the city of Rome. Finally, to whatever degree it is legitimate to apply this text beyond the local church addressed here, it certainly does not prove the Roman Catholic claim that there is a God-ordained unity in one visible church. The New Testament often refers to "churches" (Acts 16:5; Rev. 1:4) each having their own governing authorities (Acts 20:17; Phil. 1:1; Titus 1:5).[29]

1 Timothy 3:15. Catholic scholars claim this is a reference to the visible universal church, embracing the whole family on earth because of references to "the church" and phrases like "household of God" and "pillar and foundation of truth." In response, several observations are in order. First, as cosmic sounding as these phrases may be, we must keep in mind that Paul is writing to Timothy about "how to *behave*" in the church while he was "delayed" from being there personally (v. 15), which is an obvious reference to his coming to a specific local church.

---

28. Except, of course, there was the authority of living apostles (in the first century) and there is the authority of apostolic writings in the New Testament for succeeding centuries. This is precisely what Protestants believe.

29. The authority of these individual churches was, of course, subject to apostolic authority which was exercised by them personally when they were alive (2 Thess. 2:15; Titus 1:5) and which exists since their time in the apostolic writings of the New Testament (see chap. 10).

283

Second, since the letters to Timothy are pastoral in nature it is understandable that what Paul taught would be applicable to other local churches as well. The reference to public reading of the Bible (4:13) and other things not true of the universal church (5:4–16) supports this claim. Hence, the phrase "household of God" may be a collective term encompassing the various individual "churches" of which the Bible speaks elsewhere (cf. Acts 20:17; Rev. 1:4). So rather than being a reference to a universal visible church it may be only a generalization for all the individual churches collectively.

Further, even if this is a reference to a universal visible church, it in no way specifies that it is to be understood in a monolithic way, as with Roman Catholicism. It may mean no more than the collective manifestation of all believers on earth.

Finally, as already noted, there are several other important (and we believe unprovable) steps from a universal visible church in the first century to the Roman Catholic doctrine that it is the true God-ordained successor of that apostolic church on earth today.

Titus 3:5 (1 Cor. 1:10). It is true that the New Testament urges believers to deal with serious false doctrine and, "after a first and second warning, break off contact with a heretic" (Titus 3:10). However, the false teacher was in a local congregation and the action to cut off relations with them was to be taken by a local body of believers, not by a visible universal organization such as the Roman Catholic Church claims to be. Likewise, in Corinth, when church discipline was necessary in moral matters, it was the congregation that took action. Speaking to the local church "in Corinth" (1 Cor. 1:2), the apostle Paul exhorted: "in the name of [our] Lord Jesus: *when you have gathered together* . . . with the power of the Lord Jesus, *you* are to deliver this man to Satan" (1 Cor. 5:4–5, emphasis added). To be sure, apostolic authority (Paul) was behind this decision, but it was accomplished by a local body of believers. Protestants do not deny that there was living apostolic authority in the first century that was binding on all the churches. This was part of their foundational role in establishing the church (Eph. 2:20), but it in no way supports the Roman Catholic claim that there was an authoritative visible organization in place in the New Testament that was divinely authorized to exercise this authority.

Acts 15. Only once did an issue in the churches draw general interest and consultation (Acts 15), and even then the Jerusalem conference was only confirmatory of the revelation Paul had previously received directly from God. There was no new infallible declaration from God.

There are several things about the decision which indicate that it was only confirmatory of the revelation already given by and confirmed by God to an apostle (Gal. 1:11–12). First, the inquiry into the issue was a voluntary one, coming from the church in Antioch (Acts 15:2–3). Second, the nature of the event was more of a conference than a church council, since it was not only apostles and elders but also the other "brethren" who made the decision (Acts 15:22–23). Third, contrary to the Catholic claim, if anyone dominated the conference it was not Peter but James, giving as he did the last word in the discussion (15:13–21). Fourth, the language of the statement is moderate, using phrases like "it seemed good to us." Indeed, the result of the conference was only a "letter" (15:30), not a papal encyclical with the typical language of anathema. Finally, the conference recognized the supernatural confirmation of God on the message of Paul (Acts 15:12), which was the divinely appointed sign that he spoke by revelation from God (2 Cor. 12:12; Heb. 2:3–4).

RESPONSE TO ARGUMENT FROM TRADITION

The Roman Catholic argument for an organizational unity of the Christian church on the basis of tradition fails for a number of reasons. First, there was no such unity in the first few centuries. On one occasion (in the late 2nd century) the bishop of Rome, in a pompous display of power, cut Western Christians off from all of Asia Minor by assuming the right to excommunicate them from Christendom. There obviously was no organizational unity manifest here. Further, the Roman Catholic Church as we know it did not begin to develop until after the time of Constantine and Augustine (4th century). References to unity before this time are either purely confessional (e.g., the *Apostles' Creed*) or doctrinal deviations dealt with in some localized area. The first ecumenical council was not until Nicea (A.D. 325). And even here we do not see an organizational unity such as the Roman Catholic Church claims exists in its hierarchy.[30] Most orthodox Protestants accept the validity of the creeds and councils of the first five centuries but reject the Roman Catholic claim to be the one true church of Christ on earth.[31]

THE PRIESTLY AUTHORITY OF THE CHURCH

As discussed earlier (chap. 13), Catholics believe the church is an institution of salvation which dispenses grace a portion at a time by the seven sacraments from birth to death through the priesthood. Thus, the function of the priesthood is the heart of the Roman Catholic system.

30. This is not to say that Nicea did not conceive of a doctrinal unity under which umbrella it envisioned all the true Christian churches on earth to be expected to abide. But there is nothing uniquely Roman Catholic about this, since most Protestants agree as well.

31. This is not to say that there is no disagreement among Protestants over how to interpret certain phrases of the Nicene Creed like "one, holy, catholic, and apostolic Church" and "baptism for the remission of sins." Some Protestants even quibble (we believe wrongly) over the "eternally begotten" Son phrase. But these are only questions of interpretation, not questions about the acceptance of this creed.

THE NATURE OF PRIESTLY AUTHORITY

Priestly power is permanent. It "can neither be effaced nor taken away."[32] The Catholic church proclaimed "that the holy Synod [of Trent] condemned the opinion of those who assert that the priests of the New Testament have only a temporary power, and that those at one time rightly ordained can again become laymen, if they do not exercise the ministry of the word of God [can. 1]."[33] In other words, priestly power is permanent. Further, sacramental priestly function is unique only to those rightly ordained, such as the priests in the Roman Catholic Church.[34] The Council of Trent declared, "But if anyone should affirm that all Christians without distinction are priests of the New Testament . . . , or that they are all endowed among themselves with an equal spiritual power, he seems to do nothing else than disarrange [can. 6] the ecclesiastical hierarchy."[35]

THE SUCCESSION OF PRIESTLY AUTHORITY

Finally, there is a succession of priestly power under the bishop of Rome. Roman Catholic infallible dogma proclaims that "Jesus Christ instituted in the Church a living, authentic, and likewise permanent *magisterium*, which He strengthened by His own power, taught by the Spirit of Truth, and confirmed by miracles."[36] Likewise, "When the divine Founder decreed that the Church be one in faith, and in government, and in communion, *He chose Peter and his successors in whom should be the principle and as it were the center of unity*."[37]

THE ADMINISTRATION OF PRIESTLY AUTHORITY

The function of the priestly hierarchy (of priests and bishops) is to administer the seven sacraments: baptism, confirmation, Eucharist, penance, ex-

---

32. Denzinger, *Sources of Catholic Dogma*, nos. 960–61, pp. 294–95.
33. Ibid., no. 960, p. 294.
34. Roman Catholics also accept the validity of ordination in Eastern Orthodox, Old Catholics, some Anglicans, namely, the ones who have been ordained by those with valid orders.
35. Ibid. Protestants acknowledge that there are different spiritual gifts in the body of Christ but they do not believe that any of them have special priestly powers that others do not have, since we all have the same access by prayer to our one great High Priest, Christ (Heb. 4–7).
36. No alleged miracles performed by popes or priests today are of the kind the apostles performed. The apostles' miraculous healings were: (1) immediate; (2) always successful, even on incurable diseases; (3) without known relapse into the disease; and (4) confirming of the new revelation given through them (cf. Heb. 2:3–4), which even Catholic scholars admit does not exist since the days of the apostles. But if new revelation does not exist, then there is no need for supernatural confirmation; the sign and sermon go together. The new message for God was accompanied by a new miracle from God (cf. John 3:2; Acts 2:22). For further discussion, see Geisler, *Signs and Wonders*, appendix 2.
37. Denzinger, *Sources of Catholic Dogma*, nos. 1957, 1960, emphasis added.

treme unction, holy order, and matrimony.[38] "Except for Baptism and Matrimony,[39] a special priestly or episcopal power conferred by Holy Orders, is necessary for the valid ministration of the Sacraments."[40] Lay persons (e.g., nurses or doctors) and even Protestants may administer baptism in the name of the Trinity. However, the Council of Trent soundly condemned the belief that "all Christians have the power to administer all the sacraments."[41]

CATHOLIC DEFENSE OF THE PRIESTLY AUTHORITY OF THE CHURCH

Roman Catholicism is hierarchically structured. The pope, as successor to Peter, is the final and infallible authority (see chap. 11). Under him are the bishops who receive their power directly from the pope.[42] The bishops rule over all priests in their diocese and ordain new ones to the priesthood. The exercise of this priestly power includes not only the ability to administer all sacraments but, along with this, the power under God to transform the bread and wine into the actual physical body and blood of Christ and the power to forgive and retain sins. These powers are unique to the Catholic priesthood and are a serious source of conflict with Protestant belief.[43]

ARGUMENT FROM SCRIPTURE

We will concentrate here on the Catholic defense of the special priestly power to forgive sins. Several verses are crucial to the discussion. We have already discussed the verses used to support the authority of Peter as the head of the church (see chap. 11), so here we will comment on the verses used to support priestly authority.

John 20:22–23. Biblically, Catholicism stands or falls on its interpretation of certain key texts like this one. Since it holds that "The Church has received from Christ the power of remitting sins committed after Baptism,"[44]

---

38. Ibid., no. 844, p. 262.

39. Some scholars argue that technically the spouses administer the sacrament of marriage to each other, but the priest must be present as the church's official witness to the event.

40. Ott, *Fundamentals of Catholic Dogma,* p. 341.

41. Ibid.

42. See ibid., p. 290, and Denzinger, *Sources of Catholic Dogma,* nos. 1500, 2287.

43. Roman Catholicism teaches that there is a sense in which all believers are priests. In 1928 Pope Pius XI declared that "The entire Christian family . . . the prince of the apostles rightly calls 'a chosen race, a kingdom of priests'" *(Miserentissimus Redemptor).* Also, Vatican II stated that "Christ the Lord . . . made the new people [all Christians] a kingdom of priests to God, his Father" (Austin Flannery, ed., *Vatican Council II,* vol. 1, rev. [Boston: St. Paul Books and Media, 1992], p. 360).

44. See Ott, *Fundamentals of Catholic Dogma,* p. 417.

this text assumes great significance. Jesus said to his apostles after his resurrection, "Receive the holy Spirit. Whose sins you forgive are forgiven them, and whose sins you retain are retained." Catholic theology teaches that "With these words Jesus transferred to the Apostles the mission which He Himself had received from the Father. . . . As He Himself had forgiven sins on earth (Mt. 9, 2 et seq.; Mark. 2,5 . . .), He now invested the Apostles also with the power to forgive sins."[45]

Matthew 16:19. After Peter's confession that Jesus was the son of God, Jesus said: "I will give you the keys to the kingdom of heaven. Whatever you bind on earth shall be bound in heaven; and whatever you loose on earth shall be loosed in heaven." According to Catholic teaching, "'The keys of the Kingdom of Heaven' mean supreme authority on earth over the earthly Empire of God. The person who possesses the power of the keys has the full power of allowing a person to enter the Empire of God or to exclude him from it [and] . . . the power to forgive sins must also be included in the power of the keys."[46]

ARGUMENT FROM TRADITION

An early Christian writing known as the *Didache* (late 1st century A.D.) refers to "the confession of sins and the forgiveness of sins without specifying that they refer specifically to the Sacrament of Penance administered by the Church."[47] But Catholic authors refer to the late-first-century (c. A.D. 96) writing of Clement of Rome[48] as an early example of ecclesiastical penance. Early-second-century Ignatius of Antioch announced that "The Lord forgives those who do penance when they return to unity with God and to the communion with the bishop."[49] Many other early Fathers, including Justin, Eusebius, Tertullian, and Clement, also spoke of penance and forgiveness. After surveying the Fathers, Ott concludes: "From the testimony cited it is evident that Christian antiquity bears witness to the existence of an unlimited power to forgive sins conferred by Christ on His Church."[50]

PROTESTANT RESPONSE TO CATHOLIC ARGUMENT FOR THE PRIESTLY AUTHORITY OF THE CHURCH

Evangelical Protestants do not accept the inferences Catholic scholars draw from the above verses. In each case Roman Catholic scholars take the text

---

45. Ibid., p. 419.
46. Ibid., p. 418.
47. Ibid., p. 419.
48. *Epistle to the Corinthians* 57, 1.
49. *Philad.* 8, 1; cf. 3, 2. Ott, *Fundamentals of Catholic Dogma*, pp. 419–20.
50. Ott, *Fundamentals of Catholic Dogma*, p. 421.

out of its proper context and extrapolations are made that are not justified by a careful examination of the entire passage.

RESPONSE TO ARGUMENT FROM SCRIPTURE

John 20:22–23. Here the disciples are given the power to forgive and retain sin. Catholics and Protestants do not dispute this. However, the Catholic claim that this is a special power possessed only by those who are ordained under true apostolic authority, such as the Roman Catholic Church, and are true successors of the apostles, is not supported by this text for many reasons. First, no such claim is made anywhere in the text that only validly ordained priests, such as Roman Catholic priests,[51] were to possess this power.

Second, all early believers, including lay persons, proclaimed the gospel by which sins are forgiven (Rom. 1:16; 1 Cor. 15:1–4). This ministry of forgiveness and reconciliation was not limited to any special class known as "priests" or "clergy" (2 Cor. 3–5).

Third, even Philip, who was only a deacon (Acts 6:5) and not an elder or priest in the Roman Catholic sense,[52] preached the gospel to the Samaritans. This resulted in the conversion of many of them (Acts 8:1–12), which involves the forgiveness of their sins (Acts 13:38).[53]

Fourth, this passage is John's inner circle parallel to the Great Commission Jesus gave all his disciples: to take the gospel into all the world and make disciples (Matt. 28:18–20; Mark 16:15–16; Luke 24:46–49). In this mandate to evangelize Jesus promised, as he did in John, that as they "proclaimed the gospel" the result would be "the forgiveness of sins" (Luke 24:47) for those who believe and that by his Spirit he would "be with" them until the end of the age (Matt. 28:20). All three of these aspects find a parallel in Jesus giving them the Holy Spirit (John 20:22), charging them to proclaim the forgiveness of sins (John 20:23), and commissioning them to go on the authority of the Father: "As the Father has sent me, so I send you" (John 20:21). So there is no greater power given here than that which all the disciples possessed as a result of the Great Commission, which even Vatican II[54] acknowledged all Christians are obligated to help fulfill.

The documents of Vatican II make it clear that current Catholicism understands that the whole church, not just the priests, are responsible to proclaim the gospel. It declared that "The Church's mission is concerned with

---

51. See n. 36.

52. Roman Catholics believe the New Testament equivalent of the term "priest" is "elder," which is a different office than "deacon" (see Phil. 1:1; 1 Tim. 3:1, 8; Titus 1:5, 7).

53. The apostles later came to Samaria, not to convert the people, but to give them the special "gift of the Holy Spirit" (cf. Acts 2:38 and 8:14–17) and an outward ("Simon saw," 8:18) manifestations (i.e., tongues, cf. Acts 2:1–4) that accompanied this special gift (cf. Acts 1:5; 10:44–46).

54. See "Evangelization in the Modern World," *The Documents of Vatican II*, Sect. 120.

the salvation of men; and men win salvation through the grace of Christ and faith in him. Therefore, the apostolate of the church *and of each of its members* aim primarily at announcing to the world by word and action the message of Christ and communicating to it the grace of Christ. . . . *Laymen have countless opportunities for exercising the apostolate of evangelization and sanctification.*" It particularly specifies that lay persons can do this in more ways than through their life and good words. For "the true apostle is on the lookout for occasions of announcing Christ by word, either to unbelievers to draw them toward the faith, or to the faithful to instruct them . . . and in the hearts of all should the apostle's words find echo: 'Woe to me if I do not preach the Gospel' (1 Cor. 9:16)."[55]

In short, contrary to Roman Catholic claims, there is nothing in John 20:21–23 to support either the primacy or infallibility of the bishop of Rome, nor any special priestly power. It is simply an affirmation about Jesus giving to his disciples the ability to forgive sins for all who believe the message that the apostles were commissioned to proclaim.

Matthew 16:19. Here again, Protestants do not dispute that Jesus gave his disciples the power to forgive or retain sins. What they do dispute is whether this is a power that is uniquely possessed by those with proper ordination, such as Roman Catholic priests. There is absolutely nothing in this text to indicate that it is. First, it is worth noting that Jesus gave this same power to *all* the disciples (Matt. 18:18), not just to Peter.

Second, everyone who proclaims the gospel has the same power, for the gospel "is the power of God for the salvation of everyone who believes" (Rom. 1:16). Indeed, Paul defined the gospel in terms of Christ dying and rising "for our sins" (1 Cor. 15:1–4). So every preacher of the gospel, clergy or laity, has the power to, on the basis of a person accepting Christ's death and resurrection for them, forgive sins. Likewise, all who evangelize can say to those who reject the gospel that their sins are retained. For, as Paul said, messengers of Christ are "the aroma of Christ for God among those who are being saved and among those who are perishing, to the latter an odor of death that leads to death" (2 Cor. 2:15–16).

Third, the Catholic claim that the Old Testament priesthood is somehow "translated" into a New Testament priesthood on the basis of Hebrews 7:12 misses the whole point of this passage. The writer of Hebrews actually is arguing that both the law and the Old Testament priesthood are done away with by Christ, our great High Priest, for he writes: "When there is a *change* of priesthood, there is necessarily a change of law as well" (Heb. 7:12, emphasis added). He then goes on to say that "a former commandment is *annulled*" (v. 18, emphasis added). Christ did not translate Aaron's

---

55. Austin Flannery, ed., *Vatican Council II: The Conciliar and Post-Conciliar Documents* (Grand Rapids: Eerdmans, 1992), 1:772–73, emphasis added.

Old Testament priesthood into a new one for priests in the New Testament. The whole point of this section of Hebrews is to show that Christ, by perfectly fulfilling what the Old Testament priesthood prefigured (cf. 7:11, 18–19), did away with it and replaced it with his own high priestly office, after the order of Melchizedek, not after Aaron (7:17–28). Indeed, such a vivid contrast is made here between the repeated offerings of the Aaronic priests and the once-for-all sacrifice of Christ our high priest that it should cause serious pause for Roman Catholics, who believe that the priest offers up continually the (unbloody) sacrifice of the mass. Hebrews declares: "Every priest stands daily at his ministry, *offering frequently those same sacrifices that can never take away sins. But this one [Christ] offered one sacrifice for sins, and took his seat forever at the right hand of God. . . . For by one offering he has made perfect forever those who are being consecrated*" (Heb. 10:11–12, 14, emphasis added). Catholics teach the opposite of what Hebrews emphatically states, namely, that the mass is a sacrifice that is repeated over and over. Contrary to the Catholic claim that Hebrews is only speaking of a once-for-all *unbloody* sacrifice, no such qualifying word is found in the text.

Finally, while Roman Catholicism acknowledges that "the entire Christian family" is "a kingdom of priests,"[56] nevertheless in practice it denies what the New Testament clearly affirms, namely, that all believers are priests. By making such a strong distinction between the common or universal priesthood and the ministerial or hierarchical priesthood they render ineffective Peter's teaching that all believers are "a royal priesthood, a holy nation, a people of his own" (1 Pet. 2:9). In fact, there is only one priest necessary in the new covenant, our great high priest Jesus Christ (cf. Heb. 7–8). The task left for all other priests (namely, all believers) is to minister the gospel (2 Cor. 3–4). Appeal to the Old Testament to show that all Israelites were called priests (Exod. 19:6–7) even when God had established the Aaronic priesthood as a special ministerial class misses the whole point of the Book of Hebrews.[57] The Aaronic priesthood has been done away with, and every believer has direct access to the one high priest, Jesus Christ, who intercedes for us!

The fact is that nowhere in the New Testament are church leaders called "priests." They are called "elders" or "bishops" (overseers) who were exhorted by Peter himself to "Tend the flock of God in your midst, [overseeing] not by constraint but willingly, as God would have it. . . . *Do not lord it over those assigned to you,* but be examples to the flock. *And when the chief Shepherd is revealed,* you will receive the unfading crown of glory" (1 Pet. 5:2–3, emphasis added). The whole hierarchical institution of the

56. See n. 43 above.
57. See "Quick Questions," *This Rock* (September 1993): 30.

Roman Catholic priesthood as a special class of men endowed with special priestly powers to forgive sins and to transform the communion elements into the actual body and blood of Christ is contrary to the spirit of these passages. In 1 Peter 5: (1) no one is described as a priest or as having priestly powers except "the chief Shepherd" Christ himself; (2) Peter describes himself as "a fellow presbyter" (v. 1); (3) the leaders of the flock are called "elders," not priests; (4) they are depicted as undershepherds, not overlords of the church (v. 3); and (5) they have no special binding power, but are to lead by "example," not by "constraint" (vv. 2–3). The whole spirit of this passage is contrary to the priestly powers claimed by the Roman Catholic Church.

RESPONSE TO ARGUMENT FROM TRADITION

Catholic scholars go to great lengths to demonstrate a chain of succession from Peter to the present pope. This is crucial to their claim that priests today possess the same apostolic authority to forgive sins that Jesus gave to his disciples. There are, however, many good reasons for rejecting this claim.

First, even if it could be demonstrated that there was a chain from the first century to the present it would be in vain, since the crucial link is missing—the first one. For, as we demonstrated in chapter 11, there is absolutely no proof that apostolic authority was passed on to anyone after the time of the apostles. The proof that the office and authority ceased is that the gifts that confirmed the apostles ceased (cf. Heb. 2:3–4). The apostles, like Christ, could not only say "your sins are forgiven," they could also say to a man born lame, "[rise and] walk" (Acts 3:6). And when they did, "immediately" he was healed (v. 7). Like Jesus, they could and did heal *all* kinds of sickness (cf. John 9:1), exorcise demons immediately on command (Acts 16:16–18), and even raise the dead (Acts 20:7–12). No priest in his right mind claims to be able to perform "the signs of an apostle" (2 Cor. 12:12), let alone is actually able to do them. But if the signs of the apostles died with the apostles, then so did the office and its powers. What is left is a church (in fact, many churches) gifted with teachers and evangelists (Eph. 4:11–12) and in many other ways to proclaim the gospel and build up believers in the most holy faith. That is all that is necessary to accomplish God's purposes through his redeemed followers on earth.

Second, the earliest testimony is not to ecclesiastical penance but simply the need to confess sins. This falls far short of the Roman Catholic claim that this testimony "bears witness to the existence of an unlimited power to forgive sins conferred by Christ on His Church."[58]

58. Ott, *Fundamentals of Catholic Dogma*, p. 421.

Third, it is worth noting that simply because a teaching existed early in church history that does not make it true any more than a later teaching is necessarily false. It is a chronological fallacy to assume the time of a teaching's appearance proves its truth. Otherwise, recent scientific discoveries would automatically be eliminated, at least until they became very old. Many false doctrines and traditions appeared early in the history of Christianity—some even in New Testament times. Paul condemned false teaching and heresy in his day (1 Tim. 4; 2 Tim. 2), as did John (1 John 4), Jude (16–19), and Peter (2 Pet. 2). John even debunks a false tradition (which claimed that he would not die) that was current during the days of the apostles (John 21:23).

Finally, in the last analysis it is not a question of how early or how many Fathers taught something but whether it is based on the infallible written Word of God. And, as we have seen above, there is no basis in the Holy Scriptures for sacramental penance. This is not to say that Christians should not confess their sins; they should. All sins should be confessed to God (1 John 1:9) from whom alone we receive forgiveness (Mark 2:7, 10). Sins against others should be confessed to them. James exhorted: "Confess your sins *to one another* [not to a priest] and pray for one another, that you may be healed" (5:16, emphasis added). There is absolutely no evidence in the New Testament that believers should confess their sins to the priesthood (i.e., the Roman Catholic priesthood) in order to receive forgiveness.

THE CONSTITUENCY OF THE CHURCH

Historically, at least before Vatican II, there were few Catholic beliefs that caused more agitation with Protestants than the belief that the Roman Catholic Church is necessary for salvation. This doctrine has taken different forms, some more extreme than others. Some even went so far as to pronounce all non-Catholics lost. More recently, Protestants have been elevated to the status of "separated brethren." First, let us look at the traditional view.

CATHOLIC DEFENSE OF THE CONSTITUENCY OF THE CHURCH

"*The Church of Christ, therefore, is one and perpetual;* whoever go apart (from it) wander away from the will and prescription of Christ the Lord and, leaving the way of salvation, digress to destruction."[59] In short, membership in the Roman Catholic Church is necessary for salvation.

59. Denzinger, *Sources of Catholic Dogma*, nos. 1955–57, 1960, emphasis added.

CONDITIONS FOR CHURCH MEMBERSHIP

In his encyclical "Mystici Corporis" Pope Pius XII declared: "Actually only those are to be numbered among the members of the Church who have received the laver of regenerating [baptism] and profess the true faith, and have not, to their misfortune, separated themselves from the structure of the body, or for very serious sins have not been excluded by lawful authority."[60] Commenting on this, Ott says, "According to this declaration three conditions are to be demanded for membership of the Church: a) The valid reception of the Sacrament of Baptism. b) The profession of the true Faith. c) Participation in the Communion of the Church." He adds, "By the fulfillment of these three conditions one subjects oneself to the threefold office of the Church, the sacerdotal office (Baptism), the teaching office (Confession of Faith), and the pastoral office (obedience to the Church authority)."[61]

CLASSIFICATION OF THOSE EXCLUDED FROM CHURCH MEMBERSHIP

A consequence of the traditional Catholic teaching on conditions for church membership is that certain classes of people, including all orthodox Protestants, were automatically excluded from being members of the true church of Christ on earth. These included: "a) The unbaptized.[62] . . . b) Open [public or material] apostates and heretics.[63] . . . c) Schismatics, as well as those who, in good faith, fundamentally reject the Church authority. . . . d) *Excommunicati vitandi.* . . ."[64] According to many Catholic authorities, those who have been excommunicated from the church do not retain membership in it unless or until they are restored.

THE NECESSITY OF CHURCH MEMBERSHIP

For the reasons just noted, many conservative Catholic theologians believe that "Membership of the Church is necessary for all men for salvation."[65] They cite the Fourth Lateran Council (A.D. 1215), which declared that "the universal Church of the faithful is one outside of which none is saved."[66]

---

60. Ibid., no. 2286, pp. 615–16.
61. Ott, *Fundamentals of Catholic Dogma*, p. 309.
62. Those who desired to be baptized and were not are not excluded from grace (i.e., salvation), but they are excluded from church membership. See ibid., p. 311.
63. Again, material (vs. formal) heresy (that is, an error in good faith) does not disqualify one from membership in the mystical body of Christ (= salvation) but merely from membership in the church on earth.
64. Ott, *Fundamentals of Catholic Dogma*, p. 311.
65. Ibid., p. 312.
66. Denzinger, *Sources of Catholic Dogma*, no. 430, p. 169.

Thus, Ott contends that "This was the teaching also of the Union Council of Florence (D 714), and of Popes Innocent III (D 423) and Boniface VIII in the bull 'unam sanctam' (D 468), Clement VI (D 570b), Benedict XIV (D 1473), Pius IX (D 1647, 1677), Leo XIII (D 1955). Pius XII in the Encyclical "Mystici Corporis" (D 2286, 2288)."[67] Pope Pius IX declared that, "outside the Apostolic Roman Church, no one can be saved; that this is the only ark of salvation; that he who shall not have entered therein will perish in the flood."[68] He went on to say, however, that "it is necessary to hold for certain that they who labor in ignorance of the true religion, if this ignorance is invincible, are not stained by any guilt in this matter in the eyes of God."[69]

Over against this traditional conservative view many modern Catholics argue that membership in the Catholic church is not necessary for salvation. Indeed, Vatican II concluded that non-Catholics, even non-Christians, can be saved. Protestants are even called "brethren," albeit "separated brethren." Vatican II admits that "The Church knows that she is joined in many ways to the baptized who are honored by the name of Christian, but who do not however profess the Catholic faith in its entirety or have not preserved unity or communion under the successor of Peter." These "are sealed by baptism which unites them to Christ . . . [and] these Christians are indeed in some real way joined to us in the Holy spirit for they, by his gifts and graces, his sanctifying power is also active in them and he has strengthened some of them even to the shedding of their blood."[70]

According to Vatican II, even non-Christians and pagans can be saved. "Finally, those who have not yet received the Gospel are related to the people of God in various ways." This includes Jews, "the people to which the covenants and promises were made and from which Christ was born according to the flesh."[71] Furthermore, "the plan of salvation also includes those

---

67. Ott, *Fundamentals of Catholic Dogma,* p. 312.

68. Denzinger, *Sources of Catholic Dogma,* no. 1647, p. 416.

69. Ibid. In 1949, Fr. Leonard Feeney, S.J., caused a serious disruption in American Roman Catholicism. Feeney, a professor at the Jesuit seminary in Weston, Massachusetts, publicly declared Archbishop of Boston Richard J. Cushing to be guilty of heresy. Cushing's theological indiscretion—according to Feeney—was to hold that Jews and Protestants, outside of Roman Catholic jurisdiction, could be saved. Fr. Feeney demured, holding that Cardinal Cushing was going against traditional Roman Catholic teaching.

Feeney's revolt against his ecclesiastical superior caused his dismissal from the Jesuit order and four years later he was excommunicated by the direction of Pope Pius XII. As already mentioned, Vatican II has attempted to address this vexing question. For an interesting treatment of the problem, see Francis A. Sullivan, S.J., *Salvation Outside the Church? Tracing the History of the Catholic Response* (Mahwah, N.J.: Paulist Press, 1992). Sullivan attempts to reconcile the pronouncements of Vatican II with the church's traditional doctrine that has excluded non-Roman Catholics from salvation.

70. Flannery, "The People of God," in *Documents of Vatican II: The Conciliar and Post-Conciliar Documents,* vol. 1, pp. 367–68.

71. Ibid., sect. 16.

who acknowledge the Creator, in the first place amongst whom are the Moslems. . . . Nor is God remote from those who in shadows and images seek the unknown God . . . since the Savior wills all men to be saved (cf. 1 Tim. 2:4)." That is, "Those who, through no fault of their own, do not know the Gospel of Christ or his Church, but who nevertheless seek God with a sincere heart, and, moved by grace, try in their actions to do his will as they know it through the dictates of their conscience—those too may achieve eternal salvation."[72]

PROTESTANT RESPONSE TO CATHOLIC ARGUMENT FOR THE CONSTITUENCY OF THE CHURCH

Needless to say, the traditional and contemporary Catholic views on the salvation of non-Catholics are at odds. To borrow the title from Jaroslov Pelikan's excellent book, this is part of "the riddle of Roman Catholicism." Catholic scholars are quick to point out that none of these conflicting teachings are infallible, since none were pronounced *ex cathedra* by the church, even though some were in papal encyclicals and others in statements of councils they consider ecumenical. Add to this the fact that there is no infallible list of which statements by popes or councils are infallible, and one can easily see why one can question just how effective the alleged infallible guidance the church of Rome really is.

In response to the traditional conservative view, it is only necessary to point out that neither baptism (see Appendix E) nor membership in the Catholic church is necessary to be saved. All that is necessary is to "Believe in the Lord Jesus Christ and you . . . will be saved" (Acts 16:31). Indeed, Jesus said simply, "Whoever believes in the Son has eternal life" (John 3:36). Paul declared: "when one does not work, yet believes in the one who justifies the ungodly, his faith is credited as righteousness" (Rom. 4:5). Even the oft quoted passage from Mark 16 says that only "those who do not *believe*" will be condemned, not those who are not baptized.

As to the modern liberal Catholic belief that even sincere and good Jews and heathens can be saved, the words of Jesus are relevant: "I am the way and the truth and the life. No one comes to the Father except through me" (John 14:6). Peter affirms, "There is no salvation through anyone else, nor is there any other name under heaven given to the human race by which we are to be saved" (Acts 4:12).[73]

---

72. Ibid.
73. God justly condemns those who have not heard the gospel because they have rejected the light of conscience (Rom. 2:12–15) and creation so that they have "no excuse" (Rom. 1:19–20). If they seek God, however, he will provide them with the light of the gospel by which they can be saved (2 Cor. 4:3–6). For God "rewards those who seek him" (Heb. 11:6; cf. Acts 10:35).

SUMMARY AND CONCLUSION

The doctrine of the church is a significant dividing line between Catholics and evangelicals. In spite of the phrase "separated brethren," which is how Roman Catholics describe Protestants, evangelicals remain wary. In an address to the World Council of Churches (June 1984), Pope John Paul II said, "to be in communion with the Bishop of Rome is to give visible evidence that one is in communion with all who confess that same faith. . . . That is our Catholic conviction and our fidelity to Christ forbids us to give it up." Indeed, "The negative inference to be drawn from these words is that if one is not in communion with the bishop of Rome one is not giving (any? the best?) visible evidence of catholicity. Such a charge the Reformed, from the depths and reality of their ecclesial life, can only deny."[74] Of particular concern to orthodox Protestants are the Catholic claims to be the one true visible church united under the pope and the matter of the priestly power to transform the eucharistic bread and wine into the actual body and blood of Christ and the special power to forgive sins. As we have seen, there is no real support for these doctrines in Holy Scripture and there is far from unanimous consent among the Fathers. Verses used by Catholic scholars are wrenched from their context, offering no real support for the doctrine they are used to defend. Nevertheless, many of these doctrines have been proclaimed as infallible and, therefore, are irrevocable tenets of the Roman Catholic faith. As long as this is the case—and one cannot envision how it could change without Roman Catholicism losing its very essence—there is no hope for ecclesiastical unity between evangelicals and Catholics. This, of course, does not mean there cannot be personal fellowship with or social cooperation between believers in both communions (see Part Three) or even social cooperation on areas of common interest. It means that ecclesiastical separation is necessary for all evangelical Protestants who desire to be true to the Scriptures.

The words of Carl F. H. Henry, a respected evangelical theologian, sums up the authors' position nicely: "The church is not reducible to a hierarchy in Rome, Istanbul, Geneva, or Colorado Springs; its ruling head transcends all geographic location and its genuine components are not only multi-racial and multi-cultural but even superhistorical."[75]

---

74. Alan P. E. Sell, *A Reformed, Evangelical, Catholic Theology: The Contribution of the World Alliance of Reformed Churches 1875–1982* (Grand Rapids: Eerdmans, 1991), p. 133.
75. "Thirteen Theological Endnotes," no. 2, *World* (24 December 1994): 28.

15

MARIOLOGY

For many Protestants, Mariology and Mariolatry are almost synonymous. This is unfortunate, as we will see, for there are many things Catholics and Protestants hold in common on the doctrine of Mary. These include her being the most blessed among women, her virgin conception of Christ the God-man, and by virtue of that her being in this sense "the Mother of God,"[1] a title used by both Luther and Calvin. To be sure, the title was used to stress the deity of Christ, not the privileges of Mary, but it was used nonetheless.

Since this section deals with the areas of difference, we will concentrate on the major points of tension between Catholics and Protestants on Mariology. These include the Roman Catholic dogmas of the perpetual virginity, immaculate conception, sinlessness, bodily assumption, mediatorship, and the veneration of Mary and her images.

THE PERPETUAL VIRGINITY OF MARY

Of the areas of difference between Catholics and Protestants on the doctrine of Mary, some are major and some are not. Since we will concentrate on the

---

1. The controversy concerning the "Mother of Christ" (Gk: *Christotokos*) versus the "Mother of God" (Gk: *theotokos*) goes back to the fifth century, when the use of these terms caused no little disturbance in the church. "Mother of Christ" stresses Jesus' *human* nature, while "Mother of God" emphasizes his *divine* nature. Nestorius, patriarch of Constantinople, championed the term "Mother of Christ," while Cyril of Alexandria favored "Mother of God." The Council of Ephesus (A.D. 431) decided in favor of Cyril. Harold O. J. Brown comments concerning *theotokos*: "The term, which means 'God-bearing one' (not precisely 'Mother of God,' as it is frequently translated), originally was descriptive of the man Jesus, born of Mary" (*Heresies: The Image of Christ*, p. 172). *Theotokos*, therefore, was designed to say more about Jesus than to glorify Mary.

major ones we will mention only briefly a minor one first: the perpetual virginity of Mary.

The Lateran Synod of A.D. 649 was the first to stress the threefold character of Mary's virginity. As a result, Catholics believe that "Mary was a Virgin before, during and after the Birth of Jesus Christ."[2]

CATHOLIC DEFENSE OF MARY'S PERPETUAL VIRGINITY

Based on Isaiah 7:14, Matthew 1:18, and Luke 1:26 (cf. Gal. 4:4) both Protestants and Catholics believe that Jesus was conceived of a virgin. This has been universally taught in the Catholic church as a *de fide* dogma of the faith. Since all orthodox non-Catholic Christians agree we will not discuss Mary's initial virgin state further, given that our purpose in this section is to focus on the differences between Catholic and Protestant doctrine.

Catholics also believe, contrary to Protestants, that Jesus was also born in a way that left Mary a virgin.[3] Ott puts it this way: "Mary bore her son without any violation of her virginal integrity."[4] This is considered an official doctrine of Catholicism on the grounds of general proclamation. How this happened, however, is not a matter of Catholic dogma. Generally, traditional Catholic scholarship held that "Mary gave birth in miraculous fashion without opening of the womb and injury to the hymen, and consequently also without pains."[5]

Admitting that Mary's virginity was retained during Christ's birth has scant support in Scripture. Catholic scholars often point to the fact that "Holy Writ attests Mary's active role in the act of birth (Mt. 1, 25; Luke 2, 7): 'She brought forth' . . . , which does not seem to indicate a miraculous process."[6]

Catholic dogma also states that "*after* the birth of Jesus Mary remained a Virgin (*De fide*)."[7] Hence, the title "perpetual virginity" is attributed to Mary. Roman Catholics defend this belief from both Scripture and tradition.

Argument from Scripture. Catholic scholars cite several verses to support Mary's perpetual virginity. Ott summarizes them as follows: "From the question which Mary puts to the Angel, Luke 1, 34: 'How shall this be done, because I know not man?' it is inferred [by some] that she had taken the resolve of constant virginity on the ground of special Divine enlightenment." Others "note that the fact that the dying Redeemer entrusted His Mother to the protection of the Disciple John (John 19, 26), 'woman, behold thy Son,' presupposes that Mary had no other children but Jesus."[8] As to the references to

---

2. Ott, *Fundamentals of Catholic Dogma*, p. 203.
3. Ibid., p. 205.
4. Ibid.
5. Ibid. Cf. Aquinas, *Summa Theologiae* 3.28.2.
6. Ibid.
7. Ibid., p. 206, emphasis added.

Jesus' "brothers" (cf. Matt. 13:55; Mark 6:3; Gal. 1:19), Catholics generally follow Jerome's argument that these refer to Jesus' cousins, not blood brothers. Others have suggested that maybe these were Joseph's sons by a previous marriage, thus preserving Mary's perpetual virginity.

Argument from Tradition. Support for the doctrine is found in the early Fathers. Jerome claimed it was widely believed in his letter to Helvidius, and Gregory of Nyssa referred to it in A.D. 371. Pope Siricius (A.D. 393) held to Mary's virginity after Christ's birth, and the Fifth General Council at Constantine (A.D. 553) gave Mary the title of "perpetual virgin," as did many later popes and Catholic liturgies. The doctrine was affirmed at later councils, such as Chalcedon and others.

Argument from Reason. One speculative argument sometimes used by Catholics emanates from Pope Siricius (A.D. 384–399), who argued that it would be horrifying to think of another birth issuing from the same virginal womb from which the Son of God was born.

PROTESTANT RESPONSE TO MARY'S PERPETUAL VIRGINITY

While it is not a major issue among orthodox non-Catholics, there have been some significant objections to the belief that Mary was a virgin *during* Christ's birth. First, the fact that Mary "brought forth" Jesus at his birth does not indicate that it was miraculous. Rather, this is the normal way to indicate that, in the absence of a birthmaid, she delivered her own child. Second, all the descriptions of Christ's birth indicate a normal birth, such as "born of a woman" (Gal. 4:4); "brought forth" (Luke 2:7); "delivered" (Luke 2:6); "birth" (Matt. 1:18); "born" (Matt. 2:2). Third, the Bible does not use any of the normal words for a miracle (sign, wonder, power) when speaking of Jesus' birth, only of his conception (cf. Isa. 7:14 and Matt. 1:18–23). Fourth, it diminishes the humanness of the incarnational event to posit a miracle at the point of Jesus' birth rather than his conception, as the Bible does. As the God-man, Jesus was human in every way possible apart from sin (Heb. 4:15). Fifth, the idea of a miraculous birth of Christ, without coming through the birth canal or causing pain, is more Gnostic than Christian. It is more like an event found in a second- or third-century apocryphal book than a first-century inspired Book.

Some Protestants have accepted Mary's perpetual virginity, including Luther. He wrote, "She was a virgin before the birth of Christ (*ante partum*) and remained one at the birth (*in partu*) and after the birth (*post partum*)," even going so far as to affirm that "it neither adds nor detracts from faith. It is immaterial whether these men were Christ's cousins or his [half-] brothers

8. Ibid., p. 207.

begotten by Joseph."[9] However, many Protestants reject the Catholic view on the perpetual virginity of Mary.

Response to Argument from Scripture. Even Ott admits that there is no direct reference to Mary's perpetual virginity in any text of Scripture. And to infer from the above cited text that Mary was a virgin after Jesus' birth is unwarranted. First, as to the use of Luke 1:34 (that she had no relations with a man), Ott acknowledges that this supposition of a vow of virginity by Mary is contrary to the clear statement of Holy Writ that she was subsequently engaged to Joseph (Matt. 1:18).

Second, the fact that Jesus commended his mother to John at the cross need not imply that he had no brothers but only that they were not present, so he could not turn the responsibility over to them. Besides this, Jesus' brothers were not at this time believers (cf. John 7:5), so it was important that Mary be left in good spiritual hands.[10]

Third, there are clear references to Jesus' brothers and sisters in the context of his immediate family (namely, his legal father[11] and actual mother), which almost always indicate they were actual brothers, not cousins, as many Catholics believe. For example, Matthew 13:55 declares: "Is he not the carpenter's son? Is not his mother Mary and his brothers James, Joseph, Simon, and Judas? Are not his sisters all with us?" (cf. Matt. 12:46 and Gal. 1:19). There are several reasons why this text almost certainly indicates that Mary had other children after Jesus. For one thing, "brothers" and "sisters" are mentioned in the context of the family with the "carpenter's son" and "mother," which clearly indicates they are immediate blood brothers. For another, the Greek term for "brother" *(adelphos)* here is the normal word for "blood brother." In fact, there is no a single example where *adelphos* is used for "cousin" in the New Testament.[12] There is a word for "cousin"

9. Eric W. Gritsch, "The Views of Luther and Lutheranism on the Veneration of Mary," in *The One Mediator, The Saints, and Mary—Lutherans and Catholics in Dialogue* VIII, ed. H. George Anderson (Minneapolis: Augsburg, 1992), p. 239.

10. The fact that Jesus knew (in his omniscience) that one of his brothers, James, would later be converted (1 Cor. 15:7) is irrelevant since he was not there at the cross for Jesus to speak to him! Also, appealing to a natural law requirement that the closest blood relative is required to watch over her overlooks the fact that Jesus was showing his compassion for his mother in the absence of those who should have been caring for her. Further, since Jesus knew that commitment to him would separate even those with the closest blood ties (Matt. 10:34–36), it was appropriate for him to show this act of concern for his mother's care at that moment of his death.

11. That Joseph was not the actual father but only the legal father of Jesus does not change this fact, since he was the actual husband of Mary and the actual father of the other children. Further, the question is not over the use of the word "father" in this special sense but of the term "brother" in this normal sense.

12. The fact that there are not numerous New Testament examples of *adelphoi* meaning literal brothers does not diminish the argument, especially when it is remembered that (1) there are *many* such examples; (2) there are *none* using the available word "cousin"; and (3) literal brother is the *normal* meaning of the word in a family context.

(anepsios), as in Colossians 4:10, where Mark is described as "the cousin *[anepsios]* of Barnabas." But this word is not used in Matthew 13 or in any passage referring to Jesus' brothers and sisters. Finally, the words "brother" and "sister" are used many other times in the New Testament in a family connection, always meaning a literal blood brother or sister (Mark 1:16, 19; 13:12; John 11:1–2; Acts 23:16; Rom. 16:15).

Even Ott calls implausible the suggestion that these "brothers" and "sisters" of Jesus were Joseph's children from another marriage. If this were so then Joseph's oldest son would have been heir to David's throne and not Jesus, but the Bible affirms that Jesus was the heir (Matt. 1:1).[13]

Fourth, Matthew 1:25 seems to imply that Mary had sexual relations with Joseph after Jesus was born. Even the natural meaning of the Catholic translation (NAB) supports this idea when it says of Joseph, "He had no relations with her until she bore a son, and he named him Jesus."[14] Otherwise, why not say clearly that she never ever had sex with Joseph?[15]

In view of all this biblical evidence, there seems to be no real scriptural basis for the Catholic belief in Mary's perpetual virginity.

Response to Argument from Tradition. Some early Fathers opposed the concept of the perpetual virginity of Mary, including Tertullian. The first-century Jewish historian Josephus referred to James as "the brother of Jesus."[16] Further, the doctrine was neither widely accepted nor formulated by creed or even local church councils until several centuries after the time of Christ. Like many other traditions, there is no evidence to support the idea that it was an apostolic teaching, as Catholics claim. Nor is it built on any alleged "unanimous consent of the Fathers," of which the Council of Trent speaks.

Response to Argument from Reason. The idea that Mary had children after Jesus is only "horrifying," as some Catholics claim, if one presupposes some kind of Gnostic concept of virginal purity. In light of God's command to humanity to propagate children (Gen. 1:28) and God's command to Joseph, "do not be afraid to take Mary your wife to your home" (Matt. 1:20)

13. Ott, *Fundamentals of Catholic Dogma*, p. 207.

14. The *New Jerusalem Bible* obscures the natural meaning of the Greek words for "until" *(eus ou)* here by mistranslating this verse in this unlikely way: "He had not intercourse with her when she gave birth to a son"! Who would have? Even Catholic scholar Raymond Brown states: "In my judgment the question of Mary's remaining a virgin for the rest of her life belongs to post-biblical theology. . . ." *The Birth of the Messiah* (Garden City, N.Y.: Doubleday, 1977), p. 132. In other words, it is not really found in the New Testament.

15. Catholic appeal to the usage of "until" in passages like 2 Sam. 6:23 (where Michal had no children "until" the day of her death) is irrelevant, since the context (death) clearly indicates that she could not have any after her death! But Mary could have had children after she had Jesus, since she was still alive and young enough.

16. Josephus, "Antiquities," in *Josephus: Complete Works,* ed. William Shiston (Grand Rapids: Kregel, 1963), p. 423.

and the statement "He had no relations with her until she bore a son" (Matt. 1:25), there is nothing unnatural or unbiblical about Joseph having sex with Mary after Jesus was born. In fact it can be argued that it would have been unnatural and unbiblical for him not to do so, since Scripture considers sex to be an essential part of marriage (cf. Gen. 1:28; 1 Cor. 7:1–7; Heb. 13:4).

A contemporary evangelical work on Mary argues against Mary's perpetual virginity from another angle. Since there is nothing defiling about sexual relations within marriage (Heb. 13:4), to suggest that Christ would not want to be conceived in a womb that would later conceive other humans is to take away from the glory that God would afterward give him for his voluntary humility in becoming human (Phil. 2:9–11).[17]

Having said all this, Luther's comment that this doctrine "neither adds nor detracts from faith," reminds us that it is not an essential difference between Catholics and Protestants.

THE IMMACULATE CONCEPTION

Roman Catholic teaching on Mary progressively widened the gap between Catholics and Protestants. The rift began with the proclamation of Mary's immaculate conception.

CATHOLIC DEFENSE OF THE IMMACULATE CONCEPTION

In 1854, Pope Pius IX, in the bull "Ineffabilis," pronounced infallible the following doctrine to be believed firmly and constantly by all the faithful: "The Most Holy Virgin Mary was in the first moment of her conception, by a unique gift of grace and privilege of Almighty God, in view of the merits of Jesus Christ, the Redeemer of mankind, preserved free from all stain of original sin."[18] The decree went on to say that this "has been revealed by God, and on this account must be firmly and constantly believed by all the faithful."[19] This pronouncement was "To the honor of the Holy and Undivided Trinity, to the glory and adornment of the Virgin Mother of God, [and] to the exaltation of the Catholic Faith."[20]

The doctrine can be broken down into its various kinds of causes. "The efficient cause *(causa efficiens)* of the Immaculate Conception of Mary was

17. See Elliot Miller and Kenneth R. Samples, *The Cult of the Virgin* (Grand Rapids: Baker, 1992), p. 26.
18. Ott, *Fundamentals of Catholic Dogma*, p. 199.
19. Ibid., cf. Denzinger, *Sources of Catholic Dogma*, no. 1641, p. 413.
20. Denzinger, *Sources of Catholic Dogma*, no. 1641, p. 413.

Almighty God." The formal cause was the state of sanctifying grace, for "the essence of original sin consists (*formaliter*) in the lack of sanctifying grace, in consequence of the fall of Adam. Mary was preserved from this defect, so that she entered existence in the state of sanctifying grace." The meritorious cause was "the redemption by Jesus Christ," for "by reason of her natural origin, she, like all other children of Adam, was subject to the necessity of contracting original sin . . . but by a special intervention of God, she was preserved from stain of original sin." Lastly, "The final cause [purpose, end] . . . of the Immaculate conception of Mary is her Motherhood of God."[21]

Catholic scholars offer both a biblical and traditional defense of the dogma of the immaculate conception. The biblical basis is sought in several texts.

ARGUMENT FROM SCRIPTURE

Three verses are often used to defend this dogma. The first is found in Genesis 3:15. Many Catholic scholars acknowledge that the "literal sense" of this text means that "between Satan and his followers on the one hand, and Eve and her posterity on the other hand, there is to be constant moral warfare. . . . The posterity of Eve includes the Messiah, in whose power humanity will win a victory over Satan." However, they go on to insist that "the seed of the woman was understood as referring to the Redeemer . . . and thus the Mother of the Redeemer came to be seen in the woman." Even the infallible pronouncement of the immaculate conception "approves of this messianic-marianic interpretation."[22]

Luke 1:28 is also used to support the immaculate conception. "Hail, favored one!" or "one full of grace." Ott argues that "The expression 'full of grace' . . . in the angel's salutation, represents the proper name, and must on this account express a characteristic quality of Mary. . . . However, it is perfect only if it be perfect not only intensively but also extensively, that is, if it extends over her whole life, beginning with her entry into the world."[23] Thus, according to Catholic scholars, we have a reference here to Mary's immaculate conception.

Luke 1:42 is offered in defense of this doctrine. When Elizabeth said, "Most blessed are you among women," Ott says that the "blessing of God which rests upon Mary is made parallel to the blessing of God which rests upon Christ in His humanity. This parallelism suggests that Mary, just like Christ, was from the beginning of her existence, free from all sin."[24]

21. Ott, *Fundamentals of Catholic Dogma*, p. 199.
22. Ibid., p. 200.
23. Ibid.
24. Ibid., p. 201.

ARGUMENT FROM TRADITION

Catholic scholars point to a few isolated references that they believe imply Mary's immaculate conception.[25] The Lateran Council of A.D. 649 refers to her as "immaculate Mary,"[26] though it is not clear that this refers to her being conceived without a sin nature. Ott points out that "Since the seventh century a Feast of the Conception of St. Anne, that is, of the passive conception of Mary, was celebrated in the Greek Eastern Church."[27] Later, in the early twelfth century, the British monk Eadmer (c. A.D. 1060–1128) advocated the immaculate conception of Mary. John Duns Scotus (d. 1308) defended the doctrine, and in 1439 the Council of Basle declared in favor of the teaching. The Council of Trent referred obliquely to Mary as "the Immaculate Virgin" but did not pronounce on the dogma. Not until 1854 did Pope Pius IX pronounce the immaculate conception of Mary as dogma.

ARGUMENT FROM REASON

The scholastic axiom that "God could do it, He ought to do it, therefore He did it" is sometimes used to support this dogma.[28] This argument was found previously in the writings of the twelfth-century British monk Eadmer.

PROTESTANT RESPONSE TO THE IMMACULATE CONCEPTION

Protestants, like some noted Catholic theologians before them, reject the doctrine of the immaculate conception of Mary. Following Aquinas, they believe it is inconsistent with the scriptural pronouncement on the universality of sin.

RESPONSE TO ARGUMENT FROM SCRIPTURE

Generally, three texts are used to support the immaculate conception. As we shall see, they all fall far short of proving this doctrine.

Genesis 3:15. The fact that even Catholic authorities like Ott acknowledge that the "literal sense" of this text does not refer to Mary but to Eve and her offspring should be argument enough that Mary cannot be legitimately inferred from this text. Even if by extension or culmination Mary is found in this text in some indirect way, it is a gigantic leap from this to her immaculate

---

25. For example, Bishop Ambrose (A.D. 388) said that Mary was "free from every stain of sin" (*Commentary on Psalm 118*, 22:30), and Augustine (A.D. 415) exempted Mary from the universality of sin (*On Nature and Grace*, 36:42).

26. See Denzinger, *Sources of Catholic Dogma*, no. 256, p. 102.

27. Ott, *Fundamentals of Catholic Dogma*, p. 201.

28. Ibid., p. 203.

conception, which is nowhere stated or implied in this passage. The literal sense is that Eve (not Mary) and her posterity will win in their moral warfare against Satan and his offspring, culminating in the crushing victory of the Messiah over Satan and his hosts. The "woman" is obviously Eve, the "offspring" are clearly the literal offspring of Eve (cf. 4:1, 25), and the victory is the victory of Christ over Satan (cf. Rom. 16:20).

Protestants need not object to the Catholic argument that, just as the Messiah is found by extension and culmination in the term "offspring," even so Mary the mother of the Messiah is implied too. Be this as it may, the point still stands that there is no necessary or logical connection between Mary being the mother of the Messiah and her being conceived without sin.

Luke 1:28. The angel said to Mary, "Hail, favored one!" Ott's argument that the expression "full of grace" represents the proper name and therefore expresses a characteristic quality of Mary which must be understood extensively over her whole life bristles with problems. First, it is by no means necessary to take this expression as a proper name. Even contemporary Catholic versions of the Bible do not translate it as a proper name (e.g., NAB). It could refer simply to her state of being as a recipient of God's favor.

Further, even if the expression were a proper name and referred to her essential character it is not necessary to take it extensively all the way back to her birth. The only way one could conclude this is by factors beyond the text itself. Catholics believe that tradition fills in what the Scriptures do not declare here. If this is so, then why appeal to Scripture for support? Why not just admit what many contemporary Catholics are reluctant to acknowledge, namely, that this teaching is not found in Scripture but was added centuries later by tradition?

Also, even if it were taken extensively to Mary's beginning it does not necessarily mean an immaculate conception. It could simply refer to God's grace being upon her life from the point of conception. That was true of others, including Jeremiah (Jer. 1) and John the Baptist (Luke 1), who were not immaculately conceived.

Finally, as Miller and Samples note in their excellent treatment of Mariology, *The Cult of the Virgin*, the Greek term for "full of grace" is *charito.* "*Charito* is used of believers in Ephesians 1:6 without implying sinless perfection. So again there is hence nothing about Luke 1:28 that establishes the doctrine of the immaculate conception. That Mary was uniquely favored to be the mother of her Lord is the only necessary inference."[29] One must appeal to traditions outside the Bible, and late ones at that, to find support for this Catholic dogma.

Luke 1:41. Ott's reasoning that this blessing is parallel to the one on Christ and, therefore, suggests that "Mary, just like Christ, was from the be-

---

29. Miller and Samples, *Cult of the Virgin*, p. 34.

ginning of her existence, free from all sin"[30] is tenuous. The passage nowhere makes any such parallel between Mary and Christ. And even if the parallel could somehow be made, an immaculate conception would not necessarily follow from it. Jesus was conceived of a virgin. Mary was not so conceived; she had two natural parents.

RESPONSE TO ARGUMENT FROM TRADITION

Actually, the historical argument for the immaculate conception is very weak, with no conciliar reference to it until the twelfth century! The earlier possible references to it are late (4th century), scant, and indecisive, some not specifically referring to Mary's lack of original sin. There was no church-wide pronouncement on it by the church until the nineteenth century! And even when it was infallibly defined it was a dogma proclaimed solely by the authority of the pope, without the official sanction of a church council. This is scarcely early and wide support for the dogma, and it makes a sham of the "unanimous consent of the Fathers."

In point of fact, even Ott admits that many of the greatest scholastic theologians of the Catholic church flatly rejected the doctrine, including Peter Lombard, Albert the Great, Bonaventure, and Thomas Aquinas![31] They argued rightly that exempting Mary from original sin was inconsistent with the universality of original sin and the necessity of redemption for all human beings.[32] In spite of Scotus's attempt to reconcile these, this is still the most serious objection. Duns Scotus argued that Mary was in need of salvation by Christ, like any other creature, but that, unlike all other creatures, she was saved from a sin nature by way of prevention, not by way of cure as the rest of us are. There are, however, many objections to this noble but futile effort to save this extra-biblical tradition. First, even if this were theoretically possible, there is no actual evidence that it is the case. Second, it is contrary to Mary's own confession that God was her "Savior" (Luke 1:46) after her conception, not just before it, by way of prevention. Third, at best the proposed solution of Scotus is *deus ex machina,* smacking of a desperate attempt to rescue a desired but unbiblical doctrine that was locked in deadly conflict with another clear teaching of Scripture and the church.

RESPONSE TO ARGUMENT FROM REASON

The scholastic axiom that "God could do it; He ought to do it, therefore He did it" is a weak justification of the dogma of the immaculate conception. Even those who use it admit that it "gives no certainty."[33] Indeed, it is a weak

30. Ott, *Fundamentals of Catholic Dogma,* p. 201.
31. Aquinas, *Summa Theologiae* 3.27.2.
32. Ott, *Fundamentals of Catholic Dogma,* p. 201.
33. Ibid., p. 202.

argument. Possibility does not prove actuality. Nor does desirability demonstrate reality.

THE SINLESSNESS OF MARY

Not only was Mary conceived without original sin but, according to Catholic teaching, "from her conception Mary was free from all motions of concupiscence." And "in consequence of a special privilege of grace from God, Mary was free from every personal sin during her whole life." The Council of Trent declared that "no justified person can for his whole life avoid all sins, even venial sins, except on the ground of a special privilege from God such as the Church holds was given to the Blessed Virgin."[34]

CATHOLIC DEFENSE OF THE SINLESSNESS OF MARY

According to Catholic dogma, Mary had neither the tendency to sin nor did she ever actually sin during her entire life. Catholics use both Scripture and tradition to support this view.

ARGUMENT FROM SCRIPTURE

According to Roman Catholic teaching, "Mary's sinlessness may be deduced from the text: Luke 1, 28: 'Hail, full of grace!' since personal moral defects are irreconcilable with fullness of grace."[35] Grace is taken here to be both extensive and preventative.

ARGUMENT FROM TRADITION

The house of church fathers was divided on Mary's sinlessness. Nonetheless, Roman Catholic scholars point with pride to the fact that "the Latin Patristic authors unanimously teach the doctrine of the sinlessness of Mary."[36] Again, this is far short of the "unanimous consent" of all church fathers, which the Council of Trent claimed for dogma.

PROTESTANT RESPONSE TO THE SINLESSNESS OF MARY

The Bible does not support the sinlessness of Mary. To the contrary, it affirms her sinfulness. Speaking as a sinner, Mary said, "my spirit rejoices in God my savior" (Luke 1:46). An examination of the text used to prove

---

34. Ibid., p. 203 (cf. Denzinger, *Sources of Catholic Dogma*, 833, p. 260).
35. Ibid., following the Latin Vulgate.
36. Ibid.

Mary's sinlessness reveals the lack of any real support for such a doctrine. Contrary to Scotus's solution of her being prevented from needing to be saved from sin, she was confessing her present need (after her conception) of a Savior. Indeed, she even presented an offering to the Jewish priest arising out of her sinful condition (Luke 2:22–24) which was required by law (Lev. 12). This would not have been necessary if she were sinless.

RESPONSE TO ARGUMENT FROM SCRIPTURE

The Catholic argument that Mary was "full of grace" at the annunciation in no way proves sinlessness during her entire life. First, the phrase "full of grace" is an inaccurate rendering based on the Latin Vulgate that is corrected by the modern Catholic Bible (NAB), which translates it simply "favored one." The Vulgate's misleading rendering became the basis for the idea that grace extended throughout Mary's life. Second, taken in context the salutation of the angel is only a reference to her state at that moment, not to her entire life. It does not affirm that she was always and would always be full of grace but only that she was at that time. Third, the grace given here to Mary was not only limited in time but also in function. The grace she received was for the task of being the mother of the Messiah, not to prevent her from any sin. Finally, the stress on fullness of grace is misleading, since even Catholic scholars admit that Mary was in need of redemption. Why, if she was not a sinner? Ott says that Mary "required redemption and was redeemed by Christ."[37] And, as we have already seen, it is biblically unfounded to suggest that she was prevented from inheriting sins rather than being delivered from it.

RESPONSE TO ARGUMENT FROM TRADITION

Besides the lack of scriptural support for Mary's sinlessness the argument from the Fathers is weak. Even Ott admits that many "Greek Fathers (Origen, St. Basil, St. John Chrysostom, St. Cyril of Alexander) taught that Mary suffered from venial personal faults, such as ambition and vanity, doubt about the message of the Angel, and lack of faith under the Cross."[38] Likewise, almost all major scholastic fathers, including Aquinas, rejected the immaculate conception. This being so, Mary's consequent sinlessness must also be brought into question, despite scholastic protest to the contrary.[39] In spite of all the evidence to the contrary, however, the Council of Trent affirmed Mary's sinlessness as an infallible truth of the Catholic faith.

37. Ibid., p. 212.
38. Ibid., p. 203.
39. Aquinas, for example, accepted the belief that Mary was free from personal sin from the time of her birth on.

THE BODILY ASSUMPTION OF MARY

The Roman Catholic dogmas concerning Mary reveal a progressive glorification of her. According to official Catholic doctrine, Mary moved from being sinless to being immaculately conceived to being bodily assumed into heaven and even venerated as Mediatrix (a mediator of grace) and "Queen of Heaven." There is a strong cult of Mary within the Roman Catholic Church that would carry it even further. Indeed, as we shall see, in practice many folk Catholics virtually deify Mary.

CATHOLIC DEFENSE OF THE BODILY ASSUMPTION OF MARY

According to Catholic dogma, "Mary was assumed body and soul into heaven."[40] In 1950, the Roman Catholic Church spoke *ex cathedra* to proclaim infallibly that "just as the glorious resurrection of Christ was an essential part, and final evidence of the victory, so the Blessed Virgin's common struggle with her son was to be concluded with the 'glorification' of her virginal body."[41] In the bodily assumption, Mary "has finally attained as the highest crown of her privileges, that she should be immune from the corruption of the tomb, and that in the same manner as her Son she would overcome death and be taken away soul and body to the supernatural glory of heaven, where as Queen she would shine forth at the right hand of the same Son of hers, the Immortal King of Ages."[42]

Catholics defend the dogma of Mary's bodily assumption by both Scripture and tradition. Biblical support is scant, but Catholic scholars still use several texts in support of it.

ARGUMENT FROM SCRIPTURE

1 Corinthians 15:23. From this text Catholic theologians argue the "possibility" of Mary's bodily assumption on the basis of her being one of those "who belong to Christ."[43] They fail to specify just how Mary's bodily assumption before other believers is compatible with this text.

Matthew 27:52–53. Ott argues that the graves opening after Jesus' resurrection and many saints emerging shows the "probability" of the bodily assumption of Mary. For "If . . . the justified of the Old Covenant were called

40. Ott, *Fundamentals of Catholic Dogma*, p. 208.
41. Denzinger, *Sources of Catholic Dogma*, no. 2331, p. 647.
42. Ibid., no. 2332, p. 648.
43. Ott, *Fundamentals of Catholic Dogma*, p. 208.

to perfection of salvation immediately after the conclusion of the redemptive work of Christ, then it is possible and probable that the Mother of the Lord was called to it also."[44]

Luke 1:28. Scholastic theologians argue Mary's bodily assumption from her fullness of grace spoken of in this verse. Ott argues that "since she was full of grace she remained preserved from the three-fold curse of sin (Gn. 3, 16–19), as well as from her return to dust."[45]

Revelation 12:1–6. This passage speaks of a woman who gave birth to "a male child, destined to rule all the nations" (= Christ) who was "caught up to God and his throne." On this basis "scholastic theology sees also the transfigured mother of Christ."[46]

Psalm 131:8 (132:8 AV, NIV). Some Fathers refer to passages like this psalm "in a typical sense to the mystery of the bodily assumption; 'Arise, O Lord, into thy resting place; thou and the ark which thou hast sanctified,'" arguing that "the Ark of the Covenant made from incorruptible wood, [was] . . . a type of the incorruptible body of Mary."[47]

Genesis 3:15. Modern Catholic theologians often cite this text in support of the bodily assumption of Mary, "since by the seed of the woman it understands Christ, and by the woman, Mary, it is argued that as Mary had an intimate share in Christ's battle against Satan and in His victory over death."[48]

SPECULATIVE ARGUMENTS FOR
THE BODILY ASSUMPTION OF MARY

Catholic theologians infer the bodily assumption of Mary from several other dogmas about her. Each is briefly stated here.

Argument from the Freedom from Sin. Catholicism argues that, since the dissolution of the body is a punishment of sin and Mary was sinless, "it was fitting that her body should be excepted from the general law of dissolution and immediately assumed into the glory of Heaven, in accordance with God's original plan for mankind."[49]

Argument from the Motherhood of God. According to this reasoning, "As the body of Christ originated from the body of Mary . . . it was fitting that Mary's body, should share the lot of the body of Christ. As a physico-spiritual relationship the Motherhood of Mary demands a likeness to her Divine Son in body and soul."[50]

---

44. Ibid., p. 209.
45. Ibid.
46. Ibid.
47. Ibid. See also Patrick Madrid, "Ark of the New Covenant," *This Rock* (December 1991): cover and pp. 9f.
48. Ott, *Fundamentals of Catholic Dogma*, p. 209.
49. Ibid.
50. Ibid.

Argument from the Perpetual Virginity of Mary. This speculation suggests that, "As Mary's body was preserved unimpaired in virginal integrity, it was fitting that it should not be subject to destruction after death."[51] In short, Mary's perpetual virginity is used to prove her bodily immortality.

Argument from Mary's Participation in Christ's Work. Catholic theology also speculates that "As Mary, in her capacity of Mother of the Redeemer, took a most intimate share in the redemptive work of her Son it was fitting that, on the completion of her earthly life, she should attain to the full fruit of the Redemption, which consists in the glorification of soul and body."[52] This kind of argument was later to lead to Mary's role as coredemptrix and Queen of Heaven (see below).

PROTESTANT RESPONSE TO THE BODILY ASSUMPTION OF MARY

RESPONSE TO ARGUMENT FROM SCRIPTURE

Even noted defenders of Catholic dogma admit that "direct and express scriptural proofs are not to be had."[53] They speak rather of the "possibility" or "probability" of it, based on certain texts. When, however, the texts are examined closely, no such probability exists.

Matthew 27:52–53. The fact that some saints arose immediately after Jesus' resurrection in no way shows that Mary was bodily assumed into heaven. First, the text speaks only of some being raised from their graves, not of ascending into heaven. Second, many scholars believe these saints were only resuscitated like Lazarus, not resurrected in immortal bodies. Third, Mary is not mentioned in the group that was raised, nor is there any mention anywhere in Scripture of her being raised at a later time. So the belief that Mary was bodily assumed into heaven has no basis in this text whatsoever.

Luke 1:28. Scholastic theology's inference of Mary's bodily assumption from her "fullness of grace" spoken of in this verse is unjustified for two basic reasons. First, as scholastic theology admit, no such teaching is explicit in this text. Second, "fullness of grace" is not such a theologically precise term as to carry the weight of this dogma. This phrase in no way specifies that Mary was "preserved from the three-fold curse of sin (Gn. 3, 16–19), as well as from her return to dust."[54]

Revelation 12:1–6. This passage does not support the bodily assumption of Mary for several reasons. First, the "woman" does not represent Mary but the nation of Israel for whom there is "a place prepared by God, that there

---

51. Ibid.
52. Ibid.
53. Ibid., p. 208.
54. Ibid., p. 209.

she might be taken care of for twelve hundred and sixty days" (v. 6) during the tribulation period before Christ returns to earth (cf. Rev. 11:2–3).

Second, it was only Christ, not the woman who was "caught up to God and his throne" (v. 5). It is pure eisegesis (reading into the text), not legitimate exegesis (reading out of the text) to see Mary's bodily assumption here. Likewise, to argue that Mary, though not being caught up here, is pictured in heaven in the celestial imagery is equally farfetched. Nothing of the kind is stated in this text that would entail a belief in her bodily assumption, at least not before the resurrection of the rest of the saints (1 Thess. 4:13–18).

Psalm 131:8 (132:8 AV, NIV). Using verses like this one only confirms the impression that Roman Catholics are grasping for proof texts. First, it is confessedly not a literal interpretation of the text but only an alleged "typical" one which, in this case, boils down to an invalid argument from analogy. Second, the analogy between the ark and Mary is farfetched.[55] Nowhere is any such comparison stated or implied in Scripture. Nor is Mary's immaculate conception foreshadowed in the creation of the universe in an immaculate state, nor in Eve, the mother of our race. Creating analogies like these prove nothing, except that one has run out of any real biblical support for the dogma. One could prove almost anything by the same kind of argument. Third, the argument is based on another baseless belief that Mary's body was incorruptible after her death and before her alleged assumption. The Bible says this was true of Christ (Acts 2:30–31), but it nowhere affirms this of Mary.[56] Indeed, the Bible equates death with the corruption of all human beings except Christ (cf. 1 Cor. 15:42, 53). Yet most Fathers and theologians of the Catholic church believe that "Mary suffered a temporal death" like other mortals.[57] Why then should we believe she was exempted from physi-

---

55. One Catholic apologist calls this the "most compelling type of Mary's Immaculate Conception" (see Madrid, "Ark of the New Covenant," p. 12). It is only compelling if one makes the unbiblical and unjustified assumption that it is a *valid* analogy. One can note certain similarities between many things that prove nothing (e.g., there are many strong similarities between good counterfeit currency and genuine bills). Thus, even proponents of this view have to admit that none of this "proves" the immaculate conception (ibid.). The ineptness of these kinds of analogies surface in Madrid's question: "If you could have created your own mother [as God did in Mary], wouldn't you have made her the most beautiful, virtuous, perfect woman possible?" (ibid.). Sure, I would have done a lot of things differently than God did. If I were God and could have created the most beautiful and perfect place for my Son to be born it would not have been a stinky, dirty animal stable! God, however, chose otherwise.

56. Even if, as some argue, this text (via David's anticipation of his deliverance in Ps. 16:10) includes Mary's bodily resurrection, nevertheless it does not apply to her in any more special sense than it does to the resurrection of the whole human race in the endtimes (cf. John 5:28–29; 11:24; 1 Cor. 15:20–21).

57. Ott, *Fundamentals of Catholic Dogma*, p. 207. A contemporary Catholic lay apologist comments: "The Church has never formally defined whether she [Mary] died or not, but the integrity of the doctrine of the Assumption would not be impaired if she did not die, but the almost universal consensus is that she did in fact die" (Karl Keating, *Catholicism and Fundamentalism* [San Francisco: Ignatius Press, 1988], p. 273).

cal corruption any more than she was not exempted from physical death entailed by the fall (Rom. 5:12)?

Genesis 3:15. The bodily assumption of Mary is no more found in this text than is the immaculate conception. Even the Catholic authority on dogma, Ludwig Ott, admits that "It is true that the literal reference of the text is to Eve and not Mary."[58] The text is clearly speaking about Eve and her descendants, not Mary. And, as already noted, the indirect sense in which Mary is involved as the mother of the "seed" or "offspring" (Christ) who will crush the serpent in no way even implies her sinlessness or immaculate conception.

RESPONSE TO SPECULATIVE ARGUMENTS

Catholic theologians infer the bodily assumption of Mary from several other Catholic dogmas about her. Each will be briefly stated here.

Freedom from Sin Argument. Mary's bodily assumption cannot be legitimately inferred from her alleged sinlessness for many reasons. First, it assumes her sinlessness, which is not based in Scripture and even has strong arguments against it from the Fathers, such as Thomas Aquinas and others. Second, even Catholic scholars admit that there is no necessary connection here, thus settling for the weaker phrase "it is fitting." At best this would show only the possibility, not probability, of this conclusion. Third, most Catholic authorities admit that Mary died. According to Paul (Rom. 5:12), however, death is a punishment for sin. It begs the question to say that Mary did not die a *natural* death; if she was sinless, why should she die at all? She should have been taken bodily into heaven without death. The fact that Mary died shows that she was not exempt from punishment due to inherited original sin, and thus reveals that she must have had original sin.

Motherhood of God Argument. This too is a weak argument. For one thing, it depends on another assumption, namely, that Mary was the mother of God in any sense more than that she was the human channel through which the God-man was brought into this world. As we will see below, while classical Protestantism accepts the term "Mother of God," it rejects the venerational baggage with which Catholic theology had laden it. Further, the use of the phrase "it was fitting" belies the weakness of the argument's premise. There certainly is no logically necessary connection between Mary being bodily assumed into heaven and her being the earthly mother of Jesus.

Perpetual Virginity Argument. Here again we have a premise that is an assumption (not based on Scripture) and an inference that is not necessary. A lot of things are merely "fitting" that never happen. Here too we have a weak analogy and a conclusion that does not validly follow from it.

Mary's Participation in Christ's Work Argument. Two assumptions in

---

58. Ott, *Fundamentals of Catholic Dogma*, p. 209.

this argument need to be challenged. First, Mary's alleged redemptive capacity as mother of the Redeemer is not supported by Scripture (see below). In fact, even Catholic theology admits that Christ alone, not Mary, suffered for our sins on the cross. Further, a bodily assumption is a large and invalid leap from sharing with her Son in his redemptive work.

RESPONSE TO ARGUMENT FROM TRADITION

Even if one grants the validity of arguments from tradition in general, the traditional argument for the bodily assumption of Mary is weak. Catholic authorities admit that "The idea of the bodily assumption of Mary is first expressed in certain transitus-narratives of the fifth and sixth centuries." Further, they acknowledge that "these are apocryphal."[59] In fact, the bodily assumption of Mary was not held by most of the early church fathers. Ott admits that belief in this dogma did not appear until nearly the seventh century.[60] Noted Catholic theologian Karl Rahner acknowledged that "at best it can only be considered as evidence of theological speculation about Mary, which has been given the form of an ostensible historical account." He adds, "there is nothing of any historical value in such apocryphal works."[61]

As Miller and Samples aptly note, "To the Protestant, who views Scripture as the only secure anchor for theology, Catholic Mariology having cut loose from this anchor is hopelessly adrift upon a sea of splendid but dubious 'Roman logic.'" Citing Victor Buksbazen, "the non-Catholic student of Mariology who tries to follow its shaky premises and strained conclusions finds himself in a kind of theological Alice in Wonderland in which things, in spite of their seeming logic, become 'curriouser and curriouser.'"[62]

THE MEDIATORSHIP OF MARY

Another area of tension with Protestant theology is the Catholic belief in the mediatorship of Mary. This cooperative work with Christ in redemption runs headlong into conflict with the Protestant belief in the uniqueness of Christ's atonement.

CATHOLIC DEFENSE OF THE MEDIATORSHIP OF MARY

According to Catholic theology, "although Christ is the sole Mediator between God and man (I Tim. 2, 5), since He alone, by His death on the Cross,

59. Ibid., pp. 209–10.
60. Ibid., p. 210.
61. Karl Rahner, *The Mother of Our Lord* (Wheathampstead, Hertfordshire: Anthony Clarke Books, 1963), p. 16.
62. Miller and Samples, *Cult of the Virgin*, p. 43.

fully reconciled mankind with God, this does not exclude a secondary mediatorship, subordinate to Christ."[63] Aquinas stated the relationship this way: "To unite men to God perfectively (perfective) appertains to Christ according to 2 Cor. V. 19. Therefore Christ alone is the perfect mediator between God and man, inasmuch as He reconciled mankind with God by His death. . . . But there is nothing to prevent others in a certain way (secundum quid) from being called mediators between God and man, in so far as they, by preparing or serving . . . , co-operate in uniting men to God."[64]

Mary was called "mediatrix" in the 1854 bull "Ineffabilis" of Pope Pius IX, the same document that proclaimed her immaculate conception. Catholic authorities take this to mean two things: "1. Mary is the Mediatrix of all graces by her co-operation in the Incarnation. And 2. Mary is the Mediatrix of all graces by her intercession in Heaven."[65] According to Pope Leo XIII in "Magnae Dei Matris": "Nothing whatever of that immense treasure of all graces, which the Lord brought us . . . is granted to us save through Mary, so that, just as no one can come to the Father on high except through the Son, so almost in the same manner, no one can come to Christ except through his Mother."[66]

Mary's cooperation in the incarnation has earned her "the title Coredemptrix = Coredemptress, which has been current since the fifteenth century."[67] This, Catholic scholars remind us, "must not be conceived in the sense of an equation of the efficacy of Mary with the redemptive activity of Christ, the sole Redeemer of humanity (I Tim. 2, 5)." For "she herself required redemption and in fact was redeemed by Christ."[68] Indeed, "Christ alone truly offered the sacrifice of atonement on the Cross; Mary merely gave him moral support in this action. Thus Mary is not entitled to the title "Priest" (sacerdos)." Nonetheless, as Catholic scholars point out, "In the power of the grace of Redemption merited by Christ, Mary, by her spiritual entering into the sacrifice of her Divine son for men, made atonement for the sins of men, and (de congruo) merited the application of the redemptive grace of Christ. In this manner she co-operates in the subjective redemption of mankind."[69] Christ alone, of course, provided the objective basis for redemption in his death on the cross.

In addition to being the Mediatrix or channel through which Christ and

---

63. Ott, *Fundamentals of Catholic Dogma*, p. 211.

64. Aquinas, *Summa Theologiae* 3.26.1; cited in ibid., p. 211.

65. Ott, *Fundamentals of Catholic Dogma*, pp. 212–13. Other Catholic scholars claim this has not been infallibly pronounced and do not hold it to be true.

66. Quoted in Pius X, 28; cited in Miller and Samples, *Cult of the Virgin*, p. 50.

67. Ott, *Fundamentals of Catholic Dogma*, p. 212. Here again less Marian Catholic scholars contend that this is not mandatory Catholic doctrine.

68. Ibid.

69. Ibid., p. 213.

his redemption came into the world, Catholics hold that "Mary is Mediatrix of all graces by her intercession in Heaven." That is, "Since her assumption into Heaven, Mary co-operates in the application of the grace of Redemption to man. She participates in the distribution of grace by her maternal intercession which is far inferior in efficacy to that of the intercessory prayer of Christ, the High Priest, but surpasses far the intercessory prayer of all the other saints."[70] According to many Catholic theologians, Mary is the intercessory channel of all grace bestowed on God's people. However, Ott claims that "The implication of this is not that we are obligated to beg for all graces through Mary, not that Mary's intercession is intrinsically necessary for the application of the grace, but that, according to God's positive ordinance, the redemptive grace of Christ is conferred on nobody without the actual intercessory co-operation of Mary."[71]

ARGUMENT FROM SCRIPTURE AND TRADITION

Both biblical and traditional evidence have been offered for Mary's role as Mediatrix. The biblical texts cited, however, are scant. Ott summarizes the evidence this way: "Theologians seek a biblical foundation in the words of Christ, John 19, 26 et seq.: 'Woman behold thy son, son behold thy mother.' . . . The mystical interpretation . . . sees in John the representative of the whole human race. In him Mary was given as the spiritual mother of the whole of redeemed humanity that she, by her powerful intercession, should procure for her children in need of help all graces by which they can attain eternal salvation."[72]

As to the evidence from tradition for Mary's role as Mediatrix of redemption, some allusions to similar roles are found in Origen and Augustine and others to Mary's spiritual motherhood. However, "They became more numerous during the peak period of the Middle Ages." For example, Bernard of Clairvaux said, "God wished that we have nothing, except by the hands of Mary."[73]

PROTESTANT RESPONSE TO THE MEDIATORSHIP OF MARY

The way the role of Mary is carefully defined by many Catholic theologians makes it difficult to charge it with outright (formal) heresy. Be that as it may, there are some serious biblical and practical problems with it.

---

70. Ibid. Some Catholic scholars insist that this is not an infallible teaching of the church and, hence, do not accept it.
71. Ibid.
72. Ibid., p. 214.
73. Cited in ibid.

RESPONSE TO ARGUMENT FROM SCRIPTURE

The scriptural evidence for calling Mary a mediator or co-redemptrix is totally lacking. Even Roman Catholic authority Ludwig Ott confesses: "Express scriptural proofs are lacking." He says merely that "theologians seek a biblical foundation" in a "mystical" interpretation of John 19:26.[74] Such an interpretation is far removed from the actual meaning of the text and by virtue of its farfetched nature only weakens the case for the doctrine. Indeed, the clear meaning of many passages of sacred Scripture declare that there is only "one mediator between God and the human race, Christ Jesus, himself human" (1 Tim. 2:5; cf. John 10:1–11; 14:6; Heb. 1:2–3; 10:12).

The Catholic claim that "one" (Gk: *monos*) in 1 Timothy 2:5 does not mean only one *(eis)* is a false disjunction. Obviously, Paul intended to convey here that there is (only) one God and (only) one mediator between God and man. And regardless of the fact that there are other human intercessors to God on earth (2:1–2),[75] it is clear that there is only one mediator between humans and God. For if *monos* does not mean "only one," then the apostle has left open the door for polytheism too. For the same term is used of God in this text.

Finally, there is an inherent dilemma in Catholic Mariology. On the one hand, Catholic theology admits that everything we need as believers we can get from Christ. On the other hand, many Catholic theologians have exalted the role of Mary as the dispenser of all grace. For them there is a hopeless dilemma. For either the role of Mary is rendered superfluous or else the all-sufficiency of Christ's mediation is diminished.[76] The only way out of the dilemma is to hold, as do Protestants, that Mary is not the dispenser of all grace. This is not to say that Mary, as the earthly mother of Jesus, was the channel through which God's grace entered the world but only that Mary is not now, in heaven, the dispenser of God's grace to us.

RESPONSE TO ARGUMENT FROM TRADITION

Catholic scholars also admit that "express testimonies" from the early Fathers are "few in number," most being after the eighth century. O'Carroll explicitly admits that "the Fathers of the Church and early Christian writers did not so interpret the words of the dying Christ."[77] Here again, Roman Catholic scholars manifest a rather arbitrary use of the Fathers, citing them

---

74. Ibid.

75. The fact that there are human intercessors to God *on earth* in no way implies there are any *in heaven* besides Christ (Heb. 7) and the Holy Spirit (Rom. 8).

76. Miller and Samples, *Cult of the Virgin*, p. 56.

77. Michael O'Carroll, *Theotokos: A Theological Encyclopedia of the Blessed Virgin Mary* (Wilmington, Del.: Michael Glazier, 1982), s.v. "Mother of Divine Grace (the Spiritual Motherhood)."

when they favor their dogma and ignoring them when they do not. In fact, the mediatorship of Mary has never been proclaimed as an infallible dogma by the church and, therefore, can be rejected by faithful Catholics without fear of being censored.

THE VENERATION OF MARY

The Mariological doctrine that is perhaps most repugnant to Protestants is the veneration of Mary. This is based on her role as "Mother of God." This is obvious in one of the most popular of all Catholic prayers known as the "Hail Mary," which ends: "Holy Mary, Mother of God. Pray for us sinners now and at the hour of our death."

CATHOLIC DEFENSE OF THE VENERATION OF MARY

According to the teaching of the Catholic church, "Mary, the Mother of God, is entitled to the Cult of Hyperdulia," meaning that Mary may be venerated and honored on a level higher than another creature, angels, or saints. In other words, "In view of her dignity as the Mother of God and her fullness of grace, a special veneration is due to Mary."[78]

Catholic scholars are quick to point out, however, that "this [veneration due to Mary] is substantially less than the cultus latriae (= adoration) which is due to God alone, but is higher than the cultus duliae (= veneration) due to angels and to the other saints. The special veneration thus given to Mary is called cultus hyperduliae."[79] So God alone is worshiped in the sense of *latria*. Mary is venerated in the sense of *hyperdulia,* and saints and angels are honored with *dulia.*

Three kinds of arguments are offered in support of the special venerating of and prayers to Mary. Catholics argue from Scripture, tradition, and analogy.

ARGUMENT FROM SCRIPTURE

Ott summarizes the texts for honoring Mary at a level above all other creatures but below God.

The Scriptural source of the special veneration due to the Mother of God is to be found in Luke 1, 28: "Hail, full of grace, the Lord is with thee," in the praise of Elizabeth, filled with the Holy Ghost, Luke 1, 42: "Blessed art thou

78. Ott, *Fundamentals of Catholic Dogma,* p. 215.
79. Ibid.

amongst women, and blessed is the fruit of thy womb," in the prophetic words of the Mother of God, Luke 1, 48: "For behold, from henceforth all generations shall call me blessed," in the words of the woman in the multitude, Luke 11, 27: "Blessed is the womb that bore thee, and the paps that gave thee suck."[80]

ARGUMENT FROM TRADITION

According to Ott, veneration of Mary was practiced in connection with that of Christ for the first three centuries. Then, "From the fourth century onwards we find a formal veneration of Mary herself."[81] Indeed, such phrases as "Mother of God," "Co-redemptress," and even "Queen of Heaven" have been used to support the veneration of Mary down through the centuries.

ARGUMENT FROM ANALOGY

Many Catholics think of Mary as the prototypical Christian, the one to whom God gave all the blessings of redemption. They argue that, while all Christians will eventually receive complete sanctification after death, Mary received hers at conception. Likewise, while other Christians will attain bodily resurrection after Christ's return, Mary received her bodily assumption before Christ's coming again. Hence, they insist that it is appropriate to honor her more than others now, since she has attained her glorification earlier than other creatures.

PROTESTANT RESPONSE TO THE VENERATION OF MARY

RESPONSE TO ARGUMENT FROM SCRIPTURE

There is absolutely nothing in the biblical text that supports the conclusions Catholics draw from them, namely, that Mary should be venerated above all creatures but below God. The texts say nothing about veneration or prayers to Mary; they simply call Mary "blessed" of God, which she truly was. Contrary to Catholic practice, however, Mary was not blessed *above* all women but simply was the most blessed *among* all women. Even the Catholic *New American Bible* reads: "Most blessed are you *among* women" (Luke 1:42, emphasis added). This is not a distinction without a difference, for it is strange logic to argue that being the most blessed among women makes Mary worthy of more honor than all other women. Eve was the mother of all the living (Gen. 3:20), a distinctive honor held by no other person, including Mary, and yet she is not venerated by Catholics in accord with her blessed

---

80. Ibid.
81. Ibid.

status. Even great sinners who are forgiven are highly blessed but need not be most highly esteemed because of that blessing (cf. 1 Cor. 15:9; 1 Tim. 1:15). There is not a single instance in the New Testament where veneration was given to Mary. When the magi came to the manger to visit the Christ child, Matthew 2:11 declares that "they prostrated themselves and *did him homage,*" not Mary (emphasis added).

Further, Scripture forbids us to bow down in veneration before any creature, even angels (cf. Col. 2:18; Rev. 22:8–9). The Bible makes it clear that we are not to make "idols" of any creature or even "bow down" to them in an act of religious devotion (Exod. 20:4–5).[82] To call Mary "Queen of Heaven," knowing that this very phrase comes from an old pagan idolatrous cult condemned in the Bible (cf. Jer. 7:18), only invites the charge of Mariolatry. And Mariolatry is idolatry.

Finally, despite theological distinctions to the contrary, in practice there is often no real difference between the veneration given to Mary and that given to Christ. This is true for many Catholics in spite of the church's use of verses showing that we should "honor" our parents (Deut. 5:16) and our rulers (Rom. 13:1–7). Furthermore, there is clearly a difference, both in theory and in practice, in the way Catholics honor other human beings and the way they honor Mary. Consider the following book, *Novena Prayers in Honor of Our Mother of Perpetual Help,* with the Catholic Imprimatur (and nihil obstat) on it which guarantees that there is nothing heretical in it.

We have no greater help,
no greater hope than you,
O Most Pure Virgin; help us, then,
for we hope in you, we glory in you,
we are your servants.
Do not disappoint us. [83]

In the same devotional book Mary's devotees pray:

82. The case in 2 Kings 5:17–18 where Naaman was given permission by Elisha to bow down with his master (the king) in the idol temple is not in real conflict with the prohibition not to bow before idols for several reasons. First, Naaman clearly affirmed his faith that "there is no God in all the earth, except in Israel" (v. 15). Second, he was clearly not an idolater for he declared: "I will no longer offer holocaust or sacrifice to any other god except the Lord" (v. 17). Third, his presence in the idol temple was only because of his duty to assist his master, the king, not because of his own personal desire to be there (v. 18). Fourth, he made it clear that, as "army commander of the king" (v. 1), "I too, as his adjunct, must bow down in the temple of Rimmon" (v. 18). Thus, his bowing was a social obligation, not part of his religious devotion. Fifth, the fact that he asked forgiveness for the appearance of evil, reveals his heart was not in the act of bowing (v. 18). This is quite different from someone who is intentionally and freely bowing before an image in an act of religious devotion, which the Bible condemns.

83. *Novena Prayers in Honor of Our Mother of Perpetual Help* (Uniontown, Pa.: Sisters of St. Basil, 1968), p. 16.

Come to my aid, dearest Mother, for I recommend myself to thee. In thy hands I place my eternal salvation, and to thee I entrust my soul. Count me among thy most devoted servants; take me under thy protection, and it is enough for me. For, if thou protect me, dear Mother, I fear nothing: not from my sins, because thou wilt obtain for me the pardon of them; nor from the devils, because thou art more powerful than all hell together; not even from Jesus, my judge, because by one prayer from thee, He will be appeased.[84]

Numerous examples of this kind of Mary worship can be found in Alphonsus de Liguori's famous book, *The Glories of Mary* (A.D. 1750), which is published in over 800 editions! A few examples will suffice:

Shall we scruple to ask her to save us, when "the way of salvation is open to none otherwise than through Mary."

"Many things," says Nicephorus, "are asked from God, and are not granted: they are asked from Mary, and are obtained."

At the commands of Mary all obey—even God" [!!!][85]

Protestants and find such prayers repugnant, if not blasphemous, as do some less traditional Catholics.[86] The theoretical distinctions notwithstanding, on the experiential level, there appears to be little if any difference between the intensity of this devotion to Mary and the worship of God.

RESPONSE TO ARGUMENT FROM TRADITION

The evidence from tradition for venerating Mary is not solid and it is not early. While there was some earlier fascination with Mary, even Ott admits that the veneration of Mary only dates from the fourth century.[87] It was at that time that a sect (cult) formed consisting of women who worshiped the virgin Mary as a goddess. The group originated in Thrace, was also found in

84. Ibid., p. 19. Citing Scripture to show it is not wrong to pray for someone else's forgiveness (Exod. 32:30–34; Job 42:8; Acts 7:59–60) or of appeasing God's wrath on others (Gen. 20:7; 1 Sam. 12:19; Job 1:5) does not negate the near blasphemous content and tone of these Catholic prayers to Mary or their clearly unbiblical direction of praying to a dead human being rather than to the living God.

85. Alphonsus de Liguori, *The Glories of Mary,* ed. Eugene Grimm (Brooklyn: Redemptionist Fathers, 1931), pp. 169, 180, 137.

86. Less traditional Catholics, while bemoaning the extravagance in these prayers, tend to excuse it as poetic license, religious hyperbole, and/or insisting that there is an implied exception here for Christ. This, however, often does not come out in either the wording of the prayers or the religious fervor of the devotee to Mary.

87. Concerning devotion to Mary in the ante-Nicene period, Kelly states that, while not completely absent, "reliable evidence of prayers being addressed to her, or of her protection and help being sought, is almost . . . non-existent in the first four centuries" (Kelly, *Early Christian Doctrine,* p. 491).

Arabia, and baked cakes as an offering to Mary.[88] This group was condemned by Epiphanius of Salamis (c. A.D. 315–403), who became metropolitan of Constantia (Salamis) and was considered an authority on devotion to the blessed virgin Mary. On this idolatrous cult condemned by the church, he stated: "Mary should be honored, but the Father and the Son and the Holy Ghost should be adored. Nobody should adore Mary (Haer. 78,7)."[89]

Very early in church history, Epiphanius sensed the potential danger inherent in too much attention being paid to Mary. In this he reminds us of Luther's attitude many years later. Harold O. J. Brown states the concern of evangelicals: "Even if one accepts the traditional Catholic distinction between the 'extreme veneration' (hyperdouleia) offered to Mary and the worship (latreia) which is legitimately offered only to God, one fears that such a distinction becomes quite obscure in practice."[90] Indeed, when attention to Mary imperils the sufficiency of Christ, the very essence of the Gospel is threatened.

RESPONSE TO ARGUMENT FROM ANALOGY

There are many objections to the overused argument from analogy. First, it is not really an argument at all. At best, analogies only illustrate a point that must be proven some other way; they do not prove anything. Also, there is absolutely no indication in Scripture that any such comparison should be made; Mary is never referred to as the prototypical Christ. What is more, there is no evidence that Mary attained her sanctification earlier than the rest of us: she confessed being a sinner (Luke 1:46); she offered a sacrifice for her sinful condition (Luke 2:22); and, as even Catholic theologians admit, she died like the rest of us. So Mary showed no evidence of having received ultimate sanctification (glorification) while on earth. Even if Mary had attained her glorification earlier than other creatures, this still would not justify venerating her any more than we should a saint or an angel. Angels in Scripture even forbid humans to bow before them to worship God (cf. Rev. 22:8–9).

CATHOLIC DEFENSE OF THE VENERATION OF RELICS

A word should be said here about the Catholic doctrine of venerating relics of Mary and other saints. According to Catholic dogma, "It is permissible

---

88. See articles on "Collyridians," in *The Westminster Dictionary of Church History,* ed. Jerald C. Brauer (Philadelphia: Westminster, 1971), p. 220; Cross, *Oxford Dictionary,* pp. 314–15.
89. Ott, *Fundamentals of Catholic Dogma,* p. 216. On Epiphanius, see John J. Delaney and James E. Tobin, *Dictionary of Catholic Biography* (Garden City, N.Y.: Doubleday, 1961), p. 379.
90. Brown, *Protest of a Troubled Protestant,* p. 151.

and profitable to venerate the relics of saints."[91] The Council of Trent declared: "Also the holy bodies of the holy martyrs and of the others who dwell with Christ . . . are to be honored by the faithful."[92] Ott says that "the reason for the veneration of relics lies in this, that the bodies of the saints were living members of Christ and Temples of the Holy Ghost; that they will again be awakened and glorified and that through them God bestows many benefits on mankind." Further, "As well as the bodies and their parts, objects which came into physical contact with the saints are also venerated as relics."[93]

PROTESTANT RESPONSE TO THE VENERATION OF RELICS

Most Protestants find this practice repugnant. The reasons will become apparent as we critique the arguments offered by Catholics in favor of venerating relics, as well as note positive reasons against such veneration.

RESPONSE TO ARGUMENT FROM SCRIPTURE

While some Catholic apologists seek biblical support for this practice,[94] even noted Catholic authority Ludwig Ott admits that "Holy Writ does not mention the veneration of relics."[95] Neither do the so-called precedents in Scripture prove the Catholic practice, for the bones of Joseph were not venerated, but were simply preserved (Exod. 13:19). Hence, to use this verse as proof for venerating relics is to take it out of context.

Likewise, the fact that God performed a miracle through contact with Elijah's mantle (2 Kings 2:13–14) does not justify venerating them any more than it would justify venerating other physical means that God has used to convey miracles, such as the rod of Moses, the clay Jesus used to heal the blind man, or the hands or handkerchiefs of the apostles used to cure diseases!

Neither does the fact that the Old Testament ark of the Covenant was considered sacred and that Uzzah was struck dead for touching it (2 Sam.

---

91. Ott, *Fundamentals of Catholic Dogma*, p. 319.
92. Denzinger, *Sources of Catholic Dogma*, no. 985, p. 299.
93. Ott, *Fundamentals of Catholic Dogma*, p. 319.
94. Strangely, some Catholic apologists even cite the Pharisees' practice of adorning graves (Matt. 23:29) or the common Christian custom of putting flowers on a loved one's grave as proof that it is acceptable to venerate relics. This is the fallacy of noting superficial similarities and overlooking crucial differences. First, flowers in *memory* of a loved one are not the same as *venerating* them. Second, *honoring* the dead is far different from *praying to* them. Third, venerating relics of the dead ignores the biblical prohibitions against idolatry (Exod. 20:4–5) and the occult (Deut. 18:9–14). Finally, using the practice of the Pharisees as justification ignores the distinction between what the Bible *records* and what the Bible *approves*, and totally neglects the fact that Jesus here condemns the Pharisees for what they were doing, saying, "You . . . adorn the memorials of the righteous. . . . Thus you bear witness against yourselves that you are the children of those who murdered the prophets" (Matt. 23:29–31)!
95. Ott, *Fundamentals of Catholic Dogma*, p. 319.

6:7) prove that relics of dead saints should be venerated. First, Uzzah was not killed for failing to venerate the ark but for disobeying the law of God that forbade anyone but a priest to touch it (Num. 4:15).[96] Furthermore, showing respect for the ark, in which the very presence of God and his glory was manifested, is far from venerating the relics of human creatures. For one thing, the ark was a divinely appointed symbol, not the mere remains and adornment of men. Also, it was a special symbol in a unique theocracy, where God personally and visibly (in the cloud of his glory) dwelt among his specially chosen people, Israel. And, even granting this special place the ark had, they were not to venerate it (cf. Exod. 20:4–5) but simply to obey God's laws with regard to its use.

Finally, the cures achieved by clothes from the apostle do not prove that we should venerate handkerchiefs (Acts 19:12) but only that God gave special "signs of an apostle" (2 Cor. 12:12). What is conspicuously absent in all of the alleged biblical "precedents" that Catholic apologists use is the act of veneration.

THE BIBLICAL CASE AGAINST VENERATING RELICS

Not only is there a total absence of veneration of any creature or physical object in Scripture; there is an explicit condemnation of it! It is a violation of the commandments against idolatry. For God clearly commanded his people not to make graven images or to bow down to them in an act of religious devotion (Exod. 20:4–5). Paul said that this was the same error of the pagans who "revered and worshiped the creature rather than the creator" (Rom. 1:25). Even noted Catholic scholar Louis Bouyer pointed affirmed that "it is much more important to agree unreservedly with the Protestants that, if there is one error Christians must guard against more than any other, it is idolatry."[97] Unfortunately, the fine theological distinctions Catholics make between the different kinds of veneration or worship do not do this. Indeed, the Bible forbids us ever to make or even bow before an image of any creature in an act of religious devotion: "You shall not make for yourselves any carved image, or any likeness of anything that is in heaven above, or that is in the earth beneath, or that is in the waters under the earth; you shall not bow down nor serve them. For I, the Lord your God, am a jealous God . . ." (Exod. 20:4–5 NKJV).

Roman Catholics responded by saying that the prohibition against making images and bowing down to them in religious devotion is not absolute

---

96. The Bible says Uzzah was stricken dead because of his "error" (2 Sam. 6:7 NKJV). The Hebrew word *shal* occurs only here and means "a fault, an error, a crime, a transgression." It is believed to be an abbreviation of *shalal,* which occurs twice (2 Kings 4:28; 2 Chron. 29:11) and means "to be quiet, to be tranquil, to be negligent, to wander, to deceive."

97. Bouyer, *Spirit and Forms of Protestantism,* p. 92.

for two reasons: First, God himself commanded the making of images such as the cherubim in the tabernacle (Exod. 25:18) and the flowered columns in Solomon's temple (1 Kings 7:18–19). Second, there are many occasions in the Bible where bowing down before a person is not considered idolatry (e.g., Gen. 19:1; 23:7; 33:3; 2 Sam. 15:5). Both of these arguments fail, however, to observe significant differences.

First, the symbols used in the temple (e.g., cherubim) were divinely appointed symbols, not humanly contrived idols. Second, there was no chance that the people of Israel would fall down before the cherubim in the most holy place, since they were forbidden to enter the holy place at any time. Even the high priest went in only once a year on the Day of Atonement (Lev. 16). Further, the prohibition is not against making any carved image for decorative purposes, but of those used in religious worship. In other words, they were not to worship any other God or any image of any god. These cherubim were not given to Israel as images of God but as representations of angels. Nor were they given to be worshiped or even venerated. And the flowered columns in Solomon's temple were purely ornamental. They were not used for veneration, hence, they were not in violation of the commandment in Exodus 20. Finally, the Exodus 20 prohibition is not against religious art as such, which includes things in heaven (angels) and on earth (humans, animals, etc.). Rather, it was against using any image as an object of religious devotion. This is evident from the fact the people were instructed not to "bow down to them nor serve them" (Exod. 20:5). The distinction between non-religious use of images and a religious use is important.

The Use of Images or Representations of God

Forbidden	Permitted
Object of worship	Not an object of worship
Appointed by man	Appointed by God
Religious purpose	Educational or ornamental purpose
To represent essence of God	To affirm truth about Christ on earth

When Catholics argue that religiously bowing down before an image is not wrong because there are many cases in the Bible where such bowing down is approved (e.g., Gen. 18:2) they confuse two very different contexts. First, the people were not bowing before an image but a person, and they were bowing out of respect, not reverence. The Bible condemns even bowing before an angel to worship God (Rev. 22:8–9). More importantly, all the cases of approved bowing before another creature are not religious, but social.

Some contemporary Catholic theologians insist that the biblical prohibitions are only against idolatry, and venerating relics is not the same as worshiping them. One Catholic catechism even says: "Do we pray to relics or images? We do not pray to relics or images, for they can neither see, nor hear, nor help us."[98] This response misses the point. The question is not whether one should pray to an image of Mary (or any creature) but whether they should pray to the saint with or without the use of an image. As we have shown elsewhere (chap. 16), only God should be the object of prayer. The response also diverts the issue, which is not whether one should pray to an image but whether one should use an image in one's prayers. After all, even pagans do not pray to the image but to the spirit behind it. The Bible tells us clearly that there are demonic spirits behind idols (1 Cor. 10:19–20). Perhaps this accounts for many of the supernormal apparitions that are connected with using images and venerating or praying to departed persons, since the Bible speaks of demons working deceiving "signs" and "wonders" (2 Thess. 2:9; Rev. 16:14). Finally, it fails to recognize what God knows, namely, that the idolatrous tendency of the human heart will easily lead it from veneration to adoration, from honoring the relic or image to worshiping it or the person behind it. It is for this reason that even veneration of relics is prohibited.

God knows the idolatrous tendencies of the human heart. Even the bronze serpent that God designated for the healing of his snake-bitten people (Num. 21) was later worshiped by Israel in the days of the kings (2 Kings 18:4). God, knowing that even devout Israelites might be tempted to venerate the remains of Moses, buried him in an unknown place (Deut. 34:5–6) apparently to prevent idolatry that the devil desires to encourage (cf. Jude 9). And Jesus condemned the Pharisees: "Because you . . . build the tombs of the prophets and adorn the monuments of the righteous" (Matt. 23:29).

SUMMARY AND CONCLUSION

Catholics and Protestants share many beliefs about Mary. Both proclaim her to be the most blessed woman on the face of the earth. Both insist she was a virgin when she conceived Jesus. Both acknowledge that she was the mother of God, in the sense of being the earthly channel through which the God-man came into this world. Both believe she is a great model of the Christian life, a noble and virtuous woman. Both believe that she was a creature in need of redemption, which was wrought only through Jesus Christ. Some Protestants, for example, Luther, Calvin, and Zwingli, even believed in Mary's per-

---

98. *The Penny Catechism: 370 Fundamental Questions and Answers on the Catholic Faith,* reprint (Libertyville, Ill.: Prow Books, 1982), p. 33.

petual virginity and immaculate conception. The first two named Reformers even believed that she interceded for us. However, Zwingli and Luther, as well as most Protestants following them, rejected the practice of praying to Mary to make intercession for us.[99]

In spite of these areas of agreement, there are significant differences between Catholics and Protestants in the area of Mariology. Protestants take exception to the terms "mediatrix" and "co-redemptrix" being used of Mary. Despite the careful qualifications made by Catholic theologians,[100] even permitting the use of these terms tends to exalt Mary to a position far above that allotted her by Scripture.[101] Even Vatican II attempted to put the brakes on Roman Catholic enthusiasm for Mary, noting that the role of Mary is a secondary theological issue and that our salvation depends solely on the work of Christ. The Council decided against producing a special document on Mary, fearing it might emphasize her role in salvation history to excess. Instead she is discussed in the last chapter of *Lumen Gentium*, situating her role as a member of the church. It declared that the Catholic church "strongly urges theologians and preachers of the word of God to be careful to refrain as much from all false exaggeration as from too summary an attitude in considering the special dignity of the Mother of God. . . . Let them . . . carefully refrain from whatever might by word or deed lead the separated brethren or any others whatsoever into error."[102]

Protestants see no biblical basis for believing that Mary was perpetually sinless. And, despite technical distinctions to the contrary, evangelicals argue that there are no practical differences between the veneration of Mary and

99. We have taken pains to admit that the Reformers did not challenge some of the Roman Catholic beliefs concerning Mary. However, as to the doctrines which they believed could lead to a diminishing of the work of Christ, they were resolute. Concerning this danger Luther states, "We dare not put our faith in the mother but only in the fact that the child was born" (cited in Anderson, p. 241).

100. Less Marian Catholics wish to emphasize that the Catholic church only permits, not mandates, the use of terms like "co-redemptrix" of Mary. And, as stated above, they also note that Vatican II tended to downplay the Marian excesses because of their offensiveness to Protestants.

101. It is interesting to compare Marian devotion in Eastern Orthodoxy—which, as a jurisdiction, is at least as old as Roman Catholicism (see Appendix A).

Another problematic area is the difference between the measured theological pronouncements of such authorities as Augustine, Anselm, and Aquinas and the ecstatic ejaculations of a Marian devotional writer such as Alphonsus de Liguori (1696–1787). Karl Keating, director of the lay apologetics organization *Catholic Answers,* says concerning Liguori's major work, *The Glories of Mary,* that it is "precisely the kind of book one should not press into the hands of a non-Catholic . . . because it is not easy to understand." Explaining why, Keating states that "It is not easy dealing with a writer, even a saint, whose style is full of literary conceits and hyperbolic statements" (Keating, *Catholicism & Fundamentalism,* p. 281).

102. See *The Documents of Vatican II* (*Lumen Gentium,* IV). Even some traditional Catholics are disturbed by the excessive attention given to Mary; see Mark Brumley, "Putting Mary in Her Place," *The Southern Cross* (28 April 1994).

the worship of God in the minds of devout Marian Catholics.[103] Indeed, most Catholics bow in prayer before an image of Mary, which violates the prohibition against idolatry in the Ten Commandments.[104] Martin Chemnitz states the evangelical position well: "in this dispute I want nothing taken away from the dignity of the blessed Virgin Mary." He continues, "I think that the Virgin Mary is rightly proclaimed blest if those things are attributed to her which are both in agreement with the Scripture and can be proved from there, so that the name of the Lord may be Holy. No other celebration can be pleasing to her."[105]

Another form of piety involving Mary is her alleged appearances in history called "apparitions." An apparition has been defined as "the sudden appearance of a supernatural entity which directly manifests itself to a human individual or group."[106] The most recent example of this religious phenomenon has occurred at Medjugorje in former Yugoslavia. Evangelical scholar Kenneth R. Samples traveled to Medjugorje to interview persons involved in the apparition. He and his colleague, Elliot Miller, have written an excellent critique of the phenomenon.[107]

We may summarize the whole matter of Mariology in this way: one ignores Jesus at one's peril, but no one will be deprived of heaven for neglecting Mary.[108]

---

103. Of course, only God knows the heart, but judging by the fervor of Catholics' devotion and the actual words used of Mary and God there is little visible difference between their devotion to Mary and their devotion to God. And many of the folk Catholics involved in this are not even aware of the official theoretical distinction between the kind of devotion due to God alone and that due to Mary.

104. This is not the same as Protestants wearing a cross around the neck or hanging a cross on the wall of a church, since they are not (or at least should not be) bowing before the cross (a symbol of God the Son), to say nothing of an image of Mary, in devotion to a creature. Many Protestants pray with an open Bible before them, but they do not believe it is an image of God or any creature to whom they are directing their prayers.

105. Martin Chemnitz, *Examination of the Council of Trent, Part I* (St. Louis: Concordia, 1971), p. 383.

106. Miller and Samples, *Cult of the Virgin*, p. 80.

107. See Kenneth R. Samples, "Apparitions of the Virgin Mary: A Protestant Look at a Catholic Phenomenon," in Miller, pp. 77–135.

The matter of the validity of the Marian apparition at Medjugorje is an unsettled question in Roman Catholicism. Samples does a good job of describing the various categories of evaluating apparitions and reporting observations on site.

108. The virgin birth is a fundamental teaching of Scripture, but devotion to Mary is not. One must worship the Son of God to be his disciple, but one need not venerate Mary to enter the kingdom of God.

16

PURGATORY

Another area of significant difference between Catholics and Protestants re-volves around the doctrine of purgatory. It must be noted that Martin Luther did not directly reject the doctrine of purgatory early in his ministry.[1] How-ever, Luther later opposed the concept itself, as he perceived that it led to the abuses of his day. As for the Reformers in general, purgatory "was openly rejected by the Reformers, who taught that souls are freed from sin by faith in Christ alone without any works, and therefore, if saved, go straight to heaven."[2] Indeed, disputes over it and associated doctrines emerged during the Reformation. Three important topics cluster around this issue: the trea-sury of merit, prayers for the dead, and good works for the dead. First, we will consider the doctrine of purgatory itself.

THE DOCTRINE OF PURGATORY

The belief in purgatory is an essential part of the Catholic faith. The Council of Trent declared infallibly: "If anyone says that after the reception of the grace of justification the guilt is so remitted and the debt of eternal punish-ment so blotted out to every repentant sinner, that no debt of temporal pun-ishment remains to be discharged, either in this world or in Purgatory, before the gates of Heaven can be opened, let him be anathema."[3]

1. George W. Forell, ed., *Luther's Works,* vol. 32 (Philadelphia: Fortress, 1958), p. 95. Also see Paul Althaus, *The Theology of Martin Luther* (Philadelphia: Fortress, 1966), p. 4 n. 2.
2. Cross, *Oxford Dictionary,* p. 1145.
3. Henry J. Schroeder, O.P., trans., *Canons and Decrees of the Council of Trent* (Rockford, Ill.: Tan Books, 1978), p. 46.

THE DOCTRINE STATED

Before discussing purgatory it is necessary to mention that only a few teachings regarding the doctrine are considered infallible by Catholic theologians. These include the fact that: (1) there is a purification that takes place before one enters heaven; (2) this purification involves some kind of pain or suffering; and (3) this purification can be assisted by the prayers and devotions of the living. As to whether purgatory is a place,[4] what the precise nature of the pain is, or how long one remains there is not part of infallible teaching. Of course, infallible or not, many other teachings about purgatory are widely believed and practiced in Catholicism, since both noted theologians and popes have taught on the topic. Even granting room for poetic license, the current shrinking doctrine of purgatory is a far cry from that in the Roman Catholic classic, Dante's *Inferno*.

The Nature of Purgatory. In his widely distributed work on Catholic dogma, Ludwig Ott defined purgatory as follows: "The souls of the just which, in the moment of death, are burdened with venial sins or temporal punishment due to sins, enter Purgatory."[5] Since purgatory is a preparation for heaven, only believers go there. Unbelievers go directly to hell. Purgatory, then, is a period of temporal punishment for sins after death and before heaven. Many contemporary Catholic theologians downplay and even deny that purgatory is a *place*, thinking of it more as a *process* of purification which leads to heaven.

As to the "fire" of purgatory, the current tendency is to take it in a spiritual sense. One Catholic catechism states that "the talk of purgatorial fire is an image that refers to a deeper reality. Fire can be understood as *the cleansing, purifying, and sanctifying power of God's holiness and mercy.* God's power straightens, purifies, heals, and consummates whatever remained imperfect at death."[6] This is not quite what Dante had in mind.

The Object of Purgatory. The purpose of purgatory is to cleanse one from venial (not mortal) sins. Following Aquinas, Ott notes that it is for "The remission of the venial sins which are not yet remitted." Purgatory produces "contrition deriving from charity and performed with the help of grace." Thus, "The temporal punishment for sins are atoned for in the purifying fire by the so-called suffering of atonement, that is, by the willing bearing of the expiatory punishment imposed by God."[7]

The Duration of Purgatory. Two things are noted here: the punishment of purgatory is temporal, not eternal; and "the purifying fire will not con-

---

4. See Cardinal Ratzinger, *Eschatology,* p. 230.
5. Ott, *Fundamentals of Catholic Dogma,* p. 482.
6. *A Catholic Adult Catechism* by the German Conference of Bishops, p. 347.
7. Ott, *Fundamentals of Catholic Dogma,* p. 485.

tinue after the General Judgment."[8] After this there is only heaven and hell. Contemporary Catholic theologians, even conservative ones like Cardinal Ratzinger, shy away from quantifying the time one spends in purgatory. They speak, rather, of it being an "existential time" or "transforming" experience when one "encounters Christ." Ratzinger claims that it "is the inward necessary process of transformation in which a person becomes capable of Christ."[9] The more traditional view, however, is that it is a place in which one spends either longer or shorter periods of time, depending on one's sins. Even Ratzinger admits that the pronouncement at Trent implies that it is a place, since it uses the preposition "in."[10]

CATHOLIC DEFENSE OF PURGATORY

Catholic scholars use both Scripture and tradition to defend the dogma of purgatory. We will examine the arguments based on the Bible first.

Arguments from Scripture. Ott notes that "Holy Writ teaches the existence of the cleansing fire indirectly, by admitting the possibility of a purification in the other world."[11] Several Scriptures are cited in support of purgatory.

2 Maccabees 12:42–46. In this text from the Apocrypha Ott observes that "the Jews prayed for their fallen [dead] . . . that their sins might be forgiven them."[12] This indicates that there is both punishment and forgiveness beyond the grave.

Matthew 12:32. In this passage Jesus said there would never be forgiveness for blasphemy of the Holy Spirit. From this Ott infers that this "leaves open the possibility that sins are forgiven not only in this world but in the world to come."[13]

1 Corinthians 3:15. Here Paul declares that "if someone's work is burned up, that one will suffer loss; the person will be saved, but only as through fire." Ott notes that "The Latin Fathers take the passage to mean a transient purification punishment in the other world."[14]

Matthew 5:26. In this parable the judge would not release his prisoner until he paid the last penny. Ott comments, "Through further interpretation of the Parable, a time-limited condition of punishment in the other world began to be seen expressed in the time-limited punishment of the prison."[15]

8. Ibid.
9. Ratzinger, *Eschatology* p. 230.
10. Ibid., p. 220.
11. Ott, *Fundamentals of Catholic Dogma*, p. 483.
12. Ibid.
13. Ibid.
14. Ibid.
15. Ibid., p. 484.

Arguments from Tradition. Ott notes that "The main proof for the existence of the cleansing fire lies in the testimony of the Fathers." The Latin Fathers in particular are cited, Cyprian and Augustine being two cases in point.[16] In addition to tradition, Roman Catholics offer an argument from human reason in favor of purgatory.

> Speculatively, the existence of the cleansing fire can be derived from the concept of the sanctity and justice of God. The former demands that only completely pure souls be assumed into Heaven (Apoc. 21, 27); the latter demands that the punishment of sins still present be effected, but on the other hand, forbids that souls that are united in love with God should be cast into hell. Therefore, an intermediate state is to be assumed, whose purpose is the final purification and which for this reason is of limited duration.[17]

So, Catholic scholars believe that the doctrine of purgatory can be found in Scripture, especially in the references to punishment for believers after death. Further, they find support in tradition as well.

PROTESTANT RESPONSE TO CATHOLIC ARGUMENTS FOR PURGATORY

By way of introduction to our reply, two things should be observed. First, Ott admits that the Bible teaches the existence of purgatory only "indirectly," and even then it is only a "possibility" from these Scriptures. Phrases like these reveal the weakness of the biblical basis for this doctrine. Further, he acknowledges that the argument from reason is arrived at only "speculatively." In short, there is really no direct or positive proof for purgatory from Scripture. Rather, it is based on extra-biblical tradition and human speculation.

Response to Argument from Scripture. The New Catholic Encyclopedia frankly acknowledges that "the doctrine of purgatory is not explicitly stated in the Bible."[18] Neither is it taught implicitly in Scripture, since the Roman Catholic use of Scripture to support purgatory does violence to the contexts of the passages employed. A brief examination of them will suffice.

2 Maccabees 12:42–46. The Protestant response to the use of this text to prove purgatory is simple: 2 Maccabees is not part of the inspired canon of Scripture, and therefore has no authority. It, along with the rest of the Apocrypha, were not accepted as inspired by the Jewish community that wrote them. They were not accepted by Jesus and the apostles, who never quoted them in the New Testament. They were rejected by many important early Fathers of the church, including Jerome, the great biblical scholar and transla-

16. Ibid.
17. Ibid.
18. *New Catholic Encyclopedia,* 11:1034.

tor of the Roman Catholic Latin Vulgate. Indeed, they were not infallibly added to the Roman Catholic Bible until after the Reformation (A.D. 1546), in a futile attempt to support purgatory and prayers for the dead which Luther attacked. Even then this polemical anti-Reformation council inconsistently rejected some apocryphal books, including one (2 [4] Esdras 7:105) which speaks against praying for the dead (see chap. 9).

Matthew 12:32. Catholics' use of this passage to support the concept of forgiveness of sins after death fails for several reasons. First, the text is not speaking about forgiveness in the next life after suffering for sins but the fact that there will be *no forgiveness for this sin in "the world to come"* (Matt. 12:32, emphasis added). How can the denial that this sin will not ever be forgiven, even after death, be the basis for speculating that sins will be forgiven in the next life? Also, purgatory involves only venial sins, but this sin is not venial; it is mortal, being eternal and unforgiveable. How can a statement about the unforgiveness of a mortal sin in the next life be the basis for an argument that non-mortal sins will be forgiven then? What is more, the passage is not even speaking about punishment, which Catholics argue will occur in purgatory. So how could this text be used to support the concept of purgatorial punishment? Finally, even if this passage did imply punishment, it is not for those who will eventually be saved (as Catholics believe is the case with those who go to purgatory) but for those who never will be saved. Again, how can a passage not speaking about punishment for the saved after death be used as a basis for belief in purgatory, which affirms punishment for the saved? In view of these strong differences, it is strange indeed that Roman Catholic scholars cite it in support of the doctrine of purgatory. It only indicates the lack of real biblical support for the doctrine.

1 Corinthians 3:15. Here Paul is speaking of believers who will one day be given a "wage" (v. 14) for their service to Christ. The texts say nothing about believers suffering the temporal consequences for their sins in purgatory. They are not burned in the fire; only their *works* are burned. Believers see their works burn but they escape the fire. Even Ott seems to admit that this text "is speaking of a transient punishment of the Day of General Judgment, probably consisting of severe tribulations after which the final salvation will take place."[19] If so, then it is not speaking of what has traditionally been called purgatory at all.

It should be pointed out that contemporary Catholic apologists tend to reduce purgatorial pain to the scrutinizing experience of post-mortem sanctification, thus indicating their retreat from the more traditional and objectionable Roman Catholic teaching on purgatory. First, 1 Corinthians was written to those "who *have been* sanctified in Christ Jesus" (1:2, emphasis added). Since they were already positionally sanctified in Christ, they needed no fur-

---

19. Ott, *Fundamentals of Catholic Dogma*, p. 483.

ther purification to give them a right standing before God. They were already "in Christ." After listing a litany of sin, including fornication, idolatry, and coveting, Paul adds, "that is what some of you *used to be;* but *now* you *have had yourselves washed,* you *were sanctified,* you *were justified* in the name of the Lord Jesus Christ" (1 Cor. 6:11, emphasis added). From this and other Scriptures (cf. 2 Cor. 5:21) it is evident that their sins were already taken care of by Christ's suffering (cf. 1 Pet. 2:22–24; 3:18) and that they stood, clothed in his righteousness, perfect before God. They needed no further suffering for sins to attain such a standing or to get them into heaven. The fact that God desired them to improve their practical state on earth does not diminish for one moment their absolutely perfect standing in heaven. No sudden rush of practical sanctification (= purgatory) is needed to enter heaven.

Second, the context reveals that the passage is not speaking about the *consequence* of sin but of *reward* for service for those who are already saved. Paul states clearly: "If the work stands that someone built upon the foundation [of Christ], that person will receive a *wage* [or, reward]"[20] (1 Cor. 3:14). The question here is not *sin* and its punishment but *service* and its reward. Likewise, as even Catholic theology acknowledges, the "loss" (v. 15) is clearly not referring to salvation since "the person will be saved" (v. 15). Thus, the loss must be a loss of reward for not serving Christ faithfully. There is absolutely nothing here about suffering for our sins or their consequences after death. Christ suffered for all our sins by his death (1 Cor. 15:3; Heb. 1:2).

Third, the "fire" mentioned here does not purge our soul from sins; rather, it will "disclose" and "test" our "work." Verse 13 says clearly, "the *work* of each will come to light, for the Day will *disclose* it. It will be revealed with fire, and the fire [itself] will *test the quality of each one's work*" (emphasis added). There is literally nothing here about purging from sin. Contrary to the Catholic claim, the aim of the cleansing mentioned is not ontological (actual) but functional. The focus is on the crowns believers will receive for their service (2 Tim. 4:8), not on how their character is cleansed from sin.[21] It is simply a matter of revealing and rewarding our work for Christ (2 Cor. 5:10).

Matthew 5:26. Ott's "further interpretation" goes well beyond the context. First, Jesus is not speaking about a spiritual prison after death but a physical prison before death. The previous verse makes the context clear:

---

20. The Greek word *(misthos)* used here means a "payment for work done, *reward,* or recompense given (mostly by God) for the moral quality of an action" (cf. 1 Cor. 9:17; 5:46; 6:1). See William Arndt, *A Greek-English Lexicon of the New Testament* (Chicago: Chicago University Press, 1957) p. 525, emphasis added.

21. This is not to say that the experience of being reviewed for our rewards will not have a final impact on the believer's character. It will be an awesome and character-impacting experience. It is only to point out that the purpose is not to cleanse the soul from sins in order to make it fit for heaven. This is what Christ did on the cross objectively and it is subjectively applied to believers at the moment of initial justification when they are dressed in the alien righteousness of Christ.

"Settle with your opponent quickly while on the way to court with him. Otherwise your opponent will hand you over to the judge . . . and you will be thrown in prison" (v. 25). To be sure, Jesus is not speaking of mere external things but of the spiritual matters of the heart (cf. vv. 21–22). However, nothing in the context warrants the conclusion that he intended the concept of a "prison" to refer to a place (or process) of purgation for sins in the next life, which is what one would have to conclude if this passage is made to speak of purgatory. Even orthodox Catholics like Cardinal Ratzinger shy away from the prison image of purgatory, claiming it is not "some kind of supra-worldly concentration camp."[22]

Further, to make this an analogy or illustration of a spiritual prison after death (i.e., purgatory) is to beg the question, since one has to assume there is a purgatory where you "will not be released until you have paid" (v. 26) before it can be an illustration of it. Illustrations do not *prove* anything; they only *illustrate* something already believed to be true. Hence, this passage cannot be used as a proof of purgatory.

Finally, if this text is taken as a reference to purgatory it contradicts the clear teaching of Scripture that there is nothing temporal or eternal left to pay for the consequences of our sins. While Catholics acknowledge that Christ's death paid the penalty for the guilt and eternal consequences of our sins, they deny that this means there is no purgatory in which we pay for the temporal consequences of our sins. But, as we shall see below, Christ's death on the cross was both complete and sufficient for *all our sins and all their consequences*. To say there is some suffering for sins left for us insults the once-for-all finished work of Christ (cf. Heb. 10:14–15). Once Jesus suffered for our sins, there is nothing left for us to suffer, for there is "no condemnation" for those in Christ (Rom. 8:1). Indeed, even death is overcome (1 Cor. 15:54f.).

Response to Argument from Tradition. Even though Ott admits that the primary proof for the existence of purgatory comes from the testimony of the church fathers, he does not hesitate to reject the testimony of the majority of Fathers on other occasions. He notes that "the Fathers, with few exceptions, vouch for the miraculous character of Christ's birth [e.g., birth without pain or penetrating the hymen]. However, the question is whether in so doing they attest a truth of Revelation or whether they wrongly interpret a truth of Revelation."[23] This is a good question and one which we ask of the doctrine of purgatory as well. Indeed, as we have seen in examining the biblical passages used to support the dogma of purgatory, Catholic scholars have misinterpreted Scripture.

In reading through Ott, a standard Catholic authority on dogma, it is interesting to note how many times he admits that this doctrine "is not explic-

---

22. Ratzinger, *Eschatology,* p. 230.
23. Ott, *Fundamentals of Catholic Dogma,* p. 205.

itly revealed in Scripture" or that "direct and express scriptural proofs are not to be had" or "express scriptural proofs are lacking."[24] These phrases are more than a hint to the fact that purgatory has no basis in Scripture.

PROTESTANT REASONS FOR REJECTING PURGATORY

Purgatory is a denial of the sufficiency of the cross. Protestants reject the doctrine of purgatory primarily because it in effect denies the all-sufficiency of Christ's atoning death. Scripture teaches that when Christ died on the cross, he proclaimed, "It is finished" (John 19:30). Speaking of his work of salvation on earth, Jesus said to the Father, "I glorified you on earth by accomplishing the work that you gave me to do" (John 17:4). The writer of Hebrews declared emphatically that salvation by Christ's suffering on the cross was a once-for-all accomplished fact. "For by one offering he has made perfect forever those who are being consecrated" (Heb. 10:14). These verses demonstrate the completed, sufficient nature of the work of Christ. To affirm that we must suffer for our own sins is the ultimate insult to Christ's atoning sacrifice! There is a purgatory, but it is not *after* our death; it was *in* Christ's death. For "when he had accomplished *purification* from sins, he took his seat at the right hand of the Majesty on high" (Heb. 1:3, emphasis added). "Purification" or purging from our "sins" was "accomplished" (past tense) on the cross. Thank God that this is the only purgatory we will ever have to suffer for our sins. Of course, hell awaits those who reject this marvelous provision of God's grace (2 Thess. 1:5–9; Rev. 20:11–15). There are also temporal cause-effect relations in this life that what we sow, we reap (Gal. 6:8–9). There is, however, absolutely no evidence that we will have to pay for our sins in the next life, either eternally or temporally.

To argue, as Catholic scholars do, that purgatory is part of our experiential sanctification is to overlook two important points. First, all *experiential* sanctification occurs in this life before death (cf. 1 Cor. 3:10–13; 2 Cor. 5:10; Rev. 22:12). The only sanctification after death is *actual*. The Bible calls it glorification (Rom. 8:30; 1 John 3:2). Second, sanctification is not a process of *paying* for our sins. It is the process through which God, by his grace, *delivers* us from our sins, all for which (past, present, and future) Christ has already atoned. To be sure, salvation is not fully obtained at the moment of initial justification. Salvation comes in three stages: salvation from the *penalty* of sin (positional justification); salvation from the *power* of sin (practical sanctification); and salvation from the *presence* of sin (ultimate glorification). However, in none of these stages do *we* atone for our sins as a condition for entering heaven. Salvation is not something we "do" to obtain heaven. By Jesus' sacrificial death it is done! As the hymn writer put it, "Jesus

---

24. Ibid., pp. 200, 208, 214, etc.

paid it all. All to him I owe. Sin had left a crimson stain. His blood has washed it white as snow" (cf. Isa. 1:18).

Purgatory is contrary to the immediacy of heaven after death. The Bible speaks of death as the final moment of life after which one goes immediately to heaven or to hell. For "it is appointed that human beings die once, and after this the judgment" (Heb. 9:27).[25] Jesus said that "a great chasm is established to prevent anyone from crossing" the border into heaven after death (Luke 16:26). Upon death a person goes directly to one of two destinies, heaven or hell. At death believers immediately "leave the body and go home to the Lord" (2 Cor. 5:8). That Paul is not merely expressing his wish to be immediately with Christ but a reality is evident from verse 1: "For we know. . . ."

Further, the immediacy of ultimate bliss upon death for a Christian is confirmed by many other texts, including the thief on the cross who went that very day to paradise (Luke 23:43) and Paul's statement that, when he died, he would "depart and be with Christ" (Phil. 1:23). The same is true of Paul's last written words when he speaks of his "departure" to receive his "crown of righteousness" (2 Tim. 4:6–8). Likewise, the saints who will be martyred during the great tribulation will go immediately to heaven (Rev. 6:9–10), as did Enoch in the Old Testament (Heb. 11:5) and Moses and Elijah, who appeared with Christ on the Mount of Transfiguration (Luke 9:30–31). Likewise, unbelievers enter hell at the moment of death. Jesus told the story of how Lazarus died and went to heaven and "the rich man also died and was buried, and from the netherworld, where he was in torment . . . he cried out, 'Father Abraham, have pity on me'" (Luke 16:22–24).[26] There is no indication in Scripture that people will be purified from their sins after death. Scripture teaches that death is final, and a destiny of woe or bliss is immediate.[27]

---

25. Contrary to the claim of some Catholic scholars, there is no indication of a time gap between death and judgment here in Heb. 9:27, that is, reading into the text an idea not found in it. Furthermore, many Catholic scholars are conflating the "time" of purgatory and denying that any real time is involved, only "existential" time.

26. Some Catholic scholars try to spiritualize this away by claiming that it is only a "parable." Even if it were, it still describes some actual reality. Furthermore, nowhere is this called a parable, nor do parables ever use real names in them like "Lazarus" and "Abraham."

27. A doctrine closely associated with purgatory is "limbo." Roman Catholicism defines this as "the abode of souls excluded from the full blessedness of the beatific vision, but not condemned to any other punishment" (Cross, *Oxford Dictionary*, p. 823).

Two areas are distinguished: (1) the *limbus patrum*, "limbo of the fathers," which is the state in which the righteous souls of the Old Testament reposed prior to the finished redemptive work of Christ (1 Pet. 3:19 is cited); and (2) the *limbus infantium*, "limbo of children," which is the abode of "the souls of unbaptized children and adults, who die without committing grievous actual sin [and] enjoy perfect natural happiness" (Broderick, *Catholic Concise Encyclopedia*, p. 223).

Our response to this doctrine is similar to that of purgatory; there is no support for limbo in Scripture. Christ's death and resurrection suffice for all of the redeemed, including Old Testament saints and infants who die before the age of accountability.

THE TREASURY OF MERIT

Another Catholic teaching associated with the doctrine of purgatory is the treasury of meritorious works for the dead. According to Catholic theology, in addition to the merit obtained by Christ on the cross, there is a storehouse of merit deposited by the saints on which others can draw for help. The concept of merit or reward involves the dispersion of mercy over and above justice, but such merit is required for salvation nonetheless. In essence, those saints who have done more good deeds than necessary for their ultimate salvation have put money in the bank of heaven on which others in need can draw for theirs. These good works are called works of supererogation, that is, works over and above those necessary for themselves. By prayers and good deeds on behalf of the dead their stay in purgatory can be shortened as they draw on the surplus in the one big treasury of merit.

CATHOLIC DEFENSE OF THE TREASURY OF MERIT

According to Catholic teaching, "The possibility of vicarious atonement [of one believer for another] is founded in the unity of the Mystical Body. As Christ, the Head, in His expiatory suffering, took the place of the members, so also one member can take the place of another." Thus, "the doctrine of indulgences is based on the possibility and reality of vicarious atonement."[28] An indulgence is the remission of a temporal punishment for a sin whose guilt God has already forgiven. According to the Council of Trent, the Church of Rome has the power of granting indulgences.[29] There are two kinds of indulgences: partial and plenary (full). A partial indulgence frees one from only part of the temporal punishment due for sin that must be paid for, either in this life or in purgatory. A plenary indulgence frees one from the whole punishment due for that sin. The whole concept that indulgences may be obtained from the church is based on the doctrine of merit, especially that one can merit favor with God for another substitutionally by one's works or prayers.

Pope Clement VI was the first to declare in the Jubilee Bull (A.D. 1343) the doctrine of the "Treasury of the Church." According to Ott, it speaks of "the merits (= atonements) of Mary,[30] the Mother of God, and of all the chosen, from the greatest to the least of the just, [who] contribute to the increase of

---

28. Ott, *Fundamentals of Catholic Dogma*, p. 317.

29. Schroeder, *Canons of the Council of Trent.*

30. Of course, by "atonements" of Mary, Catholics do not deny the eternal atonement of Christ but add the temporal atonement of sins suffered by saints (like Mary) and thus made available for others to draw upon from the storehouse of merit.

the treasure from which the Church draws in order to secure remission of temporal punishment."[31]

At Trent the church proclaimed infallibly that the bishops are to "instruct the faithful diligently in matters relating to *intercession and invocation of the saints* . . . to invoke them and to have recourse to their prayers, assistance and support in order to obtain favors from God through His Son, Jesus Christ our Lord."[32]

Argument from Scripture. Catholic scholars claim that "Even in the Old Testament the idea of vicarious atonement by innocent persons for guilty is known. . . . Moses offers himself to God as a sacrifice for the people who sinned (Ex. 32, 32)." Further, "Job brings God a burnt offering, in order to expiate the sins of his children (Job 1, 5). Isaias prophesies [in Chap 53] the vicarious suffering of atonement of Christ as a ransom, as an offering in atonement for the sins of mankind." Likewise, "The Apostle Paul teaches that also the faithful can rend[er] expiation for one another."[33] Ott also cites 2 Corinthians 12:15, Colossians 1:24, and 2 Timothy 4:6 as proof texts.

Argument from Tradition. Catholic scholars point to early Fathers such as Ignatius and Polycarp in support of their belief in a treasury of merit. Ott also notes that "Origen teaches that the Apostles and Martyrs by their death remove the sins of the faithful" and "Cyprian says expressly that sinners can be supported with the Lord by the help of the martyrs."[34] Aquinas argued on the basis of Galatians 6:2 ("bear one another's burdens") that, "in so far as two men are one by charity, one can render [temporal] atonement for the other."[35]

PROTESTANT RESPONSE TO CATHOLIC ARGUMENT FOR THE TREASURY OF MERIT

Protestants reject the Roman Catholic doctrine of a treasury of merit by noting that it is based on a misinterpretation of Scripture and is contrary to the all-sufficiency of Christ's atonement.

Response to Argument from Scripture. The Catholic arguments for a treasury of merit are seriously lacking. Each passage cited is, on closer examination, taken out of context.

Exodus 32:30–32. In this passage Moses tells Israel, "I will go up to the LORD, then; perhaps I may be able to make atonement for your sin." Then he prays to God, "If you would only forgive their sin! If you will not, then strike

---

31. Ott, *Fundamentals of Catholic Dogma*, p. 317.
32. Schroeder, *Canons and Decrees of the Council of Trent.*
33. Ott, *Fundamentals of Catholic Dogma*, p. 317.
34. Ibid.
35. Ibid., p. 318.

me out of the book that you have written." Even a casual look at this passage reveals that it does not support a treasury of merit.

First, there is absolutely nothing about any storehouse of merit in heaven, literal or figurative, to which one can contribute through doing good deeds and upon which others can draw.[36] At best, the passage merely reveals that highly commendable desire of one person who is willing to suffer in the place of another.

Second, God did not accept Moses' offer to be blotted out of God's book for Israel's sake. What God did accept was Moses' sacrificial desire as an indication of the sincerity of his heart, as he also did in the case of Abraham (cf. Gen. 22). God did not accept Moses' offer to give up his place in God's book in exchange for the sins of Israel, his life as an atonement; God accepted Moses' *willingness* to be sacrificed for them. Moses never suffered having his name taken out of God's book, to say nothing of any temporal suffering for Israel's sins. Likewise, Paul expressed a willingness to go to hell if Israel could be saved (Rom. 9:3). This too was an admirable but unfulfillable desire. It indicated Paul's deep passion for his people.

Job 1:5. While Job did offer sacrifices for his children, here again this passages falls far short of supporting the doctrine of a treasury of merit in heaven. There is no mention of any such treasury in the text, and nowhere does it say that God actually accepted such a solicitous act of Job on behalf of his children. The passage could be descriptive, not prescriptive, informing us about what Job did but not whether this is what ought to be done. This is true of the advice of Job's friends, which is only descriptive of what they said, not of what God thought.

In any event, a careful study of the context reveals that the meaning of the passage is to show us how righteous Job was (cf. v. 1), not whether atonement can be made for someone else's sins. Certainly God hears the prayers of a righteous person (Job 42:8; James 5:16). But this in no way implies that they can help atone for the sins of another. The virtue of one human being is not transferable to another. Scripture declares that "the virtuous man's virtue shall be his own, as the wicked man's wickedness shall be his" (Ezek. 18:20).

Finally, even if the acts of one righteous person like Job were in some way efficacious for his family or friends on earth, it in no way supports the Cath-

---

36. Catholic scholars appeal to Rev. 19:8 to support the idea of a storehouse or collection of the good deeds of the saints. But speaking of the white robes of the saints in heaven as "the righteous acts of the saints" is a misunderstanding of this verse. First, it is only a symbol, as is indicated by the fact that the text interprets it for the reader and the fact that the whole book announces itself as a symbolic presentation (Rev. 1:1) and proceeds by giving and interpreting many of them for the reader (e.g., 1:20; 17:9, 15). Second, the text says nothing about there being any collection of these works but simply that each person has his own works that follow him (Rev. 22:12; cf. Rom. 14:12). Third, Holy Writ makes it clear that "each of us shall give an account of himself [to God]" for his own works (Rom. 14:12; cf. 2 Cor. 5:10). Finally, nothing in this passage suggests that the righteous acts of the saints are available for others to draw upon for their sins.

olic belief that this is effective for the departed. *Job offered sacrifices for the living, not for the dead!*

Isaiah 53. This is a great passage on the substitutionary atonement of Christ for us, but it does not teach the substitutionary atonement of one sinful human being for another. Rather, it teaches that the sinless Christ is the substitutionary atonement for a sinful world. For "he [Christ] was pierced for our offenses, crushed for our sins. Upon him was the chastisement that makes us whole. . . . We had *all* gone astray like sheep, each following his own way; But the LORD laid upon him the guilt of us *all*" (vv. 5–6, emphasis added).

Notice also that it is not simply our guilt for which Christ died but also our "chastisement" or punishment (v. 5)—which is directly contrary to the Catholic claim that we need to pay for the temporal consequences of our sins in purgatory. Why, if Christ paid for both? Either Christ did not pay for the temporal consequences, in which case his death is not all-sufficient for our sins, as this text declares, or else Christ paid for both the eternal and temporal consequences of our sins, in which case there is no need for purgatory. So either the Catholic view of Christ's death is deficient or purgatory is unnecessary.

Galatians 6:2. In this passage the apostle exhorts us to "Bear one another's *burdens*," but he does not say we can bear the *punishment* for someone else's sin. There is solidarity here but no substitution for sins. We are to bear our "own load" (v. 5) and then to help bear our brother's load. Clearly we cannot bear another's sins because Paul reminds us that "a person will reap only what *he* sows" (v. 7, emphasis added) and that "each of us shall give an account of himself (to God)" (Rom. 14:12).

Colossians 1:24. Paul speaks here of "filling up what is lacking in the afflictions of Christ on behalf of his body, which is the church," but this in no way supports the Roman Catholic dogma of purgatory. First, this does not mean that Christ's atoning sacrifice is not efficient in paying both the eternal and temporal consequences for all our sins. But if it is sufficient, as Catholics say they believe, then we cannot add to this sufficiency. If we could it would contradict the clear teaching of many other passages (e.g., John 17:4; 19:30; Heb. 10:14) discussed in chapter 13.

Second, there is a certain sense in which Christ continues to suffer. Jesus said to Paul, "Why are you persecuting Me?" Since Christ was not then literally on earth, this must be a reference to his body (the church) which Paul was persecuting (cf. Acts 8:1; 9:1–2). In a similar sense, we too can suffer for him, "For to you has been granted, for the sake of Christ, not only to believe in Him, but also to suffer for Him" (Phil. 1:29). In no sense, however, is our suffering for Christ a means of atoning for sin. Only Jesus suffered *for* sin. We suffer *because of* our sin, never *on behalf of* the sin of others. Each person must either bear the guilt of his own sin (Ezek. 18:20) or else accept the sacrifice that Christ suffered for his sin (2 Cor. 5:21; 1 Pet. 2:21; 3:18). When we "suffer" for Christ, we are undergoing pain as part of his spiritual body (cf. 1 Cor. 12:26), the church, but only what Christ suffered in his physical body on the cross is efficacious for our sins. Our suffering, then, is in *service* for Christ; it is not efficacious for the *salvation* of others.

Finally, even in the nonsalvific sense in which this verse declares that we can suffer for others, there are no verses in the canon of Holy Scripture (see chap. 9) which say we can do this on behalf of those *who are dead!* Our sacrificial lives can only be exercised on behalf of the living (cf. Rom. 5:7).

2 Corinthians 12:15. Paul does say to the Corinthians, "I will most gladly spend and be utterly spent for your sakes." One must make several significant leaps to get from here to the Roman Catholic teaching that the living can offer prayers and indulgences on behalf of those suffering in purgatory. First, neither this nor any other passage cited above speaks of purgatory. Second, the action on behalf of others in this text is for the living, not the dead. Third, the suffering is not for their *sins* or their temporal consequences but in order to bear their *burden* or help minister the grace of Christ to them. Thus, there is no real support in this text for the doctrine of purgatory.

2 Timothy 4:6. When Paul speaks of being "poured out like a libation" he is referring to his death as a martyr. Absent is any reference to purgatory, indulgences, prayers for the dead, or anything supporting the Catholic doctrine of a treasury of merit contributed to by good deeds on which those in purgatory can draw. The truth is that there is no scriptural support for this Catholic dogma. It is biblically unfounded, and, as we saw in chapter 12, it is contrary to the biblical doctrine of salvation by grace through faith.

Other Biblical Arguments against a Treasury of Merit. The most important reason to reject a treasury of merit by which one human being can do good deeds that can be credited to the account of another is the very concept of merit. As we have demonstrated in chapter 12, salvation is not merited; it is obtained by grace through faith. Paul said explicitly, "For by grace you have been saved through faith, and this is not from you; it is the gift of God; it is not from works, so no one may boast" (Eph. 2:8–9). Likewise, in Romans 4:5 the Scriptures declare: "when one does not work, yet believes in the one who justifies the ungodly, his faith is credited as righteousness." It is important to note that Paul does not speak merely of the works of the law, as Catholic scholars often claim, but of any kind of work in general. It is "not because of *any righteous deeds* we had done but because of his mercy, he saved us" (Titus 3:5, emphasis added). Merit and grace are an either/or (see Rom. 11:6).

The whole idea that one can buy[37] an indulgence, the very reason that prompted Luther's reaction against the abuses in the Church, is repugnant. The inspired words of St. Peter himself will suffice: ". . . *you were ransomed from your futile conduct . . . not with perishable things like silver or gold but*

---

37. Catholic scholars insist that indulgences are not really bought; one simply gets them by making a donation for charitable causes. But "a rose by any other name. . . ." Whatever it is called, there is still an exchange of money for merit, however unequal the exchange may be.

with the precious blood of Christ as of a spotless unblemished lamb" (2 Pet. 1:18–19, emphasis added).

Response to Argument from Tradition. Our response to the Catholic arguments from the Fathers for the treasury of merit can be brief. First, the Fathers were not unanimous on this point (a problem, considering Trent's demand that the Bible be interpreted according to the "unanimous consent" of the Fathers). Second, even great Catholic scholars, such as Augustine and Aquinas, rightly taught that the Fathers were not inspired and infallible, only Scripture is (see chap. 10). Augustine declared that "it is to the canonical Scriptures *alone* that I am bound to yield such implicit subjection as to follow their teaching, without admitting the slightest suspicion that in them any mistake or any statement intended to mislead could find a place."[38] Likewise, Aquinas affirmed that "we believe the successors of the apostles and prophets *only in so far as* they tell us those things which the apostles and prophets have left in their own writings."[39] Third, like the official Jewish traditions that grew up around the Old Testament, Roman Catholic official tradition has often strayed from the Word of God. Jesus accused the Pharisees and scribes saying, "You have nullified the word of God for the sake of your tradition" (Matt. 15:6), and the same could be said of Roman Catholics. Finally, the official (infallible) pronouncement of this doctrine at Trent is late (A.D. 1546) and ill-founded, having only scant support from the early church fathers. Thus, neither Scripture nor the unanimous teachings of the Fathers affirm a treasury of merit.

Other Reasons for Rejecting the Treasury of Merit. There are many other arguments against the Catholic doctrine of the treasury of merit. A few are briefly stated here.

First, it undermines the sufficiency of Christ's atonement. The most important reason for rejecting the Roman Catholic dogma of a treasury of merit by which the good deeds of the righteous on earth can be applied to the account of the righteous in purgatory is that it is contrary to the all-sufficiency of the atoning sacrifice of Christ on the cross. Christ not only died for the guilt of our sins but also for their consequences, eternal and temporal. His atoning sacrifice is both sufficient and efficacious, sufficient for all and efficient for those who believe. There is nothing more that needs to be done to save us from the condemnation and consequences of our sins than what Christ already did for us, which we cannot earn but must accept by faith as a free gift. "For the wages of sin is death, but the gift of God is eternal life in Christ Jesus our Lord" (Rom. 6:23). And insofar as it is a gift it cannot be worked for; only wages can. For "a worker's wage is credited not as a gift, but as something due. But *when one does not work,* yet believes in the one

---

38. Augustine, *Letters* 82.3, in Schaff, *Select Library of the Nicene and Post-Nicene Fathers,* emphasis added.
39. Aquinas, *De veritate* XIV, 10, ad 11, emphasis added.

who justifies the ungodly, *his faith is credited as righteousness*" (Rom. 4:4–5; cf. 11:6, emphasis added).

Second, it is contrary to Romans 8:1. According to the Word of God, "There is no condemnation for those who are in Christ Jesus." Catholics believe that those who go to purgatory are "in Christ," that is, they are believers. But if they are believers then no condemnation for anything having to do with their sins (their guilt or consequences) awaits them after death. Jesus took upon himself all our condemnation at the cross (2 Cor. 5:2; Col. 2:13–14; 1 Pet. 2:24; 3:18).

Third, it is inconsistent with other Catholic doctrines. Catholic theology teaches that (1) there will be no purgatory after the second coming; (2) all believers need to suffer for the temporal consequences of their sins in purgatory. But, unless we assume that of the millions of believers alive when Christ returns not even one has any unpaid consequences of his or her sins then it follows; (3) that purgatory is not necessary for those who die just before Christ returns. Indeed, we must assume further that since God is absolutely just the consequences of these sins must have been suffered for by someone else. But there are two problems with this. First, it reveals that purgatory is not really necessary for the individual who commits the sin, since someone else can substitute for that person. Second, if substitutionary atonement for the temporal consequences of one's sin is possible, why not accept the substitutionary atonement of Christ, which is precisely what Scripture affirms (Heb. 1:2–3)?

Further, those who have a deathbed conversion but die just about the time of the second coming cannot pay for the temporal consequences of their sins, since there is no purgatory after the second coming. It matters not whether they were baptized before they died since it is still true that they did not pay for the temporal consequences of their sins. Again, since God is just and must punish sin, the death of Christ must cover the temporal as well as eternal consequences of sin, and therefore there is no need for purgatory to pay for the temporal consequences of anyone's sins. Christ paid it all. Of course, this does not mean that there are no temporal consequences for sin and that God does not use events in this world to chasten and purify his own; he does (cf. 2 Cor. 4:17; Gal. 6:7; Heb. 12:4–11). It simply means that there is no need which stems from some unsatisfied justice in God that we must placate, either in this life or in the next. The sacrifice of Christ on the cross completely satisfied God's justice on behalf of the sins of the entire human race (Rom. 3:21–26; 5:18–19; 2 Cor. 5:21; 1 John 2:2).

PRAYERS TO AND FOR THE DEAD

A sixteenth-century Roman Catholic salesman of indulgences named Tetzel advertised that the moment you hear your money drop in the box, the soul of your loved one will jump out of Purgatory. Nothing was more repugnant to the great Protestant Reformer Martin Luther than the sale of indulgences. While even current Catholic scholars acknowledge that this is extreme, it did focus attention on the Catholic belief in prayers for the dead and indulgences, which are closely associated with the doctrine of purgatory and the treasury of merit. They are in fact their parasite. For there is no need to pray for the dead to be released from purgatory unless there is such a place (or condition) and unless prayers can obtain merit on their behalf.

CATHOLIC DEFENSE OF PRAYERS TO AND FOR THE DEAD

It is a matter of Catholic dogma *(de fide)* that "The living Faithful on earth can come to the assistance of the souls in Purgatory by their intercessions (suffrages)."[40] Ott explains that "suffrages are understood not only as intercessory prayers, but also indulgences, alms and other pious works, above all the Holy Sacrifice of the Mass."[41] The Council of Trent pronounced infallibly that "there is a purgatory, and that the souls there detained are aided by the suffrages [prayers] of the faithful and chiefly by the acceptable sacrifice of the altar."[42] They insisted that the bishops "instruct the faithful diligently in matters relating to intercession and invocation of the saints . . . to invoke them and to have recourse to their prayers, assistance and support *in order to obtain favors from God through His Son, Jesus Christ our Lord.*"[43]

Argument from Scripture. The Scriptures cited in support of this doctrine are scant. Other than the apocryphal text from 2 Maccabees 12:42–46, Ott gives only 2 Timothy 1:18: "May the Lord grant him to find mercy from the Lord on that day." Other Catholic scholars appeal to 1 Timothy 2:1 and even Matthew 17:3 for support. We will examine these texts shortly.

Catholic arguments from Scripture are more speculative and inferential than exegetical. For example, Patrick Madrid speculates: "(1) The Church is Christ's body; (2) Christ has only one Body; not one on earth and one in heaven. (3) Christians are not separated from each other by death. (4) Christians must love and serve each other."[44] Therefore, we must serve even those who have died by continuing to pray for them.

Argument from Tradition. The primary arguments in favor of praying for the dead are taken from tradition. Ott boasts that "tradition abounds in testimony in favor of the doctrine."[45] Strangely, he cites what he admits is the

---

40. Ott, *Fundamentals of Catholic Dogma*, p. 321.
41. Ibid.
42. Schroeder, *Canons and Decrees of the Council of Trent.*
43. Ibid., emphasis added.
44. Patrick Madrid, "Any Friend of God's Is a Friend of Mine," *This Rock* (September 1992): 8.
45. Ott, *Fundamentals of Catholic Dogma*, p. 321.

"apocryphal Acts of Paul and of Thecla" in support of praying for the dead.[46] Tertullian and Cyprian are also cited as early witnesses.

PROTESTANT RESPONSE TO PRAYERS TO AND FOR THE DEAD

Response to Argument from Scripture. Protestants reject both purgatory and prayers for the dead. They find no support for either in Scripture.

2 Maccabees 12:42–46. The dispute is not over whether this passage affirms praying for the dead—it does. It says clearly that "it was a holy and pious thought" to "pray for them in death," for "thus he made atonement for the dead that they might be freed from this sin" (vv. 44–46). The debate is over whether it belongs in the canon of Scripture. Since we have already given our objections to the Roman Catholic canonization of this and ten other apocryphal books (see chap. 9), we will not repeat them here. The dead may be praying for us (cf. Rev. 6:10), but we are not to pray for the dead.

There is no sound biblical, historical, or theological reason for accepting the inspiration of 2 Maccabees. The book does not claim to be inspired and the Jewish community that produced and preserved it never claimed it to be inspired. It also was rejected by many notable Fathers of the early church, including Jerome, the great Roman Catholic biblical scholar and translator of the Latin Vulgate. Finally, it was not infallibly proclaimed part of the canon until A.D. 1546, in an obvious attempt to support the very doctrines that Luther attacked in his reformation. To reveal the arbitrary nature of the decision, at the same time 2 Maccabees was canonized by Rome another apocryphal book, 2 (4) Esdras, which opposes prayers for the dead (see 7:105) was excluded from the canon.

2 Timothy 1:18. The fact that Paul prayed that God would have mercy on Onesiphorus on the day of his reward cannot support praying for the dead for one very fundamental reason—*he was still alive when Paul prayed for him!* Praying that someone alive will receive mercy on the Day of Judgment is a far cry from praying for a person *after* he or she has already died. There is no indication in the Bible that anyone ever prayed for another after the person died. In fact, there are, as we shall see, clear indications to the contrary.

Response to Argument from Inference. Let's consider now the speculative argument proposed by Madrid that since (1) the church is Christ's body and (2) Christ has only one body, and (3) death does not separate us from other members in it, and since (4) we have an obligation to love and serve others, (5) we must continue to ask them for help, even after they die.

From a biblical perspective there are several serious problems with this argument, a few of which will be briefly mentioned here. While a Protestant

46. Ibid.

has no objection to the first or fourth premises, there are serious objections to the others.

First, the second premise, while true, can be easily misconstrued. For example, just because there is only one body does not mean there is no real distinction between the visible and invisible dimensions of it. Likewise, it does not mean that our duties of love to each dimension can be performed in the same way. For example, I cannot (and need not) perform my duty to physically care for my departed father and mother now as I could and should were they living on earth. Nor can I perform my duty to engage in friendly conversation with a departed friend, since he is in the invisible realm, and such conversations are not possible. Likewise, prayer cannot (and should not) occur between the living and the dead.

Second, the third premise is flatly false. According to the Bible, this is precisely what death is, namely, separation from others, including believers. Paul speaks of the dead as being "away" from the visible bodily realm (2 Cor. 5:6). In Philippians 1:23 he says the dead "depart" from this world. Paul comforted the bereaved Christians at Thessalonica, assuring them that they would be "with them" again when Christ returns (1 Thess. 4:17). It is simply false to claim that we are not separated from other believers at death. With that separation comes some real differences, such as no longer being able to speak to them.

Third, the fourth premise of the argument is not true, at least in one of its major implications. For while we must love and serve one another, we should not (and cannot) always do so the same way. Even on earth, when a loved one is not available, I cannot speak with them. According to Scripture, the dead are unavailable to the living until the second coming (Luke 16:26).

Finally, there are several other mistakes made in this argument. Space only permits a brief mention of some of them. (1) The assumption that because God has revealed to the dead *some* things that transpire on earth (e.g., Luke 15:10) they therefore can hear us if we speak to them (or know our mind if we pray silently). (2) The highly debatable assumption that true *prayer* and *asking* another are the same. In fact, there is no real biblical support for this assumption, since prayer is always to God in the Bible and never to any creature, even an angel. While prayer is not identical to worship, it is part of it, and worship should always be directed to God. (3) There is the invalid inference that because the saints in heaven may be praying *for* us (Rev. 6:10) that we should be praying *to* them. There is no logical connection between the two since they would be praying *to* God, not a creature. So, if anything, this would prove just the opposite of what Catholics believe. Namely, that this is what we should do too. (4) Finally, there is a false analogy used, namely, that since Jesus' mother *on earth* interceded to him at the wedding that believers on earth should have Mary intercede to God *in heaven* on their behalf. As the underlined words reveal, there are significant differences be-tween them, to say nothing of the part that in the text even Mary pointed them to Jesus, saying, "Do whatever he tells you" (John 2:5).

Response to Argument from Tradition. Here again tradition is not always a reliable test for truth. First, there are contradictory traditions, even from other apocryphal books and the early Fathers. Second, unlike the Bible, tra-dition is not infallible; the tradition of praying for the dead is a case in point. Third, the fact that there were traditions from the second century proves nothing—there were false traditions even in the first century! The apostle John debunked a false tradition that took Jesus' words in John 21:21–23 to mean that John would never die. There were even many false teachings that the apostles condemned in their day (cf. 1 Tim. 4:1–3; 2 Tim. 2:16–18; 1 John 4:1–3). Early traditions do not necessarily prove that they were apos-tolic truths; they simply have been early errors.

As for the Roman Catholic appeal to 1 Timothy 2:1 in support of praying for the dead, the passage teaches no such thing. Paul urged believers to pray for the living, namely, "for kings and for all in authority" (v. 2). Likewise, to draw from the fact that Moses and Elijah appeared with Christ on the Mount of Transfiguration that we should pray to the dead is a misuse of the passage. For one thing, the disciples never even spoke to them, let alone prayed to them. Moses and Elijah spoke with Jesus (Matt. 17:3), not with the disciples. Indeed, the text says explicitly, "Peter said to Jesus" (v. 4), not to Moses or Elijah. For another, this was a miraculous contact, not representing a normal way we can be in contact with the dead.

Finally, it does not follow that because we should serve each other that we must do it by praying for the dead. There are other ways to serve fellow believers than talking to them. We can do many things in honor of the dead and their memory without attempting to communicate with them.

ARGUMENTS AGAINST PRAYING TO THE SAINTS

There are many reasons the Scriptures forbid praying to Mary and the saints or even venerating their images. Among these several stand out as note-worthy.

God is the only proper object of our prayers. Nowhere in Scripture is a prayer of anyone on earth actually addressed to anyone but God. In fact, *the only prayer in the Bible addressed to a saint was from hell, and God did not answer it* (Luke 16:23–31)! Prayer is an act of religious devotion, and there-fore only God is the proper object of such devotion (Rev. 4:11). There are prayers from Genesis (4:26) to Revelation (22:20), but not one is addressed to a saint, angel, or anyone other than a member of the Trinity. Jesus taught us to pray to "Our Father who art in heaven. . . ." The God of Isaiah the prophet emphatically declared: "Turn to me and be safe, all you ends of the earth, for I am God; there is no other!" (Isa. 45:22). Indeed, there is no other person but God to whom anyone anywhere in the Holy Scriptures ever turned in prayer.

Some Catholics appeal to Psalm 103:20–21 as an exception: "Bless the LORD, all you his angels. . . . Bless the LORD, all you his hosts." This passage is no more an actual prayer to angels and saints than is the poetic appeal in the doxology: "Praise Him above ye heavenly host." Both the poetic nature of the psalms and the context of this passage indicate that the psalmist is merely using a literary device to appeal to all of creation to praise God. The idea that this God-exalting text proves that angels or dead saints should be the object of our prayers is totally foreign to the meaning of this passage.

It is an idolatrous practice. Prayer is a form of worship, and only God should be worshiped (Exod. 20:3). It is idolatrous to pray to mere human beings or to bow down before them or an image of them or any other creature. The first commandment declares: "You shall not have other gods besides me. *You shall not carve idols* for yourselves in the shape of anything in the sky above or on the earth below or in the waters beneath the earth; *you shall not bow down before them or worship them*" (Exod. 20:3–5, emphasis added). Praying to saints, making images of them, or even bowing down to them are violations of this commandment.

Sophisticated distinctions about different kinds of worship (see chap. 13) will not suffice, since most devotees do not observe such distinctions in practice. Furthermore, regardless of any distinctions one makes in theory, the Bible forbids the *practice* of making images and bowing down to them or to any creature. When John bowed down to worship "at the feet of the angel" he was rebuked by the angel who said, "Don't! I am a fellow servant of yours and of your brothers the prophets. . . . Worship God" (Rev. 22:9).

It is forbidden as witchcraft. The Old Testament condemns all attempts to communicate with the dead along with other condemnations of witchcraft (Deut. 18:10–12; cf. Lev. 20:6, 27; 1 Sam. 28:5–18; Isa. 8:19–20). Those who violated this command were to be put to death. In all of Scripture there is not a single divinely approved instance of a righteous person praying to a departed believer—not one. Indeed, Saul was condemned for his attempt to contact the dead Samuel (1 Sam. 28; cf. 15:23). Given the danger of deception and the lack of faith that the practice of necromancy and idolatry evidence, it is not difficult to understand God's command.

The Catholic response to the charge of necromancy rings hollow. First, it attempts to narrow the focus of the condemnation against contacting the dead (cf. Deut. 18:11) to the practice of divination (Lev. 19:26). But God forbids communication with the dead regardless of whether it is associated with occult practices. Deuteronomy separates "divination" from one "who consults the dead" and condemns both! Second, the contention that asking a deceased believer to intercede on our behalf is no different from asking a friend here on earth to pray for us is an unsubstantiated claim. There are substantial differences. For one thing, one is in heaven and the other is on earth. Also, there is a huge difference between asking an earthly friend to pray for us and praying to a dead friend! Finally, friends on earth *are in the body* and have senses by which they can get our message, friends in heaven do not: they do not have a physical body (2 Cor. 5:8; Phil. 1:23; Rev. 6:9).

It is a practical denial of the mediatorship of Christ. Evangelicals believe that to use any mere human being to mediate with God is an insult to the all-sufficient, divinely appointed mediatorship of Jesus Christ. Paul declared emphatically, "There is also one mediator between God and the human race, Christ Jesus, himself human" (1 Tim. 2:5; cf. John 10:9; 14:6). Hebrews 4:15–16 assures us that in Jesus "we do not have a high priest who is unable to sympathize with our weaknesses, but one who has similarly been tested in every way, yet without sin." Because of this we are urged to "confidently approach the throne of grace to receive mercy and to find grace for timely help." There is no reason to go to Mary or any other saint with our requests. Indeed, it is the ultimate insult to Christ's human suffering, mediatorship, and high priestly ministry to go to anyone else for grace or help.[47]

Catholic apologists attempt to avoid the sting of this argument by distinguishing between Christ as the *sole mediator* and all believers as *intercessors*. This distinction does not, however, help their cause (of proving we should pray to saints) because all the passages they use are about direct intercession to God, not to other creatures. In Ephesians 2:18, which they cite, it says explicitly that our access in prayer is "to the Father" not to the saints. Nowhere does Scripture state or imply that we should pray to the saints, and the Roman Catholic dogma which affirms infallibly that we should is a good example of putting tradition over Scripture, thus proving how fallible the alleged "infallible" teaching magisterium really is.

It is an insult to the intercession of the Holy Spirit. Much of the practical Catholic justification for praying to the saints is based on the seemingly plausible argument that, because of their position in heaven, dead believers may be better able to intercede on our behalf. This is a practical denial of the ministry of the Holy Spirit, whose task it is to do this very thing on our behalf. And who is better able to intercede for us than another Person of the blessed Trinity? The Bible says, "we do not know how to pray as we ought, but the Spirit itself intercedes with inexpressible groanings" (Rom. 8:26). Paul adds that through Christ we "have access in one Spirit to the Father" (Eph. 2:18).

---

47. This does not mean that we ought not ask other believers on earth to pray to Jesus for us. Indeed, we should. But there are important differences here. First, we are simply asking other believers on earth to pray for us; we are not communicating with the dead which the Bible forbids. Second, we are not asking these believers to give us grace or mercy, as Catholics ask of Mary, but to ask God for grace. Finally, we are not *praying* to them but merely *asking* them to pray for us.

Since beyond our own prayers to God the Holy Spirit intercedes for us perfectly "according to God's will" (Rom. 8:27) there is no need to call on anyone else in heaven to do so. It is wrong to expect that any human being could be more efficacious with God the Father than God the Son and God the Holy Spirit (1 John 2:1–2). To think so is to insult his divinely appointed role.

PROTESTANT ARGUMENTS AGAINST PRAYING FOR THE DEAD

Not only is it unbiblical to pray *to* the dead, but we believe that it is also wrong to pray *for* the dead. There are several Protestant objections to praying for the dead. The most important ones are the following:

Praying for the dead contradicts the separation of death. The Bible speaks of death as separating the living from the departed. Paul speaks of death as "departure" from earth and being with Christ (Phil. 1:23; cf. 2 Tim. 4:6). It is when we "leave the body" (2 Cor. 5:7). Luke 16:26 speaks of a "great chasm" between the living and the dead. Paul speaks of death separating loved ones until they are reunited at the resurrection (1 Thess. 4:13–18). In all of Scripture death is a veil that seals off the living from the dead. Any attempted contacts with the dead are not only futile but forbidden (Deut. 18:11) because of the possibility of demonic deception (cf. 1 Tim. 4:1).

Praying for the dead contradicts the example of David. When David's baby was alive but seriously ill he prayed for it fervently. However, when the baby died he ceased praying for it immediately.[48] When asked why, he replied, "While the child was living, I fasted and wept, thinking, 'Perhaps the LORD will grant me the child's life.' But now he is dead. Why should I fast? Can I bring him back again? I shall go to be with him, but he will not return to me" (2 Sam. 12:22–23). It is clear that David, who as a prophet of God claimed that "the spirit of the LORD spoke through me" (2 Sam. 23:2), believed that prayers for the dead were ineffective. For if he believed that any prayer for the dead was effective, he certainly would have attempted it in his most desperate hour. In fact, in all of his many spiritual writings in the Psalms about how to communicate with God David never once even suggested that we pray for the dead.

---

48. Catholics respond that David only stopped because God turned down his request to keep the child alive, not because he believed praying for the dead was wrong. This is unconvincing for several reasons. First, David's love for the child did not cease when the child died; the natural momentum from this love would surely have led him to continue to pray for the child if he thought it was right to do so. Second, there is no record of David or any other Old Testament believer ever praying for the dead on any other occasion. Third, David states his reason for stopping, namely, he knew he would be reunited with the child at the resurrection (2 Sam. 12:23; cf. Ps. 16:10). This hope of resurrection (cf. Job 19:25–26; Isa. 26:19; Dan. 12:2) made it unnecessary to pray for the dead.

Praying for the dead contradicts the example of Jesus. When Jesus lost his close friend Lazarus by death he never prayed to God for him.[49] He simply resurrected him with the command "Lazarus, come forth!" Rather than pray for the dead, *Jesus prayed for the living.* At Lazarus's graveside Jesus prayed, "Father, I thank you for hearing me. I know that you always hear me; but because of the crowd here I have said this, that they may believe that you sent me" (John 11:41–42). Ironically, many reverse this by weeping for the living who stray and praying for the dead, while Jesus wept for the dead (John 11:35) and prayed for the living (11:41–42). The practice of praying for the dead is not the only time that humanly initiated religious practice has made void the teaching of Sacred Scripture (cf. Matt. 15:6).

Praying for the dead contradicts the sacrifice of Christ. As we have already noted, the whole idea that our prayers or works can do anything on behalf of the dead is contrary to the all-sufficiency of the completed work of Christ on the Cross. His mediation and intercession for them (1 John 2:1–2) are more than sufficient. When Jesus died and rose again the work of salvation was "finished" (John 19:30; cf. 17:4; Heb. 10:14). When he purged our sins he "took his seat" at the right hand of God (Heb. 1:3) since there was absolutely nothing more to do for our salvation. The whole concept of praying for the dead "that they might be freed from sin" is an insult to the finished work of Christ, "who freed us from our sins by his blood" (Rev. 1:5). Jesus not only obtained salvation from all our sins at one time but, as our great high priest (Heb. 7), he alone implements it for all time (see chaps. 12 and 13).

SUMMARY AND CONCLUSION

In view of the unbiblical nature of purgatory it is understandable that some contemporary Roman Catholics are de-emphasizing some aspects of traditional thinking on this doctrine. For example, one Catholic scholar insists that, "In spite of some popular notions to the contrary, the Church has never passed judgment as to whether purgatory is a place or in a determined space where the souls are cleansed."[50] And as to its importance, Catholics are con-

---

49. Some have suggested that Jesus was praying for the dead here since he acknowledged that God always hears him just before he resurrected Lazarus. However, even if true, this would not support the Roman Catholic doctrine of prayers for the dead. Jesus did not pray that Lazarus be released from his sins, as Catholics believe we should from the apocryphal book of 2 Maccabees 12:45 (46). Further, at best this is simply a prayer for God's power to raise the dead, not to deliver him from purgatory. Finally, the whole thrust of Jesus' prayer is directed toward the living, not the dead. He said his prayer was "because of the crowd . . . that they may believe" (John 11:41–42).

50. Hardon, *Catholic Catechism,* p. 274.

fessing that "In the hierarchy of revealed doctrines, purgatory does not rank as high as the Trinity or the Incarnation."[51] A popular Catholic lay-evangelist writes that some Catholics fall into the "legalism of Purgatory," thinking of it as a second chance. However, "Sacred Scripture indicates that there's really only one punishment for sin—and that's death." The Bible teaches "that we're off the hook. Jesus paid that awful price on the cross—our punishment was laid upon him. Purgatory is not a 'place' but a 'process.'"[52] These speculations, however welcomed by Protestants as a move in the right direction, are quite different from traditional Catholic teaching and practice. It is of interest to note that Eastern Orthodox theologians for the most part do not incorporate purgatory into their dogmatics (see Appendix A).

The doctrine of purgatory and its accompanying dogmas are a crucial area of difference between Catholics and Protestants. We have examined the biblical basis for these beliefs and found them seriously wanting. They are not only extra-biblical but anti-biblical, since they run contrary to fundamental teachings of Scripture, such as the all-sufficiency of the atoning sacrifice of Christ and the uniqueness of God as the sole object of all our devotion and prayer. The only real bases for pronouncing them dogma are conflicting traditions and human speculations often based on apocryphal books that have been rejected from the canon of Scripture by both Catholic and Protestant scholars (see chap. 9). These matters were at the heart of the Reformation and continue to be seemingly insurmountable theological obstacle between orthodox Catholics and orthodox Protestants today.

Perhaps we could conclude by the observations of an articulate contemporary Catholic about this practice of venerating and praying to the saints. "I visited a prominent Catholic cathedral dedicated to St. Joseph . . . and it sure seemed that one going through the cathedral could easily get the impression that St. Joseph was a Savior . . . in a way that all but obscured the unique role of Jesus as Savior and Lord."[53]

---

51. Ibid., p. 278.

52. Albert H. Boudreau, *The Born-Again Catholic* (Locust Valley: Living Flame Press, 1983), p. 139. Another well-known charismatic lay-leader mentions changes in Catholic practices that should gladden evangelical hearts: "The reform of various rites, the restoration of the catechumenate for adult baptism, the beginning restoration of baptism by immersion are all hopeful signs." And in some areas of Latin America, "infant baptism is being withheld if there is no assurance that the child will grow up in a community of faith and genuine Christian life" (Ralph Martin, *Hungry for God* [Garden City, N.Y.: Doubleday, 1974], pp. 69–70). Martin also bemoans the effect that "cultural Catholicism" has had on faith (p. 137).

53. Martin, *Hungry for God*, p. 136.

PART 3

AREAS OF
PRACTICAL
COOPERATION

Ever since I became a Christian I have thought that the best, perhaps the only, service I could do for my unbelieving neighbors was to explain and defend the belief that has been common to nearly all Christians at all times.
—C. S. *Lewis,* Mere Christianity

Since evangelicals and Roman Catholics have so much in common doctrinally and morally (see Part One), and, in spite of our significant intramural doctrinal differences (see Part Two), we believe that there are, nonetheless, many areas of common spiritual heritage and practical social and moral cooperation possible. This includes fighting our common enemies of secularism and occultism that have infiltrated our culture and public schools. In addition to this there are root moral issues that have emerged in the political arena, such as abortion, pornography, immorality, and special rights for homosexuals, that call for our common cooperation.

In this final section we wish to end on a positive note, firmly believing that a cooperative effort between Roman Catholics and evangelicals could be the greatest social force for good in America. For those who are opposed to any ecclesiastical union between Catholicism and evangelicalism, including the authors, we nevertheless plead for more personal interaction and social cooperation. Our common doctrinal and moral beliefs are too large and the need in America for a united voice on them is too great for us to dwell on our differences to the neglect of crucial cooperation needed to fight the forces of evil in our society and our world.

As one evangelical observer noted, "The real cleavage in Christendom today is . . . between biblical orthodox and heterodox world views. Even the most reactionary of Protestant fundamentalists has more in common with Cardinal John O'Connor and John Paul II than with Joan Campbell and John Spong."[1] As to the central issue, "Both Roman Catholic and Protestant churches need to take up again a serious reevaluation of the great questions of the relation between Christ as Savior and as Lord; is it forgiveness or is it change people need? Or both?"[2]

---

1. J. Daryl Charles, "Evangelical-Catholic Dialogue: Basis, Boundaries, Benefits," *Pro Ecclesia* 3, no. 3 (Summer 1994): 294.
2. D. Clair Davis, "How Did the Church in Rome become Roman Catholicism?" in Armstrong, *Roman Catholicism: Evangelical Protestants*, p. 62.

17

SOCIAL ACTION

The last forty years of discourse with our Roman Catholic friends has centered mainly on biblical and theological issues. We have examined doctrinal issues from scriptural and historical perspectives and occasionally refought the Reformation. However, during the last few decades tremendous social change and a cultural disintegration has occurred in American society. Neither informed Roman Catholics nor evangelicals are of the opinion that this country was founded to be a "Christian" nation in the theocratic sense. Nonetheless, it is true that the United States has been informed morally by what has been called the basic "Judeo-Christian ethic," and because these ethical guidelines were universal (reflected in the "natural law," if you will), they were accepted by those of other faiths as well.[1]

The cultural climate has regrettably changed in a secularistic direction. One Roman Catholic observer of the current scene identifies movement toward "religious cleansing" as an attempt to challenge the Judeo-Christian foundation of our nation. "Religious cleansing is a term I use to describe the current hostility and bigotry toward religion and people of faith that are leading to covert and overt attempts to remove any religious influence from the public arena."[2] Those who champion religious cleansing "are usually secularists bent on removing any vestige of religious influence from all places but the private sphere."[3] Some Roman Catholics and evangelicals feel it's

---

1. A recently published work, *Catechism of the Catholic Church: Libreria Editrice Vaticana* (Boston: St. Paul Books and Media, 1994), addresses the Roman Catholic response to many of the issues covered in this chapter. Consult the index for topics such as abortion, euthanasia, and homosexuality.

2. Keith A. Fournier, *Religious Cleansing in the American Republic* (Washington, D.C.: Liberty, Life and Family Publications, 1993), pp. 4–5.

3. Ibid., p. 6.

time to "circle the wagons" and face this moral relativism together whenever possible.

One issue that seems to be a major catalyst bringing our two groups together is the social and moral tragedy of abortion. The status of the unborn began to be seriously debated by large segments of society at the time of the 1973 abortion decision known as Roe v. Wade. The coming together of Catholics—laity, priests, nuns, and the occasional bishop—on one side and evangelicals/fundamentalists on the other caused a great deal of soul-searching and reevaluation by both groups. Praying together in Jesus' name helps one identify core issues.

Perhaps evangelicals felt a bit guilty when they realized they were "Johnnie-come-latelies," given the fact that Roman Catholics had been alert to the moral dimensions of the problem while their evangelical neighbors were spiritually asleep. In this chapter, we will discuss abortion and other issues that have brought Roman Catholics and evangelicals together to "stake out" common moral ground.[4]

CULTURAL DISINTEGRATION

The attack on religious values in Western culture began at least as far back as the Enlightenment. Employing tools acquired from the Renaissance, various people and movements mounted an assault against Christianity on a number of different fronts. James Turner, professor of history at the University of Michigan, has written an important book concerning this assault in America.[5] Turner develops the interesting thesis that, contrary to conventional thinking, religious belief has not collapsed under an attack from atheistic sources. "On the contrary, religion caused unbelief. In trying to adapt their religious beliefs to socioeconomic change, to new moral challenges, to novel problems of knowledge, to the tightening standards of science, the defenders of God slowly strangled Him."[6] In attempting to refashion Christianity to fit "modern" ideas, we have emasculated the gospel; "we have met the enemy and he is us."

A perceptive observer of these issues is James Hitchcock, professor of history at St. Louis University. Recognized as a leading spokesman among traditional Roman Catholics, Hitchcock has written a number of significant

4. For an insightful treatment of the subject of this chapter, see Ronald Nash, "Evangelical and Catholic Cooperation in the Public Arena," in Armstrong, *Roman Catholicism: Evangelical Protestants,* pp. 180–97. Nash is a valuable observer in that he teaches philosophy and theology at a Reformed seminary and his evangelical credentials are impeccable.

5. *Without God, Without Creed: The Origins of Unbelief in America* (Baltimore: Johns Hopkins University Press, 1985).

6. Ibid., preface, p. xiii.

books on related topics.[7] Hitchcock has lectured widely before Roman Catholic and Protestant groups and is a member of the Allies for Faith and Renewal Movement.[8] He has a special affinity for evangelicals, and sees them as allies united with believing Roman Catholics to battle unbelief in the culture. The real ecumenical task "is to begin explorations with the Protestant groups broadly called evangelical. The greatest difficulties are found here, because these groups take their own beliefs very seriously. . . . However, the greatest rewards are also to be found here because by the end of the twentieth century the liberal denominations will probably have ceased to be Christian . . . and the future of Christianity will depend on Catholics, Orthodox and evangelical Protestants."[9]

Another important figure on this scene is William Bentley Ball, a practicing Roman Catholic and distinguished "religious freedom" attorney. Ball has been lead counsel in first and fourteenth Amendment litigations before the Supreme Court and in twenty-two states. (We will say more about Ball under "Legal Issues" below.)

William Bentley Ball, like fellow Roman Catholic James Hitchcock, finds common cause with evangelicals. Ball says, "*certain* Catholics and *certain* evangelicals should be hanging together. Excluded, for example, would be those Catholics whose sentiments clustered . . . (around persons like) Fr. Richard McBrien of Notre Dame . . . whose ideological compass needle invariably point to political causes of the Left." Also excluded are "the Edward Kennedys, the Mario Cuomos, various gay-rights folks, socialists, and do-your-own thing doctrinaires."[10] In other words, if you are a "milk and water" Catholic, stay off Ball's bus.

Ball notes that cooperation between Roman Catholics and evangelicals has already begun. Catholics worked with Pat Robertson in 1988. Jerry Falwell reported that one-third of his Moral Majority membership was Catholic. Ball would like to see "Catholics and evangelicals sit down with one another to address pressing problems in the political order. For that they will both need, in the name of public duty, to suppress old suspicions and antagonisms and endeavor to see in one another brothers and sisters in Christ."[11]

Ralph Martin (discussed at length in chap. 20) is another Roman Catholic who recognizes the degree that unbelief has impacted our culture as well as Roman Catholicism and mainline Protestantism. Liberation theology has

---

7. Among them: *Catholicism and Modernity* (New York: Seabury Press, 1979); *Years of Crisis: Collected Essays, 1970–1983* (San Francisco: Ignatius Press, 1985); and *What Is Secular Humanism?* (Ann Arbor: Servant, 1982).

8. See chap. 20.

9. Hitchcock, *Catholicism and Modernity*, p. 231.

10. "Why Can't We Work Together?" *Christianity Today,* 16 June 1990, p. 22.

11. "We'd Better Hang Together," *Crisis,* October 1989, p. 21.

its tentacles in both jurisdictions.[12] Radical feminism has also worked its baleful effect in Roman Catholicism and Protestantism.[13]

Many other persons could be mentioned concerning this subject. Some are noted later in this chapter. Our cultural and societal frameworks are in spiritual and moral disarray. Both Roman Catholics and evangelicals have a vested interest in the outcome of this battle. Our yard is a mess; let's clean it up together.

RELIGION AND POLITICS

One author remembers with fondness the stimulating discussions with Fr. Coughlin of Birmingham, Michigan. We often dealt with the forbidden subjects of religion and politics. To the chagrin of secularists they have been linked closely throughout American history. In dealing with different issues such as slavery and the war in Vietnam, a well-known Catholic statesman observes that "Americans have vigorously debated how religious convictions relate to the working of government."[14]

However, a change has occurred in our culture. The moral relativists claim that "democracy itself rests on the conviction that there are no ultimate convictions . . . none about which we can know and on which we can form a public consensus to guide public policy."[15]

The idea that human government should be ordered by the norms of a transcendent moral order ("natural law") is unacceptable to "progressives." Hence, a popular governor (a "practicing" Roman Catholic) can proclaim that, while he is "personally opposed to abortion," he cannot let his religious views influence his "public deportment." Happily there are some persons in public life (Roman Catholic as well as evangelical) who resist this "value-neutral" political posture. We will mention some Roman Catholic examples below and cite other examples as we deal with topics later in this chapter.

12. For the effect that liberation theology has had in the Roman Catholic Church, see Ralph Martin, *A Crisis of Truth* (Ann Arbor: Servant, 1982), pp. 87–97.

13. For a good treatment of the debate over inclusive God-language (which springs from radical feminism), see Donald G. Bloesch, *The Battle for the Trinity* (Ann Arbor: Servant, 1985). For an evangelical treatment of feminism, see Mary A. Kassian, *The Feminist Gospel* (Wheaton: Crossway, 1992). For an investigation of Roman Catholic feminism, see Donna Steichen, *Ungodly Rage: The Hidden Face of Catholic Feminism* (San Francisco: Ignatius Press, 1992).

14. Henry J. Hyde, "Religion and Politics," in William Bentley Ball, ed., *In Search of a National Morality: A Manifesto for Evangelicals and Catholics* (Grand Rapids: Baker, 1992), p. 91.

15. Ibid., p. 92.

CONGRESSMAN HENRY J. HYDE

Henry J. Hyde has represented the Sixth District of Illinois since 1974. A devout Roman Catholic, Hyde has been an eloquent defender of traditional values in general and the rights of the unborn in particular. Henry Hyde is the author of the "Hyde Amendment" (presently under siege), which has prevented the use of federal funds to pay for abortions since 1976. He is an accomplished writer and contributed to the volume just cited, which is a "Manifesto for Evangelicals and Catholics."

GOVERNOR ROBERT CASEY

Robert Casey (Democrat) is governor of Pennsylvania. Casey, a practicing Roman Catholic, is staunchly pro-life, a position which causes him no end of difficulty in the currently structured Democratic Party. Casey was the main author of a bill (Pennsylvania's Abortion Control Act) which—concerning abortion—has some restrictions. Namely, women seeking abortions must be offered information on fetal development and alternatives to abortion, followed by a 24-hour waiting period. Also, parental or judicial consent is mandatory for minors. This act has been upheld by the U.S. Supreme Court [June 29, 1992].

Governor Casey, who is a textbook liberal on issues that do not involve social/moral questions, is about as popular in the Democratic Party as ants at a picnic. Fearing his pro-life rhetoric, the organizers of the 1992 Democratic Convention refused Casey speaking time. He cancelled a planned appearance at a local Democratic Party dinner after learning that Hillary Clinton was scheduled to be at the same event.[16] Governor Casey is a courageous man in resisting moral and spiritual relativism.

REPRESENTATIVE JIM LIGHTFOOT

Jim Lightfoot (Republican from Iowa) is another Roman Catholic who is upfront in his pro-life commitment. He defended his position on the Phil Donahue show opposite abortion advocate Representative Barbara Boxer (Democrat from California). Among the points he made were: "No one has ever listened to the people who are the product of this whole process. . . . I happen to be one of those kids. I was adopted as a baby."[17]

After speaking without notes, Lightfoot answered questions from a skep-

---

16. "Gov. Casey Refuses to Appear with Hillary Clinton," *The Wanderer,* 5 November 1992. Concerning pro-life members of the Democratic Party, see Fred Barnes, "No Womb for Debate," *The New Republic,* 27 July 1992, pp. 36–38.

17. Martin Johnson, "In 'Rape and Incest' Debate, Unborn Find New Hero," *World,* 4 November 1989.

tical audience. Among the points raised was the situation of a severely hand-icapped baby and the resulting financial and emotional stress on the family. Lightfoot responded: "I have a daughter that was born with spina bifida and the way people are thinking today, had that been identified during the preg-nancy, she would have been terminated. She's a 20-year-old kid who's got the usual problems that all 20-year-old kids have."

One woman posed a hypothetical question: "I'd like to know if your 12-year-old daughter was raped and she told you three weeks later and then you found out she was pregnant, would you make her have that baby?" Lightfoot answered, "It's very important with children to teach them values and taking an innocent life is not the value I want to teach my kids."[18] Phil Donahue—who evidently never met a perversion or an aberration he could not sympa-thize with—claimed, nevertheless, to be impressed with Representative Jim Lightfoot.

ORGANIZATIONS

There are a number of organizations and publications made up of Roman Catholics and evangelicals (and a few Orthodox Jews and Eastern Orthodox Christians). They address a myriad of issues—from America's role in the world to physician-assisted suicide here at home. Important scholars from both Roman Catholic and evangelical camps team up to address issues which threaten basic Christian values. We can mention but a few.

The Ethics and Public Policy Center. This organization publishes a news-letter and books. Also conferences and seminars are held addressing a num-ber of different issues. Michael Cromartie, George Weigel, Nicholas Wolter-storff, Terry Eastland, Fr. Richard John Neuhaus, and Carl F. H. Henry are among those who have participated with this group.

The Institute on Religion and Public Life. This group publishes a monthly journal, *First Things,* of which Richard John Neuhaus, a Lutheran turned Catholic, is editor-in-chief. Articles by the aforementioned Henry Hyde and James Hitchcock have appeared on the pages of this journal. There are also a number of Christian journalists (e.g., evangelical Cal Thomas and Catholic Pat Buchanan) who write columns and address issues from the clas-sic Christian perspective.

ISSUES OF LIFE AND DEATH

Orthodox Christians, evangelical and Roman Catholic, are united in their opposition to abortion and euthanasia. From the theological perspective the

18. Ibid.

basic reason is the *imago Dei*: "Of all his material creatures, man and man alone is made in the image and likeness of God."[19] Put in terms of common moral ground (i.e., natural law), the reason is that unborn babies are *human*, and it is morally wrong to intentionally take the life of an innocent human being, which an unborn child is.[20]

EUTHANASIA

The word *euthanasia* means "good" or "easy" death. While not as prominent as its unholy sister, abortion, it is an act condemned by the believing Christian community. The Catholic Catechism states: "Why does Catholic Christianity condemn euthanasia? Because, no matter what sentimentalists or social engineers may say, it is a grave crime against justice, both human and divine." Therefore, "the sin committed is either murder or suicide."[21]

Most of the arguments advanced against abortion also are relevant in examining the question of euthanasia. The people we will discuss who oppose abortion also regard euthanasia as unacceptable. All agree that an individual human life begins at conception, and that it is morally wrong to intentionally take such a life.

ABORTION

The Roman Catholic Church has been very clear in addressing the issue of abortion: "The tradition of the Church has always held that human life must be protected and cherished from the beginning, just as at the various stages of its development." And further, "In the course of history, the Fathers of the Church, her Pastors and her Doctors have taught the same doctrine—the various opinions on the infusion of the spiritual soul did not cast doubt on the illicitness of abortion."[22]

Traditional Roman Catholics have discovered to their dismay that the "pro-choice" movement has made inroads in the Catholic church. On May 21, 1990, Rembert Weakland, archbishop of Milwaukee ("Successor to the Apostles"), made headlines with the assertion—"Pro-Choice May Be O.K."

19. William E. May, "The Sanctity of Human Life," in Ball, *In Search of a National Morality*, p. 104.

20. Good material covering the subject of life and death issues can be found in James T. Burtchaell, C.S.C., *Rachel Weeping* (San Francisco: Harper and Row, 1982); Frank Beckwith and Norman L. Geisler, *Matters of Life and Death* (Grand Rapids: Baker, 1991), pp. 24–30, 84–92.

21. Hardon, *Catholic Catechism*, p. 330.

22. Austin Flannery, O.P., *Vatican Collection: Vatican Council II*, vol. 2, rev. (North Port: Costello Publishing Co., 1992), p. 443. Of course, modern science made the exact point of the beginning of human life more evident. But Catholics have always held that human life is sacred from its very inception in the womb.

His statement was hailed by Francis Kissling of *Catholics for Free Choice* as a "real breakthrough." This sentiment is not shared by the following people.

Dr. Jerôme Lejeune. Dr. Lejeune is a world-famous geneticist, and his credentials establish him as one of the world's foremost authorities in his field. He is Professor of Fundamental Genetics in the renowned Children's Hospital and Faculty of Medicine of Paris. He first won international fame in 1959 when he discovered the first human chromosomal abnormality—the cause of Down's Syndrome. This discovery earned him the William Allen Memorial medal, the highest prize in genetics.

Dr. Lejeune was called to testify in a case involving abortion at the Municipal Court at Morris County, New Jersey, in 1991. He stated that he sees in his practice some 2,000 children a year and keeps records on some 30,000 of them. Concerning his task Lejeune said, "Our job is really to try to understand what makes the nature of every human being; why some of them are afflicted by constitutional difficulty, and to try later to treat that, if we can; so that we would be able to someday bring them back to normal." As to the process of human reproduction, "science knows, beyond any doubt, that a new individual is formed at the moment of fertilization." Therefore, "What exists at the moment of fertilization . . . is a human, because the information on the chromosomes and in the cells is human."[23]

Dr. Lejeune described an eight-week-old fetus as being the size of his thumb. If he held "Tom Thumb" in his fist, "You would not see I had anything inside. But if I was opening my hand you would see a tiny human being with fingers, with toes, with a face and with the palm prints you could read with a microscope." Finally, in answer to the question of what happens when an abortion is performed involving an eight-week-old fetus, Lejeune replied, "It kills a member of our species."[24]

Mother Teresa. On June 6, 1988, the 200th General Assembly of the Presbyterian Church (USA) was preparing to convene. A group of evangelicals called "Presbyterians Pro-Life" hosted a presentation for over 2,000 commissioners, General Assembly officials, and members of the press. The featured speaker was Mother Teresa of Calcutta, whom Baptist layman Chuck Colson calls "the greatest living example of holiness."

As she addressed the gathering, "The softness of her voice forced a hush upon her audience as she wove the words of scripture through her plea for the life of the unborn." Mother Teresa spoke of the pregnancy of Mary and her visit to the home of her cousin, Elizabeth. Concerning the "leaping with joy" on the part of the then unborn John the Baptist, she noted that it is "Very strange that God used an unborn child to proclaim the coming of

23. Elena Muller Garcia, "Tom Thumb Is a Person," *San Diego Catholic News Notes,* July 1992 (reprinted from the *Human Life Review,* Spring 1992).
24. Ibid.

Christ. And we know today that terrible things are happening to that little unborn child; how the mother kills, destroys, murders her own child created by God Himself for greater things. . . . The mother kills two: the child and her conscience." Mother Teresa added, "When we look at the cross, we understand how much God loves us. We too must learn from Him how to love one another, so that we are ready to give our all to save life, especially the little unborn child."[25] Imagine a tiny Roman Catholic nun teaching "Ethics 101" to a group of sophisticated mainline Presbyterians![26]

Helen Alvare. Helen Alvare is pro-life but doesn't fit the media's image. She is thirty-one years old, Hispanic, Ivy League educated, a lawyer, and identifies herself as a feminist. She is the Director of Planning and Information for Pro-Life Activities for the National Conference of Catholic Bishops (NCCB). In describing her stance, she explains: "Feminism seemed natural. I do not mean the kind (of feminism) that thinks men and women must be androgynous, or in the same role in every situation. . . . I think society should accommodate the differences men and women have, as well as provide equal opportunity."

Alvare is a member of Feminists For Life (FFL) and her position is summarized by the bumper sticker on her small truck: "Real Feminists Don't Kill Babies." Her job requires her to speak regularly with members of the media. She was scheduled to appear on ABC's "Abortion: A Civil War" but was replaced at the last moment by Fr. Richard McBrien of Notre Dame. Concerning the last minute change: "Perhaps the media—80 percent of whom identify themselves as 'strongly in support of legal abortion'—hesitate to broadcast such an articulate, attractive spokeswoman, who argues so convincingly on abortion and related issues."[27]

HOMOSEXUALITY

Roman Catholics, united with evangelicals, oppose homosexuality as an acceptable Christian lifestyle. It is more accurate to say that orthodox Chris-

---

25. *The Presbyterian Layman* 21, no. 4, July/August 1988.

26. A contemporary ecumenical journal quotes a lovely story told by Mother Teresa about an act of mercy that led to the opportunity for evangelism: "Communion with Christ gives us our strength, our joy and our love. . . . The sisters care for forty-nine thousand lepers. They are among the most unwanted, unloved . . . people. . . . One of our sisters was washing a leper covered with sores. A Muslim holy man was present, standing close to her. He said, 'All the years I have believed that Jesus Christ is a prophet. Today I believe that Jesus Christ is God since he has been able to give such joy to this sister.'" *One Heart of Love* (Ann Arbor: Servant, 1984), p. 89; quoted in J. Daryl Charles, "Evangelical-Catholic Dialogue: Basis, Boundaries, Benefits," *Pro Ecclesia* 3, no. 3 (Summer 1994): 294 n. 21.

27. Susan Moran, "The Bishop's Voice," *Crisis,* July/August 1992.

tians reject homosexual *behavior,* to be distinguished from homosexual *orientation;* the latter condition is not necessarily sin in itself.[28]

Unfortunately, the Roman Catholic Church, like the Protestant mainline denominations, finds people receptive to homosexual behavior within its ranks. In a recent article in *Time* magazine, when asked just how common homosexuality among the Catholic clergy is, "a September *Washington Post* article cited the figures of a Baltimore therapist, A. W. Richard Sipe, who, after 25 years of interviewing 1,000 priests, concluded that 20% of the nation's Catholic clergy are gay, half of those sexually active." Another study concludes that "In a new anthology *Homosexuality in the Priesthood and in Religious Life,* Salvatorian priest Robert Nugent, who has worked among gay Catholics for twelve years, says estimates on the number of homosexual clergy range from 'the most conservative 10% to a more reasonable 20%' or higher." This article also makes the point that "Catholic teaching holds that all homosexual acts are sinful, though a homosexual orientation is not. There are U.S. Catholic bishops willing to ordain priests with homosexual proclivities as long as they promise to remain celibate and support church teaching on the topic."[29]

Some ecclesiastically placed officials in the Roman Catholic Church have resisted the traditional position and opted for a more "broad-minded" stance, more in keeping with this "enlightened" age. A major newspaper ran an article on the Vatican and gays: "Three Roman Catholic bishops have joined more than 1,500 Catholics in signing a statement rejecting a Vatican document that supports legal discrimination against gays and lesbians in some cases."[30] The above signers were Bishop Walter Sullivan of Richmond, Virginia; Bishop Thomas Gumbleton, Auxiliary Bishop of Detroit, Michigan; and retired Bishop Charles A. Buswell of Pueblo, Colorado. This information was released through New Ways Ministry, which describes itself as an "educational and bridge-building ministry of reconciliation between the Catholic gay and lesbian community and the Catholic Church."[31]

THE CARDINAL AND THE PRESBYTERIANS

On June 5, 1991, John Cardinal O'Connor, the 11th Bishop, the 8th Archbishop, and the 6th Cardinal of the See of New York, addressed the commissioners of the 203rd General Assembly of the Presbyterian Church (USA).

---

28. Leo IX (A.D. 1054), Alexander VII (1665–66), Innocent XI (1679), Pius XI (1929–30), Pius XII (1955), and John XXIII (1961) all issued documents concerning the problem of homosexual orientation.

29. Richard N. Ostling, "The Battle over Gay Clergy," *Time,* 13 November 1989.

30. "Three Bishops Oppose Vatican on Gays," in the *San Diego Union and Tribune,* 31 November 1992.

31. Ibid.

Sponsored by the same group (Presbyterians Pro-Life) that brought Mother Teresa to address the issue of abortion three years earlier, Cardinal O'Connor spoke to the issues of AIDS and the homosexual lifestyle. An editorial comment concerning the cardinal noted that "Because the Cardinal has stood firm where the integrity of the Church's teaching is concerned, his counsel is widely sought by leaders throughout the United States, including those who disagree with him on isolated issues."[32]

The Executive Director of Presbyterians Pro-Life, Terry Schlossberg, spoke highly of O'Connor: "John Cardinal O'Connor is at the very center of the controversy over sexual matters which is sweeping the church." She continued, "We in PPL see the obvious benefit this man can be to General Assembly Commissioners who are looking for the historical and biblical context in which to evaluate the report from the Human Sexuality Task Force."[33]

AIDS AND HOMOSEXUALITY MINISTRIES

Courage. As a result of the cultural furor over homosexuality and the emergence of the AIDS crisis, a number of support groups and ministries have come into being. One such group is *Courage.* Its founder, John F. Harvey, O.S.F.S., says:

> Let me state that I emphatically agree with the Church's teaching on sexual matters. That is why I founded *Courage,* a support group for persons tempted to homosexual behavior who seek to live chaste lives. And I realize that soft-pedaling traditional morality often only encourages persons with sexual disorders to deny their problem. Still, as Christians, we are called to love all people. With love comes responsibility, especially for those in need, as we all are, of the healing of Christ.

Fr. Harvey has been active in developing programs to deal with priests who are pedophilic, a problem which is presently of grave concern in the Roman Catholic Church in the United States. The shortage of priests is another motivator to try to restore those caught up in this serious situation.[34]

Dignity vs. Courage. Jim Johnson was a practicing homosexual who came into contact with *Courage* when he met Fr. Harvey at a conference in 1985. He opened Providence House in Long Beach, California, in 1987 as an interfaith ministry that provided hospice care for AIDS patients.

---

32. Thus we have a Roman Catholic cleric encouraging products of the Reformation to pay closer attention to biblical norms. One can only wonder what John Calvin and John Knox would say? "Cardinal O'Connor to Address Commissioners," *Presbyterian Layman,* May/June 1991.
33. Ibid.
34. John F. Harvey, "Priests Who Stray," *Crisis* (November 1992): 37–42.

Concerning the Catholic church's position on gays, Johnson says, "the church's message is that the condition of homosexuality is not sin. It's the activity bent on that disorder, a proclivity toward something unnatural and therefore intrinsically evil, that is sinful." Johnson is not a detached observer: "I've seen the results of that activity firsthand. My godfather died of AIDS. Since I started my ministry, I've buried almost 400 people."[35]

When Jim Johnson came to San Diego and established Ariel House (based on the Providence House model) he encountered people from the United AIDS Coalition of Los Angeles. "The next thing I knew, San Diego was inundated with negative letters about me." These letters were "distributed by *Dignity* people and their friends in San Diego. (*Dignity* is a national Catholic homosexual group, started in San Diego, that rejects the Church's teaching on homosexuality.)"[36]

Johnson has received death threats from those who feel the only people who are sympathetic to homosexual activity are qualified to minister to AIDS victims. He is continuing to serve this needy culture. "My recommendation to married couples and young singles is . . . devote yourselves to your family to prevent divorce, to prevent dysfunctional children. The teachings of Vatican II use the term 'the cell' that the family is the cell of society, the backbone of civilization."[37]

Other Ministries. There are a number of groups ministering to HIV positive/AIDS and homosexual persons. *Alternatives* is an organization that is committed to assisting those who want to come out of the homosexual lifestyle. *Homosexuals Anonymous* basically has the same goal: groups of men and women meet for mutual support and counsel while observing a simple, theologically sound step-program to guide the struggler out of homosexual bondage. *Spatula Ministries* is a support group for parents, friends, and loved ones who are involved one way or another with those enmeshed in this condition.

Before leaving this subject we must touch on the ministry of Dr. Joseph Nicolosi. In the late 1970s, possessing a doctorate from Los Angeles School of Professional Psychology, Nicolosi founded the Thomas Aquinas Psychological Clinic in Encino, California. His purpose was "to establish a psychological service specifically for the Catholic population . . . in harmony with Catholic teaching." His reparative therapy "has helped men—more than 200 of them—overcome their homosexual tendencies and has established him as a dissenting voice." Dr. Nicolosi has written two books: *Reparative Therapy of Male Homosexuality: A New Clinical Approach* (1991) and *Healing Homosexuality: Clinical Stories of Reparative Therapy* (spring 1993).[38]

35. Tim Ryland, "The Catholic Homosexual," *News Notes*, November 1991.
36. Ibid.
37. Ibid.
38. Tim Ryland, "A Proper Sense of Celibacy," ibid., April 1993.

Roman Catholics and evangelicals are involved in all of the programs, presentations, and ministries mentioned in this section. The common denominator is the premise that the moral prescriptions that have come from the Judeo-Christian tradition are not up for grabs; cultural norms may change but God's moral laws do not.[39]

CHRISTIANITY AND THE LEGAL SYSTEM

That Christians are to involve themselves—to some extent—in society is a truth that can be supported by numerous examples from Scripture. The Pharisees and the Herodians once attempted to draw Jesus into a church vs. state argument concerning the payment of taxes (Matt. 22:15–22). Our Lord indicated that Caesar (the state) has legitimate responsibilities and thus deserves the support of Christians. The apostle Paul taught that Christians are to be "subordinate to the higher authorities, for there is no authority except from God, and those that exist have been established by God" (Rom. 13:1). And Peter said: "Be subject to every human institution for the Lord's sake. . . . Give honor to all, love the community, fear God, honor the king" (1 Pet. 2:13, 17). Therefore, Christians are inexorably linked to the state. However, due to pressures from secular forces, some have attempted to use the state to limit the church and hamper its mission in the world. This pressure can be clearly discerned in the legal system.

In 1977, Paul Ellwanger, a Roman Catholic layman from South Carolina, formed "Citizens for Fairness in Education," a group which sponsored "balanced treatment for creation-evolution" bills in various state legislatures. In Arkansas, such a bill was signed into law by the governor in March 1981. The following May the American Civil Liberties Union (ACLU) filed a challenge to the constitutionality of the bill. A trial was held and the bill was judged to be unconstitutional. One of the authors was the first expert witness for the defense at this court case.[40]

Many such situations could be cited. We wish to draw attention to efforts in the legal arena by William Bentley Ball, already featured in this chapter. He has involved himself in numerous cases involving religious rights of Christians in the public and legal sectors. In 1992 Assistant Chief Robert Vernon of the Los Angeles Police Department was forced to retire because of

---

39. Concerning AIDS, see Franklin E. Payne, Jr., M.D., *What Every Christian Should Know about the AIDS Epidemic* (Augusta: Covenant Books, 1991). Good material on homosexuality may be found in Harry V. Jaffa, *Homosexuality and the Natural Law* (Montclair: Claremont Institute, 1990) and J. Isamu Yamamoto, ed., *The Crisis of Homosexuality* (Wheaton: Victor, 1990).

40. See Norman L. Geisler, *The Creator in the Courtroom* (Milford: Mott Media, 1982).

attacks on his Christian faith. Vernon had served the L.A.P.D. for nearly thirty-eight years and is an elder at Grace Community Church, Sun Valley, California, pastored by John F. MacArthur, Jr.

Chief Vernon has filed a lawsuit against the city of Los Angeles for this breach of his religious rights and William Bentley Ball has signed on as lead counsel in this case. Ball had stated at the time that this case might be the most significant religious liberty case of our generation. This is an example of Roman Catholic/evangelical teamwork addressing the dangerous effect of secularism and hostility leveled at those who stand for Christ in our time.[41] Ball sums up his concerns in this area: "It is time that Catholics and evangelicals sit down with one another to address pressing problems in the political order. For that they will both need, in the name of public duty, to suppress old suspicions and antagonisms and endeavor to see in one another brothers and sisters in Christ."[42]

PRISON REFORM

Throughout the Scriptures, we find references to many of God's people spending time in prison. In the Old Testament, Joseph was imprisoned for alleged improprieties with Potiphar's wife (Gen. 39) and King Zedekiah incarcerated Jeremiah for his prophetic utterances (Jer. 32:2–5). In the New Testament, John the Baptist (Matt. 11:2), the apostles (Acts 5:17–23), and Paul with Silas (Acts 16:19–24) spent time behind bars. Jesus instructed his followers to minister to those in prison (Matt. 25:31–40).

In the history of the church, God has used time spent in prison to deepen commitment and produce new insights among his people. A contemporary example of prison reform is Charles Colson, who went to jail for his involvement in Watergate, was converted, and subsequently formed *Prison Fellowship Ministries*.

PRISON FELLOWSHIP MINISTRIES

Charles Colson was a member of Richard Nixon's "inner circle." Known as Nixon's "hatchet man," Colson was tried and convicted of leaking F.B.I. documents to the press during the Watergate scandal.

The forthright testimony of Boston businessman Tom Phillips and his reading of such works as C. S. Lewis's *Mere Christianity* convinced Colson

41. For background on this incident, see Robert Vernon, "L.A. Justice Not for All," *Focus on the Family: Citizen* 7, no. 2, 15 February 1993. The case is ongoing at this time. William Bentley Ball is being assisted by the Western Center for Law and Religious Freedom.
42. William Bentley Ball, "We'd Better Hang Together," *Crisis* (October 1989): 21.

of the truthfulness of Christianity and he was subsequently converted. It was while he served a seven-month jail term that he discovered the need for programs geared to meet the spiritual needs of those in prison.[43]

In 1976, Colson founded *Prison Fellowship,* a program which seeks to rehabilitate those behind bars. Prisoners, ex-prisoners, victims, and their families are exposed to the power and healing of the gospel. *Prison Fellowship Ministries* is the largest prison outreach program in the world and is active not only in the United States but also in fifty-five countries around the world. It ministers to about 250,000 people.

Charles Colson is a widely acclaimed author, speaker, and commentator. He has recently been awarded the one million dollar 1993 Templeton Prize for Progress in Religion. This prestigious award is presented annually to a person who shows exceptional thinking in advancing humanity's understanding of God. Previous recipients include former Soviet dissident Alexander Solzhenitsyn, evangelist Billy Graham, and Mother Teresa.

The Roman Catholic Connection. It is not well known in evangelical circles that Colson receives a great amount of friendship and assistance from Roman Catholics. William F. Buckley, the host of "Firing Line" and editor of *The National Review,* is a close friend and has participated with Colson in conferences.

While Benigno Aquino was imprisoned by Ferdinand Marcos, he received a copy of Colson's book *Born Again.* Aquino was convinced of his need for salvation and gave his life to Jesus Christ. Upon his release, he was tragically gunned down as he deplaned in Manila. Colson's friendship with the dead patriot helped him obtain access for *Prison Fellowship* in the Philippines, and has gained a powerful ally there in Jaime Cardinal Sin, the leading Roman Catholic prelate in that country. Cardinal Sin, in addressing a Prison Fellowship International Conference in Nairobi in 1986, said: "Justice without mercy is tyranny, and mercy without justice is weakness. Justice without love is pure socialism, and love without justice is baloney."[44]

When *Prison Fellowship* outgrew its facilities and moved into a new headquarters, Charles Colson invited his close friend Fr. Michael Scanlan, T.O.R., president of Franciscan University of Steubenville (Ohio), to speak at the dedication. In the course of his homily, Fr. Scanlan said, "God made Jesus a felon that the rest of us felons could go free!" Indeed. (We will have more to say about Michael Scanlan in chapter 18.)

St. Francis Church and Jail Ministry. Every Tuesday evening, a team from St. Francis Roman Catholic Church minister to inmates at the jail in Vista,

43. Charles Colson wrote two books that detail these events: *Born Again* (Old Tappan, N.J.: Fleming Revell, 1976) and *Life Sentence* (Old Tappan, N.J.: Fleming Revell, 1979).

44. Quoted in Charles Colson, *Kingdoms in Conflict* (Grand Rapids: Zondervan, 1987), p. 313.

California. Led by evangelism coordinator John Clauder, the team provides music and singing for up to forty prisoners who attend the meeting.

After the singing, the team members stand and give their testimonies as to how the gospel has impacted their lives. Speakers have included former inmates, recovering drug addicts, and family members of inmates. John Clauder draws attention to the fact that Jesus mentions that he was "in prison" (Matt. 25:35–40) and when Christians minister to those in prison they are in a real sense ministering to Christ. Clauder says, "Maybe I'm selfish because I come here to see Jesus in all of you."[45]

The singing and testimonies of those committed Christians have a positive impact on the inmates. James Martin, age 26, has been in and out of prison since age 12. Martin says that the group from St. Francis, ". . . gives me peace of mind. . . . It lets you know people out there care. It helps me not to dwell on myself."[46]

A number of inmates have found Christ since coming to Vista, and John Clauder with his associates teach these new believers how to reach out and tell others about the gospel. Bible study is stressed and a support system is being formed to help released prisoners grow in Christ. The St. Francis Roman Catholics do, indeed, take Jesus' words in Matthew 25 seriously.

CONCLUSION

In this chapter we have first attempted to sketch briefly the cultural deterioration which has caused concern among Christians of all denominations. Given the purpose of this book, particular attention has been focused on the thinking and contributions of believing Roman Catholics such as William Bentley Ball. He is the editor of a current work already cited *(In Search of a National Morality)*, which addresses the areas of concern: secularization, morals, government leadership, issues of human life, family values, and the like. Contributors are equally divided between Roman Catholics and evangelicals. In the preface—entitled "Life in an Occupied Country"—Ball speaks to the moral decline we see all around. "We are assaulted by media (and, widely, through our educational institutions) in ways no less distressing to Christians than political propaganda was to people of occupied countries."[47]

As a Roman Catholic, Ball had been encouraged by the firm moral stand that his church has exhibited through the twentieth century. But a change was coming. He wrote: "in the 1970's I, along with many other Catholics, shared in the appalling experience that many evangelicals had earlier experi-

45. Tracy Walsh, "A Celebration behind Bars," *The Southern Cross,* 2 July 1992, p. 7.
46. Ibid.
47. Ball, *In Search of a National Morality,* p. 10.

enced—the entry of modernism into the church, the rise of dissentients within its body who boldly attacked the fundamental teachings of the faith and, indeed, the very teaching authority of the Church."[48] Because of this new situation and his contacts with evangelicals in the school movements and other social areas, Ball concluded that "'orthodox' Catholics and 'orthodox' evangelical Protestants should work together in the battle against rampant secularism. I defined 'orthodox' as those who hold belief in God, the Trinity, the divinity of Christ as our personal Savior, the Virgin Birth, the Holy Spirit, inerrancy of Scripture, the existence of Satan, man as created by God in His image and likeness, man's salvation through Christ."[49]

In short, William Bentley Ball is encouraging an alliance between Roman Catholics and evangelicals who, in the words of Charles Colson, "Serve in the 'little platoons' around the world, faithfully evidencing the love and justice of the Kingdom of God in the midst of the kingdoms of this world."[50]

---

48. Ibid., p. 11.
49. Ibid., p. 12.
50. Colson, *Kingdoms in Conflict,* dedication.

18

EDUCATIONAL GOALS

The educational process has been an integral part of the development of the Christian church from the beginning. As one evangelical has said, "Christian education . . . arises from the fertile soil of the Bible."[1] Vatican II declared that "The sacred ecumenical council has given careful consideration to the paramount importance of education in the life of men and its ever-growing influence on the social progress of the age."[2] Also, "For her part Holy Mother Church, in order to fulfill the mandate she received from her divine founder to announce the mystery of salvation to all men and to renew all things in Christ . . . has therefore a part to play in the development and extension of education."[3]

The Vatican II document goes on to say that parents have the primary responsibility to educate their children. This educational process requires the help of society as a whole, mainly focused in the schools. Therefore, "Parents, who have a primary and inalienable duty and right in regard to the education of their children, should enjoy the fullest liberty in their choice of school."[4]

Because many Roman Catholic children will be taught in non-Catholic schools, it is incumbent on "those priests and laymen to teach them Christian doctrine in a manner suited to their age and background and to provide them with spiritual help by means of various activities adapted to the requirements of time and circumstance."[5] This process extends to higher level

---

1. Edward L. Hayes, "The Biblical Foundations of Christian Education," in Werner C. Graendorf, ed., *Introduction to Biblical Christian Education* (Chicago: Moody Press, 1981), p. 25.
2. "Declaration of Christian Education," preface in Flannery, *Vatican Collection: Vatican Council II,* p. 725.
3. Ibid., p. 726.
4. Ibid., p. 731.
5. Ibid., p. 732.

education, where the goal is to achieve a deeper understanding of truth. The result is that "the convergence of faith and reason in the one truth may be seen more clearly. This method follows the tradition of the doctors of the Church and especially St. Thomas Aquinas."[6] Having established the importance of education in Christian formation, we now turn to its historical development.

CHRISTIAN EDUCATION IN HISTORY

The development of education in the church may be observed in several stages. The first of these occur in the Old Testament period.

THE OLD TESTAMENT

An investigation of processes of the common education roots of Catholics and evangelicals begins in the Old Testament, since "the roots of Christian education run deep into the soil of Judaism."[7] God made contact with the Jewish people through human history and the law. With this in mind, Jewish young people were taught "that they should put their hope in God, and not forget the deeds of God but keep his commands" (Ps. 78:7).

Instruction (education) was a central theme in the spiritual development of the Hebrew people. It was coupled with life itself: "Hold fast to instruction, never let her go; keep her, for she is your life" (Prov. 4:13). During the exile, the synagogue became the center of Jewish religious life. Its main purpose was to instruct. Barclay notes that "It is necessary clearly to remember that the Synagogue was very much more a place of teaching than the modern Church. The object of the Synagogue Sabbath services was not public worship in the narrower sense of the term; it was not devotion, it was religious instruction."[8]

THE NEW TESTAMENT

Because the church emerged from the Jewish milieu it utilized the same educational structures found in the Old Testament. Although Jesus remained

---

6. Ibid., p. 735. The new catechism addresses this subject: "Catechesis is an *education in the faith* of children, young people, and adults which includes especially the teaching of Christian doctrine imported, generally speaking, in an organic and systematic way, with a view to initiating the hearers into the fullness of Christian life." *Catechesi tradendae* 545, 18; quoted in *Catechism of the Catholic Church*, p. 8.

7. C. Graendorf, *Introduction to Biblical Christian Education*, p. 26.

8. William Barclay, *Educational Ideals of the Ancient World* (Grand Rapids: Baker, 1974), p. 24; quoted in ibid., p. 27.

within the Jewish framework, he raised teaching to a higher level. Indeed, he was the Master.

The Holy Spirit's coming on the day of Pentecost turned uncertain disciples into zealous preacher-teachers. The people who responded to Peter's preaching "devoted themselves to the teaching of the apostles" (Acts 2:42).

Paul's directives to Timothy and Titus include much instruction concerning the importance of building up of the "body of Christ." Teaching leads to a proper understanding of Scripture (2 Tim. 2:14–15; 3:16–17). It ensures sound doctrine (1 Tim. 4:6, 16; 6:3–5; 2 Tim. 4:3–4). In Titus, sound teaching is used to counteract heresy (Titus 1:9; 2:12) and establish order in the household. Christian education was certainly crucial in the development of early Christianity.

THE POST-APOSTOLIC PERIOD

With the death of the first generation of Christians, something was needed to replace their oral traditions. That something was a collection of literature which came to be recognized as the "canon" of the New Testament. This canon ("measuring rod") was used by the early church fathers to deal with heresy and to build up believers in the faith.

Because of the large number of converts that the church attracted, education was of paramount importance. "Catechumenal training arose to insure that those embracing Christianity understood the faith and were committed to the lifestyle expected of believers." Inquirers in the catechizing instruction classes were carefully taught, and only when they had proved competent in belief and life was baptism given.[9]

THE MIDDLE AGES

The cultural and intellectual barrenness that marked the early medieval period has caused some to characterize the entire era as the "Dark Ages," the implication being "that no gleam of light was forthcoming until the Renaissance re-lighted its torch from Greece and Rome. That generalization, ill founded in historical fact, greatly misrepresents medieval cultural and intellectual life."[10] The monastic orders which came into being in this period continued the work of literacy and instruction. They maintained libraries and labored to carry on the task of instilling a life of devotion and service in the Church.[11]

---

9. Clifford V. Anderson, "Christian Education in Historical Perspective," in Graendorf, *Introduction to Biblical Christian Education*, p. 40.

10. V. Raymond Edman, *The Light in Dark Ages* (Wheaton: Van Kampen Press, 1949), p. 123.

11. Graendorf, *Introduction to Biblical Christian Education*, pp. 41–42.

THE MODERN SCENE

The spirits of secularism and moral relativity that have permeated our culture have found a warm welcome in our educational institutions. Not only in secular circles but, sadly, in schools which formerly maintained a classic Christian stance as well one can discern movement away from orthodoxy. We will briefly touch on the cause and effect on Roman Catholic instructions and movements in the United States.

COLLAPSE OF THE SUPERNATURAL

This interesting phrase is used by Richard John Neuhaus in his provocative work on the current state of affairs in the Roman Catholic Church.[12] On Roman Catholic "progressives" he observes that "The familiar path traveled by these theologians was blazed and well beaten by Protestant liberalism in the nineteenth century."[13] Concerning this new shift: "The controlling presupposition is a general loss of belief in the supernatural and a radical turn toward humanity." It would seem that traditional Christian belief cannot survive a "plausibility collapse" with respect to the supernatural and the transcendent.[14]

Historian James Hitchcock has also addressed this shift in emphasis. He wrote: "Catholic institutions in the United States have never been able to find the proper balance between commitment and openness."[15] Hitchcock finds change has occurred philosophically: "The dominance of the Thomistic system has broken everywhere, and in many schools an extreme reaction has all but driven Thomism out."[16]

In an earlier work, Hitchcock begins by stating: "One of the great human mysteries of modern times is the amazingly swift process by which the Roman Catholic church, apparently one of the most solid, self-confident, and enduring institutions in the history of the world, was plunged into an identity crisis of cosmic proportions."[17] Its bad enough when un-Christian influences attack the church from *without* but when this comes from *within* the result is disastrous: "Many Catholics today are being victimized by ideologies they do not even know exist, proffered in pseudo-religious language

---

12. Richard John Neuhaus, *The Catholic Moment: The Paradox of the Church in the Post-modern World* (New York: Harper and Row, 1987), pp. 73–82. Neuhaus, a Lutheran pastor when he wrote this volume, has since converted to Roman Catholicism.

13. Ibid., p. 73.

14. Ibid., p. 75.

15. James Hitchcock, *Years of Crisis: Collected Essays 1970–1983* (San Francisco: Ignatius Press, 1985), p. 29.

16. Ibid., p. 216.

17. Hitchcock, *Catholicism and Modernity*, p. 1.

by persons whom they have been conditioned to respect."[18] Hitchcock goes on to describe the effect that pluralism and post-Vatican II bureaucracy has had on the modern Roman Catholic Church.

Another Roman Catholic, Dinesh D'Souza, has written an important book dealing with the educational scene.[19] In this work, D'Souza details the impact that "political correctness" has had on the American educational establishment. "Multiculturalism," "racism," "sexism," and "relativistic" forces have led to intolerance in a number of schools across this country.

Gerald Fogarty's book *American Catholic Biblical Scholarship* details the history of Roman Catholic scholarship in this country, finding that American Catholicism is moving from a "biblical fundamentalist approach" to one which is more "mature," more "insightful." This new posture is facilitated by an abandonment of biblical inerrancy for a position which extends inspiration only to matters of faith and morals.[20]

In an address by the president of the Catholic Theological Society of America we find the following evaluation: "St. Thomas Aquinas succeeded in making the Christian message relevant to the learned world of his day. . . . But this is not the day of St. Thomas Aquinas; the modern mind is not prepared to cope with the modes of Greek thought he employed."[21] What will take the place of the time honored system of Augustinian/Thomism? "[N]o age has been so blessed as ours in the development of such sciences as anthropology, sociology and psychology. Should not these disciplines now become the hand maids of the . . . new pastoral theology . . . ?"[22] In a word, believing Roman Catholics and evangelicals would say no.

We have it on good authority that when the names of John Paul II or Cardinal Ratzinger are mentioned at meetings of the Catholic Theological Society of America a good deal of wailing and gnashing of teeth ensues. So much for faithfulness on the part of Roman Catholic "progressive" theologians. What begins in the centers of ecclesiastical education usually seeps down into the teaching at the parish level. One of the authors has a daughter-in-law who is a bright, traditional Roman Catholic. She and her husband have sponsored young people's groups and taught religious education classes in their church. She has been dismayed at the presence of less than orthodox notions in the teaching materials put at her disposal. For example, the bodily resurrection of Christ is questioned, as is the virgin birth. Sin is explained away

18. Ibid., p. 72.
19. Dinesh D'Souza, *Illiberal Education: The Politics of Race and Sex on Campus* (New York: Free Press, 1991).
20. Gerald P. Fogarty, S.J., *American Catholic Biblical Scholarship* (San Francisco: Harper and Row, 1989). See chap. 1, "Revelation."
21. Richard T. Doherty, *Proceedings of the Nineteenth Annual Convention* (New York: St. Joseph's Seminary Press, 1965), p. 215.
22. Ibid., pp. 220–21.

and the Bible is said to be full of myths. And what is the source of this heterodoxy? "'The tragedy is these things are taught by master catechists and people with advanced degrees in theology,' says Janice Gray, a San Diego Catholic school teacher with 17 years of CCD experience who has taken numerous local training courses—and walked out on more than a few."[23] But in spite of all the liberalization there has been, of late, there have been some promising developments concerning these problems. After all, while the short-term prospects may be pessimistic, Jesus has promised that Satan will not, in the long run, destroy the church (Matt. 16:18).

RENAISSANCE OF ORTHODOXY

Responding to these dangerous trends in their church, orthodox Roman Catholics have accepted the challenge. Two pro-life campus groups are active in schools throughout the country. *American Collegians for Life (ACL)* was founded in 1987 and has grown to more than 300 chapters. *Collegians Activated to Liberate Life (CALL)* works throughout the Midwest and visits colleges to mobilize students to pro-life activity.

A number of journals and magazines are attempting to address the moral and ethical disarray that is occurring in our culture. *First Things,* with editor-in-chief Fr. Richard John Neuhaus, has among its contributors such traditional Roman Catholics as William B. Ball, William F. Buckley, Jr., and John Cardinal O'Connor. They are joined with such evangelicals as Elizabeth Achtemeier (Union Theological Seminary in Virginia) and Thomas C. Oden of Drew University. Another publication, *Crisis,* is a monthly journal founded by the American "god-father" of Thomistic thought, Ralph McInerny. It advertises itself as a journal of lay-Catholic opinion and its publication committee is made up of such illuminati as Zbigniew Brzezinski, J. Peter Grace, Alexander M. Haig, and Michael Novak. An occasional evangelical slips in as well.

Servant Books is the publishing outreach of *The Sword of the Spirit,* an international Christian community reflecting the Roman Catholic, Orthodox, and Protestant traditions. Servant Books has published material from "Allies for Faith and Renewal" conferences and other works that reflect on the foundational truths that all orthodox Christians hold in common. Of special interest is the series *Knowing the Truth,* co-edited by Roman Catholic Peter Kreeft and evangelical J. I. Packer. Among the titles in the series is *Knowing the Truth about Creation* (1989), written by Norman L. Geisler.[24]

---

23. Tim Ryland, "Local Lay Catholics Resist Bad Teaching," *San Diego News Notes,* March 1993.

24. Servant Publications, Dept. 209, P.O. Box 7455, Ann Arbor, MI 48107.

THE EAGLE FORUM

Eagle Forum was started in 1972 by Phyllis Schlafly. The organization "stands for the fundamental right of parents to guide the education of their own children."[25] Such systems as "Outcome-Based Education" and experimental courses in "self-esteem" or "decision-making" are opposed. Phyllis Schlafly is a practicing Roman Catholic and has been a national leader of the conservative movement since the publication of her best-selling 1964 book, *A Choice Not an Echo*. She has been active in pro-family affairs and has opposed the agendas of the radical feminist movement, often debating on college campuses.

Mrs. Schlafly writes a monthly newsletter *(The Phyllis Schlafly Report)* and her syndicated column appears in 100 newspapers, her radio commentaries are heard daily on 270 stations, and her radio talk show on educational matters is heard weekly on 45 stations. She is the author or editor of thirteen books on subjects as varied as family and feminism *(The Power of the Positive Woman)*, education *(Child Abuse in the Classroom)*, and child care *(Who Will Rock the Cradle?)*.

Phyllis Schlafly is an articulate spokesperson for orthodox Christian values and morals. As a lawyer she has testified before a number of congressional and state legislative committees. She is a graduate of Washington University and received her Masters in Political Science from Harvard University.

THE RAINBOW CURRICULUM MEETS ITS MATCH

The New York City public school system is the largest in the nation. Its chancellor, Joseph A. Fernandez, decided in 1991 to implement a program designed to teach "the positive aspects" of homosexuality to the almost one million children under his care. The curriculum, known as the Rainbow Curriculum, had among its recommended books such titles as *Daddy's Roommate, Heather Has Two Mommies,* and *Gloria Goes to Gay Pride.* Not content to teach tolerance, Fernandez insisted that his task was to enforce complete compliance and overturn social moral structures that have been in place in Western civilization for centuries. Fernandez had not counted on reaction from the likes of Mary A. Cummins.

Cummins, a feisty Roman Catholic, served in a volunteer capacity as school board president in District 24, West Queens. She told Fernandez in no uncertain terms that "We will not accept two people of the same sex engaged in deviant sex practices as 'family.'" Her protest was joined by six other school boards, and the storm of protest that resulted when the social engi-

---

25. Informational brochures, Eagle Forum, P.O. Box 618, Alton, IL 62002.

neering agenda of the Rainbow Curriculum was exposed led to Fernandez's eventual termination.

Mary Cummins has drawn support from not only evangelical parents but also orthodox Jews and Muslims. Cummins is backed by David Wilkerson *(The Cross and the Switchblade)*, pastor of Times Square Church, and that traditional values champion, John Cardinal O'Connor, archbishop of New York. Again, Roman Catholics and evangelicals are coming together to confront the encroachment of moral decay in society.

TEXTBOOK BIAS

For some time now, Christians of various persuasions have been disturbed by American public schooling in general and the textbooks in particular. Along comes Roman Catholic Paul Vitz, professor of psychology at New York University. Armed with a grant from the federal government and funded through the National Institute of Education, Vitz has examined the above charges and gathered his conclusions in a book.[26]

Vitz sees no dark plot involved in the educational revisionism in current textbooks but the result of the secular and liberal mind-set that pervades the leadership in the world of education. The results, however, are not dissimilar. One example Vitz provides is illuminating:

> One social studies book has thirty pages on the Pilgrims, including the first Thanksgiving. But there is not one word (or image) that referred to religion as even a part of the Pilgrims' life. One mother whose son is in a class using this book wrote to say that he came home and told her that *"Thanksgiving was when Pilgrims gave thanks to the Indians."* The mother called the principal of this suburban New York City school to point out that Thanksgiving was when the Pilgrims thanked God. *The principal responded by saying "that was her opinion"—the schools could only teach what was in the books!*[27]

Vitz concludes: "We are being taxed to support schools that are systematically liquidating our most cherished beliefs."[28] This is difficult to comprehend when one contemplates the battle cry of our founding fathers: "Taxation without representation is tyranny"![29]

26. Paul Vitz, *Censorship: Evidence of Bias in Our Children's Textbooks* (Ann Arbor: Servant, 1986).

27. Ibid., p. 3, emphasis added.

28. Ibid., p. 91. Paul Vitz first gained recognition with a book addressing "selfism," *Psychology As Religion: The Cult of Self-worship* (reprint; Grand Rapids: Eerdmans, 1986). He has also written an excellent work on Freud: *Sigmund Freud's Christian Unconscious* (New York: Guilford Press, 1988).

29. It was reaction to this principle that perpetrated the famous Boston Tea Party on December 16, 1773; see Samuel Eliot Morison, *The Oxford History of the American People* (New York: Oxford University Press, 1965), pp. 203–4.

A COOPERATIVE EFFORT

One of the most impressive examples of a cooperative educational effort between Roman Catholics and evangelicals is the Franciscan University of Steubenville in Ohio. It began in 1946 as the College of Steubenville, a small commuter school serving ex-servicemen. In the early 1960s land was donated and the college moved to its present location. The college originally had a Franciscan identity and in 1974 the school called a Franciscan priest, Michael Scanlan, to be its president. Fr. Scanlan had been rector at St. Francis Seminary in Loretto, Pennsylvania. The spiritual climate of most Catholic schools at the time was theologically destitute, much the same as their Protestant counterparts.[30] Concerning this situation, the distinguished Roman Catholic educator Russell A. Kirk, comments: "Now a days Catholic students, in point of both intellect and moral teaching, would be prudent to attend not the decayed 'Catholic' college but instead either the neighboring Calvinist college or state university."[31] John Henry Cardinal Newman would not be pleased.[32]

God had been preparing Michael Scanlan for his assignment at Steubenville. Following the directive of Vatican II which encouraged Catholics to enter into ecumenical dialogue with their "separated brethren," he preached in Protestant churches and held retreats for Protestant groups. Addressing differences between Roman Catholics and Protestants, Fr. Scanlan writes: "At the same time, these differences are not as great as many Christians think. Our discussions cleared up some misconceptions. Catholics do not worship Mary and the saints. Protestants *do* have appreciation for Christian tradition. Scripture *is* central in Catholic life. Protestants do not believe that 'good works' have no value."[33]

Later, in August of 1969, Michael Scanlan, at the direction of Sister Caroline, the Superior of the Discalced Carmelite Sisters, met with two charismatic priests. They laid hands on him and Scanlan relates: "The Spirit fell. It was primarily an experience of prayer, but prayer unlike any other I have experienced or studied."[34] He experienced what Pentecostal and charismatic Christians call "the baptism of the Holy Spirit." Armed with his newly found spiritual resources, Fr. Scanlan took charge of a "Catholic-in-name-only"

---

30. For a discussion of Roman Catholic educational disarray, see Ralph Martin, *A Crisis of Truth: The Attack on Faith, Morality and Mission in the Catholic Church* (Ann Arbor: Servant, 1982), pp. 99–113. Martin is especially severe on Jesuit institutions, pp. 105ff.

31. "The State of Catholic Higher Education," in Ball, *In Search of a National Morality*, p. 197.

32. Newman, the famous convert from Anglicanism to Roman Catholicism, wrote *Idea of a University* (New York: Longmans, 1947), in which he sets forth his ideals for Christian religious education.

33. Michael Scanlan, *Let the Fire Fall* (Ann Arbor: Servant, 1986), pp. 68–69.

34. Ibid., pp. 80–81.

school and turned it into a biblically based Roman Catholic institution that majors in turning "cultural" Catholics into "born again" ones. To assist him in redirecting Steubenville, Scanlan points out that "For many years, evangelical Protestants associated with the Christian Coalition have worked with our students as dorm directors. These young graduates, mostly from Covenant Presbyterian colleges, worked closely with our campus ministers in teaching our students the basics of practical Christian living and in leading them to a deeper spiritual life."[35]

Speaking of the spiritual unity that he finds with evangelicals, Fr. Scanlan writes: "I have found friends and allies in unexpected places, particularly among Protestant evangelicals. Frankly my beliefs about the essentials of the gospel are closer to those of evangelical Protestants who are culturally very different from me than they are to the beliefs of some Catholics whom I grew up with. . . . I regret this, but I am not surprised by it." Scanlan finds that the common bond which unites believing Roman Catholics and evangelicals is: "We are united by one life in Jesus Christ, not by a shared human culture. The work of God transcends cultures and nations and tongues. It takes priority over human preferences and smashes man-made barriers."[36]

Finally, in the ecumenical journal *Touchstone* one finds the following information on Steubenville: "Theology is one of the most popular fields of study, and there are more undergraduate theology majors than in any other Catholic college or university in the United States. . . . Steubenville has grown to a fully accredited university with 1,700 students, who come from 49 states and 22 foreign countries."[37]

Students from Steubenville join hands with their evangelical counterparts and during spring break evangelize hundreds of vacationing college students on Florida beaches. After fifteen years, the university is thriving and enrollment is at an all-time high. The school is mentioned in *America's Best Colleges* guide and also in the Templeton Foundation's *Honor Roll for Character Building Colleges*. Somehow we think Cardinal Newman would be happy.

AN EDUCATIONAL MINISTRY IN JERUSALEM

One author (Ralph MacKenzie) was privileged to tour the Holy Land a few years ago. It was during this trip that he met Joyce Shafer, who works for Church School Service, Inc. in Jerusalem. Shafer—originally from California—is an evangelical of the Pentecostal persuasion who works at providing

---

35. Ibid., p. 177.
36. Ibid., p. 179.
37. News release, "Franciscan University of Steubenville, Ohio," *Touchstone* 3, no. 4, winter 1990.

Christian literature for the various communions in and around Jerusalem. She takes flannel graphs and other Sunday school teaching materials such as the "Little Folk Whole Bible Visual Sets" and translates them from English into Arabic for the Arab churches and Sunday schools in the area.

Church School Service has reached out into other parts of the Middle East such as Jordan, Egypt, and Iraq. Concerning distribution of flannel graphs, Joyce comments, "This continues to be an extremely fruitful service to the Arab churches and schools in Israel and elsewhere in the Middle East. Every church denomination co-operates."[38] Church School Service is clearly nonsectarian in its ministry, serving all Protestant representations as well as numerous Eastern Orthodox and Roman Catholic churches. When thinking about the Holy Land, many people are only aware of the conflict between Muslims and Jews. However, a portion of the body of Christ exists there and attempts to witness, under dire circumstances, to the truth of Christianity. Joyce Shafer is part of this ministry and has asked Christians to " 'Pray for the peace of Jerusalem' (Ps. 122:6). Also pray that the Prince of Peace will come soon."[39]

OTHER AREAS OF COOPERATION

There are many areas of educational opportunities in which Roman Catholics and evangelicals share a common interest. One of these is in the area of parental choice in education.

PARENTAL CHOICE

Many Christians see the idea of "parental choice" as being a way to combat the sorry state of affairs in education today. In some school districts, vouchers are given so that parents of, say, differing religious and cultural backgrounds can send their children to the school of their choice. Basic educational standards are required at these institutions. This seems to be an eminently fair system in a pluralistic society that is experiencing a violent clash of values. Take, for example, the topic of the earth's origin. With vouchers, creationists could send their children to schools that teach creation and evolutionists could send their children to schools that teach evolution. Neither would *have* to send their children to schools that indoctrinate their children against their beliefs but could choose to send their children to a

---

38. "Prayer and Praise News Letter," *Church School Service,* fall 1993.

39. Ibid. Joyce Shafer's address is: Church School Service, Inc., P.O. Box 19179, Jerusalem, Israel. U.S.A. address is: Florence Christie, Church School Service, Inc., 13930 Church Place, Apt. 70-F, Seal Beach, CA 90740.

school based on Judeo-Christian, secular humanist, or New Age values, depending on their convictions.

This system causes great agitation among secular educators, however, principally because "the debate is not really about 'choice' at all; it is about 'control.' Loss of students to the private sector means loss of the government's control over them and, more importantly, over the money the state allocates for their education."[40] This issue soon will be presented to voters in a number of states. We will wait for the results.

BILL CREASY, CATHOLIC BIBLE TEACHER EXTRAORDINAIRE

Teacher, author, and lecturer Dr. Bill Creasy is a member of the English faculty at the University of California, Los Angeles. His year-long course, The English Bible, is one of the most highly rated courses at UCLA. Dr. Creasy received his bachelors and masters degrees in English from Arizona State University, *summa cum laude,* and his doctorate in medieval literature from UCLA.

Dr. Creasy is also a parishioner at St. Paul the Apostle Church in Westwood, California, where he teaches two courses. The first is a five-year program through the entire Bible and over 200 people attend the course each Monday evening. The second course is an in-depth study of the Bible, taking six to nine months per book. He also teaches a five-year "thru-the-Bible" course in Malibu, and conducts weekend Bible seminars and retreats across the country.

Creasy serves as an Adjunct Professor of Christian Spirituality at Mount St. Mary's College, and at the request of Cardinal Roger Mahoney, he is a member of the Spirituality Commission for the Archdiocese of Los Angeles. His latest books include *The Imitation of Christ, a New Reading of the 1441 Autograph Manuscript*[41] and a forthcoming book, *Mark, the Narrative Strategy of a Gospel.*

Concerning the importance of the study of Scripture, Creasy believes that "Catholics don't know how to do Bible studies. . . . I think it's very important to teach the whole Bible. . . . People duck the difficult parts. If it's the Word of God, you have to study the whole thing."[42]

The two authors were present at St. Paul the Apostle Church for a Monday evening Bible study. We sat fascinated as Creasy taught from the Gospel of John for nearly two hours non-stop. Close to two hundred people (the majority Roman Catholics) followed along attentively, taking copious notes. Chuck Swindoll and John MacArthur would have been impressed.

---

40. Robert A. Destro, "Parental Choice and Educational Equity," in Ball, *In Search of a National Morality,* p. 159.
41. (Macon, Ga.: Mercer University Press, 1989).
42. Mary Rourke, "Hitting the Book," *Los Angeles Times,* Section E, p. 2.

THE ROMAN CATHOLIC/EVANGELICAL CONNECTION IN PANAMA CITY

One author (Ralph MacKenzie) met Carli Jelenszky when both were studying in Seminary West. Jelenszky is vice-president of a large jewelry firm in Panama City, Panama, and moves in the higher socio-economic circles there. He came to faith in Christ through the witness of a Wycliffe Bible translator and the Lord led him to come to the United States for theological education.

Upon graduation, Carli returned to Panama City and has begun several Bible study classes in Roman Catholic churches there. Many Hispanics—raised in a nominal Catholic culture—upon experiencing true conversion to Christ, became very anti-Catholic. Jelenszky takes a different approach. He has used his contacts with the Roman Catholic hierarchy (including a close friendship with a Vatican official who is a lay-theologian) to develop the aforementioned Bible studies. All this while remaining a committed evangelical believer.

EXCHANGE LECTURE OPPORTUNITIES

Finally, the authors have a modest proposal to advance. Opportunity for discussion and interaction between believing Roman Catholics and evangelicals should be encouraged. Indeed, this already exists on a limited scale (see chap. 17). Might we see the day that a Roman Catholic theologian of the stature of Cardinal Ratzinger addresses the Evangelical Theological Society? Or Harold O. J. Brown lectures at the North American College in Rome? Given some of the situations mentioned in Part Three of this work, these scenarios no longer seem out of the question. Compromise of convictions is one thing, but dialogue is another. We oppose the former but favor the latter.

One author (Norman Geisler) can testify to the value of Catholic higher education, having received a doctorate in philosophy from a Catholic institution. Compared to the two secular universities he attended, there was a marked difference in their worldviews. In fact Carl Henry once proposed that there should be a Christian University based on the *Apostle's Creed* and perhaps the *Nicene Creed*. This would include Roman Catholics. Some Catholic schools are reaching out to incorporate evangelical faculty. Presently, one of the best collection of evangelical philosophers to be found in a large graduate school is at the University of Notre Dame.

As we noted in Part One, evangelicals have much in common with a Catholic world view. Both are theistic. And theologically, both are trinitarian. As for the differences, courses in a joint Catholic-evangelical university could be tailored to the various ecclesiastical preferences. In our opinion such a university would be better than what many evangelical parents presently do, namely, send their young people to secularistic universities that undermine the Christian values and beliefs of their posterity. Sadly, many evangelicals would rather have their children come under pagan influence than study with Roman Catholics.

CONCLUSION

We have briefly sketched the impact that unbelief and loosening moral constraints have had on education in general and religious instruction in particular. Also, various people (and movements) who seek to remedy this situation have been mentioned. Paul Vitz identifies "moral relativity" as a major culprit in the deterioration of the current moral climate. One model to emerge from moral relativity is "values clarification." Concerning this model, Vitz writes: "Values clarification must be contrasted with the traditional view of explicit praise for virtue and strong condemnation of wrong-doing." This traditional approach is ineffective, the progressives claim, because "today's complex society presents so many inconsistent sources of values."[43]

This spiritual laxity was not lost on the participants at Vatican II. Kevin Perrotta, a director of the *Center for Pastoral Renewal,* noted that "the bishops expressed their 'regret that the theological discussions of our day have sometimes occasioned confusion among the faithful.' "[44] Therefore, "The prospective Vatican policy regarding those who teach Catholic theology in Catholic institutions . . . must not only be academically qualified but must also communicate it faithfully and live it."[45] We have an obligation to provide our children with a Christian education. One can hardly conceive of Abraham and Sarah sending Isaac to the Canaanite University in old Salem![46]

43. "An American Disaster: Moral Relativity," in Ball, *In Search of a National Morality,* pp. 43–44.
44. "Catholic Renewal," in *Evangelical Renewal in the Mainline Churches,* ed. by Ronald H. Nash (Westchester, Ill.: Crossway, 1987), p. 152.
45. Ibid., p. 154.
46. Salem was later called Jerusalem (Gen. 14:18). See "Salem," in J. D. Douglas, ed., *New Bible Dictionary,* 2d ed. (Leicester, England: InterVarsity Press, 1962), p. 1055.

19

SPIRITUAL HERITAGE

There is a large amount of what might be called "common spiritual heritage" between Catholics and evangelicals. We use the word "common" because all communions, Roman Catholic and Protestant (as well as Orthodox) share in this rich tradition. Unfortunately, one group often is unaware of the contributions of the others. Certainly this is true of evangelicals who, on the whole, are unaware of the *source* of much spiritual and devotional material that they themselves utilize.

The cultural and moral decline which has occurred in contemporary society is reflected in the current state of literature and the arts. Evangelical theologian Carl F. H. Henry correctly observes that "The sorry fate of literature and the arts in our time likewise gives great reason for cultural concern."[1] This is not to say that the twentieth century has been completely devoid of authors writing from a Christian perspective. Henry mentions W. H. Auden, T. S. Eliot, Graham Greene, C. S. Lewis, and others who exhibit an authentic Christian stance. Concerning the ratio of evangelicals to Roman Catholics in literary contributions, he notes that "Catholics have been more successful than evangelicals in writing significant novels; they also far outnumber evangelicals as syndicated newspaper columnists. This may in part reflect the price of an excessive evangelical withdrawal from the culture."[2]

On the other side of the ecclesiastical aisle, concerning the "contemplative dimension of the life of faith, Vatican II speaks to the need for Roman Catholics to develop a personal devotional life and perspective. A Christian, therefore, should reflect "an attitude which manifests the virtue of piety, an interior fount of peace and a bearer of peace to every sphere of life and apostolate."[3] At the center of this spiritual development, "Prayer is the indispens-

---

1. Carl F. H. Henry, "Secularization," in Ball, *In Search of a National Morality*, p. 24.

2. Ibid. Also see Henry's work, *The Uneasy Conscience of Modern Fundamentalism* (Grand Rapids: Eerdmans, 1947).

3. Flannery, *Vatican Collection: Vatican Council II*, p. 246.

able breath of every contemplative dimension."[4] Priests are instructed: "Therefore, in the sometimes exhausting rhythm of apostolic commitments, there must be well ordered and sufficiently prolonged daily and weekly periods of personal and community prayer."[5] Also vital to personal Christian formation is exposure to the Word of God. Along with study of the Scriptures, a spiritual heritage is built with literature and hymnology which speaks to the trials and triumphs experienced by God's people. As charismatic Catholics can testify, Roman Catholics have a great deal to learn from evangelical hymns and devotional material.

LITERATURE

One of the reasons so many Roman Catholic lay persons are converting to evangelicalism is that they did not find a dynamic personal relationship with Christ in their Catholic church. The reality is often lost in the ritual. On the other hand, one of the reasons that a number of noted evangelical scholars (e.g., Thomas Howard and Richard Neuhaus) have converted to Catholicism is that there is a deep intellectual tradition not found in the typical evangelical church. Ironically, while Rome is losing many of its laity "out the bottom" to evangelicals, evangelicals are losing some of their intellectuals "out the top" to Catholicism. Obviously, each has something to learn from the other.

Catholic tradition is rich with literature. This section will examine some of the literature which has emerged from the Christian tradition. The content of these writings are for the most part devotional in nature with some theological implications. Space restrictions force us to be limited to a few examples out of a vast number of works.

Evangelicals, for the most part, are unaware of the origin of some Christian spiritual classics that they treasure—many of which originated from the church fathers and scholars from the Middle Ages. Our samples will be, for the most part, works written before the Protestant Reformation.

THE LIFE OF ANTONY (A.D. 357)

This was written by Athanasius (c. A.D. 296–373), who was the champion of orthodoxy against Arianism and the author of the creed that bears his name. When in exile in the West, certain Christians asked Athanasius to write concerning the life of Antony, whom Athanasius had known personally.

4. Ibid., p. 247.
5. Ibid.

Antony (c. A.D. 251–356) was born in Egypt in a Christian family. He was a shy lad, disliking school and never learning to read or write. At age 20, he retired to the desert where he devoted his life to the practice of Christian asceticism. He attracted a number of disciples and organized them into a community of hermits.

Concerning Antony's disposition, Athanasius writes that "He was never agitated or gloomy, but seemed to radiate in his countenance the joy and imperturbability of his soul."[6] Antony is represented as one who, although experiencing visions and trances, "spoke of these with reluctance, and only to those who sat with him during his ecstasy and afterwards pressed him to tell them what he had seen."[7]

Antony didn't wish to draw attention to himself and, on one occasion when a soldier asked him to heal his child, replied: "Man, why do you make all this clamor to me? I am a man just as you are. If you believe in Christ whom I serve, go and, as you believe, pray to God and it will come to pass."[8] *The Life of Antony* was translated into Latin and was influential in Roman circles. Augustine mentions the work in his *Confessions*, and Antony's subsequent victories over his spiritual trials in the desert have inspired Christians down through the centuries.

THE *CONFESSIONS* OF ST. AUGUSTINE (C. A.D. 397)

Augustine's *Confessions* is best described as a spiritual autobiography. The best known of his many works, it clearly details the personality of Augustine. In reading this book, one follows Augustine (A.D. 354–430) from his childhood in Tagaste, Northern Africa, through his investigations in Manichaeism, Platonism, and skepticism. He finally comes to faith in the God of the Bible and is baptized in A.D. 387.

Augustine often expressed his Christian convictions in Neoplatonic terms, at times even buying into their ideas. Nonetheless, his views were consciously and progressively Christian, and he always made an effort to ground them in Scripture and the great Christian teachers before him.

Augustine treated a number of different themes in this work. God is Creator and not to be confused with his creation. He is the proper object of human love and humanity acquires spiritual insight and power through conversion to Jesus Christ. Augustine's godly mother Monica never ceased to pray for her son, and when they both went to Milan he fell under the influence of the eloquent bishop Ambrose and was converted.

6. "The Life of Antony," in Frank Magill, ed., *Masterpieces of Christian Literature* (New York: Harper and Row, 1963), pp. 96–97.
7. Ibid.
8. Ibid.

The later portions of the *Confessions* deal with Augustine's struggles with the Donatists' and Pelagians' transcendent nature of God and an involved analysis of the nature and relationship of time to creation. Augustine was the first great Christian theologian to follow the Apostolic Era and one of the finest systematizers that the church has produced. The doctrines and concepts that would tax the great minds who followed him in church history were first broached by the "Bishop of Hippo."

THE CITY OF GOD (C. A.D. 413–426)

Augustine also wrote *The City of God,* which has been called the first major philosophy of history. "It seeks no less a goal than to define God, man, and the world."[9] Augustine chose the city as a model because "the city was in his day the center . . . of culture and political life."[10]

Augustine contrasted the City of God with the "city of man." Those who trust in the true God are citizens of the City of God. This "city" is temporal here on earth and will—at the eschaton—become the eternal abode. The city of man—the present world—is peopled by the just and the unjust alike. It serves as a "training ground" for the saints who experience trials and testings along with the unjust. However, "The tide of trouble tests, purifies, and improves the good, where as it beats, crushes, and washes away the wicked."[11]

Augustine here addressed the pagan charge that Christians were responsible for the sack of Rome. He argued that this distinction occurred because of evil internal reasons and was a part of God's "permissive" will. In dealing with the issue of the divine permission of oppression, Augustine offered that "a good man, though a slave, is free; but a wicked man, though a King, is a slave."[12]

Themes addressed throughout this work include the providence of God, the nature and function of philosophy, and the nature of sin—which Augustine identifies primarily as pride. His purpose was to "give a newness to historical events, and yet he relates this newness to a providential order."[13] All of this activity has as its origin and purpose the love of God which is manifested in Jesus, who is God's "co-eternal Word, the Second Person of the Trinity, who essentially serves as the instrument of creation."[14]

What is striking about Augustine is that, although a committed Catholic bishop, his writings are claimed by both evangelical Protestants and Catho-

9. Ibid., p. 141.
10. Ibid.
11. Ibid.
12. Ibid., p. 142.
13. Ibid., p. 144.
14. Ibid.

lics. Indeed, through both Luther and Calvin, Augustine is in a real sense the grandfather of the Reformation. To this day many of the best known, and best worded, theological formulations of Christian truth used by orthodox Protestants are in the words of Augustine.

CUR DEUS HOMO (A.D. 1098)

The title means "Why the God-Man" and was written by Anselm, archbishop of Canterbury (c. A.D. 1033–1109). Anselm is considered the greatest theologian between Augustine and Aquinas and has been called the father of scholastic theology. (See chap. 5 concerning his contributions.)

This famous work was written "in the form of a dialogue or debate between Anselm and an friendly interlocutor named Boso, whose duty it is to raise and pursue the questions of faithful inquirers as well as unbelievers."[15] Its main purpose is to show that the debt incurred by humanity "calls for the payment of something that is more than the whole world and all that is not God."[16] Only God could satisfy such a payment, hence, "Of necessity, then, salvation calls for the work of a God-Man."[17] As already noted, the Reformers used Anselm's "satisfaction" theory of the atonement to good effect in constructing their theological system.

THE STEPS OF HUMILITY (A.D. 1129–1135)

The author is Bernard, abbot of Clairvaux (A.D. 1090–1153), and it is considered to be "contemplative" theology. Bernard's purpose was to identify humility as a cardinal virtue and discuss the steps leading to its apprehension. He was reluctant to write this work because "To write from his own motives and to satisfy his own desires would be a violation of the virtue he intends to describe."[18]

Bernard examined the elements that make up pride, such as curiosity, frivolity, foolish mirth, and the like. Christians of all persuasions have gained insight into the practice of holiness from this godly man.

SUMMA THEOLOGIAE

Although many evangelicals are loathe to admit it, their theology is heavily influenced by one of the greatest Christian theologians of all time, Thomas Aquinas (c. A.D. 1225–74).

15. Ibid., p. 203.
16. Ibid., p. 205.
17. Ibid.
18. Ibid., p. 206.

His magnum opus, *Summa Theologiae,* is the ultimate in theological dialogue. It is one of the greatest contributions any Christian mind has ever produced. Its basic view of God, of Christ, and even of salvation is so Calvinistic that it would shock most evangelicals, were they to take time to study the angelic doctor.

Arvin Vos is one of the few contemporary evangelicals to recognize this in his excellent book, *Aquinas, Calvin, and Contemporary Protestant Thought.*[19] Since we have thoroughly discussed Aquinas's many contributions to contemporary evangelical thought in *Thomas Aquinas: An Evangelical Appraisal,*[20] we will not belabor the point here. It suffices to give the conclusion: Evangelicals should not be singing "should Ole Aquinas be forgot and never brought to mind"!

THE DIVINE COMEDY (C. A.D. 1320)

The author is Dante Alighieri (A.D. 1265–1321) and the work falls into the category of "allegorical" poetry. The poem develops on four levels: literal, allegorical, moral, and analogical. As a story, Dante is sent on an "imaginary pilgrimage which Dante made through Hell, up the mountain of Purgatory, and outward through the celestial spheres into the very presence of the Triune God."[21]

The theological and philosophical structure of the poem is borrowed from some distinctly Roman Catholic dogmas—such as "Limbo" and "Purgatory." In spite of the problematic nature of the aforementioned doctrines for evangelicals, Dante's work can serve to illuminate medieval thought and he represents the best of Christian humanism in his era. Also, he describes God's splendor thusly: "There is a light up there which makes the Creator visible to that creature who, only in seeing Him, has its peace."[22]

THE LITTLE FLOWERS OF SAINT FRANCIS (C. A.D. 1322)

This book is a number of brief anecdotes concerning Francis of Assisi (A.D. 1181–1226). The author of *The Little Flowers* is unknown. The type of work is known as "hagiography," which are writings that comment on the lives, works, and sanctity of saints.[23] Francis was born in Assisi of middle-class parents. At age 20 he contracted an illness which triggered his conversion ex-

---

19. See Arvin Vos, *Aquinas, Calvin, and Contemporary Protestant Thought* (Grand Rapids: Eerdmans, 1985).
20. Geisler, *Thomas Aquinas: An Evangelical Appraisal.*
21. Ibid., p. 259.
22. Ibid., p. 261.
23. Broderick, *Catholic Concise Encyclopedia,* pp. 179–80.

perience. He discovered his gift was preaching and founded the Order of Friars Minor, subsequently called Franciscans.

This collection relates the virtues practiced by the followers of Francis, namely poverty, simplicity, humility, charity to the poor, and joy in the Lord. Francis traveled throughout many countries and his reputation for godliness grew and his religious communities flourished.

Of benefit for the modern reader is the glimpse one gets of the moral character of Francis: "He is tender without sentimentality, gentle to all—even to his enemies—and strong beneath his gentleness."[24] Francis of Assisi was a man so revered by his contemporaries as to be designated "the second Christ," a title made official by Pope Pius XI.[25] Catholics are not alone in taking spiritual inspiration from this godly man.

THE *DIALOGUE* OF CATHERINE OF SIENA (A.D. 1370)

This is a devotional meditation composed by Catherine of Siena (A.D. 1347–80). A woman of uncommon spirituality, Catherine lived in a time of moral laxity and ecclesiastical decadence. She ministered to the sick and poor during this turbulent period and was to become a trusted advisor to the pope.

The *Dialogue* is comprised of four sections: divine providence, discretion, prayer, and obedience. Her status in the Roman Catholic Church is such that she was designated a "Doctor of the Church" in 1970, an honor shared with just one other woman, Teresa of Avila.[26]

THE *IMITATION OF CHRIST* (A.D. 1418)

One of the most widely read books in the world outside the Bible, near the top of the all-time best sellers even for Protestants, was written by Catholic monk Thomas à Kempis (c. A.D. 1380–1471). Thomas was born at Kempen, near Cologne, of poor parents. After education at a school run by the Brethren of the Common Life, he entered the house of the Canons Regular, who adopted the Rule of St. Augustine. He lived there the rest of his life and became known as a writer, preacher, and spiritual advisor of great stature.

The major purpose of this work was to instruct Christians in the need and method of modeling Christ. The inner life is examined; the need for humility, contrition, self-discipline, and submission to spiritual superiors are stressed. Concerning the quality of this spirituality, it is said that: "The noblest product of this simple, mystical, churchly piety is the *Imitation of Christ*—a book

---

24. Magill, *Masterpieces of Christian Literature*, p. 266.

25. Encyclical "Rite Expiatis" (30 April 1926); quoted in Jaroslav Pelikan, *Jesus through the Centuries* (New York: Harper and Row, 1987), p. 133.

26. Magill, *Masterpieces of Christian Literature*, pp. 280–83.

the circulation of which has exceeded that of any other product of the Middle Ages."[27]

THE *LIFE* OF ST. TERESA OF AVILA (A.D. 1562)

This is a work about the spiritual life, written by St. Teresa herself. Teresa de Cepeda y Ahumada (A.D. 1515–82) possessed a keen intellect and her *Life* is an animated personal narrative. Teresa regarded an event that occurred when she was forty as her true conversion: "A picture of the wounded Christ and a copy of St. Augustine's *Confessions* were instrumental in bringing her to a new pitch of devotion."[28]

In the monastery, Teresa experienced a number of mystical ecstasies and raptures which were interpreted by some of her advisors as being Satanic in origin. However, her careful descriptions of these experiences lead one to conclude that she remained within the borders of authentic biblical faith.

Her *Life* advances the concept that Christian devotion mainly consists of mental prayer. She distinguishes four degrees of contemplation and her work is a spiritual classic. She founded the Discalced ("barefoot") Order of Carmelites with the help of a young monk who came to be known as St. John of the Cross. Like her predecessor, Catherine of Siena, St. Teresa was declared a "Doctor of the Church" in 1970.[29]

THE DARK NIGHT OF THE SOUL (A.D. 1587)

Written by St. John of the Cross (A.D. 1542–91), this is a manual for mystical contemplation. John was born in Fontiveros, Spain, and after a rather uneventful life joined the Carmelites and subsequently was ordained in A.D. 1567. In A.D. 1572, St. Teresa called him to Avila to minister at the Convent of the Incarnation. Because of his involvement in an ecclesiastical dispute, he was imprisoned in Toledo. During this time, he experienced visions and wrote *Dark Night of the Soul*.[30]

The central theme of this work is that the goal of the human soul is union with God. The process involved may include spiritual darkness and despair,

---

27. Williston Walker, *A History of the Christian Church*, 3d ed. (New York: Charles Scribner's Sons, 1970), p. 255. For a modern translation of this classic work, see William C. Creasy, *The Imitation of Christ: A New Reading of the 1441 Latin Autograph Manuscript* (Macon, Ga.: Mercer University Press, 1989).

28. Magill, *Masterpieces*, p. 393.

29. Ibid., pp. 392–95. The title "Doctor of the Church" is bestowed on eminent scholars and leaders who display great spiritual gifts and holiness of life. See Broderick, *Catholic Concise Encyclopedia*, p. 134.

30. John J. Delaney and James Tobin, *Dictionary of Catholic Biography* (Garden City, N.Y.: Doubleday, 1961), p. 620.

which is the first stage of spiritual progress. One is reminded of Job's tribulations, which were misunderstood by his "counselors."

John does not locate sin in earthly pleasures themselves. "What possess
and harm the soul are not the things of the world but rather the will and desire for them."[31] The end result of this exercise: "Supernatural being, communicated by love and grace, overcomes the dark night of the soul."[32] The
Catholic church has proclaimed St. John of the Cross the doctor par excel-
lence of ascetical and mystical theology. Concerning John and "Calvinist
mysticism," Fr. Louis Bouyer writes: "The most striking thing about St. John
of the Cross is that he draws his teaching from exactly the same Biblical
sources as Calvin and his successors, and that the dominant themes . . . are
just those which govern what we do not shrink from . . . calling Calvinist
mysticism."[33]

INTRODUCTION TO THE DEVOUT LIFE (A.D. 1609)

This work was authored by St. Francis of Sales (A.D. 1567–1622) and concerns Christian growth in sanctification and spiritual maturity. During his
time as bishop of Geneva, Francis counseled many men and women and
wrote a number of letters dealing with problems of a spiritual nature.

Francis of Sales was concerned to point out that "The religious life is not
a special vocation for a few Christians, but a possibility and so a duty for
all."[34] Although set in a Roman Catholic framework, the *Introduction* transcends denominational boundaries, for "In all Christian bodies, thousands
have found, and still find, that this book of religious counsel is sane, wise,
deeply perceptive, and unfailingly helpful."[35]

THE PRACTICE OF THE PRESENCE OF GOD (A.D. 1692)

Brother Lawrence, born Nicholas Herman (c. A.D. 1605–91), wrote this practical guide on Christian devotion. Brother Lawrence was a lay monk in a Pa-
risian monastery. His superior gathered letters and meditations written by
Lawrence and, supplemented by personal conversations with the monk,
gives us a picture of this remarkable man.

Brother Lawrence worked for fifteen years in the monastery kitchen and
later, because of lameness, became a cobbler. He performed the simplest of
tasks to the service of God, who can be "served as well in the kitchen or on

31. Magill, *Masterpieces of Christian Literature,* p. 409.
32. Ibid.
33. Bouyer, *Spirit and Forms of Protestantism,* p. 93.
34. Magill, *Masterpieces of Christian Literature,* p. 428.
35. Ibid., p. 432.

the battlefield as in the Church while receiving the Sacrament."[36] For Lawrence, "The service of God is primarily an affair of the will and not of the understanding."[37] This unassuming monk reflected in his work and posture the biblical injunction, "Do all for the glory of God."

PENSÉES (A.D. 1670)

The *Pensées* ("Thoughts") were written by Blaise Pascal (A.D. 1623–62). Possessing one of the most towering intellects in the modern world, he also was a devout and committed Catholic, interested in Scripture as well as science. As early as age 16 he made contributions to geometry, physics, applied mechanics, and mathematic formulations which still are useful in modern science. He suffered ill health and died before reaching age 40.

The *Pensées* were notes Pascal wanted to use to write an apology for the Christian religion. As religious literature, it ranks alongside such masterpieces as Augustine's *Confessions*. One of the significant ideas advanced here by Pascal is that "Man must learn to reflect upon himself and seek to understand himself in relation to the rest of nature."[38] Another is that humanity is "characterized by a peculiar ambivalence of misery and grandeur; on the one hand, man experiences a disproportion within himself and in his relation to nature; on the other hand, he is the highest of all creatures."[39]

Pascal had little use for the utilization of pure reason in the task of understanding God's existence, preferring the "God of Abraham, Isaac and Jacob" to the God of the philosophers. This is evident in his famous statement "The heart has reasons of which the mind knows nothing." He was steadfastly Christocentric in his faith. For Pascal, "Apart from Jesus Christ we do not know what is our life, nor our death, nor God, nor ourselves."[40] Here again, his faith transcends his own religious jurisdiction and is widely embraced by Protestants.

MARTYROLOGY

A "martyr" by Christian definition is a person who, rather than deny Christ, gives up his or her life (Heb. 10:26–31). Tertullian (c. A.D. 160–225) the African church father said: "The blood of martyrs is the seed of the Church." History is replete with examples of faithful Christians who gave up their lives

36. Ibid., p. 544.
37. Ibid.
38. Ibid., p. 515.
39. Ibid.
40. Ibid., p. 518.

in witness for the gospel. While there have been numerous notable martyrs, both Catholic and Protestant, it seems fitting to mention briefly one such modern example, Fr. Maximilian Kolbe.

MAXIMILIAN KOLBE

Raymond Kolbe was born in Zdunska Wola, Poland, in 1894. He was the second of five sons whose parents labored as piecework weavers, a trade which barely provided a livelihood.

Kolbe entered the Franciscan seminary in Lwow in 1910, and was given the name Maximilian. He was a brilliant student and earned a Ph.D. in philosophy at the Pontifical Gregorian University in Rome. He would subsequently receive another doctorate, the Th.D. in theology.

As impressive as Kolbe's intellectual accomplishments were it was his deep spirituality that most commended him to his contemporaries. When he was in his early twenties he wrote to his mother: "Pray that I will love without any limits." The one who was known by his friends as "another St. Francis" would be given an opportunity to display such love.

After leaving Rome, Fr. Maximilian taught in Cracow, Poland, and in 1930 traveled to Nagasaki, Japan and established a mission. He returned to Teresin, Poland, in 1936 and became director of a work, "Niepokalanow," which he had started before his trip to Japan.

On September 1, 1939, Germany invaded Poland. Fr. Maximilian was arrested by the Nazis and was imprisoned with a number of his fellow Franciscans. Released from custody on December 10, Fr. Maximilian returned to Niepokalanow and reorganized the friary. Kolbe turned "the Franciscan friary he founded into a hospice for displaced Polish Jews, gentiles, and German invaders alike, with a sense of brotherhood that simply did not include the words 'enemy' or 'unlovable' in its vocabulary."[41]

On February 17, 1941, Kolbe was arrested by the Gestapo and imprisoned in Warsaw. On May 28 he was transferred to Auschwitz as prisoner no. 16,670. In August, as punishment for the escape of one prisoner, the S.S. chose ten prisoners to be sent to a special bunker where they were to be starved to death.

One of the chosen, Francis Gajowniczek, overcome with the realization of his fate, broke down. "My wife and my children," he sobbed. The S.S. ignored him. Then "there is movement in the still ranks. A prisoner several rows back has broken out and is pushing his way toward the front."[42] The S.S. tense and raise their weapons. The man is Maximilian Kolbe. He posi-

---

41. Patricia Treece, *A Man for Others: Maximilian Kolbe, Saint of Auschwitz* (San Francisco: Harper and Row, 1982), p. viii.
42. Ibid., p. 170.

tions himself before the officer in charge: "'Herr Kommandant, I wish to make a request, please,' he says politely in flawless German."[43] Kolbe continued, "I want to die in place of this prisoner." "Why?" the officer asked: "'I have no wife or children. Besides I'm old and not good for anything. He's in better condition,' he adds, adroitly playing on the Nazi line that only the fit should live."[44] The request was granted. Fr. Maximilian was stripped naked and put in the starvation bunker.

Kolbe ministered to his fellow prisoners, praying, hearing confessions, and singing hymns. Two weeks went by. One by one, the weakened men died; only four were left, including Fr. Maximilian. The S.S. decided that things were taking too long. A prisoner from the hospital was sent to the bunker and he gave the remaining prisoners lethal injections of carbolic acid. On August 14, 1941, Fr. Maximilian Kolbe, "the man for others," gave his life for another. His body was cremated the following day.

In 1971 the Beatification Process for Fr. Maximilian was begun by Pope Paul VI in St. Peter's Basilica, Rome, and in 1982 he was canonized a saint by Pope John Paul II. Maximilian Kolbe was but one of many Christians who suffered and gave their lives in witness for Christ. In emulating his Savior, Fr. Maximilian's sacrifice serves as an example for all believing Christians.

HYMNOLOGY

The singing of hymns has had a place of importance in Christian worship from the beginning. Here too Protestants are indebted to Roman Catholics. We sing a common heritage in many of the great old hymns.

Our common hymnic heritage is rooted in the Scriptures, which repeatedly encourage the singing of hymns and spiritual songs. In Psalm 40 David offers up a hymn of thanksgiving amidst the worshipers in the temple: "he put a new song into my mouth, a hymn to our God" (v. 4). This tradition is carried over into the New Testament. After the Lord instituted his Supper, he and the disciples sang a hymn and departed (Matt. 26:30; Mark 14:26). In the Book of Acts we find the apostle Paul and Silas imprisoned at Philippi, before their miraculous release, praying and singing hymns to God while the other prisoners listened (Acts 16:25).

In Romans, Paul encourages believers to witness among the Gentiles by singing praises to God's name (Rom. 15:9). He tells the Ephesian church to "be filled with the Spirit, addressing one another [in] psalms and hymns and spiritual songs, singing and playing to the Lord in your hearts" (Eph. 5:18–

---

43. Ibid.
44. Ibid., p. 171.

19). And in Colossians, Paul directs the believers to "let the word of Christ dwell in you richly, as in all wisdom you teach and admonish one another, singing psalms, hymns, and spiritual songs with gratitude in your hearts to God" (Col. 3:16).

MEDIEVAL CATHOLIC HYMNS

Eastern Christians in the Syrian, Byzantine, and Armenian churches placed great emphasis on the singing of hymns. Several examples illustrate this fact. Ambrose (A.D. 333/9–397), bishop of Milan, introduced the Syrian custom of singing hymns at Milan. "St. Ambrose's hymns set a simple style which persisted throughout the Middle Ages."[45] Anatolius (d. A.D. 458), archbishop of Constantinople, wrote a number of hymns, one of which is "The Day Is Past and Over."[46] Andrew (c. A.D. 660–732), archbishop of Crete, wrote several Canons for Lent and Pentecost as well as the hymn "Christian, Dost Thou See Them."[47] Bernard of Clairvaux (c. A.D. 1091–1153), a famous preacher of the Middle Ages who founded a number of monasteries of the Cistercian order, wrote several well-known hymns: "O Sacred Head, Sore Wounded," "Jesus, the Very Thought of Thee," and "Jesus, Thou Joy of Loving Hearts."[48] These are sung heartily by Protestants to this day, nearly a millennium later. Clement of Alexandria (c. A.D. 170–220), sometimes called the father of Greek theology, wrote the hymn "Sunset to Sunrise Changes Now."[49] John of Damascus (c. A.D. 696–754), considered one of the last of the Greek church fathers, organized liturgical chants and authored a number of hymns, such as "Come, Ye Faithful, Raise the Strain," "Stars of the Morning," and "So Gloriously Bright."[50] John Henry Newman (A.D. 1801–90), a convert from the Church of England to Roman Catholicism, is noted for his theological writings, but he also authored the well-known hymn "Lead Kindly Light."

REFORMATION HYMNS

The Reformation carried forward the tradition of hymnology in the church. Concerning Protestantism and the singing of hymns, Fr. Louis Bouyer comments: "The mode of devotional expression generally preferred, particularly in the Lutheran countries (Germany and Scandinavia) and the Anglo-Saxon

---

45. *The Hymnal 1940 Companion* (New York: Church Pension Fund, 1951), p. 545. Prepared for the Protestant Episcopal Church in the U.S.A.
46. Ibid.
47. Ibid., p. 546.
48. Ibid.
49. Ibid.
50. Ibid., p. 549.

ones, is the popular hymn."[51] About Luther's most famous hymn, "A Mighty Fortress Is Our God" (now sung in many Catholic churches), Bouyer comments: "This hymn has no trace of superstitious terror; its most striking feature is the virile, joyful defiance of the Christian sustained by faith."[52]

Bouyer is also appreciative of English Protestant hymns. Concerning the compositions of Charles Wesley he states: "In this form of Protestantism the grace of God in Christ is, certainly, everything. But this grace is viewed in the most orthodox light; it is a power transforming our whole life and being, not a substitute for this change."[53] Also, "Nowhere could be found more definitely stated the doctrine of salvation by grace alone in Christ."[54] Generous praise indeed from a Roman Catholic scholar regarding the spiritual worth of Protestant hymnody.

We have only touched lightly on the vast body of literature and sacred music that Roman Catholics and evangelicals share. One need only mention, for example, the Catholic composer Hayden's great oratorio, *The Creation,* to say nothing of the arts, where the name of Catholic artist Michaelangelo looms over the history of Christian art. Perhaps reading this chapter will bring awareness for the first time to some evangelicals that many literary works and hymns that they treasure have Roman Catholic origins.

OTHER ARTISTIC EXPRESSIONS

Space constraints prevent us from examining poetry in any detail. We will mention one example. Francis Thompson (1859–1907) was a Roman Catholic poet born in Lancashire, England. As a college student, he developed a drug habit and ended up in the slums as an addict. Friends put him into a hospital where he was cured of his addiction and he subsequently entered the Capuchin monastery in Pantasaph, Wales. His *Hound of Heaven* is considered one of the greatest Christian poems ever penned. In it Christ is the magnificent hound pursuing his prey—the elect—through the corridors of time.[55]

We also have said nothing about Eastern Orthodoxy and its considerable body of spirituality. For example, it is in the Russian classic *The Way of a Pilgrim* that we encounter the "Lord, Jesus Christ have mercy on me," which is repeated many times and is an integral part of devotion in some Orthodox communities.

51. Bouyer, *Spirit and Forms,* p. 24.
52. Ibid., p. 26.
53. Ibid., p. 32.
54. Ibid.
55. Delaney and Tobin, *Dictionary of Catholic Biography,* p. 1121.

COMMON INVESTIGATIVE EFFORTS

Thomas Oden, professor of theology and ethics at Drew University in Madison, New Jersey, became a member of the Evangelical Theological Society in 1990. Oden had for many years "distrusted anything that faintly smelled of orthodoxy."[56] However, a reintroduction to the literature of the Greek and Latin fathers has brought him to a place where he now has as his goal "to set forth the classical teaching of God the Father, Son, and Spirit, on which there has been substantial intergenerational agreement between traditions of east and west, Catholic, eastern orthodox, (and) classical evangelical Protestantism."[57]

Geoffrey Bromiley echoes this same theme. Concerning the study of the early church fathers "a new patristic investigation of these themes be pursued, if possible in friendly dialogue with Roman Catholic theologians."[58] Indeed, he claims that "What is needed is that evangelical and Roman Catholic theologians, preferably together, attempt a strictly objective historical study of the Fathers apart from the views and positions of a later time."[59] Thus, an investigation into our common spiritual heritage might bring insights to bear on the faith that we all—Roman Catholics, Orthodox, and evangelicals—share.

A FINAL WORD

Appreciating spiritual heritages across denominational lines is evident in the respect that traditional Roman Catholics exhibit for the contributions of C. S. Lewis (1898–1963). Lewis, born in Belfast, Ireland, was a brilliant academician and, after his conversion from agnosticism, he became a staunch defender of orthodox Christianity. He published more than forty books, many of which deal with apologetics, the defense of the faith. One of his lesser known works is a delightful little book that tells of an ongoing correspondence between Lewis and Don Giovanni Calabria of Verona, a Roman

---

56. Thomas Oden, "The Long Journey Home," *Journal of the Evangelical Theological Society* 34, no. 1, (March 1991): 85.

57. Ibid., p. 79.

58. Geoffrey W. Bromiley, "Promise of Patristic Studies," in *Toward a Theology for the Future,* ed. by David F. Wells and Clark H. Pinnock (Carol Stream, Ill.: Creation House, 1971), p. 148.

59. Ibid.

Catholic priest.[60] C. S. Lewis lived and died a practicing Anglican and is revered by orthodox Christians from all jurisdictions.[61]

Another example of respect across denominational lines is the grudging admiration that thoroughgoing Calvinist James Sauer holds for that remarkable man of letters, Roman Catholic G. K. Chesterton (1874–1936). Born in London, Chesterton, among his other achievements, was an effective apologist—much in the same strain as his successor C. S. Lewis.[62] In a journal article Sauer thanks God that "Not only did he choose me to be among his chosen people, but he also destined me to be among that other elect who have had the privilege of meeting through literature the great mind and good heart of Gilbert Keith Chesterton."[63] Sauer acknowledges that he has difficulty with some of Chesterton's Roman Catholic notions, "But where he measures up to the Word of Life, we will embrace him, we will feed upon him, we will learn from him."[64] It is important to recognize the common ingredients shared by believers who honor Scripture and recite the creeds in faith. By all means, let us defend our theological distinctions—while laboring together, when possible, "for the faith that was once for all entrusted to the saints."[65]

60. Martin Moynihan, *The Latin Letters of C. S. Lewis* (Westchester, Ill.: Crossway, 1987).

61. John D. Woodbridge, ed., *Great Leaders of the Christian Church* (Chicago: Moody Press, 1988), pp. 355–60.

62. Delaney and Tobin, *Dictionary of Catholic Biography*, p. 246.

63. "Chesterton Reformed: A Protestant Interpretation," *Antithesis* 1, no. 6, (Nov./Dec. 1990): 27.

64. Ibid.

65. Jude 3 (NIV).

20

EVANGELISM

For the past forty years, the authors have had the opportunity to dialogue with believers of the Roman Catholic persuasion, from both the clergy and the lay side of the house, of traditional as well as a charismatic bent. Indeed, we have participated in efforts to teach the Word of God to Catholic believers. As a result of this, as well as the changing landscape, the question of areas of possible cooperation between Catholics and evangelicals has emerged. Controversial as it is for many Catholics as well as evangelicals, it is our purpose here to explore some contemporary efforts in such cooperation. As Harold O. J. Brown has written, "to the extent that a Catholic and a Protestant are orthodox, there is more by far that unites them than divides them, particularly over against the monolithic secular culture of today."[1]

It is important to note that we must repeat that we are not talking about ecclesiastical union. There are, as we have seen in Part Two, apparently insurmountable obstacles for orthodox Catholics and conservative evangelicals. What we make reference to here is exploring areas of personal and social cooperation, as well as evangelistic efforts, noting some of our common spiritual heritage. We speak here of evangelistic efforts where the gospel is clearly proclaimed (1 Cor. 15:1–6), such as the Billy Graham Crusades, and in which Catholics participate.

MORE THAN SACRIFICE AND OFFERINGS

Merely participating in baptism, confirmation, the eucharistic event, and the rest of the sacramental system, without personally encountering Jesus Christ, will not save anyone. It goes without saying that this is true for all Christian systems: Baptist, Eastern Orthodox, Lutheran, Methodist, Pentecostal, Presbyterian, or Roman Catholic. It is sadly true that a person can be reared in a

---

1. Brown, *Protest of a Troubled Protestant*, p. 255.

Christian environment and never be truly converted; knowing *about* Christ, but never believing *in* him.

It may come as a surprise to some Protestants to learn that some firmly entrenched Roman Catholics have come to the same conclusion: Christian salvation involves more than cultural accretion. Léon Joseph Cardinal Suenens, a major participant at Vatican II, writes: "It was not the truth about Jesus but the truth of Jesus which was at the basis of conversion." Further, "Experiencing Christ comes of necessity before the definition of that experience. St. Thomas Aquinas, a theologian whom no one would suspect of anti-intellectualism teaches that the object of faith is not found in doctrinal propositions concerning God, but in God himself known and loved in a personal relationship." Suenens adds, "To be a true Christian means, further more, to have met Jesus personally, as Saviour, and as Lord. I must accept Jesus totally, as a reality, the Lord and Master of my life as I live and experience it day by day." For "During what we call the Christian centuries, it was commonly accepted that a Christian was, in the first place, someone who 'practiced' his religion. . . . Faith was judged by a perceptible norm: namely, the practice of one's religion."[2]

In the same volume, Cardinal Suenens quotes from a French bishop, saying, "We held the Vatican II Council in the belief it was self-evident that Christians were essentially destined to be missionaries. But that presupposes that they are believers. . . . In fact, this was true only of a few."[3] Suenens adds, "We must help Christians to become continually more aware of their faith and live it on a more personal level. Many must be helped to exchange a sociological Christianity for a full and active life of faith." Hence, "Christianity which we have inherited, which has its foundation mainly in the family and education, must mature into a Christianity of choice, based on a personal decision and embraced with full consciousness. As Tertullian said 'Christians become so, they are not born.'"[4]

Noted evangelical and Anglican Bible teacher John R. W. Stott, in a work concerning twentieth-century preaching, offers the following statement from John Chrysostom, who occupied the pulpit of the Cathedral in Antioch before becoming bishop of Constantinople in A.D. 398. Speaking of the healing of the body of Christ, Chrysostom said: "One only means and one way of cure has been given us . . . and that is teaching of the Word."[5] Stott also mentions Dominic (A.D. 1170–1221), who was the founder of the Order of Friars Preachers, and Humbert de Romans (d. A.D. 1277), a Minister General in the Dominican order, who said: "Christ only once heard Mass . . . but he laid

---

2. Léon Joseph Cardinal Suenens, *A New Pentecost?* (New York: Seabury Press, 1975), pp. 59, 63, 116, 119.

3. Bishop G. Huyghe, *L' Eglise d' Arras;* quoted in ibid., p. 120.

4. Suenens, *A New Pentecost?* p. 121.

5. Stott, *Between Two Worlds,* p. 20.

great stress on prayer and preaching, especially on preaching."[6] The Franciscan Bernardino of Siena (A.D. 1380–1444) makes this "evangelical-like" statement concerning preaching: "If of these two things you can do only one—either hear the mass or hear the sermon—you should let the mass go, rather than the sermon. . . . There is less peril for your soul in not hearing the mass than in not hearing the sermon."[7]

It seems that Suenens, Chrysostom, Dominic, and Bernardino could share the pulpit with Billy Graham and John MacArthur, and the difference in the essential message content—at least soteriologically—would be inconsequential. Having attempted to show agreement between medieval and evangelical thinking as to the need for and the purpose of preaching, let us examine some contemporary situations.

CONTEMPORARY "EVANGELICAL" CATHOLICS

In a volume edited by David F. Wells and John D. Woodbridge we find the following comment by a sociologist: "Into some evangelical groups Seventh Day Adventists, Pentecostalists, and Roman Catholics who have an evangelical spirit are accepted with open arms and a warm welcome."[8] Keith A. Fournier, an attorney who serves as General Counsel and Dean of Evangelism at Franciscan University of Steubenville in Ohio, calls himself an "evangelical Catholic" because he believes that the Christian's main task is to proclaim the good news. "I am an evangelical Catholic Christian—without contradiction in terms, logic, theology, or history."[9] Fournier continues, "We were made for God. That's why we respond to political and philosophical ideals that are greater than us." Therefore, "As Christians, we have the incredible opportunity to tell people that what they are reaching for is summed up in Jesus Christ."[10] In a later work, Fournier states, "There are times when those who profess to be Protestant, Catholic, or Orthodox are not truly followers of Christ. They need to know Him personally as their Savior and Lord."[11] It is this kind of Roman Catholic with whom many evangelicals wish to align themselves to face the unbelief of this culture.

6. Ibid., p. 22.
7. Ibid.
8. David O. Moberg, "Fundamentalists and Evangelicals in Society," in *The Evangelicals: What They Believe, Who They Are, Where They Are Changing*, ed. David F. Wells and John D. Woodbridge (Nashville: Abingdon, 1975), p. 144.
9. Keith A. Fournier, *Evangelical Catholics: A Call for Christian Cooperation to Penetrate the Darkness with the Light of the Gospel* (Nashville: Nelson, 1990), p. 21.
10. Keith A. Fournier, *Religious Cleansing in the American Republic* (Washington, D.C.: Liberty, Life and Family Publications, 1993), p. 43.
11. Keith A. Fournier with William D. Watkins, *A House United? Evangelicals and Catholics Together* (Colorado Springs: NavPress, 1994), p. 143.

COOPERATIVE EVANGELISTIC CRUSADES

When the topic of evangelism is raised, the image of Billy Graham inevitably comes to mind. Born near Charlotte, North Carolina, in 1918, Graham has preached the gospel to more people than any evangelist in history. Reaching nearly one hundred million people in his crusades, in addition to vast numbers by radio and television, two million individuals have declared their faith in Jesus Christ under his ministry.

Although Graham's efforts to keep his evangelistic meetings free of any racial segregation are well known, his acceptance of prayer and active support from Roman Catholics in his crusades is not common knowledge. He has had many Roman Catholic clerics on the platform with him, including such important national figures as Cardinal John J. O'Connor of New York and Cardinal Bernard Law of Boston.

NEGATIVE REACTION

On the Protestant side, reaction to cooperative efforts from many fundamentalists is well known. Bob Jones University and those who identify with their stand have opposed cooperative evangelism as compromise. While many are willing to admit that Graham has not compromised the basic gospel *message*, they believe his *methods* compromise the truth. They object particularly to Graham's "fellowship" with "unbelievers" in having them on the platform and even turning over "converts" to these "liberal," that is, non-fundamental, churches.

The problem with fundamentalism began with Billy Graham's New York crusade in 1957. In addition to support from local fundamentalists, Graham accepted aid and endorsement from the city's Council of Churches. This resulted in converts being directed to liberal churches and denominations. Fundamentalists such as Carl McIntire, John R. Rice, and Bob Jones, Sr., took exception to Graham's perceived capitulation with liberalism and attempted to discredit the New York campaign before it even started. Indeed, at the conclusion of the crusade, Carl McIntire stated that the effort was, "'a distinct defeat for the fundamentalists' and a victory for modernism and apostasy."[12]

The fundamentalist camp was later to split into two factions: militant fundamentalists and moderate fundamentalists. The militants "not only strictly insist on separation from denominations that tolerate theological liberalism, but also refuse fellowship even with fundamentalist individuals in such de-

---

12. "About Billy Graham," *Beacon*, 11 April 1957, p. 1; 25 April 1957, p. 3; quoted in Louis Gasper, *The Fundamentalist Movement 1930–1956* (Grand Rapids: Baker, 1963), p. 142.

nominations."[13] This approach became known as "second-degree separation." The distinction would later cause a rupture between Bob Jones III (more
militant) and John R. Rice (more moderate) because of Rice's friendly relationship with fundamentalist leaders in the Southern Baptist Convention.[14]

Most evangelicals, however, rejoice in the fact that Graham has never
compromised his basic message. They stress the good biblical follow-up material used with converts, being willing to trust them to the continuing ministry of the Holy Spirit.

Interestingly, not all traditional Catholics are as charitably inclined toward Graham's non-sectarian efforts to present the good news as the aforementioned prelates. Consider the following article of concern, which appeared in the weekly Catholic newspaper, *The Wanderer*.

"The cardinal archbishop of Philadelphia has told his people that Dr.
Billy Graham has traveled the world preaching the Gospel of Salvation."

> On the other hand, he does seem to preach some things that are not recogniz-
> able as part of Christ's Good News: the supremacy of the Scriptures as the
> sole Revelation, the necessity of "putting on Christ" by public testimony of
> commitment to Jesus, . . . indeed, the general fundamentalist Protestant
> understanding of what is involved in salvation. . . . The cardinal might have
> wished only to take advantage of Dr. Graham's generous offer to have Cath-
> olic priests present to counsel Catholics who might make themselves known
> at his "Crusade" last June. But that hardly justifies speaking of and endorsing
> Dr. Graham as a preacher of the Gospel of salvation, when he is merely one
> in a line of many Protestant revivalists. . . . It is alien to Christian tradition
> that the role of preaching the Gospel be done by laymen.[15]

We wonder if the author can be totally unaware of the valuable contributions
that lay people such as the tentmakers Priscilla and Aquila, who assisted Paul
in the formation of the church at Corinth, made in early Christianity.

POSITIVE CATHOLIC COOPERATION

Christianity Today made a much more positive statement concerning Billy
Graham's Crusade held in Budapest, Hungary, in July 1989, reported to be
the largest public evangelistic service ever held in Eastern Europe—some
90,000 people came to listen, and more than 25,000 of them responded to

13. George M. Marsden, "Fundamentalism and American Evangelicalism," in Donald W.
Dayton and Robert K. Johnston, eds., *The Variety of American Evangelicalism* (Downers
Grove, Ill.: InterVarsity Press, 1991), p. 31.

14. The two positions are detailed in ibid., n. 23.

15. Frank Morriss, "Billy Graham and the Gospel of Salvation," *The Wanderer*, 6 August
1992. Some would say that *The Wanderer* is to traditional Catholicism what John R. Rice's
magazine, the *Sword of the Lord*, was to a past generation of Protestant fundamentalists.

Graham's invitation to "come to Christ." In addition to the support of the local Protestant churches, the effort

> also attracted Catholic involvement. Catholic Bishop Endre Kovacs of Mis-kole was among 2,000 who took training classes held in both Catholic and Protestant churches for prospective counselors and follow-up workers. And the country's Catholic primate, Laszlo Cardinal Paskai, issued a strong endorsement of Graham's mission and message from the stadium platform. "We need economic renewal in Hungary," Paskai told the crowd, "but first of all we need spiritual and moral renewal from Jesus." He led in an unscheduled prayer, asking for a special divine anointing of Graham and that "many tonight might recognize Jesus as the way, the truth, and the life."[16]

Thus, we have a Roman Catholic cardinal cooperating with a Southern Baptist preacher in an evangelistic crusade—an interesting spectacle to say the least.

COMMENTS FROM ONE WHO HAS BEEN ON BOTH SIDES

Concerning Billy Graham, we will quote from a journal article written by Thomas Howard, a recent convert from evangelicalism to Roman Catholicism. Howard formerly taught English at Gordon College, a respected evangelical institution in Massachusetts. In his book *Evangelical Is Not Enough,* he describes his "pilgrimage from Evangelicalism (which he loves and reveres as the religion of his youth) to liturgical [Roman Catholic] Christianity."[17] Howard writes:

> The name of Billy Graham is virtually synonymous in the minds of most people with the word *evangelization.* Here is a man—a Protestant, to be sure—who circles the globe, decade after decade. Literally millions upon millions of men and women, in every continent now, have heard the Christian message as Graham casts it, namely, Jesus Christ is the Son of God, His death on the Cross was the sacrifice for the sins of the world, and His rising from the dead the victory over sin and death. Come to Him—believe in Him—commit yourself in total obedience to Him—accept Him as your Savior—and you will have eternal life. You will be a Christian.

Howard continues,

16. Edward Plowman, "*Glasnost* Opens Way for Graham," *Christianity Today,* 8 September 1989. One author (Ralph MacKenzie) had this event personally confirmed to him by Clifford Anderson, dean of Bethel Theological Seminary, West in San Diego, California. Dr. Anderson attended this crusade as a representative of the Baptist General Conference and witnessed the events described in the *Christianity Today* article.

17. Thomas Howard, *Evangelical Is Not Enough: Worship of God in Liturgy and Sacrament* (San Francisco: Ignatius Press, 1984), back cover.

As you know, Billy Graham appears at the hither end of a lineage which reaches back through Billy Sunday to D. L. Moody, Charles G. Finney, and thence to John Wesley and beyond. A question arises here: is this kind of evangelism a strictly Reformation phenomenon? Is it a vitiated Gospel? What, exactly, was the message which, say, Martin of Tours preached among the Gauls? Or Augustine to Ethelbert and his Kentish subjects in 597 A.D.? What did Cyril and Methodius preach on the banks of the Danube? Or St. Philip among the Ethiopians, or Thomas on the banks of the Ganges?

About evangelicals, Howard adds:

First, they love the Gospel in all of its thrilling clarity; and second, their conversions are genuine. . . . We cannot lump the evangelicals together with groups like the Jehovah's Witnesses, the Mormons, or the Reverend Sun Myung Moon's outfit, since the evangelicals are as briskly Nicene, Chalcedonian, and Constantinopolitan as the Catholics. Their critique of the cults would be identical with the Catholic critique: you people have added new and unwarranted notions to the apostolic faith.

When asked about Roman Catholics and evangelism, Howard replies:

There is no Catholic figure analogous to any of the mass evangelists that have sprung from the Reformation. In our own time, Bishop Sheen was probably the closest analogue. In the early centuries of the Church, of course, something like mass evangelism certainly took place with the preaching of figures like Martin of Tours or Augustine of Kent, when whole kingdoms converted. Do we, when we speak of evangelization, visualize some electrifying Catholic figure analogous to Billy Graham?

Howard concludes that the message Billy Graham proclaims is the one that Christians from all jurisdictions should deliver.

But surely the message to us, what with one thing and another in our own decade—the widespread slumping away of loyalty to the *Magisterium* on the part of the Catholic laity, and the plummet in vocations, and the sheer decibel-level and speed and razzle-dazzle of the messages drowning out the Christian Gospel, and the melancholy efforts at shoring up catechesis in our parishes by curricula that will undertake anything in heaven and earth *except* to hail kids abruptly with Christ Jesus the Savior—surely the message to us is, at least: Whatever else you are doing, tell your children, tell your parishioners, tell the yuppies and the paupers and the dying and the disfranchised and the complacent and the perplexed—tell them that God so loved the world that He gave His only-begotten Son that whosoever believeth in Him should not perish but have everlasting life.[18]

18. Thomas Howard, "Witness for the Faith: What Catholics Can Learn from Billy Graham," *Crisis* (April 1991): 38–41.

In contrast to Howard, we believe that "evangelical" is indeed enough, and that Howard's book can be critiqued at a number of points. However, he is irenic and attempts to avoid a triumphalistic attitude. He certainly follows C. S. Lewis who instructed about the Christian church as a whole: "When you have reached your own room, be kind to those who have chosen different doors and to those who are still in the hall."[19] At any rate, Tom Howard and Billy Graham appear to be "on the same page" concerning evangelism.

Billy Graham spoke to more than 150,000 people during three meetings in Moscow's Olympic Arena in October 1992. Unfortunately, his reception was less cordial with the Russian Orthodox leaders than it had been with Roman Catholics. Despite the Orthodox hierarchy's reluctance, Graham received support from individual priests and preached with great power.[20]

Shortly after the announcement of the Billy Graham 1993 Columbus, Ohio crusade, Roman Catholic Bishop James A. Griffin made the following editorial comment: "Dr. Graham's sermons, which emphasize the basic scriptural message of repentance, conversion and commitment to Christ, appeal to Christians of all denominations, and his crusades have proven to be effective means of reaching secularized people who have never known Christ, and reaching those who have drifted away from active religious involvement."[21]

Sterling Huston, Graham's director of crusades in North America, states that "Roman Catholic involvement has grown significantly during the past 10 to 15 years." Further, "Some Catholic leaders now serve as official representatives on crusade planning committees. And Catholics are welcome as ushers, choir members, and even counselors."[22] It should be noted that all counselors, regardless of their ecclesiological affiliation, are required to take Graham's "Christian Life and Witness" classes before participating in a crusade.[23]

The recent Catholic catechism directs Christians as follows: "Those who with God's help have welcomed Christ's call and freely responded to it are urged on by love of Christ to proclaim the Good News everywhere in the world."[24]

---

19. C. S. Lewis, *Mere Christianity* (New York: Macmillan, 1943), p. 12.

20. "Finally, for the Faithful," *World,* 31 October 1992, pp. 18–19.

21. "Catholics and the Billy Graham Crusade," *The Catholic Times* (Columbus, Ohio), 24 September 1993, p. 4.

22. David Duggins, "Evangelicals and Catholics: Across the Divide," *Moody Monthly* (November 1993): 26–27.

23. The authors wish to thank Dr. John N. Akers, special assistant to Dr. Billy Graham, for much of the information concerning Roman Catholic involvement in crusade activities.

24. *Catechism of the Catholic Church,* no. 3, p. 7.

THE CATHOLIC RENEWAL MOVEMENT

Whenever the person or work of the Holy Spirit has been ignored or under-valued the body of Christ has suffered. It is important to note that Jesus does not begin his ministry until after his anointing by the Holy Spirit, and he acts only in the Spirit's power and not his own (Luke 4:14; 5:17; 11:20; cf. parallel passage, Matt. 12:28).[25]

A BRIEF HISTORICAL BACKGROUND

The early church fathers held the Holy Spirit in high esteem. The same applies to the later Reformers; Calvin could be described as the theologian of the Spirit and the Word.[26]

The twentieth century has witnessed a great outpouring of the power and influence of the Holy Spirit concerning the kingdom of God. Not only the formation of the Pentecostal churches, but also the charismatic renewal movements in the mainline Protestant and Roman Catholic Church are a part of this outpouring, as well as many evangelistic non-charismatic groups. We should mention the Cursillo Movement which originated in 1949 in Majorca, Spain, under the direction of Bishop Juan de Hervas. A forerunner of the current charismatic renewal movement, Cursillo seeks, mainly through retreats, to motivate Christians to live an integrated Christian life. In 1957, a young Spanish-born Franciscan priest named Gabriel Fernandez gathered a group of seventeen young men on a weekend retreat in Texas for what was to be the first Cursillo in America. The movement has since been adapted by other denominations, including the United Methodist (Emmaus Walk) and the Episcopal church (Episcopal Cursillo). Many leaders of the Catholic Charismatic Renewal Movement (notably Ralph Martin) have come out of the Cursillo movement.[27]

It is unlikely that any form of charismatic activity would have been accepted by the Roman Catholic Church were it not for Vatican II. First, a decision was made that the Roman Catholic Church should participate actively in cooperation with Protestants. Second, the Catholic church recognized the importance of charismatic gifts to the life of the church (some council members resisted this premise but Cardinal Suenens and his influence carried the day). Third, Vatican II stated that holy living and spiritual activism are to be pursued by the laity as well as the clergy.

25. D. A. Tappeiner, "Holy Spirit," *International Standard Bible Encyclopedia (ISBE)*, vol. 2 (Grand Rapids: Eerdmans, 1988), pp. 733–35.

26. Ibid., pp. 742–45.

27. "Cursillo Movement," *The Concise Dictionary of the Christian Tradition* (Grand Rapids: Zondervan, 1989), p. 113.

It is generally agreed that the formation of the prayer group at Duquesne University in 1967, which consisted of faculty and students, was the beginning of the renewal movement in the Roman Catholic Church.[28] The movement soon spread to Notre Dame and Michigan State. In September 1967, Ralph Martin and Stephen Clark (both graduates of Notre Dame) were invited to the University of Michigan in Ann Arbor to work in campus ministry. Their efforts had a major impact on the Catholic Charismatic Renewal (CCR) movement; South Bend and Ann Arbor have become the main centers of influence among Roman Catholic charismatics.

The growth rate of this movement can be illustrated by the following statistics: In 1969, 450 people attended the annual CCR Conference at Notre Dame; by 1976 the number of attendants had increased to 30,000 (that year about 500 priests celebrated the Eucharist and Léon Joseph Cardinal Suenens gave the homily at this gathering). CCR has spread internationally and now is thriving in more than 100 countries. Rome has not been immune to the effect of this phenomenon. At Cardinal Suenens' request, a special audience was granted by Pope Paul VI, who warmly greeted a group of charismatic leaders. A second international congress took place in Rome in 1975, with 10,000 in attendance. One gets the impression that the CCR is firmly rooted in the Catholic church and will be around for a while.[29]

LAY CATHOLIC EVANGELIST JOHN CLAUDER

One local parish that has been influenced by the Catholic Charismatic Renewal Movement is St. Francis Church in Vista, California. The church's pastor, Fr. Douglas Regin, takes the gospel mandate seriously and employs a number of different means to that end. An important member of the St. Francis staff is lay evangelist John Clauder, preacher and drummer extraordinaire. Clauder was bitten by the rock 'n' roll bug at age fourteen and became a drummer, playing with such groups as The Mamas and the Papas, Sonny and Cher, and the Righteous Brothers. Although he had everything the world would consider important he felt empty inside.

When Clauder went on a Charismatic Renewal retreat he found God.

---

28. It is significant that this meeting took place at the home of a Presbyterian lay woman and involved people from the mainline Protestant churches.

29. We are indebted in this section to information found in F. A. Sullivan, "Catholic Charismatic Renewal," in *Dictionary of the Pentecostal and Charismatic Movements* (Grand Rapids: Regency Press, 1988), pp. 110–14; H. D. Hunter, "Charismatic Movement," in *Dictionary of Christianity in America* (Downers Grove, Ill.: InterVarsity Press, 1990), pp. 243–44; Edward D. O'Connor, C.S.C., *The Pentecostal Movement in the Catholic Church* (South Bend: Notre Dame, Ave Maria Press, 1971); Michael Scanlan, T.O.R., *Let the Fire Fall* (Ann Arbor: Servant Press, 1986); Léon Joseph Cardinal Suenens, *A New Pentecost?* (New York: Seabury Press, 1975), p. 63.

Growth in the Catholic Charismatic Renewal Movement seems to have peaked.

Clauder remembers, "All of a sudden my vision was taken away and all I could see was Jesus. The Lord touched me in a very special way."[30] He began to turn down secular jobs and play exclusively for Christian groups. In 1989, Clauder, with his wife Sandy and their eight children, moved to San Diego and began working at St. Francis Church. Among his many activities, Clauder has organized a number of Unity Rallies. "Nearly 1,000 people, most of them members of six born-again, evangelical Protestant churches, rallied to the cause of Christian Unity October 22 at St. Francis Church, Vista."[31]

Clauder has also developed a ministry to inmates at the Vista Detention Facility (see chap. 17). He recently spent three weeks in Vladivostok, Siberia, where he helped teach evangelism methods, played his drums, and witnessed for Christ in open-air meetings. We think St. Francis of Assisi would be pleased with the efforts of brother John Clauder.

THE LIGHT AND LIFE MOVEMENT IN POLAND

One of the results of the Catholic Renewal Movement was the formation of the non-charismatic Light and Life fellowships in Poland. When Fr. Franciszek Blachnicki was ordained in 1950 and sent to the town of Tychy as a vicar, he was concerned about the spiritual temperature of his parish: "Crowds filled the Church at each of the many Masses on Sunday. However, Father Franciszek saw that most people were coming to Church more out of custom and habit than anything else. To most of his parishioners, faith was not a source of happiness and strength. Nor had it any real relevance to their lives."[32] Because of his spiritual concern Fr. Franciszek began retreats first for altar boys and then young people in general. These retreats took place during the height of the Stalinist oppression; the Communists had issued a decree that the State could appoint and remove priests and bishops. The retreats became known as "an Oasis for the Children of God."

Fr. Franciszek felt that Catholic teaching over the centuries had been limited to an educational process, so he worked to introduce each young person to a personal relationship with Jesus. During the course of each retreat a practical model of Christian life was presented. By 1969, an increasing number of Oasis participants were asking for continuing spiritual instruction and the movement was growing rapidly. Following are some personal testimonies by people of all ages and walks of life: "Oasis has led to a change in my life and my behavior. I want to join a group in which we can study the Bible

30. Kim Horner, "Vistan Drums in the Lord," *North County Blade-Citizen*, 22 October 1993, p. A-1.
31. Steven Saint, "Unity Rally Joins Catholics, Evangelicals," *Southern Cross*, 4 November 1993, p. 12.
32. Grazyna Sikorska, *Light and Life: Renewal in Poland* (Grand Rapids: Eerdmans, 1989), p. 35. The foreword in this volume contains a message from John Paul II.

together. . . . I want Jesus to become my way," and "At Oasis, I discovered who Jesus really is and what a central role He can play in my life."[33] In March 1976, the movement became known as Light and Life. Retreats were designed "as a three-year programme, involving three stages of Christian maturity—(1) meeting Christ and conscious acceptance of Him as Lord and Saviour, (2) renewal of baptismal vows and (3) bearing witness to Christ in the community."[34] Fr. Franciszek made evangelism an important factor in the Light and Life movement.

EVANGELICAL SUPPORT
OF CATHOLIC RENEWAL IN POLAND

In the mid 1970s, news about this spiritual development in Poland began to reach the West. Talk about faith based on a personal relationship with Christ, systematic Bible study, and prayer brought Western evangelicals to investigate. The Light and Life Movement identified itself with the growing Catholic Renewal and contacts were later made with Polish Pentecostals, although Light and Life from its outset was non-charismatic. "To Western Protestants, Father Blachnicki's model of faith, conceived as individual encounter with Christ and total trust in Him, as well as the emphasis put on Bible studies by the Light and Life movement, were a revelation."[35] Fr. Blachnicki began to "establish contacts with Protestant evangelistic groups including 'Campus Crusade for Christ'—an American-based inter-denominational movement known also as 'Agape,' which pursues evangelistic activities in over 80 countries throughout the world with real success."[36]

It was at this time (1977) that one of the authors was privileged to go to Poland and minister. I (Norm Geisler) was asked to teach a Bible survey course to about 100 university students. We came across the border from Austria (through Czechoslovakia) incognito, traveling as campers (we actually did meet in a camp in southern Poland). I found spiritually eager young people—scarcely any of whom owned a complete Bible—eating up the Word of God day after day. Upon my return I wrote:

> Thousands of people flock to camps to hear the gospel. Young and old, factory workers, doctors, college professors, all cultivate a deep commitment to Jesus Christ. Churches are full and overflowing morning and evening. Farmers sing gospel songs at the top of their lungs. Bands of young people chant, "We are one in the Spirit, we are one in the Lord."

33. Ibid., pp. 61–62.
34. Ibid., p. 66.
35. Ibid., p. 70.
36. Ibid.

Where is all this going on? In a revival center of the United States? No. In Poland, long an overwhelmingly Roman Catholic land but dominated by Marxism for a full generation.

I saw them. I ate with them, sang with them and knelt with them in their churches and chapels. They call themselves *Oazi* (Oasis). They are an indigenous spiritual renewal group who hold retreats, publish [underground] literature and teach people to be born again by personally trusting Christ as Savior.[37]

My experience in Poland was exhilarating to say the least. Day after day, hour after hour, we presented a Christ-centered approach to Scripture, following the example of our Lord (Luke 24:27, 44; John 5:39). I shall never forget the parting words of the students: "Before you came the Bible was like a room with furniture but with no lights. You have turned on the lights for us!"

Although there were obvious ecclesiastical and doctrinal differences, I felt a continual, deep bond of spiritual unity with these brothers and sisters in Christ. We loved the same Christ, who died and rose again for our sins. They were utilizing Campus Crusade's "Four Spiritual Laws" for evangelism, although they believed also in the authority of the Catholic church. Even though they were at that time forbidden by law to witness in the streets, they sang gospel hymns—many of the same ones we sing in Protestant churches—as they walked through the streets. Catholic churches in that area were packed out—even on Sunday evening—as peasant parishioners shouted jubilant praise. What I experienced was a dynamic, joyous, Christian, and evangelistic community of believers who were more eager than most American evangelicals I know to learn and live the Word of God.

SOME NEGATIVE CATHOLIC REACTION

News of this spiritual activity in the Catholic church reached some conservative elements in the clergy. Fr. Franciszek was accused of trying to Protestantize the movement.[38] In response to the concern that arose in the Polish hierarchy over these cooperative endeavors Fr. Franciszek quoted Pope Paul VI:

We make our own the desire of the Fathers of the Third General Assembly of the Synod of Bishops for a collaboration marked by a greater commitment with the Christian brethren with whom we are not yet in perfect unity, taking as a basis the foundation of Baptism and the patrimony of faith which is common to us. By doing this, we can already give a common witness to Christ before the world in the very work of evangelization. Christ's command urges

---

37. Norman L. Geisler, "An Oasis of Living Water," *Christian Herald* (February 1978): 52.
38. Sikorska, *Light and Life*, p. 72.

us to do this, the duty of preaching and of giving witness to the Gospel requires this.[39]

Fr. Franciszek continues:

it was in this close cooperation between the Light-Life movement and the Campus Crusade for Christ that the appeal of the "Vatican Council's Fathers" was being fulfilled. "Catholics must joyfully acknowledge and esteem the truly Christian gifts of our common heritage which are to be found among our separated brethren. It is right and salutary to recognize the riches of Christ and the virtuous works in the lives of others who are bearing witness to Christ, sometimes even by shedding their blood. For God is always wonderful in His works and worthy of admiration. Nor should we forget that whatever is wrought by the Grace of the Holy Spirit in the hearts of our separated brethren can contribute to our own edification. Whatever is truly Christian never conflicts with the genuine interests of the faith, indeed it can always result in a more ample realization of the very mystery of Christ and the Church."[40]

Fr. Franciszek Blachnicki was forced to leave Poland by the Communist authorities, and on February 27, 1987, he died in exile in the small West German town of Carlsberg. In a message that was sent to be read at his funeral, Pope John Paul II said: "We have lost a devoted apostle of conversion and spiritual renewal as well as a great spiritual leader of young people. . . . He used the talents abundantly bestowed upon him . . . to build God's Kingdom."[41]

ALLIES FOR FAITH AND RENEWAL

One of the most impressive results stemming from the Catholic Renewal Movement is the formation of Allies for Faith and Renewal.[42] In 1980, under the direction of two Catholics, John C. Blattner and Kevin F. Perrotta, a notable group of Protestant, Orthodox, and Roman Catholic scholars came together to witness for the faith amidst the hostile cultural environment.

AN IMPRESSIVE LIST OF JOINT PARTICIPANTS

Advisors to and participants in Allies for Faith and Renewal include evangelical leaders such as Donald Bloesch, professor of theology, Dubuque Theo-

---

39. Ibid.
40. Ibid., p. 73.
41. Ibid., foreword.
42. Information concerning future conferences and the goals of this organization can be obtained by writing: Alliance for Faith and Renewal, P.O. Box 8229, Ann Arbor, MI 48107, or calling (313) 761-8505.

logical Seminary; Harold O. J. Brown, professor of theology, Trinity Evangelical Divinity School; Charles Colson, founder of Prison Fellowship; Richard Land, director of Christian Life Commission of Southern Baptist Convention; J. I. Packer, professor of theology, Regent College; Charles V. Simpson, pastor of Gulf Coast Covenant Church, Mobile, Alabama; John H. White, Chaplain, Geneva College; and John Wimber, founder of Vineyard Ministries.

Roman Catholics involved include William B. Ball, religious rights attorney; Francis Canavan, S.J., professor of political science, Fordham University; Stephen B. Clark, president, Sword of the Spirit; James Hitchcock, professor of history, University of St. Louis; Cardinal Bernard Law, Boston; Ralph Martin, leader, Sword of the Spirit; Michael Scanlan, T.O.R., president of Franciscan University of Steubenville; Alan Schreck, professor of theology, Franciscan University of Steubenville; Ann Shields, F.I.R.E. Evangelistic Ministries; Janet Smith, professor of classics, Notre Dame; and Paul Vitz, professor of psychology, New York University.

Eastern Orthodox participants include: Deborah Malacky Belonicki, Orthodox Church in America; Stanley Harakas, professor of ethics, Holy Cross Greek Orthodox School of Theology; Theodore Stylianopoulos, professor, Holy Cross Greek Orthodox School of Theology.

A UNITED STATEMENT

The following quotes are from the *Allies for Faith and Renewal Statement of Purpose*. They speak for themselves:

> We are Christians who want to work together for the cause of Christ. We want to see the message and teaching of Christ presented clearly in the churches and to the world, and to see individual Christians and the Christian churches renewed in a living relationship with God.
>
> We believe that the Christian people must unite in loyalty to the authority of God's word. Today faith in God's revelation and obedience to it is being attacked, both directly and indirectly, outside and inside the churches. This is an assault that all Christians must resist.
>
> As a group of Protestants, Catholics, and Orthodox, we recognize one another as brothers and sisters in Christ, separated by important differences of belief and church order but united in our desire to obey the one Lord. Many of the challenges we face in our own churches are common challenges that confront all Christians today. Therefore we want to work together for a better understanding of these challenges, fostering communication and supporting one another in our respective roles of service to the Christian people.
>
> Desiring to see a renewal of God's life in his people, we know that renewal must begin in our individual lives with repentance from sin, wholehearted commitment to Christ, and reliance on the Holy Spirit. Moreover, we

pray for God to intervene in his people's lives, pardoning us, strengthening us, and extending his kingdom through us.

It is our intention to put our commitment to Christ and his cause in the world above everything else. We want to work together in practical ways to strengthen one another as Christians, to defend Christian teaching, and to bring the world to Christ.[43]

THE CONTRIBUTION OF OTHER CONFERENCES

The allies have held a number of conferences since 1980. The fifth in the series was "Courage in Leadership," which took place near Ann Arbor, Michigan, in 1987. The major speakers were Bernard Law, Boston's Roman Catholic cardinal and evangelical (Anglican) author and speaker James I. Packer of Regent College, Vancouver. Notice their comments on the appropriateness of Catholics and Protestants coming together and making common cause. Cardinal Law told the meeting:

We gather as Catholics, Protestants, and Orthodox who are concerned to stand for historic Christian positions in dogmatic and moral theology, to work for spiritual renewal and evangelism, and to cooperate in confronting fundamental human issues. I am happy to be here, because I am convinced that there is indeed being forged a new alliance between—of all people— Catholics and Protestant evangelicals.

Packer rated the Allies conferences as

one of the most important things that is happening in the English-speaking world at the present time. I rejoice to be making common cause with those who want to build a solid wall of defense for Christian supernaturalism—the supernaturalism of the scriptures and the creed—and I rejoice doubly when those who want to do that are also folk who are seeking together the renewal of the life of Christ in his church.

Cardinal Law, in his address titled "The Problem of Faith," spoke concerning the enigmatic subject of fundamentalism.

To gather as those standing for historic Christian positions in dogmatic and moral theology takes a bit of courage these days. It is a position disdainfully dismissed by some today as "fundamentalism"—read "bad." It is interesting to observe how "fundamentalism" has recently become an ever larger net to gather together an ever wider spectrum of world views not in conformity with the wisdom of this age. I would suspect that there are not a few who would

---

43. From publicity material for the Allies for Faith and Renewal Conference, "A Society in Peril," 1988, Ann Arbor, Michigan.

characterize those of us gathered here as "fundamentalists"—and in so doing no compliment would be intended.

Since "fundamentalism" is now being defined as anti-intellectualism, we would be dismissed as nostalgic romantics at best, as obsessive and dangerous ideologues and zealots at worst. What we have to say need not be examined, then, because it denies the rigid orthodoxy of this day, that orthodoxy that proclaims there is no binding truth. We here think there is, and therefore we are not listened to or taken seriously. The notion that faith rests on truth revealed, and on truth binding on all human beings of all times, is a notion incompatible with the contemporary Western mind-set which has relativized all truth. For us, God is the source of all truth—he is truth. For the contemporary Western mind the individual human person in isolation is the source of his or her truth. . . . Those who take truth seriously are thus seen as rigid "fundamentalists"; those who take truth as relative are seen as flexible, as reasonable.[44]

Obviously, Cardinal Law recognizes that all forms of "fundamentalism" are not totally antithetical to traditional Roman Catholicism, a point the authors have often stressed to their Catholic brethren.

In 1994, a conference titled *John Paul II and the New Evangelization* was called to address "some successful models of evangelization and provide practical help for clergy and lay leaders who want to see evangelization happen in their parish or lay organization."[45] The conference also met to "consider what Catholics can learn from Evangelicals and Pentecostals about preaching the good news."[46] Roman Catholics participating in the meeting included Bishop Gabriel Ganaka, Avery Dulles, S.J., and the aforementioned charismatic lay leader Ralph Martin. Evangelicals, in addition to Charles Colson, included John Wimber of the Vineyard Fellowship Ministries. This is another example of Christian believers coming from different persuasions and banding together to enlarge the body of Christ through the proclamation of the good news.

THE IMPORTANT CONTRIBUTION OF RALPH MARTIN

Before closing this chapter, we wish to examine the writings of a Catholic layman who has perhaps more than anyone else from his jurisdiction identified the nature of the problem facing historic Christianity. Ralph Martin has also addressed the commonality of purpose and the degree of cooperation between traditional Roman Catholicism and evangelical Protestantism.

44. Law, "Center Update," *Pastoral Renewal* (September 1987): 13.
45. Announcement, *Faith and Renewal Journal* 18, no. 3 (November/December 1993): 28.
46. Ibid.

Concerning salvation in the Roman Catholic Church, Ralph Martin interviewed Maria Von Trapp of "Sound of Music" fame:

> R. Martin: How would you relate this "new Pentecost" that the Church is experiencing to the traditional Catholicism that you grew up in?
>
> M. Von Trapp: Well, I think the baptism in the Holy Spirit is what all Catholics ought to experience in confirmation but don't. . . . It's memorizing seven gifts, twelve fruits, fuss about a sponsor and a name, and trying to remember why the bishop is going to tap your cheek. . . . It's hardly ever a personally desired and experienced commitment to Jesus and release of the Spirit.
>
> R. Martin: Do you have any thoughts about why this is the case?'
>
> M. Von Trapp: Analyze how we Catholics grow up. We're baptized as babies.

Maria Von Trapp also mentions godparents, first confession, and first communion. In spite of these religious functions, she states that many Roman Catholics never meet Jesus as Savior and Lord. In fact, "We may even go to daily communion all our lives and yet never confront the great issue of whether He is my Savior and Lord."[47]

Ralph Martin believes that Vatican II has resulted in renewal in the Roman Catholic Church. For example, in some areas, "especially in parts of Latin America, infant baptism is being withheld if there is no assurance that the child will grow up in a community of faith and genuine Christian life."[48]

Martin addresses the issue of the large number of ex-Catholics he encounters in Protestant charismatic and evangelical churches: "Through my involvement in the Catholic charismatic renewal, I have frequent contact with many Protestant charismatic churches and movements. I am struck by the significant numbers of ex-Catholics I have encountered in Assembly of God churches, the Full Gospel Business Men's Fellowship International, independent Christian centers, or Hispanic Protestant churches in the Southwest."[49]

While Martin is concerned with people leaving the Catholic church he feels that the common response—to blame Protestant "fundamentalists" for using underhanded evangelization methods—is off the mark. These ex-Catholics are experiencing a more vital relationship with Christ than they had previously. Indeed: *"Many talk as if they encountered the Lord himself for the first time."* Martin states that the proper response for Catholics is to examine their own consciences as to whether they are properly reflecting Christ in such a fashion as to make him attractive to others. *"As hard as it may be to face, many Catholics who have left the Catholic Church to become part of a vital Protestant congregation may have gone to hell if they stayed, uncon-*

47. Ralph Martin, *Hungry for God* (New York: Doubleday and Co., 1974), pp. 67–68.
48. Ibid., p. 70.
49. "Why Catholics Leave," *New Covenant* (July/August 1990): 6

verted and with virtually no Christian support, in the Catholic Church!" The large number of people leaving the Catholic Church should "humble us and cause us to turn to the Lord in repentance and in seeking God, asking him to have mercy on us and to pour out his Spirit on us so that men, women, and children may encounter him in our midst."[50]

What is the remedy for this situation? Martin posits that it is "the rediscovery of the richness of the Holy Spirit that Jesus wants to pour out on his church and each individual Christian [that is] a key to meeting the 'challenge of the sects' that the Vatican is currently giving its attention to?"[51] Martin has written a major volume, *A Crisis of Truth,* in which he addresses the extent to which secular humanism and syncretism has infiltrated the Catholic church.[52] Concerning liberation theology, which plagues both Roman Catholicism and mainline Protestantism, Martin insists that "The claim that political change must precede evangelism is preposterous. Evangelical Protestants and Pentecostals have enjoyed outstanding success preaching the good news to the Latin American poor, often in the very same barrios where secularized Catholic priests and nuns are insisting that you can not preach the gospel to the poor until the revolution comes." For, "as a result of conversion to Jesus, the power of the Holy Spirit and the sustaining power of the Christian Church, those poor are better able to work together for social change. Cardinal Léon Joseph Suenens of Belgium pointed out the fallacy of the 'you can't preach the gospel to the poor unless you first improve their economic situation' approach as long ago as 1957 in his book, *The Gospel to Every Creature.*"[53]

Martin's chapter "Is Jesus the Only Way?" reads as if it was copied from some of Bill Bright's Campus Crusade for Christ literature. He contends that "It is Christianity's unique claim that in Jesus Christ, and only in Jesus Christ, all that is required for man's salvation is provided. All the requirements are met. God's Word tells us that through the incarnation, death, and resurrection of Jesus, salvation for the human race is accomplished."[54] Every

50. Ibid., pp. 6–7, emphasis added.

51. "Sects Education," *New Covenant* (October 1991): 26–27.

52. Ralph Martin, *A Crisis of Truth: The Attack on Faith, Morality and Mission in the Catholic Church* (Ann Arbor: Servant, 1982). Martin has recently produced a follow-up to this book: *The Catholic Church at the End of an Age: What Is the Spirit Saying?* (San Francisco: Ignatius Press, 1994). This volume addresses the same themes as the earlier one and indicates the positive contributions of Protestant evangelicals and charismatics in "cultural" Catholic settings.

53. Martin, *Crisis of Truth*, p. 97.

54. Ibid., p. 77. In an article on marriage, Martin observes, "Many couples desiring to receive the sacrament of matrimony have been sacramentalized, but neither evangelized to a basic Christian conversion nor adequately catechized to know even the fundamentals of Christian faith" (Ralph Martin, "Catholic Marriage: An Institution in Crisis," *The Southern Cross*, 12 January 1995, p. 20).

In the same article, Martin quotes philosophy professor Peter Kreeft: "Perhaps [one reason] God allows the Protestant Catholic division to persist is . . . because many Catholics have never been taught the most precious truth of all: that salvation is a free gift of grace, accepted by faith" (ibid.).

Roman Catholic (and indeed every evangelical) would do well to ponder a copy of this excellent book.

ROMAN CATHOLIC AND EVANGELICAL DIALOGUE

There have been several attempts to bring Roman Catholics and evangelicals together for dialogue. The Evangelical-Roman Catholic Dialogue on Mission first met at Venice in 1977, again at Cambridge in 1982, and lastly at Landévennec in France in 1984. Participants were Roman Catholic and evangelical theologians and missiologists from many parts of the world. Evangelicals will recognize such names among the participants as Harvie M. Conn of Westminster Seminary, Anglican John R. W. Stott, David Hubbard of Fuller Theological Seminary, and David F. Wells of Gordon-Conwell Theological Seminary. Two documents made the dialogue possible: the "Lausanne Covenant" produced by the Evangelical International Congress on World Evangelization (1974) and Pope Paul VI's "Evangelization in the Modern World" (1975). Because of perceived commonalities found in these two statements, the two groups came together, not "as a step towards Church unity negotiations," but in "search for such common ground as might be discovered between Evangelicals and Roman Catholics as they each try to be more faithful in their obedience to mission."[55]

After exploring such subjects as the nature of Christian mission, revelation, authority and the Gospel, and culture, the participants addressed the possibilities of common witness.[56] Speaking about common witness in evangelism, the members confessed that "substantial agreement continues to elude us, and therefore common witness in evangelism would seem to be premature. Although we are aware of situations in some parts of the world in which Evangelicals and Roman Catholics have felt able to make a common proclamation."[57] We have detailed in this chapter some of these situations.

Another attempt to address the issue of evangelism was the General Assembly of the World Evangelical Fellowship (WEF) which met in Hoddesdon, England in 1980.[58] The purpose of the gathering was to examine the relationship between evangelicals and Roman Catholics with regard to faith and practice. Two Roman Catholic observers—Ralph Martin, a leader in the

55. Basil Meeking and John Stott, eds., *The Evangelical-Roman Catholic Dialogue on Mission* (Grand Rapids: Eerdmans, 1986), p. 10.
56. Ibid., chap. 7.
57. Ibid., pp. 88–89.
58. The conference is recorded in Paul G. Schrotenboer, ed., *Roman Catholicism: A Contemporary Evangelical Perspective* (Grand Rapids: Baker, 1987).

Catholic charismatic renewal movement, and Msgr. Basil Meeking, a Vatican official—were also invited.

A number of evangelicals, principally from Italy, Spain, and parts of Latin America, took exception to the inclusion of Roman Catholics in this gathering. They felt that they have been mistreated by Roman Catholic officials for their evangelical stance and found it impossible to feel comfortable in this situation.[59] Therefore, the WEF General Assembly addressed a number of issues which evangelicals find problematic, including Mariology, authority, and papal infallibility. Although the volume is for the most part critical of Roman Catholic doctrine and practice, it suggests that cooperation and fellowship with Roman Catholics is by no means impossible.

Acknowledging the difficulties of dialogue, the document states: "This does not mean that dialogue between evangelicals and Roman Catholics should continue to be discouraged."[60] As to the presence of God in Roman Catholicism: "As evangelicals, we should not be closed to the power of God's Spirit and God's Word operating in the lives of people within the Roman Catholic Church."[61] Addressing theological trends in contemporary Roman Catholicism: "The basic thrust in the writings of Roman Catholic thinkers such as Rahner, Teilhard de Chardin, Küng, Schillebeeckx and Schoonenberg do not differ substantially from those of their secular Protestant counterparts."[62] While the above statement is true, it also must be pointed out that the liberal posture of the aforementioned Roman Catholic scholars *does* significantly differ with the thinking of Pope John Paul II and his premier theologian Joseph Cardinal Ratzinger.[63] On a more positive note, lay-theologian Ralph Martin reports that concerning the contemporary Roman Catholic Church in Canada "of the 39 percent who attend church weekly or monthly, 21 percent reported experiencing a profound conversion experience or awaking and considered themselves to be evangelicals." And even more startling, "31 percent of the more faithful Catholics considered themselves to be fundamentalist Christians."[64]

---

59. One author, Ralph MacKenzie, faced a similar problem when studying at seminary. The school is located in San Diego and thus a significant number of students come from Mexico and Latin America. Having been reared in a sub-culture of Catholicism which stresses human merit and having not understood Jesus Christ in a personal way, these recent converts to evangelicalism were very suspicious of any positive comments concerning Roman Catholicism.

60. Schrotenboer, *Roman Catholicism*, p. 11.

61. Ibid., p. 49.

62. Ibid., p. 59.

63. For an objective examination of Roman Catholic/Protestant differences, see Peter Toon, *Protestants and Catholics: A Guide to Understanding the Differences among Christians* (Ann Arbor: Servant, 1983).

64. "Special Report: The Religion Poll," *Macleans*, 12 April 1993, pp. 34, 36, 48, 49. Cited in Martin, *Catholic Church at the End of an Age*.

The most recent example of this sort of endeavor is a document released at a New York news conference during Holy Week 1994. The statement, entitled "Evangelicals and Catholics Together: The Christian Mission in the Third Millennium," was produced primarily by Fr. Richard John Neuhaus (formerly Lutheran), Charles Colson (Prison Fellowship founder), Kent Hill (president of Eastern Nazarene College) and George Weigel (Roman Catholic scholar and writer). They were aided in drafting the document by a number of other Roman Catholic and evangelical leaders.[65]

The joint statement has been criticized by some evangelicals (including Carl F. H. Henry, David Wells, R. C. Sproul, and the present authors) for imprecise theological formulation at points. Indeed, even justification by faith alone was not listed as a significant difference between evangelicals and Catholics. This occasioned some evangelicals to charge that the joint statement had given away the Reformation (for a fuller discussion see Appendix F). In spite of its significant problems, the document makes a number of positive statements. In the section "We Affirm Together," the paper states: "Jesus Christ is Lord. That is the first and final affirmation that Christians make about all reality." And "All who accept Christ as Lord and Savior are brothers and sisters in Christ."[66] Also, the Scriptures are declared to be "the infallible Word of God" and the Apostles Creed is declared to be ". . . an accurate statement of Scriptural truth."[67]

WHAT THEN SHALL WE DO?

The magnanimity of the apostle Paul is not always reflected in conservative Protestant circles when he said, "Of course, some preach Christ from envy and rivalry, others from good will. . . . What difference does it make, as long as in every way, whether in pretense or in truth, Christ is being proclaimed? And in that I rejoice" (Phil. 1:15, 18). One author of this book was asked by a parish priest to teach the gospel to the young people in a particular Catholic church and even to preach at a mass. Billy Graham has set the example for evangelical cooperation with Catholics in mass evangelism without compromising the basic gospel message. Despite ecclesiastical and doctrinal differences (see Part Two), there are some important things many Catholics and evangelicals hold in common not the least of which is the good news that Jesus died for our sins and rose again. Thus, there seems to be no good reason

65. Arthur H. Matthews, "Cooperation, Not Communion," *World*, 9 April 1994, pp. 10–13.

66. *Evangelicals and Catholics Together*, final draft, 29 March 1994, p. 5.

67. Ibid., p. 6. We wait to see what final impact this statement has on Roman Catholic/evangelical relationships.

why there should not be increased ways of mutual encouragement in fulfilling our Lord's Great Commission (Matt. 28:18–20). Catholics and evangelicals do not have to agree on everything in order to agree on some things—even something important. We do not need to agree on the authority of the church before we can cooperate in proclaiming the power of the uncompromised gospel (Rom. 1:16).

Epilogue

The purview of this book is immense; beginning with the Apostolic Era, through the patristic and medieval periods, touching the Reformation events and the current situation. It has been a daunting task and one that we readily admit has not been exhaustive. We ask the readers' indulgence for any historical slights or oversights.

Our primary task has been an honest evaluation of the agreements and differences between evangelicals and orthodox Roman Catholics, being irenic about areas of agreement and yet realistic about areas of differences. Centuries of suspicion and mistrust, fueled by misconceptions on both sides, make this a formidable project.

In Part One, we addressed the areas of agreement among orthodox Christians of all jurisdictions. These are doctrinal truths emerging from the councils and creeds of classic Christianity. Chapter 5 on salvation is crucial in that we developed the thesis that Augustinianism was the major soteriological framework that informed Western Christianity. Both Roman Catholics and Protestants are indebted to the Bishop of Hippo. This chapter should be read in connection with chapter 12 on justification.

Part Two was more difficult. We realize that genuine differences exist between our two groups and that nothing is achieved by failing to face the issues. Efforts of this type by evangelicals have been flawed, erecting straw men and utilizing stereotypes. In our desire to avoid this we have attempted to use official Roman Catholic sources in developing our arguments and have called on our years of experience dialoguing with Roman Catholic brethren of various persuasions. While being rigorous in examination, we have attempted not to be rancorous in spirit.

In Part Three we endeavored to stress commonalities. Cooperative efforts of believing Roman Catholics and evangelicals facing the great moral and cultural declension of our society have been detailed. Both message and method, from Chrysostom "the golden mouthed" to Billy Graham the evangelist, have been mentioned.

Concerning this matter evangelicals might benefit from some observations from J. Gresham Machen, founder of Westminster Seminary. In the midst of his analysis of liberalism he wrote:

431

> Far more serious still is the division between the Church of Rome and evangelical Protestantism in all its forms. Yet how great is the common heritage that unites the Roman Catholic Church . . . to devout Protestants today! [As great as the difference is] . . . it seems almost trifling compared to the abyss which stands between us and many ministers of our own church.[1]

We are convinced that much confusion exists because of unfamiliarity with the Holy Scriptures. On that subject, a well-known spokesman of orthodox Roman Catholicism has said: "I am firmly convinced that some erroneous doctrines of present day theology would have been impossible if the author (or authors) had regularly and attentively read the complete New Testament."[2] Harold O. J. Brown echoes this sentiment: "The question of the reality of a personal God, or of Christology, divides believers from unbelievers, Christians from non-Christians. The question of the authority of Scripture divides sound teaching and good theology from false teaching and bad theology."[3]

Concerning the nature of the church Brown says, "The true church is an *invisible* fellowship, but it is not an *imaginary* one. To be in it, you do not step inside four walls, but you accept a whole framework and orientation towards truth, by entering into it with your whole understanding as well as your will." And as to the doctrinal and moral integrity of the church: "In the final analysis, the purity of the church cannot be guaranteed by decrees—it can only be guaranteed by church members who know their faith, both its vital elements and its secondary ones, and the difference between them."[4]

In closing, we quote from a theologian who, to use his own words, was "raised in the bosom of the liberal ecumenical tradition." Upon reexamination of the church fathers, he came to see the powerlessness of current liberal ecumenicism and embraced evangelicalism. Concerning interfaith dialogue he writes: "Evangelicals are more ready for serious dialogue with Eastern Orthodoxy and with Roman ecumenical initiatives than with a Geneva pan-Protestant voice that only faintly echoes Reformation teaching on Scripture, sin and grace."[5]

---

1. J. Gresham Machen, *Christianity and Liberalism* (New York: Macmillan, 1923), p. 52; quoted in J. Daryl Charles, "Evangelical-Catholic Dialogue: Basis Boundaries, Benefits," *Pro Ecclesia* 3, no. 3, p. 304.

2. Cardinal Joseph Ratzinger, *The Catholic World Report*, November 1992; quoted in *Touchstone* (Fall 1992): 47.

3. Brown, *Protest of a Troubled Protestant*, p. 133.

4. Ibid., p. 248. As to the controversy between Roman Catholics and Protestants, one would be hard-pressed to find an evangelical more perceptive than Harold O. J. Brown. For a masterful discussion, see "Unhelpful Antagonism and Unhealthy Courtesy," in Armstrong, *Roman Catholicism: Evangelical Protestants*, pp. 163–78.

5. Thomas C. Oden, "How Should Evangelicals Be Ecumenical?" *Christianity Today*, 5 April 1993, p. 40.

THE CHURCHES OF THE EAST

If evangelicals know little about Roman Catholicism they know even less about Eastern Orthodoxy. There are more than 225 million adherents to Orthodoxy worldwide. Still, the Orthodox Church is virtually unknown in this country. The impact Eastern Orthodoxy has had in America is due to faithful immigrants who maintained their faith within ethnic boundaries. Metropolitan Philip, Primate of the Antiochian Orthodox Christian Archdiocese of North America, has said that Orthodox Christianity is "the best kept secret in America."[1]

In this appendix we will briefly consider the history of Eastern Orthodoxy: its early development, subsequent estrangement from Western (or Latin) Christianity, and particular doctrinal differences with Western Christianity. Special effort will be made to understand the Orthodox equivalent of justification (and sanctification), which they call "deification."

ORTHODOX HISTORY

It is an undeniable fact of history that Christianity was Eastern before it was Western. It was an Eastern Christian Ananias from Damascus, Syria, who baptized the apostle Paul (Acts 9:1–19). Followers of "the Way" were first called "Christians" at Antioch (Acts 11:19–26). Antioch, Alexandria, and Jerusalem were more important than Rome during the early years of church history, and "Even in the West, the theological leadership of the church was in North Africa, which produced such figures as Tertullian, Cyprian, and Augustine."[2] For a time both branches of the church—East and West—were

---

1. Peter E. Gillquist, *Becoming Orthodox: A Journey to the Ancient Christian Faith* (Brentwood: Wolgemuth and Hyatt Publishers, 1990), p. 62. The title "metropolitan" is applied to a bishop who has spiritual jurisdiction over a province or nation.

2. Justo L. González, *The Story of Christianity*, vol. 1 (San Francisco: Harper and Row, 1984), p. 242.

one. Then a number of events, such as the Muslim conquests in the East and the disintegration of the empire in the West, led to events that would result in the final schism, which occurred in A.D. 1054.

THE CHURCH OF THE SEVEN COUNCILS

John II, Metropolitan of Russia (A.D. 1080–89), said: "All profess that there are seven holy and Ecumenical Councils, and these are the seven pillars of the faith of the Divine Word."[3] The early Byzantine church was informed and directed by the first seven general councils. The doctrines which all Orthodox Christians acknowledge to be central to their faith—the Trinity and the incarnation—emerged from these councils.

I Council of Nicea (A.D. 325). This first council condemned Arius, who taught that Jesus was of a "different substance" from the Father. It also produced the Nicene Creed.

I Constantinople (A.D. 381). This Council reaffirmed the pronouncements of Nicea and proclaimed the divinity of the Holy Spirit.

Ephesus (A.D. 431). The theological question raised here was: In what sense is Jesus Christ fully divine and completely human at the same time? Nestorius from Antioch was pitted against Cyril from Alexandria. The former taught the *diversity* and the latter pressed the *unity* of Christ's person. Cyril carried the day, affirming of Jesus Christ that "What Mary bore was not a man loosely united to God, but a single and undivided person, who is God and man at once."[4]

Chalcedon (A.D. 451). Monophysitism, the doctrine that the incarnation resulted in a single nature in the person of Christ, appeared on the scene. The council reacted to this formulation and declared that in Christ the two natures—human and divine—are clearly separated. Monophysitism would continue to plague the Eastern church for some time to come.[5]

II Constantinople (A.D. 553). The fifth Ecumenical Council carried forward the work of its predecessor. Using the Alexandrian perspective, this council explains *how* the two natures of Christ unite to form a single person.

III Constantinople (A.D. 680–681). This council condemned the heresy of Monothelitism, which taught that while Christ had two natures, he had but one will. The council disagreed and stated that, "Since Christ is true man as well as true God, He must have a human will as well as a divine."[6]

---

3. Quoted in Timothy Ware, *The Orthodox Church*, rev. (New York: Penguin, 1983), p. 26.
4. Ibid., p. 33.
5. Evangelicals agree with the theological formulations found in these first four councils. Eastern Orthodoxy adds three more, and Roman Catholics—with the potentiality for more development—are open-ended.
6. Ibid., p. 37.

II Nicea (A.D. 787). This last ecumenical council pronounced for iconodules and against the iconoclasts. The former accepted veneration dulia directed toward icons; the later rejected this devotion as idolatry. Since one of the distinctives of Orthodoxy is the attention it pays to icons, the decisions of the Council are very important. While God cannot be represented in his eternal nature (John 1:18), Orthodoxy believes that because "the Incarnation has made a representational religious art possible: God can be depicted because He became man and took flesh."[7]

The first seven councils are very important to Eastern Orthodoxy. They are a theological guide "and, next to the Bible, it is the Seven Councils which the Orthodox Church takes as its standard and guide in seeking solutions to the new problems which arise in every generation."[8]

THE GREAT SCHISM

In the year A.D. 1054, at the Church of the Holy Wisdom (Gk: *Hagia Sophia*) in Constantinople, an event took place that would perpetrate the first major rupture in the Christian church. A representative of the pope, Cardinal Humbert, placed a Bull of Excommunication upon the altar. This was the culmination of a long and complicated process, involving a number of causes. In the last analysis however, the quarrel was not over cultural but theological themes.[9] Two matters in particular were at issue: the claims of the papacy and the filioque, to which issues we now turn.

The Papal Claims. Eastern Orthodoxy accepts the proposition that, from the beginning, Peter was the acknowledged leader among the apostles. After the death of the apostles and the spread of Christianity westward, the church at Rome became more important. Although all bishops were equal in authority, the Bishop of Rome was considered "first among equals."

However, trouble was on the horizon. For, "after nearly three hundred years, the Bishops of Rome slowly began to assume to themselves a role of superiority over the others. And without consensus, they ultimately claimed to be the only true successors to St. Peter."[10] The vacuum caused by the decline of secular power in the Roman Empire was filled by religious power, namely, the church of Rome. In addition, "In the West . . . there was only one great see claiming Apostolic foundation—Rome—so that Rome came to be regarded as the Apostolic see."[11]

---

7. Ibid., p. 41.
8. Ibid., p. 43.
9. A move to address this ancient rupture was made by the Vatican II Council. See Appendix D.
10. Gillquist, *Becoming Orthodox*, p. 54.
11. Ware, *Orthodox Church*, p. 55.

There were many churches in the East, however, that traced their ancestry back to the apostles. Also, four of the five patriarchates were located there. Collegiality (decision making among equals) was the rule in the East, while the Western church became highly centralized and "was seen less as a college and more as a monarchy—the monarchy of the Pope."[12] This situation was (and still is) rejected by Eastern Orthodoxy.[13]

The Filioque. The other problem identified at the time of the great schism was the term *filioque* (Latin: "And the Son"). This word was added by the Western church to the Nicene-Constantinopolitan Creed, thus affirming that the procession of the Holy Spirit is not "from the Father through the Son" but "from the Father and the Son." The purpose of this change was to safeguard against Arianism.

The Eastern wing of the church objected to the change on two grounds. First, the creed belongs to the whole church and any change must have the consent of all parties; and second, the Orthodox believe the *filioque* to be theologically incorrect. They believe its inclusion tends to "destroy the balance between the three persons of the Holy Trinity: it leads also to a false understanding of the work of the Spirit in the world."[14]

This is a complicated problem which we cannot fully explore in this limited treatment. Eastern Orthodoxy's motives were sound: the protection of the person and work of the Holy Spirit. However, evangelicals are united with Roman Catholics on this issue. Ecumenically oriented theologian John Warwick Montgomery, speaking in support of the inclusion of the filioque, writes, "Scripture calls the Holy Spirit not only the Spirit of the Father (Matt. 10:20) but also the Spirit of the Son (Gal. 4:6); . . . and the sending of the Spirit to the New Testament church is ascribed both to the Father (John 14:16) and the Son (John 15:26; 16:7, 13–14)."[15]

POST-SCHISM EVENTS

Tensions increased between East and West following A.D. 1054. Power plays on the part of the politically stronger Latin church further drove the wedge between the two branches of the church. The rape and pillage of the Byzantine capitol of Constantinople by the Roman Catholic crusaders is a dark blot on the history of the church and prompted the following lamentable

12. Ibid.
13. We have explored this problem in chap. 11. It can be noted that evangelicals—while siding with their Western Roman Catholic brethren on many things—on this issue agree with Eastern Orthodoxy.
14. Ibid., pp. 59–60. We will examine the Orthodox position of the work of the Holy Spirit in the next section on "Doctrines."
15. John W. Montgomery, *Ecumenicity, Evangelicals and Rome* (Grand Rapids: Zondervan, 1969), p. 29 n. 32.

statement by the Grand Duke Lucas Notaras: "I would rather see the Moslem turban in the midst of the city than the Latin mitre."[16]

CATHOLIC CHURCHES—EASTERN RITE

The churches which occupy the same territories as the Orthodox churches but are in communion with Rome are called Eastern Rite Catholic churches. They retain their original languages, have liturgies and dispense communion in both species, baptize by immersion, and allow clergy (excepting bishops) to be married. The term "Uniat" or "Uniate" was used by the opponents of the Eastern Rite Catholic churches and is considered a pejorative one.

Eastern rite churches include Armenians, Chaldeans, Copts, Ethiopians, Marianites, and Syrians. As one might expect, tensions arose between the two groups and consequently the Roman Catholic Church founded the "Congregation of Eastern Rites" in 1862 in order to address problems. Eastern Rite Catholics now number over 12 million worldwide. The churches were represented at Vatican II and subsequent events will be considered in the conclusion of this appendix.[17]

DOCTRINES

We now turn to an examination of the differences between the Eastern and Western churches. This involves differing principles or motifs.

GUIDING PRINCIPLES

Western theology has been informed by a rational framework in an attempt to understand Christian truth. The East, on the other hand, has been guided by a different principle: "This motif can be summed up in a single word: Mystery. The entire theology and church life of Eastern Christendom is an effort to give organic expression to the unfathomable, mysterious life of the Godhead."[18] In fact, what the West calls "sacraments," the East calls "mysteries." This motif of mystery can be seen in the theological language used—that of metaphor and symbolism. The symbol "becomes the language of mystery; i.e., a vehicle to represent the hidden divine realities."[19]

16. Ware, *Orthodox Church*, p. 81.
17. For material on the Eastern Rite Churches, see Broderick, *Catholic Concise Encyclopedia*, pp. 138–39; Cross, *Oxford Dictionary*, p. 1407; and González, *Story of Christianity*, 2:316.
18. Montgomery, *Ecumenicity, Evangelicals and Rome*, p. 28.
19. Stanley M. Burgess, *The Holy Spirit: Eastern Christian Traditions* (Peabody, Mass.: Hendrickson, 1989), p. 5.

Eastern Orthodoxy also tends to be "pneumatological" (guided by the Holy Spirit) rather than "Christological" (guided by Christ), as is the case in the West. A good deal of the controversy surrounding the disagreement concerning the origin and procession of the Holy Spirit arises out of Orthodoxy's concern to preserve the integrity and office of the Holy Spirit. As to the work of the persons within the Trinity: "No member of the Triune God functions without the involvement of the other Two."[20] Hence, the persons within the Godhead are "blended, though not confounded; distinct, though not divided."[21]

Montgomery, drawing on the insights of Belgian Jesuit theologian G. Dejaifve, presents a number of contrasting motifs that differentiate between the theology of the East and that of the West. They may be placed in the following form:

Western Church	Eastern Church
Earthly	Heavenly
Present Focus	Future Focus
Rational	Mystical
Essentialistic	Existential

These distinctions may be helpful for Western Christians who wish to understand the nature of Eastern Orthodoxy.

OTHER DOCTRINAL DISTINCTIONS

We now turn to some differences concerning other doctrines.

Deification. In chapter 5 we attempted to show that, in spite of important differences, Roman Catholics and evangelicals share a common Augustinian framework concerning salvation. The Eastern church, on the other hand, develops the doctrine of salvation from a different perspective. The concept is called "deification," and it is found in both Eastern and Western theologians prior to Augustine. An Anglican scholar states: "The idea of deification or divinization as taught in the patristic period has often been misunderstood by Protestants."[22]

Deification has been defined as follows: "*Theosis* in the Greek. The goal of Eastern Christian life. The term does not imply that a human ever can have the divine essence, but rather that it is possible to become God-like."[23] Dei-

---

20. Ibid., p. 2.
21. *The Athanasian Creed 4*; quoted in ibid., p. 4.
22. Toon, *Justification and Sanctification*, p. 46.
23. Burgess, *Holy Spirit*, p. 228. The Scripture most often used in describing deification is 2 Pet. 1:4: "so that through them you may come to share in the divine nature."

fication has also been called "Christification." Peter speaks of becoming partakers of the divine nature in 2 Peter 1:4. Paul instructs every man to become "mature in Christ" (Col. 2:10).[24] Therefore, deification or Christification began with "The assumption of human nature by the Logos of God from the womb of the Virgin." And it "is the foundation and starting-point of His incarnation and of the deification of humanity."[25]

In his two-volume work examining the history of the Christian doctrine of justification Alister McGrath comments on the differences in the views of salvation between East and West: "The West has tended to subordinate the work of the Holy Spirit to the concept of grace," whereas in the East we find the "stress upon the immediacy of the divine, and the direct encounter of man with the Holy Spirit."[26] Also, the concept of deification meshes well with Neoplatonic thought, which has been influential in the formation of Orthodox theology. Finally, the Western interest in developing "Roman law" themes in soteriological concerns is absent in the East.[27]

One criticism of the Eastern Orthodox understanding of salvation as "deification" is that it sounds perilously close to pantheism (God is all and all is God). However, "The idea of deification must always be understood in the light of the distinction between Creator and creative activity, between God's essence and His energies. Union with God means union with the divine energies, not the divine essence: the Orthodox Church, while speaking of deification and union, rejects all forms of pantheism."[28] Also, "When the teachers of the early Church spoke of deification or divinization, there was no intention of claiming cosubstantiality with God, for, in the words of the Creed, only Christ is one in substance with the Father."[29]

There is no question that Orthodoxy uses images and concepts that are different from those used in the West. However, the basis for the idea of deification springs from the central truths of Christology, the person and work of Christ. Therefore, concerning salvation, the Orthodox are "orthodox."[30] Another Orthodox distinction is the use of "icons" in worship. Icons are "flat pictures . . . to represent the Lord, the BVM, or another saint, which are

---

24. See Panajiotis Nellas, *Deification in Christ* (Crestwood: St. Vladimir's Seminary Press, 1987), p. 39.

25. Georgios I. Mantzaridis, *The Deification of Man* (Crestwood: St. Vladimir's Seminary Press, 1984), p. 31.

26. McGrath, *Iustitia Dei*, 1:3.

27. Ibid., pp. 3–4.

28. Ware, *Orthodox Church*, p. 237. Also, for a helpful discussion of God's essence versus his energies, see Mantzaridis, *Deification of Man*, pp. 104–15. Also for an evangelical assessment, see Daniel B. Clendenin, "Partakers of Divinity: The Orthodox Doctrine of Theosis," *Journal of the Evangelical Theological Society*, vol. 37, no. 3 (September 1994): 365–79.

29. Toon, *Justification and Sanctification*, p. 46.

30. See William G. Rusch, "How the Eastern Fathers Understood What the Western Church Meant by Justification," in Anderson, *Justification by Faith*, pp. 131–42.

used and venerated in the Greek Church."[31] The use of icons caused a serious problem within the Eastern Church itself. This was termed the "Iconoclastic Controversy" and was to resurface during the Protestant Reformation.[32]

Differences with Roman Catholicism. We will only briefly touch on some differences between Roman Catholicism and Eastern Orthodoxy. We already stated that the East prefers to accept "mystery" more readily than does the West. Hence, the explanation of how Christ is present in the Eucharist is not as precisely reasoned as the Roman Catholic position, the East preferring to stay with mystery and incomprehensibility.[33] In Eastern Orthodoxy, the laity as well as the clergy receive communion "under both kinds," the bread as well as the cup. Concerning purgatory, "Today most if not all Orthodox theologians reject the idea" because "Christ the Lamb of God who takes away the sin of the world, is our only atonement and satisfaction."[34] As to Mariology, Orthodoxy honors Mary as "most blessed among God's creatures." Most Eastern theologians reject the doctrine of the immaculate conception (in rare agreement with Thomas Aquinas!), but all accept the bodily assumption dogma.[35]

It is of some interest to note that, concerning what some say is the most important difference between Roman Catholics and evangelicals—infallibility (see chap. 11)—the Orthodox side with evangelicals against the infallibility of the church (and the pope). As to the status of the Apocrypha, "most Orthodox scholars at the present day, . . . following the opinion of Athanasius and Jerome, consider that the Deutero-Canonical Books, although included in the Bible, stand on a lower footing than the rest of the Old Testament."[36]

CONCLUSION

The status of the Eastern Orthodox Church came up at Vatican II, which had ecumenicity as one of its goals. Whenever Roman Catholic triumphalism would emerge some Uniate participant would rush to the defense of Orthodoxy. One stated "that all this talk about the Eastern Church 'returning to the true fold' was ridiculous. Many of them regarded their Churches as older than the Church of Rome, so that, if anyone had wandered away and needed

31. Cross, *Oxford Dictionary,* p. 686.
32. Ibid., pp. 687–88. A good account of the place and history of icons may be found in Daniel B. Clendenin, *Eastern Orthodox Christianity: A Western Perspective* (Grand Rapids: Baker, 1994), pp. 71–93, 152–55.
33. Ware, *Orthodox Church,* pp. 290–95.
34. Ibid., p. 259.
35. Ibid., pp. 261–65.
36. Ibid., pp. 208–9.

to be recalled, it was the Romans rather than they."[37] In fact, the Uniates "were men who lived side by side with members of the eastern Churches. . . . They knew . . . what holy lives many of them led. The Roman Church had no right to be . . . patronizing to the Church of S. Basil, S. Cyril, and S. Chrysostom."[38]

Eastern Orthodox participation in the National and World Council of Churches—never solid—is now more tenuous than ever. Controversial issues such as the ordination of women, the acceptability of a homosexual lifestyle, and abortion are causing Orthodox Christians to rethink their commitment to these organizations.

We only briefly touch on the significant move of some evangelicals to Eastern Orthodoxy. Seeking a more liturgical element in their worship experience, a number of people with backgrounds in Campus Crusade, Youth for Christ, and Young Life have joined Orthodox churches.[39]

Recently, an agreement of historic proportions came into being. "Representatives of two Orthodox branches that split in the fifth century over presumed differences about the nature of Christ have agreed on a joint statement of common faith."[40] The statement brings together the Orientals, who did not participate at Chalcedon, with the Greeks who did. They agree that Christ has two natures; however, they comprise an inseparable, indivisible union.

Although Eastern Orthodox participation and dialogue with evangelicals is not well known, there are interesting examples. One is when Metropolitan Anthony of the Russian Orthodox Church in England consented to become the Chairman of the Trustees of the C. S. Lewis Centre in London. This leader—whose office is one of the highest in the Orthodox Church—assumed this position because "of his conviction that despite the divorce of East and West, and the internal divisions of Western Christianity, historic orthodoxy is still there as a sweet savor, a common smell of true faith."[41] The Centre's promotional material has the following quote from Metropolitan

37. John Moorman, *Vatican Observed* (London: Darton, Longman and Todd, 1967), p. 57.
38. Ibid., p. 58.
39. See Gillquist, *Becoming Orthodox*, as well as his articles "Evangelicals Turned Orthodox," *The Christian Century*, 4 March 1992, and "Orthodoxy," *Faith and Renewal*, July/August 1992.

A recent convert to Orthodoxy is Frank Schaeffer. He is the son of Francis Schaeffer, who was well known in evangelical circles as a Reformed author and theologian. Frank Schaeffer's spiritual journey is chronicled in *Dancing Alone: The Quest for Orthodox Faith in the Age of False Religions* (Brooklyn: Holy Cross Orthodox Press, 1994).

For a recent treatment of Eastern Orthodoxy from an evangelical perspective, see Clendenin, *Eastern Orthodox Christianity*. Clendenin has served as a visiting professor of Christian Studies at Moscow State University.

40. "Orthodox Branches Take Step toward Communion," *San Diego Union and Tribune*, 26 August 1989.
41. Andrew Walker, "In Defense of Ecumenical Orthodoxy," *Touchstone: A Journal of Ecumenical Orthodoxy*, vol. 7, no. 1 (winter 1994): 13.

Anthony: "At the Centre we like to think that affirming the central tenets of historic Christianity—while remaining ourselves, with all our unresolved differences—offers a way forward for Christians of goodwill who are bored with or feel betrayed by institutional ecumenism."[42] Anglican C. S. Lewis would be pleased by these words in defense of "mere Christianity."

Evangelicals would do well to familiarize themselves with this most ancient of Christian jurisdictions. Eastern Orthodoxy has many desirable tenets—historicity, continuity, and doctrinal steadfastness being the most noticeable. We should indeed become acquainted with our brethren in the "Church of the Seven Councils."

42. Ibid.

APPENDIX B

THE COUNTER-REFORMATION AND LATER DEVELOPMENTS

The Counter-Reformation (also known as the Catholic Reformation) is usually dated from the middle of the sixteenth century to the beginning of the Thirty Year War (A.D. 1618). That the Roman Catholic Church was in a state of moral and spiritual disarray is acknowledged by Catholic authorities. The papacy had lost territories north of the Alps and popes had been forced to negotiate treaties with the secular authorities who in turn controlled the church. Simony (the selling of spiritual merits and church offices) was widely practiced. Indulgences (pledges of freedom from the punishment for sin granted to individuals) were sold like merchandise.[1] Most clergy were poorly educated and many lived with women in violation of their vows of celibacy.

As to the spiritual condition of the average Roman Catholic layperson, a contemporary Catholic historian writes: "Their Christian life often focused on external devotions to saints or Mary, going on pilgrimages, and gaining indulgences, without an understanding of the more basic truths of the Catholic faith."[2] This state of moral declension, coupled with the theological differences that were to surface with the Protestant Reformers, sets the stage for the Counter-Reformation. We will begin with the formation of the Society of Jesus, the Jesuits.

THE JESUITS

The theologians who emerged from the Jesuit order proved to be highly influential in the Counter-Reformation. Due in part to centuries of conflict

---

1. Indulgences were of primary concern to Martin Luther. See Roland H. Bainton, *Here I Stand: A Life of Martin Luther* (Nashville: Abingdon, 1978), pp. 54–64.
2. Alan Schreck, *The Compact History of the Catholic Church* (Ann Arbor: Servant, 1987), pp. 61–62.

with Islam, Spain became known for its orthodox militancy and obedience to the papacy. The Inquisition found fertile ground there for its investigations of heresy. Spain, therefore, was called "the hammer of heretics" and the "sword of Rome."[3] The Society of Jesus was to become a product of Iberian spirituality.

IGNATIUS LOYOLA (A.D. 1491/95–1556)

Ignatius Loyola was born in the Spanish province of Guipúzcoa, of a well-to-do Basque family. As a young man he acquired a reputation as a ne'er-do-well, joined the army, and was seriously wounded in combat against the French.

During a long convalescence, Loyola became acquainted with some books on the life of Christ and the saints and was converted. He set out on a pilgrimage to Montserrat and while in retreat developed the outline which would become his *Spiritual Exercises,* a manual designed to lead one into a deeper spiritual life. This work became the text book of the Jesuits.

After making a pilgrimage to Jerusalem in A.D. 1523, Loyola returned to Spain and attended several universities before enrolling at the University of Paris. There he determined to become a "soldier for Christ" and the Society of Jesus was born. Loyola recruited six of his brightest fellow students (one of which, Francis Xavier, became a famous missionary to India, Japan, and China) to establish what would become the Jesuit order. The Society of Jesus was officially established in 1540 by Pope Paul III.

JESUIT DISTINCTIONS AND MISSION

In addition to the usual vows of poverty, chastity, and obedience, the Jesuits took a vow of direct obedience to the pope. Concerning their reputation, "The Jesuits became known for their discipline and sacrifice and the society reflected Loyola's military spirit and organizational talent."[4] Loyola was also very concerned with education. Colleges and universities were formed for laity as well as clergy, the most famous being the Roman College (founded in 1551, now called the Gregorian University).

Although mention of the Jesuits often conjures up images of ecclesiological intrigue, casuistry, and the like (especially among evangelicals), their original mission concerned preaching Christ to the unconverted in the world. They became great missionaries, winning many to Christ in Africa, Asia, and the New World. Many were martyred for their faith.

3. Lewis W. Spitz, *The Renaissance and Reformation Movements,* vol. 2, rev. (St. Louis: Concordia, 1987), p. 477.

4. Robert D. Linder, "Ignatius Loyola," in John D. Woodbridge, ed., *Great Leaders of the Christian Church* (Chicago: Moody Press, 1988), p. 228.

Jesuit theologians were active in the Council of Trent and have been called "the shock troops of the Counter-Reformation."[5] We will meet them again at the Council of Trent and the Molinist and Jansenist controversies. Jesuits have also had considerable impact (some would say not always positive) on nineteenth- and twentieth-century theological development.[6]

THE COUNCIL OF TRENT

The Council of Trent (A.D. 1545–63) was the most important council since Nicea (A.D. 325). There would not be another council for 300 years—Vatican I. Trent's purpose was twofold: to address disciplinary reform (which admittedly was much needed), and to deal with doctrinal issues that had been raised by the Reformers.[7]

The Tridentine proceedings were as follows: Period I (A.D. 1545–47) set the basic agenda; Period II (A.D. 1551–52) was concerned with repudiating Reformed views on the Eucharist; and Period III (A.D. 1562–63) saw the influence of the Jesuits increase and any hope of repairing the breach with the Reformers disappeared.[8] Humor was not totally absent from these august proceedings: "One skeptical father at the Council observed that the Holy Spirit would no doubt come to them from Rome in the courier's bag."[9]

The Council of Trent dealt with a number of concerns, both of a disciplinary and theological nature. We will restrict our examination here to the most crucial issue: the nature, purpose, extent, and results of justification by faith.

PRE-TRIDENTINE DEVELOPMENTS

We have already examined in chapter 5 the nature of Augustine's thought on soteriological issues. Concerning justification, "Augustine has an all-embracing understanding of justification, which includes both the *event* of justification (brought about by operative grace) and the *process* of justification (brought about by cooperative grace)."[10]

The conflict Augustine had with Pelagianism involved the question of the human will: to what extent is it free to choose good and eschew evil? He be-

5. Spitz, *Renaissance and Reformation Movements,* p. 478.

6. Material on Ignatius Loyola and the Jesuit Order may be found in Cross, *Oxford Dictionary;* and Delaney and Tobin, *Dictionary of Catholic Biography.*

7. One of the major works used in this treatment is McGrath, *Iustitia Dei,* vol. 2. In chap. 7, "The Tridentine Decree on Justification," McGrath carefully details the existing theological schools that participated at Trent and the complex doctrinal formulations that were debated.

8. Cross, *Oxford Dictionary,* pp. 1392–93.

9. Spitz, *Renaissance and Reformation Movements,* p. 486.

10. McGrath, *Iustitia Dei,* vol. 1, p. 31.

lieved that "the power of sin is such that it takes hold of our will, and as long as we are under its sway we cannot move our will to be rid of it."[11] The II Council of Orange (A.D. 529) affirmed the Augustinian view.

Another group of doctrines emerged in the fourth and fifth centuries that has been called "semi-Pelagianism." It should be noted that the term itself is modern and was originally used to designate the teachings of the Jesuit Luis de Molina (A.D. 1535–1600). The earlier version of semi-Pelagianism was a position midway between Augustine and Pelagius, maintaining that, while divine grace was needed for salvation, "the first steps toward the Christian life were ordinarily taken by the human will and that Grace supervened only later."[12] These doctrines continued to be championed, especially in France, and finally were condemned by the II Council of Orange (A.D. 529).[13] The findings of Orange were confirmed by Boniface II (A.D. 530–532) in A.D. 531.[14]

That semi-Pelagian tendencies reappeared in pre-Reformation theology is admitted by both Roman Catholic and Protestant historians. Contemporary Roman Catholic scholar Hans Küng states: "Major significance for the history of dogma attaches to the fact that, because the Council [II Orange] was not contained in the majority of medieval collections or compilations, it was unknown to theologians between the 12th century and the second-third of the 16th century. In general, these theologians do not distinguish between Pelagianism and semi-Pelagianism."[15] Küng identifies Peter Abelard (A.D. 1079–1142) as "neo-Pelagian."[16]

Concerning the freedom of the will during this period, "This emphasis on human freedom was strong especially . . . among those influenced by Ockham's nominalism and the *via moderna* at the end of the Middle Ages."[17] A Roman Catholic historian writes of the late Middle Ages: "There was even a new approach to theology and philosophy called Nominalism, first championed by Englishman William of Ockham (A.D. 1280–1349), that separated the realms of faith and reason instead of seeing them as complementary as Thomas Aquinas and the other great scholastics had done."[18]

In spite of the popularity of the *via moderna*, the period witnessed the re-

---

11. González, *Story of Christianity*, 1:214.
12. Cross, *Oxford Dictionary*, p. 1258.
13. Denzinger, *Sources of Catholic Dogma*, nos. 1736–2000, pp. 75–81.
14. Ibid., pp. 81–82.
15. Küng, *Justification*, p. 177.
16. Ibid., p. 216.
17. H. George Anderson, ed., *Justification by Faith: Lutherans and Catholics in Dialogue VII* (Minneapolis: Augsburg, 1985), p. 19.
18. Schreck, *Compact History of the Catholic Church*, p. 58. Roman Catholics have pointed out that Martin Luther was trained in Nominalism (e.g., Bouyer, *Spirit and Forms of Protestantism*). While this may be true, Luther nevertheless rejected the view that a person's *unaided* will could move toward God.

birth of Augustinianism. Within this movement were a group of theologians who have been characterized as "Reform Catholics."[19] While these men cannot be understood as "Protestants," they were not impervious to the Reformed insights on justification by faith. Their thought was represented at the Council of Trent, but unfortunately (from the evangelical perspective) it could not make any headway.

EXISTING THEOLOGICAL SCHOOLS

The major doctrine that Trent was to investigate was the Protestant understanding of justification. As to the existing theological schools, "we are concerned with the identification of the main schools present at Trent, as this has an important bearing upon the relation of the final decree to late medieval Catholic theology in general."[20] While Alister McGrath is reluctant to rigidly classify the positions represented at Trent, he does identify three schools: the Thomists who had experienced a revival in the fifteenth century; the Scotist school, both the early (Bonaventure) and later (Duns Scotus) varieties; and Augustinianism was present in several forms as was the *via moderna* of Gabriel Biel.[21]

PROCEEDINGS AND DECREE ON JUSTIFICATION

The first doctrinal discussions concerned the topics of Scripture, tradition, and original sin. We will consider the outcome of debates surrounding the doctrine of justification only briefly here, since a fuller discussion is found in chapter 12.

In 1547 the council participants agreed on a final formula for justification. The process had been long and arduous and all of the theological schools weighted in with opinions on a great variety of complicated scholastic theological distinctions. Although several council members recognized an extrinsic element in justification (thereby approaching the Reformers on this point), the consensus view rejected "the opinion that a sinner may be justified solely as a matter of reputation or imputation."[22] Therefore, "Justification is thus defined in terms of a man becoming, and not merely being reputed as, righteous."[23] Trent understood justification in two senses (the second corresponding to the Reformed doctrine of sanctification), this second justifica-

---

19. Two of which were Gasparo Contrarini (1483–1542) and Johann Gropper (1503–59).
20. McGrath, *Iustitia Dei*, vol. 2, p. 63.
21. For a chart on various groups involved at Trent, see Table 7.1 in ibid., pp. 65ff.
22. Ibid., p. 72.
23. Ibid.

tion requiring a person's cooperation. Hence, "It is thus both possible and necessary to keep the law of God."[24]

The council, taking into account original sin, stated that sin has affected the human race. Therefore, "man is incapable of redeeming himself. Freewill is not destroyed, but is weakened and debilitated by the Fall."[25] However, "The sinner indeed cooperates with this grace, at least in the sense of not sinfully rejecting it."[26] Trent understood justification in two ways: "first" and "second" phases. Baptism is operative in "first" justification, where grace to overcome original sin is "mediated" to us.[27] The Eucharist and penance pertain to "second" justification, such justification being said to "increase" by participation in these sacraments.

Because the Reformers laid such stress on the concept of assurance of salvation Trent was forced to deal with the subject. Subsequently, they issued "An explicit condemnation of the Lutheran doctrine of assurance as an assertion contrary to proper Christian humility."[28] However, "In many ways Roman dogmatics has pointed out that Rome's rejection of personal assurance of salvation does not mean the proclamation of a religion of uninterrupted anxiety."[29] Thus, for the Roman Catholic "There is an intermediate position between the assurance of faith and doubt. This position is that of moral certainty which excludes any anxiety and despair."[30] Since grace is cooperative—at least concerning the second phase of justification—one can forfeit one's salvation. Thus, Christians can be said to have "relative," not absolute, certainty of salvation. A contemporary Dominican scholar, Stephanus Pfürtner, states that "it must be observed that the faith of the Church is not by any means exhaustively stated in its dogmas." Further, "we are in no way forbidden to ask what the Council properly means by 'certainty of grace,' in other words, what it condemned when it rejected this notion."[31]

Trent seems to state that our justification must be seen as a "gift" rather

24. Ibid., p. 84.
25. Ibid., p. 81.
26. Anderson, *Justification by Faith*, p. 34.
27. A detailed treatment of the sacrament of baptism is beyond the scope of this appendix. There are differences concerning it not only between Roman Catholics and evangelicals, but also in the Protestant community. It should be noted that Luther had difficulties formulating his understanding of baptism in light of his concept of forensic justification. On Luther and baptism, see Althaus, *Theology of Martin Luther*, pp. 353–74.
28. McGrath, *Iustitia Dei*, vol. 2, p. 78.
29. G. C. Berkouwer, *The Conflict with Rome* (Philadelphia: Presbyterian and Reformed, 1958), p. 114.
30. Bartmann, *Lehrbuch der Dogmatik, II*, p. 109; quoted in ibid., p. 115.
31. Stephanus Pfürtner, O.P., *Luther and Aquinas—a Conversation: Our Salvation, Its Certainty and Peril*, trans. by Edward Quinn (London: Darton, Longman and Todd, 1964), p. 31. Fr. Pfürtner suggests that the Fathers of the Council of Trent may have misunderstood what Luther actually taught concerning the "certainty of grace."

than a "reward." Thus, it comes as a surprise to many Protestants that
Roman Catholics believe that "If anyone shall say that man can be justified
before God by his own works which are done . . . without divine grace
through Christ Jesus: let him be anathema."[32] On the other hand, Trent says,
"If anyone shall say that man's free will moved and aroused by God does not
cooperate by assenting to God who looses and calls, . . . let him be anathema."[33] As to Luther's understanding of the total corruption of human nature and Trent's reaction to it, Roman Catholic scholar Michael Schmaus
comments, "It is questionable whether Luther actually advocated the doctrine to which the council's condemnation alludes."[34] Contemporary evangelical scholar Harold O. J. Brown notes that "Trent went so far in rejecting
everything that Luther taught that it impoverished Catholicism, and made it
unnecessarily rigid, even from the point of view of its own tradition. Valuable elements of the common Christian heritage were eliminated for no better reason than because Luther praised them."[35] Thomas Nettles summarizes it this way: "The evangelical error comes in spite of a confessional
history to the contrary; the Roman error purposefully canonized a historical
aberration at the sixteenth century Council of Trent and has maintained it
since."[36]

EVANGELICAL EVALUATION

The results flowing from the Council of Trent are complex and require
close study and evaluation. Our limited examination leads to the following
observations. First, Trent addressed and corrected many moral and disciplinary problems that had plagued the medieval church. Bishops were ordered to
live in their sees, the holding of several ecclesiastical offices at one time was
condemned, and the use of relics and indulgences was regulated. Second, the
charge of semi-Pelagianism is often made against Roman Catholicism by
Protestants; this is incorrect. The condemnation of semi-Pelagianism first
made at the II Council of Orange was reaffirmed at the Council of Trent.[37]
Third, the Council of Trent encouraged the study of Aquinas, who was
strongly Augustinian and thus anti-Pelagian. His theological system was de-

---

32. Trent, *Denz.,* 811, p. 258.
33. Ibid., p. 814. For a good treatment of the Council of Trent from a Roman Catholic perspective, see H. Jedin, *History of the Council of Trent,* trans. by F. C. Eckhoff (St. Louis and
London, 1947). The standard Protestant work is Martin Chemnitz, *Examination of the Council
of Trent* (St. Louis: Concordia, 1971).
34. Michael Schmaus, *Dogma 6: Justification and the Last Things* (London: Sheed and
Ward, 1977), p. 24.
35. Brown, *Protest of a Troubled Protestant,* p. 123.
36. Nettles, "One, Holy, Catholic, Apostolic Church," in Armstrong, *Roman Catholicism:
Evangelical Protestants,* p. 27.
37. See "Canons on Justification," in Denzinger, *Sources of Catholic Dogma,* pp. 258–61.

clared the official and dominant theology of Roman Catholicism. Lastly, there are real differences in areas such as justification, infallibility, the extent of the canon, the nature of the church, and sacramentalism. (These issues are addressed in Part Two.)

POST-TRIDENTINE DEVELOPMENTS

Earlier we developed the thesis that the Western Church owes its soteriology to Augustine (see chap. 5). Both Roman Catholics and evangelicals acknowledge their debt to the Bishop of Hippo.

However, the Pelagian system which Augustine bested reoccurred throughout church history. The debate usually revolves around the relationship between God's sovereignty and human responsibility; how God's grace is mediated to sinful human beings. We will look briefly at Molinism, the subsequent Augustinian reaction, and Blaise Pascal and Jansenism.

LUIS DE MOLINA (A.D. 1535–1600)

Molina was born in Cuenca, New Castile, Spain. He joined the Society of Jesus and became a theologian. The theology that bears his name claims to protect the integrity of human free will better than any other system. Among other things, Molinism affirmed that predestination follows God's foreknowledge. Thus, "the efficacy of grace has its ultimate foundation, not within the substance of the Divine gift of grace itself *(ab intrinseco),* but in the Divinely foreknown fact of free human cooperation with this gift."[38] This was perceived as a species of Pelagianism and was vigorously opposed by followers of Augustinianism.[39] If God's predestination depended on his knowledge of human free choice, then God's knowledge is dependent on contingent happenings and he is not truly an Independent Being. As the noted Thomist authority Garrigou-Lagrange put it, citing the Council of Orange: "If anyone maintains that God waits upon our will to cleanse us from sin, and does not rather acknowledge that even our willingness to be cleansed is brought about in us through the infusion and operation of the Holy Ghost, he resists the Holy Spirit Himself, who declares. . . : 'It is God who worketh in you both to will and to accomplish, according to His good will' (Phil. 2:13)."[40]

38. Cross, *Oxford Dictionary,* p. 928.
39. Material on Molina can be found in Delaney and Edward, *Dictionary of Catholic Biography,* pp. 814–15.
40. Reginald Garrigou-Lagrange, *Grace: Commentary on the Summa Theologica of St. Thomas, 1a 2ae, g. 109–14* (St. Louis: B. Herder Book Co., 1952), p. 208.

DOMINGO BÁÑEZ (A.D. 1528–1604)

Like Molina, Báñez was born in Spain. He joined the Dominican order and became known as one of the best Catholic theologians of his day. It is important to note that Báñez was interested in practical spiritual matters as well as theological issues, as he served as director and confessor of Teresa of Avila (see chap. 19).[41]

Báñez became the primary adversary of Molinism, which he claimed made "the power of divine grace subordinate to the human will."[42] Instead, Báñez claimed that "God knows the future, including conditional future free acts, in virtue of his divine decrees, which predetermine all events."[43] McGrath notes that "the term 'semi-Pelagian' was introduced during the course of this dispute by the followers of Báñez to describe the teachings of their Molinist opponents."[44]

This dispute between the Dominicans and the Jesuits became so severe that Pope Clement VIII intervened and decided to permit both viewpoints. The Dominicans were forbidden to call the Jesuits "Pelagians" and the Jesuits were not to refer to Dominicans as "closet Calvinists"! Both views exist in the Roman Catholic Church to this day.

BLAISE PASCAL AND JANSENISM (A.D. 1623–1662)

Blaise Pascal was born at Clermont-Ferrand, France, and is regarded as one of the greatest scientific geniuses that ever lived. As a teen he developed skills in geometry, physics, and mathematical theory that are still valid today. What is not so well known is his deep faith in Jesus Christ and his consciousness of sinful human nature. His theological insights naturally inclined him toward Jansenism, a group within French Roman Catholicism that professed to follow Augustine. This made them natural foes of the Jesuits, "who appeared to them to make Christianity too easy and accessible."[45]

The center of Jansenism was at the Convent of Port Royal in Paris. Pascal's sister Jacqueline was to later become a nun there and he maintained contact with the men and women of Port Royal all his life. A leading Jansenist, Antoine Arnauld, had been condemned by the Jesuit establishment and Pascal came to his defense by writing the *Provincial Letters*. These were published anonymously to avoid imprisonment and were a devastating critique

---

41. Material on Báñez can be found in Cross, *Oxford Dictionary*, p. 125.
42. Colin Brown, *Christianity and Western Thought*, vol. 1 (Downers Grove, Ill.: InterVarsity Press, 1990), p. 162.
43. Ibid.
44. McGrath, *Iustitia Dei*, vol. 2, p. 95.
45. Toon, "Blaise Pascal," in Woodbridge, *Great Leaders of the Christian Church*, p. 258.

of Jesuit casuistry, which they believed employed "situationalism" to arrive at moral decisions.[46]

CONCLUSION

We have examined some important events that occurred in Christendom from the Council of Trent through the post-Tridentine period. We have paid special attention to soteriological concerns, namely, justification by faith. Some observations follow.

1. Just as in church history prior to the Reformation, Augustinianism was never completely absent from the theological scene.
2. Although forms of Pelagianism (or semi-Pelagianism) can be detected in this time frame, these doctrines were condemned by official Roman Catholic pronouncements. This condemnation was first issued by the II Council of Orange, which "approved by Boniface II, obtained such authority in the Church that it is worthily held as an infallible norm of faith."[47]
3. The problem of how to reconcile the sovereignty of God and human freedom is an issue with which both Roman Catholics and evangelicals wrestle. May we humbly suggest considering the following quotation from the *Westminster Confession of Faith:*

> God from all eternity did by the most wise and holy counsel of his own will, freely and unchangeably ordain whatsoever comes to pass, *yet so as thereby neither is God the author of sin, nor is violence offered to the will of the creatures, nor is the liberty or contingency of second causes taken away, but rather established.*[48]

4. The doctrinal investigations of the Council of Trent seem to have been predicated on a number of misconceptions—chief of which is an erroneous belief that the Reformers were indifferent at best and antinomian at worse concerning faith and good works.

We have already quoted Luther on the subject of the need for a "good tree" to be present in order to produce "good fruit." In addition he said, "Our faith in Christ does not free us from works, but

---

46. A good treatment of Blaise Pascal can be found in Emile Cailliet, *Pascal: The Emergence of Genius* (New York: Harper and Brothers, 1961).

47. "Council of Orange II (A.D. 529)," Denzinger, *Sources of Catholic Dogma*, p. 75 n. 1.

48. "Of God's Eternal Decrees," in *The Constitution of the Presbyterian Church (U.S.A.),* Part 1, Book of Confessions (New York: Office of the General Assembly, 1983), emphasis added.

from false opinions concerning works. . . . For faith redeems, corrects, and preserves our consciences, so that we know that righteousness does not consist in works, although works neither can nor ought to be wanting."[49] John Calvin and the major Reformers agreed with Luther that while works are not the *grounds for* salvation they are the *result of* the believers justification. Peter Kreeft has this interesting observation about the Reformation: "How do I resolve the Reformation? Is it faith alone that justifies, or is it faith and works? Very simple. No tricks. On this issue I believe Luther was simply right; and this issue is absolutely crucial. As a Catholic I feel guilt for the tragedy of Christian disunity because the church in the fifteenth and sixteenth centuries was failing to preach the gospel."[50]

5. Roman Catholic and Lutheran scholars in the United States have engaged in dialogue for twenty-seven years. The issues discussed involve the doctrinal differences that led to the Reformation. These theologians have petitioned the Vatican to lift the anathema issued at the Council of Trent against justification by faith alone. The statement, among other things, says: "The goal is to declare by 1997 that the condemnations on justification 'are no longer applicable,' according to a joint statement issued here February 18–21."[51] The year 1997 will mark the 450th anniversary of the anathema issued by the Council of Trent. Such a declaration seems unlikely since infallible declarations are irrevocable. Nonetheless, real differences remain with Protestants affirming (and Catholics denying) that salvation is "by grace alone through faith alone" (see chap. 12).

6. Lastly, we have attempted to accurately describe the events and theological formulations that occurred during this interest period. Evangelicals and orthodox Roman Catholics should investigate the issues frankly and fairly, and not forget to emulate the godly Bereans, who "received the word with all willingness and examined the scriptures daily to determine whether these things were so (Acts 17:11)."

---

49. *Works of Martin Luther,* vol. 2, p. 344; quoted in Faculty of Union Theological Seminary in Virginia, *Our Protestant Heritage* (Richmond: John Knox, 1948), p. 176.

50. Kreeft, *Fundamentals of the Faith,* p. 290.

51. "Revocation of Condemnation Sought," *San Diego Union and Tribune,* 27 February 1993.

APPENDIX C

MODERN/LIBERAL CATHOLICISM

Protestantism was not the only branch of Christendom weakened by the Enlightenment. At the beginning of the twentieth century, ideas that had infiltrated many Protestant churches began to surface in Roman Catholicism. Catholic modernism was informed by two principal ideas: first, it desired to bring Roman Catholic belief into conformity with modern notions of philosophy and science; and second, it was subjectivistic—intuition was preferred to intellect. One Catholic source analyzes the situation this way: Because the criticism of Christian faith that came from some quarters was embarrassing, some "opted for a faith without knowledge. . . . They began with the premise that the human mind is entirely restricted to phenomena, the external, sensible properties of things."[1]

MODERNISM

Among the Modernist tendencies were:

1. A destructive critical approach to Bible study was employed. This often exceeded the skepticism found in their Protestant counterparts.[2] The Roman Catholic Church's position on the inerrancy of the Scripture had been clear cut: "The Council of Trent, though reacting strongly against the Reformation's formal principle of *Sola Scriptura*, stated in no uncertain terms the full inspiration of the Bible."[3] Mod-

1. Hardon, *Catholic Catechism*, p. 34.
2. For a treatment of how this has impacted Catholic Scripture teaching, see Fr. William G. Most, *Free from All Error* (Libertyville, Ill.: Franciscan Marytown Press, 1985).
3. Montgomery, *Ecumenicity, Evangelicals and Rome*, p. 74. Also see chap. 1, "Revelation."

ernism began to undermine this by limiting the infallibility of Scripture to only truths about salvation.

2. Scholastic theology was rejected. The systems of Augustine, Anselm, and especially Aquinas were declared invalid. "Deed" was stressed over "creed." The Modernists "sought the essence of Christianity in life rather than in an intellectual system or creed."[4]

3. In Modernism, history is understood as teleological; what it is *doing* is more important than where it *comes from*. In doctrine, this approach proved very destructive. The divinity of Jesus Christ was challenged and among other things they believed Jesus was in error concerning the time of his second coming (Gk: *parousia*).[5]

One authority calls Modernism "the synthesis of all heresies."[6] Among the leaders in the movement were Alfred Loisy (1857–1940), a Frenchman who was excommunicated in 1908; Friedrich Von Hügel (1852–1952); and George Tyrell (1861–1909)—the last two from England. Although Pius X (pope, 1903–14) condemned Modernism in 1907, its baleful effects are still with us. We will encounter it again in Appendix D.

THE OXFORD MOVEMENT AND JOHN NEWMAN

Space limitations force us to leave the effects of the Reformation in England untouched. As with the Reformation in Europe, political action and state policy—along with theological considerations—were active in the English ecclesiological rupture. Lutheran ideas, dating from at least A.D. 1520, were finding their way into the common culture and the universities. Also, humanism was in full swing; its most famous proponent was Erasmus, who lectured at Cambridge from A.D. 1509 to 1514.

The English revolt really emerged with the reign of Henry VIII (A.D. 1491–1547), which began in 1509. Henry has been described as "a man of remarkable intellectual abilities and executive force, well read and always interested in scholastic theology, sympathetic with humanism, popular with the mass of people, but egotistic, obstinate, and self-seeking."[7] When Henry's wife Queen Katharine was unable to provide him with a male heir and the papacy would not provide him with a divorce, the official breach with Rome occurred.

The Church of England is an interesting mix of theological stances; one

---

4. Cross, *Oxford Dictionary*, p. 926.

5. See Hardon, *Catholic Catechism*, pp. 144–45.

6. Broderick, *Catholic Concise Encyclopedia*, p. 243. For positions on various doctrines, see Ott, *Fundamentals of Catholic Dogma*, Index, "Modernism."

7. Walker, *History of the Christian Church*, p. 358.

can find the very liberal as well as the thoroughly orthodox within its ranks. Anglicanism has been called "half Catholic and half Protestant" in its doctrinal understandings. Many great Christian leaders have been nurtured in its bosom; the brothers Wesley, the social reformers Shaftsbury and Wilberforce, and the apologist C. S. Lewis to name but a few.

THE OXFORD MOVEMENT (1833–1845)

The "high church" tradition (also known as the Anglo-Catholic party) in the Church of England produced the Oxford, or Tractarian Movement. Also, the spread of "liberalism" in theology and increasing Roman Catholic influence were major factors in the birth of the Oxford Movement. This group of devout and intensely self-conscious believers had for their goal the restoration of primitive and medieval Christianity. Their main objective was to defend the Anglican communion as a legitimate branch of the Christian church and they argued for the validity of "Apostolic Succession" within the Church of England. The acknowledged leaders within the movement were John Keble (1792–1866), E. B. Pusey (1800–1882), and John Henry Newman (1801–90), to whom we now turn our attention.[8]

JOHN HENRY NEWMAN

The most important figure to emerge from the Oxford Movement was John Henry Newman. Born in London of well-to-do parents, he graduated from Oxford and was ordained to the Anglican priesthood in 1825. He was appointed vicar of St. Mary's, the university church where he ministered for fifteen years. In addition to his work in the Oxford Movement, Newman wrote a number of books: *The Arians of the Fourth Century* (1833) and *Tracts for the Times* (1833–41), the latter being statements of his religious positions. A number of them "defended his thesis of the 'Via media,' i.e. the belief that the Church of England held an intermediate position, represented by the patristic tradition, as against modern Romanism on the one hand and modern Protestantism on the other."[9]

Of special interest to us in this book is the fact that Newman finally became disillusioned with the claims of the Anglican Church and in 1845 he was received into the Roman Catholic Church. Soon after his conversion he wrote his *Essay on the Development of Christian Doctrine*, and in 1852 the *Idea of a University*. Although Leo XIII made Newman a cardinal in 1879, he was viewed with suspicion in conservative Catholic circles and his genius

---

8. For background on the Oxford Movement and its leaders, see Cross, *Oxford Dictionary,* pp. 1019–20; Walker, *History of the Christian Church,* pp. 497, 499; and John A. Griffin, *John Keble: Saint of Anglicanism* (Macon, Ga.: Mercer University Press, 1987).

9. Cross, *Oxford Dictionary,* p. 965.

was not recognized until after his death. He was also to play an important role in Vatican I, which will be discussed shortly.[10]

Newman and Justification. Newman's *Lectures on Justification,* published before his conversion to Roman Catholicism, is well regarded by modern Roman Catholic scholars. Küng writes, "Though too little known, this book is one of the best treatments of the Catholic theology of justification."[11] In *Justification,* Newman addressed the primary sense of the term by setting forth three principles: (1) justification is a *declaration* of righteousness; (2) it is to be *distinguished from* renewal; and (3) it is the *ground* or efficient cause of renewal.

The essence of Newman's understanding of justification "is his insistence upon the real presence of the Trinity within the soul of the justified believer, . . . which undoubtedly reflects his interest in and positive evaluation of the Greek fathers, such as Athanasius."[12] In *Justification* "Newman defined what he took to be a *via media* understanding of justification, which allowed an authentically *Anglican* concept of justification to be defended in the face of the distortions of both Protestantism and Roman Catholicism.[13] However, according to McGrath, "Newman's historico-theological analysis appears to be seriously and irredeemably inaccurate."[14] In particular "Newman's critique of Luther in the *Lectures* appears to rest upon the quite fallacious assumption that the Reformer regards faith as a human work."[15]

Luther understood human beings to be passive in justification, which is God's work completely. Concerning Luther's position McGrath writes: "Luther does not understand 'justification by faith' to mean that man puts his trust in God, and is justified on that account . . . rather, it means that God bestows upon that man faith and grace, without his cooperation, effecting within him the real and redeeming presence of Christ as the 'righteousness of God' within him, and justifying him on *this* account."[16]

McGrath feels that Newman misunderstood the actual Lutheran and Reformed position on justification. Concerning the Reformer from Geneva, he comments: "Had Newman studied Calvin seriously, he could hardly have failed to notice the remarkable similarities between them on the nature of justification."[17] Both believed that justification and renewal are part and parcel of God's great gift to us.

10. For background on Newman, see "John Henry Newman," in Delaney and Tobin, *Dictionary of Catholic Biography,* pp. 847–48.
11. Küng, *Justification,* p. 212.
12. McGrath, *Iustitia Dei,* 2:123.
13. Ibid., p. 122.
14. Ibid.
15. Ibid., pp. 125–26.
16. Ibid., p. 126.
17. Ibid., p. 130.

Newman's "Doctrine of Development." Almost immediately after his conversion to Roman Catholicism in 1845, Newman released his *Essay on the Development of Christian Doctrine.*[18] This theological treatise was to have implications for Roman Catholic doctrinal development.

Newman began his thesis with two convictions: first, the fourth- and fifth-century Fathers were the rightful successors of the apostolic church, and second, any revelation from God must of necessity be in some way associated with God's church.[19] Also, he was aware of the possibility of corruption (heresy) concerning the development of doctrine. Thus, he stated a number of characteristics of true development: the preservation of the idea or type, the continuity of principles, the power of assimilation, early anticipation, logical sequence, preservative additions, and chronic continuance.[20]

Evangelicals may critique Newman's development model at several points: first, his identification of the Roman jurisdiction as being *the* authentic, "true" church, and second, his use of his theory to develop dogmas (i.e., concerning the virgin Mary, the sacraments, etc.), which are rejected by non-Roman Catholic Christians. Some evangelicals, however, have overstated the case against Newman's theory of development. A penetrating critique of Newman's theory is found in the classic refutation of infallibility by George Salmon, *The Infallibility of the Church.*[21]

Newman is accused of providing the historical/theological framework that would become the "warp and woof" of Roman Catholic Modernism in the early years of the present century. Further, it is claimed that Newman's theory makes any appeal to earlier sources or authorities (such as Augustine, Aquinas, Trent, and Vatican I) dated and irrelevant. This may be the view of liberal Roman Catholic theologians but it is firmly rejected by traditionalists.

Concerning Newman's orthodoxy Pope Pius X, who was very critical of Modernism, stated: "Be assured that we strongly approve of your pamphlet proving that the works of Cardinal Newman, far from being at variance with our Encyclical are actually in close agreement with it."[22] In 1993, John Paul II

---

18. (Notre Dame: University of Notre Dame Press, 6th ed., 1989).

19. Newman felt that he had to choose between the Roman Catholic Church and the Protestant denominations. He seems not to have considered Eastern Orthodoxy an option (see Appendix A).

20. Peter Toon, *The Development of Doctrine in the Church* (Grand Rapids: Eerdmans, 1979), pp. 8–15. Also see "John Henry Newman," *New Catholic Encyclopedia,* vol. 10 (New York: McGraw-Hill, 1967), p. 418. Evangelicals will notice the similarity between Newman's theory and that of "progressive revelation" mentioned in chap. 1.

21. (E. P. Dutton & Company, 1914 [1st ed. 1888]).

22. From a private letter to Bishop O'Dwyer of Limerick, Ireland; quoted in Christopher Hollis, "The Achievements of Vatican II," *The Twentieth-Century Encyclopedia of Catholicism,* ed. by Henri Daniel-Rops (New York: Hawthorn Books, 1967), p. 13. For an examination of the similarity between Newman's theory of development and the Protestant understanding of "progressive Revelation," see Henri Rondet, S.J., "Do Dogmas Change?" ibid., pp. 7–9.

issued an encyclical, *Veritatis Splendor* ("The Splendor of Truth"). Among its purposes is to affirm "the universality and immutability of the moral commandments," to which most evangelicals would bid the pope "Godspeed." This encyclical contains 184 footnotes. Of those, thirty-six (or one in five citations) contain references to patristic writers (sixteen from Augustine), and nineteen footnotes reference Aquinas, principally from the *Summa Theologiae*.[23] Evangelical criticism of Roman Catholicism in other areas notwithstanding, traditional Catholicism cannot be accused of jettisoning the pronouncements of its forerunners. Concerning the essay on development, David Wells states: "To be sure, John Henry Newman would have been appalled to see the use to which his formulation had been put by the Modernists."[24]

VATICAN I (1869–70)

Pope Pius IX convoked the First Vatican Council to address a number of issues, including faith and dogma, church discipline, foreign missions, and church-state relations. Two schools of thought concerning church and papal authority were present. The majority party defended the authority of the pope and for this reason were called "ultramontane," for "they looked for authority 'beyond the mountains'—that is, beyond the Alps."[25] The minority party (represented, among others, by John Henry Newman) wished to see infallibility linked to the bishops as well as the pope. This is known as "conciliarism." The two views clashed on various issues throughout the council proceedings.

The council opened on December 8, 1869, with nearly 700 bishops in attendance. Various stances such as rationalism, materialism, and pantheism were examined and condemned. Of the remaining topics, it was decided to first deal with the question of papal infallibility (see chap. 11), to which we now turn.

PAPAL INFALLIBILITY

The council debated infallibility in heated discussion. The minority party objected to papal authority being defined apart from the rest of the magisterium (the councils and bishops). The vote on infallibility was taken two months after the debate began and the measure passed.

23. John Paul II, "Veritatis Splendor," *Origins: Catholic News Service,* vol. 23, no. 18, 14 October 1993.

24. David F. Wells, *No Place for Truth: Or Whatever Happened to Evangelical Theology?* (Grand Rapids: Eerdmans, 1993), p. 120.

25. González, *Story of Christianity,* 2:165.

The definition of the dogma contained a number of elements, one of the most crucial being that infallibility is operative only when the pope speaks *ex cathedra* ("from the chair"), which is to say "when in discharge of the office of Pastor and Doctor of all Christians, by virtue of his supreme Apostolic authority he defines a doctrine regarding faith or morals."[26] Evangelicals, of course, reject the Catholic claim to infallibility. What is more, others (including the Eastern Orthodox) contend that this formulation is objectionable because there is no sure way to determine which papal statements are "from the chair" and which are not (see chap. 11).[27]

John Henry Newman's opposition to the dogma of papal infallibility is noted by the anti-Roman Catholic Reformed scholar Loraine Boettner.[28] Concerning Newman's position, contemporary Roman Catholic apologist Karl Keating states: "He opposed not the content of the definition given at Vatican I, but the wisdom of promulgating the definition at that time; he thought the promulgation was inopportune, not inaccurate."[29] Even granted that Boettner could be injudicious in method and strident in temperament when addressing Roman Catholicism, Keating's contention is difficult to accept. The historical evidence seems to indicate that Newman opposed restricting the authority of the church to the papal office. Nevertheless, the infallibility of the pope was promulgated on July 18 and war broke out the following day between France and Prussia, bringing the council to an end.[30] As a faithful Catholic, Newman was obliged to accept the dogma he fought against.

CONCLUSION

We have examined events and people who have, for good or ill, prepared the Catholic church for the twentieth century. When the first church council in almost 300 years convened, solidifying the authority of the pope, the breach between Protestants and Roman Catholics widened. But perhaps the most ominous development to occur in this time frame is the foothold that Mod-

26. Cross, *Oxford Dictionary,* p. 1428.

27. Several cases in church history illustrate this problem. One of the best known is the trial of Galileo (1564–1642) in 1616 when the Copernican theory was condemned at Rome and Galileo was ordered not to teach it. Galileo's condemnation recently has been lifted, which raises the interesting question concerning the original "infallible" pronouncement (see chap. 11). Background on the incident can be found in Charles E. Hummel, *Galileo Connection* (Downers Grove, Ill.: InterVarsity Press, 1986), pp. 81–125.

28. See Loraine Boettner, *Roman Catholicism* (Philadelphia: Presbyterian and Reformed, 1962), p. 243.

29. Keating, *Catholicism and Fundamentalism,* p. 226.

30. The official texts of the dogma of the infallibility of the pope can be found in Denzinger, *Sources of Catholic Dogma,* nos. 1832–40, pp. 455–57.

ernism established in the Roman Catholic Church. The antecedents of this movement can be identified at least as far back as Erasmus and his dispute with Luther over the freedom of the will. They probably date back further to the Augustinian and Pelagian controversy. Humanism of this ilk, with its tolerant, syncretistic framework, has been and always will be the enemy of authentic Christianity, of whatever variety. We will encounter its negative influences in Appendix D, which concerns the contemporary situation.

Concerning heretical teachers—either Roman Catholic or Protestant—Harold O. J. Brown offers wise counsel, "It is repugnant to every concept of human liberty and dignity to say that a man should be punished or persecuted for his ideas and opinions—but it is also repugnant to reason to say that a church cannot dismiss a teacher who is undermining its own intellectual foundations. It has no right to persecute him, but it certainly has no obligation to furnish him with a salary and a pulpit."[31]

31. Brown, *Protest of a Troubled Protestant,* p. 127.

Appendix D

Vatican II and the Current Situation

Introduction

Before we address the Second Vatican Council some introductory remarks are in order. The period between Vatican I and Vatican II saw some developments that had a profound impact on Christianity.

British Roman Catholic historian Paul Johnson has chronicled a definite philosophical shift in Western culture beginning in the twentieth century. Johnson notes, "At the end of the Second World War, there was a significant change in the predominant aim of secular intellectuals, a shift of emphasis from utopianism to hedonism."[1] Johnson identifies three English writers, all born in 1903, who illustrate this philosophical re-direction: George Orwell, Evelyn Waugh, and Cyril Connolly. Hedonism and its close relative, existentialism, had a sizable effect on Christianity in the twentieth century.

Modernism Resurfaced

We dealt with the origins of Modernism in Appendix C. As a movement, it was condemned by Pope Pius X in 1907.[2] Modernism wreaks havoc first in the study of Scripture. Since the Bible is the source of and plumb line for Christian belief, any diminishing of its authority and authenticity is fatal. This destructive approach which had found fertile ground in mainline Protestantism surfaced in Roman Catholic Bible studies and theological systems.

1. Paul Johnson, *Intellectuals* (New York: Harper & Row, 1988), p. 306.
2. By the decree "Lamentabili" and the encyclical "Pascendi." See Denzinger, *Sources of Catholic Dogma*, nos. 2001–2178, pp. 508–59.

Roman Catholics were warned not to be swayed by "the old war-cry of Protestantism, 'the Bible and the Bible only.'"[3] Such notions led Roman Catholics to embrace an "unCatholic super-exaltation of the Bible."[4] "Bibliolatry" is to be avoided at all costs.

The same liberalizing tendencies were encouraged in theology and societal concerns. Stephen Duffy paints the scene: "What is being played out in contemporary Catholic life is the effort to come to terms with modernity."[5] Contemporary traditional Roman Catholics have lamented this slide into unbelief. An editor of a Catholic publishing house wrote, "I don't pray any more. I've given it up for Lent. Also for Advent and Pentecost." He said "My prayer life is a room with no furniture in it," and concerning saying grace, "How can I maintain, without lying, that God has a hand in the meal?"[6] Jesuit scholar John O'Malley explained the meaning of this "new," "progressive" Catholicism is that "we are freed from the past. We are free to appropriate what we find helpful and to reject what we find harmful."[7]

Evangelical scholar John Montgomery perceptively calls this approach "new shape" Catholicism. It infuriates orthodox Roman Catholics, but some Protestants find it appealing. "One must not be afraid to look deeper—to the motif that underlies the New Shape. This is the substitution of a 'dynamic,' 'personalistic' category of doctrinal interpretation for the formalistic, propositional, Aristotelian—Thomistic categories of 'efficient causality.'"[8] This "new shape" avant garde tendency in Roman Catholic theology looks suspiciously like Bultmannian demythologization, which wreaked such havoc in twentieth-century Protestantism.[9]

LIBERATION THEOLOGY

One movement to emerge from the new theological climate in Catholicism is liberation theology. Also known as "Marxist Christianity," its basis is Chris-

---

3. Gerald P. Fogarty, S.J., *American Catholic Biblical Scholarship: A History from the Early Republic to Vatican II* (San Francisco: Harper & Row, 1989), p. 150.

4. Ibid. Fogarty's work is an interesting history of biblical and theological development in American Roman Catholic "progressive" circles.

5. Stephen Duffy, "Catholicism's Search for a New Self-Understanding" in Gerald M. Fagin, S.J., ed., *Vatican II: Open Questions and New Horizons* (Wilmington, Del.: Michael Glazier, 1984), p. 9.

6. Don Brothy, "Why I Don't Pray Anymore," *National Catholic Reporter,* 1 March 1974, p. 9; quoted in Hitchcock, *Catholicism and Modernity,* p. 12.

7. John W. O'Malley, S.J., "Report, Historical Consciousness, and Vatican II's Aggiornamento," *Theological Studies,* 32, 1971, pp. 575, 590, 597, 600; quoted in ibid., p. 20. Also see Martin, *Crisis of Truth.*

8. Montgomery, *Ecumenicity, Evangelicals and Rome,* p. 34.

9. Ibid., p. 37.

tian social action aimed at bettering the lot of the poor and oppressed. Liberation theology is best known for its effect in the "third world," Latin America in particular, where it also has the support of some mainline Protestant groups.

Liberation theologians synthesize between Marxism and Christianity, making two assertions: one economic, the other theological.[10] The economic thesis states that "Democratic capitalism . . . is responsible for the poverty of the third world."[11] Concerning the situation in South America, "Traditional Catholic ignorance about modern economics may, in fact, have more to do with the poverty of Latin America than any other single factor."[12] The theological thesis of liberation theologians assumes a new and different source of revelation than that which has informed historic Christianity. "Neither the *sola Scriptura* of Reformation Protestantism nor the 'two sources' of Tridentine Catholicism . . . , namely Scripture and sacred tradition, is sufficient to justify so fundamental an assumption."[13] Their Marxist hermeneutic is flawed, however, because "Instead of first focusing on Christ and the Bible as the revelational center of human history and destiny, . . . liberation theologians . . . make existing social and political conditions the necessary lens for viewing and interpreting scriptural data."[14] Brown warns that "When even committed Marxists join the ostensibly 'neutral' secular press in their praise of the course the Roman Church is taking, all those who are concerned about her fate and destiny, Catholics and Protestants alike, had better take notice."[15]

Finally, let us say clearly that orthodox Roman Catholics and evangelicals agree that Christians have a duty to care for the poor and to promote justice among the world's oppressed. Our approach to this issue has several concerns. First, a true liberation theology must be faithful to the biblical doctrines of the historic Christian faith. Second, it should be evangelistic. Third, it ought to give priority to the vertical aspect of the gospel (God to humanity) rather than the horizontal (person to person).[16]

---

10. Nash, *Social Justice and the Christian Church*, p. 156.

11. Michael Novak, "A Theology of Development for Latin America," in Ronald H. Nash, ed., *Liberation Theology* (Milford: Mott Media, 1984), p. 22. Novak is a Roman Catholic scholar in philosophy, religion, and public policy at the American Enterprise Institute. He has written extensively on liberation theology and modern economic theories.

12. Ibid., p. 24.

13. Harold O. J. Brown, "What Is Liberation Theology?" ibid., p. 10.

14. Carl F. H. Henry, "Liberation Theology and the Scriptures," ibid., p. 196.

15. Brown, *Protest of a Troubled Protestant*, p. 142.

16. In addition to works already quoted, see Jacques Ellul, *Jesus and Marx* (Grand Rapids: Eerdmans, 1988). The French sociologist and lay theologian brilliantly dissects the unholy alliance between Christianity and Marxism. One of his most fascinating insights is that the word "poor" in Scripture has a wider context than popularly assumed. The wealthy publicans were "poor"; the high paid call-girl prostitutes were "poor" (p. 145ff.). Also see Martin, *Crisis of Truth*, pp. 88, 96ff., where he discusses liberation theology in Latin America.

RADICAL FEMINISM

Radical feminism is closely related to liberation. In addition to the impulses that influence liberation theology in general, New Age concepts also have been incorporated in radical feminism. This movement is especially active in Roman Catholicism. Concerning the make-up of one feminist convention: "A startling majority of the women in attendance appeared to be Catholics: nuns, ex-nuns, students and faculty members from Catholic women's colleges, parochial school teachers."[17] A quote from the "godmother" of Catholic feminism, Rosemary Radford Ruether, immediately locates her on the theological spectrum: "A lot of evil had been done in the name of Christ, but no crusades or pogroms had been sent in the name of Ba'al, Isis or Apollo."[18] Small wonder that orthodox Roman Catholics are exercised about this movement.[19]

VATICAN II (A.D. 1962–65)

In January 1959 Pope John XXIII made public his intention to summon a council. It is important to note at the outset that the council neither claimed nor made any infallible pronouncements. Hence, while Catholics must accept it as authoritative, nothing stated in it is irrevocable. People everywhere asked themselves what motivated this move to call a council and how would it effect the Roman Catholic Church and other Christian jurisdictions? The pope defined the task of the council to be the renewing of the religious life of the church and asked Catholics to pray for the council: "Renew in our day O Lord, your wonders, as in a new Pentecost." The portrayal of Jesus as the "Good Shepherd" deeply impressed him, indeed, "every description of John XXIII calls attention to this single ambition; he wanted first of all and genuinely to be a pastor."[20] Pope John's vision extended beyond his own communion to the Christian church worldwide.

Vatican II developed as follows:

Session I (October 11–December 8, 1962). Participants elect their own commission, thus distancing themselves from the Roman curia. John XXIII dies on June 3, 1963; he is succeeded by Paul VI on June 21, who announces his intention to continue the council.

---

17. Donna Steichen, *Ungodly Rage: The Hidden Face of Catholic Feminism* (San Francisco: Ignatius Press, 1992), p. 31.

18. Ibid., p. 32.

19. In addition to Steichen's excellent volume for an evangelical critique of feminism, see Kassian, *Feminist Gospel.*

20. G. C. Berkouwer, *The Second Vatican Council and the New Catholicism* (Grand Rapids: Eerdmans, 1965), p. 12.

Session II (September 29–December 4, 1963). Delegates vote to support the collegiality of the bishops, the divine right of the Episcopal College, and the reinstating of the Diaconate order. On May 17, 1964, the secretariat for non-Christian religions is formed.

Session III (September 14–November 21, 1964). This session results in the promulgation of the Dogmatic Constitution on the Church, the Decrees on Ecumenism and the Eastern Catholic churches. The Virgin Mary is also proclaimed to be the "Mother of the Church."

Session IV (September 14–December 8, 1965). In this session a number of documents are drawn up, involving church discipline, religious renewal, and Christian education. On December 4, a service for the "Promotion of Christian Unity" takes place, and observers and guests as well as delegates take part. The council closes on December 8, 1965.[21]

THEOLOGICAL MAKEUP OF THE PARTICIPANTS

Delegates of Vatican II represented the whole of the theological spectrum, from the most liberal to the most conservative. This variety was also present in the non-Roman observers and guests.[22] Indeed, so diverse were the participants at Vatican II that David Wells says the documents that Vatican II produced "officially embraced mutually incompatible theologies."[23] One theology represented was traditional, the other progressive. "The first was championed by the conservatives in general and the Curia in particular, while the second found its proponents among a school of thinkers who in general represent the New Catholicism."[24]

One area of difficulty was the doctrine of inerrancy. On the one hand, "Without doubt, it would seem, the Roman Catholic church wants to say it still believes in biblical inerrancy, at least as it was defined in 1870."[25] However, an English bishop and progressive theologian explains the council's view in such a fashion as to distinguish between "salvation truths" in Scripture that are inerrant and non-salvific material (historical and scientific statements) that are not.[26] This definition breaks with the historic position of the church.

21. Cross, *Oxford Dictionary*, pp. 1428–29.

22. See John Moorman, *Vatican Observed: An Anglican Impression of Vatican II* (London: Darton, Longman & Todd, 1967). Moorman (bishop of Ripon) indicates that there was as much disagreement among the observers as between the council's participants.

23. David F. Wells, *Revolution in Rome* (Downers Grove, Ill.: InterVarsity Press, 1972), p. 27.

24. Ibid., p. 28.

25. Ibid., pp. 30–31.

26. Ibid., pp. 31ff. For the view of the British Roman Catholic scholar who left the church because it was not progressive enough, see Charles Davis, *A Question of Conscience* (New York: Harper & Row, 1967).

LIBERAL BIAS CONCERNING INERRANCY

Evangelicals will remember the controversy that occurred in our community surrounding the understanding of what it means to declare that the Bible is "inerrant." Some evangelicals held to "limited inerrancy," meaning the Scriptures are inerrant when addressing salvific matters, but not necessarily so when non-salvific statements are made. Liberal Protestants have the same agenda as their Catholic compatriots.

Vatican II dealt with the issue of inerrancy in the "Dogmatic Constitution on Divine Revelation."[27] One translation from the Latin text is found in a volume edited by Walter M. Abbott, S.J., and is the one preferred by liberal scholars.[28] The translation that Roman Catholic traditionalists believe best represents the original text is the one edited by Austin Flannery, O.P.[29] The Abbott treatment of the text in question is misleading in that it *relocates* a key phrase in the Latin text, transforming it from a purposive, explanatory clause "for the sake of our salvation" to a restrictive clause. The Flannery translation following the Latin text, renders the sentence as follows:

> Since, therefore, all that the inspired authors, or sacred writers, affirm should be regarded as affirmed by the Holy Spirit, we must acknowledge that the books of Scripture firmly, faithfully and without error, teach that truth which God, *for the sake of our salvation,* wished to see confided to the sacred Scriptures.[30]

In this rendering, the placement of the clause makes it explanatory; it explains the purpose for which God recorded his truth in sacred Scripture. It was to facilitate our salvation.

The Abbott translation, however, renders the sentence as follows:

> Therefore, since everything asserted by the inspired authors or sacred writers must be held to be asserted by the Holy Spirit, it follows that the books of Scripture must be acknowledged as teaching firmly, faithfully, and without error that truth which God wanted put into the sacred writings *for the sake of our salvation.*[31]

Notice that the relocation of the clause in question changes its purpose from an explanatory sense and becomes instead a restrictive clause, indicating that Scripture teaches without error only that truth that is salvific in nature. Other assertions made by Scripture are not guaranteed to be true.

---

27. *Dei Verbum*, 18 November 1965.
28. Walter M. Abbott, S.J., *The Documents of Vatican II* (New York: Guild Press, 1966).
29. Austin Flannery, *Vatican Council II*, vol. 1, rev. (Boston: St. Paul's Books and Media, 1992).
30. Ibid., p. 757, emphasis added.
31. Abbott, *Documents of Vatican II*, p. 119, emphasis added.

We have examined this problem at length to prove a point that some evangelicals overlook in their zeal to refute Roman Catholics. The official position of traditional Roman Catholicism concerning the authority of Holy Writ is that everything Scripture asserts is asserted by God, and since God cannot assert falsehood, everything Scripture asserts is automatically inerrant (see chap. 1). Just as we would take offense if someone confused the theological position of Henry Emerson Fosdick with that of B. B. Warfield, so we should realize that Hans Küng is informed by a different theological impulse than, say, Cardinal Ratzinger.[32]

SOME RESULTS OF VATICAN II

We will touch briefly on a few topics that were addressed in the Council under "Separated Brethren." Here a more tolerant and open attitude was displayed at Vatican II concerning non-Roman Catholic Christians. "The relationship between Rome and non-Catholic Christians has for sometime not been the same as it was at Florence, for instance, where the Church was distinguished from heretics and schismatics as sheep from goats."[33] The exclusiveness of the Roman Catholic church was down played; people could be "members of the Church *in a certain sense* without being members of the institution."[34] Thus, non-Roman Catholic believers could belong to the "soul" while being absent from the "body."

Liturgical Renewal. Efforts were also made to emphasize that the "church" is not only the pope and the hierarchical structure but all the people of God—laity as well as clergy. Lay ministry (women as well as men) was expanded and encouraged.

Collegiality. Further, there was an increased awareness of shared authority or "collegiality." The bishops have an important role to play in the directing of the church. This function, however, is not to be understood as diluting the authority of the papacy.

Non-Christian Religions. There has been some confusion as to what the council determined concerning the salvific status of non-Christian religions. With regard to *Nostra Aetate* (NA), the document dealing with this subject, a Lutheran scholar observes that, "For the first time, there is a recognition of non-Christian religions as entities that the church should respect and with

---

32. We are indebted to James Akin, staff member of *Catholic Answers*, for insights concerning this issue.

In the encyclical, "Humani Generis," (1950), Pope Pius XII addressed the error of "limited inerrancy." Speaking of certain "progressive" theologians, "they put forward again the opinion, already often condemned, which asserts that immunity from error extends only to those parts of the Bible that treat of God or of moral and religious matters" (p. 22).

33. Berkouwer, *Second Vatican Council and the New Catholicism*, p. 196.

34. Ibid., p. 197.

which Christians should enter into dialogue."[35]

Many commentators on NA maintain that it recognized non-Christian religions as ways of salvation. Traditional scholars disagree, believing that this line of interpretation reflects more the presuppositions of the individual thinkers than the direct teaching of the council. Their view is that, while the council did not recognize the salvific *efficacy* of other religions, it did find the general salvific *presence* of God's grace in all of God's universe (the concept of "general revelation").

The Blessed Virgin Mary. There was a concerted effort on the part of some traditionalists at Vatican II to devote a special document to Mary, to emphasize her unique role in salvation and in Catholic tradition. This effort failed. The council decided not to elevate Mary's status at this time. Instead, she is discussed in the last chapter of *Lumen Gentium,* the document dealing with the church.

EVALUATION OF VATICAN II

Evangelicals are faced with a bewildering amount of conflicting opinions concerning the determinations of Vatican II. Roman Catholic liberals (of the Curran, Hunthausen, McBrien variety) have interpreted Vatican II to permit changes in theology and morals that exercise not only their more conservative colleagues but evangelicals as well. Views on the ordination of women, abortion, and the homosexual life-style come to mind. Also, evangelicals are rightly concerned about any trend to diminish the doctrine of the complete inerrancy of Scripture. In addition, any reflection of a inclusivistic/universalistic notion of salvation being present in non-Christian religions is of serious import.[36]

---

35. Miikka Ruokanen, "Catholic Teaching on Non-Christian Religions at the Second Vatican Council," *International Bulletin of Missionary Research*, October 1985, 9:154–58. Ruokanen is a professor of theology at University of Helsinki. Vatican Council II also attempted to address that most ancient of disruptions in Christendom—the East/West schism. In the "Decree on Ecumenism," we find a common statement from Pope Paul VI and Patriarch Athenagoras, leader of the Orthodox Church of Constantinople.

The spiritual leaders of both jurisdictions "regret the offensive words . . . and the reprehensible gestures which on both sides marked or accompanied the sad events of that period." Further, "They also regret and wish to erase from the memory and midst of the Church the sentences of excommunication which followed them" ("The Common Declaration of Pope Paul VI and Patriarch Athenagoras," December 7, 1965. Flannery, *Vatican Council II*, p. 471).

36. Official Roman Catholic positions have been informed by both "traditional" and "progressive" perspectives. Dietrich von Hildebrand *(Trojan Horse in the City of God)* was a close friend of Pope Pius XII. A traditionalist, he was an erudite but blunt-speaking scholar who became concerned after the Second Vatican Council with certain "renewal" innovations. Among other charges, he accused some bishops of tolerating "the drivel of heretics."

Issues such as the reception of communion in the hand, the "new" vs. the Latin/Tridentine mass, and currently the use of "altar girls" during the Eucharist feast have been cause for concern amongst traditionalists. Pope John Paul II is attempting to return the church to a more orthodox perspective.

Orthodox Roman Catholics take issue with the usual "progressive" interpretation of Vatican II. An associate director of the Center for Pastoral Renewal (a Catholic charismatic group) writes: "The overriding purpose of the Vatican Council was to enable the Catholic Church to bear more effective witness to Christ in the modern world."[37] But the message was misunderstood, and "Catholic magazines and books carried the message that while official Catholic teaching on various issues had not changed, it was no longer binding, since Vatican Council II supposedly had promulgated a new view of conscience (an instance of appealing to the 'spirit' of the Council rather than to what was actually said)."[38]

John Cardinal O'Connor is probably the premier example of traditional, orthodox Roman Catholicism in the United States. He has joined forces with evangelicals to combat the moral laxity in our culture. In a meeting between American archbishops and curial officials, he addressed the misconceptions that issued from Vatican II: "We are still trying to recover from the chaos of misunderstanding and deliberate distortions. Suddenly all the old certainties seemed to be in question."[39] Our orthodox friends in the Roman Catholic Church are attempting to fight unbelief and pluralism in their communion. While we remain vigilant to biblical norms, evangelicals should stand with them whenever possible.

THE CURRENT SITUATION

In March 1990, John Cardinal O'Connor took on heavy-metal rock music in general and rocker Ozzy Osbourne in particular. He warned that "Violence is on the rise and heavy metal rock can trap people, especially teenagers." The cardinal also affirmed the existence of Satan and his influence in the world. Father Richard McBrien (then chairman of the theology department at the University of Notre Dame) disagrees. McBrien considers the idea of a personal Satan to be "premodern and precritical."[40] Here again we are faced with the riddle of Roman Catholicism.

There is a new appreciation on the part of Roman Catholics concerning the thinking of the Reformers. An example of this "rethinking" is a fascinating little volume by Dominican scholar Stephanus Pfürtner. He finds Martin Luther and Thomas Aquinas much closer in their understanding of the Chris-

---

37. Kevin Perrotta, "The U.S. Catholic Church," in Ronald H. Nash, ed., *Evangelical Renewal in the Mainline Churches* (Westchester, Ill.: Crossway, 1987), p. 141.

38. Ibid., p. 147.

39. Steichen, *Ungodly Rage*, p. 17. For accounts of Cardinal O'Connor's involvement with evangelicals, see chaps. 17 and 20.

40. Philip Elmer-De Witt, "No Sympathy for the Devil," *Time,* 19 March 1990, pp. 55–56.

tian's hope of salvation than has been commonly held. Concerning the ground of this hope, it was for Aquinas, "no less than for Luther a vital relationship to God and 'the experience' of his personal faith." Pfürtner believes that Luther's understanding of Aquinas's theological method was flawed and prevented him from appreciating the work of the "Doctor Angelicus."[41]

As to his "new" direction, Harold O. J. Brown states, "It is significant that Roman Catholic scholars in two fields, biblical studies and church history, have been at the forefront of his development. Roman Catholics, turning more readily to the Bible itself instead of their traditional commentaries, have discovered it to be the legitimate source of some 'Protestant' ideas."[42] However, this "new spirit" is not without its dangers. "Unfortunately, precisely because such scholars have stimulated a new openness, Roman Catholicism may be dangerously naive vis-à-vis Protestantism today. The Protestantism of Robinson is not that of Luther, nor is Pike's anti-Catholicism anything like that of Calvin."[43]

Concerning Luther and his understanding of the work of the Holy Spirit in sanctification, contemporary Roman Catholic scholar Jared Wicks concludes that "anyone who deals with ecclesiological topics can be positively stimulated and enriched by Luther's insights."[44]

On the evangelical side, there has been a revived appreciation of the work of Thomas Aquinas. Reformed thinker Arvin Vos's book, *Aquinas, Calvin, and Contemporary Protestant Thought*, is a case in point.[45] One of the authors (Norman Geisler) has produced a major tome on the angelic doctor titled, *Thomas Aquinas: An Evangelical Appraisal*.[46] There are also many young evangelical thinkers who have a great appreciation for Aquinas, including Winfried Corduan, Douglas Givett, Terry Miethe, and J. P. Moreland. Indeed, Miethe is now the co-editor of the authoritative work on Thomistic writings.[47] In fact, having read Aquinas more carefully, even the noted Reformed philosopher Alvin Plantinga is more friendly to Aquinas.

Also, some evangelicals are renewing their interest in liturgy. In a contemporary Roman Catholic magazine, a P.C.A. (Presbyterian Church of American) pastor writes that many evangelical congregations are "entertainment-drenched." The purpose of worship is "not entertainment for believers. Worship is designed to be entertaining to God, to please and delight Him. God is

41. Pfürtner, *Luther and Aquinas—a Conversation*, pp. 39–40.
42. Brown, *Protest of a Troubled Protestant*, pp. 124–25.
43. Ibid.
44. Jared Wicks, S.J., "Insights for Luther's Instructions on the Faith," *Pro Ecclesia* 2, no. 2, pp. 150–72.
45. See Arvin Vos, *Calvin, Aquinas, and Contemporary Protestant Thought* (Grand Rapids: Eerdmans, 1985).
46. See Geisler, *Thomas Aquinas: An Evangelical Appraisal* (Grand Rapids: Baker, 1991).
47. Terry Miethe and Vernon J. Bourke, eds., *Thomistic Bibliography* (Westport, Conn.: Greenwood Press, 1980).

the audience in worship."[48] Therefore, these Presbyterians have "tested the traditional liturgies of the Church by the standard of Scripture and have found them sound in many important respects."[49]

What then does the face of modern Roman Catholicism look like? Just as it is possible to distinguish different varieties within Protestantism, so it is within the Roman Catholic Church. Allowing for some overlap, first, there are the *traditionalists.* These devotees have been said to be "more Catholic than the pope." Indeed, they oppose the pope whenever they perceive that he is blurring the parameters of Roman Catholic orthodoxy. The ultra-traditionalists are firm in their defense of Tridentine Catholicism and prefer that the mass be recited in Latin. They are few in number and not very influential and may be compared in demeanor with the more radical wing of the Protestant fundamentalist movement.[50]

Next are the *conservatives.* This is historic Roman Catholicism and most of the scholars and clergy we have quoted with approval belong to this group. They resist all forms of revisionism and liberalism in theological matters and have joined forces with evangelicals in opposing a number of secularist trends in our culture.[51]

Liberal Catholics have adapted positions common to their liberal counterparts in mainline Protestantism. In addition to reinterpreting particular Catholic dogmas, they often go further and reject basic Christianity, such as the authority of Scripture and the orthodoxy of the councils and creeds. They are outspoken in their criticism of Pope John Paul, who has attempted to curtail their influence.

48. Peter J. Leithart, "The Biblical Way to Worship," *Crisis* (October 1992): 32.

49. Ibid., p. 30.

50. The concerns of this group are reflected in the journal *The Latin Mass: Chronicle of a Catholic Reform,* published bi-monthly by the Foundation for Catholic Reform, Fort Collins, Colorado.

51. Each day seems to unveil a new controversy that impacts Roman Catholic communion. Altar girls have already been mentioned and when the Holy See responded positively to the request of the American bishops to allow female altar servers orthodox Catholics were nonplussed. See Joseph Fessio, S.J., "How Did It Happen? A Canonical Investigation," *The Catholic World Report* (June 1994): 42–48.

On the other hand, on May 30, 1994, Pope John Paul II clearly reaffirmed the Church's ban on women priests. See *"Ordinatio sacerdotalis"* commented on in *The Southern Cross,* 9 June 1994, p. 6. Also, the English translation of the *Catechism of the Catholic Church* (which we have quoted throughout this work) was held up by a dispute between Cardinal Ratzinger and Cardinal Bernard Law, archbishop of Boston. Law, previously known as a conservative and extremely orthodox prelate, wanted to use "inclusive" (gender-neutral) language in the document while Ratzinger held out for traditional terminology. Although the "inclusivists" were addressing language referring to people traditional Catholics feared it would be extended to titles concerning God. Cardinal Ratzinger prevailed. See Cindy Wooden, "Catechism: Getting English to Match French," Catholic News Service, *The Southern Cross,* 9 June 1994, pp. 4, 24. Also see Lucio Brunelli, "That Strange Translation: Made in America," *30 Days,* no. 4, 1994, pp. 10–12; and "Comparative Translations," *The Catholic World Report* (June 1994): 38–41.

We have alluded to the fact that many (if not most) American Roman Catholic theologians are of the liberal/progressive persuasion. Robert B. Strimple is professor of systematic theology at Westminster Seminary West. He is also one of the few non-Catholic members of the Catholic Theological Society of America (CTSA). Professor Strimple has related to one author (Ralph MacKenzie) that mention of John Cardinal Ratzinger's name elicits hoots and hisses at the CTSA meetings.[52]

Concerning ecumenicism, Harold O. J. Brown has sound advice: "If Roman Catholicism is to avoid poisoning itself on the new ecumenical diet, it must be very careful not to ingest the radical theologies which are destroying Protestant church life and doctrine."[53] And, "Roman Catholics ought to be aware that if they take Protestantism en masse, they will be buying some kind of a radical pig in a voluminous poke."[54] Brown says, "For any kind of Catholic, a liberal Protestant is a more companionable and agreeable dialogue partner, but for a believing Catholic, it is only the evangelical Protestant who can be a *Christian* dialogue partner."[55]

Charismatic Catholics are "evangelical" and share characteristics with their Pentecostal and charismatic brethren in Protestantism. The "Baptism of the Holy Spirit" and the exercise of gifts such as tongues and healing are central to their spiritual experience. They also cooperate with evangelicals in various efforts.

Cultural Catholics make up the majority of Catholics, and are sometimes referred to as "cradle Catholics." These are people who, due to circumstances of birth and rearing, have a cultural attachment to Catholicism but have little or no religious conviction. Unfortunately, this group, coupled with the aforementioned liberal Catholics, presents the only portrait that the person on the street sees. It is also tragic that many clergy (including some bishops) are guided by this mentality.

Lastly, we may identify *folk Catholics,* who are found in abundance in places such as Latin America and Haiti. A combination of primitive beliefs of an animistic nature with traditional Catholicism produces an eclectic religious mix. An example of the cultic nature of "folk" Catholicism was reported by the Associated Press. On Good Friday 1994, nineteen people reenacted the death of Jesus Christ by being crucified in Capitangan, Philippines. The report stated that, "Fourteen of the devotees were nailed to

---

52. For a detailed treatment of the American Roman Catholic theological scene, see Robert B. Strimple, "Roman Catholic Theology Today," in Armstrong, *Roman Catholicism: Evangelical Protestants,* pp. 85–117.

53. Brown, *Protest of a Troubled Protestant,* p. 137. Harold O. J. Brown addresses this group in "Catholic Loyalists vs. Traditionalist," *The Religion & Society Report,* December 1994, vol. II, no. 12, pp. 6–7.

54. Ibid., p. 138.

55. Ibid., p. 157.

crosses while the others were tied to them. Attendants dressed as Roman centurions used slender aluminum nails soaked in alcohol to prevent infection." The account went on to say that the local Roman Catholic hierarchy disapproves of such activity, but that "the events are so popular among rural peasants that the church makes little effort to discourage them."[56] Many folk Catholics are guilty of idolatry in the worship of the virgin Mary and the saints. This group is particularly susceptible to proselytism by zealous (often charismatic) evangelicals. These new believers tend to be passionately anti-Catholic, and it is difficult to convince them that authentic faith can be found in the Roman Catholic Church. This probably more than any other factor is the reason that evangelicals and charismatics have been so successful evangelizing in the "third world" nominally Catholic areas.[57]

In a contemporary journal, Fr. Avery Dulles, S.J., states that there are "four fronts" comprising American Catholicism. They are:

The Traditionalists. These include authors such as Ralph Martin and James Hitchcock. While not advocating a "ghetto mentality," they favor environments that transmit Catholic faith and morals.

Neo-Conservatives. These include Catholics such as Richard John Neuhaus and George Weigel, who are democratic capitalists and resist statism.

Liberal Catholics. These are thinkers such as Richard McBrien, who favor a restructuring that would include married priests and women in clerical office.

Radical Catholics. This position is typified by Dorothy Day and Daniel Berrigan, and reflects such stances as voluntary poverty, radical feminism, and support for inclusive language referring to God as well as persons.[58]

The good news is that there is a new spirit of reaching out to Protestants based on shared moral and biblical convictions. We conclude this discussion with a quote from one Roman Catholic, James Hitchcock:

> The real ecumenical task, which presents both the greatest difficulties and possibly the greatest rewards, is to begin explorations with the Protestant groups broadly called evangelical. The greatest difficulties are found here, because these groups take their own beliefs very seriously and will not compromise easily.[59]

---

56. "Faith Healer, Others Undergo Crucifixion," *San Diego Union & Tribune,* 2 April 1994.

57. We wish to acknowledge that the source of this basic classification is Kenneth R. Samples, "What Think Ye of Rome?" *The Christian Research Journal* (winter 1993). Also, see the editorial "What Separates Evangelicals and Catholics?" *Christianity Today,* 23 October 1981.

58. "Catho-cliques: The U.S. Catholic Fronts," *30 DAYS,* no. 11 (1993): 21–22. Fr. Dulles is a valuable resource in that he occupies a mediating position between liberal/progressive and traditional American Roman Catholics. Some Roman Catholics chide Protestants for the proliferation of denominations within Protestantism. This seems a bit disingenuous given the various and diverse stances found within their own jurisdiction.

59. Hitchcock, *Catholicism and Modernity,* p. 231.

And from Peter Kreeft:

The agreements between orthodox Protestants and orthodox Catholics are far more important than the agreements between orthodox Catholics and liberal, or Modernist, or demythologized Catholics, and far more important than the agreements between orthodox Protestants and liberal Protestants.[60]

---

60. Kreeft, *Fundamentals of the Faith*, p. 294.

Appendix E

Baptismal Regeneration

While not unique to Catholicism, the sacrament of baptismal regeneration has a unique role in the Catholic faith. Some Protestants (such as Lutherans, Anglicans, and Methodists) hold to the *fact* of baptismal regeneration, but not in the same way that Catholics do, since they believe it is a cause of grace (see chap. 13). These differences make the criticism of baptismal regeneration more damaging for Catholics.

Why Baptismal Regeneration Is Crucial to Catholicism

There are many reasons why the rejection of baptismal regeneration is more fatal to Roman Catholicism as a system. First, only Catholicism institutionalizes baptism in a unique way (see chap. 13). Second, only Catholicism sees baptismal regeneration as the way adults receive initial justification. Third, Catholicism sees no necessity for forensic justification in contrast to baptismal regeneration. Fourth, there is no tension in Catholicism between baptismal regeneration and initial justification by faith alone, as there is in Lutheranism. Finally, only Catholicism proclaims this doctrine infallibly; therefore they have more to lose if it is wrong. Thus, while the following critique applies to some forms of Protestantism, it is even more damaging for Catholicism. Baptismal regeneration is not an essential belief for those Protestants who hold it; in fact, they find significant tension between it and their basic Protestant principle of "faith alone." However, baptismal regeneration naturally fits with and is essential to Catholicism. That is, Protestantism can live without it (e.g., Reformed and Baptist churches), but Catholicism cannot. For this reason the following criticisms apply uniquely to Catholicism.

Catholic theology insists on the necessity of baptismal regeneration. This is evident both from the official pronouncements on the topic and from the biblical text Catholics use to support it.

ARGUMENT FOR THE NECESSITY OF BAPTISM

The Council of Trent declared: "If anyone shall say that natural water is not necessary for baptism, and on that account those words of our Lord Jesus Christ: 'Unless a man be born again of water and the Holy Spirit' (John 3:5), are distorted into some sort of metaphor; let him be anathema."[1] And, according to the same council, "If anyone shall say that baptism is optional, that is, not necessary for salvation: let him be anathema."[2] Baptism properly administered is a once-for-all act, not to be repeated.[3] However, like some Protestants (e.g., Arminians), Catholics believe baptism is not a guarantee of salvation, for even the regenerate can lose their salvation.[4]

What is more, the Council of Trent declared that "If anyone shall say that infants, because they have not actual faith, after having received baptism are not to be numbered among the faithful, and therefore, when they have reached the years of discretion, are to be rebaptized . . . let them be anathema."[5] This is crucial to the debate between Catholics and evangelicals. For, according to Catholics, "Baptism confers the grace of justification."[6] But for Protestants, justification is by faith alone apart from baptism or any other righteous work (act).[7] Since baptismal regeneration is a *de fide* pronouncement of the Catholic faith it is not negotiable. The Council of Trent declared: "If anyone denies that by the grace of our Lord Jesus Christ which is conferred in Baptism, the guilt of original sin is remitted; or even assert that the whole of that which has the true and proper nature of sin is not taken way . . . let him be anathema."[8] This, of course, does not mean that one becomes sinless at baptism but that all of the *guilt* of original sin and actual sin are forgiven at baptism. The *desire* to sin (which is the stain of sin), however, remains and will result in future sinful *behavior*.

1. Denzinger, *Sources of Catholic Dogma*, no. 858, p. 263.
2. Ibid., no. 861, p. 264.
3. Ibid., no. 867, p. 264.
4. Ibid., no. 862, p. 264.
5. Ibid., no. 869, p. 264. It should be noted that Roman Catholic theology does not believe that all unbaptized infants go to hell. Older Catholic theologians speculated that they went to limbo (neither heaven nor hell). Currently, most Catholic theologians reject limbo in favor of a mysterious way in which God reveals himself to infants with the offer of salvation and they express implicit "faith."
6. Ott, *Fundamentals of Catholic Dogma*, p. 354.
7. Christian baptism is a righteous act or deed done in obedience to God's command. Jesus called his baptism an act that fulfilled "righteousness" (Matt. 3:15). In this sense it is properly called a righteous work. Since it is a divinely appointed work prompted by his grace it is considered a good deed and not one done by purely human effort in an attempt to please God. These kinds of self-righteous works are condemned by Scripture (Rom. 10:3; 1 Cor. 13:3).
8. Denzinger, *Sources of Catholic Dogma*, no. 792, p. 247.

Elaborating on the Catholic dogma of justification by baptism, noted Catholic authority Ludwig Ott comments:

> As justification consists, negatively, in the remission of sin, positively, in the sanctification and renewal of the inner man (D 799), so Baptism, provided that the proper dispositions (Faith and sorrow for sin) are present, effects: a) the eradication of sins, both original sin and, in the case of adults, also all personal moral or venial sins; b) inner sanctification by the infusion of sanctifying grace, with which the infused theological and moral virtues and the gifts of the Holy Ghost are always joined.[9]

ARGUMENT FROM SCRIPTURE

Catholics offer a host of texts to support their belief in salvation by baptism, which includes infant salvation, since infants are considered proper candidates of baptism. Ott summarizes the case this way:

> According to the testimony of Holy Writ, Baptism has the power both of eradicating sin and of effecting inner sanctification. Acts 2, 38: "Do penance: and be baptized every one of you in the name of Jesus Christ for the remission of your sins. And you shall receive the gift of the Holy Ghost." I Cor. 6, 11: But you are washed: but you are sanctified: but you are justified: in the name of our Lord Jesus Christ and the Spirit of our God." Acts, cf. 22, 16 [sic]; Rom. 6, 3 et seq.: Tit. 3, 5: John 3, 5; I John 3, 9; 5, 18.[10]

ARGUMENT FROM TRADITION

In addition to the argument from Scripture, Catholic scholars appeal to tradition in support of baptismal regeneration. Ott claims that "From the very beginning Tradition ascribes to Baptism the same effects. The author of the Barnabas Letter says: 'We descend into the water full of sins and filth and we arise from it bearing fruit as we have in our hearts the fear of God, and in our spirits hope in Jesus' (II,II)."[11] Justin, Tertullian, and Cyprian are also cited in support of salvation through baptism.

PROTESTANT RESPONSE TO CATHOLIC ARGUMENT FOR BAPTISMAL REGENERATION

Since Catholics offer many Scriptures in support of their belief in baptismal regeneration, we will respond to them first before arguing that salvation is

9. Ott, *Fundamentals of Catholic Dogma*, p. 354.
10. Ibid., p. 355.
11. Ibid.

by faith alone, apart from baptism.[12] Since many of the same points can be made from different texts we will concentrate on the most important ones.

RESPONSE TO ARGUMENT FROM SCRIPTURE

Since Protestants believe that the Bible alone is sufficient for faith and practice, they take seriously any attempt by Catholics to support their doctrines from Scripture. And while the authors acknowledge that some Protestants (e.g., Anglicans and Lutherans) believe in baptismal regeneration, we believe the Reformed/Baptist rejection of this doctrine is a more consistent Protestant approach.

Acts 2:38. Ludwig Ott uses this often cited text (from the Douay version) in support of baptismal regeneration: "*Do penance:*[13] and be baptized every one of you in the name of Jesus Christ for the remission of your sins. And you shall receive the gift of the Holy Ghost." Several points should be made in response to the use of this verse.

First, the outmoded and inaccurate translation "do penance" (following the Latin Vulgate) has been corrected by almost all modern and contemporary translations, including those done or approved by Catholics. The *New American Bible,* St. Joseph Edition, which is approved by the National Conference of Catholic Bishops, renders it correctly as "Repent and be baptized," as do the Catholic *New Jerusalem Bible* and the *Revised Standard Version Catholic Edition.* This eliminates the mistaken idea that any works are necessary as a condition for receiving the gift of the Holy Spirit.

Second, people are "born again" by receiving God's word (cf. 1 Pet. 1:23), and Peter's audience "accepted" his word before they were baptized (Acts 2:41).

Third, elsewhere in Acts those who believed Peter's message clearly received the Holy Spirit *before* they were baptized. Peter said, "Can anyone

12. One must be careful not to overstate the conclusion here, since many Protestants hold baptismal regeneration too, including the Lutheran *Book of Concord* (Philadelphia: Fortress, 1978) which affirms: "What gifts or benefits does Baptism bestow? Answer: It effects forgiveness of sins, delivers from death and the devil, and grants eternal salvation to all who believe, as the Word and promise of God declare" (Small Catechism, "The Sacrament of Holy Baptism," pp. 348–49). See also the Large Catechism which affirms that "the power, effect, benefit, fruit, and purpose of baptism is to save [which] . . . is nothing other than to be delivered from sin, death, and the devil and to enter into the kingdom of Christ and live with him forever" ("Baptism," p. 439).

13. Contemporary Catholics are embarrassed by this mistranslation of the Greek word *metanoia* as "do penance" and have dropped it. What they forget, however, is that the Vulgate was the official translation of the Catholic church and this very text was cited by Trent and used as a basis for their (false) teaching on penance. At best this is scarcely a good example of the alleged infallible guidance Catholics claim for the church, especially one gathered at an ecumenical council!

withhold the water for baptizing these people who have received the holy Spirit even as we have?" (Acts 10:47).[14]

Fourth, Acts 2:41 speaks of "those who accepted his message" (i.e., believed) as having been baptized later on. Receiving (believing) the message is the means by which one is saved (John 1:12; 12:48; Rom. 1:16). And verse 44 speaks of "those who believed" as being constituents of the early church, not all of whom were baptized. Likewise, Mark says "Whoever believes and is baptized will be saved" (Mark 16:16), because baptism should follow belief. Nowhere does it say, "whoever is not *baptized* will be condemned." Yet Jesus said emphatically that "whoever does not *believe* has already been condemned" (John 3:18, emphasis added).[15]

Fifth, Paul separates baptism from the gospel, saying, "Christ did not send me to baptize but to preach the gospel" (1 Cor. 1:17).[16] But it is the

---

14. Catholic scholars sometimes appeal to a "dispensational shift" here, claiming that this passage is not normative but a special case to assure the Jewish believers that Gentiles also were to be accepted into the church. This creative evasion of the obvious is insufficient for several reasons: First, the fact that it happened at all proves the evangelical point that water baptism is not necessary for salvation. If it were, then they could not have received the Holy Spirit before baptism. Second, the Jews would have been just as convinced that God accepted Gentiles if they had miraculously received the Holy Spirit and tongues *after* being baptized; doing it before was no more miraculous. Third, reversing the order to convince the Jews of Gentile acceptance would more likely to have had a different effect on the Jews. It probably would have convinced them that there was no necessity to be baptized first, rather than the subtle "dispensational" point that Gentiles should be accepted too.

15. Some Catholic apologists argue unconvincingly that if the text said "whoever believes and repents will be saved" everyone would understand that there were two conditions for salvation stated here. This is purely hypothetical since the text does not say this. However, since the Bible does list both belief and repentance as the means of receiving salvation, the illustration is a good one—unfortunately, not for the Catholic position. For both belief and repentance are two aspects of *one and the same act* of receiving Christ (Acts 17:30, 34), sometimes being used in the same verse (Acts 20:21). Repentance stresses the turning from sin and faith stresses the turning to God (cf. 1 Thess. 1:9), but both are part of one true act of faith. Baptism, however, is clearly a separate act from believing (whichever comes first). Nonetheless, even if a text were to read: "Whoever believes and repents will be saved. But whoever does not believe will not be saved" we would know that repentance, as a separate act from believing, is not necessary for salvation. We could easily conclude from such a statement that belief was the only necessary condition and that repentance was put there as a synonym or for emphasis to make explicit that true faith involved a turning from sin as well as a turning to God. Finally, in texts where the meaning is not as clear as we may like it, we should never use them to build a dogma. In fact, these difficult texts should be interpreted in the light of the clear ones which call for only one condition for receiving salvation—belief (e.g., John 3:16, 36; 5:24; Acts 16:31; Rom. 1:17; 4:5).

16. The Catholic retort that Paul is only putting conceptual distance between baptism and the gospel is unconvincing for several reasons. First, he makes a strong contrast between the two in this passage, insisting that his call was only to preach the gospel, not to baptize. If baptism is part of the gospel by which we are saved, as Catholics believe, then such a statement by St. Paul would mean that he did not understand or preach the true gospel, since he claimed it was not part of what God sent him to do! Second, even though it is understandable that a busy itinerant preacher like Paul could not take time to baptize all his converts, nonetheless, it is still true that

gospel that saves us (Rom. 1:16). Therefore, baptism is not part of what saves us.

Sixth, Jesus referred to baptism as a work of "righteousness" (Matt. 3:15), but the Bible declares clearly that it is "not because of any righteous deeds we had done but because of his mercy, he saved us" (Titus 3:5). Hence, we are not saved by baptism.[17]

Seventh, the Gospel of John, written explicitly so that people could believe and be saved (John 20:31), cites only belief as the condition of salvation. It simply states over and over that people need to "believe" and they will be saved (cf. John 3:16, 18, 36). If more were necessary, then the entire Gospel of John misleads on the central purpose for which it was written.[18]

Eighth, the word "for" (Gk: *eis*) can also mean "with a view to" or even "because of." In this case, water baptism would be called for *because* they had been saved, not *in order to* be saved. Even in the broader sense of "with a view to" the view could be backwards to the fact that they had been saved, baptism being a later outward manifestation of it.[19]

Finally, even if "for" is taken in the sense of "in order to" this text does

---

he affirmed that baptism is not part of the gospel. And it is the gospel that saves us (Rom. 1:16). Hence, baptism is not part of what saves us. Third, baptism in the New Testament, at least in the case of adults, always followed, as a separate act, believing the gospel that was preached (e.g., Acts 2:38; 10:44–47; 16:31–33). So it was not part of the gospel. The fact that the gospel and baptism are often mentioned in the same text does not prove they are the same, especially when they are mentioned as two separate acts, as they are. Finally, there are instances of those who were never baptized but still were saved, such as the thief on the cross (Luke 23:43).

17. It is unconvincing to argue that Jesus' baptism was a special case and our baptism is not like his. First, Catholics believe that Jesus is our great moral example (1 Cor. 11:1). Peter said that Christ left "an example that you should follow in his footsteps" (1 Pet. 2:21). Second, even if Christ's baptism is not a paradigm of Christian baptism, nonetheless, ours is still a work of righteousness in the sense that it is a physical act performed in obedience to his command. But this by definition is a work of righteousness. Certainly no Christian would call Christian baptism an unrighteous act. It is a righteous act! It makes no difference whether it is a means of receiving grace or not. It still would be a work by which this grace was received. Of course, it should be done in faith, opening one's self to God's blessing. That is what true obedience is. But that does not make it any less a righteous work.

18. No appeal to one isolated text (John 3:5) which is subject to disputed interpretations (see below) can contradict the repeated and clear teaching that belief is the only condition for salvation. Otherwise, Jesus was deceiving his audience on all those other occasions when he said that only belief, not belief and baptism, was necessary for salvation.

19. It has been argued that *eis* meant "for" (i.e., in order to bring about) to the authors of the Nicene-Constantinopolitan Creed and, therefore, to deny this meaning here is to reject orthodoxy. But this does not follow. The word *eis* can and often does mean "for" in other contexts, and even if it means "for" in Acts 2:38 baptismal regeneration does not necessarily follow. What the authors of the creed believed on other points is irrelevant to what they affirmed in the creed. Nowhere in this creed do they affirm baptismal regeneration. It merely connects baptismal forgiveness in the same associational and symbolic way they are in Scripture (cf. Acts 22:16; 1 Pet. 3:20–21).

not prove baptismal regeneration for two reasons: first, the apostles were already believers by this time (cf. Matt. 16:16–18; John 20:30–31). It was not a question of their getting saved; they already were saved. What they were promised here after water baptism as Christians was "the gift of the Holy Spirit," not the gift of salvation or eternal life (cf. Rom. 6:23) which is received only by faith (Eph. 2:8–9; Titus 3:5–7). They were already regenerate, but they were not yet equipped with gifts by which they would have the "power" to serve Christ (cf. Acts 1:8).[20] Indeed, it was only after they received the gift of the Spirit (Acts 2) and gave it to others (Acts 8, 10, and 19) that the church grew in great numbers (Acts 2:41, 47). The converts of the evangelist Philip are a case in point. Even though he had preached to them and they believed and were baptized (Acts 8:12), they had not received the Holy Spirit until the apostles came down and laid hands on them (Acts 8:15–17). But they were obviously saved before they received this special gift of the Holy Spirit.[21] So, it is entirely possible that Peter was not referring to being justified (or regenerated) in Acts 2:38, but rather of their repentance and baptism as a Christian. This was a condition of their receiving the special gift of the Holy Spirit that empowered them to speak supernaturally in languages unknown to them (cf. Acts 2:4, 8) and to witness with great boldness (Acts 1:8; cf. 4:1–20).

In brief, this oft cited text does not support the Roman Catholic doctrine of baptismal regeneration. Rather, consistent with the rest of Scripture, it teaches that people have to "repent" or "accept the message" in order to be saved. Baptism is merely an outward sign of an inward reality that came "by grace through faith" and not by any "works of righteousness," including baptism.

John 3:5. Jesus said, "no one can enter the kingdom of God without being born of water and Spirit." Although this is a favorite text of those who believe in baptismal regeneration, it says nothing about baptism or it being a condition of salvation.

20. Nor can one argue that the apostles were already baptized and therefore "grandfathered" out of this command. There is no indication that baptism before Pentecost was the same as this baptism. We know, for example, that those who were baptized by John before Pentecost had to be rebaptized after Pentecost (Acts 19:4–5). And even if the apostles were exempted here on the basis of an earlier proleptical Christian baptism, there were over one hundred others there who were believers (Acts 1:15). Indeed, many in the crowd were "devout Jews" (Acts 2:5) who believed in the Messiah and had come to worship at this Jewish feast. Even though they were saved, as any other devout Jew was saved before Christ, they would still have to be baptized here.

21. The fact that Paul later said that no one can be saved who does not have the *presence* of the Holy Spirit (Rom. 8:9) is not in conflict with the promise to receive the special *gift* of the Holy Spirit here. The Holy Spirit *indwelt* the apostles (John 14:16) before they were later *baptized* by the Spirit (Acts 1:5, 8). These are different acts of the Holy Spirit.

First, baptism is not necessary for salvation. Salvation is by grace through faith and not by works of righteousness (Eph. 2:8–9; Titus 3:5–6). But baptism is a work of righteousness (cf. Matt. 3:15). So, baptism is no more necessary for being saved than is any other "work of righteousness."

Whatever Jesus meant by this disputed text, he clearly did not mean that infant baptism was a condition of salvation. For one thing, he was speaking here to an adult—Nicodemus the Pharisee—and not to or about children. Infants cannot consciously "accept" or "believe" as Jesus called on Nicodemus to do (John 3:11–12, 15–16).[22] Furthermore, if baptism is specified here as a condition of salvation, then it is contradictory to everything else in the entire Gospel of John which says "that everyone who believes in him [Christ] might not perish but might have eternal life" (John 3:16; cf. vv. 18, 36). What is more, all of the believe-only verses are not limited to this sermon. They are scattered throughout the whole of John's Gospel (e.g., John 5:24; 6:35; 7:38; 8:24; 9:35; 10:38; 11:26; 12:44–48; 20:31). By any good rule of interpreting Scripture one unclear and disputed text should not be taken in any sense contrary to that conveyed clearly over and over by the same author and the rest of Scripture.

There are three basic ways to understand this text, none of which involve baptismal regeneration of anyone and certainly not of children. Some believe Jesus was speaking of the water of the womb, since Nicodemus had just mentioned a mother's womb in the preceding verse. If so, then Jesus was saying "unless you are born once by water (at your physical birth) and then again by the Spirit at your spiritual birth, you cannot be saved." This also fits with his statement that "what is born of flesh is flesh [physical birth] and what is born of the spirit is spirit [spiritual birth]" (3:6).

Others take "born of water" spiritually to refer to the washing of "water with the word" (cf. Eph. 5:26). They note that Peter refers to being "born anew . . . through the living and abiding word of God" (1 Pet. 1:23), the very thing John is speaking about in John 3:3–7. So this interpretation is possible both in the immediate context and in the broader context of usage of "water" as the Word of God elsewhere in Scripture.

Still others think that "born of water," while not referring to Christian baptism, refers to the baptism of John mentioned earlier (John 1:26). John said he baptized with water, but Jesus would baptize by the Spirit (cf. Matt. 3:11), saying "repent, for the kingdom of heaven is at hand" (Matt. 3:2). If

---

22. There is heaven for those who *cannot* believe but who would have if they could have (e.g., infants). There is no heaven for those who *will not* believe when they could have believed (e.g., adults who reject Christ). See Robert Lightner, *Heaven for Those Who Cannot Believe* (Shaumburg, Ill.: Regular Baptist Press, 1977). Appealing to Old Testament circumcision will not help the Catholic argument, since circumcision was only a sign of an earthly covenant they inherited as Jews, not of eternal salvation. Furthermore, girls were not circumcised, yet they were part of the covenant.

this is what is meant, then when Jesus said they must be "born of water and Spirit" (John 3:5) he meant that the Jews of his day had to undergo the baptism of repentance by John and also the baptism of the Holy Spirit (Acts 1:5) before they could "enter the kingdom of God." Being "born of water" (i.e., being baptized by John) was not enough, for John's baptism was not Christian baptism, as is proven by the fact that those who were baptized by John were rebaptized as Christians by the apostles (Acts 19:1–5). So, whatever this passage means, it does not mean that Christian baptism is a necessary condition for regeneration.

Finally, the fact that many of the early Fathers understood this as a reference to baptism is not decisive for numerous reasons. First of all, only the Bible is infallible, not the Fathers; the Fathers had many mistaken and conflicting interpretations of Scripture. Second, even if baptism is meant, it may be a reference to the baptism of John and not to any Christian baptismal regeneration. Third, since baptism was so closely associated with belief, following immediately upon it, it is understandable that many of the Fathers would speak of it in salvific terms. Finally, the tendency to identify the ritual with the reality, the symbol with substance, is a common error in religion. The New Testament constantly warned against it (Matt. 15:3–6; 23:23–28; 2 Tim. 3:5). It is understandable that as Christianity became more institutionalized errors like this would occur (cf. 2 Tim. 3:5).

Titus 3:5–7. Paul's reference here to the "washing of regeneration" (AV) is clearly not a reference to water baptism. First, contrary to the mistranslation of the Catholic *New American Bible,* the word "baptism" (Gk: *baptizo*) does not occur in this text. Here the word *loutrou* is used, which means "washing or cleansing." Second, the clue that it is a figurative use of the term "washing" is that it is the "washing of *regeneration.*" That is, a regeneration kind of washing, namely, a spiritual washing. Third, this passage makes it absolutely clear that we are saved by God's mercy and not by any "righteous deeds" which we have done (vv. 5–6). Fourth, baptism is a righteous act or deed. Hence, it could not be part of what saves us. Fifth, Paul is borrowing an image from the Old Testament laver which was used for cleansing of the priest before he entered the Holy Place, an image that here refers to a believer's spiritual cleansing before he enters the presence of God and not to the regeneration of an unbeliever.

Acts 22:16. When Ananias told Paul to "be baptized at once and wash away your sins" he could not have been referring to any actual washing away of sins but only to a symbolic cleansing from them. First, the apostle was already converted earlier on the road to Damascus (cf. Acts 9). At this point he had acknowledged Jesus as his "Lord," something he told the Roman Christians was the means of salvation (Rom. 10:9–10; cf. 1 Cor. 12:3).

Second, the reason God gave for going to Ananias was not to be *saved* but to be *sent.* It was not to be *converted* but to be *commissioned.* The text says clearly, "get up and go into the city and you will be told what you must do" (Acts 9:6). And this is precisely what happened, for here Ananias told Saul, "for you will be his witness before all" (Acts 22:15).

Third, the manner and wording of Paul's repeated testimony of his conversion experience make it clear that it was here that he was regenerated and justified, not at his baptism (cf. Acts 9:3–6; 22:6–8; 26:13–18). Indeed, in the last reference Paul even mentions that his message to the nations about what happened to him should be one about "the forgiveness of sins" (Acts 26:18), something he could scarcely testify about unless he himself had received it in his conversion experience.

Fourth, since Paul's actual forgiveness of sins took place on the road to Damascus, the reference to forgiveness of sins later at his baptism must be symbolic or figurative. This fits perfectly with what Paul later told the Roman Christians about baptism, namely, that it is a figure or likeness of what takes place to us at the moment of salvation. "We have grown into union with him through a death like his, we shall also . . . in the resurrection" (Rom. 6:5). Since it is Jesus' actual death and resurrection by which we are saved (Rom. 4:25; 10:9–10; 1 Cor. 15:1–4), then baptism can only be a representation of this salvation; it cannot be the moment of the salvation itself. Baptism is an outward sign of an inward reality. It is a figurative representation of the washing away of our sins. It symbolically does to the body outwardly what the blood of Christ actually does to the soul inwardly. Finally, whenever there is any question as to whether or not a passages like this should be taken figuratively, one must appeal to other clear passages. But these, as we have seen, inform us emphatically that salvation is by faith alone.

1 Peter 3:21. Peter's reference to a "baptismal bath" by which we are "saved" is often used to support the Catholic dogma of baptismal regeneration. However, the text taken in its proper context yields no such conclusion. For one thing, Peter makes no reference to being saved from original sin in this passage, which is what Catholics claim occurs in baptism. Further, it is evident that what one is being saved from in baptism is a bad "conscience." Since baptism is a command of Christ (Matt. 28:18–20), any Christian who knowingly remains unbaptized is living in disobedience to Christ. The only thing that will save that person from a bad conscience resulting from this disobedience is baptism. Finally, the prototype (Noah in the ark) of which baptism is said to be the antitype here is contrary to baptismal regeneration. For Noah was regenerated (i.e., received initial righteousness) long before he went into the ark (Gen. 6:9; Heb. 11:7). In point of fact, Noah is called a "truly just" or "righteous" man before the flood (Gen. 7:1). Since baptism is the antitype of the waters of the flood, it is clear that it came after one is saved, not before, in Noah's case.

Other Texts. Most other texts offered by Catholics actually say nothing about water baptism. Indeed, often the word "baptism" does not even appear in the text. The term "washing" is used figuratively or symbolically (e.g., 1 Cor. 6:11). At other times neither baptism nor washing of any kind is mentioned in the text, so there is no need to even reply to their use in support of Catholic teaching on this point (e.g., 1 John 3:9; 5:18).

The use of Romans 6:3–6 calls for brief comment, since it refers to baptism "into Christ," a phrase often referring to the status of the saved in the New Testament. It should be noted first that not all scholars agree that water baptism is in view here. They note the absence of any reference to water, the reference to baptism with the Spirit elsewhere (Acts 1:5; 1 Cor. 12:13), and the fact that Paul is here speaking of our position in Christ, namely, one that denotes a true believer.

However, even if the text is referring to water baptism (as it seems to be), the Roman Catholic view that baptism justifies does not follow. First, as already noted, it speaks of being baptized in the "likeness" of Christ's death and resurrection, which would indicate a figurative event. Further, "into" (Gk: *eis*) can mean "unto" or "with a view to" (not literally "into"), and it is used elsewhere simply of identification *with* (not salvation *by*). For example, Paul also said the children of Israel were "baptized into *(eis)* Moses" (1 Cor. 10:2), which does not mean they were thus saved by Moses[23] but rather that they were identified with him as they passed through the Red Sea. It is important to observe that noted Catholic authority Ludwig Ott believes that girls were saved in the Old Testament without circumcision, which they believe to be the Old Testament correlative of baptism, even though he affirmed that "During the period from Abraham to Moses, circumcision (Gn. 17, 19 et seq.) was for the male Israelite the ordinary means of purification from original sin."[24] In fact, even Abraham, with whom God first instituted circumcision, was saved by faith (Gen. 15:6; cf. Rom. 4:9) before he was circumcised (Gen. 17).

CONCLUSION

Baptism is not absolutely essential to salvation—as acknowledged by the Catholic concept of baptism by desire. Salvation is obtained by faith and

23. Their "salvation" came earlier when they offered, in type, Christ their Passover Lamb (cf. John 1:29; 1 Cor. 5:7).
24. Ott, *Fundamentals of Catholic Dogma*, p. 347. Ott cites Pope Innocent III and scholastic theology in favor of this point. He admits that some early fathers (e.g., Justin, Irenaeus, Tertullian) "saw in circumcision only a Sign of the Covenant and a model of Baptism, not a means for attaining salvation." This view, however, would favor the non-baptismal regeneration position, which Catholic theology rejects.

faith alone. To be sure, justification by faith alone causes some tension for Protestants who believe in infant baptism.[25] Martin Luther, for example, believed that it has been "practiced since the beginning of the church" and originates "from the apostles and has been preserved ever since their time."[26] However, "Luther freely admitted that infant baptism is neither explicitly commanded nor explicitly mentioned in Scripture."[27] It is difficult to apprehend clearly Luther's thinking on baptism and the presence of faith in infants. At first "Luther declares that children are baptized on the basis of the faith and confession of the sponsors, who in the baptismal liturgy are asked to answer in the place of the child being baptized whether he believes."[28] However, to preserve the idea that we are saved not by another's faith but by our own, he later began to teach that infants themselves believe when they are baptized. For instance, he refers to "John the Baptist who believed while in the womb of his mother."[29]

In the Large Catechism (A.D. 1529), Luther changed his view again. "In complete opposition to the statements of 1525, Luther now says that it is not decisive for baptism whether the baptized person believes or does not believe; that does not make baptism invalid but everything depends on God's word and commandment."[30] On this point of doctrine, Martin Luther was much closer to the Roman Catholic view than that of the other Reformers and he vigorously opposed the Anabaptists who rejected infant baptism, insisting that New Testament baptism was only for those old enough to believe (Mark 16:15–16; Acts 2:38; 10:45–47).

The Reformed view of infant baptism is closely linked with the Old Testament idea of covenant. While the New Testament neither directly commands nor forbids infant baptism, "The debate centers on questions surrounding the meaning of baptism and the degree of continuity between the

---

25. It is understandable, even if it is not justifiable, how early Catholic reformers (i.e., Protestants) would not obtain a perfect harmony with all their previously held Catholic beliefs and their newfound principle of *sola fide* (faith alone). However, it appears to be inconsistent with the Protestant principle of faith alone as a means of salvation to affirm that an infant, not yet able or willing to believe, could be regenerated or justified. Augustine, who believed in baptismal regeneration, distinguished between "regeneration" and "conversion," recognizing "the need of infants to be converted at a later age even if they have been baptized" (Toon, *Born Again*, p. 83). Augustine continues, "We all know that if one baptized in infancy does not believe when he comes to years of discretion . . . then he will have no profit from the gift he received as a baby" (Augustine, "A Treatise on the Merits and Forgiveness of Sins, and on the Baptism of Infants"; quoted in Toon, *Born Again*). In *Born Again* Anglican scholar Peter Toon gives a good account of the theological development of the doctrine of regeneration from the biblical, Patristic, Medieval, and Reformation perspectives.

26. Althaus, *Theology of Martin Luther,* p. 359.

27. Ibid., p. 361.

28. WA 7, 321; LW 32, 14, ibid., p. 364.

29. Ibid., p. 368.

30. Ibid., p. 369.

Old Covenant and the New Covenant."[31] Reformed Christians find a parallel between infant baptism and circumcision in the Old Testament. The point is made that in the case of Abraham he came to faith *prior* to his circumcision while his son Isaac "received the sign of his faith before he had the faith that the sign signified."[32] Thus, the purpose of infant baptism is to introduce the baby into the believing community (the local church).[33] But baptism is not the *means* of faith, only a sign of it—even though it is done in advance.

The following quote summarizes the matter:

> If the convert is fit for baptism he already knows what God's friendship means, and being justified by faith he already has peace with God through our Lord Jesus Christ. Baptism will assure him afresh of these highest of all blessings, but it does not create them.[34]

---

31. R. C. Sproul, *Essential Truths of the Christian Faith* (Wheaton: Tyndale House, 1992), p. 227.

32. Ibid.

33. It must be noted that not all Christians who claim to be "Reformed" accept infant baptism. Baptists, and others believe that baptism is something that must *follow*, not *precede* the presence of faith in the individual. For a defense of infant baptism, see Geoffrey W. Bromiley, *Children of Promise: The Case for Baptizing Infants* (Grand Rapids: Eerdmans, 1979). For a critique of infant baptism, see Paul K. Jewett, *Infant Baptism & the Covenant of Grace* (Grand Rapids: Eerdmans, 1978).

34. Robert MacKintosh, *Proceedings of the International Congregational Council*; quoted in Alan P. F. Sell, *A Reformed, Evangelical, Catholic Theology: The Contribution of the World Alliance of Reformed Churches, 1875–1982* (Grand Rapids: Eerdmans, 1991), p. 153.

THE COLSON–NEUHAUS DECLARATION

INTRODUCTION

When the document in question was published, it caused a furor in evangelical and Roman Catholic circles. The statement, *Evangelicals and Catholics Together: The Christian Mission in the Third Millennium* (ECT), March 29, 1994, was drafted by Richard John Neuhaus, Charles Colson, George Weigel, and Kent Hill. Neuhaus is a former Lutheran pastor who is now a Catholic priest; Colson, a Southern Baptist who founded Prison Fellowship; Weigel, a Catholic philosopher; and Hill, president of Eastern Nazarene College.

CONTENTS OF THE DECLARATION

The introduction of the statement makes clear that while crafted by evangelicals and Roman Catholics, it cannot "speak officially for our communities." However, since secularism presents such a threat in the modern world, areas of spiritual commonality and moral cooperation need to be explored.

SECTION I

"We Affirm Together" states "Jesus is Lord. . . . And there is salvation in no one else (Acts 4)." Further, "We affirm together that we are justified by grace through faith because of Christ." And "All who accept Christ as Lord and

Saviour are brothers and sisters in Christ." The *Apostles' Creed* "we can and hereby do affirm together as an accurate statement of Scriptural truth."

SECTION II

"We Hope Together" indicates the common desire that "all people will come to faith in Jesus Christ as Lord and Savior." Further, "Unity and love among Christians is an integral part of our missionary witness to the Lord whom we serve (John 13)." Thus, "As evangelicals and Catholics, we pray that our unity in the love of Christ will become even more evident as a sign to the world of God's reconciling power. Our communal and ecclesial separations are deep and long standing. We acknowledge that we do not know the schedule nor do we know the way to the greater visible unity for which we hope. . . . We do know that God . . . intends that we also be in communion with one another."

SECTION III

"We Search Together" is a joint venture "for a fuller and clearer understanding of God's revelation in Christ and his will for his disciples." The signatories confess: "We do not presume to suggest that we can resolve the deep and long standing differences between evangelicals and Catholics. . . . [However] Not all differences are authentic disagreements, nor need all disagreements divide."

"Among points of difference in doctrine, worship, practice, and piety that are frequently thought to divide us are these":

- "The church as an integral part of the Gospel or the church as a communal consequence of the Gospel.
- The church as visible communion or invisible fellowship of true believers.
- The sole authority of Scripture *(sola scriptura)* or Scripture as authoritatively interpreted in the church.
- The sole freedom of the individual Christian or the Magisterium (teaching authority) of the community.
- The church as local congregation or universal communion.
- Ministry ordered in apostolic succession or the priesthood of all believers.
- Sacraments and ordinances as symbols of grace or means of grace.
- The Lord's Supper as eucharistic sacrifice or memorial meal.
- Remembrance of Mary and the saints or devotion to Mary and the saints.
- Baptism as sacrament of regeneration or testimony to regeneration."

This list is by no means complete and the differences have, in some cases been misstated.

SECTION IV

"We contend together" states that "In the exercise of these public responsibilities there has been in recent years a growing convergence and cooperation between Evangelicals and Catholics. We thank God for the discovery of one another in contending for a common cause. Much more important, we thank God for the discovery of one another as brothers and sisters in Christ." So, "Together we contend for the truth that politics, law, and culture must be secured by moral truth." Thus, "Christians individually and the church corporately also have a responsibility for the right ordering of civil society," such as opposing pornography, homosexual practices, abortion, and "Together we contend for the truth that politics, law, and culture must be secured by moral truth."

SECTION V

"We Witness Together" states that "the achievement of good will and cooperation between Evangelicals and Catholics must not be at the price of the urgency and clarity of Christian witness to the Gospel." However, "There is a necessary distinction between evangelizing [non-Christians] and what is today commonly called proselytizing or 'sheep stealing.'" For "in view of the large number of non-Christians in the world and the enormous challenge of our common evangelistic task, it is neither theologically legitimate nor a prudent use of resources for one Christian community to proselytize among the active adherents of another Christian community." Thus, "We condemn the practice of recruiting people from another community for purposes of denominational or institutional aggrandizement."

The "Conclusion" states that "We do not know, we cannot know, what the Lord of history has in store for the Third Millennium." However, "We do know that this is a time of opportunity—and . . . responsibility—for Evangelicals and Catholics to be Christians together in a way that helps prepare the world for the coming of him to whom belongs the kingdom, the power, and the glory forever. Amen."

Signatories to the declaration included noted persons across the evangelical spectrum, such as Elizabeth Achtemeier, Bill Bright, Os Guinness, Thomas Oden, J. I. Packer, and Pat Robertson. Among Roman Catholic signatories were William Bentley Ball, James Hitchcock, Peter Kreeft, Ralph Martin, and John Cardinal O'Connor.

REACTION TO THE DECLARATION

THE DAVE HUNT STATEMENT

Response to this document was immediate and spirited. From the far right sector of the evangelical/fundamentalist spectrum came the reactions of Dave Hunt. In an article titled "The Gospel Betrayed," he states, "The document overturns the Reformation and does incalculable damage to the cause of Christ." Further, "the document represents the most devastating blow against the gospel in at least 1,000 years." Finally, "The most tragic result of this historic development will be to prevent the gospel from being presented to lost millions who have now been wrongly reclassified by evangelical leaders as Christians."[1]

THE CURE EVALUATION

Closer to the center of the evangelical spectrum came a more measured but critical evaluation. In their journal *Modern Reformation,* Christians United for Reformation (CURE) produced a critical review of ECT.

Opening on a positive note, the review states that "Protestants have much to learn from Rome's mature reflections in the realm of moral philosophy, metaphysics, epistemology, and the like." Negatively, the Decrees and Canons of the Council of Trent, which are authoritative for Roman Catholics, take a stance in opposition to the unchanging gospel of Christ.

Each affirmation in ECT is examined and found wanting. For example in Section I, "We affirm together that we are justified by grace through faith because of Christ" is incomplete because the Reformed qualifier *sola* ("only" or "alone") is missing. They insist that "The doctrine of justification by grace alone through faith alone because of Christ alone has since the Reformation been acknowledged by mainstream Protestants as 'the article by which the church stands or falls,' and the tenet that distinguishes a true from a false church. . . . The Council of Trent anathematized those who embrace this doctrine." They add, "[W]e see justification by faith alone as an essential of the Gospel on which radical disagreement continues, and we deny the adequacy of any version of the Gospel that falls short at this point."

Section II presents Christ as *example* while Reformed theology under-

---

1. "Current Issues," *Voice, Journal of the Independent Fundamental Churches of America* (July/Aug. 1994): 21–24. An equally severe, but better documented critique, came from well-known pastor and author John F. MacArthur, Jr., in *Reckless Faith: When the Church Loses Its Will to Discern* (Wheaton: Crossway, 1994). Relevant material is found in chap. 5: "Evangelicals and Catholics Together" and Appendix 1: "Is Roman Catholicism Changing?" MacArthur condemns the ECT declaration and any attempt to effect a rapprochement between Roman Catholics and evangelicals.

stands him first as *mediator*. In Section III is found a list of ten major differences that the CURE evaluation pronounces to contain "false dilemmas" and deals with "secondary issues." One problem addressed is the confusion between "baptistic" and Reformed/Lutheran distinctives. Hence, "The reformers and their descendants were set in opposition not only to Rome's magisterial authority, but also to the individualistic and subjective claims of the Anabaptist radicals."

In Section IV there are "many shared assumptions" that may lead to cooperation. Indeed, they acknowledge that "The extent of the creedal consensus that binds orthodox Evangelicals and Roman Catholics together warrants the making of common cause on moral and cultural issues in society. . . . Yet it is incorrect to regard such cooperation among Christians as common ecclesial action in fulfilling a common ecclesial mission." For "We believe that cultural issues must be clearly distinguished from the mission of the church." The CURE reaction to Section V accuses ECT of slighting the Reformed emphasis on "the objective Gospel message" for a "conversion experience." Indeed, "To the extent that Evangelicals have replaced the objective emphasis . . . with the subjective . . . to that extent Evangelicals have become more closely linked to the Roman emphasis on justification as a process of conversion."

In the "Conclusion" of the CURE critique, evangelicals may profit from and cooperate with Roman Catholic moral theologians even while they carefully reject Rome's errors of systematic and biblical theology. The major error of Rome's soteriology is that the righteousness of God "is a 'gift,' not in the sense of imputation of an alien righteousness, but in the sense of a revelation of communication of divine goodness somehow infused into us through Jesus."

CURE's final word is that in spite of an attempt to differentiate between the Council of Trent and Vatican II, Rome remains unchanged on these crucial doctrines. The review then presents "Ten Theses for Roman Catholic-Evangelical Dialogue," which will be commented on in the following section.[2]

THE HORTON–PACKER REVISION

Some months after the CURE evaluation, Michael Horton, director for CURE, and Anglican scholar J. I. Packer produced a revised Reformed statement. The basic thrust of the original "Ten Theses" is softened: "We deny that there can be any fellowship with those [Roman Catholics] who openly oppose the Gospel" is replaced by a milder one—"we deny the adequacy of any version of the Gospel that falls short at this point."

Other weaker statements are made too, such as "We deny that this [the fact that some Catholics are 'brothers and sisters' in Christ despite the official

---

2. Reprint from *Modern Reformation* (Jan./Feb. 1994): 23–24.

teachings of their church] allows for joint communion or similar expressions of visible ecclesial union." Also, "We deny such cooperation [on 'moral and cultural issues'] is sufficient to declare that both communions are engaged in a common mission, part of a common church, and witness to a common Gospel" is weakened to "Yet it is incorrect to regard such cooperation among Christians as common ecclesial action in fulfilling a common mission."

The Horton–Packer revision includes an introduction and seven points, which can be summarized as follows:

- The agreement of both parties concerning the creeds does not mean that complete agreement on the essentials of the gospel has been achieved.
- Disagreement over justification by grace *alone* through faith *alone* because of Christ *alone* remains a serious obstacle.
- The Vatican II statements that unbelievers may be saved by their good works is extremely problematic for evangelicals.
- Consensus on moral and cultural matters are not to be understood as indicating a common ecclesial mission.
- The Roman Catholic claim on infallibility is rejected; dogmas such as justification according to Trent, transubstantiation, and the various doctrines surrounding the person and mission of the Virgin Mary remain serious differences between the two groups.
- While individual Roman Catholics can be our brethren in Christ, this does not mean that the Roman Catholic Church "in its present confession . . . is an acceptable Christian communion."
- The mission stemming from the Great Commission of our Lord requires not only conversion, but "catechesis, nurture and discipline of converts." Biblically based ecclesiastical structures are essential to Christian formation.[3]

THE *TABLETALK* POSITION

A severe critique was also forthcoming from *TABLETALK,* the monthly magazine of the Ligonier Ministries. In the introduction, the editor states that Roman Catholics, "if they believe the doctrines of their Church, are not Christians."[4] In an article titled, "After Light, Darkness," Ligonier founder R. C. Sproul writes: "The Colson–Neuhaus document did not cause disunity

---

3. "Resolutions for Roman Catholic and Evangelical Dialogue," drafted by Michael Horton; revised by J. I. Packer. "Christians United for Reformation," 1994. Signatories of the statement include such noted evangelicals as James Boice, R. C. Sproul, *J. I. Packer, David Wells, John W. Montgomery, Roger Nicole, Robert Preus, Edmund Clowney, *John White, *Richard Land, and Michael Horton. (Those with a * signed both this and the earlier ECT statement.)

4. R. C. Sproul, Jr., "Coram Deo," *TABLETALK* (Nov. 1994): 2.

but *exposed* a serious rift within evangelicalism."[5] Sproul continues: "This [God's grace, imputed to us when we are still sinners] the Reformers believed, is the biblical Gospel . . . the denial of which was worthy of anathema. This is the very Gospel Rome anathematized at Trent, thereby condemning the biblical Gospel."[6]

In the same periodical, John Armstrong writes that "Rome does not confess the Gospel." Further, "The fuzziness of this [ECT] document should trouble us precisely because we remain diligent for the Gospel itself."[7] Others in this issue of *TABLETALK* are equally critical of the Colson–Neuhaus Declaration.[8]

OTHER REACTIONS

In an editorial that appeared in *Christianity Today*, senior editor Timothy George writes a fairly positive evaluation of the ECT document.[9] However, two months later, a more critical appraisal of ECT appeared in the same magazine, which warns that "we dare not gloss over certain essential doctrines that still separate evangelicalism and Catholicism. While this document addresses some of these distinctions, it presents them in ways that do not always accurately reflect Protestant or evangelical convictions."[10]

In May 1994 the ECT document was published in its entirety in *FIRST THINGS*, of which Fr. Richard John Neuhaus is editor in chief. In the journal's "Letters to the Editor" (Nov. 1994), two communications reflect both sides of the issue. A Catholic nun writes, "I was amazed at the compromising attitude of the Catholic participants toward Evangelicals." Indeed, "Protestants are not one with the Catholic Church." Therefore, "The Catholic Church does not compromise its doctrine to accommodate Protestants—or shouldn't."[11]

From the evangelical side comes the following: "Thus, acknowledging

---

5. Ibid., p. 6.

6. Ibid., p. 52.

7. Ibid., p. 12.

8. It is of some interest to note that an earlier edition of *TABLETALK* (May 1994) titled "Should Old Aquinas Be Forgot?" attempted to make the case that Thomas Aquinas (the premier theologian of the Roman Catholic Church—designated the "Doctor of Angels") can be safely embraced by evangelicals. Evangelical and Reformed scholars such as R. C. Sproul, Norman L. Geisler, and Ronald Nash contribute positive evaluations of Aquinas. John H. Gerstner, who is adamant in his belief that Roman Catholicism is apostate, even writes an article titled, "Aquinas Was a Protestant"!

9. "Catholics and Evangelicals in the Trenches," *Christianity Today*, 16 May 1994, pp. 16–17.

10. "Should Roman Catholics and Evangelicals Join Ranks?" *Christianity Today*, 18 July 1994, p. 17.

11. Sister Winifred Bauer, C.P.P.S., "Catholics & Evangelicals (Cont.)," pp. 5–6.

joyfully the numerous points in common presented in this document . . . I must confess deep reservations on behalf of my evangelical brethren in regions where this distinctly American Christian experience is not their own." These evangelicals "frequently encounter a virulent nationalistic Catholicism that is actually quite fundamentalist in the world-religious sense."[12]

Several of the Protestants who signed the ECT document have received censure from the groups they represent. John H. White, president of Geneva College and past president of the National Association of Evangelicals, was persuaded by his denomination (the Reformed Presbyterian Church of North America) to withdraw his name from the ECT statement.

Another signer who received heat from his denomination was Richard D. Land, executive director of the Southern Baptist Christian Life Commission (CLC). The Foreign Mission Board trustees of the Southern Baptist Church, on June 16, 1994, "by unanimous resolution, expressed concern that the Evangelical-Catholic document is subject to interpretations harmful to Southern Baptist work of global witness and missionary outreach."[13] Land defended his endorsement of the document in question but, according to sources close to him, he privately regrets signing it.[14]

The quarterly *Touchstone* has been very supportive of the ECT document. The statement was reproduced by them in Vol. 7.2, Spring 1994, and has been commented on often in the journal.

An associate editor of *Touchstone,* Patrick Henry Reardon, wrote an editorial interacting with *Christianity Today*'s editorial warning of July 18, 1994 (reported above). Reardon, a priest in the Antiochian Orthodox Church, commenting on reactions to ECT, claimed the rumblings were "entirely Protestant rumblings. Not a whisper of complaint was heard in Roman Catholic quarters."[15] This is incorrect.

In fact, CATHOLIC ANSWERS, a lay-run Catholic apologetics and evangelization organization, is very concerned that the Colson–Neuhaus statement is loaded *against* the Roman Catholic position.[16] Reardon is criti-

---

12. Kurt A. Richardson, Southeastern Baptist Theological Seminary, ibid., p. 6.

13. "Report of Committee on Resolutions on Southern Baptists and Roman Catholics," meeting in Orlando, Florida, June 14–16, 1994.

14. "Perspective: Evangelicals and Catholics?" *Light,* a publication of the Southern Baptist Christian Life Commission, May/June 1994.

15. "Editorial: Evangelicals & Catholics Together?" *Touchstone: A Journal of Ecumenical Orthodoxy,* Fall 1994, vol. 7, no. 4, p. 6.

16. One Catholic team engaged Michael Horton (president of CURE), W. Robert Godfrey (president and professor of church history at Westminster Theological Seminary in California), and Lutheran scholar and lecturer Rod Rosenbladt in a public debate on the topic, "What Still Divides Us?" on March 3 and 4, 1995, in Pasadena, California. *Sola scriptura* and *sola fide* were the topics addressed.

For a positive treatment of ECT from a Roman Catholic perspective, see Keith A. Fournier with William D. Watkins, *A House Divided? Evangelicals and Catholics Together* (Colorado Springs: NavPress, 1994), pp. 330–32, 337–49.

cal not only of Kenneth Kantzer of Trinity Evangelical Divinity School but also of Michael Horton's evaluation of ECT, which appeared in *Modern Reformation* (No. 26). He states, "I am convinced that the doctrine of external justification as described by Horton is a serious distortion of Holy Scripture."[17] Further, Reardon understand Horton to believe "that . . . in order to be saved, I must have not only faith but also a correct doctrine ('some recognition') of justification by faith." Reardon rejects Horton in this point and states, "I believe that a man is justified by faith, not by entertaining a correct view on justification."[18]

An extensive examination of the question of Roman Catholic-evangelical cooperation appeared in *Pro Ecclesia*, vol. 3, no. 3.[19] The author concludes, "Evangelicals are not called to view other streams within broader Christendom with an uncritical eye. Neither are they constrained to dissolve their confessional differences. God is not interested in a merger between Rome and Wheaton." However, "Those claiming to be a part of the Body of Christ stand nevertheless under the divine mandate to promote reconciliation—as far as it lies within their power—with all who profess and worship Jesus Christ as Lord (John 17)."[20]

The Christian Research Institute (CRI) has monitored developments stemming from the Colson–Neuhaus statement. Indeed, its president, Hank Hanegraaff, a friend of Charles Colson, refused to sign the Colson–Neuhaus statement. While believing that some of the evangelical criticisms of ECT are too harsh, CRI nevertheless voices concern about the statement in a number of areas.[21] Indeed, they have published a number of articles by the present authors critical of Roman Catholic doctrine.[22]

Discussions surrounding the ECT document and those who crafted it have continued. One such meeting produced a statement drafted by J. I. Packer and carrying the signatures of Packer, Bill Bright and Charles Colson. It was offered to the other original Protestant signers of ECT for their approval as well.

We will summarize the points which emerged from this statement:

17. *Touchstone*, ibid., p. 7.
18. Ibid. The authors are in agreement with Horton against Reardon on the definition of justification, but concede that Reardon may have a point with the second comment.
19. J. Daryl Charles, "Evangelical-Catholic Dialogue: Basis, Boundaries, Benefits," pp. 289–305.
20. Ibid., p. 305.
21. Memorandum from Elliot Miller to Hank Hanegraaff, "Evangelicals and Catholics Together," June 16, 1994. CRI's president Hank Hanegraaff did not sign the ECT document as erroneously reported.
22. See Norman L. Geisler and Ralph MacKenzie, "The Catholic Protestant Debate on Papal Infallibility" and "The Protestant Catholic Debate on Biblical Authority" in *Christian Research Journal* (fall 1994 and spring 1994).

1. Evangelical cooperation with orthodox Roman Catholics to advance the goals mentioned in ECT "does not imply acceptance of Roman Catholic doctrinal distinctives or endorsement of the Roman Catholic church system."
2. "We understand the statement that 'we are justified by grace through faith because of Christ,' in terms of the substitutionary atonement and imputed righteousness of Christ, leading to full assurance of eternal salvation. . . ."
3. Those who profess to be Christian—Protestant, Catholic and Orthodox—should in addition to an orthodox creed, exhibit signs indicating new life in Christ.
4. The signatories "hold that evangelism and church planting are always legitimate, whatever forms of church life are present already."
5. Further theological discussions stemming from the ECT document should reflect the above clarifications to prevent misunderstandings of basic evangelical concerns.

As a result of this meeting and this new addendum to the ECT document, Dr. John F. Ankerberg (a participant in the discussion) feels that the ambiguity that existed in the original document has been addressed and "this new statement . . . reaffirms and clarifies the gospel, which is the life of the church." It appears that this addendum goes a significant way toward clearing up confusion that the original ECT document generated.[23]

EVALUATION AND CONCLUSION

POSITIVE EVALUATION

- Because Roman Catholics and evangelicals share the same view on a number of societal and moral issues, the document is right to call for cooperation in these situations.
- It correctly points to a common core of theological beliefs that unite *believing* Roman Catholics and evangelicals. (This is the thesis of Part One of this volume).
- Common ideological foes of Catholics and evangelicals are identified (see Part Three of this volume).
- An attempt is made to find some common ground concerning salvation by grace through faith (see chap. 5 of this volume).

23. "News Release," Dr. John F. Ankerberg, Ankerberg Theological Research Institute, January 27, 1995.

NEGATIVE EVALUATION

- A serious problem is the document's equating the term "Roman Catholics" (without a qualifier, such as "believing" or "traditional") and evangelicals. It would be equally inappropriate to link the terms "Protestants" (in general, which includes nonorthodox members) and "*believing* Roman Catholics.*"
- The document overlooks the crucial disagreements concerning the nature and extent of justification: grace *alone,* through faith *alone,* based on Christ *alone.*
- The question of the extent of the canon should not be overlooked, since the Apocryphya (accepted by Catholics) supports purgatory and prayers for the dead (see chap. 9).
- Questions concerning the idolatrous implications surrounding the worship of the consecrated host are not addressed.
- Evangelical concern over inappropriate attention involved in the veneration of saints, images, and especially Mary is not addressed.
- The statement is in many places is somewhat theologically unsophisticated.
- A visible *ecclesial* union with Rome is encouraged.
- The document confuses the *cultural* mandate (Gen. 1) with the *Gospel* mandate (Matt. 28).
- Evangelization between the two groups is prohibited.

CONCLUSION

A number of crucial questions remain to be resolved.

- How is the gospel to be defined? If belief in the "forensic" aspect of justification is demanded as a condition for receiving salvation, then how could people between the time of Paul and the Reformation be saved?
- To what extent is the gospel found in official Roman Catholicism? Even the severest evangelical critics of the Roman Catholic Church admit that individual Catholics can and are saved. Is this *because of* or *in spite of* their church's official teaching?
- Does Catholicism officially deny the saving gospel in principle or only detract from it in practice?
- Were the Reformers correct in believing that after Trent Roman Catholicism was an apostate church, since it infallibly defined a false gospel (one that included meritorious works as a condition for receiving the gift of eternal life) as the true gospel?

In the final analysis, then, the question is this: is Roman Catholicism (since Trent) a false church with significant truth in it, as the Reformers believed, or is it a true church with significant error in it? Since "a true church" must proclaim the "true gospel" (Gal. 1:8; 2:4), the answer will depend on what is essential to the true gospel.

In an attempt to respond to this question three important distinctions must be made. First, there is a difference between whether Catholics can be truly saved inside their system and whether their system officially proclaims the true gospel. Virtually everyone recognizes that one can be saved by believing the gospel in spite of being part of a system that may officially deny essential parts of the gospel.

Second, there is a difference between what is essential to the gospel itself and what is essential for people to believe about the gospel in order to be saved. For example, we believe that imputed righteousness is essential to the true gospel, but we also hold that one can be saved without believing that imputed righteousness (or forensic justification) is an essential part of the true gospel. Otherwise, few people were saved between the time of the apostle Paul and the Reformation, since scarcely anyone taught imputed righteousness (or forensic justification) during that period! That is, God has to impute Christ's righteousness (and make a forensic declaration of justification) to people in order for them to be saved, even if they do not believe that he has to do so. Likewise, God can only save people "by grace alone through faith alone based on Christ alone," even if they do not believe this is necessary to the way God does it.

Third, it is important to distinguish between what the Roman Catholic Church fails to affirm as essential elements of the gospel and what it actually denies is an essential element of the gospel. We suggest that the simple failure to affirm an element (say, forensic justification) is not the equivalent of affirming a false gospel. Rather, it is merely proclaiming an incomplete gospel. It seems to us that this charge is justly laid at Rome's door.

The bottom line, then, is whether there is anything in what Roman Catholicism has infallibly proclaimed that denies an essential element of the true gospel. According to the Reformers, the answer was affirmative, since Catholicism denies salvation is "by grace alone through faith alone, based on Christ alone." For Trent demanded that meritorious works are a necessary condition for receiving the gift of eternal life (= entering heaven). Thus, while affirming the necessity of grace, Catholicism denies the exclusivity of grace as a condition for receiving the gift of eternal life (see chap. 12). This, in the eyes of historic Protestantism, is a false gospel. Whether this assessment is correct depends on whether the classical or Reformation standard is employed as the minimal test for orthodoxy. The authors favor the former—it is not anachronistic or exclusivistic, and is more in accord with the broad sweep of church history.

BIBLIOGRAPHY

ARTICLES AND CHAPTERS

Akin, James. "Material and Formal Sufficiency." *This Rock*, vol. 4, no. 10 (Oct. 1993).

———. "A Tiptoe Through TULIP." *This Rock* (Sept. 1993).

Ball, William Bentley. "We'd Better Hang Together." *Crisis* (Oct. 1989).

Barnes, Fred. "No Womb for Debate." *The New Republic* (27 July 1992).

Brothy, Don. "Why I Don't Pray Anymore." *National Catholic Reporter* (1 March 1974). Quoted in James Hitchcock, *Catholicism and Modernity*. New York: Seabury Press, 1979.

Brunelli, Lucio. "Comparative Translations." *The Catholic World Report* (June 1994).

Charles, J. Daryl. "Evangelical-Catholic Dialogue: Basis, Boundaries, Benefits." *Pro Ecclesia*, vol. III, no. 3 (1994).

Chesterton, G. K. "A Crisis of Truth: The Attack on Faith, Morality and Mission." In *Saint Thomas Aquinas*. Garden City, N.Y.: Image Books, 1956.

Duggins, David. "Evangelicals and Catholics: Across the Divide." *Moody Monthly* (Nov. 1993).

Dulles, Fr. "Catho-cliques: The U.S. Catholic Fronts." *30 DAYS*, no. 11 (1993).

Elmer-De Witt, Philip. "No Sympathy for the Devil." *Time* (19 March 1990).

"Encyclical Letter of John Paul II." *The Splendor of Truth: Veritatis Splendor*. Boston: St. Paul Books and Media, 1993.

"Evangelicals and Catholics Together" (29 March 1994).

Fessio, Joseph, S.J. "How Did It Happen? A Canonical Investigation." *The Catholic World Report* (June 1994).

Garcia, Elena Muller. "Tom Thumb Is a Person." *San Diego Catholic News Notes* (July 1992). Reprinted from the *Human Life Review* (Spring 1992).

Geisler, Norman L. "The Extent of the Old Testament Canon." *Current Issues in Biblical and Patristic Interpretation*. Edited by Gerald F. Hawthorne. Grand Rapids: Eerdmans, 1975.

———. "An Oasis of Living Water." *Christian Herald* (Feb. 1978).

———. "A Pre-Millennial View of Law and Government." *Bibliotheca Sacra* (July–Sept. 1985).

———. "Purpose and Meaning: The Cart and the Horse." *Grace Theological Journal* 5 (1984).

———. "To Die or Not to Die: That Is the Fatal Question." Paper presented at Naval Hospital, San Diego (7 December 1992).

Gillquist, Peter. "Evangelicals Turned Orthodox." *The Christian Century* (4 March 1992).

———. "Orthodoxy." *Faith and Renewal* (July/Aug. 1992).

Harvey, John F. "Priests Who Stray." *Crisis* (Nov. 1992).

Horner, Kim. "Vistan Drums in the Lord." *The North County Blade-Citizen* (22 October 1993).

Howard, Thomas. "Witness for the Faith: What Catholics Can Learn from Billy Graham." *Crisis* (April 1991).

"John Paul II/Encyclical: *Veritatis Splendor.*" *Origins: Catholic News Service,* vol. 23, no. 18 (14 October 1993).

"John Paul II/Encyclical on Missionary Activity." *Origins: CNS Documentary Service,* vol. 20, no. 34 (31 January 1991).

Johnson, Martin. "In 'Rape and Incest' Debate, Unborn Find New Hero." *World* (4 November 1989).

Jurgens, William A. *Faith of the Early Church.* Quoted in "The Fathers Know Best." *This Rock* (Dec. 1992).

Law, Cardinal. "Center Update." *Pastoral Renewal* (Sept. 1987).

Leithart, Peter J. "The Biblical Way to Worship." *Crisis* (Oct. 1992).

———. "A Presbyterian Appreciation of Liturgy." *Crisis* (Oct. 1992).

Madrid, Patrick. "Any Friend of God's Is a Friend of Mine." *This Rock* (Sept. 1992).

Mansoor, Menahem. "The Dead Sea Scrolls." *New Catholic Encyclopedia* 2:390. Prepared by the editorial staff of Catholic University of America, Washington, D.C. New York/Washington, D.C.: McGraw-Hill, 1967, 1974, 1979.

Mar, Gary. "What Evangelicalism Needs." *New Oxford Review* (June 1994).

Martin, Ralph. "Sects Education." *New Covenant* (Oct. 1991).

———. "Why Catholics Leave." *New Covenant* (July/Aug. 1990).

Merrill, Eugene H. "Ebla and Biblical Historical Inerrancy." *Bibliotheca Sacra* (Oct.–Dec. 1983): 302–21.

Moran, Susan. "The Bishop's Voice." *Crisis* (July/Aug. 1992).

Morriss, Frank. "Billy Graham and the Gospel of Salvation." *The Wanderer,* vol. 125, no. 32 (6 August 1992).

Oden, Thomas C. "How Should Evangelicals Be Ecumenical?" *Christianity Today* (5 April 1993).

Plowman, Edward. "Glasnost Opens Way for Graham." (8 September 1989).

Potterie, Ignace de la. "Exegesis: Truth As Event." *30 Days,* no. 2 (1993).

———. "And the Word Became Flesh." *30 Days,* no. 12 (1992).

Ratzinger, Cardinal Joseph. *The Catholic World Report* (Nov. 1992).

Rourke, Mary. "Hitting the Book." *Los Angeles Times,* Section E.

Ruokanen, Miikka. "Catholic Teaching on Non-Christian Religions at the Second Vatican Council." *International Bulletin of Missionary Research,* vol. 9 (Oct. 1985).

Ryland, Tim. "Local Lay Catholics Resist Bad Teaching." *San Diego News Notes* (March 1993).

Saint, Steven. "Unity Rally Joins Catholics, Evangelicals." *The Southern Cross* (4 November 1993).

Samples, Kenneth. "Does the Bible Teach the Principle of *Sola Scriptura?*" Unpublished paper (1993).

———. "What Think Ye of Rome?" *Christian Research Journal,* Parts 1 and 2 (winter/spring 1993).

Sauer, James. "Chesterton Reformed: A Protestant Interpretation." *Antithesis,* vol. 1, no. 6 (Nov./Dec. 1990).

Shafer, Joyce. "Prayer and Praise News Letter." *Church School Service* (fall 1993).

Vernon, Robert. "L.A. Justice Not for All." *Focus on the Family: Citizen,* vol. 7, no. 2 (15 February 1993).

Walker, Andrew. "In Defense of Ecumenical Orthodoxy." *Touchstone: A Journal of Ecumenical Orthodoxy,* vol. 7, no. 1 (winter 1994).

Walsh, Tracy. "A Celebration behind Bars." *The Southern Cross* (2 July 1992).

Wells, David F. "Tradition: A Meeting Place for Catholic and Evangelical Theology?" *Christian Scholar's Review,* vol. 5, no. 1 (1975).

Wicks, Jared, S.J. "Insights for Luther's Instructions on the Faith." In *Pro Ecclesia,* no. 2.

Wilson, James Q. "'Calvin and Hobbes' and the Pope's Case for Morality." *The San Diego Union-Tribune* (29 November 1993), Opinion.

BOOKS

Abbott, Walter M., S.J., ed. *The Documents of Vatican II.* New York: Guild Press, 1966.

Althaus, Paul. *The Ethics of Martin Luther.* Translated by Robert C. Schultz. Philadelphia: Fortress Press, 1972.

———. *The Theology of Martin Luther.* Philadelphia: Fortress, 1984.

Anderson, H. George, ed. *Justification by Faith: Lutherans and Catholics in Dialogue,* vol. 7. Minneapolis: Augsburg, 1985.

———, ed. *The One Mediator, the Saints, and Mary.* Minneapolis: Augsburg, 1992.

Ankerberg, John, and Weldon, John. *Protestants and Catholics: Do They Now Agree?* Eugene: Harvest House Publishers, 1995.

Anselm. *Cur Deus Homo.* Translated by S. W. Deane. In *St. Anselm: Basic Writings.* La Salle, Ill.: Open Court Publishing, 1962.

———. "Why God Became Man." *The Library of Christian Classics,* vol. 10. Edited and Translated by Eugene R. Fairweather. Philadelphia: Westminster, 1951.

Aquinas, Thomas. *Commentary on Saint Paul's Epistle to the Ephesians by St. Thomas Aquinas.* Translated by Matthew L. Lamb. Albany, N.Y.: Magi Books, 1966.

———. *Compendium of Theology.* Translated by Cyril Vollert. St. Louis: B. Herder Book Co., 1949.

———. *Light of Faith: The Compendium of Theology.* Manchester: Sophia Institute, 1993.

———. *Philosophical Texts.* Edited by Thomas Gilby. New York: Oxford University Press, 1960.

———. *Summa contra Gentiles,* vols. 1–4. Translated by Anton C. Pegis. Garden City, N.Y.: Hanover House, 1955.

————. *Summa Theologiae*. In *The Basic Writings of Thomas Aquinas*. Edited by Anton C. Pegis. New York: Random House, 1944.

————. *On Truth*, vols. 1–2. Translated by Robert W. Mulligan. Chicago: Henry Regnery Co., 1952.

Aristotle. *Metaphysics*. In *The Basic Works of Aristotle*. Translated by Richard Mckeon. New York: Random House, 1941.

Armstrong, John, gen. ed. *Roman Catholicism: Evangelical Protestants Analyze What Divides and Unites Us*. Chicago: Moody Press, 1994.

Arndt, Stephen W., and Mark Jordan. *A Catholic Catechism for Adults: The Church's Confession of Faith*. San Francisco: Ignatius Press, 1987.

Arndt, William. *A Greek-English Lexicon of the New Testament*. Chicago: Chicago University Press, 1957.

Atkinson, James. *Martin Luther: Prophet to the Church Catholic*. Grand Rapids: Eerdmans, 1983.

Aulén, Gustaf. *Reformation and Catholicity*. Edinburgh and London: Oliver and Boyd, 1962.

Augustine. *Against the Epistle of Manichaeus*.

————. *On Baptism*.

————. *On Christian Doctrine*.

————. *The City of God*.

————. *Confessions*.

————. *Correction of the Donatists*.

————. *Enchiridion*.

————. *The Epistle of John*.

————. *On Forgiveness of Sins and Baptism*.

————. *On Free Will*. In *The Fathers of the Church*. Edited by Ludwig Schopp et al. New York: CIMA, 1948–54.

————. *On Grace and Free Will*.

————. *On the Grace of Christ*.

————. *Letters*.

————. *On Lying*.

————. *On Marriage and Concupiscence*.

————. *On the Morals of the Catholic Church*.

————. *On the Nature of Good*.

————. *Rebuke and Grace*.

————. *Reply to Faustus*.

————. *On the Trinity*.

————. *Of True Religion*.

Bahnsen, Greg L. *Theonomy in Christian Ethics*. Nutley, N.J.: Craig Press, 1979.

Bainton, Roland H. *Here I Stand: A Life of Martin Luther*. Nashville: Abingdon, 1978.

Ball, William Bentley, ed. *In Search of a National Morality: A Manifesto for Evangelicals and Catholics*. Grand Rapids: Baker, 1992.

Baram, Robert, ed. *Spiritual Journeys* (Revised). St. Paul: St. Paul Books and Media, 1988.

Beckwith, Roger. *The Old Testament Canon of the New Testament Church and Its Background in Early Judaism*. Grand Rapids: Eerdmans, 1986.

Berkhof, Louis. *The History of Christian Doctrine.* Grand Rapids: Eerdmans, 1953.

———. *Systematic Theology.* Grand Rapids: Eerdmans, 1939–41.

Berkouwer, Gerrit C. *The Conflict with Rome.* Philadelphia: Presbyterian and Reformed, 1958.

———. *The Second Vatican Council and the New Catholicism.* Grand Rapids: Eerdmans, 1965.

Bloesch, Donald G. *The Battle for the Trinity.* Ann Arbor: Servant, 1985.

———. *Essentials of Evangelical Theology,* vols. 1–2. San Francisco: Harper and Row, 1978.

Boettner, Loraine. *Roman Catholicism.* Philadelphia: Presbyterian and Reformed, 1962.

Boudreau, Albert H. *The Born-Again Catholic.* Locust Valley: Living Flame Press, 1983.

Bouyer, Fr. Louis. *The Spirit and Forms of Protestantism.* Translated by A. V. Littledale. Westminster: Newman Press, 1961.

Braaten, Carl E. *Justification: The Article by Which the Church Stands or Falls.* Minneapolis: Fortress Press, 1990.

Brauer, Jerald C., ed. *The Westminster Dictionary of Church History.* Philadelphia: Westminster, 1971.

Bray, Gerald. *Creeds, Councils and Christ.* Downers Grove, Ill.: InterVarsity Press, 1984.

Broderick, Robert C., M.A., ed. *The Catholic Concise Encyclopedia.* St. Paul: Simon and Schuster, 1956.

Bromiley, Geoffrey W. "The Book of Revelation." *God's Word Today.* St. Paul: University of St. Thomas Press, 1993.

———. *Children of Promise: The Case for Baptizing Infants.* Grand Rapids: Eerdmans, 1979.

———, ed. *International Standard Bible Encyclopedia,* 4 vols. Grand Rapids: Eerdmans, 1988.

———. "Promise of Patristic Studies." In *Toward a Theology for the Future.* Carol Stream, Ill.: Creation House, 1971.

Brown, Colin. *Christianity and Western Thought: A History of Philosophers, Ideas and Movements,* vol. 1. Downers Grove, Ill.: InterVarsity Press, 1990.

Brown, Harold O. J. *Heresies: The Image of Christ in the Mirror of Heresy and Orthodoxy from the Apostles to the Present.* Grand Rapids: Baker, 1984.

———. *The Protest of a Troubled Protestant.* New Rochelle: Arlington House, 1969.

Bruce, F. F. *The New Testament Documents: Are They Reliable?* Downers Grove, Ill.: InterVarsity Press, 1960.

———. *Paul: Apostle of the Heart Set Free.* Grand Rapids: Eerdmans, 1977.

———. *Peter, Stephen, James and John.* Grand Rapids: Eerdmans, 1979.

Bruner, Frederick Dale. *A Theology of the Holy Spirit.* Grand Rapids: Eerdmans, 1970.

Burgess, Stanley M. *The Holy Spirit: Eastern Christian Traditions.* Peabody, Mass.: Hendrickson, 1989.

Burroughs, Millar. *More Light on the Dead Sea Scrolls.* New York: Viking, 1958.

Burtchaell, James T., C.S.C. *Rachel Weeping.* San Francisco: Harper and Row, 1982.

Buswell, James Oliver, Jr. *A Systematic Theology of the Christian Religion.* Grand Rapids: Zondervan, 1962–63.

Cailliet, Emile. *Pascal: The Emergence of Genius.* New York: Harper and Brothers, 1961.

Calvin, John. *Calvin: Theological Treatises.* In *The Library of Christian Classics.* Translated by J. K. S. Reid, vol. 22. Philadelphia: Westminster, 1954.

————. *The Epistles of Paul the Apostle to the Romans and to the Thessalonians* (2:14). Edited by David W. Torrance and Thomas F. Torrance, vol. 8. Grand Rapids: Eerdmans, 1979.

————. *Institutes of the Christian Religion.* Philadelphia: Westminster, 1960.

Carey, George. *A Tale of Two Churches: Can Protestants and Catholics Get Together?* Downers Grove, Ill.: InterVarsity Press, 1984.

Chemnitz, Martin. *Examination of the Council of Trent.* St. Louis: Concordia, 1971.

Clendenin, Daniel B. *Eastern Orthodox Christianity: A Western Perspective.* Grand Rapids: Baker Book House, 1994.

Clouse, Robert. *The Meaning of the Millennium: Four Views.* Downers Grove, Ill.: InterVarsity Press, 1977.

Colacci, Mario. *The Doctrinal Conflict between Roman Catholic and Protestant Christianity.* Minneapolis: T. S. Denison and Co., 1962.

Colson, Charles. *The Body.* Dallas: Word, 1992.

————. *Born Again.* Old Tappan, N.J.: Fleming Revell, 1976.

————. *Kingdoms in Conflict.* Grand Rapids: Zondervan, 1987.

————. *Life Sentence.* Old Tappan, N.J.: Fleming Revell, 1979.

Conway, Msgr. J. D. *What the Church Teaches.* Garden City, N.Y.: Doubleday, 1962.

Coughlin, Fr. Charles E. *Bishops Versus the Pope.* Bloomfield Hills: Helmet and Sword Publishers, 1969.

Creasy, William C. *The Imitation of Christ: A New Reading of the 1441 Latin Autograph Manuscript.* Macon, Ga.: Mercer University Press, 1989.

Cross, F. L., ed. *The Oxford Dictionary of the Christian Church.* Oxford: Oxford University Press, 1983.

Cullmann, Oscar. *Peter: Disciple-Apostle-Martyr.* Translated by Floyd V. Filson. Philadelphia: Westminster, 1953.

Cyril of Jerusalem. *Catechetical Lectures.* In *A Select Library of the Nicene and Post-Nicene Fathers of the Christian Church.* Edited by Philip Schaff. Grand Rapids: Eerdmans, 1983.

Davis, Charles. *A Question of Conscience.* New York: Harper and Row, 1967.

Davis, John J. *Foundations of Evangelical Theology.* Grand Rapids: Baker, 1994.

Dayton, Donald W., and Robert K. Johnston, eds. *The Variety of American Evangelicalism.* Downers Grove, Ill.: InterVarsity Press, 1991.

Delaney, John J., and James Edward Tobin. *Dictionary of Catholic Biography.* Garden City, N.Y.: Doubleday, 1961.

Denney, James. *The Atonement and the Modern Mind.* New York: A. C. Armstrong and Son, 1903.

Denzinger, Henry. *The Sources of Catholic Dogma.* Translated by Roy J. Deferrari. St. Louis: B. Herder Book Co., 1957.

Doherty, Richard T. *Proceedings of the Nineteenth Annual Convention.* New York: St. Joseph's Seminary Press, 1965.

Dorr, Darrell R., ed. *Perspectives on the World Christian Movement.* Pasadena: William Carey Library, 1981.

Douglas, J. D., ed. *New Bible Dictionary,* 2d ed. Wheaton: Tyndale House, 1982.

D'Souza, Dinesh. *Illiberal Education: The Politics of Race and Sex on Campus.* New York: Free Press, 1991.

Duffy, Stephen. "Catholicism's Search for a New Self-Understanding." In Gerald M. Fagin, S.J., ed., *Vatican II: Open Questions and New Horizons.* Wilmington, Del.: Michael G. Lazier, 1984.

Dulles, Avery. "Infallibility: The Terminology." In *Teaching Authority.* Edited by Empie.

———. "Justification in Contemporary Catholic Theology." In *Justification by Faith: Lutherans and Catholics in Dialogue VII.* Edited by H. George Anderson. Minneapolis: Augsburg, 1985.

Durant, William. *The Reformation.* New York: Simon and Schuster, 1957, Part 6 of "The Story of Civilization" series.

Edman, V. Raymond. *The Light in Dark Ages.* Wheaton: Van Kampen Press, 1949.

Ellul, Jacques. *Jesus and Marx.* Grand Rapids: Eerdmans, 1988.

Empie, Paul C., and T. Austin Murphy. *Eucharist and Ministry.* Minneapolis: Augsburg, 1979.

———, eds. *Papal Primacy and the Universal Church.* Minneapolis: Augsburg, 1977.

Empie, Paul C., T. Austin Murphy, and Joseph A. Burgess. *Teaching Authority and Infallibility in the Church.* Minneapolis: Augsburg, 1978.

Erickson, Millard J. *Christian Theology.* Grand Rapids: Baker, 1986.

———. *Concise Dictionary of Christian Theology.* Grand Rapids: Baker, 1986.

Fagin, Gerald M., S.J. *Vatican II: Open Questions and New Horizons.* Wilmington, Del.: Michael Glazier, 1984.

Flannery, Austin, O.P. *Vatican Collection: Vatican Council II,* vol. 1. Revised. North Port: Costello Publishing Co., 1992.

———, ed. *Vatican Council II: The Conciliar and Post-Conciliar Documents.* Grand Rapids: Eerdmans, 1992.

Fletcher, Joseph. *Situation Ethics: The New Morality.* Philadelphia: Westminster, 1966.

Fogarty, Gerald P., S.J. *American Catholic Biblical Scholarship: A History from the Early Republic to Vatican II.* San Francisco: Harper and Row, 1989.

Forell, George W., ed. *Luther's Works,* vol. 32. Philadelphia: Fortress, 1958.

Foster, Frank Hugh. *The Fundamental Ideas of the Roman Catholic Church.* Philadelphia: Presbyterian Board of Publication and Sabbath-School Work, 1898.

Fournier, Keith. *Evangelical Catholics: A Call for Christian Cooperation to Penetrate the Darkness with the Light of the Gospel.* Nashville: Nelson, 1990.

———. *Religious Cleansing in the American Republic.* Washington, D.C.: Liberty, Life and Family Publications, 1993.

Fournier, Keith A., with Watkins, William D. *A House Divided? Evangelicals and Catholics Together.* Colorado Springs: Navpress, 1994.

Frame, John M. *Evangelical Reunion.* Grand Rapids: Baker, 1991.

French, R. M., trans. *The Way of a Pilgrim and the Pilgrim Continues His Way*. San Francisco: Harper, 1973.

Fulgentius. *Letter to Donatus*. Post A.D. 512–ante A.D. 527.

Garrigou-Lagrange, Reginald. *Grace: Commentary on the Summa Theologica of St. Thomas*. St. Louis: B. Herder Book Co., 1952.

Gasper, Louis. *The Fundamentalist Movement 1930–1956*. Grand Rapids: Baker, 1963.

Geisler, Norman L. *The Battle for the Resurrection*. Nashville: Nelson, 1989.

Against Faustus. In Norman L. Geisler, *Decide for Yourself*. Grand Rapids: Zondervan, 1982.

———. *The Creator in the Courtroom*. Milford: Mott Media, 1982. Later purchased and distributed by Baker Book House.

———. *In Defense of the Resurrection*. Chico, Calif.: Witness, 1993.

———, ed. *Inerrancy*. Grand Rapids: Zondervan, 1979.

———. *Is Man the Measure?* Grand Rapids: Baker, 1983.

———. *Signs and Wonders*. Wheaton: Tyndale House, 1988.

———. *Thomas Aquinas: An Evangelical Appraisal*. Grand Rapids: Baker, 1991.

———. *To Understand the Bible, Look for Jesus*. Grand Rapids: Baker, 1979.

———, ed. *What Augustine Says*. Grand Rapids: Baker, 1982.

Geisler, Norman L., and Francis Beckwith. *Matters of Life and Death*. Grand Rapids: Baker, 1991.

Geisler, Norman L., and Ron Brooks. *When Skeptics Ask*. Wheaton: Victor, 1990.

Geisler, Norman L., and W. E. Nix. *General Introduction to the Bible, Revised and Expanded*. Chicago: Moody Press, 1986.

Gerstner, John H. *Jonathan Edwards: A Mini-Theology*. Wheaton: Tyndale House, 1987.

Gilby, Thomas. *St. Thomas Aquinas: Philosophical Texts*. New York: Oxford University Press, 1964.

Gilles, Anthony E. *Fundamentalism: What Every Catholic Needs to Know*. Cincinnati: St. Anthony Messenger Press, 1984.

Gillquist, Peter E. *Becoming Orthodox: A Journey to the Ancient Christian Faith*. Brentwood: Wolgemuth and Hyatt Publishers, 1990.

González, Justo L. *The Story of Christianity*, vols. 1–2. San Francisco: Harper and Row, 1984.

Graendorf, Werner C., ed. *Introduction to Biblical Christian Education*. Chicago: Moody Press, 1981.

Green, Michael. *Evangelism in the Early Church*. Grand Rapids: Eerdmans, 1970.

Griffin, John R. *John Keble: Saint of Anglicanism*. Macon, Ga.: Mercer University Press, 1987.

Grisez, Germain. *The Way of Our Lord*, vol. 1. Chicago: Franciscan Herald Press, 1983.

Gritsch, Eric W. "The Views of Luther and Lutheranism on the Veneration of Mary." In *The One Mediator, the Saints, and Mary-Lutherans and Catholics in Dialogue*. Edited by H. George Anderson. Minneapolis: Augsburg, 1992.

Hand, Thomas A., O.S.A. *Augustine on Prayer*. New York: Catholic Book Publishing, 1986.

Hanegraaff, Hank. *Christianity in Crisis*. Eugene, Oreg.: Harvest House, 1993.

Hardon, John A., S.J. *The Catholic Catechism: A Contemporary Catechism of the Teachings of the Catholic Church.* New York: Doubleday, Image Books, 1966.

Harris, Murray. *Raised Immortal.* Grand Rapids: Eerdmans, 1985.

Harrison, Everett F., ed. *Baker's Dictionary of Theology.* Grand Rapids: Baker, 1960.

Hase, Karl Von. *Handbook to the Controversy with Rome,* 2 vols. London: Religious Tract Society, 1906.

Hayes, Edward L. "The Biblical Foundations of Christian Education." In *Introduction to Biblical Christian Education.* Edited by Werner C. Graendorf. Chicago: Moody Press, 1981.

Henry, Carl F. H. "Secularization." In *In Search of a National Morality.* Edited by William Bentley Ball. Grand Rapids: Baker, 1992.

———. *The Uneasy Conscience of Modern Fundamentalism.* Grand Rapids: Eerdmans, 1947.

Herbermann, Charles G. et al., eds. *The Catholic Encyclopedia.* New York: Robert Appleton Co., 1909.

Hitchcock, James. *Catholicism and Modernity: Confrontation or Capitulation?* New York: Seabury Press, 1979.

———. *What Is Secular Humanism?* Ann Arbor: Servant, 1982.

———. *Years of Crisis: Collected Essays 1970–1983.* San Francisco: Ignatius Press, 1985.

Hodge, Charles. *Systematic Theology,* 3 vols. Reprint. Grand Rapids: Eerdmans, 1975.

Hoekema, Anthony A. *Saved by Grace.* Grand Rapids: Eerdmans, 1989.

Hollis, Christopher. "The Achievements of Vatican II." In *The Twentieth-Century Encyclopedia of Catholicism.* Edited by Henri Daniel-Rops. New York: Hawthorn Books, 1967.

Hopfe, Lewis M. *Religions of the World.* New York: Macmillan, 1991.

Horton, Michael, ed. *The Agony of Deceit: What Some TV Preachers Are Really Teaching.* Chicago: Moody Press, 1990.

———. *Christ the Lord: The Reformation and Lordship Salvation.* Grand Rapids: Baker, 1992.

Howard, Thomas. *Evangelical Is Not Enough: Worship of God in Liturgy and Sacrament.* San Francisco: Ignatius Press, 1984.

Hummel, Charles E. *The Galileo Connection: Resolving Conflicts between Science and the Bible.* Downers Grove, Ill.: InterVarsity Press, 1986.

Hunter, H. D. "Charismatic Movement." In *Dictionary of Christianity in America.* Downers Grove, Ill.: InterVarsity Press, 1990.

The Hymnal 1940 Companion. 3d ed. New York: The Church Pension Fund, 1951.

Interdicasterial Commission, *Catechism of the Catholic Church: Libreria Editrice Vaticana.* Boston: St. Paul Books and Media, 1994.

Irenaeus. *Against Heresies.* In *The Ante-Nicene Fathers.* Edited by Rev. Alexander Roberts and James Donaldson. Grand Rapids: Eerdmans, 1885.

Jafa, Harry V. *Homosexuality and the Natural Law.* Montclair: Claremont Institute, 1990.

Jedin, Hubert. *History of the Council of Trent.* Translated by F. C. Eckhoff. St. Louis and London, 1947.

Jerome. Preface to *Jerome's Commentary on Daniel*. Translated by Gleason Archer. Grand Rapids: Baker, 1977. *Against Rufinus*.

Jewett, Paul K. *Infant Baptism and the Covenant of Grace*. Grand Rapids: Eerdmans, 1978.

John Paul II. *Catechesi Tradendae* (16 October 1979).

Johnson, Paul. *A History of Christianity*. New York: Atheneum-Macmillan Publishing, 1976.

———. *Intellectuals*. New York: Harper and Row, 1988.

Johnston, Robert K, ed. *The Use of the Bible in Theology/Evangelical Options*. Atlanta: John Knox, 1985.

Jones, R. Tudor. *The Great Reformation*. Downers Grove, Ill.: InterVarsity Press, 1985.

Jordan, Mark, ed. *The Church's Confession of Faith*. San Francisco: Ignatius Press, 1985.

Josephus. *Antiquities*. In *Josephus*. Translated by William Whiston. Grand Rapids: Kregel, 1963.

Kant, Immanuel. *Critique of Practical Reason*. Translated by Lewis White Beck. New York: Bobbs-Merrill Co., 1956.

Kantzer, Kenneth. *John Calvin's Theory of the Knowledge of God and the Word of God*. Cambridge, Mass.: Harvard Divinity School, 1981.

Kassian, Mary A. *The Feminist Gospel*. Wheaton: Crossway, 1992.

Keating, Karl. *Catholicism and Fundamentalism*. San Francisco: Ignatius Press, 1988.

Kelley, Fr. Bennet, C.P. *God and His Perfections*. New York: Catholic Book Publishing, 1964.

Kelly, J. N. D. *Early Christian Doctrine*. San Francisco: Harper, 1978.

Kik, J. Marcellus. *Ecumenism and the Evangelical*. Philadelphia: Presbyterian and Reformed, 1958.

Kreeft, Peter. *Fundamentals of the Faith*. San Francisco: Ignatius Press, 1988.

Kuiper, B. K. *The Church in History*. Grand Rapids: Eerdmans, 1955.

Küng, Hans. *Infallible? An Inquiry?* Translated by Edward Quinn. Garden City, N.Y.: Doubleday, 1971.

———. *Justification*. New York: Nelson, 1964.

Ladd, George E. *A Theology of the New Testament*. Grand Rapids: Eerdmans, 1974.

Lécuyer, Joseph, C.S.Sp. *What Is a Priest?* New York: Hawthorn Books, 1959.

Lehmann, Karl, and Wolfhart Pannenberg, eds. *The Condemnations of the Reformation Era: Do They Still Divide?* Translated by Margaret Kohl. Minneapolis: Fortress, 1989.

Lewis, C. S. *Mere Christianity*. New York: Macmillan, 1943.

Liguori, Alphonsus de. *The Glories of Mary*. Edited by Eugene Grimm. Brooklyn: Redemptionist Fathers, 1931.

Linder, Robert D. "Ignatius Loyola." In *Great Leaders of the Christian Church*. Edited by John D. Woodbridge. Chicago: Moody Press, 1988.

Locke, John. *An Essay*. In *The Great Books*. Chicago: Encyclopedia Britannica, 1952.

Lohse, Bernhard. *Martin Luther: An Introduction to His Life and Work*. Philadelphia: Fortress, 1986.

———. *A Short History of Christian Doctrine*. Translated by F. Ernest Stoeffler. Revised American Edition. Philadelphia: Fortress Press, 1985.

Luther, Martin. *The Babylonian Captivity of the Church*. In *Three Treatises*. Translated by A. T. W. Steinhäuser. Revised by Frederick C. Ahrens and Abdel Ross Wewtz. Philadelphia: Fortress Press, 1960.

———. *Explanations of the Ninety-five Theses*, 1518.

Macquarrie, John. *Mary for All Christians*. Grand Rapids: Eerdmans, 1990.

Magill, Frank, ed. "The Life of Antony." In *Masterpieces of Christian Literature*. New York: Harper and Row, 1963.

Mantzaridis, Georgios I. *The Deification of Man*. Crestwood: St. Vladimir's Seminary Press, 1984.

Marsden, George M. "Fundamentalism and American Evangelicalism." In *The Variety of American Evangelicalism*. Edited by Donald W. Dayton and Robert K. Johnston. Downers Grove, Ill.: InterVarsity Press, 1991.

Martin, Ralph. *A Crisis of Truth: The Attack on Faith, Morality and Mission in the Catholic Church*. Ann Arbor: Servant, 1982.

———. *Hungry for God*. Garden City, N.Y.: Doubleday, 1974.

Martyr, Justin. *On the Resurrection, Fragments*. In *The Ante-Nicene Fathers: The Apostolic Fathers*.

McGavran, Donald A. *Understanding Church Growth*. Grand Rapids: Eerdmans, 1970.

McGrath, Alister E. *Iustitia Dei: A History of the Christian Doctrine of Justification*. Cambridge: Cambridge University Press, 1986.

———. *Understanding the Trinity*. Grand Rapids: Zondervan, 1990.

McGrath, Joanna, and Alister McGrath. *The Dilemma of Self-Esteem: The Cross and Christian Confidence*. Wheaton: Crossway, 1992.

McManners, John, ed. *The Oxford Illustrated History of Christianity*. Oxford: Oxford University Press, 1990.

McSorley, Harry. *Luther: Right or Wrong?* Minneapolis: Augsburg, 1969.

Meeking, Basil, and John Stott, eds. *The Evangelical-Roman Catholic Dialogue on Mission*. Grand Rapids: Eerdmans, 1986.

Mercati, A. "The New List of the Popes." In *Medieval Studies*. 1947.

Metzger, Bruce. *An Introduction to the Apocrypha*. New York: Oxford University Press, 1957.

Miceli, Vincent P., S.J. *The Antichrist*. Harrison, N.Y.: Roman Catholic Books, 1981.

Miethe, Terry. "Natural Law: The Synderesis Rule." In *Augustinian Studies*. 1980.

Miethe, Terry, and Vernon J. Bourke. *Thomistic Bibliography*.

Miller, Elliot, and Kenneth R. Samples. *The Cult of the Virgin: Catholic Mariology and the Apparitions of Mary*. Grand Rapids: Baker, 1992.

Milne, Bruce. *Know the Truth*. Downers Grove, Ill.: InterVarsity Press, 1982.

Moberg, David O. "Fundamentalists and Evangelicals in Society." In *The Evangelicals: What They Believe, Who They Are, Where They Are Changing*. Nashville: Abingdon, 1975.

Montgomery, John W. *Ecumenicity, Evangelicals and Rome*. Grand Rapids: Zondervan, 1969.

———. *The Shape of the Past*. Minneapolis: Bethany Fellowship, 1975.

Moorman, John. *Vatican Observed: An Anglican Impression of Vatican II*. London: Darton, Longman and Todd, 1967.

Moran, Bob. *A Closer Look at Catholicism*. Waco: Word, 1986.

Morison, Samuel Eliot. *The Oxford History of the American People*. New York: Oxford University Press, 1965.

Most, G. *Catholic Apologetics Today: Answers to Modern Critics*. Rockford, Ill.: Tan Books and Publishers, 1986.

———. *Free from All Error*. Libertyville: Prow Books, 1985.

Moynihan, Martin. *The Latin Letters of C. S. Lewis*. Westchester, Ill.: Crossway, 1987.

Nash, Ronald H., ed. *Evangelical Renewal in the Mainline Churches*. Westchester, Ill.: Crossway, 1987.

———. *Social Justice and the Christian Church*. Milford: Mott Media, 1984.

The Navarre Bible, 2d ed. Dublin: Four Courts Press, 1991.

Nellas, Panajiotis. *Deification in Christ*. Crestwood: St. Vladimir's Seminary Press, 1987.

Neuhaus, Richard John. *The Catholic Moment: The Paradox of the Church in the Postmodern World*. New York: Harper and Row, 1987.

Neuner, J., S.J., and J. Dupuis, S.J., eds. *The Christian Faith: Doctrinal Documents of the Catholic Church*. 5th rev. New York: Alba House, 1990.

The New American Bible. St. Joseph Edition. New York: Catholic Book Publishing, 1991.

New Catholic Encyclopedia, 17 vols. New York: McGraw-Hill, 1979.

Newman, John Henry. *An Essay on the Development of Christian Doctrine*. Notre Dame: University of Notre Dame Press, 1989.

———. *Idea of a University*. New York: Longmans, 1947.

Novak, Michael. "A Theology of Development for Latin America." In *Liberation Theology*. Edited by Ronald H. Nash. Milford: Mott Media, 1984.

Novena Prayers in Honor of Our Mother of Perpetual Help. Uniontown, Pa.: Sisters of St. Basil, 1968.

O'Brien, John A. *The Faith of Millions*. Huntington: Our Sunday Visitor, 1974.

O'Carroll, Michael. *Theotokos: A Theological Encyclopedia of the Blessed Virgin Mary*. Wilmington, Del.: Michael Glazier, 1982.

O'Connor, Edward D., C.S.C. *The Pentecostal Movement in the Catholic Church*. South Bend: Notre Dame, Ave Maria Press, 1971.

Oberman, Heiko A. *The Dawn of the Reformation*. Grand Rapids: Eerdmans, reprinted 1992.

Oden, Thomas C. *Corrective Love: The Power of Communion Discipline*. St. Louis: Concordia Press, 1995.

Orchard, Dom Bernard, et al., eds. *A Catholic Commentary on Holy Scripture*. Nashville: Nelson, 1953.

Orlandis, Jose. *A Short History of the Catholic Church*. Dublin: Four Courts Press, 1985.

Osterhaven, M. Eugene. *The Faith of the Church*. Grand Rapids: Eerdmans, 1982.

Ott, Ludwig. *Fundamentals of Catholic Dogma*. Edited by James Canon Bastible. Translated by Patrick Lynch. Rockford, Ill.: Tan Books and Publishers, 1960.

Packer, J. I. "*Sola Scriptura:* Crucial to Evangelism." In *The Foundations of Biblical Authority.* Edited by James M. Boice. Grand Rapids: Zondervan, 1978.

Payne, Franklin E., Jr., M.D. *What Every Christian Should Know about the AIDS Epidemic.* Augusta: Covenant Books, 1991.

Pelikan, Jaroslav. *Jesus through the Centuries.* New York: Harper and Row, 1987.

———. *The Riddle of Roman Catholicism.* New York: Abingdon, 1960.

Penaskovic, Richard, ed. *Theology and Authority: Maintaining a Tradition of Tension.* Peabody, Mass.: Hendrickson, 1987.

Perrotta, Kevin. "The U.S. Catholic Church." In *Evangelical Renewal in the Mainline Churches.* Edited by Ronald H. Nash. Westchester, Ill.: Crossway, 1987.

Perrotta, Kevin, and John C. Blattner, eds. *Courage in Leadership.* Ann Arbor: Servant, 1988.

Pesch, Otto Hermann. *The God Question in Thomas Aquinas and Martin Luther.* Translated by Gottfried G. Krodel. Philadelphia: Fortress, 1972.

Pfürtner, Stephanus, O.P. *Luther and Aquinas—A Conversation: Our Salvation, Its Certainty and Peril.* Translated by Edward Quinn. London: Darton, Longman and Todd, 1964.

Pieper, Franz. *Christian Dogmatics,* 4 vols. St. Louis: Concordia, 1950–57.

Pius XII. Encyclical letter. *Humani Generis* (12 August 1950).

Proceedings of the Nineteenth Annual Convention: The Catholic Theological Society of America. Yonkers: St. Joseph's Seminary, 1965.

Rahner, Karl. *The Mother of Our Lord.* Wheathampstead, Hertfordshire: Anthony Clarke Books, 1963.

Ramm, Bernard. *The Pattern of Religious Authority.* Grand Rapids: Eerdmans, 1959.

Ratzinger, Joseph Cardinal. *Introduction to Christianity.* San Francisco: Ignatius, 1990.

Reardon, Bernard M. G. *Religious Thought in the Reformation.* London: Longman, 1981.

Rondet, Henri, S.J. *Do Dogmas Change?* New York: Hawthorn Books, 1961.

Rudolph, Kurt. *Gnosis: The Nature and History of Gnosticism.* Edinburgh: T. and T. Clark, 1984.

Rupp, Gordon. *Luther's Progress to the Diet of Worms.* Reprint. New York: Harper and Row, 1964.

Salmon, George. *The Infallibility of the Church.* London: John Murray Publishing, 1914.

Scanlan, Michael. *Let the Fire Fall.* Ann Arbor: Servant, 1986.

Schaeffer, Frank. *Dancing Alone: The Quest for Orthodox Faith in the Age of False Religions.* Brookline: Holy Cross Orthodox Press, 1994.

Schaff, David S. *Our Father's Faith and Ours.* New York: G. P. Putnam's Sons, 1928.

Schaff, Philip. *The Creeds of Christendom: With a History and Critical Notes.* Grand Rapids: Baker, 1983.

———, ed. *A Select Library of the Nicene and Post-Nicene Fathers of the Christian Church.* 9th ed. Grand Rapids: Eerdmans, 1956.

Schillebeeckx, Edward. *Jesus: An Experiment in Christology.* Translated by Hubert Hoskins. New York: Seabury, 1979.

Schmaus, Michael. *Dogma 6: Justification and the Last Things.* London: Sheed and Ward, 1977.

Schouppe, F. X., S.J. *Purgatory.* Rockford, Ill.: Tan Books and Publishers, 1986.

Schreck, Alan. *The Compact History of the Catholic Church.* Ann Arbor: Servant, 1987.

Schroeder, Rev. Henry J., ed. *Canons of the Council of Trent.* Canon 30, Session t, 1547. Rockford, Ill.: Tan Books and Publishers, 1978.

Schrotenboer, Paul G. *Roman Catholicism: A Contemporary Evangelical Perspective.* Reprint. Grand Rapids: Baker, 1988.

Second Vatican Council. *Dogmatic Constitution on the Church.*

Sell, Alan P. F. *A Reformed, Evangelical, Catholic Theology: The Contribution of the World Alliance of Reformed Churches 1875–1982.* Grand Rapids: Eerdmans, 1991.

Sheed, Frank. *Theology and Sanity.* Enlarged ed. Huntington: Our Sunday Visitor, 1978.

———. *Theology for Beginners.* Ann Arbor: Servant, 1981.

Sikorska, Grazyna. *Light and Life: Renewal in Poland.* Grand Rapids: Eerdmans, 1989.

Spitz, Lewis W. *The Renaissance and Reformation Movements.* Revised. St. Louis: Concordia, 1987.

Steichen, Donna. *Ungodly Rage: The Hidden Face of Catholic Feminism.* San Francisco: Ignatius Press, 1992.

Stott, John R. W. *Between Two Worlds: The Art of Preaching in the Twentieth Century.* Grand Rapids: Eerdmans, 1982.

———. *The Cross of Christ.* Downers Grove, Ill.: InterVarsity Press, 1986.

Stravinskas, Peter M. J., Ph.D., S.T.L., ed. *Our Sunday Visitor's Catholic Encyclopedia.* Huntington: Our Sunday Visitor, 1991.

Strimple, Robert B. *Anselm and the Theology of Atonement.* Unpublished thesis. Philadelphia: Westminster Theological Seminary, 1964.

Suenens, Léon Joseph Cardinal. *A New Pentecost?* New York: Seabury Press, 1975.

Sullivan, F. A. "Catholic Charismatic Renewal." In *Dictionary of the Pentecostal and Charismatic Movements.* Grand Rapids: Regency Press, 1988.

Tappeiner, D. A. "Holy Spirit." In *International Standard Bible Encyclopedia.* Grand Rapids: Eerdmans, 1988.

Tavard, George H. *Holy Writ or Holy Church.* New York: Harper and Brothers, 1959.

Toon, Peter. *Born Again: A Biblical and Theological Study of Regeneration.* Grand Rapids: Baker, 1987.

———. *The Development of Doctrine in the Church.* Grand Rapids: Eerdmans, 1979.

———. *Foundations for Faith: Justification and Sanctification.* Westchester, Ill.: Crossway, 1983.

———. *Protestants and Catholics: A Guide to Understanding the Differences among Christians.* Ann Arbor: Servant, 1983.

Treece, Patricia. *A Man for Others: Maximilian Kolbe, Saint of Auschwitz.* San Francisco: Harper and Row, 1982.

Turner, James. *Without God, without Creed: The Origins of Unbelief in America.* Baltimore: Johns Hopkins University Press, 1985.

Vatican Council II, vol. 1. Revised. Boston: St. Paul's Books and Media, 1992.

Vitz, Paul. *Censorship: Evidence of Bias in Our Children's Textbooks.* Ann Arbor: Servant, 1986.

———. *Psychology as Religion: The Cult of Self-worship.* Reprint. Grand Rapids: Eerdmans, 1986.

———. *Sigmund Freud's Christian Unconscious.* New York: Guilford Press, 1988.

Vos, Arvin. *Aquinas, Calvin and Contemporary Protestant Thought.* Grand Rapids: Eerdmans, 1985.

Walker, Williston. *A History of the Christian Church.* 3d ed. New York: Charles Scribner's Sons, 1970.

Walvoord, John, ed. *Lewis Sperry Chafer: Systemic Theology,* vol. 2. Abridged edition. Wheaton: Victor, 1988.

Ware, Timothy. *The Orthodox Church.* Revised. New York: Penguin Books, 1983.

Warfield, Benjamin B. *Calvin and Augustine.* Philadelphia: Presbyterian and Reformed, 1956.

Webster, William. *Salvation, the Bible, and Roman Catholicism.* London: Banner of Truth, 1990.

Wells, David F. *No Place for Truth: Or Whatever Happened to Evangelical Theology?* Grand Rapids: Eerdmans, 1993.

———. *Revolution in Rome.* Downers Grove, Ill.: InterVarsity Press, 1972.

———. *Turning to God: Biblical Conversion in the Modern World.* Grand Rapids: Baker, 1989.

Wells, David F., and Clark H. Pinnock, eds. *Toward a Theology for the Future.* Carol Stream, Ill.: Creation House, 1971.

Wells, David F., and John D. Woodbridge, eds. *The Evangelicals: What They Believe, Who They Are, Where They Are Changing.* Nashville: Abingdon, 1975.

The Westminster Confession of Faith. Philadelphia: Great Commission Publications, n.d.

White, James R. *Answers to Catholic Claims.* Southbridge, Mass.: Crowne Publications, 1990.

———. *The Fatal Flaw.* Southbridge, Mass.: Crowne Publications, 1990.

Williamson, Peter, and Kevin Perrotta, eds. *Christianity in Conflict.* Ann Arbor: Servant, 1986.

Woodbridge, John D., ed. *Great Leaders of the Christian Church.* Chicago: Moody Press, 1988.

Yamauchi, Edwin M. *Pre-Christian Gnosticism: A Survey of the Proposed Evidence.* 2d ed. Grand Rapids: Baker, 1983.

Yamamoto, J. Isamu, ed. *The Crisis of Homosexuality.* Wheaton: Victor, 1990.

Zwingli, Ulricht. *Apolegeticus Architeles.*

Index of Persons

INDEX OF SUBJECTS